Communications in Computer and Information Science 2671

Series Editors

Rationale
The CCIS series is devoted to the publication of proceedings of computer science conferences. Its aim is to efficiently disseminate original research results in informatics in printed and electronic form. While the focus is on publication of peer-reviewed full papers presenting mature work, inclusion of reviewed short papers reporting on work in progress is welcome, too. Besides globally relevant meetings with internationally representative program committees guaranteeing a strict peer-reviewing and paper selection process, conferences run by societies or of high regional or national relevance are also considered for publication.

Topics
The topical scope of CCIS spans the entire spectrum of informatics ranging from foundational topics in the theory of computing to information and communications science and technology and a broad variety of interdisciplinary application fields.

Information for Volume Editors and Authors
Publication in CCIS is free of charge. No royalties are paid, however, we offer registered conference participants temporary free access to the online version of the conference proceedings on SpringerLink (http://link.springer.com) by means of an http referrer from the conference website and/or a number of complimentary printed copies, as specified in the official acceptance email of the event.

CCIS proceedings can be published in time for distribution at conferences or as post-proceedings, and delivered in the form of printed books and/or electronically as USBs and/or e-content licenses for accessing proceedings at SpringerLink. Furthermore, CCIS proceedings are included in the CCIS electronic book series hosted in the SpringerLink digital library at http://link.springer.com/bookseries/7899. Conferences publishing in CCIS are allowed to use our online conference service (Meteor) for managing the whole proceedings lifecycle (from submission and reviewing to preparing for publication) free of charge.

Publication process
The language of publication is exclusively English. Authors publishing in CCIS have to sign the Springer CCIS copyright transfer form, however, they are free to use their material published in CCIS for substantially changed, more elaborate subsequent publications elsewhere. For the preparation of the camera-ready papers/files, authors have to strictly adhere to the Springer CCIS Authors' Instructions and are strongly encouraged to use the CCIS LaTeX style files or templates.

Abstracting/Indexing
CCIS is abstracted/indexed in DBLP, Google Scholar, EI-Compendex, Mathematical Reviews, SCImago, Scopus. CCIS volumes are also submitted for the inclusion in ISI Proceedings.

How to start
To start the evaluation of your proposal for inclusion in the CCIS series, please send an e-mail to ccis@springer.com

Maxim Bakaev · Radomir Bolgov ·
Anna Chizhik · Andrei Chugunov ·
Valeriia Demareva · Yury Kabanov ·
Roberto Pereira · Elakkiya R. · Wei Zhang
Editors

Internet and Modern Society

28th International Conference, IMS 2025
St. Petersburg, Russia, June 23–25, 2025
Proceedings, Part I

Springer

Editors
Maxim Bakaev
Novosibirsk State Technical University
Novosibirsk, Russia

Radomir Bolgov
St. Petersburg State University
St. Petersburg, Russia

Anna Chizhik
St. Petersburg State University
St. Petersburg, Russia

Andrei Chugunov
ITMO University
St. Petersburg, Russia

Valeriia Demareva
Lobachevsky State University of Nizhny Novgorod
Nizhny Novgorod, Russia

Yury Kabanov
HSE University
St. Petersburg, Russia

Roberto Pereira
Federal University of Paraná
Curitiba, Paraná, Brazil

Elakkiya R.
Birla Institute of Technology and Science
Pilani Dubai Campus
Dubai, United Arab Emirates

Wei Zhang
Huazhong University of Science and Technology
Wuhan, China

ISSN 1865-0929 ISSN 1865-0937 (electronic)
Communications in Computer and Information Science
ISBN 978-3-032-04957-5 ISBN 978-3-032-04958-2 (eBook)
https://doi.org/10.1007/978-3-032-04958-2

This Springer imprint is published by the registered company Springer Nature Switzerland AG
The registered company address is: Gewerbestrasse 11, 6330 Cham, Switzerland

Preface

On June 23–25, 2025, the International Conference "Internet and Modern Society" (IMS 2025) was held in St. Petersburg (Russia), preceded by its Dubai (UAE) section. This was the 28th edition of the conference, which has been held without interruption since 1998.

The current proceedings contain the 56 papers in the field of Collaborative Information Systems that were selected by the IMS 2025 Program Committee and presented at the conference. In total there were 135 submissions from over 10 countries. After the preliminary screening of the 135 submissions by the editors, 104 were sent for reviewing. Of these, 44 were accepted as full papers, and 12 as short papers. The submissions were evaluated by about 90 reviewers, each of whom on average produced 3.64 reviews. The average number of reviews received per submission was 3.05. The double-blind review process was supported by the licensed Microsoft Conference Management Toolkit (CMT) software. Overall, there were over 400 registered participants in the conference.

These two proceedings volumes address the topical issues of computer and information science and engineering, providing experts in related fields with a platform for discussion and collaboration. In them, authors from all over the world consider the impact of the recent drastic changes caused by the introduction of Large Language Models and the AI-supported "intent-based" interaction paradigm and their lasting effects on social, economic, educational, and technological aspects of human life. The main areas of the conference this year included Human-Computer Interaction, Natural Language Processing, Collaborative and Social Computing, E-Governance, Interactive Systems, Cyber Psychology, etc. The papers of the current proceedings were presented in the following sessions of IMS 2025:

Vol. 1 (2671):

- Computational Linguistics & Machine Learning (CompLing);
- Cyberpsychology & Post-AI Education (PsyAI);
- Digital Transformation in Governance and Society (DTGS);

Vol. 2 (2672):

- Art and Innovation in Museums (AIMs);
- Interactive Systems & Information Society Technologies (InterSys).

The conference also involved several keynote talks, including:

- Development of the Unified Card of St. Petersburg: Prospects and Challenges (Valentina R. Kozyreva, Candidate of Historical Sciences, Deputy Director of St. Petersburg Information Support Center);

- The Use of Artificial Intelligence for Improving the Quality of Digital Management Services Urban Environment (Sergey V. Ivanov, Candidate of Technical Sciences, Head of the Laboratory "Artificial Intelligence in Urban Planning" of ITMO University and Moscow Department of Urban Planning Policy);
- An Ecosystem of Services for Working with Scientific and Technical Information as a Development Tool a New Generation of Researchers (Anton V. Mayevsky, Candidate of Physical and Mathematical Sciences, Director of Products and Technologies of INVENTORUS LLC).

Overall, the contents of these proceedings may be of interest both to academics working in the related fields and to IT industry practitioners.

ITMO University was the main organizer of IMS 2025, which was held in cooperation with the partner universities:

- Birla Institute of Technology and Science, Pilani – Dubai Campus, United Arab Emirates;
- Novosibirsk State Technical University, Russia;
- Federal University of Paraná, Brazil.

We would like to thank those who made this event possible and successful. We especially express our gratitude to the Program Committee members and additional reviewers for their contribution to the selection of the papers, and to the Session Chairs for their invaluable help in the organization. We thank the authors for submitting their manuscripts. We are proud of having attracted a great team of scholars from different countries and disciplines and will work further to sustain and expand the IMS community through joint research and collaboration.

June 2025

Maxim Bakaev
Radomir Bolgov
Anna Chizhik
Andrei Chugunov
Valeriia Demareva
Yury Kabanov
Roberto Pereira
Elakkiya R.
Wei Zhang

Organization

General Chair

Dmitry Prokudin	St. Petersburg State University, Russia

Program Committee Chairs

Maxim Bakaev	Novosibirsk State Technical University, Russia
Radomir Bolgov	St. Petersburg State University, Russia
Anna Chizhik	St. Petersburg State University, ITMO University, Russia
Andrei Chugunov	ITMO University, Russia
Katarina Cokrlic	University of Bologna, Italy
Valeriia Demareva	Lobachevsky State University of Nizhny Novgorod, Russia
Yury Kabanov	HSE University, Russia
Roberto Pereira	Federal University of Paraná, Brazil
Elakkiya R.	BITS Pilani Dubai Campus, United Arab Emirates
Wei Zhang	Huazhong University of Science and Technology, China

Steering Committee

Nikolay Borisov	St. Petersburg State University, Russia
Andrei Chugunov	ITMO University, Russia

Program Committee

Mikhail Bundin	Lobachevsky State University of Nizhny Novgorod, Russia
Thiago Campos	Federal University of Technology – Paraná, Brazil
Wei Dai	Huazhong University of Science & Technology, China
Saravanan Devadoss	Sri Manakula Vinayagar Group of Institutions, India

Ruben Elamiryan	Russian-Armenian University, Armenia
Olga Filatova	ITMO University, Russia
Julian Grigera	National University of La Plata, Argentina
Anna Guminskaia	National Research Nuclear University MEPhI, Russia
Deógenes Junior	Federal University of Paraná, Brazil
Pavel Konyukhovskiy	Herzen University, Russia
Igor Kuprienko	ITMO University, Russia
Irina Mamonova	St. Petersburg State University, Russia
Olga Mitrofanova	St. Petersburg State University, Russia
Radka Nacheva	University of Economics – Varna, Bulgaria
Prabir Panda	Motilal Nehru National Institute of Technology, India
Olga Razumnikova	Novosibirsk State Technical University, Russia
Aleksandr Riabushko	Independent Researcher, Russia
Bogdan Romanov	University of Tartu, Estonia
Dmitry Ryumin	St. Petersburg Federal Research Center of the RAS, Russia
Anna Smoliarova	Hebrew University, Israel
Leonid Smorgunov	St. Petersburg State University, Russia
Alexander Sokolov	P. G. Demidov Yaroslavl State University, Russia
Evgeny Styrin	HSE University, Russia
Anna Sytnik	St. Petersburg State University, Russia
Irina Tolstikova	ITMO University, Russia
Dmitrii Trutnev	ITMO University, Russia
Subramaniyaswamy Vairavasundaram	Vellore Institute of Technology, India
Lyudmila Vidiasova	ITMO University, Russia
Daniil Volkovskii	Paris 1 Panthéon-Sorbonne University, France
Can Yang	Chongqing University, China
Yulia Zherebtsova	ITMO University, Russia

Additional Reviewers

Shivang Agarwal	Hussain Ahmed Chowdhury
Mark Athugodage	Deepak Dasaratha Rao
Olga Babina	Natalia Fomina
Olga Blinova	Anna Glazkova
Victoria Blokhina	Aditya Gupta
Natalia Bogdanova-Beglarian	Ashish Gupta
Chiranjeevi Bura	Daria Guseva
Anna Bykova	Balaji Ingole

Anna Izmalkova
Olga Kamshilova
Margarita Kirina
Marina Kogan
Anastasia Kolmogorova
Evgeny Kotelnikov
Andrew Krizhanovsky
Ksenia Kunnikova
Natalia Loukachevitch
Ivan Mamaev
Mohan Krishna Mannava
Tojo Mathew
Dmitry Morozov
Anna Moskvina
Praveen Kumar Myakala
Anton Pashkov
Pranav Pawar
Tamizharasan Periyasamy
Lada Petrushenko
Ravikumar S.
Thylashri S.
Isan Sahoo
Ilya Seletkov
Ulka Shirole
Suyash Shukla
Valery Shulginov
Amit Singh
Kseniia Studenikina
Mariya Timofeeva
Valeriia Viakhireva
Zicheng Wang
Vibhas Mohan Zanpure

Contents – Part I

Digital Transformation in Governance and Society

Contents – Part II

Computational Linguistics and Machine Learning

Mapping Effective Teaching with Topic Modeling

Ivan Mamaev[1,2](✉)

[1] Department of Mathematical Linguistics, Saint Petersburg State University, Universitetskaya Emb. 11 199034, Saint Petersburg, Russia
i.mamaev@spbu.ru, mamaev_id@voenmeh.ru

[2] Department of Theoretical and Applied Linguistics, Baltic State Technical University "Voenmeh" Named After D.F. Ustinov, 1-Ya Krasnoarmeyskaya Street, 1, 190005 Saint Petersburg, Russia

Abstract. Teacher effectiveness is of utmost importance with respect to educational quality, and determines levels of student accomplishment and societal outcomes in general. Through the Latent Dirichlet Allocation (LDA) topic modeling of Russian language lessons, this study investigates how well the observed teaching practices align with Federal State Educational Standards (FSES, FGOS in Russian) and contrasts the findings for more and less effective teachers. More effective teachers design their lessons around central topics within the curriculum, they have greater coherence and alignment with FSES goals. Less effective teachers pick generic topics the lessons hardly ever touch upon. The proposed procedure not only yields insights on teaching strategies but also provides a template for the development of data-driven tools for assessing instructional quality in various educational settings. The results confirm the ability of topic modeling to advance the appraisal of actual educational practices in Russia and beyond.

Keywords: Corpus Linguistics · Topic Modeling · Pedagogical Practices

1 Introduction

Teacher effectiveness is a pillar of educational quality and directly affects student achievement, student engagement, and social and economic consequences for the wider community. For decades, research has focused on discerning which pedagogical practices correspond with high-quality instruction [7, 8, 21], but the difficulty of systematic evaluation arises from the subjectivity of teaching as well as its acute contextuality. Traditional methods of assessing an instructional event, for example, classroom observations [20], student surveys [6], or analyses of standardized test score distributions [9], have characteristics of being manpower-intensive and methodologically weak because they take a snapshot of an isolated event that is highly prone to rater bias and scalability issues. Within the Russian context, where a centralized curricular framework collides with a highly diverse educational landscape on the regional level, there is now an increasing urgency for developing data-driven instruments for assessing instructional quality.

M. Bakaev et al. (Eds.): IMS 2025, CCIS 2671, pp. 3–17, 2026.
https://doi.org/10.1007/978-3-032-04958-2_1

Advances in computational linguistics provide an enterprising avenue in this regard. Unsupervised machine learning methods enable researchers to extract latent patterns from mostly unstructured data in textual format, such as lesson transcripts, which can be used as evidence for inference about classroom interaction and pedagogical strategies. In particular, topic modeling (TM) algorithms have shown promise in extracting thematic structures from different corpora such as social networks corpora [10, 14], fiction corpora [4, 5], etc.

Topic modeling remains to be scarcely explored in non-English-speaking educational contexts, where linguistic, cultural, and institutional factors might have different impacts on the design of teaching practices. This study bridges this gap by employing topic modeling to examine lesson transcripts from Russian secondary schools, aiming to identify language markers distinguishing more and less effective educators.

2 Related Works

In the educational research field, topic modeling procedures have demonstrated a very similar methodology when applied to different teaching challenges, including teacher self-evaluation and environmental impact on student learning. The common thing here is the application of Latent Dirichlet Allocation (LDA), although its adaptations differ across linguistic and institutional settings.

Most studies stress the need for a rigorous preprocessing pipeline consisting of tokenization, stop-word removal, and lemmatization to deal with noise, especially for morphologically rich languages like Spanish [3] or Chinese [31]. The importance of human validation has been recognized in each of the frameworks, whether for the purpose of refining algorithmically generated topics [24] or to make sense of the polarity of sentiment in climate-impacted classrooms [12]. Pioneering hybrids like in [31], which pursue the integration of term-frequency matrices (QTFM) with hierarchical Dirichlet processes (HDP), indicate the recognition of a tension between scalability and semantic precision. Much like text network modeling [3] and sentiment analysis [12], topic modeling shows the compatibility with other techniques so as to enrich insights.

Competency-based education (CBE) has seen a global surge in attention, driven by the need for 21st-century skills and the evolving demands of modern society. The research [16] highlighted that international organizations like the OECD have played a pivotal role in steering educational discourses toward sustainability and inclusivity. The findings emphasized themes such as "learning skills" and "teacher training," signaling a fundamental shift from traditional knowledge-based models to frameworks that prioritize competencies. This growing interest reflects a broader understanding that education must prepare individuals not merely for rote knowledge retention but for adaptable, real-world application.

In parallel, the flipped classroom model has emerged as a transformative pedagogical approach. Ozyurt [15] conducted a comprehensive analysis that revealed sixteen key themes, with topics like "Performance and perception," "Nursing education," and "Effectiveness and motivation" standing out. This approach, characterized by its emphasis on student-centered learning environments, has proven highly adaptable during the pandemic. By shifting traditional in-class instruction to pre-class activities and using classroom time for engagement and reinforcement, the flipped model has offered a dynamic and effective solution for many educational contexts.

The COVID-19 pandemic itself became a watershed moment for educational research. Vijayan [26] studied topical landscape studies and distilled six major themes, the effects on higher education institutions, the implementation of digital tools, and the mental health conditions of students. The pandemic exposed and deepened the pre-existing inequalities in education; technological inequality arose as one issue of concern, especially in lower-income areas and some parts of the developed world. As much as these challenges surfaced, the pandemic also offered opportunities for educators and institutions to think creatively about ways of being and implement digital models that may have a lasting impact to beyond the pandemic.

A notable trend in physics education research, as explored in [29], highlights the dual identity of physics education as both a scientific and pedagogical field. By applying topic modeling to extensive journal archives, this study identified shifts in research focus over decades. Topics such as pedagogical content knowledge (PCK), assessment methodologies, and gender-related educational outcomes have gained prominence, while traditional themes like introductory physics and problem-solving have seen relative declines. The reliance on LDA facilitated a broad yet nuanced categorization of research themes, enabling insights into evolving pedagogical priorities and underexplored areas.

In a broader educational context, Weng et al. [28] employed topic modeling to examine peer interaction in online and mobile learning environments within higher education. Their study spanned nearly three decades and utilized sophisticated clustering methods to synthesize diverse research themes. The findings underscored the growing role of digital peer assessment, engagement innovations, and collaborative learning technologies. Notably, the study revealed an increasing emphasis on asynchronous peer feedback mechanisms, anonymity in assessments, and the integration of artificial intelligence in learning management systems. The topic modeling approach not only categorized research trends but also highlighted the interplay between technological advancements and pedagogical strategies.

The integration of topic modeling in education research offers a powerful means of systematically analyzing vast educational datasets. However, current studies face challenges in balancing scalability with semantic precision, addressing linguistic complexities, and ensuring meaningful human validation. To move forward, we propose using topic modeling approaches for detecting more and less effective teaching practices by describing common topics that were mentioned within specific classes and comparing them with existing secondary school curricula.

3 Experimental Design

The corpus described in [11] is used for this study. At first, a dataset of more than 50 video-recorded secondary school lessons was provided by SberObrazovanie LLC (see the Acknowledgments Section), the textual data was obtained for further analysis. Nevertheless, it is important to note that the compiled corpus is not limited to textual data alone. The research team led by E.I. Riekhakainen is developing a multi-level annotation of the corpus of teaching practices, including, in particular, the annotation of pauses [27]. Building on this dataset, SberObrazovanie LLC identifies more effective teachers as a group of people that share certain features: linguistic markers and patterns, metaphors and means to regulate the mental condition of students. In this paper, the leading linguistic feature under study is word representations of LDA topic models.

Subject subcorpora of more and less effective teachers are selected, with each subject subcorpus containing at least two transcribed lessons. Thus, for topics modeling, a dataset with a total volume of about 77,000 words was compiled for topic modeling. The Russian Language (5th, 6th and 7th grades) and Literature (5th grade) are taken as subjects for the experiment as the most representative ones in different levels of secondary education. The second reason for choosing these subjects lies in the homogeneity of lessons of The Russian Language and Literature in Russian schools. The subjects share the same role in fostering national identity and cultural understanding. In future research, it is necessary to develop a topic modeling methodology for lessons of different domains, e.g., biology, mathematics and literature.

The developed Python script is designed to perform topic modeling on the pedagogical dataset using Latent Dirichlet Allocation (LDA). It continues to find traction because it derives meaningful topics from large documents with the least amount of supervision, thus making it useful for exploratory analysis in many fields, ranging from text mining to social sciences [1, 2]. Interpretability, simplicity, and scalability are the reasons for the sustained popularity of LDA in research and applications [23].

To prepare the data for analysis, several preprocessing steps are applied: tokenization, lemmatization using the Stanza library [17], and removal of stopwords. After this, the cleaned and lemmatized text is converted into a bag-of-words format through the creation of a Gensim dictionary [18]. Next, the script performs topic modeling by applying the LDA algorithm to the processed text corpus. It experiments with different numbers of topics, ranging from 3 to 15, to evaluate the optimal configuration. During this process, the model's perplexity and coherence scores are computed for each topic count. Perplexity serves as a measure of how well the model generalizes to unseen data, with lower values signifying better generalization [25]. The coherence score assesses the semantic consistency of topics, with higher values indicating more meaningful and interpretable topics [13]. These evaluation metrics are visualized using Matplotlib, providing a clear indication of the optimal number of topics. Some results are presented in Figs. 1 and 2. Figure 1 shows suggests moderate topic structure in the lessons of less effective teachers, though with signs of topical redundancy. The lack of sharp coherence peaks may indicate topical overlap. Figure 2 demonstrates a clearer peak in coherence and lower perplexity values around 5 topics, it may indicate more stable topics from semantic point of view.

Once the best model is selected based on the highest coherence score, the script outputs the identified topics, displaying their topical terms. The set of words are presented in Table 1. To improve readability, the table is split into subtables by grade, subject and effectiveness parameters, with resultant models highlighting key differences between more and less effective teaching patterns.

Additionally, an interactive visualization is generated using pyLDAvis [22]. It allows for a deeper exploration of topic distributions; an example is presented in Fig. 3. The relatively even spacing and non-overlapping nature of the circles show a set of distinct topics in the discourse of more effective teachers. Another important finding in Fig. 3

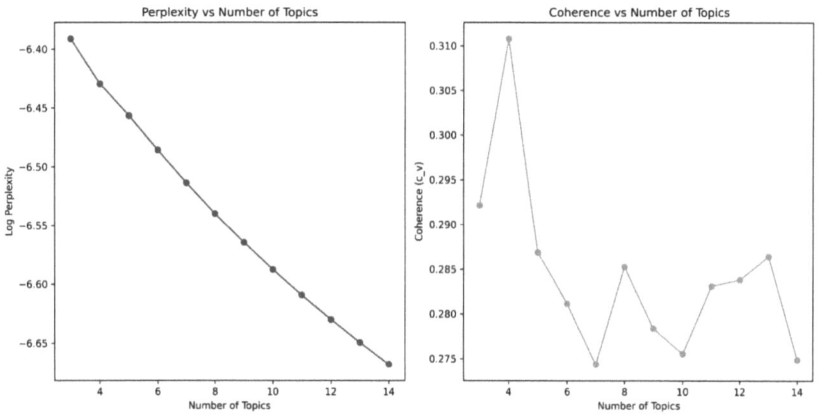

Fig. 1. The perplexity and coherence scores for less effective teachers of the Russian Language (the 7th Grade).

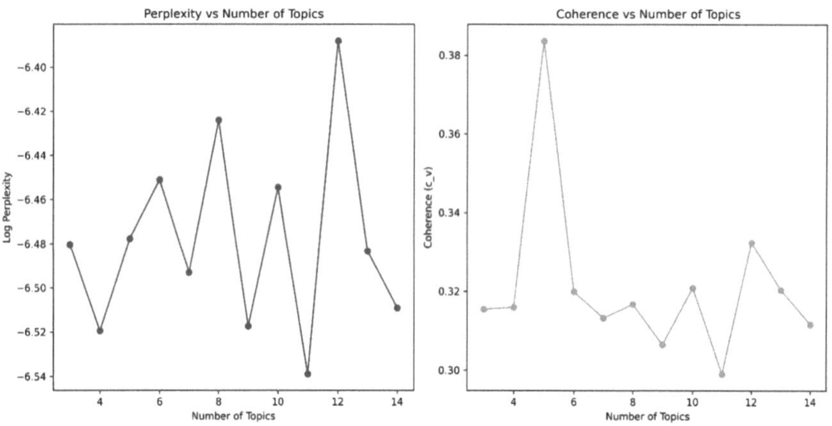

Fig. 2. The perplexity and coherence scores for more effective teachers of the Russian Language (the 5th Grade).

is that the Stanza lemmatizer output has several erroneous forms such as "*padekhoy*" and "*pristavky*". These artifacts stem from limitations in lemmatization accuracy for Russian as a morphologically rich language, especially when there are colloquial words in transcribed data.

Table 1. The resultant sets of topic models for more and less effective teachers.

Grade	Subject	Effectiveness	Topic Number	LDA Topics
5	Literature	More Effective	0	byt' (to be), voyna (war), rebyata (children), mal'chik (boy), stikhotvoreniye (poem), moch' (can), god (year), mal'chishka (little boy), verny (correct)
			1	byt' (to be), Vasyutkiy (Vasyutka), rebyata (children), verny (correct), les (forest), davat' (to give), pravil'no (correctly), ozero (lake), pervy (first)
			2	byt' (to be), otets (father), Vasya (Vasya), khoroshiy (good), moch' (can), vnimanie (attention), schitat' (to consider), chelovek (person), khotet' (to want)
5	Literature	Less Effective	0	byt' (to be), rebyata (children), Nikita (Nikita), khoroshiy (good), moch' (can), rasskaz (story), govorit' (to speak), molodets (well done),
			1	rebyata (children), byt' (to be), god (year), Robinzon (Robinson), Kruzo (Crusoe), ostrov (island), chetyre (four), Defo (Defoe), zhizn' (life)
			2	byt' (to be), rebyata (children), Nikita (Nikita), god (year), Robinzon (Robinson), ostrov (island), Kruzo (Crusoe), moch' (can)
5	Russian	More Effective	0	prilagatel'noye (adjective), byt' (to be), rod (gender), pisat' (to write), okonchaniye (ending), chislo (number), khoroshiy (good), slovo (word), vopros (question)
			1	glagol (verb), byt' (to be), vremya (tense), govorit' (to speak), delat' (to do), proyti (now we know), suffiks (suffix), okonchaniye (ending), forma (form)
			2	prilagatel'noye (adjective), kratkiy (short), khoroshiy (good), pisat' (to write), myagkiy (soft), znak (sign), shipyashchiy (hissing), byt' (to be), vopros (question)

(*continued*)

Table 1. (*continued*)

Grade	Subject	Effectiveness	Topic Number	LDA Topics
			3	slovo (word), byt' (to be), predlozheniye (sentence), koren' (root), khoroshiy (good), rech' (speech), moch' (can), delat' (to do), zvuk (sound)
			4	rod (gender), prilagatel'noye (adjective), okonchaniye (ending), chislo (number), byt' (to be), pisat' (to write), padezh (case), sushchestvitel'ny (noun), sushchestvitel'noye (noun)
6	Russian	More Effective	0	chislitel'ny (numeral), prostoy (simple), byt' (to be), sostavnoy (compound), slovo (word), zapisyvat' (to write down), dva (two), poryadkovy (ordinal), kolichestvenny (quantitative)
			1	byt' (to be), chislitel'ny (numeral), davat' (to give), zapisyvat' (to write down), god (year), padezh (case), sorok (forty), pyat' (five), okonchaniye (ending)
			2	tsely (whole), chislitel'ny (numeral), devyat' (nine), davat' (to give), pribavit' (to add), tri (three), devyanosto (ninety), drobny (fractional), chetyre (four)
			3	pisat' (to write), suffiks (suffix), slovo (word), byt' (to be), khoroshiy (good), okonchaniye (ending), defis (hyphen), slity (merged), narechiy (adverb)
7	Russian	More Effective	0	byt' (to be), predlozheniye (sentence), soyuz (conjunction), chast' (part), prilagatel'noye (adjective), tekst (text), podchinitel'ny (subordinating), vopros (question), khoroshiy (good)
			1	byt' (to be), prilagatel'noye (adjective), tekst (text), stil' (style), tema (theme), olen' (deer), dvadtsat' (twenty), pisat' (to write), moch' (can)

(*continued*)

Table 1. (*continued*)

Grade	Subject	Effectiveness	Topic Number	LDA Topics
			2	soyuz (conjunction), chast' (part), byt' (to be), predlozheniye (sentence), podchinitel'ny (subordinating), vopros (question), khoroshiy (good), rebyata (children), davat' (to give)
5	Russian	Less Effective	0	prilagatel'noye (adjective), byt' (to be), padezh (case), vopros (question), rebyata (children), slovo (word), imya (name), predlozheniye (sentence), delo (matter)
			1	byt' (to be), padezh (case), vopros (question), prilagatel'noye (adjective), rebyata (children), slovo (word), okonchaniye (ending), predlozheniye (sentence), delo (matter)
			2	byt' (to be), slovo (word), vopros (question), padezh (case), rebyata (children), prilagatel'noye (adjective), delo (matter), predlozheniye (sentence), imya (name)
			3	byt' (to be), vopros (question), padezh (case), delo (matter), slovo (word), okonchaniye (ending), rebyata (children), verny (correct), molodets (well done), zapisat' (to write down)
			4	byt' (to be), padezh (case), vopros (question), rebyata (children), slovo (word), okonchaniye (ending), predlozheniye (sentence), delo (matter), davat' (to give)
			5	prilagatel'noye (adjective), byt' (to be), kratkiy (short), rod (gender), predlozheniye (sentence), chestny (honest), bely (white), prekrasny (beautiful), okonchaniye (ending)
			6	prilagatel'noye (adjective), kratkiy (short), predlozheniye (sentence), byt' (to be), rod (gender), bely (white), chislo (number), yasny (clear), prekrasny (beautiful)

(*continued*)

Table 1. (*continued*)

Grade	Subject	Effectiveness	Topic Number	LDA Topics
			7	prilagatel'noye (adjective), rebyata (children), imya (name), rod (gender), pravil'no (correctly), chislo (number), zapyataya (comma), byt' (to be), predlozheniye (sentence)
6	Russian	Less Effective	0	[Low-weight topic: byt' (to be), slovo (word), predlozheniye (sentence), narechiy (adverb), mestoimeniye (pronoun), moch' (can), delat' (to do), pisat' (to write), sleduyushchiy (next)
			1	byt' (to be), slovo (word), sposob (method), narechiy (adverb), moch' (can), suffiks (suffix), sufliksal'ny (suffixal), pristavochny (prefixal)
			2	byt' (to be), narechiy (adverb), khoroshiy (good), predlozheniye (sentence), priznak (feature), dva (two), nayti (to find), slovo (word), chast' (part)
			3	os'minozhkiy (octopus-like), predlozheniye (sentence), bank (bank), byt' (to be), variant (variant), delat' (to do), proveryat' (to check), mestoimeniye (pronoun), stavit' (to put)
			4	byt' (to be), predlozheniye (sentence), narechiy (adverb), nayti (to find), mestoimeniye (pronoun), slovo (word), khoroshiy (good), rod (gender), chislo (number)
			5	predlozheniye (sentence), mestoimeniye (pronoun), voprositel'ny (interrogative), otnositel'ny (relative), slozhny (complex), byt' (to be), khoroshiy (good), pravil'no (correctly), vtoroy (second)
7	Russian	Less Effective	0	byt' (to be), zapyataya (comma), slitny (together), nuzhny (needed), predlozheniye (sentence), pisat' (to write), dva (two), slovo (word), razdel'no (separated), stavit' (to put)

(*continued*)

Table 1. *(continued)*

Grade	Subject	Effectiveness	Topic Number	LDA Topics
			1	predlozheniye (sentence), byt' (to be), slitny (merged), zapyataya (comma), pisat' (to write), deeprichastny (adverbial participle), moch' (can), nuzhny (needed), oborot (construction)
			2	byt' (to be), predlozheniye (sentence), oshibka (mistake), moch' (can), deeprichastny (adverbial participle), smotret' (to look), oborot (construction), nepravil'ny (incorrect), pravil'no (correctly)
			3	byt' (to be), predlozheniye (sentence), oshibka (mistake), zapyataya (comma), nuzhny (needed), moch' (can), pravil'no (correctly), oborot (construction), pisat' (to write)

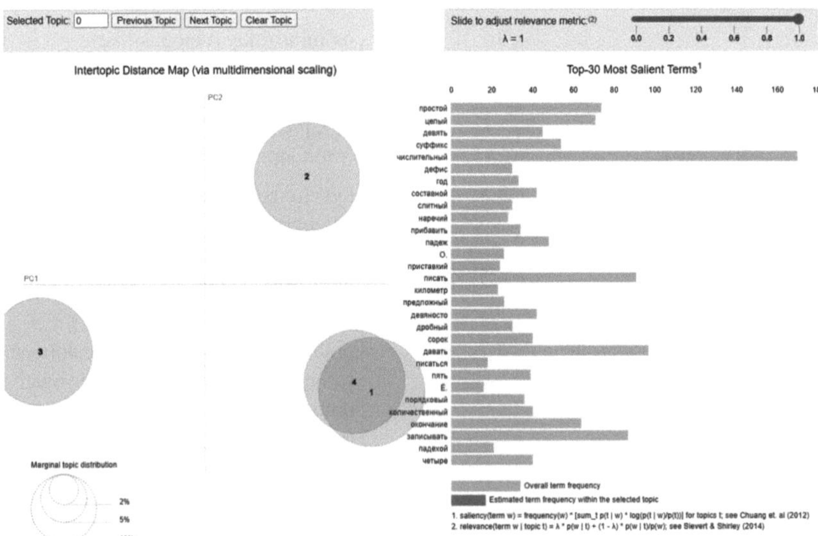

Fig. 3. The visualization of topic models for more effective teachers of the Russian Language (the 6th Grade).

4 Results and Discussion

4.1 The Russian Language, the 5th Grade

The comparative analysis of LDA topic modeling results for more effective (ME) and less effective (LE) Russian language teachers in Grade 5 reveals significant differences in curricular alignment with Federal State Educational Standards (FSES, FGOS in Russian), as outlined in [19] proposed by the Institute for Education Development Strategy of the Russian Academy of Education, a pivotal authority in shaping evidence-based Russian educational policies and conducting advanced research. Although Federal Working Programs (FWP, FRP in Russian) are generally assumed to play a role in operationalizing educational standards by providing recommended content sequencing and timelines, it is FSES that sets these standards and expected outcomes. It is the main reason for referring to FSES in the current paper.

The ME teachers' topics demonstrate structured adherence to FSES thematic planning, particularly in core linguistic domains such as morphology, syntax, and orthography. For instance, high-coherence ME topics like Topic 1 (*"glagol", "vremya", "suffiks"—verb, tense, suffix*) and Topic 4 *("rod", "padezh", "chislo"—gender, case, number)* explicitly reflect FSES objectives for noun declension, verb conjugation, and grammatical gender, mirroring the curriculum's emphasis on systematic progression from phonetics to syntax. Conversely, the LE teacher's topics exhibit fragmentation, with redundant themes such as Topics 0–2 and 4 *("vopros", "padezh", "rebyata"—question, case, children)* lacking specificity and failing to address advanced FSES requirements like complex sentence structures or direct speech punctuation. This divergence may suggest that effective teachers prioritize FSES-mandated content sequencing, whereas less effective ones rely on generic or repetitive terminology.

A critical distinction lies in semantic coherence and pedagogical focus. The ME model's topics, such as Topic 2 (*"kratkiy", "myagkiy", "shipyashchiy"—short, soft, hushing*), align with FSES orthography units on spelling rules and phonetic analysis, while Topic 3 (*"slovo", "rech'", "zvuk"—word, speech, sound*) correlates with text composition and editing standards. These topics reflect a hierarchical structure, progressing from foundational concepts to applied skills. In contrast, the LE model's low-coherence themes, including Topic 3 *("verny", "zapisat'", "molodets"—correct, write down, well done)*, reveal an overemphasis on procedural language and classroom management rather than linguistic content, deviating from FSES's content-driven goals.

Temporal relevance analysis, considering the modeling data was collected at the end of School Term 3 (the end of March in the Russian Federation), underscores the ME teachers' alignment with FSES pacing. By this stage, FSES expects advancement to applied grammar and text analysis, reflected in ME topics like Topic 1 (*"proyti", "form"—now we know, form*) on verb forms and Topic 3 on phonetic and textual linkages. In contrast, LE topics stagnate in basic vocabulary reinforcement (e.g., Topic 7: *"imya", "chislo", "predlozheniye"—name, number, sentence*), failing to address School Term 3 goals such as *"redaktirovaniye teksta" (text editing)* or *"intonatsionnye normy" (intonation norms)*. This misalignment suggests that less effective teachers lag in curricular progression and may leave students underprepared for Year 5 final assessments.

4.2 The Russian Language, the 6th Grade

From the FSES thematic planning document, the curriculum for the sixth-grade Russian language includes topics such as types of speech (narrative, description, reasoning), functional varieties of language (official, scientific), and deep engagement with linguistic structures like nouns, adjectives, numerals, pronouns, and verbs. Activities focus on developing skills in creating and analyzing various text forms, understanding lexical nuances, and applying grammatical norms.

In the LDA topics derived from the more effective teachers' lessons, there is a strong emphasis on numerals, word formation, and syntax. Topical words such as *"chislitel'ny" (numeral)*, *"prostoy" (simple)*, *"sostavnoy" (compound)*, *"slovo" (word)*, and *"suffiks" (suffix)* suggest a focus on understanding structural aspects of language, particularly in relation to numbers and word formation rules. This aligns well with the FSES emphasis on morphological analysis and syntactic functions, indicating that these teachers' lessons are closely following the curriculum goals.

In contrast, the LDA topics from the less effective teachers' lessons (LE) are characterized by more generic and less focused terms. While topical words like *"byt'" (to be)*, *"slovo" (word)*, *"predlozheniye" (sentence)* touch on fundamental aspects of language, they do not reflect the detailed engagement with linguistic categories and structures expected by the FSES standards. This suggests that the lessons might not be as rigorously aligned with the curriculum's targeted learning outcomes.

4.3 The Russian Language, the 7th Grade

The comparative analysis of LDA topic modeling results for effective and less effective 7th grade Russian language teachers reveals nuanced differences in their alignment with the FSES thematic planning. The FSES curriculum emphasizes blocks such as morphology (participles, adverbs), functional language varieties (styles, text analysis), and syntax (conjunctions, sentence structure), alongside practical activities like text creation, error correction, and grammatical application. ME teachers' topics (0, 1, and 2) broadly align with these areas, focusing on conjunctions (*"soyuz", "podchinitel'ny"—conjunction, subordinating*), text analysis (*"tekst", "stil'"—text, style*), and parts of speech (*"prilagatel'noye"—adjective*). However, the lack of specificity in these topics, such as limited emphasis on morphological details (e.g., participles) or stylistic nuances, raises questions about depth.

At the same time, less effective teachers' topics (0, 1, 2, and 3) highlight practical challenges: frequent references to punctuation (*"zapyataya"—comma*), spelling (*"slitny", "razdel'no"—together, separated*), and error analysis (*"oshibka", "nepravil'ny"—mistake, incorrect*), particularly in deeprichastie (*"deeprichastny"—an adverbial formed from a Russian verbal part of speech called 'deeprichastie'*) and sentence construction. These topics reflect a reactive focus on correcting common mistakes, aligning with FSES emphasis on applied skills but suggesting fragmented coverage of the curriculum's broader thematic goals. The presence of error-centric terms in LE topics may indicate prioritization of remedial instruction over holistic thematic mastery, potentially linked to addressing student difficulties observed by the third quarter's end. While both groups touch on FSES elements, ME's alignment with structural components (e.g., conjunctions, text types) versus LE's emphasis on error correction suggests effectiveness correlates not with mere coverage of curriculum topics but with how comprehensively and proactively these topics are integrated into pedagogical practice. ME's approach appears more congruent with FSES integrative goals, whereas less effective teachers focus on troubleshooting specific issues, though relevant, may reflect a less systematic implementation of the planned curriculum.

4.4 Literature, the 5th Grade

In the subcorpus of more effective teachers, the frequent occurrence of terms like *"voyna" (war), "mal'chik" (boy)*, and *"stikhotvoreniye" (poem)* suggests a focus on core literary themes and texts from the curriculum, such as patriotism and childhood narratives. This alignment implies that they offer lessons reflecting structured literary analysis and foster a deeper understanding of literature. Conversely, less effective teachers often mention *"Robinzon" (Robinson)* and *"ostrov" (island)*, indicating an overemphasis on Daniel Defoe's "Robinson Crusoe", a text not directly prescribed by the curriculum, which may lead to deviations from the thematic objectives set by FSES. However, this interpretation (and many of them) should be approached with caution. The presence of topical words such as *Robinzon" (Robinson)* and *"ostrov" (island)* in LDA output does not unambiguously indicate disproportionate instructional focus. It may result from isolated lessons or even model noise.

Furthermore, their reliance on conversational terms such as *"molodets"* (*well done*) and *"govorit'"* (*to speak*) suggests a classroom approach more focused on interaction than literary analysis. Although these results suggest that teacher effectiveness correlates with curriculum adherence, the variety of fiction works in literature may inherently bias the thematic analysis. It is not true for teachers of the Russian Language since students are often offered a limited set of rules to learn. Nevertheless, the resultant models indicate that more effective teachers present a more cohesive and planned thematic approach, closely reflecting curriculum objectives.

5 Conclusion and Future Work

The present study underscores the potential of topic modeling as a methodological tool for examining the relationship between teacher effectiveness and adherence to curriculum planning within lessons. The analyses reveal notable distinctions between the instructional approaches of more and less effective teachers and suggest that pedagogical effectiveness may be linked to the structured integration of curricular topics. To build on these findings, future research should investigate the influence of teacher training programs and the availability of educational resources on lesson coherence and topical alignment. Moreover, expanding the scope of analysis to include other educational levels and subject areas could offer a broader perspective on the relationship between curriculum adherence and teaching effectiveness.

Although basic LDA procedures are used in the paper, it is worth mentioning that future work could explore more advanced topic modeling approaches, such as neural topic models (NTMs) or models with contextual embeddings. According to [30, p. 4720], "...although the marriage between NTMs and language models is still an emerging area, we expect to see more developments in this important direction." In this regard, there is a chance to enhance the current results, as well as depth of pedagogical analysis.

Acknowledgments. The author acknowledges Saint-Petersburg State University for a research project 96806302 (123042000132-6) and SberObrazovanie LLC for a research No. 230712-107-YUL.

References

1. Blei, D.M., Lafferty, J.D.: A correlated topic model of science. Ann. Appl. Stat. **1**, 17–35 (2007)
2. Blei, D.M., Ng, A.Y., Jordan, M.I.: Latent Dirichlet allocation. J. Mach. Learn. Res. **3**, 993–1022 (2003)
3. Buenano-Fernandez, D., González, M., Gil, D., Luján-Mora, S.: Text mining of open-ended questions in self-assessment of university teachers: an LDA topic modeling approach. IEEE Access **8**, 35318–35330 (2020)
4. Chu, K.E., Keikhosrokiani, P., Asl, M.P.: A topic modeling and sentiment analysis model for detection and visualization of themes in literary texts. Pertanika J. Sci. Technol **30**(4), 2535–2561 (2022)
5. Dahllöf, M., Berglund, K. Faces, fights, and families: topic modeling and gendered themes in two corpora of Swedish prose fiction. In: DHN 2019, 4th Digital Humanities in the Nordic Countries 2019, University of Copenhagen, Copenhagen, Denmark, 6–8 March 2019, pp. 92–111 (2019)
6. Ferguson, R.F.: Can student surveys measure teaching quality? Phi Delta Kappan **94**(3), 24–28 (2012)
7. Fischer, C., et al.: Investigating relationships between school context, teacher professional development, teaching practices, and student achievement in response to a nationwide science reform. Teach. Teach. Educ. **72**, 107–121 (2018)
8. Hill, H.C., Umland, K., Litke, E., Kapitula, L.R.: Teacher quality and quality teaching: examining the relationship of a teacher assessment to practice. Am. J. Educ. **118**(4), 489–519 (2012)
9. Ho, A.D., Yu, C.C.: Descriptive statistics for modern test score distributions: skewness, kurtosis, discreteness, and ceiling effects. Educ. Psychol. Measur. **75**(3), 365–388 (2015)
10. Hu, B., Ester, M. Spatial topic modeling in online social media for location recommendation. In: Proceedings of the 7th ACM Conference on Recommender Systems, pp. 25–32 (2013)
11. Mamaev, I. Towards the issue of creating linguistic pedagogical profiles. In: NLPIR '24: Proceedings of the 2024 8th International Conference on Natural Language Processing and Information Retrieval, pp. 225–234 (2025)
12. Miranda, J.P.P., Penecilla, E.M., Gamboa, A.B., Hernandez, H.E., Dianelo, R.F.B., Simpao, L.S.: The shifting classroom: impact of heightened seasonal heat in education through sentiment and topic modeling. Int. J. Eval. Res. Educ. **13**(4), 2269–2278 (2024)
13. Morstatter, F., Liu, H.: In search of coherence and consensus: measuring the interpretability of statistical topics. J. Mach. Learn. Res. **18**(169), 1–32 (2018)
14. Nolasco, D., Oliveira, J.: Subevents detection through topic modeling in social media posts. Futur. Gener. Comput. Syst. **93**, 290–303 (2019)

15. Ozyurt, O.: Empirical research of emerging trends and patterns across the flipped classroom studies using topic modeling. Educ. Inf. Technol. **28**(4), 4335–4362 (2023)
16. Paek, S., Um, T., Kim, N.: Exploring latent topics and international research trends in competency-based education using topic modeling. Educ. Sci. **11**(6) (2021)
17. Qi, P., Zhang, Y., Zhang, Y., Bolton, J., Manning, C. D. Stanza: a python natural language processing toolkit for many human languages. In: Proceedings of the 58th Annual Meeting of the Association for Computational Linguistics: System Demonstrations, pp. 101–108. Association for Computational Linguistics (2020)
18. Řehůřek, R., Sojka, P. Sofware framework for topic modelling with large corpora. In: Proceedings of the LREC 2010 Workshop on New Challenges for NLP Frameworks, pp. 45–50 (2010)
19. Sample Programme of the General Basic Education. The Russian Language (Primernaya rabochaya programma osnovnogo obshchego obrazovaniya. Russkij yazyk), p. 146 (2021)
20. Schoenfeld, A.H.: Classroom observations in theory and practice. ZDM **45**, 607–621 (2013)
21. Sheridan, S.: Discerning pedagogical quality in preschool. Scand. J. Educ. Res. **53**(3), 245–261 (2009)
22. Sievert, C., Shirley, K. LDAvis: a method for visualizing and interpreting topics. In: Proceedings of the Workshop on Interactive Language Learning, Visualization, and Interfaces, pp. 63–70 (2014)
23. Steyvers, M., Griffiths, T. Probabilistic topic models. In: Handbook of Latent Semantic Analysis, pp. 439–460 (2007)
24. Sun, J., Yan, L.: Using topic modeling to understand comments in student evaluations of teaching. Disc. Educ. **2**(1), 1–12 (2023)
25. Vayansky, I., Kumar, S.A.: A review of topic modeling methods. Inf. Syst. **94**, 1–31 (2020)
26. Vijayan, R. Teaching and learning during the COVID-19 pandemic. a topic modeling study. Educ. Sci. **11**(7) (2021)
27. Vinogradova, Y.S., Prokaeva, V.O., Riekhakainen, E.I.: There are different kinds of pauses: multidimensional classification of pauses for annotating corpora of russian spoken speech. Russ. Speech **6**, 7–23 (2023)
28. Weng, A.K.W., Chang, H.Y., Lai, K.K., Lin, Y.B.: Topic modeling on peer interaction in online and mobile learning of higher education. 1993–2022. Educ. Sci. **14**(8) (2024)
29. Yun, E.: Review of trends in physics education research using topic modeling. J. Balt. Sci. Educ. **19**(3), 388–400 (2020)
30. Zhao, H., Phung, D., Huynh, V., Jin, Y., Du, L., Buntine, W. Topic modelling meets deep neural networks: a survey. In: International Joint Conference on Artificial Intelligence, Association for the Advancement of Artificial Intelligence (AAAI), pp. 4713–4720 (2021)
31. Zhu, J.: Text mining and topic modelling in English teaching: extracting key themes and concepts for effective curriculum development. J. Comput. Methods Sci. Eng. 1–13 (2024)

Profiling the Corpus of Tutor Advertising Texts: A Statistical and Linguistic Analysis

Nadezhda Ogorodova(✉)

Baltic State Technical University "VOENMEH" Named After D.F. Ustinov, Street 1st Krasnoarmeyskaya, 1, 190005 St. Petersburg, Russia
marinnett.2004@gmail.com

Abstract. Modern linguistics witnesses a growing interest in the problem of profiling the authors of written texts. At the same time, advertising materials published by tutors have received little scholarly attention. The paper presents the results of studying such texts published on the VK social network. The experimental corpus comprises more than 30,000 tokens. Statistical regularities that demonstrate dependencies between various parameters of texts and tutors' age are supplemented with Python-scatter plots in the Google Colab environment. The analysis of the collected data reveal correlations between age and specific textual features, such as word length and emoticon concentration. For instance, tutors aged 20 to 40 use emoticons more frequently compared to those in other age groups. Perspectives for future research include expanding the study to incorporate patterns related to the number of 'Like' marks on posts, which could provide insights into the popularity of specific advertising content. This approach may contribute to modeling an 'ideal' promotional text in the field of education.

Keywords: linguistic corpus · promotional texts · linguistic profiling

1 Introduction

In the modern digital space, where informational resources are continuously expanding, the process of choosing educational materials becomes increasingly complex. This presents additional challenges for educators who seek to attract the attention of potential students to their courses. Despite the rise of multimedia formats, text remains an important tool for communication and promotion of educational services. For consumers, text serves as a source of information about the characteristics and benefits of the offered services, while for educators, it provides an opportunity to present their services in the most favorable light. Linguistic trends change rapidly due to the dynamic nature of language itself. By observing the development of educational products and analyzing the lexical and stylistic features of various teaching professionals, it is possible to identify several linguistic characteristics that influence the perception and evaluation of the materials being offered.

The sample size enables a more comprehensive analysis of the linguistic features present in tutor advertising texts, offering deeper insights into the language used by

M. Bakaev et al. (Eds.): IMS 2025, CCIS 2671, pp. 18–34, 2026.
https://doi.org/10.1007/978-3-032-04958-2_2

educators from different backgrounds. This expansion allows for a more nuanced understanding of the factors that influence the effectiveness of educational advertising, making the findings more reliable and applicable to a wider range of contexts.

2 Related Works

In the field of linguistic profiling, several studies have examined the characteristics and structures of various text types, including online personalities, advertisements, and genre-specific texts. However, few studies have focused on the profiling of educational advertising texts, particularly those created by tutors or educators.

For example, some authors explore the broader domain of profiling internet users' language, but do not address the specifics of pedagogical or advertising texts [1]. Similarly, others analyze genre differences [2], yet do not focus on educational advertising content. Other studies explore advertising language but do not address the particularities of educational advertising or the creation of a corpus centered around tutors' texts [3, 4] These works contribute significantly to the field of linguistic profiling but do not cover the specific context of pedagogical texts aimed at attracting potential students. Therefore, my research represents a novel contribution by focusing on the linguistic characteristics of advertising texts produced by tutors and educators, thus providing fresh insights into the language of educational marketing.

The study by Vinogradova, Prokaeva, and Riekhakaynen [5] provides a corpus-based analysis of teachers' spoken discourse, focusing on the classification and functions of pauses. The researchers examined speech samples from history lessons, identifying both universal and speaker-specific patterns of hesitation, rhythmic, and emphatic pauses. The study highlights the complexity of categorizing teachers' speech as either fully prepared or spontaneous, as it exhibits characteristics of both. While this research significantly contributes to the understanding of spoken educational discourse, it does not address the linguistic features of written texts used for advertising educational services. The focus remains on oral communication within a classroom setting rather than the promotional discourse employed by tutors. In contrast, the present study applies a corpus-based approach to analyzing written tutor advertisements. By examining linguistic variations across different age groups, it extends the field of educational discourse analysis and offers insights into the relationship between language use and the professional self-presentation of educators.

Gabidullina [6] examines evaluative statements in pedagogical discourse, analyzing their linguistic, psychological, and pedagogical aspects. The study specifically focuses on speech genres such as praise and criticism, highlighting their role in teacher-student communication. The findings contribute to a broader understanding of how teachers use language to influence students' motivation and behavior. Although this research provides valuable insights into the communicative strategies of educators, it does not explore the advertising discourse of tutors. The focus remains on interpersonal classroom interactions rather than self-promotional language. In contrast, the present study investigates how evaluative language is employed in tutor advertisements, particularly in different age groups. By analyzing linguistic markers of persuasion and authority, it expands the discussion on evaluative statements beyond the classroom, offering a new perspective on their function in professional self-presentation.

Pochebutova's research examines expressive syntactic constructions in the speech of modern teachers [7]. The study is based on the linguistic analysis of two educators from Taganrog, both possessing over twenty years of experience, higher education, and a PhD in philology. Their speech is characterized by a high frequency of question-answer structures (35.3%), which serve as a tool for engaging students, facilitating material comprehension, and maintaining interest in educational topics. These constructions focus students' attention on key issues, creating a foundation for better assimilation of subsequent explanations. Additionally, expressive syntactic structures contribute to the segmentation of speech, enhancing emotional appeal and emphasizing significant elements. The use of such constructions in pedagogical discourse reflects a high level of linguistic proficiency and professional communicative competence. While this study provides insights into the interactive nature of teachers' speech in the classroom, it does not address linguistic strategies in advertising discourse. The present research, however, extends the focus to how tutors employ similar syntactic techniques in self-promotional texts, exploring whether expressive syntax plays a role in attracting potential students.

The study conducted by Andewi and Waziana (2019) examines speech acts in classroom interaction, focusing on the types and functions of speech acts used by teachers during the teaching and learning process [8]. Using a qualitative approach, the research analyzes the speech of an English teacher from SMAN 1 Kalirejo, with data collected through recordings and processed through three analytical stages: data reduction, data display, and conclusion drawing. The findings indicate that directive speech acts dominate the teacher's discourse, accounting for 71.8% of all recorded utterances. In contrast, representative speech acts constitute 21.2%, expressive speech acts 3.8%, and commissive speech acts only 3.2%. The study further classifies directive speech acts into categories such as need statements, bald imperatives, embedded imperatives, permission directives, and question directives. These results highlight the central role of directive speech acts in structuring classroom communication, emphasizing teachers' authority, instructional control, and engagement strategies. While this research provides valuable insights into teacher-student interactions within classroom discourse, it does not extend its scope to non-classroom contexts, such as self-promotional materials. The current study, in contrast, explores whether similar directive strategies appear in tutors' advertising texts and how such linguistic features influence audience engagement and perception.

The analysis of existing papers demonstrates that extensive research has been conducted on pedagogical discourse, including studies on teachers' speech characteristics, evaluative statements, expressive syntax, and speech acts in classroom interactions. These works provide valuable insights into how teachers communicate within educational settings, revealing patterns of linguistic structuring, engagement strategies, and discourse effectiveness. Additionally, research on advertising texts has explored their linguistic and structural features, offering a foundation for understanding persuasive and promotional language. However, a noticeable gap remains in the study of peripheral texts produced by educators—particularly in self-promotional and advertising contexts. While pedagogical discourse and advertising discourse have been examined separately, little research has been dedicated to the intersection of these two domains, specifically focusing on how tutors construct their online advertisements to attract students.

This study aims to bridge that gap by analyzing the linguistic strategies employed in tutor advertisements, thereby contributing to a more comprehensive understanding of educators' language use beyond traditional classroom and academic settings.

3 Data Collection

The process of data collection for the research corpus was multifaceted and involved several stages. Initially, it was essential to define specific criteria for selecting educator profiles and their corresponding texts. These criteria were based on the relevance, authenticity, and quality of the content, ensuring that only those profiles that met particular conditions were included in the study. Once the selection criteria were established, the next step involved conducting a comprehensive search for educator profiles that fit the predefined parameters. This search was carried out by manually exploring social media platforms, specifically targeting educational content, and identifying profiles that were active in posting educational materials.

Following the identification of suitable profiles, the texts associated with these profiles were gathered. The selected texts were carefully examined to ensure they met the established requirements, such as content length and topical relevance. Afterward, the texts were systematically organized and collected in two formats for ease of further analysis: plain text files (TXT) and structured spreadsheets (XLSX). This dual-format approach facilitated efficient data handling and analysis, providing a robust foundation for subsequent linguistic and statistical profiling.

The corpus was manually collected from the VK social network. To find tutor advertisements, various search phrases were used that were characteristic of such posts, such as "open for lessons," "message to sign up," or simply subject names related to tutoring services. I searched both through the general search and within groups where tutors post their advertisements. The criteria for the texts were as follows:

- Language: Only Russian-language texts were included.
- Length: Advertisements had to be longer than 100 characters to ensure sufficient linguistic content for analysis.

As for the selection of tutor profiles, a key challenge in this study was determining authorship. Over recent years, social media groups have become increasingly popular for advertising educational materials, which complicates the identification of the individual tutor as the author due to the involvement of marketing teams. Therefore, this research focused exclusively on personal tutor profiles, excluding group pages.

Additionally, the profiles were evaluated subjectively for activity. Only those that had been active for at least five years, with regular and varied posts, were included. For instance, a profile that only posted about lesson schedules and prices once every three months was excluded, as the lack of textual diversity made it unsuitable for identifying linguistic trends.

Once the necessary data was collected in two formats, a document processing stage was undertaken. Specifically, five posts from a single educator were combined into one TXT file, and subsequently, all 15 files were processed through an electronic environment. Profiling-UD is a linguistic processor capable of analyzing texts and identifying their linguistic features [9]. The automated processing of texts is carried out on the platform of the electronic environment, enabling efficient analysis of large volumes of data. After the data was uploaded, users could access the accompanying legend, which includes a wide range of categories for text description. However, for the purposes of this study, it was decided to focus on the most relevant and informative categories, ensuring a more in-depth understanding of the linguistic characteristics of the analyzed materials (Table 1).

Table 1. Statistics of the corpus.

Feature	Value
Number of tutors observed	40
Number of texts by each of the author	5
Total number of texts	200
Words in total	31,651
Average length of a text in words	160
Number of tutors observed	40

4 Statistical and Linguistic Methods

For the analysis of the corpus, no manual processing was done. Instead, the corpus was analyzed using the Profiling-UD linguistic processor. This tool automatically extracts a wide range of linguistic features from various levels of annotation, capturing numerous linguistic phenomena (Table 2).

Table 2. Key areas

Characteristics	Explanation
Raw Text Properties	This feature analyzes basic textual characteristics, such as the total word count, sentence length, and the occurrence of punctuation marks. It provides an initial overview of the text's structure
Lexical Variety	Lexical variety refers to the range and diversity of vocabulary used within the text. This feature measures how many unique words (types) appear in relation to the total number of words (tokens) in the corpus. Higher lexical variety indicates a broader and more diverse vocabulary, which can reflect the stylistic richness of the text

(continued)

Table 2. (*continued*)

Characteristics	Explanation
Morphosyntactic Information	This component provides information about the morphological and syntactic structure of words and sentences. It includes part-of-speech (POS) tagging, which identifies whether a word is a noun, verb, adjective, etc.
Verbal Predicate Structure	This feature focuses on the syntactic role and structure of verbs in the sentences. It identifies verbal predicates and their arguments. Understanding the verbal predicate structure is key to analyzing sentence complexity and sentence types (declarative, interrogative, imperative, etc.)
Global and Local Parse Tree Structures	This feature involves the syntactic parsing of sentences. A parse tree is a hierarchical representation of the syntactic structure of a sentence, showing how different words are related to one another through grammatical rules. Global parse tree structure examines the overall syntactic structure of the sentence, while local parse tree structures focus on specific phrases or substructures within a sentence
Syntactic Relations	Syntactic relations refer to the grammatical connections between words in a sentence
Use of Subordination	This feature analyzes the use of subordinate clauses in the corpus. Subordination refers to the use of dependent clauses that are connected to a main clause by conjunctions or relative pronouns

During the data analysis process, it became apparent that not all available categories in the dataset could serve as appropriate criteria for further analysis. Based on the conducted study, it was decided to focus on those characteristics that have already proven to be significant in the context of crafting persuasive texts.

The selected categories must meet several key requirements, with the primary importance being their relevance to the specific sample, ensuring the informativeness of each criterion. After a thorough review of the available criteria in the legend and their comparative analysis, several parameters were identified as most significant: sentence count; word count; word length; word form and lemma diversity; noun count; numeral count; symbol saturation; and lexical density [10].

Python libraries—matplotlib, pandas, and numpy—were used for data visualization and analysis in Google Colab. Graphs were created with matplotlib to show how tutor characteristics, such as age, relate to text complexity. Data was managed with pandas, allowing for filtering and analysis of features like sentence count. Numerical calculations and statistical analysis were performed using numpy. Google Colab was used to process data efficiently and adjust the analysis in real time.

The generated graphs, such as the one displaying the relationship between tutor age and sentence count, served as useful tools in interpreting the linguistic data. They enhanced the overall understanding of the corpus, providing insights into the textual complexity and stylistic features present across the collected advertisements.

5 Results and Discussions

While this study has provided valuable insights into the linguistic features of tutor advertisements, it is important to recognize its limitations. The research was focused on the textual analysis of tutor advertisements, but it did not take into account the influence of other factors such as the visual design of advertisements or the role of social media algorithms in promoting certain content.

5.1 Sentence Count and Age Correlation

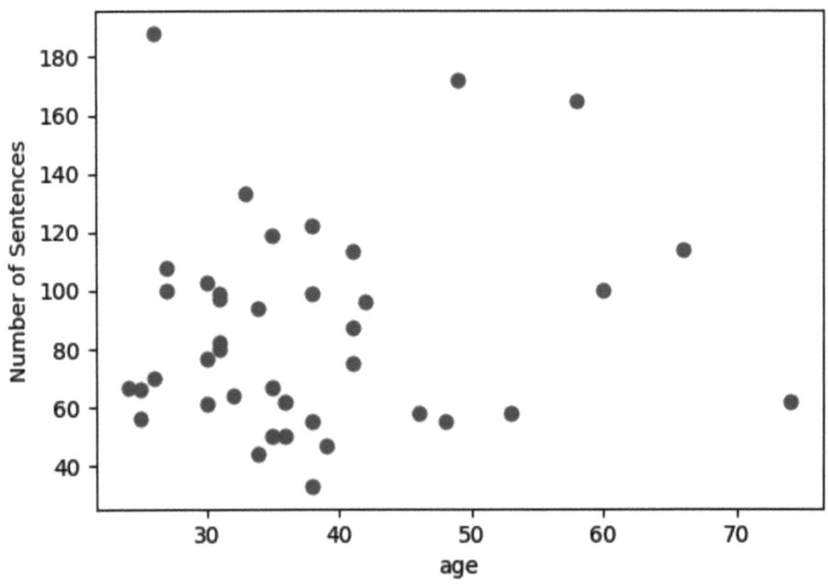

Fig. 1. The dependence of the number of sentences on age.

The analysis of sentence count across tutor advertisements, as can be seen in the graph, revealed a positive correlation with age. Specifically, when tutors are older, they tend to write longer advertisements with more sentences. This trend suggests that experienced tutors provide more detailed texts because they need to convey more information to potential clients (Fig. 1).

Most tutors, regardless of age, write advertisements that contain between 12 and 24 sentences. This length is common because it includes enough detail but does not overwhelm the reader. It also helps balance informativeness and readability [11]. The fact that many tutors follow this pattern may indicate their shared understanding of the optimal advertisement length. They likely aim to provide clear and concise information while keeping the text engaging.

5.2 Word Count Variation

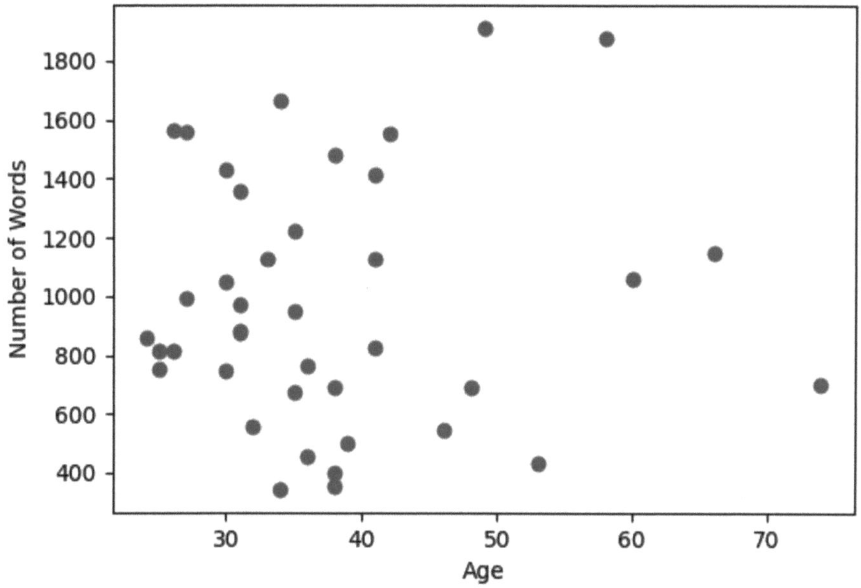

Fig. 2. The dependence of the number of words on age.

The word count of tutor advertisements demonstrates significant variability, ranging from 200 to 360 words per text. This wide range suggests that tutors adapt the length of their advertisements depending on the amount of information they wish to convey and their communication style (Fig. 2).

Interestingly, the highest word counts were observed among tutors aged 50 and 60. This may indicate a tendency for older tutors to provide more comprehensive descriptions of their services, possibly reflecting their greater experience or a preference for offering detailed insights into their teaching methods, qualifications, and success rates. The extended length of their texts could also serve to reassure potential clients, offering more persuasive and convincing arguments.

5.3 Word Length

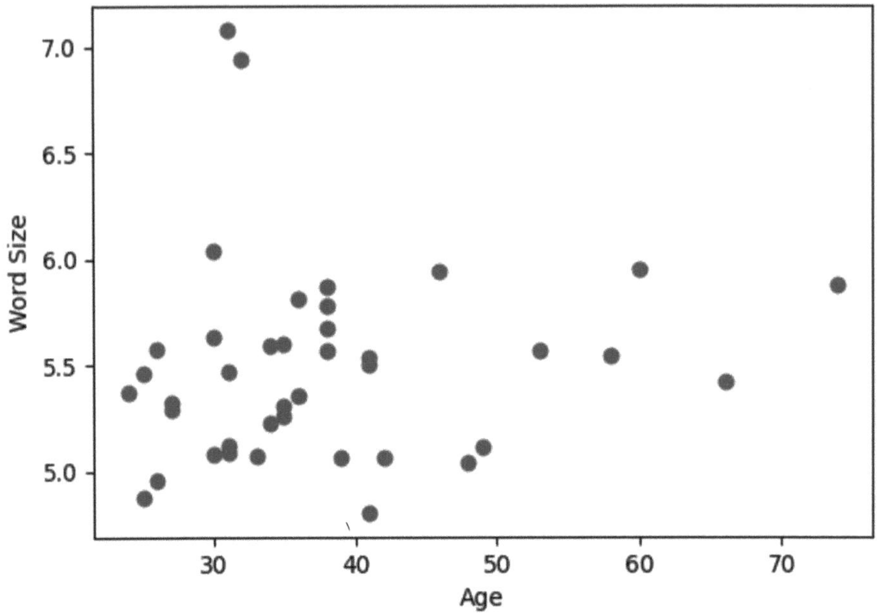

Fig. 3. The dependence of word size on age

The average word length across all tutor advertisements ranges from 5 to 6 characters, with a few examples extending to 7 to 7.5 characters. The concept of "long" words, however, does not have a universally agreed-upon definition and cannot be strictly quantified [12]. Despite this, words that are considered "long" are often those consisting of up to four morphemes and/or syllables. These words typically tend to be more complex and may reflect a higher level of linguistic sophistication or a more formal tone in the tutor's communication (Fig. 3).

This distribution suggests that tutors generally use words of average length, balancing clarity and expressiveness in their advertisements. The few occurrences of longer words may reflect an attempt to convey professionalism or to use specific terminology that resonates with the target audience.

For example, in the sentence *«Khochu sdelat' etu temu prostoi i ponjatnoi dlja rebat 👶»* (*id34280154*), (*I want to make this topic simple and understandable for the kids* 👶), the words are of average length, using simple, accessible language. The use of an emoji helps to add an informal and friendly tone, which is characteristic of a more relaxed pedagogical style. On the other hand, the sentence *«Do vstrechi na Predbannike* ❤️ 🧖 🌿 *P.S. OGE—eto zharko = BANJA»* (*id556912405*), (*See you in the 'Pre-Banya'* ❤️ 🧖 🌿 *P.S. The OGE is hot = BATH*), introduces more specialized terms and playful references (like 'Pre-Banya'), showcasing a blend of creativity and informality. Here, the inclusion of both emojis and an informal phrase likely aims to engage the target audience in a more casual, approachable manner, which may appeal to younger learners.

These examples reinforce the notion that tutors strike a balance between professional language and relatable, engaging content designed to attract students. While most words remain simple and concise, occasional use of longer or more creative expressions, often accompanied by emojis, helps to establish a connection with the audience in a manner that is both engaging and accessible.

5.4 Noun Count

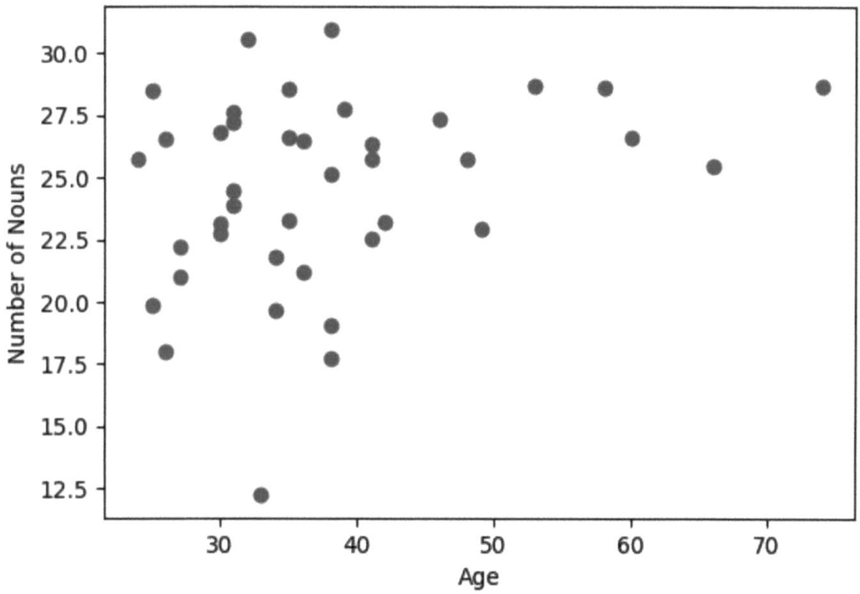

Fig. 4. The depenence of the number of nouns on age

The majority of tutor advertisements contain more than three nouns per text, indicating a strong emphasis on naming objects, subjects, and concepts related to the tutoring services [13]. The highest noun counts are observed in texts with an average of six nouns, which reflects a more detailed and specific approach to describing the tutor's offerings (Fig. 4).

This tendency suggests that tutors often prioritize clarity and specificity, using nouns to outline the subjects taught, the qualifications of the tutor, and the overall educational experience. The higher noun count may also indicate an effort to establish authority and expertise by clearly defining key concepts and services offered.

For example, in the sentence *Kak uchitel' (osobenno v gruppakh malyshej) moja radost' - kogda rebenok vdrug neozhidanno umestno ispol'zoval frazu, kotoruju my uchili v odnom kontekste, na sovsem drugoj kontekst* (*id30233*), *As a teacher (especially in groups of little ones), my joy is when a child suddenly and appropriately uses a phrase we learned in one context, in a completely different context*, the use of nouns like *uchitel'* (*teacher*), *gruppy malyshej* (*groups of little ones*), *radost'* (*joy*), and *fraza* (*phrase*) emphasizes the subject matter, the role of the teacher, and the educational outcomes. These nouns reflect the importance of teaching and the tutor's connection to the students' learning process.

The inclusion of such specific nouns highlights the tutor's expertise and their commitment to tangible educational goals. In addition, the example reveals an emphasis on the student's learning journey, helping to build a clear, relatable image of what is being taught and how it impacts the learner.

5.5 Numeral Count

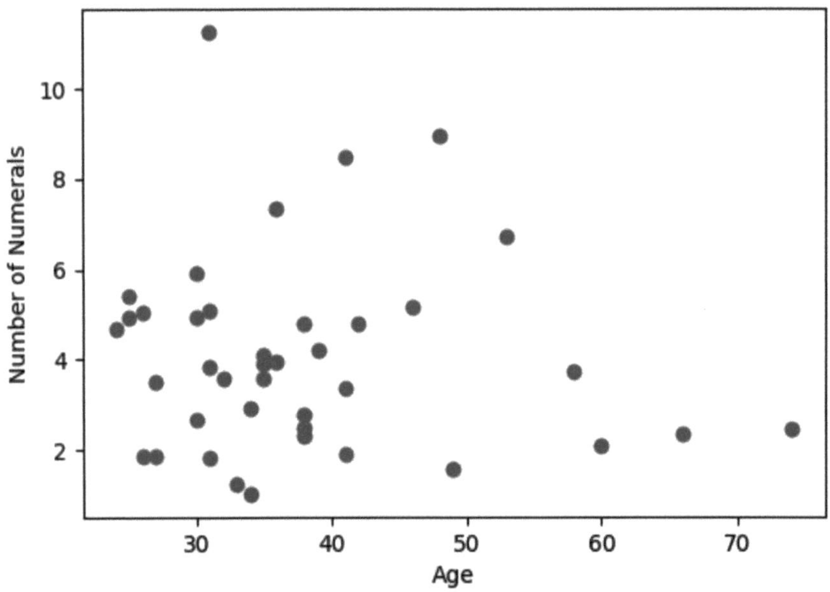

Fig. 5. The dependence of the number of numerals on age

The use of numerals in tutor advertisements decreases with age. Tutors in the age group between 35 and 50 tend to use numerals more frequently, with an average of over 8 numerals per text. This increase may be attributed to the younger tutors' tendency to provide specific numerical information related to their teaching methods, pricing, or success rates (Fig. 5).

However, a notable decline in numeral usage occurs among tutors aged 50 and above, with an average of fewer than 4 numerals per 5 texts. This shift may reflect a change in how older tutors present their services, focusing less on quantitative data and more on qualitative descriptions, which could be associated with their experience and established reputation.

For instance, in the advertisement example: *Novogodnie master-klassy "ROSPIS' GIPSOVOJ FIGURY" SUBBOTA 13.00–14.00 15.00–16.00 17.00–18.00 Dlitel'nost': 60 minut Stoimost': 300 rub.* (id180735744), *New Year's master classes 'PAINTING A PLASTER FIGURE' SATURDAY 13:00–14:00 15:00–16:00 17:00–18:00 Duration: 60 min Cost: 300 rubles*, the frequent use of numerals such as "13.00," "14.00," "60," and "300" emphasizes the key logistical and pricing details of the class. These numerals serve to present clear, concrete information, aiming to attract potential customers with specific and easily understandable data.

The prevalence of numerals in this example highlights the direct and pragmatic approach typical of younger tutors who focus on quantifiable elements of their services. This use of numerals contrasts with the style of older tutors who might opt for more descriptive, less data-heavy language in their advertisements.

5.6 Emoji Usage and Text Multimodality

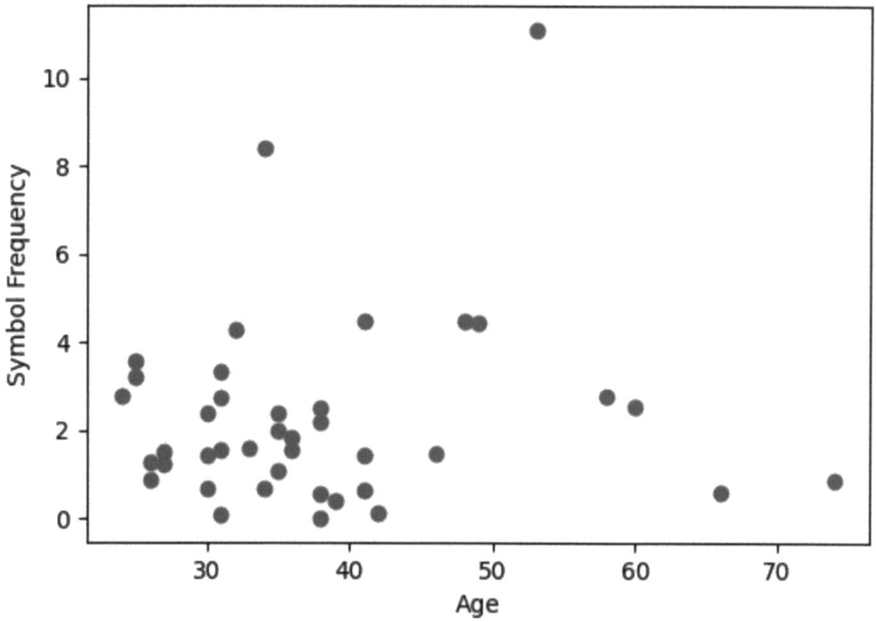

Fig. 6. The dependence of symbol frequency on age

The use of emojis in tutor advertisements is fairly consistent across all age groups. Tutors employ between 0 and 4 emojis per 5 texts on average, indicating a moderate and balanced approach to incorporating visual elements into their advertisements. However, there are instances where tutors, particularly those aged 50, use more than 10 emojis in their texts. This increased use of emojis suggests a more pronounced attempt to engage the audience through multimodal communication, where the visual elements (emojis) complement the verbal text to enhance emotional appeal and readability (Fig. 6).

or instance, in the advertisement example: *Sdelaj repost etogo posta v storis i ja otpravlju tebe v podarok 🎁chek-list po samostojatel'noj podgotovke k EGE 2025, kotoryj pomozhet tebe splanirovat' svoju rabotu i sdat' ekzamen na vysokij ball 💯(id62270628), Repost this post in your stories and I'll send you as a gift 🎁 a check-list for self-preparation for the 2025 Unified State Exam, which will help you plan your work and score high 💯*, the use of emojis like 🎁and 💯adds a playful, personal, and emotionally engaging element to the text.

Emojis, as non-verbal cues, help create a more dynamic and accessible representation of information, adding nuance to the textual content and allowing the message to resonate more strongly with the audience [14]. This multimodal approach not only adds an emotional dimension to the text but also serves as a means to break the monotony of written language, potentially making the advertisement more attractive and memorable to potential clients. The inclusion of visual elements reinforces the idea of a gift and success, making the text feel more engaging and appealing.

5.7 Content vs. Function Words: Lexical Density

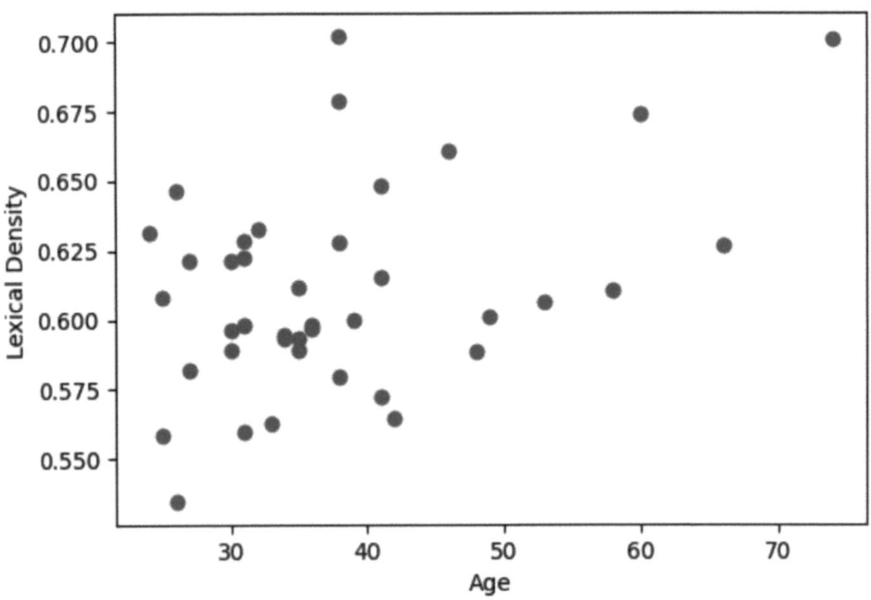

Fig. 7. The dependence of lexical density on age

The ratio of content words to function words, often referred to as lexical density, plays a crucial role in identifying the informative value of the text. Content words, which carry the core meaning of a sentence, are key in conveying the essential information about the tutor's services. In contrast, function words, such as articles, prepositions, and conjunctions, are used primarily for syntactic structure and are critical for analyzing the author's style within the framework of stylometry (Fig. 7).

Across all age groups, content words occupy a larger proportion of the text compared to function words, as tutors aim for maximum information density. This trend aligns with the general principle in educational marketing, where texts designed to promote services tend to maximize informativeness to appeal to potential clients. In the context of tutor advertisements, the goal is to ensure the text is as informative as possible, with an ideal approach approaching 100% lexical density.

Interestingly, the lexical density of the texts increases with age, rising from 0.55 to 0.7 on average. This suggests that older tutors tend to use a higher proportion of content words, reflecting a more concise and information-rich style. It may also indicate a growing confidence in their ability to deliver clear and direct messages to potential clients, further supporting the idea of maximizing the informational content of the advertisements.

For instance, the advertisement by a tutor aged 66 states: *V nojabre 2022 goda ko mne obratilsja uchenik 11 klassa po podgotovke k EGE. Posle pervogo zanjatija on podelilsja s mamoj vpechatleniem ot pervogo zanjatija. I uzhe na sledujushchij den', po pros'be mamy, stala zanimat'sja s mladsjim bratom, uchenikom 8 klassa. So slov mal'chika, problema byla v geometrii. Posle zanjatij uspevaemost' povysilas' s 3,0 do 3,4 po algebre i geometrii. V etom godu prodolzhim gotovit'sja k OGE.* (*id164115944*), *In November 2022, an 11th-grade student approached me for preparation for the Unified State Exam. After the first lesson, he shared his impression with his mother. The very next day, at his mother's request, I started tutoring his younger brother, an 8th-grade student. According to the boy, the problem was with geometry. After the lessons, his grades improved from 3.0 to 3.4 in algebra and geometry. This year, we will continue preparing for the OGE.*, This example clearly demonstrates the higher lexical density typical of older tutors. The advertisement focuses on concrete details, such as the specific academic achievements of the student, improvements in grades, and the subjects being taught. The use of technical terms like *EGE* (*Unified State Exam*), *algebra* (*algebra*), and *geometrija* (*geometry*) not only enhances the informational value but also contributes to the authoritative tone of the text. The inclusion of exact numbers and tangible outcomes (improvement from 3.0 to 3.4) reflects the tutor's intent to provide potential clients with clear, measurable evidence of success, showcasing their professional competence.

In contrast, a 26-year-old tutor's advertisement states: *Zadanija na audirovanie, grammatiku, chtenie, pis'mo v zavisimosti ot klassa. Kogda gotovit'sja? Eshchjo vchera* 😨 *Nu a esli ser'jozno, to zdes' zavisit ot iskhodnogo urovnja uchenika.* (*id289750441*), *Tasks for listening, grammar, reading, and writing depending on the grade level. When to start preparing? Yesterday* 😨 *Well, seriously, it depends on the student's initial level.*

This advertisement exhibits a lower lexical density, as it is less focused on providing specific academic information and more on creating a casual, engaging tone. The use of emoticons, such as the shocked face 😨, adds a sense of informality and approachability. The vocabulary here is primarily composed of function words, such as "когда" (when), "зависит" (depends), and "уровень" (level), which serve to keep the text fluid and conversational. Although this style may attract a broader audience, it lacks the detailed, evidence-based information that the older tutor's advertisement provides. The text here does not emphasize tangible results or specific learning outcomes but instead invites the reader to engage with a more playful and less formal tone.

These examples illustrate the variation in lexical density between younger and older tutors. While older tutors tend to adopt a more formal and informative approach with a focus on measurable achievements and specific content, younger tutors often use more informal language and expressions to create a friendly, approachable tone. This distinction highlights the different ways in which tutors tailor their advertisements to appeal to potential clients, with older tutors placing a greater emphasis on authority, credibility, and evidence of success, while younger tutors prioritize engagement, relatability, and accessibility.

6 Conclusion

The primary objective of this research was to examine the linguistic features of texts written by tutors from various age groups, and to explore how these features correlate with the tutors' age. Based on the analysis of the tutor advertisements, the following key linguistic features were found to be the most prominent.

Sentence Count: The number of sentences in the tutors' texts showed a noticeable increase with age. Tutors aged 35 and older tended to use longer texts, with the average sentence count rising from 12 to 24 sentences. This trend indicates that older tutors often provide more detailed and structured descriptions of their teaching services. The use of longer sentences may suggest a preference for clarity and thoroughness, as more experienced tutors often seek to communicate the depth of their expertise and create a professional impression. Moreover, older tutors might be more confident in elaborating on their offerings, making their advertisements more informative for potential clients. This higher sentence count is not merely a stylistic choice but reflects the tutors' experience in articulating their knowledge in a well-organized manner, demonstrating their ability to engage and inform prospective students.

Noun Usage: The analysis showed that the majority of tutor advertisements contained more than three nouns per text, with some texts reaching an average of six nouns. This suggests that tutors, particularly those in older age groups, place a strong emphasis on naming objects, subjects, and concepts relevant to their services. Nouns, in this context, are employed to define specific subjects (e.g., "math," "English," "history") or concepts (e.g., "methodology," "approach," "technique") that help structure the message and communicate the tutor's qualifications. Older tutors, in particular, tend to use more nouns to establish authority and expertise. This lexical choice serves a dual purpose: it not only clarifies what the tutor teaches but also strengthens the perceived professionalism and specificity of the advertisement. The consistent use of nouns helps shape a clear and precise image of the tutor's offerings, ensuring that prospective clients fully understand what is being proposed.

Lexical Density: Lexical density, defined as the ratio of content words (nouns, verbs, adjectives, adverbs) to function words (prepositions, articles, conjunctions), increased with age, rising from 0.55 to 0.7 on average. This higher lexical density in older tutors' texts suggests that they tend to use a greater proportion of content words in their advertisements. This pattern reflects a more information-dense style, where every word serves a functional role in delivering clear and substantive information. The increased lexical density may indicate that older tutors have developed a style focused on delivering direct and concise information to potential clients. It reflects a greater emphasis on providing value in the form of useful, clear content. The shift towards higher lexical density may also indicate greater confidence in the ability to convey information effectively, relying more on substantial content rather than filler words or vague language.

In addition to these linguistic features, it is essential to consider thematic and pragmatic aspects of the texts – such as rhetorical strategies, genre structure, and forms of audience engagement – to fully understand the communicative function of advertising discourse. For instance, how tutors appeal to credibility (ethos), structure their messages to emphasize benefits, or directly address prospective students can significantly affect the persuasiveness and accessibility of their advertisements. These dimensions open new directions for analysis and can be crucial in interpreting how language choices function within the broader context of tutor-client interaction. This perspective will be valuable in future research to further deepen the understanding of tutor advertisement effectiveness.

To deepen the research, it is also worth considering the use of ANOVA (Analysis of Variance) for feature analysis. This statistical method can help identify significant differences in linguistic features across age groups with greater precision. In future stages of this research, I intend to apply ANOVA to explore more nuanced patterns in the data, strengthening the reliability of the conclusions and enabling a more robust quantitative interpretation.

Further studies could investigate how multimodal elements, such as images or video content, interact with the linguistic features of tutor advertisements to influence their effectiveness. In addition, future research could expand the scope of analysis by incorporating data on engagement metrics such as likes, shares, and comments, as well as examining how these factors correlate with the linguistic features identified in the current study. By analyzing user feedback, researchers could gain a better understanding of what makes certain tutor advertisements more popular or successful in attracting students. This would allow for the modeling of an "ideal" tutor advertisement based on both linguistic features and audience engagement. Furthermore, it would be beneficial to consider additional variables, such as the tutors' subject areas, teaching methods, and pricing strategies, to explore how these factors influence language use in advertisements. This broader approach could provide a more comprehensive understanding of the marketing strategies that are most effective in the educational field.

The practical implications of this study are significant for understanding the linguistic features that influence the effectiveness of tutor advertisements. By analyzing how different age groups use language, this research provides insights into how tutors can tailor their advertisements to be more effective in attracting potential clients. For instance, the findings suggest that older tutors tend to use more detailed and structured texts, which may be more appealing to clients looking for experienced and authoritative figures. On the other hand, younger tutors, who may rely more on numerical data or a less formal tone, might appeal to clients who prioritize a more approachable or results-oriented teaching style.

These insights are valuable for educational marketers and platform developers, enabling them to refine the presentation of tutoring services based on linguistic patterns associated with age. By integrating such knowledge into marketing strategies, platforms can optimize the impact of tutor advertisements, ensuring that they align with the preferences and expectations of their target audiences. Furthermore, the findings may assist in the development of personalized marketing campaigns, helping tutors refine their approach to attract specific student demographics.

References

1. Potapova, R.K., Potapov, V.V., Nefedova, K.A.: Lingvisticheskoe profilirovanie internet-lichnosti [Linguistic profiling of an internet personality]. Vestnik Moskovskogo gosudarstvennogo lingvisticheskogo universiteta. Gumanitarnye nauki **6**(887), 78–83 (2024)
2. Solnyshkina, M.I., Kupriyanov, R.V., Shoeva, G.N.: Linguistic profiling of text genres: adventure stories vs. textbooks: research result. Theor. Appl. Linguist. **10**(1), 115–132 (2024). https://doi.org/10.18413/2313-8912-2024-10-1-0-7
3. Litvinova, A. P.: Lingvisticheskie osobennosti reklamnykh tekstov: perevod i sokhranenie pragmaticheskogo komponenta. [Linguistic features of advertising texts: translation and preservation pragmatic component]. Aktual'nye voprosy sovremennoi nauki (4–2), 62–71 (2008)
4. P'yadisheva, T.G.: Advertising language: structural features of advertising texts. Neofilologiia **8**(29), 154–162 (2022)
5. Vinogradova, Yu.S., Prokaeva, V.O., Riekhakaynen, E.I.: A corpus-based analysis of pauses in teachers' speech: first results. Terra Linguistica **14**(4), 25–38 (2023)
6. Gabidullina, A. R.: Evaluative utterances in the pedagogical discourse. Vestnik Rossiiskogo universiteta druzhby narodov. Seriia: Teoriia iazyka. Semiotiika. Semantika (3), 36–45 (2013)
7. Pochebutova, S. V.: Konstruktsii ekspressivnogo sintaksisa v rechi sovremennogo uchitelia [Expressive syntax constructions in the speech of a modern teacher]. In: Golubeva, I.V., Senina, N.A. (eds.) Rech', Rechevaia deiatel'nost', Tekst: Materialy Vserossiiskoi mezhvuzovskoi nauchnoi konferentsii, posviashchennoi pamyati professora G. G. Infantovoi [Materials of the All-Russian Interuniversity Scientific Conference in Memory of Professor G. G. Infantova], pp. 361–366. Taganrog (2012)
8. Andewi, W., Waziana, W.: An analysis of teacher's speech acts in teaching and learning process. Teknosastik **17**(1), 29–34 (2019)
9. Brunato, D., Cimino, A., Dell'Orletta, F., Venturi, G., Montemagni, S.: Profiling-ud: a tool for linguistic profiling of texts. In: Proceedings of the Twelfth Language Resources and Evaluation Conference, pp. 7145–7151 (2020)
10. Solnyshkina, M.I., Kiselnikov, A.S.: Slozhnost' teksta: etapy izucheniia v otechestvennom prikladnom iazykoznanii [Text complexity: stages of study in Russian applied linguistics]. Vestnik Tomskogo gosudarstvennogo universiteta. Filologiia (6(38)), 86–99 (2015)
11. Shurak, A.D., Tikhonov, D.V.: Optimizing the content of the educational organization's community in order to expand the target audience. Terra Linguistica (2021)
12. Tiraspol'skii, G.I.: Dlinna slova i evoliutsiia grammaticheskogo stroia. [Word length and the evolution of grammatical structure]. Chelovek. Kul'tura. Obrazovanie (2014)
13. Antonova, L.G., Zhdanova, T.A.: New model of Internet communication in social networks. Sotsial'nye i gumanitarnye znaniia **3**(1), 63–68 (2017)
14. Tapilin, T.: Narrative multimodal texts in digital educational resources for learning foreign languages: purposes and principles of use. Prepodavatel' XXI vek (4-1) (2023)

Measuring Public Satisfaction with Service Quality: Customer-Oriented Approach

Svetlana Sheremetyeva(✉), Olga Babina, and Andrew Polev

South Ural State University, 76 Prospekt Lenina, Chelyabinsk 454080, Russia
{sheremetevaso,babinaoi}@susu.ru

Abstract. The focus of this research is on assessing the public perception of service quality with a multi-aspect sentiment analysis technique and visualizing the assessment results by means of a customer-oriented web application. Both the methodological and development issues are covered. The methodology includes two main steps: 1) creating digitalized linguistic resources and 2) developing a web application based on the pipelined precreated resources. The first step includes raw data acquisition and data specificity analysis, preprocessing to eliminate public induced linguistic mistakes, as well as creation of a gold standard annotated corpus based on a domain- and task-oriented lexical and ontological knowledge base and disambiguation rules. The second step describes specific methods for the automatic calculation of sentiment scores for multiple service aspects prioritized by general public. The calculations are performed by means of a web application that works on the pipelined gold standard annotated corpus and specific knowledge for template-based natural language generation (NLG). The methodology is tested as applied to measure public satisfaction with medical services in the city of Chelyabinsk (the capital of the South Ural). Practical results of the methodology application are presented. Both the methodogical issues and practical results of the current work are to be used for further research and may also deserve the attention of both computational linguists and sociologists.

Keywords: Public Service Quality · Multi-Aspect Sentiment Analysis · Lexical-Ontological Knowledge · Web Application · Russian Language

1 Introduction

We live in an age, where the ever increasing amount of data demands novel tools to effectively extract, analyze, and understand the data content. One of the most important types of data is customer reviews that are valuable resource for analyzing customer satisfaction with different types of institution services. Ultimately, the goal of providing high quality services is to meet customer needs and expectations and improve their satisfaction with the services they receive [1, 2]. The objectives here is to find out what factors construct service quality and customer service satisfaction, as well as to understand which aspects of service quality is perceived as the most important by customers. Institution service quality is reflected by public satisfaction and comprises multiple factors that are prioritized differently by customers. It is a complex and multi-dimensional concept that is challenging to measure and evaluate.

M. Bakaev et al. (Eds.): IMS 2025, CCIS 2671, pp. 35–45, 2026.
https://doi.org/10.1007/978-3-032-04958-2_3

The focus of this research is on assessing the public perception of service quality with a multi-aspect rule-based sentiment analysis technique and visualizing the assessment results by means of a customer-oriented web application to help people compare medical institutions and select the best one addressing their needs. Both the methodological and development issues are covered. The calculation is done over the space of gold standard annotated corpus. The explicit aspect-sentiment annotation allows for a rather straight forward calculation procedure based on tag statistics that, taken in different combinations, provides for a) extraction and comparative prioritization of clinic service aspects (i.e., which service aspects are most important for people), b) public perception measurement of a clinic in general, c) extraction and comparison of the clinic service aspect qualities, d) comparison of different clinic public perceptions in general and e) comparison of different clinic perceptions along one or several service aspects.

The rest of the paper is organized as follows. Section 2 gives an overview of related work. In Sect. 3, the methodology of the current research is presented. Practical results of the methodology application to assessing public satisfaction with medical services in the city of Chelyabinsk (the capital of the South Ural) are given in Sects. 4 and 5. Section 4 describes knowledge acquisition and digitalizing, while Sect. 5 describes the development of the web application LinguaMetrics. Conclusions summarize the research results and outline future work.

2 Related Work

Many scientists interpret essence and substance of quality perception in a different way. The earlier developed methods that are widely used by today combine qualitative research conducted using focus group discussions, and quantitative research based on customer surveys [3]. There are a lot of survey guides and questionnaires that can easily be found online[1]. This can be illustrated by the survey based research on the analysis of the Russian public service quality described in [4], and the research targeted to assess customer satisfaction with healthcare systems in Russia and Romania presented in [5]. The latter is based on electronic surveys and a special questionnaire. Quite popular is the SERVQUAL model according to which, customers evaluate service's quality along five distinct dimensions: reliability, responsiveness, assurance, empathy, and tangibles [6]. Some of the commonly used metrics to go about measuring customer satisfaction use the Customer Satisfaction Score (CSAT) which is calculated by gathering feedback through surveys and calculating the percentage of satisfied customers based on their responses. CSAT formulas are based on a 5- or 10-point Likert scale, a rating system to measure customer expectations, attitudes, behaviors, and opinions. The highest scores (5 on a 5-point scale or 9 or 10 on a 10-point scale) indicate "very satisfied" customers, while the lowest scores indicate "very dissatisfied" customers.

One of the modern approaches to analyze and classify data is to use sentiment analysis. A detailed study conducted on different sentiment analysis applications, methods, tools, and challenges that can be applied on document, sentence, phrase and aspect levels is described in [7]. Sentiment analysis and related to it more refined multi-aspect

[1] https://contentsquare.com/fr-fr/survey-templates/csat-customer-satisfaction/

sentiment analysis have come in focus of many NLP areas and can be realized in the frames of different aspect-sentiment analysis technologies: rule-based, statistical, neural or hybrid [8]. Each of the technologies involves establishing a correspondence between texts and hidden factors (tone scores and assessment aspects), all based on annotated data.

Data annotation (or "labeling") is the process of adding metadata, or tags, to raw data and is a corestone of most information processing projects that contributes essentially to the accuracy of analysis results. Annotation is extremely effort and time consuming, and the need to automate the annotation process is obvious. However, in many sentiment related studies, the stage of data annotation is often overlooked or lacks the description of annotation [9]. Literature attending to data/corpus annotation relevant for our research covers both, sentiment and aspect-sentiment analysis, and, in general, share all or a combination of the following stages: corpus acquisition, preprocessing, extraction of sentiment/ aspect relevant lexica and annotation proper. The annotation schemes differ from work to work depending upon the type of corpus and analysis task. In reality, the most popular annotation approaches are

a) in-house manual or automated mark-up, either with computer interfaces like BRAT [10], or based on some heuristics, such as tag assignment based on emoticons [11];
b) crowdsourcing through platforms, like Yandex.Toloka (https://toloka.ai/);
c) outsourcing annotation to freelancers. Quite often, annotation comes in the form of numerical values (scores or weights) showing discrete or gradual degrees of sentiments [12, 13]. In much fewer works other approaches to formalize and annotate aspect sentiment data are used. For example, in the research presented in [14], a domain and task oriented ontological formalism is suggested to complement the values of numerical weights.

3 Methodology

The public perception measurement approach used in this research falls in the frame of a rule-based multi-aspect sentiment analysis technique that relies on a pre-constructed lexical-ontological knowledge base and rules. This resource is used for corpora annotation with aspect and sentiment categories, a must and most problematic step of all sentiment evaluation techniques. The specificity of our methodology is as follows:

- knowledge acquisition and perception measurement are task- and domain-driven and are highly automated with tools developed by the authors;
- annotation procedure following the most recent tendencies in computational linguistics is the realization of ontological analysis based on the domain and task-oriented ontology, which in practical terms consists in mapping textual units into ontology concepts; we here follow the definition of "ontology" as "the network of concepts underlying linguistic coding across natural languages" [15];
- the set of lexical units that fall into particular categories (i. e., whose meaning could be represented/annotated by ontological concepts) are called «annotation units»; the annotation units thus specified form what we call "ontolexicon" and in addition to single words, include multicomponent phrases;

The listed methodological principles conditioned the following steps and workflow of computing general and aspect related sentiment scores as perceived by general public:

- raw data acquisition and pre-annotation analysis to improve data linguistic quality as the authentic public created reviews (unlike published papers) are full of spelling and grammar mistakes that distort opinion calculation, the problem that is neglected in most of the related research;
- development of rules and tools to automate the data linguistic check
- corrected data categorization and creation of ontology and ontolexicon tuned to aspect-sentiment analysis in a limited domain
- data annotation with aspect-sentiment codes of ontology concepts
- development of rules and tools for concept disambiguation
- creation of a gold annotated data (corpus)[2];
- calculation of public satisfaction with service quality;
- development of web user- friendly application for general public use.

4 Measuring Public Satisfaction with Medical Service Quality in the South Ural

4.1 Data

The original data used for this study include a corpus of 200 000 word tokens that was used to create the lexical-ontological knowledge base. The corpus was created using the continuous sampling method and acquired from the 2GIS electronic directory website. Out of this initially acquired and processed corpus, 1,601 reviews of eight most popular medical centers of the city of Chelyabinsk (the capital of the South Ural) amounting to 113,606 word tokens were extracted and further used to test the developed methodology. The pre-created linguistic and information resources to achieve the study objectives are described further.

4.2 Pre-constructed Resources

Ontology. The ontology constructed in the course of the current study is domain- and task-tuned. It has the following three level structure:

ALL [SENTIMENT [POS NEG POSX NEGX] MODIFIER [MAG ANT REV] ASPECT [Q CH EQ ... L] OTHER],

where ALL is a first-level concept (the root of the ontological tree); SENTIMENT, MODIFIER, ASPECT and OTHER are the second-level concepts, third-level concepts, POS - positive, POSX - extremely positive, NEG - negative, NEGX - extremely negative are third-level concepts which are sub-classes of the SENTIMENT concept, MAG - strengthening, ANT - weakening, REV - changing the context-independent sentiment a lexeme to the opposite one are third-level concepts that are subclasses of the MODIFIER concept.

The list of the third-level ontology concepts that are subclasses of the ASPECT concept, their definitions (conceptual meanings) and examples of corpus lexemes whose meaning is described by these concepts are given in table 1.

[2] A gold annotated data (corpus) means data (corpus) with an absolutely correct annotation.

Table 1. Conceptual meanings of ASPECT ontology concepts

ASPECT CONCEPTS (meaning) *Examples of Russian lexemes linked to the ontology ASPECT concepts*
Q (doctor qualification, treatment quality) *Большая эффективность, верх профессионализма, высший класс, дикий непрофессионализм, некомпетентность, европейский уровень, побочка* CH (doctor human features, attention to patients) *вежливый доктор, доброжелательный специалист, врач - грубиян*
T (waiting time, consultation/examination time table) *короткий прием, долгое ожидание, плохое расписание, быстрые ответы*
COM (booking ease, online communication) *неработающий чат, онлайн-связь, ответное письмо, смс, автоответчик,*
EQ (availability, state and quality of equipment) *томограф, аппарат МР, флюорограф, Мас-компьютер, каталка*
L (clinic location, accessibility, dedicated parking) *неудобное место, большая парковка, велопарковка, доступная среда* M (cost of services and possibility of money back) *адекватная цена, баснословные деньги, возврат денег, выкачивание денег*
INT (interior, wardrobe, children's playground) *аккуратная палата, бункер, весёлый интерьер, гардероб, детский уголок*
S (friendliness of medical and administrative staff) *адекватный персонал, безграмотный работник, бестолковая девочка*
F (availability and quality of food) *вкусное питание, выпечка, ароматный кофе, сырой рис, хорошее меню*

Ontolexicon. Ontolexicon created within the frame of our study is a set of typed lexemes relevant for the domain-tuned aspect-sentiment analysis. In addition to individual words, as in most related projects, it also contains multi-component lexical groups (nominal, verbal, prepositional, adverbial, adjective groups), and, when practically feasible, clauses, which reduces the polysemy of lexemes and facilitates subsequent aspect-sentiment analysis. The meanings of the ontolexicon units are represented by related ontological concepts. The attribution of ontolexicon units to specific ontological concepts is not straight forward and was done in such a way as, on the one hand, to make corpus aspect-sentiment annotation as explicit as possible and, on the other hand, to allow for the facilitation of automated aspect-sentiment calculation procedures be applying special rules. In our approach, lexical categorization accounts for such phenomena as conceptual syncretism and conceptual ambiguity. Conceptual syncretism can be illustrated, for example, by the Russian lexeme *неработающий чат* that conveys both the aspect (COMMUNICATION), and sentiment (NEGATIVE) meanings, and therefore, is related to the two mentioned ontological concepts. Conceptual ambiguity is manifested, for example, by the Russian lexeme *детский уголок* that in addition to the aspect meaning INTERRIOR is sentiment ambiguous. When used in different contexts, it can have either POSITIVE (*порадовался. когда увидел детский уголок*), or NEGATIVE (*этот бардак называется детский уголок*) meaning, and is therefore related to all the three ontological concepts.

In constructing ontolexicon, special attention was paid to the textual units (normally linked to the MODIFIER concept), in the context of which (1) neutralization, (2) weakening, (3) strengthening, or (4) complete change of the sign of context-independent sentiment tonality of lexemes can happen.

Rules. Pre-created linguistic resources include disambiguation rules a) to resolve ambiguity of multiple tags that occur due to the possible one-to-many relations between ontolexicon and ontology and b) to take care of the influence of contextual factors on the context-independent tonality of the ontolexicon units. Such rules were created and formalized based on a deep analysis of the contextual factors (lexical modifiers) and their specific modifying influence on the context-independent tonality of ontolexemes. Both, a narrow context within one or two steps to the left and right of the tonal unit, and a broad context of the entire medical review were investigated.

Gold Standard Annotated Corpus. The gold standard annotated corpus has been built by combining automatic annotation with subsequent manual post-editing. It contains 1,601 reviews of eight most popular medical centers of the city of Chelyabinsk (the capital of the South Ural) and amounts to 113,606 word tokens. Inter-annotator agreement was provided by detailed guidelines and weekly discussions held by the project participants throughout the whole annotation period. The workflow of the annotation procedure is as follows:

1. Raw corpus preprocessing that includes
   a) automatic spellchecking with an in-house developed spellchecker based on the JamSpell library[3] that offers an out-of-the-box model for the Russian language and the Peter Norvig's algorithm[4] complemented with an n-gram model; our spellchecker was trained on the pre-corrected original reviews corpora for medical and avia service domains (the latter is under development for our future work) and 29,000 articles from the Russian-language Wikipedia[5] collected by an in-house web crawler. After training, the spellchecker copes quite well with typos in medical reviews and features a high operating speed;
   b) automatic grammar checking for such mistakes as **не мало важно* (*немаловажно*), **не в коем случае* (*ни в коем случае*) **на изнанку* (*наизнанку*), **ни куда* (*никуда*), etc., with a grammar checker module of the annotation tagger;
2. Automatic conceptual tagging with an annotation platform [16] that consists of an e-lexicon (digitalized lexical-ontological knowledge base that currently contains 13 747 entries) and a conceptual tagger that performs
   a) ontolexicon look-up

[3] https://github.com/bakwc/JamSpell?ysclid=m8tsfbz853940984971.

[4] https://www.norvig.com/spell-correct.html.

[5] See the file train_data at.https://drive.google.com/drive/folders/1rd1tcrTVJkECrS0fBO4A24IfM0sJYL0V?usp=sharing

   b) automatic tag disambiguation with an in-house developed tag disambiguation module of the annotation tagger
3. Interactive annotation post-editing to the gold standard annotation with the tagger post-editor interface.

In assessing the efficiency of the posteditior, we used the temporal post-editing effort quantitative measure that was successfully used in [16]. The annotators were given same-size portions of raw and automatically annotated texts and reported on the time they spent on gold annotations of each text. Post-editing time for the automatically annotated texts was ~ 40% less than the time needed to gold-annotate a raw text.

5 LinguaMetrics Web Application[6]

5.1 Interface Overview

In the current research, the main purpose of computing patient's perception is to provide general public with the information on the medical institution quality and thus to help people compare their city medical institutions so that they could select the best one addressing their needs. To make computational results available to general public, a special web application, which we called LinguaMetrics, with a user-friendly interface is developed[7]. At the start up page of the interface, the user is presented with a menu that allows either getting an evaluative information on one of the clinics, or comparative information on two or more clinics.

In the first case, by selecting the name of a clinic of interest in the menu and clicking on different buttons, the user is given a chance to either get access to evaluative information on the clinic as such, or to see the ratings of individual "raw" patient's reviews. See the right screenshot in Fig. 1 where individual review ratings are marked with yellow stars.

In the second case, after clicking on a corresponding button, the user is presented with the information on what aspects of the clinic service are prioritized by the patients (see the left screenshot in Fig. 2). This information is visualized with a hypertext and a pie chart. Interactive phrases in the hypertext and a menu of aspects on this interface page allow for further navigation along pop-up windows and getting evaluative information on the clinic as a whole, or on one or several aspects of its service, the latter is given in the right screenshot in Fig. 2. From every current window, the user can return to the start-up page and make a new selection in the menu.

By selecting several clinics on the start-up page, the user gets comparative information on the public perception of the selected clinics in general, or evaluative information on patient satisfaction/unsatisfaction with the different clinic service aspects (see Fig. 3). The evaluation scores are visualized with vertical bar charts. A click on a particular colored bar section displays a pop-up hint with an exact percentage number (see the window screenshot on the right of Fig. 3).

---

[6] This application version works on the data acquired and preprocessed by the authors to work out its design and functionalities. A web console application that will allow users acquiring and processing new texts is under development.

[7] http://37.75.248.254/qa-medicine

5.2 LinguaMetrics Development Issues

The patient perception scores are computed over the tag space of the gold standard annotated corpus that is pipelined to LinguaMetrics. The explicit aspect-sentiment annotation allows for a rather straight-forward computing procedure based on tag statistics that, taken in different combinations, provides for a) the extraction and comparative prioritization of clinic service aspects (i.e., which service aspects are most important for people), b) public perception measurement of a clinic in general, c) extraction and comparison of the clinic service aspect qualities, d) comparison of different clinic public perceptions in general and e) comparison of different clinic perception scores along one or several service aspects. Depending on the computing task, LinguaMetrics calculator uses one or several selected parts of the gold standard annotated corpus as input.

The algorithm for comparing several medical centers is a follows. First of all, the parts of annotated corpus that contain all the annotated reviews on each individual medical center are input to the LinguaMetrics calculator. Then aspect-sentiment tags are extracted from each input corpus part, the proportion of each type of tags is calculated and a data frame with the information on each tag is created. The results are further used to visualize evaluation graphs in the user interface.

The algorithm for calculating and visualizing the scores of people's satisfaction with the service of one clinic is similar to that used for multiple institutions, but it is applied to the annotated data related to one selected clinic only and in this case, a hypertext generation step is added. The hypertexts like the one displayed in the left screenshot in Fig. 2 is generated with the template-based NLG technique [17], which is also called a mail-merge. This method consists in filling pre-defined text templates with appropriate content and is widely used in many applications that differ in text templates and content sources. For example, in [18], this method is used to create personalized questionnaires where the content consists in words extracted from source articles. The specificity of our approach is that our knowledge includes a content template whose slots are aspects, a list of glosses, each related to a certain aspect slot, a text template with "holes" to be filled with aspect glosses, and a merge algorithm, which in addition to filling the text template with content glosses, also ranges the resulting text sentences depending on the pre-calculated data on the extracted tags.

An individual review rating (visualized with yellow stars in Fig. 1) is computed by the following formula.

$$r_i = 0{,}6108 - 0{,}4574 \times p_i^{NEGX} - 0{,}3301 \times p_i^{NEG} + 0{,}3939 \times p_i^{POS} + 0{,}3937 \times p_i^{POSX},$$

where r_i is the rating value for the i-th review, $p_i^{NEGX}, p_i^{NEG}, p_i^{POS}, p_i^{POSX}$ are relative frequencies of the sentiment tags extracted from the review. The formula is based on a ridge regression model trained on our data. According to the experimental results, the model achieved a mean squared error of 0.0226. Details on the experimental setup and further information about the model's performance can be found in [19]. The overall rating of the clinic based on all individual reviews is calculated as the arithmetic mean of all. r_i.

The programming languages used for LinguaMetrics development are Python and JavaScript, hypertext markup language HTML, style sheet language CSS and Python

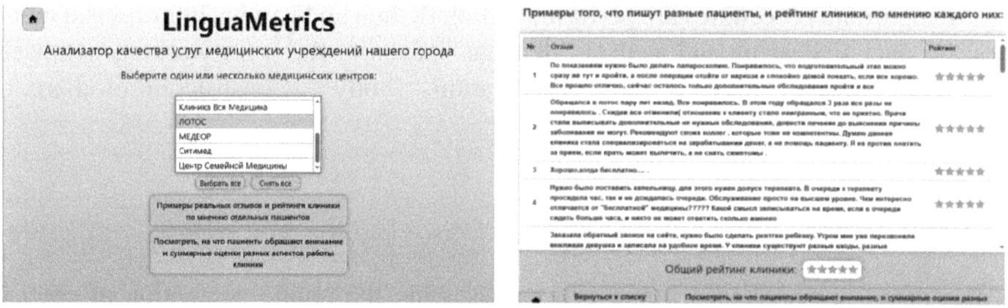

Fig. 1. The start-up interface window and a page with original patient reviews on individual medical centers.

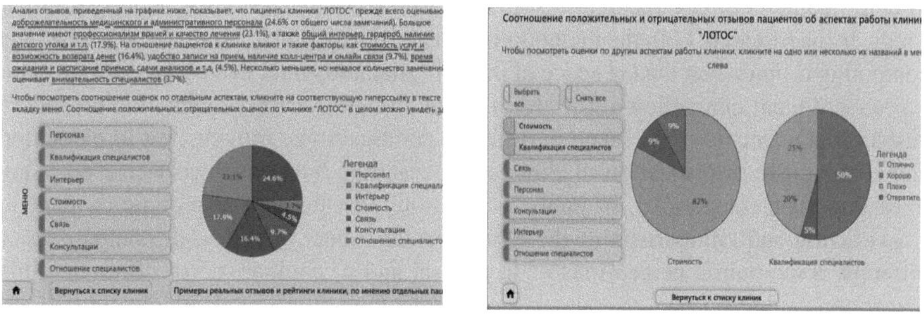

Fig. 2. Selected interface windows that display measurements related to one medical center.

framework Django[8]. The SQLite DBMS[9] is used as a database where all texts displayed in the LinguaMetrics are stored and can be edited. The texts can be configured using the admin panel such as a Django tool, while the main text blocks can be edited interactively right on the page itself. For this, a special JavaScript script was written.

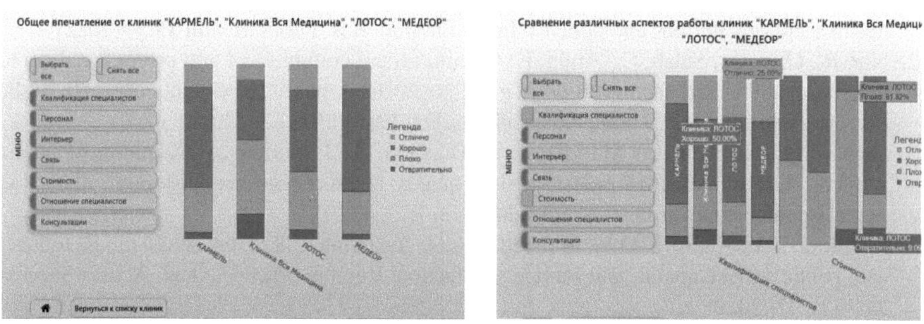

Fig. 3. Selected interface windows that display perception measurement results related to several medical centers.

---

[8] https://www.djangoproject.com
[9] https://www.sqlite.org

All algorithm procedures are performed using Python and various libraries and modules: for data processing and analysis - Pandas[10], Json[11], Re[12], for working with web requests to the server - urllib[13], for visualization - Plotly[14]. Construction of charts is carried out using the Python library Plotly.

6 Conclusion

In this paper, we presented a research on assessing the public perception of service quality with a multi-aspect rule-based sentiment analysis technique and described the development of a customer-oriented web application LinguaMetrics that computes and visualizes the assessment scores in a user friendly interface. The application is meant to help people compare medical institutions and select the best one addressing their needs. In the research, both the methodological and development issues are covered. The computing is done over the tag space of the gold standard annotated corpus. The explicit aspect-sentiment annotation allows for a rather straight forward calculation procedure based on tag statistics that, taken in different combinations, provides for a) extraction and comparative prioritization of clinic service aspects (i.e., which service aspects are most important for people), b) public perception measurement of a clinic in general, c) extraction and comparison of the clinic service aspect qualities, d) comparison of different clinic public perceptions of in general and e) comparison of different clinic perceptions along one or several service aspects. Our future work is four-fold: (1, 2) to port the developed methodology and LinguaMetrics application to new domains and languages other than Russian, (3) to develop a web console application that will allow users acquiring and processing new reviews, and (4) to augment LinguaMetrics with a researchers' module to access its calculator.

References

1. Rastoka, J., Petkovic, S., Radicic, D. Impact of entrepreneurship on the quality of public health sector institutions and policies. Int. J. Environ. Res. Public Health **19**(3) (2022)
2. Nor, R., Gani, A., Saleh, C., Amin, F.: Organizational commitment and professionalism to determine public satisfaction through good governance, public service quality, and public empowerment. Int. Rev. Public Nonprofit Market. **19**(1), 191–217 (2022)
3. Gayatri, G., Astuti, R.D., Martdianty, F., Daryanti, S.: Performance evaluation of public services: a development of public services quality measurement and customer satisfaction model on three cities in Java. ASEAN Mark. J. **1**(2), 4 (2013)
4. Matraeva, L.V., Kaurova, O.V., Maloletko, A.N., Vasiutina, E.S.: Conceptual model to measure public service quality and service satisfaction: Russian practice. Qual. Access Success **21**(177), 77 (2020)

[10] https://pandas.pydata.org
[11] https://docs.python.org/3/library/json.html
[12] https://docs.python.org/3/library/re.html
[13] https://docs.python.org/3/library/urllib.html
[14] https://plotly.com/python/

5. Bulatnikov, V., Constantin, C.P.: Assessing customer satisfaction to support future improvement strategies of healthcare systems: evidences from Russia and Romania. Sustainability **15**(19), 14534 (2023)
6. Zeithaml, V.A., Parasuraman, A., Berry, L.L.: Delivering Quality Service. The Free Press, New York (1990)
7. Wankhade, M., Rao, A.C.S., Kulkarni, C.: A survey on sentiment analysis methods, applications and challenges. Artif. Intell. Rev. **55**(7), 5731–5780 (2022)
8. Alqurafi, A., Alsanoosy, T.: Measuring Customers' Satisfaction Using Sentiment Analysis: Model and Tool (2023). https://thescipub.com/pdf/jcssp.2024.419.430.pdf. Accessed 30 Jan 2025
9. Smetanin, S.: RuSentiTweet: a sentiment analysis dataset of general domain tweets in Russian (2022). https://www.ncbi.nlm.nih.gov/pmc/articles/PMC9454938/
10. Stenetorp P., Pyysalo S., Topic G., Ohta T., Ananiadou S., Jun'ichi Tsujii J. BRAT: a Web-based Tool for NLP-Assisted Text Annotation. In: Proceedings of the 13th Conference of the European Chapter of the Association for Computational Linguistics, pp.102–107. Avignon, France (2012)
11. Rubtsova, Yu.: Automatic construction and analysis of a corpus of short texts (microblog posts) for the tone classifier development and training (2014). https://study.mokoron.com/wp-content/uploads/2014/02/rubtsova-kesw_paper-21.pdf. Accessed 10 Mar 2024
12. Swarnalatha, S., Kesavarthini, I., Poornima, S., Sripriya, N.: Med-recommender system for predictive analysis of hospitals and doctors. In: International Conference on Computational Intelligence in Data Science (ICCIDS), Chennai, India, 2019, pp. 1–5 (2019). https://doi.org/10.1109/ICCIDS.2019.8862121
13. Koltsova, O., Nikolenko, S., Alexeeva, S., Nagornyy, O., Koltcov, S.: 'Detecting interethnic relations with the data from social media. In: Alexandrov, D.A., Boukhanovsky, A.V., Chugunov, A.V., Kabanov, Y., Koltsova, O. (eds.) Digital Transformation and Global Society, pp. 16–30. Springer, Cham (2017)
14. Loukachevitch, N., Blinov, P., Kotelnikov, E., Rubtsova, Y., Ivanov, V., Tutubalina, E.: SentiRuEval: testing object-oriented sentiment analysis systems in Russian. In: Computational Linguistics and Intellectual Technologies: Proceedings of the International Conference "Dialogue" 2015; Russian State University for the Humanities; pp. 3–13 (2015)
15. Schalley, A.C.: Ontologies and ontological methods in linguistics. Lang. Linguist. Compass **13**(11), 1–19 (2019)
16. Sheremetyeva, S.: An interoperable platform for multi-grain text annotation. In: International Conference "Internet and Modern Society" IMS-2021, 24–26 June 2021, ITMO University, St. Petersburg, Russia. Proceedings. CEUR Workshop Proceedings, vol. 428, pp. 56–67 (2021). ISSN 1613–0073
17. Gatt, A., Krahmer, E.: Survey of the state of the art in natural language generation: Core tasks, applications and evaluation (2018). https://arxiv.org/pdf/1703.09902. Accessed 30 Jan 2025
18. Taljaard, M., Chaudhry, S., Brehaut, J., Weijer, C., Grimshaw, J.: Mail merge can be used to create personalized questionnaires in complex surveys. BMC Res. Notes **8**, 574 (2015). https://doi.org/10.1186/s13104-015-1570-5
19. Babina, O.I.: Regression-based sentiment analysis model for predicting customer satisfaction. Bull. South Ural State Univ. Ser. Linguist. **21**(4), 63–70 (2024). (In Russ.)

AI-Related Public Discourse Analysis via Emotion and Topic Modeling in Telegram Conversations

Anna Chizhik(✉)

ITMO University, Kronverksky Prospekt 49, 197101 Saint Petersburg, Russia
chizhik@itmo.ru

Abstract. This study explores public attitudes towards artificial intelligence (AI) by analyzing user discussions on Telegram chats. The analysis integrates Latent Dirichlet Allocation (LDA) for topic discovery and an emotion classificator that was initially trained on a labeled subset of the data. Thus, the sentiment analysis process involved a two-stage method, starting with preliminary data annotation using GPT-4o followed by emotion classification through supervised learning. The paper reports on experimental comparisons of different vectorization techniques and classification models to identify the most effective approach for emotion recognition within AI-related conversations. The findings uncover five primary themes in the discourse about AI, including general opinions, accessibility issues, creative uses, and technical performance evaluations. Sentiment analysis indicates a prevalent sense of surprise and curiosity toward AI technologies, coupled with persistent undertones of sadness and fear. The approach demonstrates the utility of combining language models with interpretable classifiers and highlights the potential of discourse-based methods for understanding affective engagement with emerging technologies.

Keywords: AI · sentiment analysis · topic modeling · embeddings · telegram discourse · public perception

1 Introduction

The integration of artificial intelligence (AI) into quotidian existence has fundamentally altered its status from a specialized instrument to a ubiquitous digital aid. AI models are now extensively employed in the generation of textual content, visual representations, and video productions, thereby cultivating novel avenues for creative expression, automated processes, and enhanced efficiency. Contemporary studies have commenced to illuminate the AI assimilation in everyday life and user interaction with it. Despite the allure of AI a recent survey conducted by the Pew Research Center demonstrated that 52% of American citizens articulate a higher degree of apprehension than enthusiasm regarding the escalating influence of AI in their daily routines, with a mere 10% expressing predominantly positive sentiments [1, 2]. Within the corporate domain, a global survey undertaken by McKinsey & Company indicates a notable surge in the practical

M. Bakaev et al. (Eds.): IMS 2025, CCIS 2671, pp. 46–56, 2026.
https://doi.org/10.1007/978-3-032-04958-2_4

application of AI technologies, with 78% of organizations documenting the deployment of AI in a minimum of one functional area, representing an increase from the 72% reported in preceding assessments [3]. This discernible trend underscores the increasingly pivotal role of AI in augmenting operational efficacy and refining decision-making protocols within contemporary business enterprises.

Across Europe, AI adoption trends reveal both enthusiasm and skepticism. According to a survey conducted by the IE University Center for Change Management, 34% of Europeans under the age of 35 would trust AI to vote on their behalf, indicating a high level of confidence in AI among younger demographics. However, concerns about AI's impact remain prevalent: 67% of respondents fear potential election manipulation using AI, particularly in the United Kingdom (54%) and Spain (51%) [5]. At the same time, 85% of Europeans report limited familiarity with AI applications in daily life, with only 17% of Spaniards and 23% of Poles actively using AI tools [6]. These findings highlight the gap between AI's rapid technological progress and the general public's ability to integrate it effectively into daily activities. Age appears to be a significant factor in AI adoption. Data indicates that individuals over 61 constitute the largest percentage (30.8%) of weekly virtual assistant users, closely followed by the 18–25 age bracket (29.9%) [4]. This suggests that both older and younger demographics are integrating AI into their routines, albeit potentially for different purposes. Furthermore, findings from a similar study suggest that factors such as age, educational background, and field of study significantly influence how individuals engage with AI technologies, emphasizing the importance of tailoring AI tools to diverse user needs [7].

Beyond the U.S. and Europe, Russia has also demonstrated significant developments in AI adoption. According to a survey by the Russian Public Opinion Research Center (VTsIOM), 94% of Russians are aware of AI technologies, with the proportion of respondents able to explain AI increasing from 36% to 50% over the past two years. More than half (52%) trust AI technologies, although 26% express concerns about AI potentially becoming uncontrollable [8]. AI usage is becoming prevalent in everyday life: six out of ten Russians permanently use AI tools, with 31% interacting via voice assistants and neural networks. Applications extend across various domains. For example, individuals use AI for financial management, budgeting, and expense tracking, and also AI-driven technologies are actively implemented in education and healthcare. Moreover, industrial sectors employ AI to enhance efficiency and service quality. Currently, 72% of Russian companies employ AI to optimize business processes, particularly in finance, IT, and energy sectors [9].

Despite its widespread adoption, the social composition of AI users remains highly heterogeneous and underexplored. Evidently, user engagement with AI technologies varies based on age, profession, and digital literacy. While IT professionals use AI mainly for coding and data analysis, younger people experiment with it in creative and experimental contexts, whereas the general public shows a more mixed response and interaction cases. Moreover, the aforementioned studies underscore the heterogeneity of AI adoption worldwide. This trend is shaped by demographic differences, digital literacy levels, and regional policies. While AI is becoming an integral part of everyday life, its adoption patterns are largely chaotic and require study.

Survey-based studies are inherently constrained by their methodological design – respondents are prompted by predefined questions that may lead them to think in idealized categories rather than express emotional and spontaneous reactions, moreover this strategy limits the range of topics discussed. In contrast, analyzing spontaneous user discussions removes these constraints and allows for a more organic and unfiltered exploration of the fenomena. This approach is particularly valuable for two reasons. First, in natural conversations within their social groups, individuals express emotionally genuine reactions, free from the potential priming effects of survey questions. Unlike structured surveys, where the respondent is placed within a trigger-response framework, spontaneous discussions provide an opportunity to capture raw, context-driven emotional expressions related to AI. Second, in open discussions, it is not a researcher who dictates the agenda by selecting predefined aspects of AI to be explored; rather, users themselves decide which facets of AI to discuss. This shifts the analytical focus from externally imposed concerns to organically emerging topics, offering a broader and more authentic perspective on public discourse.

Thus, the aim of this study was to conduct a preliminary analysis of the perception of AI in society through the analysis of public correspondence of Telegram-users including detection key themes discussed in relation to its use. Special attention was paid to the connotations of the discussions, which allowed for determining the emotional context in which AI technologies are perceived, and which aspects generate the most interest or concern among different user groups.

This study applies computational linguistic methods to analyze Telegram discussions about AI technologies, using LDA for topic modeling and a hybrid GPT-assisted emotion classification pipeline combining semantic embeddings with machine learning.

2 Methodology

2.1 Data Collection and Preprocessing

To ensure a comprehensive analysis of public discussions on artificial intelligence, we examined 70 AI-focused Telegram channels, ranging from general AI news aggregators to specialized discussions on machine learning and generative models. The most popular channels within this selection collectively amassed over one million subscribers. However, auditory engagement levels varied considerably across these channels. Some exhibited highly active user discussions, while others functioned primarily as broadcast platforms with limited or completely disabled commenting features. Given the research objective of analyzing organic user discourse, two large Telegram channels were highlighted based on active user engagement: GPT News (340,646 subscribers, https://t.me/gpt_news) and Neironavt (7,855 subscribers, https://t.me/GreenNeuralRobots). These channels stood out due to their significant user involvement.

Despite its smaller audience size, Neironavt demonstrated a higher citation index (22.77), indicating that its content is more frequently referenced across other AI-related discussions, including user-generated chats. Additionally, engagement statistics revealed that the percentage of readers performing actions such as sharing, commenting, or reacting was consistently 2–3 times higher in this channel compared to larger AI channels, including GPT News. This suggests that its audience is not only more interactive but also more influential in shaping AI-related discourse. Given these factors, we selected Neironavt as the primary source for this study, hypothesizing that analyzing discussions within an engaged and participatory AI community would yield richer insights into user perceptions within the framework of preliminary research. Thus, the dataset comprises 14,323 messages collected from January 2022 to January 2025, ensuring a sufficient temporal range for analyzing both short-term fluctuations and long-term trends in AI discussions. The average message length is approximately 150 characters. However, the length distribution is highly variable, ranging from 1 character (short reactions or emojis) to 2,040 characters. The longest messages typically represent detailed explanations or comprehensive discussions about a topic. The median message length is 69 characters. Figure 1 shows the dynamics of user messages in the selected Telegram channel. The message volume remained relatively low and sporadic throughout 2022, followed by a gradual increase in activity during 2023. A significant surge is observed in 2024, with more frequent peaks and higher overall activity levels, suggesting a rising public interest in AI. This growth correlates with major technological advancements, increased AI adoption, or significant industry events that stimulated discussions.

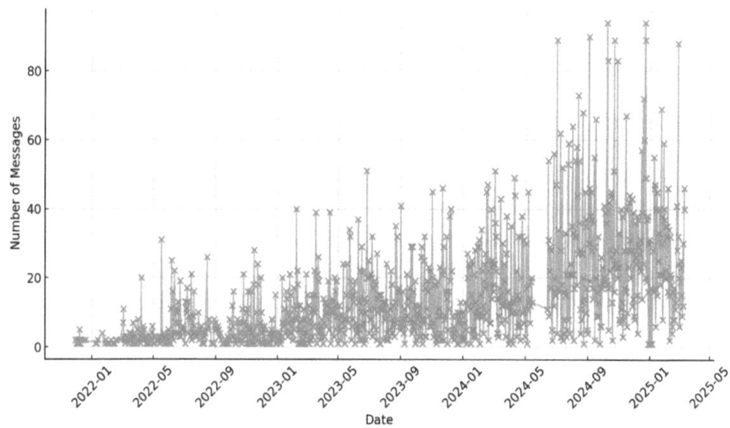

Fig. 1. Dynamics of Daily Message Volume

Each message entry in the dataset is characterized by eight attributes: a unique Message ID, the Date and Time, and the Text, which contains the content of the message and serves as the primary unit of analysis. To enhance interpretability and accuracy, preprocessing steps were applied, including lemmatization, stop-word removal, and collocation identification. Given the domain-specific nature of AI-related discussions, a custom stop-word list was developed to improve text processing efficiency. In addition to standard stop-words (e.g., conjunctions, prepositions, and common function words), a domain-specific stop-word list was manually curated to remove non-informative elements while retaining meaningful AI-related terminology. This process involved filtering out technical artifacts and structural noise, such as hyperlinks (e.g., «https», «t.me»), system messages, and metadata artifacts, which frequently appeared in Telegram conversations but did not contribute to thematic content.

At the same time, key AI-related technical terms that, despite their frequent appearance, carried semantic value for discussions were carefully preserved. For instance, terms like «API», «GPT», «fine-tuning» and «dataset» were retained, as they often indicated hands-on work with AI models rather than generic mentions. This selective approach ensured that the preprocessing step removed irrelevant noise while preserving content indicative of real AI-related engagement.

Furthermore, to account for multilingual terminology usage, cross-linguistic variations of commonly used AI-related terms were identified and standardized. As AI discourse often blends English and Russian terms, users frequently alternate between transliterated, original English, and fully adapted Russian versions of the same words (e.g., «prompt» vs. «промпт», «fine-tuning» vs. «финетюнинг», «dataset» vs. «датасет»). Rule-based normalization and dictionary were applied to make sure similar terms were mapped to a unified representation. This preprocessing step was important step for improving the subsequent robustness of topic modeling and sentiment analysis, preventing the fragmentation of thematically similar discussions due to orthographic variations.

Additionally, collocation identification was performed to retain meaningful multi-word expressions frequently occurring in AI-related contexts (e.g., «deep_learning», «write_text», «generate_image», «improve_quality»).

2.2 Topic Modeling

To analyze the thematic structure of discussions, Latent Dirichlet Allocation (LDA), a probabilistic generative model, was applied. This model identifies latent topics based on word co-occurrence patterns. Given the conversational nature of the data and its high lexical variability, we tested two vectorization methods: TF-IDF (Term Frequency-Inverse Document Frequency) and Laser (the deep contextual embedding model). To assess the effectiveness of each method, parallel experiments were conducted using both vectorization approaches. The key observations were:

- LDA with TF-IDF: This approach yielded more interpretable topics characterized by clear semantic separation. The effectiveness of LDA when paired with TF-IDF can be attributed to the method's emphasis on word frequency patterns, which are well-aligned with LDA's probabilistic assumptions. The good results largely depended on the preprocessing pipeline described above.
- LDA with LASER: In contrast, the use of deep embeddings to generate dense vector representations proved less effective in the context of LDA for topic modeling. This method resulted in topic overlap and a less distinct categorization of content.
- Additionally, further experiments were conducted using the Dostoevsky tool for sentiment analysis, where LASER demonstrated good performance in detecting and interpreting sentiments while TF-IDF provided more mediocre results.

Thus, TF-IDF was selected as the primary vectorization method for LDA-based topic modeling.

The best number of topics was determined by analyzing coherence scores, which assess the semantic similarity of words within each topic, and perplexity, which measures the model's ability to handle new data. Balancing these metrics, five discussion topics were identified, which were then manually analyzed and interpreted:

- Topic 0: General discussions about AI and ChatGPT (models, accessibility, new capabilities).
- Topic 1: Image generation using AI (model specifics, examples, effectiveness, Stable Diffusion).
- Topic 2: Discoveries and experiments (model testing results, unexpected outcomes).
- Topic 3: Performance and coding (model quality, code examples).
- Topic 4: Video and visual content (video processing, 3D generation, AI-based animation).

Figure 2 illustrates the distribution of topics in discussions over time.

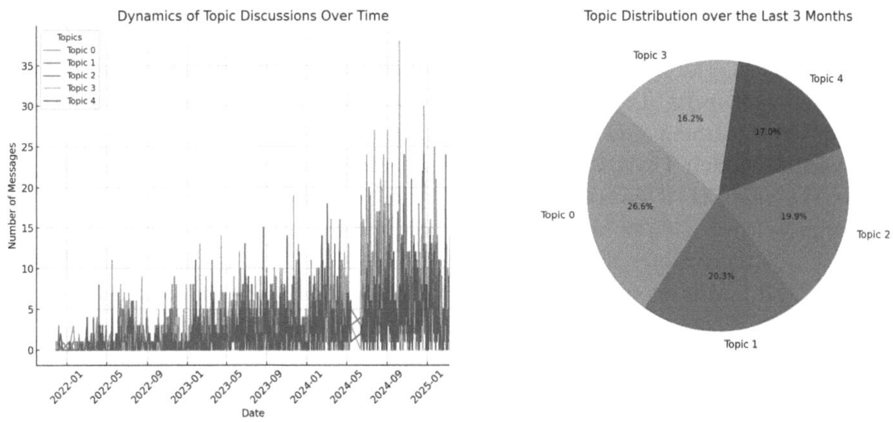

Fig. 2. Temporal and Proportional Analysis of Discussion Topics

The results confirm that public discourse around AI is diverse, spanning practical applications, experimentation, and technical performance evaluations, as well as philosophical discussions. The thematic structure provided the basis for further sentiment analysis. Thus it became possible to examine how emotional engagement varies across different AI-related topics. It is worth noting that the study period from 2022 to 2025 was chosen due to the active development and adoption of artificial intelligence technologies at this time. Technological advancements, including the launch and refinement of large language models (GPT-4, GPT-4o), the evolution of generative neural networks (DALL-E, Stable Diffusion), was observed in the timeframe. This led to the growing public discourse on ethics, regulation, and the impact of AI on the labor market. Therefore, the left graph illustrates the trend of shaping a new technological agenda. The distribution of topics discussed over the past three months shows a relatively even representation of discussion areas. This indicates that there is no clearly defined trend, no more important topic of discussion. All five thematic clusters are developing in parallel. The analysis revealed the periodic nature of discussions, characterized by sharp peaks in activity. This uneven pattern of discourse visualizes the reactive nature of public attention, which is shaped in response to news trends, regulatory initiatives, and societal debates concerning artificial intelligence.

Thus, the results of the discussion dynamics analysis for the period 2022–2025 indicate a rapid growth of public interest in AI, the formation of a multi-layered discussion environment, and a strong dependence of discussion topics on external events (news agenda and company releases).

2.3 Sentiment Analysis

At the next stage, a sentiment analysis of the texts was conducted. The method involved annotating a portion of the data, training a machine learning model on this sample, analyzing the entire dataset, and subsequently aggregating the results by thematic categories.

In the first step, a small sample of 1,000 messages was annotated using GPT-4o. Each text was assigned one of seven emotion labels: neutral, surprise, sadness, fear, joy, anger, or disgust. The segment of data annotated using GPT was subsequently validated by two human experts. The remaining 13,323 messages were automatically classified using machine learning models trained on this labeled dataset.

Baseline Model: TF-IDF + Random Forest

As a baseline, TF-IDF vectorization was combined with a Random Forest Classifier. This approach was chosen based on its demonstrated effectiveness in text classification tasks, particularly for short-form content, its robustness to noise inherent in user-generated text, and its interpretability, as feature importance analysis enables insights into the key lexical elements influencing predictions. Furthermore, TF-IDF was convenient for reuse in light of the previously conducted topic modeling, ensuring methodological consistency across analytical tasks.

The model got an F1-score of 0.76, doing better at recognizing clear emotions like joy and anger but struggling more with subtle ones like fear, surprise, and sadness due to overlapping expressions. Since emotions in text are often context-dependent, an alternative approach was explored by employing semantic vectorization through sentence embeddings.

Two vectorization techniques were examined. The first used LASER embeddings with a Support Vector Machine (SVM) classifier, which provides dense, context-aware sentence representations. This method was chosen because SVMs are effective for multi-class classification, especially with high-dimensional data. The second technique involved fine-tuning the efficient transformer-based model Tiny RuBERT. This model was also assessed with a SVM classifier. It should be noted that the transition from using Random Forest to SVM occurred due to its better ability to handle large feature spaces and its high efficiency in creating separating hyperplanes, which improved the accuracy and generalization emotion classification capability.

The Laser + SVM method did better than the baseline, achieving an F1-score of 0.85, with precision at 0.86 and recall at 0.84. It was particularly good at distinguishing similar emotional categories by using deep semantic embeddings to understand context. However, this accuracy increase made the model slower (35ms per message) and more computationally intensive compared to the TF-IDF-based model.

The RuBERT-tiny + SVM model presented a trade-off between accuracy and efficiency, achieving an F1-score of 0.81, with precision at 0.80 and recall at 0.82. While slightly less precise than Laser + SVM, it maintained faster inference (20ms per message).

Overall, the results confirm that Laser embeddings significantly enhance emotion classification accuracy, particularly for nuanced sentiment categories, but at the expense of processing speed. The RuBERT-tiny model provided a reasonable middle ground, balancing accuracy and efficiency. The choice between these models depends on the trade-off between interpretability, computational cost, and classification precision, with Laser + SVM being the best choice for high-accuracy sentiment differentiation. Figure 3 presents the evaluation results for each model in terms of precision, recall, and F1-score.

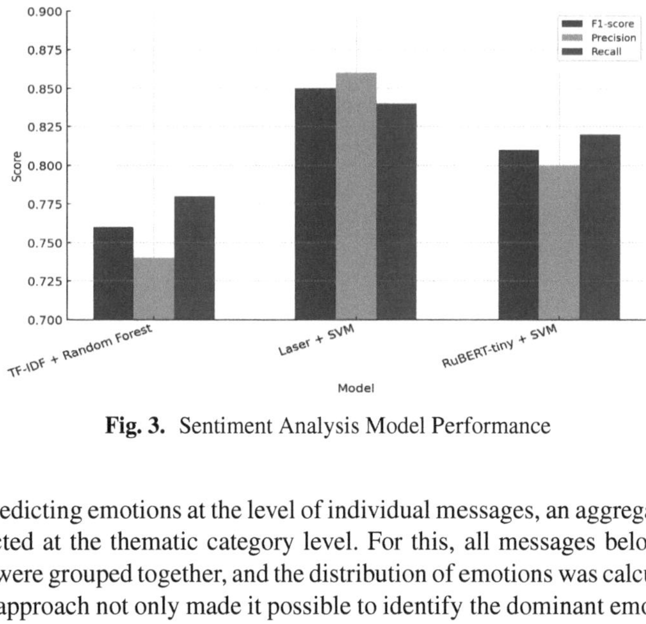

Fig. 3. Sentiment Analysis Model Performance

After predicting emotions at the level of individual messages, an aggregated analysis was conducted at the thematic category level. For this, all messages belonging to the same topic were grouped together, and the distribution of emotions was calculated across them. This approach not only made it possible to identify the dominant emotions within each topic but also allowed for an assessment of the degree of their emotional polarization (Fig. 4).

The analysis of emotion distribution in AI-related thematic discussions indicates that these discussions are predominantly informational and analytical in nature. Notably, the emotion of surprise appears across all categories, reflecting a generally positive perception of AI technologies and demonstrating user interest with a favorable connotation. However, the significant presence of sadness and fear, particularly in topics related to AI's generative capabilities, highlights existing concerns among users.

A detailed examination of texts containing these emotions revealed that discussions tend to focus on unsuccessful use cases, ethical risks, technological limitations, and the potential impact of AI on professional fields.

Further time-series analysis (Fig. 5) showed that surprise exhibits distinct spikes correlating with major releases and significant AI-related announcements. In contrast, sadness remains relatively stable without abrupt changes, indicating a persistent level

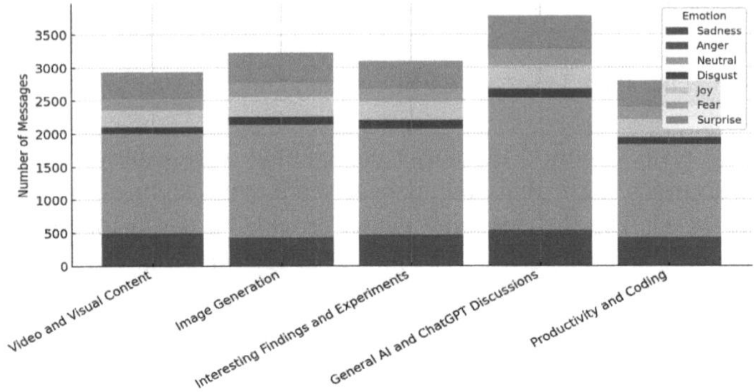

Fig. 4. Emotion Distribution by Topic

of skepticism and concern in discussions. Peaks in sadness often coincide with peaks in surprise, as new releases tend to trigger reflections on issues such as job displacement and similar socio-economic implications.

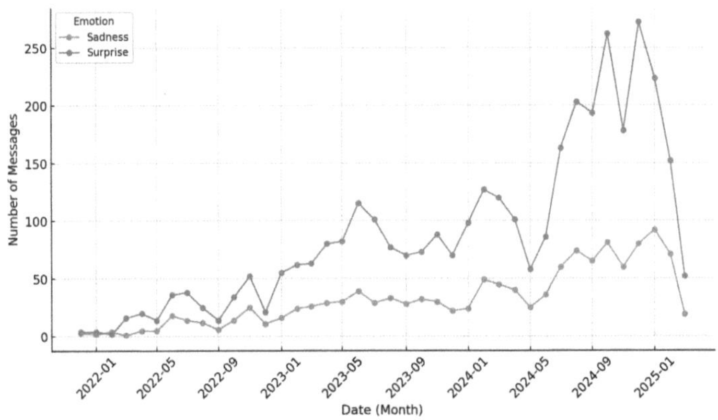

Fig. 5. Dynamics of «Surprise» and «Sadness» Emotions Over Time

3 Results and Discussion

This study offers a perspective of using computational linguistic methods for detection of AI public perception. Our pipline demonstrate how a combination of topic modeling and sentiment analysis can uncover patterns of engagement, emotional polarization, and thematic emphasis in discussions. Thus, research into the discourse of such debates can become an important component in analyzing trends in the use and understanding of AI. Findings indicate that while AI generates excitement and curiosity, it also triggers anxieties, particularly in creative and IT fields where automation is perceived as a disruptive force. The five identified topics reflected diverse dimensions of engagement with AI, ranging from general accessibility to technical performance and creative applications. This thematic diversity highlights the multiplicity of roles AI plays in users' daily lives and professional contexts. These insights complement prior survey-based research by providing access to spontaneous, non-prompted expressions, offering a more grounded perspective on the affective dynamics of AI adoption.

Sentiment analysis of AI discussions indicates a generally informational tone, punctuated by point episodes of heightened emotionality. The prevalence of surprise across various themes highlights a widespread curiosity and receptiveness towards AI. Peaks in surprise correlated with significant technological advancements, wich are often released by media. Thus these peaks illustratie the influence of release cycles and media coverage on public sentiment and attention to the theme. Concurrently, the sustained presence of sadness and fear, especially concerning generative AI, reveals underlying anxieties, often linked to implementation failures, ethical considerations, and anticipated job displacement. The consistent, rather than acute, presence of sadness suggests that apprehension towards AI is structurally integrated into public discourse. Comparative modeling showed that context-aware semantic embeddings (Laser, RuBERT-tiny) significantly improved emotional subtlety capture compared to lexical models. The Laser + SVM model's high F1-score (0.85) demonstrates its utility for detailed sentiment analysis, though its inference speed may limit scalability. RuBERT-tiny offers a balanced solution, providing computational efficiency and reliable accuracy. The combined topic modeling and sentiment analysis pipeline, utilizing distinct vector representations, optimizes performance by leveraging the strengths of each method while mitigating their weaknesses.

The pipeline that combines topic modeling and sentiment analysis on separate vector representations appears optimal, as it leverages the strengths of each method while minimizing their respective limitations.

In this study, GPT-4o was employed to annotate an initial subset of 1,000 messages with seven emotion categories. The decision to use GPT-4o was based on two key considerations. First, manual annotation of thousands of messages is labor-intensive and time-consuming, whereas GPT provides rapid, consistent labeling. Second, GPT-4o is capable of understanding contextual semantics.

However, despite its capacity, GPT-4o remains a black-box model – it does not offer transparent reasoning behind each labeling decision. This introduces an uncertainty regarding the validity of annotations. While the model performs well on canonical emotional expressions, it may misinterpret irony, slang, or culturally specific idioms, particularly in multilingual or informal settings like Telegram chats. These limitations are difficult to detect without manual auditing or comparative expert annotation.

To mitigate overreliance on GPT's outputs, the annotated sample was not used directly for full-scale emotion assignment. Instead, we adopted a hybrid strategy: using GPT to create an initial training set, then applying a traditional supervised classifier to predict emotions in the remaining 13,000 + messages. This approach offered several advantages. First, it allowed us to evaluate and quantify classification quality using standard metrics such as F1-score, precision, and recall. Second, it enabled model tuning and cross-validation, which are not feasible with an opaque system like GPT. Third, by transferring emotion recognition to a replicable classifier, we preserved methodological transparency and ensured that downstream analysis (e.g., topic-emotion correlations) relied on interpretable, testable models.

The application of GPT for large-scale data analysis remains uncertain, highlighting the need for automated methods to validate its annotations. However, at this stage of the research, GPT-4o played a fundamental role in the sentiment analysis pipeline, providing the basis for a nuanced understanding of individuals' affective responses to AI.

Acknowledgements. This research is supported by Russian Science Foundation, grant No. 25-28-00217 «Differentiation of practices in the use of artificial intelligence technologies among metropolitan residents: sociological analysis».

References

1. Pew Research Center: Views of Artificial Intelligence Methodology (2023). https://www.pewresearch.org/wp-content/uploads/2023/08/SR_23.08.28_views-of-ai_methodology.pdf. Accessed 20 Mar 2025
2. Pew Research Center: Views of Artificial Intelligence Topline (2023). https://www.pewresearch.org/wp-content/uploads/2023/08/SR_23.08.28_views-of-ai_topline.pdf. Accessed 20 Mar 2025
3. McKinsey & Company: The State of AI: How Organizations are Rewiring to Capture Value (2025). https://www.mckinsey.com/capabilities/quantumblack/our-insights/the-state-of-ai. Accessed 20 Mar 2025
4. AIPRM: AI Statistics. Available online at https://www.aiprm.com/ai-statistics/. Accessed 20 Mar 2025
5. IE University: European Tech Insights 2024 (2024). https://www.ie.edu/cgc/research/european-tech-insights/. Accessed 20 Mar 2025
6. Samsung: Vida inteligente: cómo la IA está mejorando nuestras experiencias diarias. https://news.samsung.com/ch/wp-content/themes/btr_newsroom/download.php?id=fyeijloTwkDF8oe16z7swQ%3D%3D. Accessed 20 Mar 2025
7. Atadika, D., Anim, A.N., Segbenya, M.: Antecedents of artificial intelligence and learners demographic characteristics in higher education: implication for human resource managers. Curr. Psychol. **43**(40), 31542–31558 (2024)
8. VTsIOM: Trust in AI. https://wciom.ru/analytical-reviews/analiticheskii-obzor/doverie-k-ii. Accessed 20 Mar 2025
9. Russian Government: Official Portal of Artificial Intelligence of Russia. https://ai.gov.ru. Accessed 20 Mar 2025

What Officials Talk About? Extracting Topics from Russian Civil Servants' Interviews with LDA and NMF

Sofiia Chepovetskaia[1,2](✉)

[1] Saint-Petersburg State University, Universitetskaya Embankment 7-9, 199034 Saint-Petersburg, Russia
schepovetskaya@hse.ru

[2] National Research University Higher School of Economics, Soyuza Pechatnikov 16, 190121 Saint-Petersburg, Russia

Abstract. This study applies non-negative matrix factorization (NMF) and latent Dirichlet allocation (LDA) to extract topics from interviews with Russian civil servants. This study aims to identify and analyze the predominant topics in Russian officials' public oral speech during the first quarter of the 21st century. Using a corpus-based approach, the research examines both the unified corpus and its four sub-corpora – each representing distinct occupational groups – to detect overarching topics as well as unique, role-specific ones. The analysis seeks to determine the most effective model for topic extraction and comparative assessment across these datasets. The material of the study is represented by transcripts of 90 randomly sampled interviews containing 252.225 words. We conducted lemmatization via pymystem3, developing two configurations for each method: one incorporating all denominative parts of speech except numerals and another restricted to nouns. To estimate the optimal number of topics and training epochs, we used the logarithm of perplexity for LDA and the coherence score for both methods. We concluded that both NMF and LDA perform better when trained on denominative parts of speech than on nouns only. For both data preprocessing techniques, the strongest results were achieved through the utilization of NMF. The average coherence score increased by 14.6% (from 0.363 to 0.425) for LDA and by 4% (from 0.611 to 0.638) for NMF. The application of both models allowed us to identify 6 main topics within the entire interview corpus: 'citizenship', 'justice', 'real estate', 'arbitration', 'state body operations' and 'finance'.

Keywords: Topic Modelling · NMF · LDA · Text Preprocessing · Interview Analysis · Public Oral Speech

1 Introduction

Topic modelling is one of the most discussed methods of semantic text analysis in the last two decades. It allows clustering fragments of a single document or a text corpus into categories, identifying the most relevant lexemes for each of them. The goal of this

M. Bakaev et al. (Eds.): IMS 2025, CCIS 2671, pp. 57–69, 2026.
https://doi.org/10.1007/978-3-032-04958-2_5

method in computational linguistics is to automatically determine the thematic structure of a text dataset, followed by human analysis of the results. Besides classical algorithms based on unsupervised or semi-supervised learning, methods based on pre-trained models have been developed and tested in recent years. Due to the fact that the application of both probabilistic (e. g. LDA, PLSA) and non-probabilistic approaches (e. g. LSA, NMF) implies vectorization using bag-of-words (BOW) or continuous bag-of-words (CBOW) architectures and the absence of both training data and pre-trained models [1], such methods are language-independent and do not require the development of special language packages, in contrast to the new topic modelling algorithms BERTopic and Top2Vec, which use Universal Sentence Encoder [2]. Other topic modelling methods based on unsupervised machine learning provide research opportunities regardless of the language of the material, which, in particular, is the reason for the fruitful discussion about the results of applying these methods in different languages. It should be noted that topic modelling is used to identify themes in genre-specific datasets. In particular, these include corpora of fiction texts [3], twitter posts [2], literary interviews [4] and legal texts [5].

This study compares two distinct approaches to topic modelling: LDA, a probabilistic method, and NMF, a matrix decomposition-based algorithm. Unlike neural network-based approaches, the aforementioned ones do not consider word order and grammatical characteristics [6], which provides more freedom in defining model configurations. A number of studies have found higher interpretability scores for sets of terms upon the utilization of LDA compared to NMF [7, 8]. However, it has been noted that the former algorithm may be more effective for identifying general topics within thematically diverse datasets, while NMF excels in generating "specific and granular topics" [7]. The primary interpretability metric used in this study is the coherence score. It evaluates "the degree of semantic similarity between high scoring words in the topic" in the range from 0 to 1 [9], with higher values indicating better topic quality. By employing this metric, the research aims to evaluate the effectiveness of LDA and NMF-algorithms in generating coherent and interpretable topics.

In addition to evaluating algorithms themselves, studies compare coherence scores when different text preprocessing techniques on distinct sub-corpora are applied. These involve variability in the set of lexemes of different parts of speech (POS). For instance, research conducted on Russian-language fiction texts [10] found that the highest coherence scores were achieved when no POS-categories were excluded during preprocessing. The second-best results were observed when only verbs and nouns were retained, as measured by the average percentage of "unambiguously interpreted topics", while the lowest scores were associated with preprocessing configuration that included only nouns. Due to the fact that the present study analyzes Russian-language interviews, we anticipate to see similar observations on the behavior of POS-configurations. Furthermore, it is worth noting that interviews with officials suggest the presence of topics related to politics and public administration. Since these themes are likely to recur across the entire corpus, it should be assumed that the application of the NMF algorithm will be more effective than LDA. Moreover, we expect to observe distinct topics specific to the sub-corpora: from more general ones related to the federal level to specific ones involving regional issues, which is explained by the principle of sub-corpora formation described in the next section of this paper.

The material under study was chosen since it bridges oral speech and formal legal discourse. Analyzing its thematic patterns will help identify prevailing topics in contemporary Russian institutional communication. It should be noted that texts belonging to legal discourse have recently garnered significant interest in the context of natural language processing applications. For instance, researchers have developed metrics for assessing the complexity of legal texts [11] and employed dynamic topic modeling to examine thematic evolution in diachronic perspective, thereby revealing fundamental properties of Russian legal texts [12]. However, hybrid genres such as oral public speech of civil servants remain understudied, particularly concerning automated semantic feature extraction. This study aims to address this research gap.

2 Data

2.1 Collection

The data are represented by 90 transcripts of interviews in Russian containing 252,225 words before pre-processing. The transcripts were collected from the websites of the legal information and reference systems ConsultantPlus [13] and GARANT.RU [14], as well as from the website of the information and talk radio station Echo of Moscow[1]. The primary criterion for selecting the interviews was the time frame, which spanned from 2004 to 2021. Additionally, efforts were made to ensure that no more than two interviews from a single official were included. Beyond these constraints, the sample was assembled randomly. Thus, the corpus[2] consists of 90 interviews featuring 89 distinct officials. The average length of the interviews was 2,802.5 words, with a median length of 1,886.5 words. In addition, we formed 4 sub-corpora within the corpus, allocated according to the position of the official in the structure of the official hierarchy, defined on the basis of the Federal Law "On General Principles of Organisation of Public Power in the Subjects of the Russian Federation" from 21.12.2021 N 414-FZ [15], the Federal Constitutional Law from 21.07.1994 N 1-FKZ (ed. From 01.07.2021) "On the Constitutional Court of the Russian Federation" (with amendments and additions, effective from 01.12.2021) [16] and the Federal Constitutional Law of 05.02.2014 N 3-FKZ (ed. From 14.07.2022) "On the Supreme Court of the Russian Federation" [17]. Thus, the sub-corpora are structured as follows: the first sub-corpus comprises interviews with top federal officials and governors; the second includes interviews with deputy top federal officials and heads of secondary federal bodies; the third consists of interviews with mid-level federal officials; and the fourth encompasses interviews with officials from the federation's constituent entities, their deputies, and individuals capable of influencing political and legal developments. The descriptive statistics for all sub-corpora before preprocessing are presented in Table 1.

---

[1] Disabled 2022/03/04 at the request of the Prosecutor General's Office of the Russian Federation.

[2] The materials of the collected corpus are currently under restricted access and will undergo further processing before publication.

Table 1. Descriptive statistics for sub-corpora according to the officials' hierarchy

	Top Federal Officials (1)	Heads of Minor Federal Bodies (2)	Mid-level Federal Officials (3)	Non-federal Officials (4)
Number of documents	11	20	42	17
Number of words	45,857	52,328	102,498	51,542
Mean length of an interview	4,168.8	2,616.4	2,440.4	3,031.9
Median length of an interview	3,436	1,949.5	1,709.5	2,353

2.2 Preprocessing

Data preprocessing was performed using the library nltk [18] and the morphological analyser MyStem [19] for the Python programming language - pymystem3 [20]. Via nltk it was possible to perform tokenization as well as to clean the text from punctuation marks and stop words, while pymystem3 was used for lemmatisation and identification of POS-tags. As noted earlier, we used two preprocessing methods in this study to prepare the data for vectorisation: (1) including lemmas for all denominative parts of speech except numerals; (2) including only nouns. The necessity of excluding numerals is conditioned by the fact that the speech of officials is accompanied by references to dates, numbers of laws and other indicators that have no relation to the content of statements. Table 2 demonstrates the counts of the number of lemmas in the sub-corpora as a result of both preprocessing methods.

Table 2. Statistics for words in sub-corpora (after preprocessing)

	Top Federal Officials (1)	Heads of Minor Federal Bodies (2)	Mid-level Federal Officials (3)	Non-federal Officials (4)	Total
All POS	24,228	30,462	58,161	29,017	141,868
Nouns only	14,318	21,131	39,835	18,104	93,388

After applying preprocessing options, we vectorized both corpus and each of the sub-corpora by selecting the Word2Vec model and setting the parameters as follows: vector_size = 200, window = 7, min_count = 5, workers = 4. The selection of Word2Vec for text vectorization is conditioned by its superior ability to capture semantic components of words and their contextual relationships, while accounting for word order, compared to TF-IDF [21]. Although TF-IDF may exhibit marginally better performance on certain datasets, particularly for long texts, its computational inefficiency presents a significant drawback. Specifically, processing sparse TF-IDF matrices requires calculation time exceeding those of Word2Vec by a factor of 200 [22].

3 Methods

3.1 LDA

The study uses two of the most common topic modelling methods, one of which is LDA, developed by Blei et al. in 2003 for automated semantic analysis of large text collections [23]. As a probabilistic model, LDA operates through a three-step process. The core principle is that each document can perform as a mixture of topics, which in turn are represented as probabilistic distributions of words. For every word within a document, a topic is assigned based on probability scores. Once the topics are formed, the most probable words involved in the formation of these topics are selected [Ibid].

Despite its widespread adoption in fields such as linguistics, journalism, and social sciences for analyzing diverse datasets, LDA is known to exhibit sensitivity to hyper-parameters, such as the number of topics and training epochs. Improper selection of these parameters can lead to distorted results. In addition, some researchers note that this method demonstrates insufficiently accurate outcomes for short documents [24].

3.2 NMF

NMF is an alternative method of topic modelling based on decomposing text into components using matrix multiplication, described by the following formula:

$$\mathrm{V} \approx \mathrm{W} \times \mathrm{H} \tag{1}$$

where V represents the input term-document matrix, W denotes the document-topic matrix, and H corresponds to the topic-term matrix, all of which are constrained to contain only non-negative values [25]. The imposition of the non-negativity constraint facilitates a "part-based representation", which aligns more closely with the human perception of topics [26]. Matrix multiplication results in a linear combination of semantic features for each document, which facilitates the consideration of all feature combinations and leads to the discovery of the underlying topic structure of the text. Nevertheless, the application of NMF can come with a number of problems related to factorisation ambiguity, since for a single input matrix V, there may exist multiple decompositions into W and H. This leads to the possibility that the same data may be explained by different sets of topics [27].

In this study, each of the algorithms was implemented using a script in the Python programming language using the libraries gensim [28] for LDA and scikit-learn [29] for NMF.

4 Results

4.1 LDA Passes Optimization

Due to the fact that the implementation of LDA in gensim requires selecting the optimal number of not only topics but also passes (epochs), we trained two models according to the data preprocessing options, limiting the number of passes to 1000. We used the logarithm of perplexity to estimate the optimal number of passes, lower values of which indicate less "uncertainty" of the model in predicting words forming topics [30]. Figures 1 and 2 demonstrate the results of training with the number of topics equal to 6, since a larger number of topics led to higher extremes of log perplexity values.

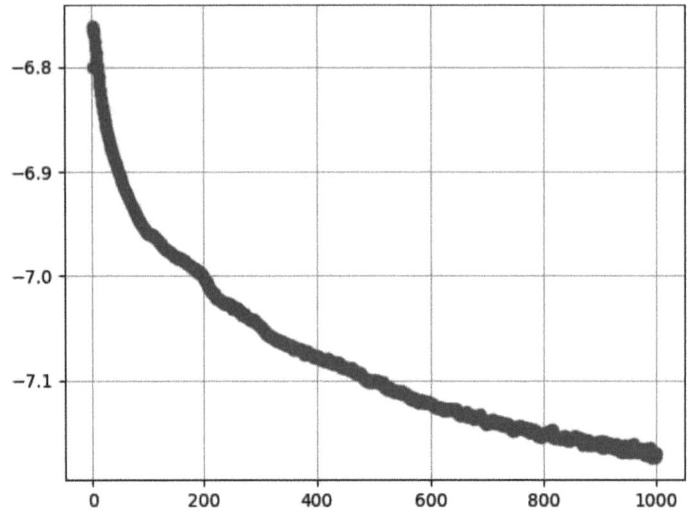

Fig. 1. Dynamics of the logarithm of perplexity when training the LDA model on lemmas of all parts of speech

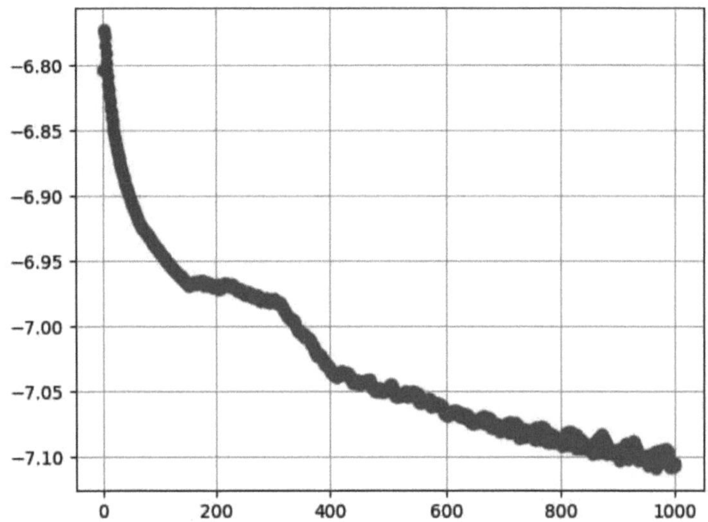

Fig. 2. Dynamics of the logarithm of perplexity when training the LDA model on nouns

As can be seen from the graphs, the perplexity ranges from -6.75 to -7.2, ceasing to decrease significantly in both cases after 400 passes. Hence, we selected this number as optimal for training both LDA models.

4.2 Performance of the Models for the Entire Corpus

When generating topics using both preprocessing options, coherence scores were estimated for different number of topics from 2 to 10 when applying LDA and NMF. Table 3 shows descriptive statistics of the coherence scores evaluation for the 4 models.

Table 3. Coherence scores for 4 models trained on the entire interview corpus

	NMF		LDA	
	all POS	nouns only	all POS	nouns only
mean	0.638794	0.611055614	0.424874	0.362872
median	0.644177	0.609672339	0.428179	0.370246
range	0.57–0.66	0.55–0.65	0.38–0.45	0.33–0.39

Based on the table, the best result is demonstrated by the model based on NMF and lemmas of all parts of speech. The preprocessing option including only nouns is accompanied by worse coherence scores when both topic modeling algorithms are applied. It should be noted that NMF also shows greater robustness to the POS-factor, as its performance is reduced by 5.4% on average. LDA, on the other hand, is more dependent on parts of speech, as evidenced by a more noticeable decrease in the average coherence score – 14.6%. The difference in the robustness of the methods to the POS-factor is also confirmed by the results of the correlation analyses conducted for coherence scores for the number of topics from 2 to 10. The counts indicate that there is no correlation between the values in the *all POS* and *nouns only* columns for LDA ($r \approx 0.087$, p-value ≈ 0.824). According to Chaddock scale, we detected a strong correlation between the values in the same columns for NMF ($r \approx 0.847$, p-value ≈ 0.0039).

The labels presented in the first column (in brackets) were assigned through a manual annotation process, involving systematic analysis of the top-terms identified by the models, to ensure each label reflects the semantic coherence and conceptual unity of the corresponding term set. Tables 4 and 5 show 6 topics for both methods, with Table 4 displaying the results obtained after applying POS-filtering and Table 5 containing the results prior to filtering.

Table 4. Results for NMF and LDA with POS filtering (nouns only)

Topic	NMF	LDA	Match (in terms)
Topic 1 (citizenship)	*federacija* (*federation*), *grazhdanin* (*citizen*), *rossija* (*Russia*), *grazhdanstvo* (*citizenship*), *organ* (*body*)	*federacija* (*federation*), *grazhdanin* (*citizen*), *rossija* (*Russia*), *zakon* (*act*), *grazhdanstvo* (*citizenship*)	4/5

(continued)

Table 4. (*continued*)

Topic	NMF	LDA	Match (in terms)
Topic 2 (justice)	*sud (court), delo (case), reshenie (judgement), pravo (law), rf (rf – Russian Federation)*	*sud (court), delo (case), reshenie (judgement), pravo (law), rf (rf – Russian Federation)*	5/5
Topic 3 (real estate)	*ob"ekt (object), nedvizhimost' (real estate), uchjot (accounting), uchastok (plot), kadastr (inventory)*	*ob"ekt (object), uchastok (plot), pravo (law), nedvizhimost' (real estate), dokument (document)*	3/5
Topic 4 (finance)	*kaznachejstvo (inventory), federacija (federation), bjudzhet (budget), organ (body), sredstvo (money)*	*organ (body), federacija (federation), uchrezhdenie (institution), kaznachejstvo (treasury), bjudzhet (budget)*	4/5
Topic 5 (state body operations)	*federacija (federation), situacija (situation), bezopasnost' (safety), ob"ekt (object), organ (body)*	*zakon (act), federacija (federation), ob"ekt (object), bezopasnost' (safety), organizacija (organization)*	3/5
Topic 6 (arbitration | taxes)	*arbitrazh (arbitration), reshenie (judgement), spor (dispute), arbitr (arbitrator), storona (party)*	*organ (body), lico (entity), nalogoplatel'shhik* (taxpayer), *nalog (tax), rossija (Russia)*	0/5

Table 5. Results for NMF and LDA without POS-filtering

Topic	NMF	LDA	Match
Topic 1 (real estate)	*ob"ekt (object),* nedvizhimost' *(real estate), uchjot (accounting), zemel'nyj (land.ADJ), uchastok (plot)*	*ob"ekt (object), zemel'nyj (land.ADJ), uchastok (plot),* nedvizhimost' *(real estate), uchjot (accounting)*	5/5
Topic 2 (justice)	*sud (court), delo (case), reshenie (judgement), pravo (law), rf (rf – Russian Federation)*	*sud (court), sudebnyj (court.ADJ), delo (case), pravo (law), zakon (act)*	3/5
Topic 3 (citizenship)	*federacija (federation), grazhdanin (citizen), rossija (Russia), grazhdanstvo (citizenship), organ (body)*	*federacija (federation), grazhdanin (citizen), zakon (act), rossija (Russia), pravo (law)*	3/5
Topic 4 (arbitration)	*arbitrazh (arbitration), reshenie (judgement), spor (dispute), arbitr (arbitrator), sud (court)*	*arbitrazh (arbitration), spor (dispute), moch' (can), reshenie (judgement), storona (party)*	4/5
Topic 5 (finance | taxes)	*kaznachejstvo (treasury), federacija (federation), bjudzhet (budget), bjudzhetnyj (budgetary), organ (body)*	*nalogoplatel'shhik (taxpayer), nalog (tax), organ (body), lico (entity), rossija (Russia)*	1/5
Topic 6 (state body operations)	*federacija (federation), organ (body), zakon (act), sluzhba (service), stat'ja (article)*	*federacija (federation), organ (body), delo (case), zakon (act), sotrudnik (officer)*	3/5

The original terms are presented outside the brackets, while their English translations are inside them, accompanied by POS-tags if necessary. Each set of terms was assigned a name based on the concept that best encapsulates the resulting collection. A single title was allocated to both sets of terms if at least 3 out of 5 matches were detected. Upon analyzing the corpus topics generated by the four models, we observed that 5 out of 6 topics are characterized by similar lemma sets across both preprocessing options. The exception is the sets of terms related to the topic of taxes, which is only emphasized by the LDA-models. In addition, the topic *arbitration* is detected by both topic modeling methods only when applying the preprocessing option that does not involve POS-filtration. When both preprocessing options are utilized, two topics - justice and real estate - are identified with entirely matching term sets. It is also important to note that, contrary to the obtained coherence scores for distinct preprocessing techniques, the overall interpretability of the topics remains largely unaffected. The decrease in coherence scores during POS-filtering can be attributed to the exclusion of relevant cognates associated with other parts of speech, such as *bjudzhetnyj* (*budgetary*) for the finance topic and *zemel'nyj* (*land.*ADJ) for real estate. Nevertheless, even in the absence of POS-filtering, the term sets predominantly consist of nouns.

It should also be pointed out that LDA-models produce less topic-specific sets of terms compared to NMF. For example, the LDA-generated set of terms for *justice* contains the lemma *pravo* (*law*), which is also present in the lists for *citizenship* and *real estate* topics. The model based on the NMF-algorithm with POS-filtering includes the word *kadastr* (*inventory*) in the set for *real estate* topic, which presumably enhances analytical precision, as the term constitutes a specific legal concept, offering greater semantic specificity than *zemel'nyj* (*land.*ADJ) – a polysemous term that can occur in non-legal contexts.

4.3 Performance of the Models for Sub-corpora

Keeping the model parameters outlined in the previous part of this section, we calculated coherence scores for the four sub-corpora as a result of applying the four models. The descriptive statistics of the resulting values are presented in Tables 6 and 7 for LDA and NMF, respectively.

Table 6. Results of LDA-models utilization for sub-corpora

	All POS			Nouns only		
	Mean	Median	Range	Mean	Median	Range
1	0.421	0.424	0.39–0.45	0.380	0.376	0.33–0.44
2	0.402	0.422	0.32–0.47	0.354	0.358	0.28–0.42
3	0.360	0.351	0.28–0.45	0.379	0.379	0.31–0.44
4	0.364	0.374	0.30–0.44	0.352	0.352	0.32–0.39

Table 7. Results of NMF-models utilization for sub-corpora

	All POS			Nouns only		
	Mean	Median	Range	Mean	Median	Range
1	0.594	0.590	0.55–0.64	0.556	0.553	0.52–0.59
2	0.637	0.636	0.61–0.65	0.613	0.611	0.58–0.63
3	0.657	0.650	0.64–0.68	0.621	0.620	0.60–0.64
4	0.637	0.635	0.62–0.68	0.602	0.599	0.56–0.64

To evaluate the significance of the changes in mean values, we conducted a paired two-sample t-test for the values of the whole corpus and each of the four sub-corpora. The findings reveal that the mean coherence scores of the LDA-model without POS-filtering exhibited a significant decline for the third and fourth sub-corpora compared to the results obtained for the full corpus, at a significance level of $\alpha = 0.05$ (p-values ≈ 0.0078 and 0.0052, respectively). In contrast, the LDA-model with POS-filtering demonstrated higher stability with respect to the change in values, as no significant differences were observed between coherence scores for the corpus and sub-corpora. Regarding the NMF-models, both of them demonstrated a significant decrease for the first sub-corpus (p-value ≈ 0.0004 and 0.0002 for models without and with POS-filtering, respectively), while no significant changes were found for the remaining sub-corpora. These results indicate that the LDA model with POS-filtering is the most robust in terms of formal performance. Although both NMF models outperformed LDA-models overall, their performance was notably weaker for the first sub-corpus.

Among the topics unique to each of the sub-corpora and identified by at least one model implemented by each algorithm are:

1. 'housing law' – dom (house), sobstvennik (proprietor), pravo (law), rf (rf – Russian Federation), zhilishhnyj (housing), 'smoking' – sigareta (cigarette), kurenie (smoking), pachka (packet), zakon (act), akciz (excise) for the first sub-corpus;
2. 'education' – obrazovanie (education), zakon (act), uchrezhdenie (institution), programma (program), vuz (hei), 'labour' – trud (labour), uslovie (condition), ocenka (assessment), provedenie (conduction), mesto (place) for the second one;
3. 'benefits' – posobie (benefit), vyplata (payment), pensionnyj (pension.ADJ), rebjonok (child), fond (fund), 'Afghanistan' – talib (talib), afganistan (Afghanistan), sila (force), pravitel'stvo (government), govorit' (to say) for the third one;
4. 'ownership' – pravo (right), rf (rf – Russian Federation), pravoobladatel' (right holder), sud (court), stat'ja (article), 'family law' – rebjonok (child), sem'ja (family), rabota (job), chelovek (human), problema (problem) for the fourth one.

This topic distribution likely reflects the influence of civil servants' groups and the degree of their involvement in political processes. For instance, the prominence of housing law and smoking among top federal officials may stem from legislative developments addressing critical issues in these domains. Specifically, 'housing law' could relate to mortgage and housing affordability issues, while 'smoking' may be tied to excise tax policies and anti-tobacco legislation. In contrast, heads of minor federal bodies appear more focused on enforcing existing laws rather than drafting new ones, which aligns with the prevalence of 'labour' and 'education' topics. Their responsibilities likely include maintaining workplace or educational standards and monitoring compliance with occupational safety assessments. Mid-level federal and non-federal officials concentrate on regional concerns, prioritizing the social and legal challenges faced by individuals rather than broader state functions. This is confirmed by the presence of the words *rebjonok* (*child*) and *human* (*chelovek*) in the sets of terms for the topics 'benefits' and 'family law'. Overall, the identified topics correspond to the hierarchical structure of bureaucratic responsibility: the lower the official's job position, the more localized, citizen-centric issues appear in the interviews.

It should also be noted that the topic 'judgement' was detected in all sub-corpora, indicating its importance for Russian civil servants regardless of the level of their job position.

5 Conclusions

The study allowed us to assess the thematic diversity of the corpus of interviews with officials, as well as to identify the model that performs best in terms of automated evaluation for this purpose. Contrary to the fact that the LDA-model with POS-filtering demonstrates stable coherence scores when applied on sub-corpora, the choice was made in favor of the NMF-model without POS-filtering, as it demonstrates the highest scores both for the whole corpus and for sub-corpora. The NMF-based models also showed a higher specificity as we observed more topic-specific words in the term sets. Nevertheless, in identifying topics for the whole corpus, the compared methods show high consistency, which testifies to the accuracy of the obtained results and gives the right to assert that the most relevant topics in the public speech of officials for the 21st century are arbitration, justice, state body operations, real estate, finance and citizenship, as well as topics specific to particular groups of officials' job positions. By comparing the performance of LDA- and NMF-models, the study provides insights into the strengths and limitations of these approaches, particularly in handling genre-specific language and thematic structures. Overall, this study contributes to a clearer understanding of topic modeling in specialized contexts and provides a methodological framework for future research in similar areas. The future work in this field should consist in determining precise criteria for expert topic evaluation, followed by a comparison of the results of automated and human assessments.

Acknowledgement. The author acknowledges Saint-Petersburg State University for a research project 123042000068-8.

References

1. Kherwa, P., Bansal, P.: Topic modeling: a comprehensive review. ICST Trans. Scalable Inf. Syst. **0**, 159623 (2018). https://doi.org/10.4108/eai.13-7-2018.159623

2. Egger, R., Yu, J.: A topic modeling comparison between LDA, NMF, Top2Vec, and BERTopic to demystify twitter posts. Front. Sociol. **7**, 886498 (2022). https://doi.org/10.3389/fsoc.2022.886498
3. Zamiraylova, E., Mitrofanova, O.: Dynamic topic modeling of Russian prose of the first third of the XXth century by means of non-negative matrix factorization. In: 3rd International Conference on R. Piotrowski's Readings in Language Engineering and Applied Linguistics, PRLEAL 2019, pp. 321–339 (2020)
4. Greene, D., O'Sullivan, J., O'Reilly, D.: Topic modelling literary interviews from the Paris review. Digital Sch. Humanit. **39**, 142–153 (2024). https://doi.org/10.1093/llc/fqad098
5. Vianna, D., De Moura, E.S., Da Silva, A.S.: A topic discovery approach for unsupervised organization of legal document collections. Artif. Intell. Law **32**, 1045–1074 (2024). https://doi.org/10.1007/s10506-023-09371-w
6. Kirina, M.A.: A comparison of topic models based on LDA, STM and NMF for qualitative studies of Russian Short Prose. jour. **20**, 93–109 (2022). https://doi.org/10.25205/1818-7935-2022-20-2-93-109
7. Nanyonga, A., Wasswa, H., Wild, G.: Topic modeling analysis of aviation accident reports: a comparative study between LDA and NMF Models. In: 2023 3rd International Conference on Smart Generation Computing, Communication and Networking (SMART GENCON), pp. 1–2. IEEE, Bangalore (2023)
8. Turan, S.C., Yildiz, K., Büyüktanir, B.: Comparison of LDA, NMF and BERTopic topic modeling techniques on amazon product review dataset: a case study. In: García Márquez, F.P., Jamil, A., Ramirez, I.S., Eken, S., Hameed, A.A. (eds.) Computing, Internet of Things and Data Analytics, pp. 23–31. Springer Nature Switzerland, Cham (2024)
9. Stevens, K., Kegelmeyer, P., Andrzejewski, D., Buttler, D.: Exploring topic coherence over many models and many topics (2012)
10. Sherstinova, T., et al.: Topic modeling of literary texts using LDA: on the influence of linguistic preprocessing on model interpretability. In: 2022 31st Conference of Open Innovations Association (FRUCT), pp. 305–312. IEEE, Helsinki (2022)
11. Blinova, O., Tarasov, N.: Complexity metrics of Russian legal texts: selection, use, initial efficiency evaluation. Computat. Linguist. Intellect. Technol., 1–12 (2022)
12. Mitrofanova, O.A., Athugodage, M.M.: Dynamic topic modelling of the Russian legal text corpus. Terra Linguistica **14**, 70–87 (2023)
13. ConsultantPlus. https://www.consultant.ru/. Accessed 16 Mar 2025
14. GARANT.RU. https://www.garant.ru/. Accessed 16 Mar 2025
15. The Federal Law "On General Principles of Organisation of Public Power in the Subjects of the Russian Federation" from 21.12.2021 N 414-FZ. https://www.consultant.ru/document/cons_doc_LAW_404070/. Accessed 16 Mar 2025
16. The Federal Constitutional Law from 21.07.1994 N 1-FKZ (ed. from 31.07.2023) "On the Constitutional Court of the Russian Federation". https://www.consultant.ru/document/cons_doc_LAW_4172/. Accessed 16 Mar 2025
17. The Federal Constitutional Law of 05.02.2014 N 3-FKZ (ed. from 14.07.2022) "On the Supreme Court of the Russian Federation". https://www.consultant.ru/document/cons_doc_LAW_158641/. Accessed 16 Mar 2025
18. Bird, S., Klein, E., Loper, E.: Natural Language Processing with Python: Analyzing Text with the Natural Language Toolkit. O'Reilly Media, Inc. (2009)
19. Segalovich, I., Titov, V.: MyStem (2014). https://yandex.ru/dev/mystem/
20. Sukhonin, D., Panchenko, A.: pymystem3 (2014). https://github.com/nlpub/pymystem3
21. Kramer, K.: Comparative analysis of document-level embedding methods for similarity scoring on Shakespeare sonnets and Taylor swift lyrics (2024). https://arxiv.org/abs/2412.17552

22. Meijer, H.J., Truong, J., Karimi, R.: Document embedding for scientific articles: efficacy of word Embeddings vs TFIDF (2021). http://arxiv.org/abs/2107.05151
23. Blei, D., Ng, A., Jordan, M.: Latent Dirichlet allocation. In: Dietterich, T., Becker, S., и Ghahramani, Z. (eds.) Advances in Neural Information Processing Systems. MIT Press (2001)
24. Babalola, O., Ojokoh, B., Boyinbode, O.: Comprehensive evaluation of LDA, NMF, and BERTopic's performance on news headline topic modeling. J. Comput. Theor. Appl. **2**, 268–289 (2024). https://doi.org/10.62411/jcta.11635
25. Lee, D.D., Seung, H.S.: Learning the parts of objects by non-negative matrix factorization. Nature **401**, 788–791 (1999). https://doi.org/10.1038/44565
26. Wang, Y.-X., Zhang, Y.-J.: Nonnegative matrix factorization: a comprehensive review. IEEE Trans. Knowl. Data Eng. **25**, 1336–1353 (2013). https://doi.org/10.1109/TKDE.2012.51
27. Wang, J., Zhang, X.-L.: Deep NMF topic modeling. Neurocomputing **515**, 157–173 (2023). https://doi.org/10.1016/j.neucom.2022.10.002
28. Rehurek, R., Sojka, P.: Gensim–python framework for vector space modelling. NLP Centre, Faculty of Informatics, Masaryk University, Brno, Czech Republic. 3, (2011)
29. Pedregosa, F., et al.: Others: Scikit-learn: machine learning in Python. J. Mach. Learn. Res. **12**, 2825–2830 (2011)
30. Gualberto, E.S., De Sousa, R.T., De B. Vieira, T.P., Da Costa, J.P.C.L., Duque, C.G.: From feature engineering and topics models to enhanced prediction rates in phishing detection. IEEE Access **8**, 76368–76385 (2020). https://doi.org/10.1109/ACCESS.2020.2989126

Do LLMs Understand Why We Write Diaries? A Method for Purpose Extraction and Clustering

Valeriya Goloviznina([✉]), Alexander Sergeev, Mikhail Melnichenko, and Evgeny Kotelnikov

European University at Saint Petersburg, St. Petersburg, Russia
{v.goloviznina,a.sergeev,mmelnichenko,e.kotelnikov}@eu.spb.ru

Abstract. Diary analysis presents challenges, particularly in extracting meaningful information from large corpora, where traditional methods often fail to deliver satisfactory results. This study introduces a novel method based on Large Language Models (LLMs) to identify and cluster the various purposes of diary writing. By "purposes," we refer to the intentions behind diary writing, such as documenting life events, self-reflection, or practicing language skills. Our approach is applied to Soviet-era diaries (1922–1929) from the Prozhito digital archive, a rich collection of personal narratives. We evaluate different proprietary and open-source LLMs, finding that GPT-4o and o1-mini achieve the best performance, while a template-based baseline is significantly less effective. Additionally, we analyze the retrieved purposes based on gender, age of the authors, and the year of writing. Furthermore, we examine the types of errors made by the models, providing a deeper understanding of their limitations and potential areas for improvement in future research.

Keywords: LLM · Diaries Analysis · Clustering · Archival Documents · Digital Humanities

1 Introduction

Large Language Models (LLMs) are widely used in Digital Humanities (DH) and Computational Social Sciences (CSS) for tasks such as analyzing archives and forums, topic modeling, cultural analytics, text classification, summarization, and generating human-like text with interpretable explanations across fields such as sociology, psychology, literature, history, and linguistics [1–3].

One of the important fields of application of LLMs is the analysis of archival documents such as diaries, letters, journals, etc. It is difficult or impossible to read huge text corpora if it is necessary to extract some important elements from the texts. Simple template-based methods do not work efficiently enough. This is where LLMs come to the rescue.

However, in practice, DH and CSS researchers face the following challenges:

1. uncertainty in model selection and in the accuracy of the model for a particular problem;

M. Bakaev et al. (Eds.): IMS 2025, CCIS 2671, pp. 70–85, 2026.
https://doi.org/10.1007/978-3-032-04958-2_6

2. difficulty in using standard interfaces to LLMs to analyze large corpora;
3. the need for programming skills to access the APIs and handle the results;
4. the high cost of inference.

In this paper, we propose a method to analyze the large diary corpora. In the human sciences, the diary is used as a qualitative research tool [4]. The diary analysis allows researchers to study people's experiences, behaviors, and life circumstances in a natural setting. This research area has been actively explored from the 1990s to the present [5]. Among other things, researchers are interested in the purposes of keeping a diary [6].

In our work, we extract the purposes of diary writing using LLMs. By purposes, we mean the intentions with which people keep diaries – both the reasons why a person started writing (for example, inspiration from someone else's diary, boredom, free time) and the purposes for doing so (for example, writing memoirs, tracking your condition, practicing foreign languages).

As data we use the corpus of diaries of the post-revolutionary Soviet era (1922–1929) from "Prozhito", the Center for the Study of Ego-Documents of the European University at St. Petersburg, which has been collecting and publishing personal diaries in Russian and other languages since 2015 and actively developing a digital archive[1].

The contributions of our work are as follows:

1. we test different proprietary and open-source models for identifying diary entries that contain purposes and for extracting these purposes;
2. we evaluate the performance of these models on both tasks – identification and extraction – based on manual annotation of the results;
3. we propose an iterative algorithm that leverages LLMs to cluster the extracted purposes and evaluate the results for various LLMs;
4. in addition to advancing Computational Linguistics, our study contributes to Digital Humanities and Computational Social Sciences by proposing a scalable and accessible methodology for quantitative research on personal narratives;
5. this study contributes to the humanities by examining the diverse motivations behind diary writing. By analyzing gender, age, and temporal factors, we uncover the significance of diary entries as tools for self-expression and cultural documentation.

2 Previous Work

LLMs are often used to extract structured data from unstructured documents. For instance, in materials science and chemical research, LLMs are employed to extract chemical knowledge, such as formulas or bandgap values [7, 8]. In agriculture, they are applied for pest identification [9], and in medicine, they are used to extract symptoms of pulmonary embolism [10]. Baddour propose using LLMs to search for phenotypes in clinical reports related to medical research [11]. The integration of a novel LLM-based span detector component in their work improves results.

In addition to these applications, LLMs are utilized for diary analysis [6, 12, 13]. Diary analysis involves collecting qualitative information about individuals' daily lives

[1] https://prozhito.org

and is applied in fields such as psychology, education, and healthcare to study human behavior [14].

However, processing such data is challenging, as it requires substantial time and effort. Modern technologies, including LLMs, can streamline this process by accelerating data analysis and providing deeper insights into diary content.

Pooley investigated the reasons why individuals begin and cease diary-keeping [6]. However, their study relied on labor-intensive manual analysis rather than leveraging LLMs. In contrast, Shin et al. used diary analysis to identify depression, employing the GPT-3.5 and GPT-4 models [12]. Using 428 diaries from 91 participants, the fine-tuned GPT-3.5 demonstrated higher performance in detecting depression, achieving an accuracy of 0.902 and an F1-score of 0.685.

Li et al. introduced DiaryHelper, a tool that utilizes generative AI techniques to assist diary writers in capturing event details with minimal effort, thereby reducing bias in the note-taking process [13]. DiaryHelper predicts five dimensions of information critical for episodic memory – time, place, emotion, people, and activity – for each recorded event. The GPT-3.5 model is used to generate possible labels for these dimensions.

A related application of LLMs is in social networking analysis. Alhamed et al. used the LLaMA-2-7B-Chat model to detect evidence of suicidal tendencies in Twitter posts, achieving an accuracy of 0.96 [15].

The reviewed studies demonstrate the effectiveness of LLMs in extracting data from unstructured documents and analyzing diary entries. However, none of the studies address the extraction of diary purposes. Furthermore, unlike the reviewed works, our study employs different state-of-the-art LLMs, enabling a comparative evaluation of their performance in extracting data from unstructured documents.

3 Methodology

Our methodology includes three steps – purpose extraction by different models, annotation and evaluation of the extracted sets, and purpose clustering.

Step 1. Purpose Extraction. We process the entire corpus using multiple models with the same prompt (see Appendix A). On each run, 10 text diary entries are fed (no more than 15,000 tokens[2]), from which models extract potential purposes.

Step 2. Annotation and Evaluation of Extracted Sets. The union of the extracted sets was given to the three annotators for labeling. Annotators had to answer the question, "Is the purpose(s) of diary writing present in this diary entry, and if so, did the model(s) correctly extract that purpose(s)?"[3] A binary answer was implied in both questions. As a result, a set of diary entries containing purposes was identified, relative to which performance scores were computed. Also, for such entries, scores of the purposes extracted by the models were obtained.

We used Precision, relative Recall, and relative F1-score as performance scores. Precision, defined as the proportion of correct answers given by the model to the total

[2] The minimum of the limits of the used models.

[3] Annotators were shown extracted purposes only if they indicated that the entry had a purpose.

number of answers provided by the model, serves as an objective measure in this context. Recall, as the proportion of correct answers of a model to the total number of correct answers in the whole corpus, cannot be properly computed because we are not able to label the whole corpus. This limitation arises from the labor-intensive of annotating.

To achieve a more comprehensive evaluation, we compute relative Recall and relative F1-score, following the approach used in studies [16, 17], for example. In our case, we consider the set of all correct answers to be the set of correct answers labeled by the annotators.

In addition to evaluating individual models, we also assess unions of these models, hypothesizing that merging their answers may improve the performance of purpose extraction.

Step 3. Purpose Clustering. The number of purposes extracted by the models turns out to be quite large (hundreds of purposes), so it is necessary to combine them into categories (clusters). We evaluate how well LLMs cope with purpose clustering.

In the simplest case, the model is given all purposes as input and asked to cluster them. However, none of the models was able to successfully cluster the purposes in one run because a large number of purposes did not belong to any cluster.

Therefore, we used the following algorithm.

1. Clustering Initialization: provide the model with a complete list of purposes and ask it to generate cluster names (see the prompt in the Appendix B).
2. Purpose Assignment: provide the model with a current list of purposes (initially including all purposes) along with the generated cluster names. Ask the model to assign the purposes to the clusters (see the prompt in the Appendix C). Check which purposes have been assigned to clusters – exclude them from the list of purposes.
3. Repeat step 2 until the list of purposes is empty.

To evaluate the quality of the clustering, we manually partitioned each set of purposes into clusters and used these partitions as references. As a performance measure, we used the Rand index [18] and averaged it over all sets of purposes.

4 Data and Models

4.1 Data

The texts of 40,222 personal diaries of 247 authors written in Russian between January 1, 1922 and December 31, 1929 were used as the corpus. Entries that were too short (consisting of 1–2 words) and too long (exceeding 1,400 tokens for any of the tested models) were removed from this set. The value of 1,400 was derived from the context limitations of the LLM – the prompt included 10 entries, the lower bound on the context limit was 15,000 tokens (DeepSeek V3 model, provided by DeepInfra[4], at the time of the experiments). This leaves 38,332 diary entries.

Distributions of diary entries gender, author age category, and period of entries writing presented in Tables 1, 2 and 3.

[4] https://deepinfra.com

The corpus is unbalanced by gender. Experts offer the following explanations for this imbalance: women destroyed their diaries; women kept fewer diaries due to the large number of daily responsibilities, including those related to childbirth.

The time period of entries writing from 1922 to 1929 is divided into three parts: the early years of the decade (1922–1923), the middle years (1924–1926), and the late years (1927–1929).

To determine age categories, we rely on Levinson's stages: pre-adulthood (under 17 years old), early adulthood (ages 18–39), middle adulthood (ages 40–59), and late adulthood (60 years old and older) [19].

Table 1. Distribution of entries by gender.

Gender	# entries
Male	32,371
Female	5,961

Table 2. Distribution of entries by author age category.

Age category	# entries
under 17 years old	2,514
18–39	14,381
40–59	15,323
over 60 years old	5,287

Table 3. Distribution of entries by period of entries writing.

Period of writing	# entries
early 1920s (1922–1923)	8,302
mid 1920s (1924–1926)	14,021
late 1920s (1927–1929)	16,009

4.2 Models

The following models were considered:

- **OpenAI GPT-4o** (v. 2024–08-06) – a proprietary chat model;
- **OpenAI o1-mini** (v. 2024–09-12) – a proprietary reasoning model;
- **DeepSeek-V3** – an open-source chat model with MoE architecture, has 671B total parameters and 37B active parameters to generate each token [20]. Hereafter, we will refer to DeepSeek-V3 simply as DeepSeek.

For the OpenAI models their own provider was used, for the other models the DeepInfra provider was used.

Statistics of the corpus processing for each model are presented in Table 4.

Table 4. Statistics of the corpus processing for each model. Number and average number of tokens are the parameters of the corpus with respect to model tokenizers. The number of entries and purposes shows for how many diary entries the model indicated the presence of purposes and how many total purposes the model extracted. The cost includes processing of the entire corpus and clustering of purposes (for OpenAI – using BatchAPI).

Model	# tokens	Avg. Tokens	# entries	# purposes	Processing cost
baseline[a]	3,868,282	100.9 ± 114.4	177	177	$0
GPT-4o	8,111,474	211.6 ± 226.6	108	172	$9.81
o1-mini	8,111,474	211.6 ± 226.6	71	118	$16.70
DeepSeek	9,183,438	239.6 ± 256.3	290	443	$5.81

[a] In baseline, tokens are words.

We also tried to use other models – OpenAI GPT-4o-mini, DeepSeek-R1-Distill-Llama-70B, Qwen-2.5-72B-Instruct – but the number of entries in which they found purposes was too large (GPT-4o-mini – 2,983, DeepSeek-R1 – 685, Qwen-2.5 – 13,405) and preliminary analysis showed a large number of incorrectly selected entries, so it was decided not to analyze them in more depth.

Besides LLMs, we tested a simple template-based model (baseline). We created lists of nouns ("diary", "record", "purpose", etc.) and verbs ("keep", "write", "help", etc.) indicating the purpose of keeping a diary. An entry was considered to potentially contain a purpose if any of the possible morphology-aware noun + verb pairs occurred in it. In this case, the purpose was defined as the sentence in the entry that contained this pair. Using the baseline, we identified 177 entries, corresponding to 177 purposes.

5 Results

Step 1. Purpose Extraction. We obtained results from 4 models for 38,332 diary entries. The number of entries for which the models extracted purposes is shown in Table 5. The union of the four sets includes 460 entries. These entries were given to three annotators for labeling.

Table 5. Results of the models (first four rows) and the union of the models (last four rows). *Entries* is the number of diary entries in which the model identified purposes, *Correct entries* is the number of diary entries labeled by annotators as actually containing purposes.

Model	# entries	# correct entries	Precision	Rel. Recall	Rel. F1-score
baseline	177	35	0.1977	0.2059	0.2017
GPT-4o	108	83	**0.7685**	0.4882	0.5971
o1-mini	71	48	0.6761	0.2824	0.3983

(continued)

Table 5. *(continued)*

Model	# entries	# correct entries	Precision	Rel. Recall	Rel. F1-score
DeepSeek	290	140	0.4828	0.8235	0.6087
Continuation of Table 5					
Model	# entries	# correct entries	Precision	Rel. Recall	Rel. F1-score
GPT-4o ⋃ o1-mini	153	107	0.6993	0.6294	**0.6625**
GPT-4o ⋃ DeepSeek	306	147	0.4804	0.8647	0.6177
o1-mini ⋃ DeepSeek	319	156	0.4890	0.9177	0.6380
GPT-4o ⋃ o1-mini ⋃ DeepSeek	333	161	0.4834	**0.9471**	0.6402

Step 2. Annotation and Evaluation of Extracted Sets. From 460 diary entries, the annotators identified 170 entries by majority voting as actually containing the purpose(s). The performance scores of the individual models, as well as their union[5], are shown in the Table 5. The inter-annotator agreement was quite high: Krippendorff's alpha = 0.895.

The best result for Precision is shown by GPT-4o, o1-mini lags behind by 10 p.p. DeepSeek extracts a lot of entries (290), but only 140 of them are correct, which results in low Precision. However, this is compensated by high relative Recall, so relative F1-score is even slightly higher than GPT-4o. Among the model union, the best result is the union of GPT-4o and o1-mini in terms of Precision and relative F1-score. This union represents the optimal balance of Precision and relative Recall.

For diary entries that annotators labeled as containing purposes (170 entries), the purposes extracted by the models were also labeled. The results are shown in Table 6. GPT-4o and o1-mini show comparable results, with DeepSeek lagging behind by 5–6 pp.

Table 6. Results of the purpose extraction. *Purposes* refers to the number of purposes extracted by the model, considering only those diary entries that annotators labeled as containing a purpose. *Mean* is the average number of extracted purposes per entry. *Correct purposes* is the number of purposes labeled by annotators as valid purposes.

Model	# purposes	mean	# correct purposes	Precision
GPT-4o	141	1.70	126	0.8936
o1-mini	85	1.77	77	**0.9059**
DeepSeek	221	1.58	187	0.8462

Inter-annotator agreement was much lower: Krippendorff's alpha = 0.598. It is because model-generated purpose statements are often ambiguous and perceived differently by annotators.

Examples of the purposes are shown in the Appendix D and typical errors are given in the Appendix E. The errors were related to diary entries:

- mentioning other people's diaries: error in identifying the author (e.g., "to familiarize oneself with Korolenko's true experience");

[5] Union with baseline are not given as they show low performance.

- mentioning other types of entries: error in identifying the type of entry (e.g., "writing on canvas", "writing down objections to an article");
- mentioning plans, reasoning or style of keeping a diary, but not the purpose: error in identifying the purpose (e.g. "keep a diary neatly").

Step 3. Purpose Clustering. Each LLM clustered all three sets of extracted purposes (separately) according to the proposed algorithm. The number of clusters allocated by each model for each set of purposes is shown in Table 7.

Table 7. The number of clusters. The rows correspond to the models that performed clustering of the purpose sets, the columns correspond to the models that generated these purpose sets.

Clustering model	Purpose extraction model		
	GPT-4o (141 purposes)	o1-mini (85 purposes)	DeepSeek (221 purposes)
GPT-4o	13	9	10
o1-mini	10	10	10
DeepSeek	10	9	12
manual	11	9	16

We compared the resulting partitions with the manual partitions and calculated the Rand index (Table 8). The Rand index quantifies the similarity between data clusterings by measuring the proportion of pairs of elements that are either assigned to the same cluster or assigned to different clusters. The best results are again GPT-4o and o1-mini, although DeepSeek is not far behind, apart from the case of clustering a large number of purposes (221) extracted by DeepSeek itself. Examples of the clusters are given in the Appendix F.

Table 8. Results of the clustering. The rows correspond to the models that performed clustering of the purpose sets, the columns correspond to the models that generated these purpose sets. The values in the cells are the Rand indices (↑).

Clustering model	Purpose extraction model		
	GPT-4o	o1-mini	DeepSeek
GPT-4o	**0.8693**	**0.8333**	0.8490
o1-mini	0.8398	0.8076	**0.8537**
DeepSeek	0.8367	0.8280	0.7956

6 Discussion

We analyze GPT-4o clusters based on GPT-4o purposes as the best option for clustering the identified purposes (see the first row and first column in Table 8), specifically 13 clusters that contain 126 correctly identified purposes. During this clustering process, the total number of purposes was reduced to 109, as some purposes allocated within a single entry were grouped into the same cluster; such purposes were not considered in further analysis. The name of these clusters and examples of purposes for each cluster are provided in the Appendix F.

Figure 1 shows the distribution of purposes among the clusters identified by GPT-4o. In the following diagrams, the order of clusters is preserved as in Fig. 1, specifically by their frequency of occurrence.

Three clusters – "Preservation of Memories," "Personal History and Memoirs," and "Memory of Other People" – are related to memories. They differ as follows: "Preservation of Memories" refers to keeping personal memories for oneself. "Personal History and Memoirs" involves preserving personal memories for others. "Memory of Other People" pertains to preserving memories of other individuals. Examples of diary entries from these clusters are shown in Appendix G.

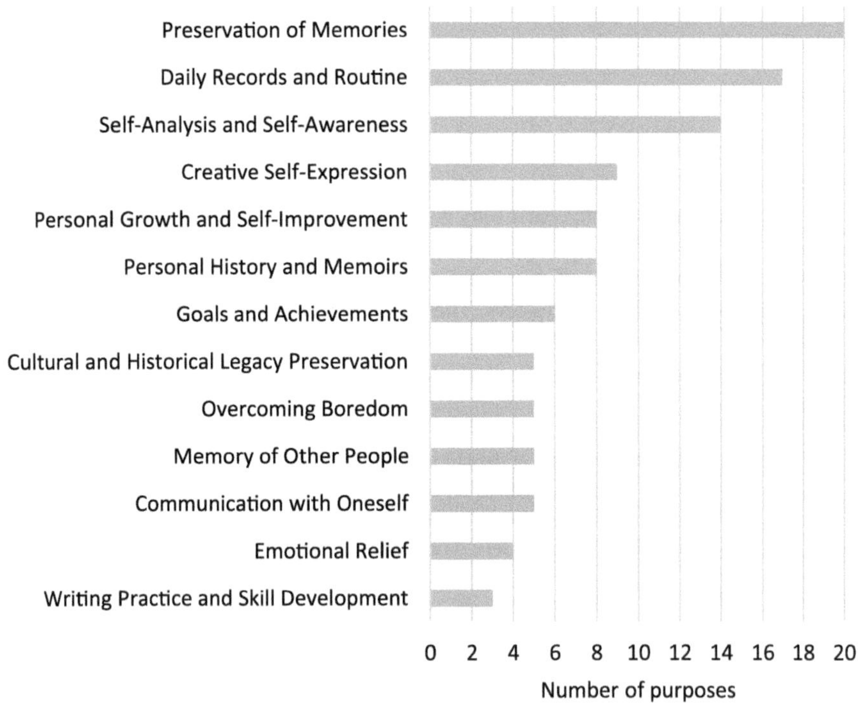

Fig. 1. Distribution of purposes among the clusters identified by GPT-4o.

We consider the composition of the clusters by gender, author age category, and period of entries writing (Figs. 2, 3 and 4).

The original corpus contained 5.4 times more male diary entries than female diary entries (Table 1). The manually annotated part of the corpus (460 entries) consists of 284 male and 176 female entries. When examining entries that specified a purpose, the ratio shifted to 1.6, still favoring male entries. This indicates that women were more inclined to articulate the purpose behind their diary-keeping.

Due to the imbalance in the original corpus, we consider not the number of male and female entries, but the proportion of these entries with purposes in each cluster relative to the total number of male and female entries with purposes in the labeled part of the corpus. Specifically, out of 109 labeled purposes, there were 67 male and 42 female entries. Among the 20 entries containing purposes, the cluster "Preservation of Memories" included 14 male and 6 female entries. Thus, the proportion of male entries in this cluster was 0.21 (14 out of 67), while the proportion of female entries was 0.14 (6 out of 42). Similar calculations were performed for all clusters, and the results are shown in Fig. 2.

Fig. 2. The proportions of male and female entries with purposes in clusters. After the #, the chart legend indicates the number of purposes for each category.

The proportions in Fig. 2 allow us to hypothesize that the purposes of "Personal History and Memoirs" holds equal significance for both genders. Men tend to focus more on retaining memories, personal growth and recording daily events, while women are more likely to emphasize emotional release, achievement and self-analysis in their diary entries.

The analysis of purposes by the author's age category is shown in Fig. 3 (we also use proportions rather than absolute numbers).

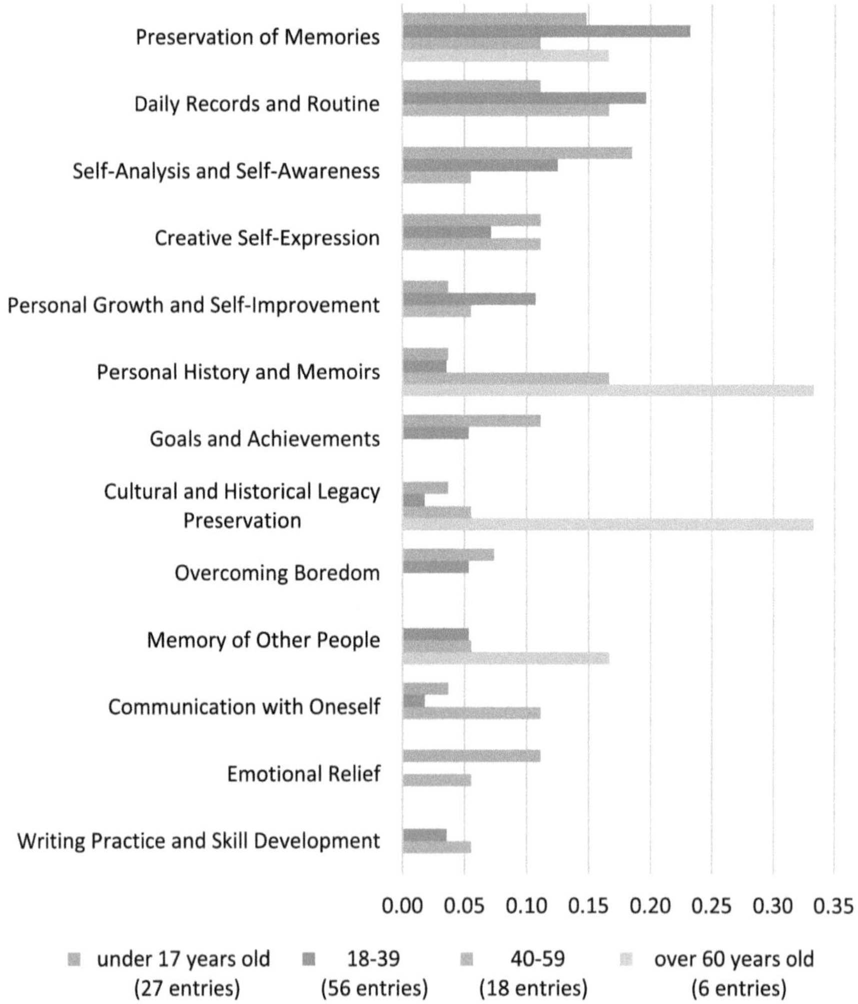

Fig. 3. The proportions of age categories in clusters. After the #, the chart legend indicates the number of purposes for each category.

It is worth noting that in the diaries of the age category over 60, only purposes about preserving memories were identified. The under-17 age category focuses on entries related to self-analysis. Interestingly, the cluster "Goals and achievements" and "Overcoming Boredom" is divided among two young age categories (under 17 and 18–39).

The analysis of purposes by the period of writing the entries is shown in Fig. 4.

Fig. 4. The proportions of periods in clusters. After the #, the chart legend indicates the number of purposes for each category.

The cluster "Preservation of Memories" remains consistently popular across all three periods. Meanwhile, the cluster "Self-Analysis and Self-Awareness" experiences a decline during the mid-1920s. In contrast, the cluster "Daily Records and Routine" sees an increase in frequency during the same timeframe. The "Memory of Other People" decreases from 11% to 0% over three periods, while the "Overcoming Boredom" cluster increases in the later period.

7 Conclusion

In this study, we propose a method for extracting and clustering purposes in diary entries using LLMs. We evaluated three state-of-the-art LLMs alongside a template-based baseline. GPT-4o and o1-mini demonstrated the best performance, while the baseline performed poorly.

Our experimental results suggest the following recommendations. If precision is the primary concern, GPT-4o is the best choice. However, if the purpose is to retrieve the maximum number of potentially relevant entries at a lower cost, followed by manual labeling, DeepSeek is preferable. A balanced approach is to combine the results of GPT-4o and o1-mini, offering a trade-off between precision and recall.

We also highlight common model errors found in the extraction of purposes from diary entries, such as misidentifying the author by referencing other people's diaries, confusing diary entries with other types of writing, and mentioning plans or styles of diary-keeping without clearly stating the actual purpose.

The use of LLMs allows to save a lot of time while obtaining acceptable quality of the analysis. According to our experts' estimates, the time one person would spend reading the entire corpus is on the order of 300 h (37.5 working days), while LLM processed in an hour.

Our analysis of diary-keeping purposes provides insights into the motivations behind personal writing across different demographics. We found that both genders appreciate "Personal History and Memoirs", but men are more focused on memory retention and personal growth, while women place greater emphasis on emotional release and self-analysis.

Age also plays a significant role; individuals over 60 primarily write to preserve memories, whereas those under 17 engage more in self-reflection.

Notably, the "Preservation of Memories" cluster remains consistently popular across all three examined time periods (1922–1923, 1924–1926, 1927–1929). In contrast, "Self-Analysis and Self-Awareness" experiences a decline in the mid-1920s, while the frequency of "Daily Records and Routine" increases during the same timeframe.

Limitation

It should be noted that the study encounters certain limitations. The main difficulty lies in the ambiguous definition of the concept of "purpose of keeping a diary". This led to the need to write a more detailed prompt and provide examples. This ambiguity was also the main reason for the disagreement between the annotators.

Another limitation was the chosen time period for the diary entries – the 1920s. Misunderstanding of the historical context could lead to hallucination of the models and incorrect labeling by the annotators.

The reasons mentioned above, as well as the small number of annotators (three persons), could lead to bias in the quality assessments of the considered models.

Another issue is that we lack information about the complete set of diary entries in our corpus that contain purposes, as labeling the entire corpus is too time-consuming.

Therefore, we utilize relative Recall (and consequently relative F1-score) since we only consider the set of entries extracted by all four models.

Ethics Statement
This study was conducted with careful consideration of ethical principles. A diary entry may contain sensitive information that the author may not have intended to share. In our work, we relied on the principles of the "Prozhito" diary corpus[6]. In particular, diaries were not used unless the author or their heirs provided permission for publication. The diary entries were also anonymized: neither the models nor the annotators had information about the author of the diary.

The diary corpus was compiled by both professional publishers and interested volunteers. The original diary entry could be edited by the author, an editor during publication, or a center staff member at the center for annotation. Each participant in the process could have contributed their own personal beliefs and biases, which could have distorted the research results. Like any other personal text, a diary requires critical interpretation from the reader – it is essential to understand that the author may have various motivations for keeping a diary, including the desire to distort or alter the description of events.

The authors were in close contact with the "Prozhito" Center for the Study of Ego-Documents of the European University at St. Petersburg, and regular consultations were held.

Appendix A. Prompt for Purpose Extraction

Prompt for purpose extraction is available at the repository, Appendix A.

Appendix B. Prompt for Generating Cluster Names

Prompt for generating cluster names is available at the repository, Appendix B.

Appendix C. Prompt for Purpose Clustering

Prompt for purpose clustering is available at the repository, Appendix C.

Appendix D. Examples of Purposes

Examples of purposes is available at the repository, Appendix D.

Appendix E. Errors in Extracting Diary-Keeping Purposes by LLMs

Errors in extracting diary-keeping purposes by LLMs is available at the repository, Appendix E.

[6] https://prozhito.org/page/corpus/

Appendix F. Examples of Clusters

Examples of clusters is available at the repository, Appendix F.

Appendix G. Examples of Diary Entries

Examples of diary entries is available at the repository, Appendix G.

References

1. Ziems, C., Held, W., Shaikh, O., Chen, J., Zhang, Z., Yang, D.: Can large language models transform computational social science? Comput. Linguist. **50**(1), 237–291 (2024)
2. Cigliano, A., et al.: The impact of digital analysis and large language models in digital humanity. In: ICYRIME 2024: 9th International Conference of Yearly Reports on Informatics, Mathematics, and Engineering, p. 1. CEUR Workshop Proceedings (2024)
3. Kataishi, R.: The technological trajectory of semantic analysis: a historical-methodological review of NLP in social sciences (2024). SSRN 5022988
4. Hyers, L.L.: Diary Methods. Oxford University Press, New York, NY (2018)
5. Lischetzke, T., Könen, T.: Daily diary methodology. encyclopedia of quality of life and well-being research, pp. 1563–1570, Springer International Publishing, Cham (2023)
6. Pooley, C. G., Pooley, M. E.: The value of diary writing. everyday mobilities in nineteenth- and twentieth-century British diaries, pp. 21–53, Springer International Publishing, Cham (2022)
7. Schilling-Wilhelmi, M., et al.: From text to insight: large language models for chemical data extraction. Chem. Soc. Rev. **54**, 1125–1150 (2025)
8. Patiny, L., Godin, G.: Automatic extraction of FAIR data from publications using LLM. Preprint, ChemRxiv (2023)
9. Peng, R., Liu, K., Yang, P., Yuan, Z., Li, S.: Embedding-based retrieval with LLM for effective agriculture information extracting from unstructured Data. Preprint, arXiv:2308.03107
10. Wiest, I.S., et al.: LLM-AIx: An open source pipeline for Information extraction from unstructured medical text based on privacy preserving large language models. medRxiv (2024)
11. Baddour, M., Paquelet, S., Rollier, P., De Tayrac, M., Dameron, O., Labbe, T.: Phenotypes extraction from text: analysis and perspective in the LLM Era. In: 2024 IEEE 12th International Conference on Intelligent Systems (IS), pp. 1–8 (2024)
12. Shin, D., Kim, H., Lee, S., Cho, Y., Jung, W.: Using large language models to detect depression from user-generated diary text data as a novel approach in digital mental health screening: instrument validation study. J. Med. Internet Res. **26**, e54617 (2024)
13. Li, J., He, C., Hu, J., Jia, B., Halevy, A.Y., Ma, X.: DiaryHelper: exploring the use of an automatic contextual information recording agent for elicitation diary study. In: Proceedings of the 2024 CHI Conference on Human Factors in Computing Systems, CHI '24. Association for Computing Machinery, New York (2024)
14. Pezzato, L. M., Bragança, I. F. de S., Prado G. do V. T.: What can a diary do? A look at the academic literature. Revista Brasileira de Educação, 19 (2024)
15. Alhamed, F., Ive, J., Specia, L.: Using large language models (LLMs) to extract evidence from pre-annotated social media data. In: Proceedings of the 9th Workshop on Computational Linguistics and Clinical Psychology (CLPsych 2024), pp. 232–237. Association for Computational Linguistics, St. Julians, Malta (2024)

16. Lagisz, M., Yang, Y., Young, S., Nakagawa, S.: A practical guide to evaluating sensitivity of literature search strings for systematic reviews using relative recall. Res. Synth. Methods, 1–14 (2025)
17. Hanneke, R., Brunskill, A.: Searching for the social determinants of health: observations from evidence synthesis publications. Syst. Rev. **13**, 134 (2024)
18. Rand, W.M.: Objective criteria for the evaluation of clustering methods. J. Am. Stat. Assoc. **66**(336), 846–850 (1971)
19. Levinson, D.J.: A conception of adult development. Am. Psychol. **41**, 3–13 (1986)
20. Liu A., et al.: DeepSeek-AI DeepSeek-V3 Technical Report. Computing Research Repository, arXiv:2412.19437

Dialog Flow Analytics Toolkit for a Contact Center Platform

Alena Zhivotova(✉) and Valeria Zarembo

Erllecta LLC, Moscow, Russia
zhivotova.aa@erllecta.ru

Abstract. The paper is dedicated to crucial tasks of communication analysis in high-load contact centers, including structured data collection, key events identification, and automation of speech pattern analysis. Emphasis is placed on the optimization of dialog scripts through topic-based graph modeling to discover the most effective pathways for agent-customer communication, as well as dynamic classification of long multi-intent conversations to identify subtasks and improve the accuracy of complex communication analysis. The authors suggest a methodology that combines graph algorithms for identifying standard scenarios and extracting anomalies in dialog corpora, as well as n-gram segmentation of dialogs with adaptive overlapping for context preservation and dynamic classification by using lightweight Large Language Models and aggregation rules. The developed toolkit was tested on real-life technical support chat and call data. Results have shown its effectiveness for monitoring and analyzing agent-customer interactions, allowing for up to 100% coverage of dialogs analyzed. Practical significance of the study is attested by use cases such as common speech pattern extraction, event-topic context analysis, and retrieval of similar dialogs based on visual representations of task type dynamics.

Keywords: dialog flow analysis · graph models · topic modelling · large language models · speech analysis · natural language processing

1 Introduction

Contact centers are the key element of company-customer interaction, providing support and service through various communication channels. In high-load contact centers handling over 400,000 monthly omnichannel dialogs (voice, chat, messengers), traditional methods of monitoring and supervising agents' (both human operators and digital assistants) performance become ineffective. Supervisors can physically analyze only 0.5%–1.5% of all communications, leading to a loss of valuable insights and missed optimization opportunities. Customer-initiated dialogs contain unique data on needs, service efficiency, and areas for improving the company's operations. Analysis of this information significantly enhances customer service, decreases operating expenses and increases profits.

Therefore, *speech analytics* – a set of methods for automated analysis of dialog records using natural language processing (NLP), has become an essential instrument

M. Bakaev et al. (Eds.): IMS 2025, CCIS 2671, pp. 86–100, 2026.
https://doi.org/10.1007/978-3-032-04958-2_7

for scaling up monitoring, analyzing interaction content, and identifying key topics, trends, potential problem areas, and anomalies of various types.

The market offers numerous comprehensive solutions for contact center automation, many of which incorporate speech analytics modules. These include products from tech giants like Google, Microsoft, Amazon, and IBM, as well as specialized companies developing conversational AI solutions for businesses, such as Kore.ai, Omilia, Ada, Yellow.ai, and Cognigy. In Russia, key providers of speech analytics tools are Speech Technology Center group, companies BSS and 3iTech, while MTS AI and others are developing proprietary solutions. During the development of a contact center platform, we analyzed client requirements and market-tested solutions, concluding that beyond basic speech analytics tasks, there is a critical demand for functionality to detect typical dialog scenarios; analyze agent-customer conversational patterns; perform advanced searches across large dialog datasets with flexible tagging and filtering (e.g., identifying dialogs related to video surveillance systems where a customer intended to terminate a contract but reconsidered after interacting with an agent, without the agent offering a discount); as well as to identify semantically and structurally similar interactions. Such capabilities are essential for comprehensive communication monitoring, extracting insights into products, agent performance, and customer responses to specific speech patterns, as well as detecting both successful and anomalous interaction scenarios.

In this context, the key objective is the development of methods for annotating communications to automate data collection and extraction of key dialog events, while representing semantic attributes of dialogs both statically and dynamically. This is particularly crucial for long dialogs with multiple intents and critical events.

Thus, the research aims to develop a toolkit for the effective collection, analysis, and visualization of dynamically changing interaction data between customers and contact center agents. The toolkit is designed to enable scalable processing of communications and extract actionable insights for the further optimization of dialog scripts.

2 Related Work

The task of automated analysis of dialog structure, typical scenarios discovery and visual model creation is a widely discussed research topic. Most studies propose methods for representing dialogs as graph-based structures, including: trajectories, modeled as a stochastic finite state machine [1]; transitions between dialog phases [2]; utterance-level transitions [3], followed by clustering utterances using bigrams, trigrams, and frequent collocations, and extracting subtasks based on agent-side cluster combinations. Negi, Joshi, Chalamalla, and Subramaniam achieved an 80% match between automated and expert-annotated subtask labels. Bangalore, Di Fabbrizio, and Stent [4] used statistical analysis of utterance transitions in dialog graphs to predict dialog acts basing on trigrams of previous and current utterances.

Patricia Ferreira [5] describes a method for constructing dialog graphs through clustering utterances by topics. Meanwhile, Bouraoui and Lemaire [6] propose using topics obtained by co-clustering a bipartite graph of utterances from both dialog actors.

The methodology in Unsupervised Flow Discovery from Task-Oriented Dialogs [7] involves generating utterance embeddings using sentence encoder *all-MiniLM-L6-v2*, clustering utterances via *k-means* algorithm, and constructing a graph of transitions between clusters, where edge weights are transition probabilities. Prediction accuracy for topic transitions is calculated as a ratio of transitions in a dialog flow to transitions in a test set. The authors reported 82.2% accuracy for graphs with edges weighted above 0.05, noting that accuracy decreases as the weight threshold increases.

Ferreira, Carvalho, Alves, Silva, and Gonçalo Oliveira [8] enhanced the dialog flow extraction framework by integrating sentiment analysis. The authors tested the method on five multilingual datasets (English and Portuguese) of diverse domains, with various interaction goals and agent types. Their algorithm operates in three stages: utterances clustering using *k-me*ans on sentence embeddings (keywords per cluster were extracted via *Key-BERT*), dialog flows extraction and graph-based representation, and classification by sentiment. Sentiment scores are averaged for each topic, with standard deviation metrics calculated to assess variability.

Graph representation is used for both speech analytics tasks and typical scenario extraction, driving the development of specialized frameworks and tools [9].

The implementation of described methods faces a number of limitations when applied in high-load contact centers:

Limitation 1: graph-based dialog visualization becomes exceedingly complicated for long, multi-thread dialogs. As the number of dialogs and intents grows, the number of topics increases accordingly and can reach 300 topics and more, which complicates dialog visual analysis.

Limitation 2: most methods focus on task-oriented dialogs with well-defined structure and predictable patterns but real dialogs often contain deviations from a script, mixed intents, and unstructured conversations.

Limitation 3: existing approaches prioritize textual content of a dialog, ignoring important paralinguistic features (e.g., intonation, speech rate, pauses) that reveal actor's intent and emotional state.

Limitation 4: described methods primarily analyze utterances in isolation, disregarding dialog history and contextual dependencies, leading to misinterpretation, particularly in multi-intent dialogs.

Limitation 5: in discussed papers, the methods are validated on English and other languages, however, Russian implementation requires addressing rich morphology, free word order, and diversity of language patterns.

Methods and algorithms developed as part of current research make it possible to use the advantages of a graph-based approach to semantic and structural dialog representation while adapting them to the Russian language and reducing the influence of identified limitations.

3 Methodology and Algorithms

3.1 Model of a Dialog Flow Graph Based on Utterance Features

The objects of study in this work are transcribed and textual records of dialogs between customers and agents, represented as directed graphs, in accordance with taken terms and definitions:

Agent is an employee or digital assistant who performs the role of a contact center operator. Set of contact center agents: $A = \{a_0, a_1, \ldots, a_m\}$.

Customer is an individual initiating contact with an agent to obtain information, assistance, or resolution of issues related to products or services offered by an organization that the contact center serves. Set of customers: $U = \{u_0, u, \ldots, u_l\}$.

Dialog is a record of verbal communication between actors, represented as time-ordered sequence of utterances in plain-text format, labeled as per the role of an actor.

Let C be set of dialogs $C = \{c_0, c_1, \ldots, c_k\}$, and R be set of utterances $R = \{r_0, r_1, \ldots, r_i\}$, where each utterance is defined as $r_i = (t_i, s_i, text_i, (v_{i,0}, v_{i,1}, \ldots, v_{i,n}))$, in which: t_i is utterance timestamp (start time of the utterance); s_i is actor identifier (agent or customer); $text_i$ is utterance text; $(v_{i,0}, v_{i,1}, \ldots, v_{i,n})$ is a tuple of utterance feature values, where $v_{i,n} \in V_n$ and V_n are sets of feature $f_n \in F$ values; and $F = \{f_0, f_1, \ldots, f_n\}$ is a set of all utterance features identified by speech analytics tools, such as topic, sentiment, and others.

Then each dialog $c_k \in$ C can be represented as

$$c_k = (R_k^{u_1}, R_k^{a_m}, E_k), \tag{1}$$

where $R_k^{u_l} = \{r_i \in R | r_i \in c_k \wedge s_i = u_l\}$ means customer utterancesu_l; $R_k^{a_m} = \{r_i \in R | r_i \in c_k \wedge s_i = a_m\}$ means agent utterancesa_m; $E_k \subseteq \left(R_k^{u_l} \times R_k^{a_m}\right) \bigcup (R_k^{a_m} \times R_k^{u_l})$ means directed edges representing utterance sequence, with edge $(r_p, r_q) \in E_k$ if$t_p < t_q$.

Using this model, we can represent dialog flow in a formalized form and visualize graphically (Fig. 1).

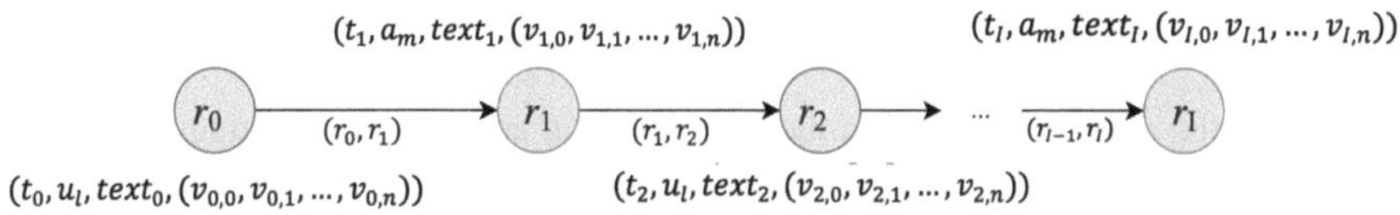

Fig. 1. Dialog graph, I is utterance quantity

Using definitions of dialog and utterance, let us describe a model for graph representations based on utterance features. For this, a set of dialogs is transformed into directed graph:

$$G_{f_n} = \left(V_n, E_{f_n}, w\right), \tag{2}$$

where vertices $V_n = \{v_0, v_1, \ldots, v_x\}$ represent values of selected feature f_n used for graph construction, and edges E_{f_n} are a set of edges, where each edge (v_i, v_j) has weight $w_{i,j}$ equal to the frequency of transitions between utterances with values of corresponding feature f_n.

For each dialog $c_k \in$ C, a transition matrix between utterances P_k is created, where each element $p_{i,j}$ is the number of transitions from an utterance with feature value v_i to an utterance with feature value v_j:

$$p_{i,j} = \sum\nolimits_{(r_p, r_q) \in E_k} \delta(f_n(r_p) = v_i \bigwedge f_n(r_q) = v_j), \tag{3}$$

where δ is the function equal to 1 if the condition is met and 0 otherwise.

Next, transition matrices of all dialogs are merged into one graph by summing edge weights:

$$w_{i,j} = \sum_{k=0}^{K} p_{i,j}^{(k)}, \tag{4}$$

where K is the total number of analyzed dialogs.

Graph visual representation of dialogs in the context of feature f_n state change is shown in Fig. 2.

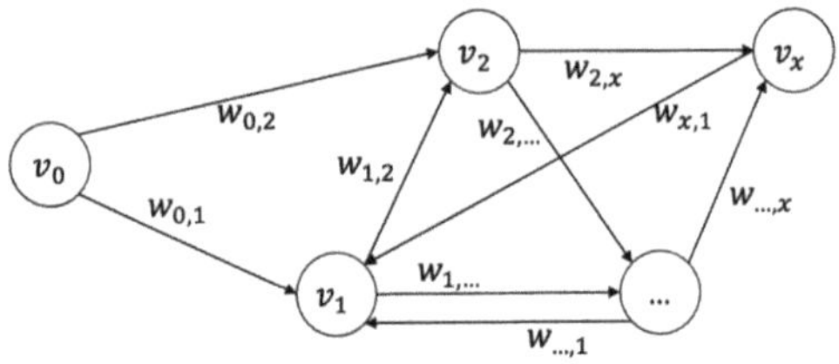

Fig. 2. Dialog graph in the context of feature f_n state change

The model described allows analyzing interactions between different states represented by features $f_n \in F$, and identifying patterns in dialogs between customers and agents in dynamics.

3.2 Topic Modeling-Based Optimal Path Identification

Considering the described model, a method based on agent topic dynamics for identifying optimal paths was proposed. It consists of three main stages: clustering of dialog utterances based on topic modeling results; dialog graph construction within the context of an *utterance topic* feature dynamics; and optimal paths search to retrieve typical communication patterns ang generate standard dialog scripts. In this context, an *optimal path* is a sequence of transitions between agent topic clusters that minimizes the number of steps required to successfully conclude a dialog.

Topic Modeling and Utterance Clustering. Dialog tagging is performed using topic modeling – a method that processes a combined corpus of utterances from all dialogs into a collection of topics and clusters utterances based on their semantic similarity. Before clustering, utterances are preprocessed with segmentation, as a single customer request may contain multiple data (e.g., intents, problem symptoms, or questions); and removal of numbers, emojis, and special symbols to avoid skewing clustering results.

After preprocessing, vector representations of utterances are generated. To address *Limitation 5*, multiple transformer models were tested: *paraphrase-multilingual-mpnet-base-v2* and *paraphrase-multilingual-MiniLM-L12-v2* [10] from *SentenceTransformers* library; and *FRIDA*. For each model, an expert assessment was conducted on the technical-support chat corpus. The resulting topics were evaluated for homogeneity and logical coherence, and the percentage of valid topics (those meeting predefined criteria) was calculated. Table 1 presents transformer models' performance on *ruMTEB* benchmark [11, 12] alongside the expert assessment results. Based on these findings, *FRIDA* model is chosen as the most fitting for topic modeling.

Table 1. Transformer Models Performance for the Russian Language

Model	ruMTEB	Expert Assessment
FRIDA	67.49	98.05
paraphrase-multilingual-mpnet-base-v2	49.18	95.12
paraphrase-multilingual-MiniLM-L12-v2	47.76	94.48

The next step is clustering of vector representations using *HDBSCAN* algorithm [13, 14]. Unlike *k-means*, it automatically estimates the optimal value of k; moreover, due to its hierarchical nature, it allows the identification of relationships between clusters, thereby simplifying the task of cluster reduction. Finally, *HDBSCAN* algorithm is able to identify outliers – texts that cannot be attributed to any of the clusters found in the data. These clustering algorithm features contribute to overcoming *Limitation 1* and *Limitation 2*.

Building Graph Based on Utterance Topic Dynamics. In order to build graph (2), utterances of each dialog are mapped to topics from the dataset obtained after topic modeling and utterance clustering. Since the agent plays a leading role in agent–customer communication, information about both actors is redundant for the task of standard script extraction; therefore, separate agent/customer graphs are built. In addition, sequences of identical topics and "noisy" topics (e.g., greetings, politeness formulas, repeated inquiries) determined by expert assessment are to be removed.

Searching Optimal Paths. The inputs for the task of paths search are: graph $G_{fn} = (V_n, E_{fn}, w)$ built using formula (2); edge weight threshold w_{th} (determined through statistical analysis of the weight distribution); range of valid path length $[l_{min}, l_{max}]$ (initial values correspond to an average number of steps an agent takes to solve a problem). The solution includes the following steps:

1. Edge filtering by threshold w_{th} in order to eliminate the influence of rare and insignificant transitions and reduce the computation load. For that purpose, subgraph $G'_{f_n} = (V_n, E'_{f_n}, w)$ is built, where:

$$E'_{fn} = \{(v_i, v_j) \in E_{fn} | w_{i,j} \geq w_{th}\}. \quad (5)$$

2. Generation of all possible paths in a given length range, i.e. for graph G'_{f_n}, simple paths set P is defined so that it fulfils a condition:

$$P = \{ p_z = (v_0, v_1, \ldots, v_k) | v_i \in V_n, (v_i, v_{i+1}) \in E'_{fn}, k \in [l_{min}, l_{max}]\} . \quad (6)$$

3. Computation of a cumulative weight for each path $p_z \in P$:

$$f(p_z) = \sum\nolimits_{i=1}^{k-1} w(v_{i,}v_{i+1}), \tag{7}$$

where $w(v_i, v_{i+1})$ is the weight of edge (v_i, v_{i+1}), calculated according to formula (4).

4. Selection of optimal path P_{opt} that maximizes cumulative weight $f(p_z)$:

$$P_{opt} = \underset{p_z \in P}{\text{argmax}} f(p_z). \tag{8}$$

Given algorithm formalizes the process of searching for the most probable and relevant transition sequence between topics of agent utterances. If the algorithm results in an empty set P, it can be repeated with relaxed w_{th} and expanded $[l_{min}, l_{max}]$.

Result Analysis. The proposed method can be applied to both retrospective analysis and the synthesis of adaptive dialog strategies, providing solutions for two complementary tasks. First, it enables dialog clustering based on structural patterns: dialogs are grouped based on the presence of specific paths P detected in graph G_{f_n}. This facilitates the identification of dialog classes with similar actor strategies and allows for cluster comparison against performance metrics. Second, the method solves the problem of paths search in pre-annotated dialogs. When dialogs are annotated with specific features (e.g., intent type), class-specific optimal paths P_{opt} can be identified to establish a causal relationship between dialog structure and its outcome.

3.3 Dynamic Classification of Long Dialogs

In contact centers, dialog classification is carried out using various methods that may be based on customer or agent features, dialog session metadata, or a system of labels developed by an analyst or supervisor. One of the primary classification methods is by the type of problem being solved or the customer's intent. At the same time, long dialogs (lasting more than 6 min or consisting of more than 150–500 utterances) are characterized by high structural complexity, as they may include several intents, multiple context shifts, parallel resolution of several subtasks, or problem escalation. Analyzing such dialogs requires breaking them down into semantic segments with subsequent dynamic classification. We propose using an approach that includes the following steps.

Partition into Semantic Segments by splitting a dialog into overlapping N-gram utterances (set of windows S of fixed-length N) with step size s, i.e.

$$S_i = (r_i, r_{i+1}, \ldots, r_{i+N-1}), \text{ with } i = 1, 1 + s, 1 + 2s, \ldots, l - N + s, \tag{9}$$

where $S_i \in S$; $s = N/2$ is N-gram overlap step rounded up; $(r_i, r_{i+1}, \ldots, r_{i+N-1}) \in c_k$; l is dialog length c_k in utterances; if $l \leq N$, the dialog is classified as a single window.

Classification of Obtained Windows, where for each S_i class $y_i \in Y$ is determined, with Y being the set of classes specified by an analyst.

For classification, an approach using open-source lightweight generative LLMs is chosen. This provides the optimization of resource usage while maintaining classification accuracy. The models can be deployed locally without the need for expensive computing clusters, which reduces implementation costs and ensures the security of personal data.

Moreover, generative models can handle typos, abbreviations, and colloquial speech typical for live dialogs, and unlike traditional ML models, effectively capture semantic relations between utterances even if key words or phrases are not explicitly mentioned. For example, in the window of utterances (*"I cannot log into my account", "Check your password", "That password doesn't work"*), generative models recognize the context as "Authentication problem". LLM is selected based on the ranking of open-source models [15], taking into account hardware capabilities of the speech analytics server.

Aggregation of Sequential Windows S_i belonging to the same class y_i to form semantically coherent sub-dialogs $D_j^{(y)}$:

$$D_j^{(y)} = \bigcup_{S_i \in S_y} \left(r_{start(S_i)}, r_{end(S_i)} \right), \tag{10}$$

where $r_{start(S_i)}$ is the first utterance of window S_i; $r_{end(S_i)}$ is the last utterance of window S_i; the merging is carried out for all consecutive S_i that satisfy the continuity condition

$$\forall S_p, S_q \in D_j^{(y)} \left| start\left(S_p\right) - end\left(S_q\right) \right| \le s. \tag{11}$$

Sub-dialogs obtained can be used both for finding optimal paths, thereby allowing dialogs to be normalized by length, and for retrieving sub-dialogs with similar dynamics in class variation. Moreover, classifying N-gram windows instead of individual utterances enables contextual consideration and overcomes *Limitation 4.*

4 Implementation of Dialog Flow Analytics Toolkit

4.1 Dialog Graph Analysis and Paths Search

To analyze dialog flow, tools for dialog text processing, clustering, topic chains annotation, building and visualization of topic relations as a graph, optimal paths discovery and path frequency calculation are developed. Additionally, tools for path querying in dialogs are also implemented. Figure 3 shows the toolkit architecture.

In order to process a dialog corpus with the toolkit, the following pipeline is implemented:

Step 1. In Text Preprocessing Module, utterances with metadata (timestamp, actor, dialog ID) are extracted from corpus *RawDialog* represented by XML files, using *beautifulsoup4* library. Then, they are segmented by *natasha* tools and cleared of emoji and numbers. The result is recorded in *Dataset_Chats.*

Step 2. Dataset_Chats is filtered by actor and unique values of *Sentences* column are passed to the Clustering Module being vectorized and clustered with *BERTopic.* At this stage, a toolkit user can choose an actor of utterances to be clustered and minimal allowable number of texts per topic. After clustering, topics can additionally be edited by changing their amount or merging specified topics. Two datasets: *Dataset_[actor]Docs* with sentence-to-topic relations and *Dataset_[actor]Topics* with topic definitions; and trained classification model *TM_[actor]Model* are the output of this stage.

Step 3. Dataset_Chats is filtered by actor, and a list of sentences is created for each dialog Then, each sentence is assigned a topic from *Dataset_Docs.topic* and a topic

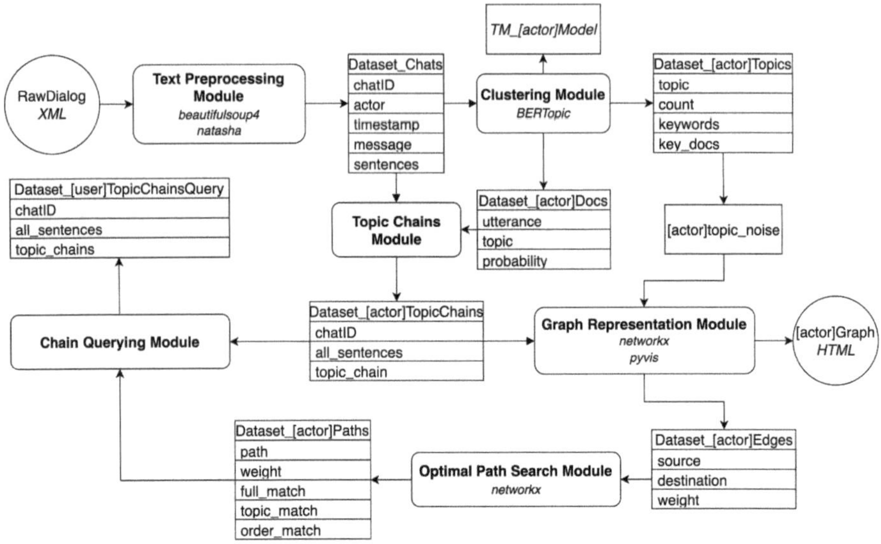

Fig. 3. Architecture of dialog flow analytics toolkit

chain is created. As an option, topic chains can be augmented with information about dialog beginning and/or end. Chains are recorded in *Dataset_[actor]TopicChains*. If both *Dataset_agentDocs* and *Dataset_customerDocs* are present, full topic chain and the chain of customer-agent pairs can be created. Full topic chains are recorded in *Dataset_fullTopicChains*.

Step 4. List *[actor]topic_noise* is created based on *Dataset_[actor]Topics* data. Topic chains *Dataset_[actor]TopicChains.topic_chain* are filtered from *[actor]topic_noise* and consecutive identical topics; after that, *Dataset_[actor]Edges* with topic relations and their weights is created. From *Dataset_[actor]Edges*, all relations with weight lower than the specified threshold are dropped, and the resulting dataset is used for *[actor]Graph* or *[actor]Tree* construction. Results are *Dataset_[actor]Edges* and an HTML page with interactive visualization of *[actor]Graph* or *[actor]Tree*. Libraries *networkx* and *pyvis* are used for graph construction and visualization.

Step 5. For *[actor]Graph*, all simple paths between specified vertices are listed. For each path, edge weights are summarized, and the final list with paths and weights is recorded in *Dataset_[actor]Paths* with descending sort. Additionally, chains from *Dataset_[actor]TopicChains.topic_chain* are checked for the presence of resulting paths by three queries: full match, topic occurrence, and topic occurrence with order retention. Results for each query are joined to *Dataset_[actor]Paths*.

As an option, *Dataset_[actor]TopicChains* can be filtered by the presence of paths from *Dataset_[actor]Paths*. For the search, list of desired paths *[actor]query* and a query type from step 5 must be provided. Search results are in *Dataset_[actor]TopicChainsQuery*.

4.2 Classifying Long Dialogs by Request Type

In addition to graph analysis tools for dialogs, a module for processing long dialogs is developed to reduce their complexity and break them into manageable subtasks for agents. The classification criterion was chosen as the high-level request type, aligned with TM Forum standards [16]. Customer intents, based on agent actions, can thus be divided into six main categories: Request-to-Answer (consultations), Request-to-Change (contract operations), Termination-to-Confirmation (contract termination), Problem-to-Solution (setup and diagnostics), Complaint-to-Solution (complaints), and Other.

By studying approaches to clustering and classifying long texts based on dynamically changing parameters [17, 18], we adapt these methods for dialog text analysis and colored visualization of task dynamic during agent-customer interactions.

The dialog processing pipeline includes the following steps: defining classes and assigning color labels; extracting and preprocessing dialog utterances; splitting dialogs into overlapping N-gram windows; summarizing utterances for each window and classifying windows using *glm-4-9b-chat* model; visualizing results graphically using *matplotlib* library. Processing results for each dialog are saved to dataset *Dataset_end2end_call[callID]* and file *callID.png*.

Examples of colored visualization of dialogs are shown in Fig. 4.

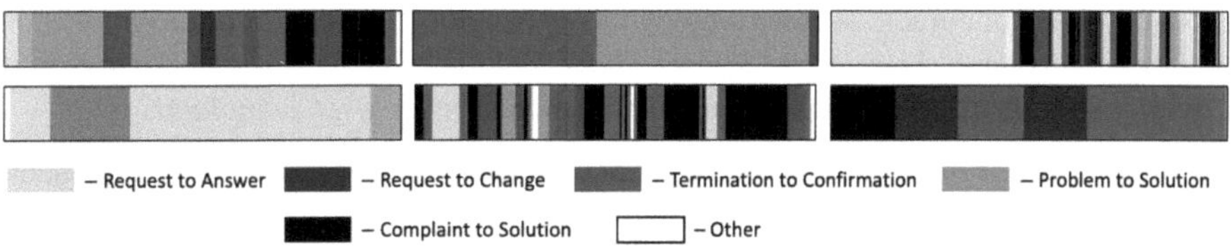

Fig. 4. Colored Dialog Visualization

A color is assigned to each class, and if the class changes during overlapping n-gram windows, the colors are blended. This approach simplifies the analysis of long dialog dynamics and filtering, as analysts can visually identify trends or anomalies requiring heightened attention. To filter samples from the dialog corpus, a tool for clustering dialog images is developed, enabling the detection of similar patterns in dynamics and task types without processing the text itself.

5 Testing and Practical Cases

In order to test the developed toolkit, three corpora were collected: *dataset_chats_24K* – 24,000 technical support chats on the subject of low internet speed with dialog lengths of 2–347 utterances; *dataset_calls_200K* – 200,000 technical support calls on the subject of low internet speed with dialog length of 2–721 utterances (average call duration: 5 min., 24 s.); and *dataset_complaints_1K* – 1095 technical support chats with keywords "complaint" or "termination" with dialog length of 10–1335 utterances. As part of the testing, individual test cases were analyzed and load testing was conducted to determine the hardware capabilities for processing a large volume of dialogs using the described methods.

Testing has shown that applying the described methodology and implemented graph analysis tools allows processing 200,000 dialogs in 3.5 h using up to 16 GB of GPU memory, which accounts for approximately 18% of the contact center's load (based on an average monthly workload of up to 700,000 calls and 400,000 chats, with a total peak daily load of up to 100,000 dialogs). Additionally, the ability to classify new data using trained topic model *TM_[actor]model* further reduces dialog processing time, while scaling hardware resources could increase the share of processed calls to 100%.

The current study focuses on validating the architecture and maximizing the number of processed dialogs. Deeper results of metric analyses, such as classification and clustering accuracy, will be comprehensively detailed in future work to provide a holistic validation of the employed models and algorithms. A large-scale quantitative evaluation of dialog processing stages, leveraging accumulated and annotated operational data, is in preparation. Preliminary expert assessments of dynamic request-type classification performed by *glm-4-9b-chat* model for a subset of test samples, demonstrated an accuracy of 84%, surpassing the manual annotation accuracy by human agents (75%). The highest accuracy was observed for Problem-to-Solution (91%) and Termination-to-Confirmation (94%) classes.

5.1 Cases of Dialog Flow Analysis

Let us consider four practical cases employing the developed toolkit: optimal path search and community analysis in corpus *dataset_chats_24K*; pauses analysis for calls in corpus *dataset_calls_200K*; clustering of long dialogs in corpus *dataset_complaints_1K*.

Optimal Paths for Solving Low Internet Speed Problem. The task involves representing dialog paths as a graph and finding optimal paths for problem solution in 4–9 steps; it is decided that only agent utterances are to be used for the experiment, as agent's speech has less variety and is more structured, which simplifies its generalization. Experiment has shown that optimal path has a following structure: *[Conversation Start]–[Problem Clarification]–[Router Reset]–[Router Setup]–[Do you still have a problem?]–[Solution Explanation]–[Conversation End]*. Additionally, there exist variations of the path in question: namely, an agent might perform a preliminary diagnostic or end dialog without explaining the solution.

Another result of the experiment is the discovery of multiple possible beginnings and ends of a dialog. Based on this, topic chains were augmented with start ("Greeting", "Problem Report", "Problem Report with Symptoms", "Complaints") and end ("Successful Resolution", "Timeout", "Technician Call", "Other") nodes. Paths for combinations of dialog classes were analyzed separately. Figure 5 provides an example of the dialog graph for *Successful Resolution* class.

In order to decrease the number of graph edges and keep the most important dialog phases, only topics pertaining to speed diagnostics and router setup and reset were retained. Splitting dialogs into categories has allowed identifying successful and unsuccessful paths and finding ways to improve the existing scripts, namely, by taking into consideration a variety of possible dialog beginnings.

Community Analysis in Dialogs. The analysis of graphs from the case on finding optimal dialog paths allows proposing a solution for shortening topic chains to overcome

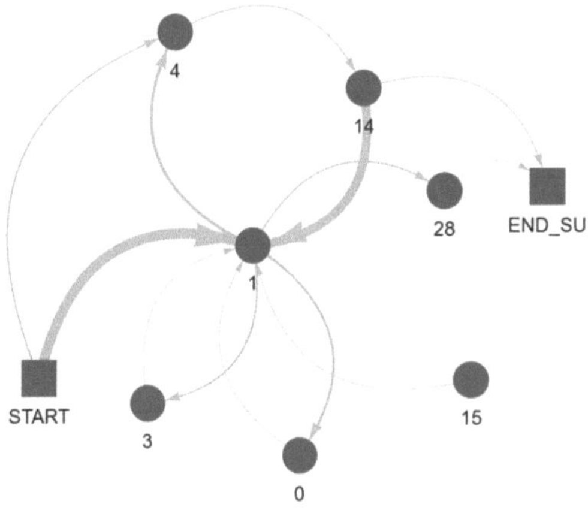

Fig. 5. Graph for *Successful Resolution* class

Limitation 1. Namely, it was hypothesized that agent speech contains patterns of frequent combinations of topics. A community analysis helped testing this hypothesis. Two algorithms were used to conduct an experiment: greedy modularity maximization [19] and the Louvain algorithm [20]. Later, based on expert evaluation, the latter has been chosen.

As the result of experiment, a number of topic combinations was obtained, e.g. "*Signal level and network check*" (includes topics "Signal level detection", "Distance from the router", "Internet speed measurement near the router", "Network on other devices"), "*Internet speed measurement*" (topics "Devices connected to the router", "Instruction on internet speed measurement", "Site for internet speed measurement", "Internet speed measurement screenshot") and "*Cable test*" ("Connecting the internet cable to LAN port", "Connecting the internet cable to WAN port", "Signal from cable to router check", "Router photo"). Communities, like topics, can be used for graph construction; furthermore, existing topic relation graphs can be filtered by communities.

Pauses in Calls. The next case is the analysis of dialog paths with regard to pauses. Input data for the experiment were 200,000 samples of calls on the subject of low internet speed (*dataset_calls_200K*). The experiment aimed to identify agent actions with the highest time expenditure that cause a subsequent increase in customer waiting time. Pauses were split into four categories (short, medium, long and abnormal) and added to topic chains as separate vertices. Resulting topic chains were used to build trees for pause contexts. An example of a context tree for long pause is depicted in Fig. 6.

Analysis of the context tree helped identify bottlenecks in dialogs: router diagnostics, client data retrieval and completion of an application form for a technician call. Furthermore, the experiment has shown that dialog graphs can be successfully augmented with other information about dialog flow, thus weakening the impact of *Limitation 3*.

Similar Dialog Retrieval. As a distinct case study, the task of retrieving similar long dialogs based on its colored codes was explored. Corpus *dataset_complaints_1K* were used as experiment data. Images of dialog colored codes generated using the dynamic

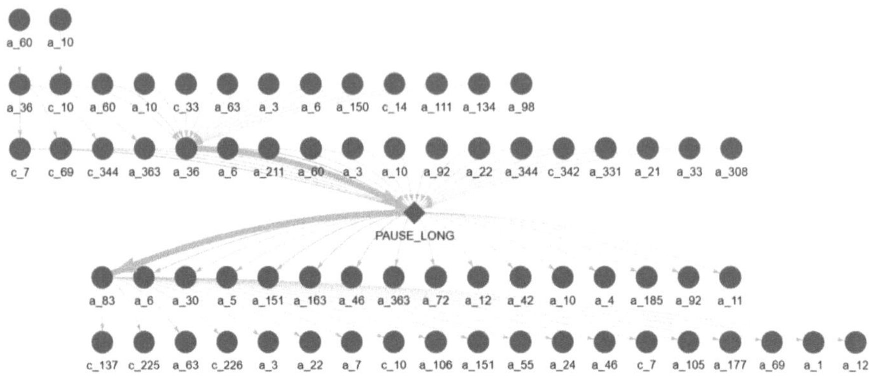

Fig. 6. Long pauses context

image classification module were vectorized and clustered via *k-means*; *k* was determined by *HDBSCAN* algorithm; clustering was additionally verified by assessing clusters coherence basing on semantic similarity of initial dialogs. Four distinct dialog clusters were identified for corpus *dataset_complaints_1K* (Fig. 7a). Resulting clustered dialog images are shown in Fig. 7b. Thus, subsets of dialogs with similar dynamic were retrieved for further analysis through graph-based method and path search modules.

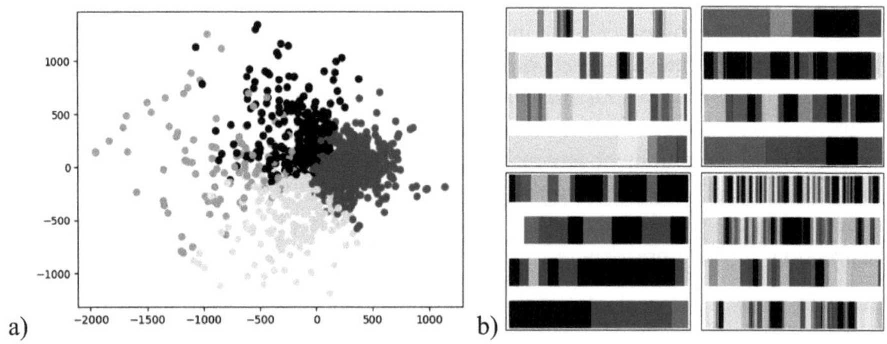

Fig. 7. a) Clustering results for *corpus dataset_complaints_1K*, b) Examples of clustered dialogs (4 classes)

6 Conclusion

Within this work, we have developed a toolkit for dialog flow analytics in high-load contact centers that combines methods of graph modeling, topic clustering and dynamic classification. In addition, the limitations of existing methods are addressed by incorporating transformer models and adding options for dialog filtering based on graph analysis augmenting graph with paralinguistic parameters, analyzing utterances within its context, and implementing alternative dialog visualizations. Tests demonstrates that even in its baseline implementation, the toolkit significantly expands the coverage of analyzed dialogs, identifies semantically or dynamically similar dialogs, and extracts actionable insights about contact center operations – such as optimal dialog paths, variations in customer behavior, dialog problem points, and more.

Promising directions for further research include graph optimization using graph neural networks for clustering and structural compression; LLM integration for utterance normalization and unified template generation; real-time adaptive strategy development based on topic transition prediction, enabling dynamic adjustments to dialog scripts for contact center agents.

References

1. Abella, A., Wright, J., Gorin, A.L.: Dialog trajectory analysis. In: 2004 IEEE International Conference on Acoustics, Speech, and Signal Processing, pp. 1–441. IEEE (2004)
2. Vakulenko, S., Revoredo, K., Di Ciccio, C., de Rijke, M.: QRFA: a data-driven model of information-seeking dialogues. In: Advances in Information Retrieval: 41st European Conference on IR Research, ECIR 2019, Cologne, Germany, 14–18 April 2019, Proceedings, Part I 41, pp. 541–557. Springer, Cham (2019)
3. Negi, S., Joshi, S., Chalamalla, A.K., Subramaniam, L.V.: Automatically extracting dialog models from conversation transcripts. In: 2009 Ninth IEEE International Conference on Data Mining, pp. 890–895. IEEE (2009)
4. Bangalore, S., Di Fabbrizio, G., Stent, A.: Learning the structure of task-driven human-human dialogs. In: Proceedings of the 21st International Conference on Computational Linguistics and 44th Annual Meeting of the Association for Computational Linguistics, pp. 201–208. Association for Computational Linguistics (2006)
5. Ferreira, P.: Automatic dialog flow extraction and guidance. In: Proceedings of the 17th Conference of the European Chapter of the Association for Computational Linguistics: Student Research Workshop, pp. 112–122. Association for Computational Linguistics (2023)
6. Bouraoui, J. L., Lemaire, V.: Cluster-based graphs for conceiving dialog systems. In: Workshop DMNLP at European Conference on Machine Learning (ECML) (2017)
7. Ferreira, P., Martins, D., Alves, A., Silva, C., Oliveira, H.G.: Unsupervised flow discovery from task-oriented dialogues. arXiv preprint: arXiv:2405.01403 (2024)
8. Ferreira, P. S. P., Carvalho, I., Alves, A., Silva, C., Oliveira, H. G.: Sentiment-aware dialogue flow discovery for interpreting communication trends. In: Proceedings of the 25th Annual Meeting of the Special Interest Group on Discourse and Dialogue, pp. 274–288. Association for Computational Linguistics (2024)
9. Bouraoui, J.L., Le Meitour, S., Carbou, R., Barahona, L.M.R., Lemaire, V.: Graph2Bots, unsupervised assistance for designing ChatBots. In: Proceedings of the 20th Annual SIGdial Meeting on Discourse and Dialogue, pp. 114–117. Association for Computational Linguistics (2019)
10. Reimers, N., Gurevych, I. Sentence-BERT: sentence Embeddings using siamese BERT-networks. In: Proceedings of the 2019 Conference on Empirical Methods in Natural Language Processing. Association for Computational Linguistics (2019)
11. Muennighoff, N., Tazi, N., Magne, L., Reimers, N.: MTEB: massive text embedding benchmark. In: Proceedings of the 17th Conference of the European Chapter of the Association for Computational Linguistics, pp. 2014–2037. Association for Computational Linguistics (2023)

12. Snegirev, A., Tikhonova, M., Maksimova, A., Fenogenova, A., Abramov, A. The Russian-focused embedders' exploration: ruMTEB benchmark and Russian embedding model design. arXiv preprint: arXiv:2408.12503 (2024)
13. Campello, R.J.G.B., Moulavi, D., Sander, J.: Density-based clustering based on hierarchical density estimates. In: Pei, J., Tseng, V.S., Cao, L., Motoda, H., Xu, G. (eds.) Advances in Knowledge Discovery and Data Mining. PAKDD 2013. Lecture Notes in Computer Science, vol. 7819, pp 160–172. Springer, Berlin, Heidelberg (2013)
14. Campello, R.J.G.B., Moulavi, D., Zimek, A., Sander, J.: Hierarchical density estimates for data clustering, visualization, and outlier detection. In: ACM Transactions on Knowledge Discovery from Data (TKDD), vol. 10, no. 1, pp. 1–51 (2015)
15. SuperCLUE Rating. www.superclueai.com. Accessed 26 Dec 2024
16. Business Process Framework (eTOM): End-to-End Business Flows (release 24.0.0). https://www.tmforum.org/resources/standard/gb921-business-process-framework-processes-excel-v24-0-0/. Accessed 20 Sep 2024
17. Gao, J., Jockers, M.L., Laudun, J., Tangherlini, T.: A multiscale theory for the dynamical evolution of sentiment in novels. In: 2016 International Conference on Behavioral, Economic and Socio-cultural Computing (BESC), pp. 1–4. IEEE (2016)
18. Zarembo, V., Sherstinova, T.Y.: The dynamics of extensive text variables in Russian short stories. In: Workshop on Cognitive Modeling and Computational Linguistics, pp. 102–114. CEUR-ws.org (2020)
19. Clauset, A., Newman, M.E., Moore, C.: Finding community structure in very large networks. In: Physical Review E—Statistical, Nonlinear, and Soft Matter Physics, vol. 70, no. 6, p. 066111 (2004)
20. Blondel, V.D., Guillaume, J.L., Lambiotte, R., Lefebvre, E.: Fast unfolding of communities in large networks. J. Stat. Mech: Theory Exp. **2008**(10), P10008 (2008)

Emotion-Sentiment Profiling of Customer Feedback Through Cluster-Driven Analysis

Olga Babina(✉) and Svetlana Sheremetyeva

South Ural State University, 76 prospekt Lenina, Chelyabinsk 454080, Russia
{babinaoi,sheremetevaso}@susu.ru

Abstract. The study proposes a methodology for constructing emotion-sentiment profiles of customer reviews based on cluster analysis. The approach employs k-means clustering to group reviews into distinct emotion clusters. For each review, a multidimensional vector representation is generated by calculating centroid vectors of emotion-related parameters (valence, arousal, and five discrete emotions) across sentiment categories (positive, negative, their intense variants, and also neutral). The emotion parameters are derived from the lexical database ENRuN-2, where words are annotated with mean and standard deviation scores for emotion dimensions. The sentiment category reference is derived from the corpus annotation capturing sentiment related phrases in the text. The generated text profile integrates both global text characteristics and localized patterns within sentiment-marked phrases, facilitating correlation analysis between emotion and sentiment categories. Using a kNN algorithm, a test review is mapped to the relevant document cluster. Further, aggregated emotion scores from the closest neighboring datapoints within the cluster are calculated for each sentiment category individually, thereby the emotional load of the review under analysis is identified. The proposed approach was validated on a corpus of healthcare service reviews, comprising more than three thousand reviews of 200,000 tokens in total. The corpus was divided into sentiment-annotated training and unannotated test splits. The results highlight the utility of cluster-based profiling in maintaining interpretability through dimensional approach to emotion and sentiment-related text representation, while enabling scalable analysis of customer feedback within the chosen domain.

Keywords: Sentiment Analysis · Emotion Recognition · Emotion-Sentiment Profiling · ENRuN-2 · Cluster Analysis · k-Means · kNN · Data Visualization

1 Introduction

Understanding emotions and sentiments expressed in customer feedback is crucial for businesses seeking to improve their services and customer satisfaction. Automated sentiment analysis techniques have evolved to address these needs, ranging from lexicon-based approaches to machine learning models. However, many traditional sentiment analysis techniques struggle to capture, besides sentiment polarity, human emotions. Emotion models are broadly categorized into categorical (discrete) and dimensional

M. Bakaev et al. (Eds.): IMS 2025, CCIS 2671, pp. 101–116, 2026.
https://doi.org/10.1007/978-3-032-04958-2_8

(continuous) models. Categorical models, distinguishing from 6 to more than 20 basic emotions [5, 7, 16, 17], define emotions as distinct categories (fear, anger, joy, surprise, etc.). In contrast, dimensional models represent emotions in continuous spaces, using the dimensions like valence, arousal and dominance [19].

Approaches to automating emotion recognition in texts can be divided into knowledge-based and computational. Knowledge-based methods rely on lexicon empowered reasoning to extract emotion clues from texts [6]. The core of this approach is sentiment lexicons, which are curated lists of words annotated with emotional or sentiment scores. Resources like SentiWordNet [2], WordNet-Affect [23], SenticNet [4], NRC Word-Emotion Association Lexicon [14] and others provide valuable information about the semantic orientation of words, including the emotional dimension distributed scores. While extensive English language lexicons providing detailed information on polarity, sentiment intensity, specific emotion categories, for sentiment and emotion analysis are available, comparable resources for the Russian language are scarce [3, 9, 12, 24]. Furthermore, sentiment lexicons tailored to specific domains are often necessary to capture the unique expressions of evaluation within those contexts, which may require domain-specific lexicons, e.g., [11, 21].

Computational methods typically involve machine learning with large datasets, specifically, recent advancements in the field are increasingly leveraging the power of large language models (LLMs). Emotion recognition is often approached here as a classification task, requiring annotated datasets to train effective models. Recent research on emotion recognition using large language models (LLMs) is increasingly focused on applications in emotional support during dialogue interactions [8, 10, 27]. Parallel efforts involve the distillation of LLMs to optimize their application to emotion support conversations [28]. Additionally, there is a growing emphasis on creating comprehensive datasets for training emotion classifiers using neural network models [26], and also benchmarks used to evaluate the emotional intelligence of LLMs [20]. These text collections require investigating the methods to optimize the annotation of emotional datasets aimed at improving the accuracy and reliability of emotion annotation [25].

The lack of high-quality annotated data for certain languages, including Russian, limits the applicability of supervised machine learning methods. Moreover, existing methods often fail to provide interpretable insights into the emotional underpinnings of customer feedback. Therefore, there is a need for novel hybrid approaches that combine the strengths of lexicon-based methods, machine learning techniques, and contextual information to enable more accurate and interpretable emotion-sentiment analysis.

In this paper, we present a methodology for constructing emotion-sentiment profiles of customer reviews. Our approach leverages a clustering model trained on the text embeddings generated by FRIDA [1], a state-of-the-art language model for Russian, to capture semantic similarity and context. We then enhance this representation by incorporating information from the ENRuN-2 lexical database [24], which provides detailed emotional annotations for Russian words, within both dimensional and categorical approaches to emotion categorization. By combining these resources, we aim to create a visual representation of customer emotions and sentiments of the text.

2 Materials

2.1 Emotion Space Lexicon

This study adopts an exploratory approach to emotion-sentiment profiling, leveraging the ENRuN-2 lexical database [24] as a source of emotion-related data. The database contains 1,800 nouns with frequencies ranging from 0.4 to 1131.8 ipm according to [13], which was constructed based on experiments where respondents evaluated the words across emotion-related parameters. In the experiments two key approaches to understanding the structure of the emotional sphere were employed. According to the multidimensional approach, the words were mapped onto Valence and Arousal dimensions, using scales from −3 to 3 for Valence and from 1 to 7 for Arousal. The categorical approach focused on basic emotions, including Happiness, Sadness, Fear, Anger, and Disgust. For each word, respondents evaluated the presence of these emotions category evaluated on a scale from 0 to 5. The ENRuN-2 database encompasses aggregated rating scores for lexical items provided by the respondents belonging to different age groups. For each word, the database includes mean, standard deviation, minimum, and maximum scores for the emotion-related parameters. Thus, the lexicon items are located within a space defined by rated emotion categories and dimensions.

In this study, only the mean and standard deviation scores were used, aggregated across all respondents without differentiation by gender. The head of the ENRuN-2 database with some of the emotion space parameters used in this study is shown in Fig. 1.

	Word	Valence_Mean_All	Valence_Std_All	Arousal_Mean_All	Arousal_Std_All	Happy_Mean_All	Happy_Std_All	Sad_Mean_All	Sad_Std_All
0	абсолютизм	-0.100	0.718	2.800	1.852	0.720	1.137	1.360	1.604
1	абсурд	-0.650	0.813	3.400	1.465	1.545	2.017	0.727	1.241
2	абсурдность	-0.450	1.191	3.450	1.468	0.538	1.363	0.500	0.860
3	аванс	1.625	1.245	4.292	2.136	4.409	0.854	0.727	1.120
4	аварийность	-1.381	1.024	3.524	2.040	0.077	0.392	1.269	1.638

Fig. 1. A fragment of the ENRuN-2 database with emotion-related category scores associated with lexical items

The database provides a well-annotated resource for analyzing the emotion facet in the customer feedback.

2.2 Sentiment-Annotated Corpus

For the purpose of the research, we utilize a corpus of 3247 Russian-language customer reviews, collected from the 2GIS local business directory, focusing on healthcare services in private medical centers. The corpus consists of approximately 200,000 tokens.

In this research, we utilized the gold standard subcorpus with a semi-automatic aspect-sentiment annotation as a training dataset. The remining texts were reserved for testing.

The training split comprises 1605 texts with the total length of 100, 000 tokens. The steps of the gold standard creation included:

(1) lexicon extraction and conceptualization into sentiment and aspect categories,
(2) tagset definition, based on the conceptualized categories, resulting in the formulation of a sentiment-related tagset including POS for positive, NEG for negative, POSX for extremely positive, and NEGX for extremely negative sentiment, alongside aspect-related tags indicating features of the service being reviewed,
(3) a domain-specific e-lexicon compilation for sentiment detection, comprising one- and multi-word units labeled with aspect- and sentiment-related tags,
(4) automated text annotation using a platform equipped with the compiled e-lexicon to facilitate the process, and
(5) verification of the annotated texts by trained annotators.

The annotated training dataset may be exemplified by the following (English translation is provided for comprehension):

Original: {*У*}~UNK {*клиники*}~C {*много плюсов*}~POS: {*удобная парковка*}~L~POS, {*дистанционная запись*}~COM~POS, {*приветливый персонал*}~S~POS ({*очень симпатичные администраторши*}~S~POSX). {*Минусов*}~NEG {*два*}~UNK: {*заоблачные цены*}~M {*и*}~UNK {*то*}~UNK, {*что*}~UNK {*при*}~UNK {*оформлении заявки через интернет*}~COM {*запись*}~COM {*сорвалась*}~NEG.

Translation: {*The clinic*}~C (has) {*many advantages*}~POS: {*comfortable parking*}~L~POS, {*remote appointment*}~COM~POS, {*friendly staff*}~S~POS *(*{*very cute receptionists*}~COM~POSX*).* {*Disadvantages*}~NEG (include) {*two*}~UNK: {*exorbitant prices*}~M {*and*}~UNK {*the fact*}~UNK {*that*}~UNK, {*when*}~UNK {*making an appointment online*}~COM, {*the appointment*}~COM {*failed*}~NEG.

In the given example, text tokens are enclosed in curly brackets. ~POS, ~NEG, ~POSX, and ~NEGX are used to denote sentiment-related lexical units indicating sentiment polarity, in particular, positive, negative, strong positive, and strong negative respectively. Other tags refer to aspects (~C, ~COM, etc.) or out-of-domain (~UNK, ~O) words, being irrelevant for this study. While lexicon units in the gold standard may exhibit multiple syncretic tags (e.g., S~POS, ~COM~POSX, etc.), the gold annotation protocol prescribes an unambiguous and consistent sentiment assignment.

The gold standard annotation serves as an empirical knowledge base for modeling the sentiment facet of the customer feedback profiling in this study. Consequently, further analysis focuses solely on sentiment-related tags from the gold standard annotation, enabling the extraction of sentiment.

3 Methods

3.1 Emotion Lexicon Profiling

Our analysis starts from the profiling of emotion-bearing words from the ENRuN-2 lexical database, focusing on their correlation with sentiment tags in the training dataset represented by the gold standard annotated corpus.

Step 1. We begin with identifying the relevant tokens (words of ENRuN-2 lexicon) within the sentiment-annotated phrases in the corpus. We perform a morphological analysis and lemmatization of the words within each labeled phrase in the corpus using standard *spaCy*'s morphological tagger, with the *ru_core_news_sm* model applied to provide the necessary linguistic features. This yields lemmas of the words in the corpus, which are then matched against the words in the ENRuN-2 dictionary.

For each matching word, we count the frequency of its occurrence within the phrases labeled with four sentiment tags (POS, POSX, NEG, NEGX) and outside of such phrases (NEUT). The dimensions defined by these five categories constitute the basis of the word's multidimensional representation. The counts in the five dimensions are then subjected to L1 normalization, ensuring that the sum of all vector coordinates equals a unity.

Step 2. As part of our comprehensive approach, we cluster the words based on the features derived at Step 1 from the ENRuN-2 lexicon. This involves grouping words according to their dimensional emotion features, including valence and arousal, for which we consider both mean and standard deviation values. These features are then standardized using the *StandardScaler* from the *scikit-learn* library to ensure that all variables are on the same scale.

We apply the K-Means clustering algorithm to group the words into clusters based on the standardized features. We chose the number of clusters equal to 5 as our sentiment framework consists of five components (POS, POSX, NEG, NEGX, and NEUT), and we aim to verify whether the vocabulary naturally segregates into clusters that align with these sentiment categories. This involves validating whether the emotional lexicon can be meaningfully divided into clusters that correspond to the sentiment categories. We assess whether the vocabulary naturally aligns with the sentiment framework through manual analysis of the resultant clusters.

3.2 Customer Feedback Profiling

Profile Construction. Our approach to constructing a sentiment profile of customer feedback involves a multi-step procedure that combines semantic embedding generation using a large language model with unsupervised clustering of text representations from a gold standard training dataset, enabling the application of these clusters for subsequent analysis of customer feedback. The embeddings are clustered using the k-means algorithm into five groups, which, as we assume, align with the sentiment-related tagset (POS, POSX, NEG, NEGX, NEUT). Each datapoint in the training dataset is defined by emotion vectors tailored to individual sentiment categories and a total emotion vector, derived from the lexicon data for tokens within the datapoint and the distribution of these tokens across sentiment-tagged phrases in that datapoint. The emotion vectors from the training dataset collectively form a knowledge base for subsequent text profiling.

To represent the profile of a test datapoint, we first identify the cluster to which the text datapoint belongs. Next, we extract emotion data from the knowledge base that is distributed across sentiment clusters, focusing on the nearest neighbors within the same cluster as the test datapoint. Finally, we aggregate these data to construct the test datapoint's profile.

We further detail the specific models and parameters employed in our experiments to provide a comprehensive understanding of our methodology.

Feature Extraction. We apply a Sentence Transformer framework [18] to generate dense embeddings for each text sample in the training dataset. Sentence Transformers are optimized for tasks like semantic search and clustering, providing superior performance in capturing semantic similarity, which motivated our choice.

Specifically, we utilize the FRIDA model [1], selected for its top performance for clustering tasks according to the MTEB leaderboard [15] involving Russian language models [22]. FRIDA has approximately 823 million parameters, produces embeddings of 1536 dimensions, and can process up to 512 tokens, with a score of 67.49% for the clustering task. The embeddings are created by encoding each text sample into a dense vector representation, preserving the contextual meaning of the text.

Clustering. We apply the K-Means clustering algorithm to group similar text samples based on their semantic embeddings. In our implementation, we utilize the *KMeans* class from the *sklearn* module in Python, with the number of clusters set to 5, a random state of 42 and default values for other parameters. Our choice of the number of clusters equal to 5 is motivated by the desire to align with the underlying sentiment structure, as informed by our earlier analysis of sentiment tags.

Profiling Customer Feedback. The stage of profile creation involves analyzing a test datapoint by identifying its cluster and finding its nearest neighbors within the same cluster in the training data using the k-nearest neighbors (kNN) algorithm. This is achieved using the *NearestNeighbors* class from *sklearn*, configured with a Euclidean distance metric and a k-value. The selection of k equal to 5 to 20 balances computational efficiency with capturing a representative set of neighbors.

After applying the kNN model, the sentiment-related emotion vectors from these neighbors are then aggregated to generate a distribution. The aggregation is made as follows:

1. The emotion-bearing tokens (words present in ENRuN-2) are extracted from all the nearest neighbouring reviews of a training dataset;
2. Based on the parameters of the relevant tokens (ENRuN-2 words), the vector representation of emotional load in the test review is found using weighted emotion vector representations for each of the 5 sentiment categories c_j, where $j \in [1..5]$, $c_j \in \{POS, NEG, POSX, NEGX, NEUT\}$. A total emotion load for the review is also computed.

Specifically, if the emotion information for a given token T includes features, denoted as $f_i(T), i \in [1,7]$, then the token vector $V(T)$ may be represented as $[f_1(T), f_2(T), \ldots, f_7(T)]$, where the i-th dimension corresponds to (1) valence, (2) arousal, (3) happiness, (4) sadness, (5) anger, (6) fear, and (7) disgust mean values stored for the target token T in the ENRuN-2 lexicon.

The weight $w\left(T_{cj}^{R}\right)$ of each token T within a phrase labeled with a sentiment category c_j in a given review text R of the gold standard training dataset is determined by its frequency within this review. The total weight W_j^R of the j-th sentiment category within the customer review R is found as a total occurrence of all relevant token T_{cj}^{R} within the phrases of the gold standard labeled with c_j in this review R:

$$W_j^R = \sum\nolimits_{\forall T_{c_j}^R} w\left(T_{c_j}^R\right), j \in [1..5] \tag{1}$$

Then, the category vector $V^{c_j^R}$ for the sentiment category c_j in the given review R is found as follows:

$$V\left(c_j^R\right) = \frac{1}{W_j^R} \cdot \sum\nolimits_{\forall T_{c_j}^R} w\left(T_{c_j}^R\right) \cdot V\left(T_{c_j}^R\right), j \in [1..5] \tag{2}$$

The total weight $W(R)$ of the review text R is found as a total of the occurrences $w\left(T^R\right)$ of the relevant tokens T^R in the review:

$$W(R) = \sum\nolimits_{\forall T^R} w\left(T^R\right), \tag{3}$$

Then the total emotion load distribution for the review R is found as follows:

$$V(R) = \frac{\sum_{\forall T^R} w\left(T^R\right) \cdot V\left(T^R\right)}{W(R)}, \tag{4}$$

where $V\left(T^R\right)$ is an emotion vector derived from the ENRuN-2 lexicon values for the term T^R, used in the current review R.

Profile Evaluation. The resulting distributions, alongside the lexical profile for text emotions derived directly from the test point, are visualized using *matplotlib*. The visualization consists of a line plot displaying the mean emotion values for each sentiment category, with shaded regions representing the standard deviation. This visualization provides a comprehensive representation of the sentiment and emotional tone of the text, with the confidence in the values discernable from standard deviation values.

To evaluate the robustness of emotion-sentiment profiles, we systematically analyzed how variations in neighborhood size k influenced profile consistency. For each test data point, we computed profiles using k values ranging from 5 to 20 (step size equal to 5). Then, treating each profile as a vector representation of emotion-sentiment distribution, we calculated pairwise cosine similarities between all pairs of k-derived profiles for each test datapoint. The mean and standard deviations of these similarities were then computed across all test points to quantify the stability.

To further enhance the profiling of customer feedback, we leverage the word clustering model trained during Step 2 of emotion token analysis. From a customer review, we extract all relevant words from the ENRuN-2 database and create visualizations based on the emotional dimensions of valence and arousal, as well as each of the five discrete emotions (happiness, sadness, anger, fear, and disgust). Each point in the visualization is represented by a color and shape corresponding to its cluster membership, providing a comprehensive visual profile of the emotional content in the text. This approach enables an understanding of how different words contribute to the emotional tone of customer feedback, facilitating a deeper insight into customer opinions and experiences.

This methodology can also be applied to a collection of texts related to a specific organization to analyze the profile of the organization based on the customer reviews.

4 Results

4.1 Emotion Word Cluster Analysis

In the sentiment-annotated training corpus, 311 distinct words from the ENRuN-2 lexicon were identified, with a total of 2720 word occurrences across all phrases in the training dataset. Figure 2 presents a fragment of 10 randomly selected words, illustrating their frequency distributions across phrases labeled with five sentiment-related categories (POS, NEG, POSX, NEGX, NEUT) in the training corpus and contributions of the sentiment polarities into the semantics of each word after L1-normalization of the sentiment category counts.

word	frequency	POS count	NEG count	POSX count	NEGX count	NEUT count	POS	NEG	POSX	NEGX	NEUT
кушетка	6	0	0	0	0	6	0.000000	0.000000	0.00	0.000000	1.000000
половина	8	0	1	0	0	7	0.000000	0.125000	0.00	0.000000	0.875000
стол	6	1	1	0	0	4	0.166667	0.166667	0.00	0.000000	0.666667
фраза	13	0	3	0	0	10	0.000000	0.230769	0.00	0.000000	0.769231
выяснение	3	0	2	0	0	1	0.000000	0.666667	0.00	0.000000	0.333333
раз	246	4	5	0	3	234	0.016260	0.020325	0.00	0.012195	0.951220
место	100	22	18	4	2	54	0.220000	0.180000	0.04	0.020000	0.540000
поход	12	0	2	0	0	10	0.000000	0.166667	0.00	0.000000	0.833333
впечатление	70	16	11	7	6	30	0.228571	0.157143	0.10	0.085714	0.428571
выбор	20	9	1	0	0	10	0.450000	0.050000	0.00	0.000000	0.500000

Fig. 2. A fragment of the words of the ENRuN-2 lexicon mapped onto sentiment phrases in the training corpus. Column frequency contains total occurrence of a word in the corpus; columns POS/NEG/POSX/NEGX/NEUT count are word frequencies in phrases labeled with the respective tags; columns POS/NEG/POSX/NEGX/NEUT are L1-normalized tag counts.

Figure 2 shows that the lexical units from ENRuN-2 feature neutral contexts alongside sentiment-tagged expressions within the corpus. As the lexicon focuses on nouns that typically denote participants in evaluative situations (e.g., objects or subjects of evaluation) rather than explicit evaluative predicates that often align with sentiment expressions, their primary association with neutral contexts is a rather expected phenomenon. However, the ENRuN-2 annotations of these words enable the extraction of latent emotional load employing the words outside sentiment-labeled expressions, including those that convey factual information. This amplifies sentiment analysis in contexts devoid of overt affective vocabulary, where emotional undertones might otherwise remain undetected.

The resultant vector representations of ENRuN-2 lexicon words enable their visualization in coordinate systems, facilitating analysis of how lexicon-derived emotion dimensions (valence, arousal) align with corpus-derived sentiment categories. Specifically, we plot mean and standard deviation of valence/arousal against L1-normalized contextual frequencies for each sentiment category (POS, NEG, etc.), revealing their interplay. Figure 3 displays a random sample of 30 lexicon words, where each dimension (valence, arousal, sentiment category) only includes words with non-zero occurrences in the corresponding category's contexts.

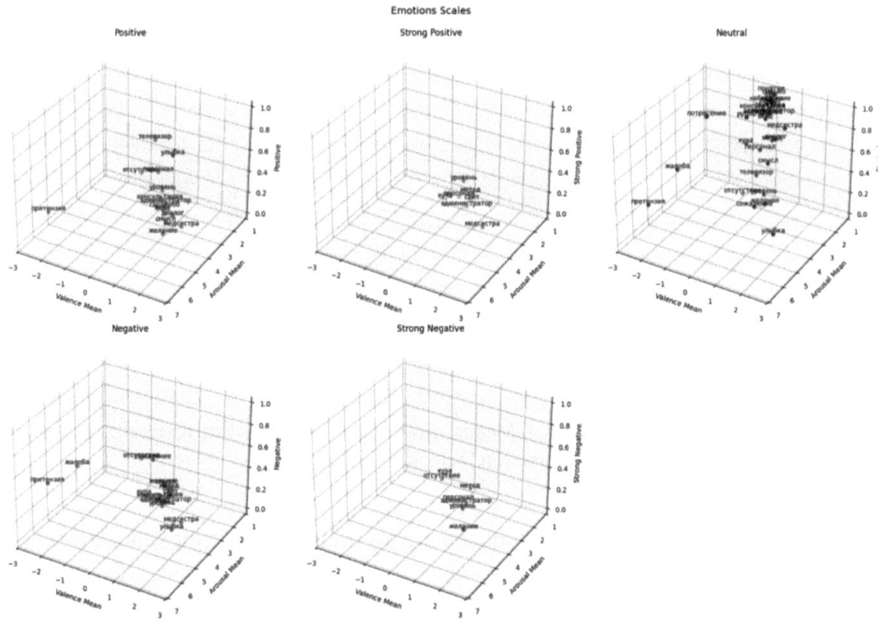

Fig. 3. Random 30 words of the lexicon plotted for each sentiment category across valence mean and arousal mean dimensions.

Figure 3 reveals a correlation between sentiment categories and valence, with positive sentiment categories (e.g., POS, POSX) exhibiting a tendency toward positive valence scores and negative categories (e.g., NEG, NEGX) toward negative valence scores. High mean arousal values characterize affective words explicitly expressing emotions or sentiments, while low arousal values correspond to words weakly associated with evaluative scales. The sentiment-axis values quite appropriately reflect the degree of typicality in word-sentiment associations. For example, *жалоба* (*complaint*) occupies the extreme negative end of the mean valence spectrum while displaying one of the highest NEG-axis values, aligning with its intuitive classification as a definitely negative term. The token *желание* (desire) demonstrates the highest arousal value in the POSX graph, as it most closely aligns with emotional connotations among all units occurring in the corresponding sentiment contexts (cf. *персонал* (staff), *метод* (method), etc. that exhibit minimal affective connotations). Neutral words hardy exhibit discernible patterns in their distribution.

The automatically identified clusters, derived from 311 emotion lexicon units, are visualized in Fig. 4.

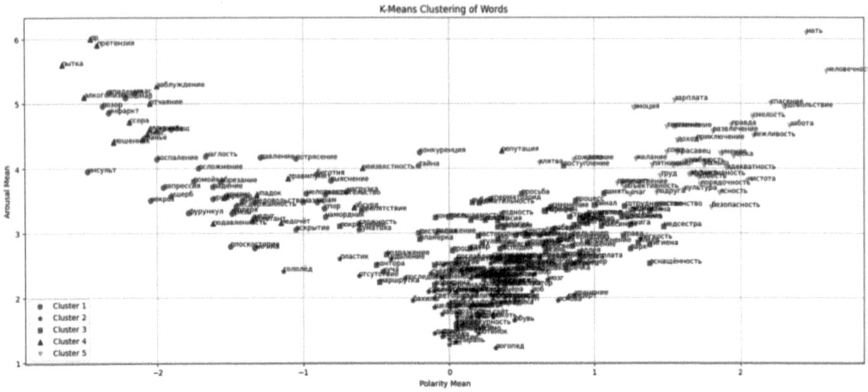

Fig. 4. Word-clusters obtained from k-Means modeling based on word representation using valence and arousal values from the emotion lexicon

The quality of word clustering was quantitatively evaluated using the silhouette score. The resulting silhouette score of 0.369 indicates moderate partitioning, reflecting that clusters are reasonably well separated but not entirely distinct. As illustrated in Fig. 4, clusters 0 and 3 in particular exhibit considerable overlap and are less clearly delineated. This moderate clustering performance is consistent with the inherent properties of sentiment annotation in the corpus, where the same ENRuN-2 nouns frequently appear in a range of affective contexts, leading to graded rather than strictly categorical emotion associations. Nevertheless, clusters 2, 3, and 5 are relatively more distinct, although their boundaries remain somewhat blurred.

Based on the semantic analysis of the identified clusters, the lexical units may be distributed into the following categories:

Cluster 1: Words with negative valence and middle values of arousal, reflecting intense negative emotions. E.g., *потрясение* (shock), *конкуренция* (competition), *давление* (pressure), *падение* (fall), *потеря* (loss), *эпидемия* (epidemic), *кошмар* (nightmare), *шрам* (scar), etc. This cluster contains terms clearly associated with phenomena or objects traditionally perceived as negative, which elicit unambiguous negative emotional responses.

Cluster 2: Neutral terms with minimal valence and arousal, devoid of affective associations. E.g., *стол* (table), *метод* (method), *персонал* (staff), *сайт* (site), *пластик* (plastic), etc.

Cluster 3: Words with weak positive valence and low to middle values of arousal. E.g., *выбор* (choice), *согласие* (agreement), *пожелание* (wish), *щепетильность* (fastidiousness), *сахар* (sugar), *альтернатива* (alternative), *сотрудничество* (collaboration), etc. These terms exhibit subtle connotative associations with positive qualities, positioning them as neutral-positive rather than overtly emotional.

Cluster 4: Extremely negative terms with high negative valence and high arousal, indicating strong emotional load. E.g., *жалоба* (complaint), *абсурд* (absurdity), *мошенник* (scammer), *пытка* (torture), *упадок* (decline), *неизвестность* (uncertainty), *ожог* (burn), *алкоголизм* (alcoholism), *враньё* (pack of lies). The cluster includes words with pronounced negative emotional components, aligning well with the NEGX category.

Cluster 5: Words with middle to high positive valence and high arousal. E.g., *впечатление* (impression), *улыбка* (smile), *желание* (desire), *вежливость* (politeness), *чистота* (cleanliness), *тело* (body), *эмоция* (emotion), *принцип* (principle), *человечность* (humanity), *забота* (care), *безопасность* (safety), etc. These terms are confidently associated with positive situations.

Thus, the clusters broadly map to sentiment categories, capturing negativity and reflecting positivity, though the positive clusters reflect rather explicitness or subtlety of positive connotations rather than the polarity intensity. As a result, the semantic analysis of words in the clusters substantiates their alignment with the established sentiment categories as follows: Cluster 1 ⇔NEG, Cluster 2 ⇔NEUT, Cluster 3 ⇔POS, Cluster 4 ⇔NEGX, and Cluster 5 ⇔POSX.

For all words in the ENRuN-2 lexicon, clusters were predicted using the trained clustering model. The distribution of the resultant cluster distribution is visualized in Fig. 5.

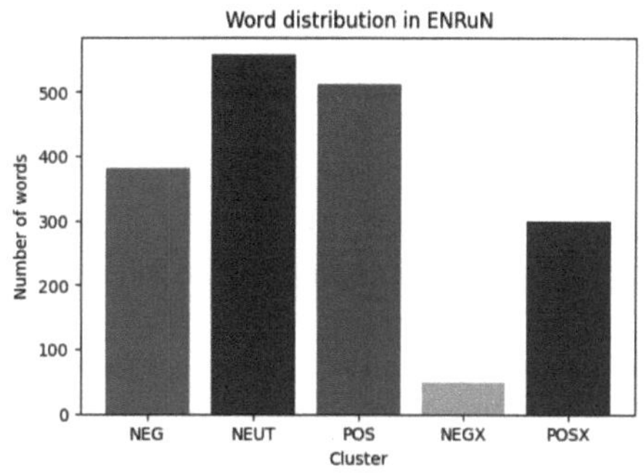

Fig. 5. Emotion lexicon word distribution across the learned clusters

4.2 Customer Feedback Profile Analysis

The clusters derived from text embeddings generated by the FRIDA language model are visualized in Fig. 6, separately for the training and test datasets, projected onto a three-dimensional scale using the first three principal components (PCA). The visualization reveals two quite distinct clusters, separated by values above and below zero along the first principal component. Each of these clusters exhibit sub-clusters with fuzzier boundaries, though PCA provides a simplified interpretation, and semantic relationships present in higher dimensions may be masked.

Clusters serve as the foundation for identifying training data that inform the construction of emotion-sentiment profiles for texts from the test dataset. Figure 7 visualizes the profile of a randomly selected test text (datapoint 917), derived from its alignment with training clusters based on the number of neighbors *k* from 5 to 20.

Text of datapoint 917:

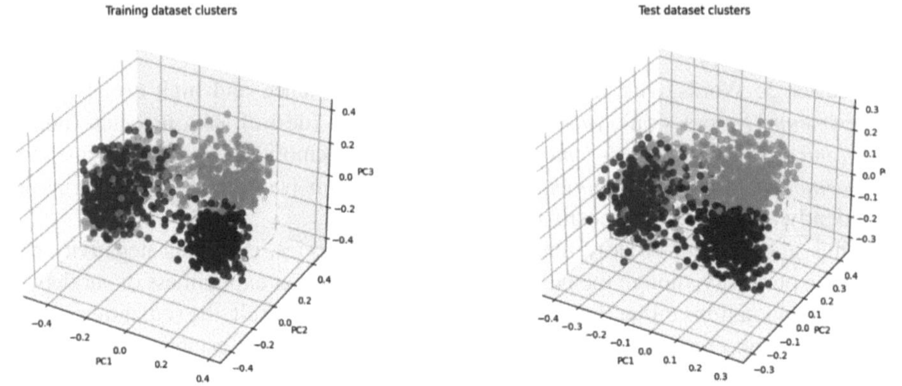

Fig. 6. Datapoint k-means clusters based on LLM text representations (k equals to 5)

Orginial: *Посоветовали этот медицинский центр, позвонила и записалась на прием к стоматологу, мне нужна была консультация специалиста. На входе встречает приветливый персонал, все чисто, красиво, без очереди, консультация стоматолога 200 рублей, если вам нужен снимок то можно его сделать в соседнем кабинете, быстро без очереди. Цены намного ниже, чем в других центрах.*

Translation: *I was advised this medical center, so I called and scheduled an appointment with a dentist, I needed a specialist consultation. Upon arrival, I was greeted by friendly staff, everything was clean, beautiful, and no queues. The dentist consultation cost 200 rubles, and if you need an X-ray, it can be done in the adjacent room, quickly and without waiting. Prices here are significantly lower than at other centers.*

The graph in Fig. 7 demonstrates stable emotion distribution overall, though increasing k from 5 to 20 reveals smoothing effects. Thus, in the shown example, when k increases, *Happiness* becomes more dominant, while *Fear* (manifested through disease-related lexicon) diminishes in prominence, indicating reduced significance. Profiles constructed this way show two key findings:

(1) profiles remain consistent across the number of neighbors (k) variations;
(2) an adequate emotional representation emerges at quite low k values (10 and above), validating the method's robustness.

The mean cosine similarity between profiles of the test datapoints constructed for the k values ranging from 5 to 20 was 0.979, indicating high stability of emotional-sentiment patterns. The mean standard deviation of similarity between profiles was 0.016, confirming minimal variability in results. These values demonstrate that the method is robust to changes in the k parameter and maintains consistency even with variations in the neighborhood size.

The representation of the test datapoint through the words from a subcluster of 10 nearest neighbours to the target review is illustrated in Fig. 8. The visualization demonstrates a general tendency toward positive sentiment, inferred from the distribution of emotionally relevant words across sentiment categories in similar reviews.

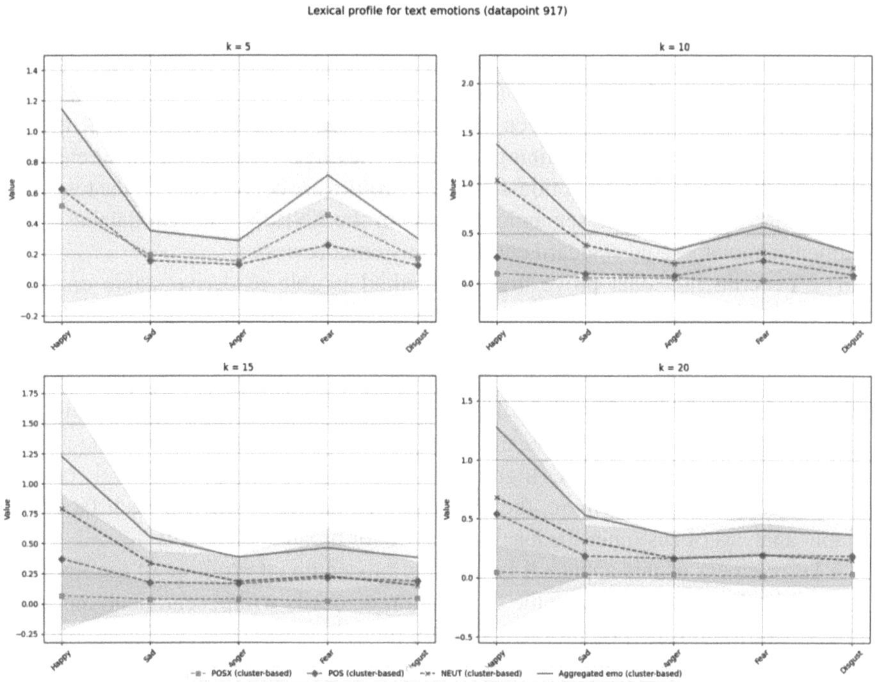

Fig. 7. Emotion-sentiment profile of a customer feedback for a test datapoint.

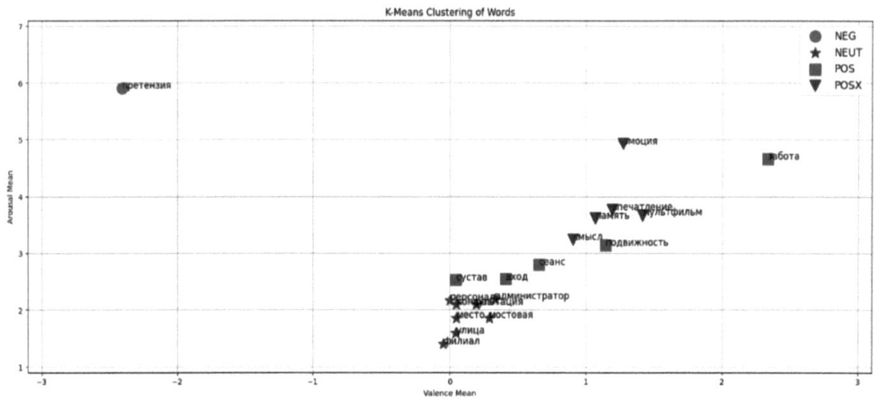

Fig. 8. Cluster word representation: sentiment distribution of emotionally relevant terms in similar reviews

5 Conclusion

This study introduced a methodology for constructing emotion-sentiment profiles of customer reviews by leveraging cluster analysis on text embeddings generated by the FRIDA language model. At its core, the method initially enhances a base lexicon of emotionally labeled nouns by extracting sentiment polarity associations from a gold-standard annotated corpus. This expanded knowledge base then forms the foundation for profiling texts in the training dataset. The training set profiles, in turn, act as a knowledge base for profiling unseen text in the test dataset. By analyzing *k* nearest neighbors within clusters in the training data and retrieving information from the enriched lexicon for those neighbors, emotion-sentiment profiles are constructed for the test texts. This approach combines the semantic richness of the ENRuN-2 lexical database with sentiment-annotated gold standard corpus of customer reviews.

The experimental data prove that the method is able to derive stable emotion-sentiment profiles, a finding validated through variations in the k parameter used in the k-NN algorithm, highlighting the method's robustness on unseen data. Adequate representation of emotions was achieved with relatively small values of *k* (equal to 10). The approach also provides a clear identification of distinct emotional categories, although boundaries between certain clusters are fuzzy. The use of FRIDA, a state-of-the-art language model for Russian, ensures high-quality text embeddings that effectively capture semantic similarity. Furthermore, the cluster-driven nature of the approach facilitates scalable analysis of customer feedback, allowing for broad applicability.

A key element of this approach is the emotion-sentiment profiling of the ENRuN-2 lexical database. By analyzing the distribution of words within sentiment-annotated phrases in the training corpus, the method builds multidimensional vector representations for each term, capturing its association with positive, negative, and neutral sentiment categories. This creates a foundation for understanding how specific words contribute to the overall emotional tone of a text. Thanks to this foundation, which relies on the Russian word source labeled with emotion-related categories, hidden emotions can be detected, something that is not always possible through direct sentiment analysis techniques. We admit that evaluation of affective words including verbs, adjectives, modal forms, or idiomatic expressions, which are explicit indicators of evaluative meaning, is also valuable but requires to involve further lexical resources of different origin.

Compared to purely unsupervised techniques, this approach is more resource-intensive, given the need for a sentiment-annotated training dataset to drive the profiling process. Additionally, manual analysis of the resultant clusters, undertaken to ensure the vocabulary naturally aligns with the sentiment framework, introduces a degree of subjectivity into the process.

Moving forward, research should focus on addressing these limitations. Exploring methods to reduce the dependence on large annotated datasets, such as active learning or transfer learning techniques, would enhance scalability. Furthermore, automating the cluster analysis validation could mitigate the potential for subjective bias. Despite these caveats, the proposed methodology provides a valuable and interpretable approach for understanding the emotional load of customer feedback. The generated profiles enable rapid visual summarization of emotional patterns across feedback corpora, aligning with growing demands for intuitive, non-textual data representations. While operational deployment would require integration with dashboard systems, the methodology's output format directly supports trend-spotting and comparative analysis without granular text review – a critical advantage in resource-constrained business intelligence workflows.

References

1. Ai-forever/FRIDA. https://huggingface.co/ai-forever/FRIDA. Accessed 22 Mar 2025
2. Baccianella, S., Esuli, A., Sebastiani, F.: SentiWordNet 3.0: an enhanced lexical resource for sentiment analysis and opinion mining. In: Proceedings of the Seventh International Conference on Language Resources and Evaluation (LREC 2010), pp. 2200–2204. ELRA, Valletta (2010)
3. Bochkarev, V.V., Achkeev, A.A., Savinkov, A.A., Shevlyakova, A.V., Solovyev, V.D.: Large sentiment dictionary of Russian words. In: Calvo, H., Martínez-Villaseñor, L., Ponce, H. (eds.) MICAI 2023. LNCS, vol. 14392, pp. 68–82. Springer, Cham (2024). https://doi.org/10.1007/978-3-031-47640-2_6
4. Cambria, E., Poria, S., Bajpai, R., Hussain, A.: SenticNet 4: a semantic resource for sentiment analysis based on conceptual primitives. In: Proceedings of COLING 2016, the 26th International Conference on Computational Linguistics: Technical Papers, pp. 2666–2677. ACL, Osaka (2016)
5. Ekman, P.: Chapter 3. Basic emotions. In: Dalgleish, T., Power, M. (eds.) Handbook of Cognition and Emotion, pp. 45–60. Wiley, New York (1999)
6. Hu, D., Wei, L., Huai, X.: DialogueCRN: contextual reasoning networks for emotion recognition in conversations. In: Proceedings of the 59th Annual Meeting of the Association for Computational Linguistics and the 11th International Joint Conference on Natural Language Processing (Volume 1: Long Papers), pp. 7042–7052. Association for Computational Linguistics, Online (2021)
7. Izard, C.E.: The Psychology of Emotions. Plenum, New York (2012)
8. Kang, D., et al.: Can large language models be good emotional supporter? Mitigating preference bias on emotional support conversation. In: Proceedings of the 62nd Annual Meeting of the Association for Computational Linguistics (Volume 1: Long Papers), pp. 15232–15261. ACL, Bangkok (2024)
9. Koltsova, O.Yu., Alexeeva, S.V., Kolcov, S.N.: An opinion word lexicon and a training dataset for Russian sentiment analysis of social media. In: Computational Linguistics and Intellectual Technologies: Proceedings of the International Conference "Dialogue-2016", pp. 277–287. RSUH, Moscow (2016)
10. Kotov, A., Zaidelman, L., Zinina, A., Arinkin, N., Filatov, A., Kivva, K.: Conceptual processing system for a companion robot. Cogn. Syst. Res. **67**, 28–32 (2021)
11. Loughran, T., McDonald, B.: When is a liability not a liability? Textual analysis, dictionaries, and 10-Ks. J. Financ. **66**(1), 35–65 (2011)
12. Loukachevitch, N., Levchik, A.: Creating a general Russian sentiment lexicon. In: Proceedings of Language Resources and Evaluation Conference (LREC-2016), pp. 1171–1176. ELRA, Portorož (2016)
13. Lyashevskaya, O.N, Sharoff, S.A.: Frequency dictionary of modern Russian: based on the national Russian corpus. Azbukovnik, Moscow (2009). (In Russ.)
14. Mohammad, S., Turney, P.: Crowdsourcing a word-emotion association lexicon. Comput. Intell. **29**(3), 436–465 (2013)
15. MTEB/leaderboard. https://huggingface.co/spaces/mteb/leaderboard. Accessed 25 Mar 2025
16. Ortony, A., Clore, G.L., Collins, A.: The Cognitive Structure of Emotions. Cambridge University Press, Cambridge (1990)
17. Plutchik, R.: Emotions and Life: Perspectives from Psychology, Biology, and Evolution. American Psychological Association, Washington, DC (2002)
18. Reimers, N., Gurevych, I.: Sentence-BERT: sentence embeddings using siamese BERT-networks. In: Proceedings of the 2019 Conference on Empirical Methods in Natural Language Processing and the 9th International Joint Conference on Natural Language Processing (EMNLP-IJCNLP), pp. 3982–3992. ACL, Hong Kong (2019)

19. Russell, J.A., Mehrabian, A.: Evidence for a three-factor theory of emotions. J. Res. Pers. **11**(3), 273–294 (1977)
20. Sabour, S., et al.: EmoBench: evaluating the emotional intelligence of large language models. In: Proceedings of the 62nd Annual Meeting of the Association for Computational Linguistics (Volume 1: Long Papers), pp. 5986–6004. ACL, Bangkok (2024)
21. Sheremetyeva, S.O., Babina, O.I.: Digital analysis of poetic text emotions. Bull. South Ural State Univ. Ser. Linguist. **19**(1), 58–65 (2022). (In Russ.)
22. Snegirev, A., Tikhonova, M., Maksimova, A., Fenogenova, A., Abramov, A.: The Russian-focused embedders' exploration: ruMTEB benchmark and Russian embedding model design. In: Computing Research Repository (2022). https://arxiv.org/abs/2210.07316. Accessed 22 Mar 2025
23. Strapparava, C., Valitutti, R.: WordNet-affect: an affective extension of WordNet. In: Proceedings of the Fourth International Conference on Language Resources and Evaluation (LREC 2004), pp. 1083–1086. ELRA, Lisbon (2004)
24. Sysoeva, T.A., Lyusin, D.V. Development of the extended database ENRuN-2 with emotional assessments of nouns: achievements, problems and prospects. In: Vladimirov, I.Yu., Korovkin, S.Yu. (eds.) Psychology of Cognition: Materials of the All-Russian Scientific Conference, pp. 316–320. Filigran, Yaroslavl (2024). (In Russ.)
25. Wu, W., et al.: Handling ambiguity in emotion: from out-of-domain detection to distribution estimation. In: Proceedings of the 62nd Annual Meeting of the Association for Computational Linguistics (Volume 1: Long Papers), pp. 2078–2093. ACL, Bangkok (2024)
26. Zhang, E., Trujillo, R., Poellabauer, Ch.: The MERSA dataset and a transformer-based approach for speech emotion recognition. In: Proceedings of the 62nd Annual Meeting of the Association for Computational Linguistics (Volume 1: Long Papers), pp. 13960–13970. ACL, Bangkok (2024)
27. Zhang, T., Zhang, X., Zhao, J., Zhou, L., Jin, Q.: ESCoT: towards interpretable emotional support dialogue systems. In: Proceedings of the 62nd Annual Meeting of the Association for Computational Linguistics (Volume 1: Long Papers), pp. 13395–13412. ACL, Bangkok (2024)
28. Zheng, Zh., Liao, L., Deng, Y., Qin, L., Nie, L.: self-chats from large language models make small emotional support chatbot better. In: Proceedings of the 62nd Annual Meeting of the Association for Computational Linguistics (Volume 1: Long Papers), pp. 11325–11345. ACL, Bangkok (2024)

An Experimental Study of Automating Explanatory Dictionary Compilation with Language Models

Timur Garipov[1], Dmitry Morozov[1,5](✉), Yana Gubarkova[2], Anastasia Kozerenko[3], and Anna Glazkova[4]

[1] Novosibirsk State University, 1 Pirogova str., Novosibirsk 630090, Russia
t.garipov@g.nsu.ru, morozowdm@gmail.com
[2] Yandex LLC, Lva Tolstogo str., 16, Moscow 119021, Russia
[3] Institute of the Russian Language named after V. V. Vinogradov RAS, 18/2 Volkhonka str., Moscow 119019, Russia
[4] University of Tyumen, 6 Volodarskogo str., Tyumen 625003, Russia
[5] Russian National Corpus, Moscow, Russia

Abstract. The creation of explanatory dictionaries has long been a cornerstone of classical linguistics. For the Russian language alone, dozens of such dictionaries have been compiled. However, the process of dictionary compilation is highly labor-intensive, requiring significant time and expertise. Moreover, the emergence of new words and the evolution of existing ones necessitate continuous updates to keep dictionaries relevant. Existing dictionaries are not without flaws; for instance, it is not uncommon for definitions to include terms that are more complex than the word being defined. Meanwhile, generative language models have reached a level of sophistication that allows them to tackle a wide range of applied tasks with near-expert proficiency. In this study, we explored whether the task of compiling a modern explanatory dictionary can be addressed using machine learning. We focused on two specific subtasks: 1) generating definitions for words not yet included in dictionaries, and 2) producing generalized definitions based on multiple existing dictionaries. We conducted a series of experiments that involved both fine-tuning and prompt-based approaches with language models. The quality of the generated definitions was evaluated using both automated metrics and human assessment. Our results demonstrate that while traditional sequence-to-sequence models like T5 and BART struggle with producing clear and accurate definitions, large language models (LLMs) yield significantly better results. At the same time, generating definitions from scratch works noticeably worse than generalizing existing ones. Our findings highlight the potential of LLM-based methods for automating dictionary compilation and suggest promising directions for further research in AI-assisted lexicography.

Keywords: Explanatory Dictionary · Large Language Models · Natural Language Processing

M. Bakaev et al. (Eds.): IMS 2025, CCIS 2671, pp. 117–131, 2026.
https://doi.org/10.1007/978-3-032-04958-2_9

1 Introduction

Explanatory dictionaries have long served as foundational tools in linguistics, preserving the semantic richness of languages and providing authoritative references for speakers and learners alike. For the Russian language numerous dictionaries have been compiled over centuries, reflecting evolving lexicons and cultural shifts. Yet, despite their historical significance, traditional lexicography faces critical challenges in the modern era. Existing dictionaries are inherently incomplete, struggling to keep pace with the rapid emergence of neologisms—driven by technological advancements, social change, and cross-cultural exchange—while updates to legacy entries remain labor-intensive and slow. Compounding these issues, many dictionaries suffer from structural flaws: definitions often rely on overly complex terminology or circular reasoning (e.g., using cognates or synonymous phrases), rendering them inaccessible to non-experts.

Recent breakthroughs in generative language models (LLMs), such as GPT [1] or LLaMA [2], have demonstrated remarkable proficiency in text generation tasks, from summarization to creative writing. These models exhibit near-human fluency and adaptability, raising the question: Can the difficult process of dictionary compilation be automated or augmented by modern AI systems? This study posits that LLMs hold significant potential to address the dual challenges of lexicography—expanding coverage to include new words and refining existing entries to improve clarity and consistency. Specifically, we propose a framework for developing a next-generation explanatory dictionary through two interrelated tasks:

1. **Definition Generation from Scratch:** Generating coherent, accurate definitions for words absent from existing dictionaries (e.g., neologisms like "cryptocurrency" or dialect-specific terms).
2. **Definition Generalization and Enhancement:** Synthesizing and improving definitions for words already documented in multiple sources, resolving inconsistencies and simplifying overly technical language.

To evaluate these tasks, we conducted experiments using both fine-tuned sequence-to-sequence models (e.g., T5, BART) and prompt-based approaches with LLMs. For the first task, the models were tasked with generating definitions from scratch, with outputs assessed through automated metrics (i.e. ROUGE and BERTScore) and human evaluations focusing on clarity, accuracy, and conciseness. For the second task, we explored methods for summarizing and paraphrasing existing dictionary definitions while preserving their meaning and improving readability. This involved LLM-based iterative refinement approaches. To assess the quality of the summarized and paraphrased definitions, we employed human evaluations opinion polls. The annotators rated the rewritten definitions based on semantic preservation, readability, and linguistic correctness. Additionally, we experimented with multi-step refinement, where LLMs iteratively improved definitions based on critique and feedback loops.

The paper is structured as follows: Sect. 2 reviews related work in natural language processing (NLP)-driven lexicography; Sects. 3 and 4 detail methodologies and experiments for the two tasks; our results are presented in Sect. 6, and the discussion in Sect. 7; and Sect. 8 outlines future directions for AI-assisted dictionary development. By bridging classical linguistic rigor with modern generative AI, this research aims to catalyze a paradigm shift in how dictionaries are created, maintained, and democratized in the digital age.

2 Related Work

The intersection of NLP and lexicography has garnered increasing attention as language models advance in sophistication. This section surveys prior research in three key areas: (1) NLP-driven dictionary compilation, (2) definition generation, and (3) definition simplification and unification. We also highlight gaps in existing work that motivate our approach.

2.1 NLP in Lexicography

Traditional lexicography has long relied on manual curation, with early computational methods primarily focusing on corpus analysis to identify word frequencies or collocations [3]. Initial attempts to automate dictionary creation involved extracting definitions from structured resources such as WordNet [4], yet these methods struggled to handle open-ended, context-aware explanations. With the advent of neural networks, more dynamic approaches have emerged that leverage large-scale data and machine learning techniques to generate and refine definitions—thereby reducing the reliance on manual expert. However, fully automated methods still face challenges in producing definitions that are both precise and accessible.

2.2 Definition Generation

LLMs have revolutionized the field of definition generation. GPT-3 [5] demonstrated the potential for zero-shot definition generation, though its outputs often suffered from issues of precision and included hallucinated details. Multilingual models such as mT5 [6] have been adapted for many languages; however, their performance still lags behind English-centric systems.

In addition, definition generation approaches, such as that proposed by Noraset et al. (2017) [7], learn to generate definitions from word embeddings. While innovative, these methods typically do not address the need for clarity and often produce outputs that lack the succinctness of expert-authored definitions.

LLM-based methods have also been applied to generate plausible definitions for neologisms [8], demonstrating that these models can infer meanings for new words by leveraging morphological and contextual patterns. However, a common finding is that such models tend to produce semantically unstable or culturally biased definitions when handling low-frequency terms. The work of August et al. (2022) [9] introduced a framework for generating definitions with tunable complexity using control tokens to adjust technicality and length. Although their method achieved human-level ratings for clarity in scientific terminology, it still struggled with domain-specific jargon, highlighting the challenge of balancing accessibility and precision—a tension central to our work.

2.3 Definition Simplification and Unification

An equally important challenge is the simplification and unification of definitions to make them more accessible. The research of Glavaš and Štajner (2015) [10] proposed vector-based methods for shortening definitions while preserving core semantics. Although their approach was effective for many cases, it encountered difficulties with idiomatic expressions and context-specific usage. This underscores the inherent complexity of rephrasing dictionary entries to maintain both clarity and accuracy, and motivates further research in this area.

3 Generation from Scratch

To evaluate the feasibility of generating dictionary-quality definitions from scratch without leveraging existing lexical resources during inference, we conducted experiments across two paradigms: 1) fine-tuned sequence-to-sequence models, 2) and prompt-based LLMs. This section details our methodology and evaluation framework.

3.1 Test Dataset

We collected a test set of 200 Russian words across three categories:

1. **Median-frequency words**: 50 words with median frequency from the frequency dictionary of the Main corpus of the Russian National Corpus (RNC) [11].
2. **High-frequency queries**: 50 most viewed words from the "Word at a Glance" RNC service[1].
3. **Genre-specific words**: Having consulted experts, we prepared words from five thematic categories (20 words per category, 100 words in total):
   a. common vocabulary (e. g. *абсурд* 'absurd');
   b. archaisms (e.g. *фатоватый* 'foppish');
   c. neologisms (e.g. *мерч* 'merchandising');
   d. technical terms (e.g. *демаркация* 'demarcation');
   e. slang (e.g. *расслабон* 'chill/relax').

3.2 Sequence-to-Sequence Models

For fine-tuning the sequence-to-sequence models, we utilized a dataset based on the Russian-language Wiktionary[2]. This dataset, comprising 251,314 definitions, was selected for fine-tuning because it is one of the biggest existing dictionaries and is available in a machine-readable format with minimal tagging and linguistic annotations. The input sequence followed the pattern: *Определение слова «WORD»* 'Definition of the word *«WORD»*'. The simplicity of the prompt ensures that the models focus on producing dictionary-style definitions without additional constraints or stylistic guidance.

[1] https://ruscorpora.ru/en/word/main.
[2] https://ru.wiktionary.org/

3.3 Prompt-Based Models

To evaluate the ability of modern LLMs to generate dictionary-style definitions without relying on existing lexical resources, we conducted a series of zero-shot experiments using five distinct prompts:

1. Дай определение слову «*WORD*» 'Define the word «*WORD*»';
2. Дай краткое понятное определение слову «*WORD*» 'Provide a concise, clear definition of the word «*WORD*»';
3. Что значит «*WORD*» 'What does the word «*WORD*» mean?';
4. Объясни простыми словами, что значит «*WORD*»? 'Explain the word «*WORD*» in simple terms';
5. Дай определения всем значениям слова «*WORD*» 'Give definitions to all meanings of the word «*WORD*»'.

3.4 Automated Evaluation

To automatically calculate the quality of the generated definitions, we compared them with dictionary definitions. For evaluation, we used the ROUGE [12] and BERTScore [13] metrics. ROUGE measures lexical overlap between generated definitions and reference texts, providing insight into surface-level similarity. In contrast, BERTScore evaluates semantic similarity by computing cosine similarity between contextualized embeddings generated by a BERT model (in our case, bert-base-multilingual-cased[3] [14]), capturing deeper meaning alignment beyond mere word overlap. These metrics complement each other, offering a comprehensive assessment of both lexical and semantic fidelity.

Ground-truth definitions were extracted from the "Large Explanatory Dictionary of the Russian Language" [15]. In total, we were able to obtain definitions for 159 of the 200 words. Automated metrics were calculated only for them. The exceptions were mainly neologisms and slang words.

3.5 Human Evaluation

To rigorously assess the quality of generated definitions, we designed a Telegram bot-based evaluation involving both linguistic experts and native speakers. Each word was assessed in two stages. After receiving a word, the user assessed whether it was familiar to him/her. If the word was familiar to the user, he/she was asked to evaluate the quality alongside the following criteria (multiple selections allowed):

1. Не соответствует действительности 'Factually incorrect';
2. Непонятно 'Unclear';
3. Неграмотно написано 'Contains grammatical errors';
4. Содержит лишние слова 'Contains redundant words';
5. Неполное 'Doesn't describe all meanings';
6. Просто не понравилось 'Disliked'.

For each definition, we collected 5 responses from different people.

[3] https://huggingface.co/google-bert/bert-base-multilingual-cased.

4 Generation Based on Existing Dictionaries

While generating definitions for new words is critical, refining and unifying entries from existing dictionaries is equally vital to address inconsistencies, archaic language, and accessibility barriers. An LLM may not know all the meanings and contexts of use of a word. As a result, it can profitable to use existing definitions from explanatory dictionaries. This section details our methodology for synthesizing and enhancing definitions by leveraging heterogeneous lexical resources.

4.1 Sources of Definitions

We have researched modern explanatory dictionaries of the Russian language and interviewed linguists and lexicographers about how such dictionaries are compiled. Due to the availability of machine-readable form, markup within definitions and a greater coverage of the main number of lemmas from the Main corpus of the RNC, the following dictionaries were selected: the "Large Explanatory Dictionary of the Russian Language" [15] with 40% coverage of the RNC and Russian Wiktionary[4] with 87% coverage.

4.2 Definitions Summarization

Since fine-tuning of sequence-to-sequence models showed results significantly inferior to the prompt-based approach in the preliminary experiments, we decided to use only prompt-based models in this task. To guide the model in synthesizing definitions from multiple sources, we crafted prompts during preliminary experiments. In this experiment, we considered only those words that were present in at least one of the sources. The final prompt consists of 1) a set of rules describing the required definition format, 2) a few-shot block with a number of definition examples manually prepared by experts based on definitions from both dictionaries, 3) and a list of definitions from one or two sources:

```
You are an experienced copywriter in Russian. Your task is to create simple and clear summaries of definitions of words for the school dictionary. REMEMBER: 1. Write definitions in natural language, without tracing from other languages. 2. Preserve the original meaning of each expert definition. 3. Combine similar meanings into one definition, avoiding repetitions, but covering each meaning. 4. Number each meaning and start a new definition on a new line. 5. Use the same part of speech as the original word being defined. 6. Avoid including minor variations or redundant phrases unless they add significant information. 7. Write only the definitions, without any explanations. Your definitions will be used in the school dictionary, and children's lives depend on it. Provide only rewritten definitions point by point as a response.
-
Examples of Russian language definition summaries:
```

[4] https://ru.wiktionary.org.

```
—
Write a definition summary for the "WORD":
—
Summary of definitions for the WORD:
```

This multi-strategy approach enabled systematic quality improvement while maintaining computational feasibility in just one generation.

4.3 Human Evaluation

To validate the safety, coherence, and formatting of the definitions generated via our few-shot summarization approach, we conducted a structured human evaluation.

For the evaluation, the definitions were distributed to seven annotators via a Telegram bot. Each annotator was provided with the lemma and its corresponding generated definition. The annotators were asked to classify each definition into one of six categories based on predefined criteria:

1. **All Good:** No issues were detected.
2. **Offensive:** The definition contained language that could be considered obscene or offensive.
3. **Broken Tokens:** The output included non-sensical character sequences or formatting errors.
4. **Hallucinations:** The definition exhibited loops, repetitions, or included information not presented in the source.
5. **Bad Format:** The definition deviated from the established format (e.g., inclusion of examples or extraneous linguistic markers).
6. **Proper Noun:** The definition incorrectly provided an explanation for a proper name.

A definition was removed from the evaluation pool if it received a total of three ratings, irrespective of the label, or if it garnered two "All Good" ratings, signifying early approval. This rigorous annotation protocol ensured that only definitions that met high-quality standards were ultimately retained.

Initial experiments with prompts and temperature settings were conducted on a subset of 70 words, selected to represent all lexical categories (archaisms, neologisms, etc.). After achieving satisfactory quality ($\geq$80% "All Good" ratings in pilot rounds), we scaled to 7000 definitions for full evaluation. The 70-word experimental dataset and a sample of the 7000 generated definitions are publicly available in the GitHub repository[5].

5 Models

For fine-tuning sequence-to-sequence models, we selected two widely used models—facebook/mbart-large-50 [16] and google/mt5-base [17]. These models were fine-tuned on a Russian Wiktionary corpus consisting of word-definition pairs. For fine-tuning, we used a batch size of 8, a learning rate of 3e-5, and trained for 3 epochs with early stopping based on validation loss. During inference, temperature sampling was applied with values set to 0.25, 0.5, 0.75, 1.0.

[5] https://github.com/Qishna/compling-2025.

For the definition generation stage from stratch, we conducted a number of experiments with both locally run models and models available via API. Based on the results of the preliminary experiment, we settled on the proprietary YandexGPT model (version as of April 1, 2024).

At the same time, for the task of generating definitions based on explanatory dictionaries, we were limited to local launch of models, since the final scenario for using the algorithm involved marking definitions for several tens of thousands of words. Our experiments with locally run prompt-based models were limited to models with up to 12 billion parameters due to computational limitations. In preliminary experiments, we considered the following 12 models spanning three distinct architectural families:

1. meta-llama/Meta-Llama-3-8B-Instruct[6] [18],
2. AnatoliiPotapov/T-lite-instruct-0.1[7],
3. google/gemma-2-9b-it[8] [19],
4. Vikhrmodels/Vikhr-Nemo-12B-Instruct-R-21–09-24[9] [20],
5. Qwen/Qwen2.5-7B-Instruct[10] [21],
6. CohereForAI/aya-expanse-8b[11] [22],
7. IlyaGusev/saiga_mistral_7b_gguf[12].

All local inferenced models generated outputs at the same set of temperatures: {0.25, 0.5, 0.75, 1.0}, with quantized variants {FP16, Q8, Q4} tested for memory efficiency. After a series of preliminary experiments with draft expert evaluation of generated data, we selected the CohereForAI/aya-expanse-8b model with temperature of 1.0 in FP16 mode for a large-scale experiment.

6 Results

6.1 Generation from Scratch

Table 1 summarizes the ROUGE and BERTScore metrics when comparing model outputs to definitions from "The Large Explanatory Dictionary of the Russian Language".

During the draft analysis of the generated data, we found that the coherence and literacy of the definitions generated by sequence-to-sequence models do not allow us to consider them a promising option for further use. Several examples in Table 2 from fine-tuned mT5 and mBART models illustrate the shortcomings of generating from scratch. These examples clearly highlight the deficiencies of generating definitions with relatively small generative models. The generated outputs are prone to semantic errors, redundancy, and lack the necessary clarity and factual accuracy. In this regard, during the human evaluation, we assessed only the definitions generated by YandexGPT and the definitions from the "The Large Explanatory Dictionary of the Russian Language".

[6] https://huggingface.co/meta-llama/Llama-3-8B-Instruct.
[7] https://huggingface.co/AnatoliiPotapov/T-lite-instruct-0.1.
[8] https://huggingface.co/google/gemma-2-9b-it.
[9] https://huggingface.co/Vikhrmodels/Vikhr-Nemo-12B-Instruct-R-21-09-24.
[10] https://huggingface.co/Qwen/Qwen2.5-7B-Instruct.
[11] https://huggingface.co/CohereForAI/aya-expanse-8b.
[12] https://huggingface.co/IlyaGusev/saiga_mistral_7b_gguf.

Table 1. Automated Metrics for Generation from Scratch

	ROUGE-1	ROUGE-2	ROUGE-L	BERTScore
mT5 vs Dictionary	0.447	0.157	0.447	0.607
mBART vs Dictionary	0.419	0.085	0.419	0.590
YandexGPT vs Dictionary	0.074	0.028	0.072	0.629

Table 2. Examples of definitions generated by the mT5 and mBART models

Word	Model	Definition
музыка 'music'	mT5	1. *В музыке—мелодия, играющая роль персонажа в музыкальном инструменте или в музыкальной игре* 'In music—a melody that plays the role of a character in a musical instrument or a musical game.'
	mBART	*1. Музыкальное произведение, музыкальное произведение 2. В переносном значении,, музыкальное произведение 3. В переносном значении,, музыкальное произведение 4. В переносном значении,, музыкальное произведение* '1. A musical piece, a musical piece. 2. In a figurative sense, a musical piece. 3. In a figurative sense, a musical piece. 4. In a figurative sense, a musical piece.'
космос 'space'	mT5	1. *Земная организация, занимающаяся освоением океанов* 'A terrestrial organization engaged in the exploration of oceans.'
	mBART	*1. Устаревшее слово, земля 2. Устаревшее слово, земля 3. Устаревшее слово, земля*} '1. An outdated word, earth. 2. An outdated word, earth. 3. An outdated word, earth.'

The human evaluation involved 53 participants, yielding 3,247 annotations across definitions, with each word evaluated by an overlap of five annotators. The histogram in Fig. 1 shows the grouped user ratings for both types of definitions. The results show that dictionary definitions are, on average, more popular with native speakers than generated by the neural network ones. The key problem with generated definitions is their incompleteness. At the same time, dictionary definitions were more often unclear or contained unnecessary words, which highlights the fact that existing dictionaries are not perfect.

In conclusion, our results demonstrate that the approach of generating definitions without external dictionary references suffers from multiple shortcomings, including incomplete content, semantic distortions, and formatting issues, which collectively render the outputs less acceptable to native speakers. These findings underscore the necessity of leveraging existing lexicographic resources to paraphrase and refine definitions, rather than relying solely on direct generation by LLMs.

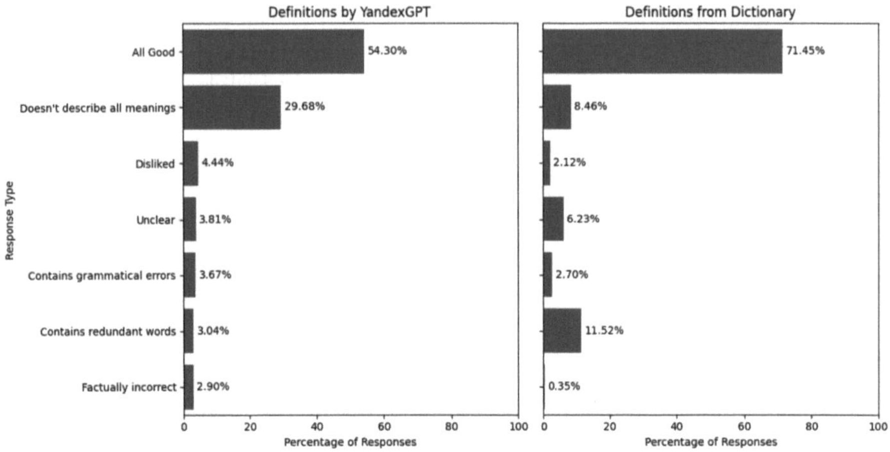

Fig. 1. Feedback from native speakers on generated and dictionary definitions

6.2 Generation Based on Existing Dictionaries

An example of summarized definition is given in Table 3 (LED stands for the "Large Explanatory Dictionary of the Russian Language"). For the resource-augmented approach, we conducted a comprehensive evaluation on 7,000 words via a Telegram bot. The generated definitions were subjected to both automated filtering and rigorous human evaluation. Overall, over 80% of the definitions were accepted as having the correct format, demonstrating that the incorporation of external lexical resources significantly aids in producing syntactically coherent outputs. The error analysis revealed that:

1. 9.4% of the generated definitions deviated from the desired format, often due to improper alignment with the prescribed template.
2. 4.5% of the outputs contained hallucinated information or semantic inconsistencies that did not reflect any of the source definitions.
3. 3.5% of the definitions exhibited issues with broken tokens or nonsensical character sequences, which were largely attributed to limitations in the decoding process.
4. 2% of the cases erroneously included proper nouns, where definitions for non-proper names were expected.
5. Only 0.1% of the definitions were flagged as containing offensive content.

These results indicate that while the resource-augmented generation approach generally produces high-quality, dictionary-style definitions, several areas remain for improvement. In particular, further tuning is needed to reduce hallucinations and ensure strict adherence to formatting guidelines.

6.3 Additional Experiments

After receiving the results, we tried several approaches aimed at improving the quality of the generated definitions. The lack of large-scale human evaluation for these approaches does not allow us to consider the obtained results as a complete study. Nevertheless, we will briefly describe our experiments.

Table 3. An example of summarized definition

Word	Source	Definition
обезьяна 'monkey'	Wiktionary	*1. Высокоорганизованное млекопитающее из отряда приматов 2. Человек, склонный к слепому, бездумному копированию, подражательству или кривлянию 3. Человек с тёмным цветом кожи; негр, мулат 4. Символ «@»* '1. A highly organized mammal from the order of primates 2. A person prone to blind, thoughtless copying, imitation or grimacing 3. A person with dark skin, mulatto 4. The symbol "@"'
	LED	*1. Животное из отряда высших млекопитающих (приматов), по строению тела наиболее близкое к человеку. 2. Разг. О человеке, который подражает другим, передразнивает других, гримасничает, кривляется. 3. Разг. Об очень некрасивом человеке.4. Спец. Мех нутрии, выделанный под обезьяний.* '1. An animal from the order of higher mammals (primates), closest to humans in body structure. 2. Colloquial. About a person who imitates others, mocks others, grimaces, makes faces. 3. Colloquial. About a very ugly person. 4. Special. Nutria fur dressed to look like monkey fur.'
	Generated	*1. Высокоорганизованное млекопитающее из отряда приматов, близкое по строению тела к человеку. 2. Человек, склонный к подражанию, гримасничанию или некрасивому поведению. 3. Символ «@».* '1. A highly organized mammal from the primate order, similar in body structure to humans. 2. A person prone to imitation, grimacing, or ugly behavior. 3. The symbol «@».'

1. **Adding contexts and part of speech.** We tried to experiment with the prompt, making it more complex and adding additional information to it. The word was supplemented with its part of speech and a few usage contexts from the Main corpus of the RNC. This approach should theoretically allow the model to take into account variants of word meanings that are not yet listed in existing explanatory dictionaries.
2. **LLM-as-Judge.** To enhance definition quality via automated quality control, we implemented a two-stage pipeline. In the first stage, for each word, two candidate definitions are generated with distinct few-shot prompts using the AnatoliiPotapov/T-lite-instruct-0.1 model. In the second stage, a separate LLM, nousresearch/hermes-3-llama-3.1-405b [23], accessed via the OpenRouter API, automatically evaluates and ranks these candidate definitions by comparing them against the original source definition. The final definition is then produced by combining the highest-rated candidate with further LLM-suggested improvements. This pipeline should theoretically ensure that the output is refined iteratively based on clear quality metrics such as semantic preservation, clarity, and linguistic correctness.

3. **Actor-Critic.** We implemented an iterative refinement system based on an actor–critic framework to improve definition quality. In our approach, the "actor" model initially generates a candidate definition for a given word, aiming to produce a simplified and natural description that preserves the core meaning. Subsequently, a separate "critic" model evaluates both the original and the candidate definitions according to a set of predefined criteria—assessing semantic preservation, clarity and linguistic correctness. Based on the critic's evaluation, which includes detailed feedback and recommendations, the actor model then refines its output in an iterative manner. We experimented with multiple iterations (from one to three cycles) to determine the optimal number of refinement steps. This actor–critic approach should theoretically allow the system to progressively enhance definition quality by integrating automated quality control and guided refinement, ultimately yielding outputs that are more precise, readable, and aligned with expert standards.

According to the draft analysis, additional experiments did not allow us to achieve a noticeable improvement in the quality of the generated interpretations. However, this may be due to the insufficient number of experiments, so research in this area should be continued.

7 Discussion

A key observation from our study is that resource-augmented approaches, where definitions are synthesized from multiple existing dictionaries, consistently outperform models tasked with generating definitions from scratch. This outcome aligns with previous research, where models such as GPT-3 and its contemporaries have struggled with semantic consistency when operating in a zero-shot scenario [5]. Our results corroborate these findings: definitions generated without leveraging existing lexical resources were frequently incomplete, contained hallucinated information, or diverged from established semantic nuances. Conversely, by incorporating curated sources, our system was able to produce outputs that were both syntactically coherent and more closely aligned with expert-defined standards.

The error analysis highlights several challenges inherent to both approaches. For instance, a notable proportion of generated definitions exhibited formatting issues, semantic inconsistencies, and, in rare cases, hallucinations. These issues suggest that current LLMs are still limited in their ability to fully capture the breadth of meanings associated with Russian words, particularly when cultural and dialectal nuances are considered. However, the success of the resource-augmented method in achieving an 80% acceptance rate among evaluators suggests that with further refinement, these systems can serve as valuable tools for modernizing legacy dictionaries.

When compared to other works in the field, our study underscores a critical paradigm: while LLMs can act as powerful augmentation tools, they are not yet ready to replace human lexicographers. Previous studies have similarly noted that automated systems often sacrifice clarity or precision for breadth of coverage [8]. Our approach, which emphasizes the synthesis of multiple definitions and the iterative improvement of outputs via an actor-critic framework, represents a step towards addressing these shortcomings. Moreover, the integration of human evaluation via a Telegram bot-based system allowed us to capture qualitative feedback that automated metrics alone could not provide, thereby offering a more nuanced picture of model performance.

8 Conclusion

This study addresses the challenge of automating the creation of a next-generation explanatory dictionary by leveraging modern language models. We divide the task into two complementary subtasks: (1) generating definitions for unregistered words and (2) refining and unifying entries from existing dictionaries. Our experiments reveal insights into the capabilities and limitations of current AI-driven approaches to lexicography.

For generation from scratch, we demonstrate that while LLMs outperform traditional sequence-to-sequence architectures like mT5 and mBART, their outputs remain insufficient for practical deployment. Native speakers consistently rated generated definitions as less accurate and incomplete compared to dictionary definitions. This underscores the challenges of grounding models in real-world semantics without curated references.

For generation based on existing dictionaries, we demonstrate that at least in most cases it is possible to achieve definitions that human experts consider acceptable. These results validate the potential of AI to modernize legacy dictionaries by resolving inconsistencies, simplifying complex terms, and harmonizing multiple sources.

At the same time, our study should be considered only the first step towards a large-scale analysis of the applicability of AI in lexicography, and our conclusions should be considered preliminary. This is primarily due to the impossibility of adequately automating the assessment of the quality of generation. Our ability to attract annotators during this study was quite limited. In order to ensure a large-scale testing of the generated definitions from a wide sample of native speakers, we agreed with the Russian National Corpus to conduct a study of the quality of definitions using the previously mentioned service “Word at a Glance”. Conducting such a study will allow us to iteratively improve the model in the future and eliminate its shortcomings.

In summary, our work reinforces the notion that while current generative models exhibit strong potential, their optimal use in lexicography is as augmentative aids rather than standalone solutions. Future work should focus on reducing semantic inconsistencies and further refining prompt engineering techniques, while also exploring the integration of additional external resources such as etymological databases and corpus-based usage statistics. Search engines and Perplexity-like agents can play a crucial role in this context, especially for handling neologisms, slang, and other lexical items that are absent from existing dictionaries. Such directions are likely to further bridge the gap between machine-generated definitions and the precision of human-authored lexicons, ultimately advancing the democratization of authoritative linguistic resources in the digital age.

Acknowledgments. The article was prepared with the support of the Center for Technologies for Society of the Yandex Cloud platform.

References

1. Achiam, J., et al.: GPT-4 technical report. arXiv preprint arXiv:2303.08774 (2023)
2. Touvron, H., et al.: Llama: open and efficient foundation language models. arXiv preprint arXiv:2302.13971 (2023)
3. Kilgarriff, A., et al.: The sketch engine: ten years on. Lexicography 2197-4306 **1**, 7–36 (2014). https://doi.org/10.1007/s40607-014-0009-9
4. Miller, G.A.: WordNet: a lexical database for English. Commun. ACM **38**, 39–41 (1995). https://doi.org/10.1145/219717.219748
5. Brown, T.B., et al.: Language models are few-shot learners https://arxiv.org/abs/2005.14165 (2020)
6. Xue, L., et al.: MT5: a massively multilingual pre-trained text-to-text transformer. In: Proceedings of the 2021 Conference of the North American Chapter of the Association for Computational Linguistics: Human Language Technologies, pp. 483–498. Association for Computational Linguistics, Online (2021). https://doi.org/10.18653/v1/2021.naacl-main.41
7. Noraset, T., Liang, C., Birnbaum, L., Downey, D.: Definition modeling: learning to define word embeddings in natural language. In: Proceedings of the Thirty-First AAAI Conference on Artificial Intelligence, pp. 3259–3266. AAAI Press, San Francisco, California, USA (2017)
8. Malkin, N., Lanka, S., Goel, P., Rao, S., Jojic, N.: GPT perdetry test: generating new meanings for new words. In: Proceedings of the 2021 Conference of the North American Chapter of the Association for Computational Linguistics: Human Language Technologies, pp. 5542–5553. Association for Computational Linguistics, Online (2021). https://doi.org/10.18653/v1/2021.naacl-main.439
9. August, T., Reinecke, K., Smith, N.A.: Generating scientific definitions with controllable complexity. In: Proceedings of the 60th Annual Meeting of the Association for Computational Linguistics (Volume 1: Long papers), pp. 8298–8317. Association for Computational Linguistics, Dublin, Ireland (2022). https://doi.org/10.18653/v1/2022.acl-long.569
10. Glavaš, G., Štajner, S.: Simplifying lexical simplification: do we need simplified corpora? In: Proceedings of the 53rd Annual Meeting of the Association for Computational Linguistics and the 7th International Joint Conference on Natural Language Processing (Volume 2: Short Papers), pp. 63–68. Association for Computational Linguistics, Beijing, China (2015). https://doi.org/10.3115/v1/P15-2011
11. Savchuk, S.O., et al.: Russian national corpus 2.0: new opportunities and development prospects. Voprosy Jazykoznanija **2**, 7–34 (2024)
12. Lin, C.-Y.: ROUGE: a package for automatic evaluation of summaries. In: Text Summarization Branches Out, pp. 74–81. Association for Computational Linguistics, Barcelona, Spain (2004)
13. Zhang, T., Kishore, V., Wu, F., Weinberger, K.Q., Artzi, Y.: BERTScore: evaluating text generation with BERT. CoRR. abs/1904.09675 (2019)
14. Devlin, J., Chang, M.-W., Lee, K., Toutanova, K.: BERT: pre-training of deep bidirectional transformers for language understanding. CoRR. abs/1810.04805 (2018)
15. Kuznetsov, S.A. (ed.) Large explanatory dictionary of the Russian language. Norint, Saint Petersburg (2003)
16. Tang, Y., et al.: Multilingual translation with extensible multilingual pretraining and finetuning (2020)
17. Xue, L., et al.: mT5: a massively multilingual pre-trained text-to-text transformer. CoRR. abs/2010.11934 (2020)
18. AI@Meta: Llama 3 model card (2024)
19. Team, G.: Gemma (2024). https://doi.org/10.34740/KAGGLE/M/3301
20. Nikolich, A., Korolev, K., Bratchikov, S., Kiselev, I., Shelmanov, A.: Vikhr: constructing a state-of-the-art bilingual open-source instruction-following large language model for Russian.

In: Proceedings of the Fourth Workshop on Multilingual Representation Learning (MRL 2024), pp. 189–199 (2024)
21. Yang, A., et al.: Qwen2 technical report. arXiv preprint arXiv:2407.10671 (2024)
22. Dang, J., et al.: Aya expanse: combining research breakthroughs for a new multilingual frontier. https://arxiv.org/abs/2412.04261 (2024)
23. Teknium, R., Quesnelle, J., Guang, C.: Hermes 3 technical report. https://arxiv.org/abs/2408.11857 (2024)

The Influence of Language Typological Features on Neural Summarization Performance

Mark Athugodage[1] and Olga Mitrofanova[2(✉)]

[1] Higher School of Economics, Saint-Petersburg, Russia
mathugodage@hse.ru
[2] Saint-Petersburg State University, Saint-Petersburg, Russia
o.mitrofanova@spbu.ru

Abstract. While summarization remains one of the most prominent fields in NLP with hundreds of articles a year that focus on many aspects of multilingual summarization and seq2seq at all, little research has been conducted on the influence of typological features on the Transformer performance. In this study we tried to fill this gap, offering an extensive analysis of multilingual models for abstractive summarization (T5, FLAN-T5 and BART). To implement this task we collected non-machine-generated datasets for 15 languages, including BBC News Summary for English, Gazeta Summaries for Russian, OrangeSUM for French and many others. To evaluate the model performance we used the full range of ROUGE metrics, BLEU and BERTScore. We focused on the influence of language typological characteristics on model performance, paying much attention to morphological and syntactic features. As regards to metrics used for evaluation of summarization models, we provided evidence in favor of correlation between certain metrics. Cluster analysis of their values allowed to obtain 2 groups of similar metrics (N-gram ROUGE metrics and skip-gram ROUGE metrics). Experiments proved that models for agglutinative languages perform better due to Byte-Pair Embeddings in T5 tokenizer.

Keywords: Multilingual summarization · Typological features · mT5 · mBART · FLAN-T5 · Metrics clustering

1 Introduction

It will not be a surprise to anyone to learn out that the efficiency of language models differs depending on linguistic properties of the texts processed by these models. E.g., LLaMA works much better in English than in low-resource languages (and even in other world languages, like Spanish or Russian). This is usually explained by the fact that languages are distributed unequally in training datasets. In the above mentioned LLaMA about 90% of the training set belongs to English, so it is reasonable that the model may work worse on other languages and that language performance depends on the typological features. The most obvious criterion here is a script: it is expectable that language models will work better on languages with Latin or similar to Latin script. But there are even more important criteria – one of them is the morphological type of a language. In [1]

M. Bakaev et al. (Eds.): IMS 2025, CCIS 2671, pp. 132–144, 2026.
https://doi.org/10.1007/978-3-032-04958-2_10

the authors showed that: (1) mBERT transfer learning is possible even for languages in different script (thus making a script less important), (2) mBERT transfer learning works best for typologically similar languages. Moreover, in [2] researches described correlation between the morphological richness of a language and the performance of a model. These works show us that language typological features indeed play a key role in model quality.

In our work we would like to show how language typological features affect state-of-the-art summarization models. We see also that the script is not such an important criterion as morphological features. Thus, in this work we decided to focus on three criteria: language family, morphology, word order. Overall, our goal in this work is to find the dependency between multilingual models' performance and the language type. Following our primary task to compare multilingual encoder-decoder Transformers we restricted the set of models to three of them (T5, FLAN-T5 and BART) under consideration as having open-source multilingual versions. We selected different summarization datasets for 15 languages, generated summaries using the chosen models and then evaluated using sets of metrics. We then made an extensive analysis of obtained results.

2 Related Work

Before talking about multilingual summarization, we will make a brief revision of contemporary research in the field of summarization. Summarization is usually defined as a process of compressing a large text into a smaller one [3].

There are two approaches to this task.

1. *Extractive summarization* means that we rank sentences in the original text and choose the most important ones. TextRank, a graph based algorithm, is the classic implementation of this approach. Other implementations include fine-tuned BERT models.
2. *Abstractive summarization* implies generating a new text from scratch. Recently Transformers encoder-decoder models like T5 [4] and BART became mainstream solutions in this approach [5].

Alongside with T5, T5-FLAN and BART, many other models are applied for summarization task, but they do not have multilingual versions. PEGASUS, a model which was specially developed for summarization, and Longformer Encoder-Decoder (LED) do not have multilingual versions. Another model that was deliberately created for summarization is PRIMERA, however it is focused on multi-document summarization, which is not of interest in our paper.

Most recently scholars and developers started to apply Large Language Models (LLMs, primarily, GPT) for summarization with prompt-engineering [6]. Some researchers even claim that classic summarization 'is almost dead' since users prefer LLMs. LLMs, they say, demonstrate higher factuality. Nonetheless, we believe that not all hope is lost for smaller specially fine-tuned models.

Most previous works focused on two points: either evaluating summarization itself, or evaluating multilingual Transformers. An extensive work on mBERT for different tasks (NER, POS, etc.) showed up that the model does not work equally in different languages. Authors have cast doubt on the fact that it possible to get a reliable model for all 104 mBERT languages. Still, authors came to conclusion that bilingual BERT outperforms monolingual BERT. Similarly, [7] found out that monolingual BERT is more effective in fine-tuning a model for minor languages, similar to the language of the monolingual model. Authors prove it by fine-tuning German BERT to Gronings and West Frisian. Research described in [8] also took into account similarities between Indo-European languages by comparing document vectors of the Bible text in different languages. As of our knowledge, the only study of multilingual summarization was carried out in [9], focusing just on a limited number of European languages.

We have already mentioned the abundance of evaluation algorithms for our task. However there is still a problem that existing metrics neither evaluate faithfulness of the generated summary nor check how much the generated summary is human alike. In [10] the authors proposed using ChatGPT to evaluate the extent of a generated summary being human-like. The authors adopted standard human evaluation scoring systems like Likert, pairwise comparison and prompted ChatGPT to score the generated summary. The faithfulness of generated summaries was studied in [11], where ChatGPT was also adopted for this task.

One of the keystones in multilingual summarization, which we cannot pass, is certainly multilingual summarization datasets. The most famous and biggest of them is XLSum – a dataset with summaries for 44 languages [11]. Another interesting project is EUR-Lex-Sum dataset, which covers 24 official languages of European Union [12]. Most of other multilingual datasets cover less than 10 languages. The Multilingual Amazon Reviews Corpus includes the most wide-speaking human languages. What is interesting, this dataset is based on reviews, not news as the majority of datasets do [13]. Many other multilingual datasets are based on the popular English summarization dataset CNN/Daily Mail [14]. The idea is that one takes the original English dataset and translates it to the language needed. So does MLSUM which provides machine-translated summaries to five languages [15]. Machine-translated datasets seem to be of low quality as regards our task, so we will evade them in course of dataset processing.

3 Datasets

We focused our attention on specific datasets for particular languages, cf. Table 1, and intentionally did not use multilingual datasets as XLSum. Most of the datasets are domain-specific, namely, news texts. It is worth mentioning that that the Vietnamese dataset was made up with ‘summa’ library for extractive summarization. Although we understand that evaluation on Wikipedia dataset (since many pages in Wikipedia are just machine-translated) and automatically generated summaries is not correct in our case, we mention them here since we wanted to cover as much languages as possible. There are no other datasets for Tamil or Vietnamese (except for XLSum subset). Since they both belong to specific language families (Dravidian and Austroasiatic respectively), we wanted to compare various language groups. Noticeably, for Norwegian we used two datasets: VG and SNL. We randomly selected 500 samples from each dataset.

Table 1. Experimental datasets.

Dataset	Train set (texts)	Domain	Language	Family	Morphol. Type	Word order
BBC [16]	2225	News	English	Ind.-Eur.	Analytic	SVO
Gazeta summaries [17]	~52K	News	Russian	Ind.-Eur.	Fusional	FREE
OrangeSUM [18]	~21K	News	French	Ind.-Eur.	Fusional	SVO
News summaries [19]	~102K	News	Italian	Ind.-Eur.	Fusional	SVO
SNL and VG [20]	~47K	News	Norwegian	Ind.-Eur.	Analytic	SVO
Hindi summarization [21]	~55K	News	Hindi	Ind.-Eur.	Fusional	SOV
Bengali [22]	~19K	News	Bengali	Ind.-Eur.	Fusional	SOV
Farsnews-1399 [23]	~266K	News	Persian	Ind.-Eur.	Fusional	SOV
Indosum [24]	~20K	News	Indonesian	AN	Agglutinative	SVO
Arabic [25]	~5K	News	Arabic	Semitic	Fusional	VSO
TR-News [26]	~278K	News	Turkish	Turkic	Agglutinative	SOV
ThaiSum [27]	~350K	General	Thai	Kra-Dai	Analytic	SVO
TamilWiki [28]	~557K	Wiki	Tamil	Dravidian	Agglutinative	SOV
1700Vietnews [29]	1779	News	Vietnam	AA	Analytic	SVO
Naver [30]	~22K	News	Korean	Koreanic	Agglutinative	SOV

[1] 'Ind.-Eur.' stands for Indo-European, 'AN – Austronesian, 'AA – Austro-Asiatic.

4 Experiments

We tried the following multilingual models on summarization: mT5, FLAN-T5, mBART. We generated summaries with mT5 and mBART using standard parameters and only defining specific maximum length for tokenizer – 512. It is important to note that we generated summaries on different sets of languages for each model. The reason is that mBART and FLAN-T5 models support less languages than T5. T5 model is the only one that supports the full range of languages we offer. To evaluate the models we used the following metrics: ROUGE-1, ROUGE-2, ROUGE-L, ROUGE-S, ROUGE-SU, ROUGE-W, BLEU, BERTScore and additionally compression rate to see how much texts are compressed in different languages. Results are available on Table 2.

The first model we tried was an mT5 model [31], fine-tuned on XLSum dataset. Authors evaluated the model on different languages from XLSum test set – this is one of the reasons we did not collect multilingual datasets. We evaluated this model on all datasets at our disposal. Further, we tried multilingual FLAN-T5-base [32], which is basically a T5 model trained on multiple tasks. Since the model is multi-task, we wrote the following prompt for English: 'Please, summarize the following text:...'. For other languages we typed: 'Please, summarize the following text in [LANGUAGE]:...', where [LANGUAGE] is the name of a specific language we tested. Although in the model card it is claimed that the FLAN-T5 is available on a wide range of languages (including Korean and Vietnamese), we succeeded in generating coherent summaries only for following ones: Indonesian, Italian, English, French and Russian. For other languages the model generated random sequences. A more elaborated study gave us conclusion that though the authors claimed that the model can work with Korean, Chinese and Sinhalese, in reality the model's tokenizer can process well only languages with Latin script. Finally, we tried an mBART model [33] fine-tuned for summarization task. Original mBART model, presented by Facebook, is more intended for machine translation.

Table 2. Evaluation results.

Language	ROUGE						Other metrics		
	R-1	R-2	R-L	R-S	R-SU	R-W	BLEU	BERT-Score	CP
T5 evaluation results									
Arabic	28.1	19.0	26.5	10.5	11.6	14.7	8.3	0.74	6.2
Turkish	23.3	11.5	22.3	7.3	9.2	14.4	8.2	0.74	19.7
Persian	36.0	18.4	31.3	13.6	15.6	18.4	13.1	0.77	17.5
Bengali	18.0	5.5	17.1	3.6	6.0	14.3	2.3	0.73	2
Hindi	34.5	20.3	30.0	16.4	17.9	17.6	16.1	0.74	26
Tamil	14.3	6.7	13.4	4.1	5.9	9.4	0.5	0.67	16.1
Indonesian	40.0	26.2	37.3	18.9	21.2	21.9	19.9	0.79	2
Vietnamese	27.4	15.4	23.2	7.6	8.8	12.4	7.7	0.74	105
Thai	18.1	9.1	17.5	5.7	8.0	12.7	12.2	0.74	26.5
Korean	12.9	5.9	12.0	13.3	18.0	5.9	0.7	0.71	25.2
Norvegian	8.0	0.9	7.5	0.5	1.23	4.5	0.31	0.62	22.1
Russian	15.5	4.5	13.9	1.8	2.6	7.6	1.8	0.7	39.2
French	21.4	6.7	17.4	4.0	5.4	9.6	3.8	0.71	23.3
Italian	9.7	2.2	8.8	4.1	0.6	0.9	0.003	0.63	31.3
English	11.3	4.0	8.8	0.7	0.9	2.9	0	0.67	24.7
FLAN-T5 evaluation results									
Indonesian	44.7	30.3	42.7	25.6	26.7	26.2	29.4	0.77	1.1
Italian	28.7	10.9	26.1	12.5	10.3	11.0	6.3	0.66	6.1

(continued)

Table 2. (*continued*)

Language	ROUGE						Other metrics		
	R-1	R-2	R-L	R-S	R-SU	R-W	BLEU	BERT-Score	CP
English	16.8	9.5	13.9	2.0	2.3	4.9	0	0.69	7
French	12.1	2.1	10.5	1.0	1.9	5.7	0.4	0.65	39.6
Russian	0.5	0	0.5	24	0.02	0.3	0	0.49	32
BART evaluation results									
Russian	11.7	3.1	10.7	1.5	2.1	5.9	0.4	0.6	304
French	23.8	7.7	19.1	5.7	7.0	11.2	7.5	0.69	125
English	28.8	20.4	25.8	8.2	8.6	9.9	1.2	0.78	125
Turkish	27.6	15.6	26.4	10.6	12.2	18.1	12.1	0.72	172

5 Metrics Clustering

Most common evaluation metric, designed particularly for summarization is ROUGE. ROUGE offers a number of metrics. Researchers most frequently mention N-gram metrics: ROUGE-1, ROUGE-2, ROUGE-L and ROUGE-LSUM. Other ROUGE metrics are almost forgotten in NLP. We would like to revise them.

1. ROUGE-W is based on statistics of the appearance of Longest Common Sequence in the text.
2. ROUGE-S is a skip-bigram-based metric, which analyzes any pair of words, allowing a possible gap between them.
3. ROUGE-SU is an extension of ROUGE-S, which allows to adequately score sentences with inversion.

Other evaluation algorithms applicable for summarization include common seq2seq metric BLEU, which was initially proposed for machine translation task, and metrics based on language models BERTScore and BARTScore. Sometimes researchers also mention compression rate $CP = len_{text}/len_{summary}$.

In the presented paper we use extensive linguistic typology to compare multilingual models: morphological types (analytic, fusional), syntactic word order (SVO vs. SOV) and languages families (Indo-European, Semitic, etc.). This will help us understand how the nature of the specific language influences model performance. We have decided to compare different evaluation metrics to figure out how they correlate between each other? Finding a stable correlation between two metrics can help to choose just of the one group in order to get rid of evaluations that are based on resembling criteria.

According to Figs. 1, 2 and 3, there are two groups of similar metrics. The first group combines the so-called N-gram ROUGE metrics: ROUGE-1, ROUGE-2 and ROUGE-L. The second one consolidates skip-gram ROUGE metrics: ROUGE-S and ROUGE-SU. We have found the following unique metrics: ROUGE-W, BLEU, BERTScore. Taking into account Pearson correlation matrix, we can further analyze the results of the following evaluation metrics: ROUGE-L (which also resembles ROUGE-1, ROUGE-2), ROUGE-S (which resembles ROUGE-SU), ROUGE-W, BLEU, BERTScore.

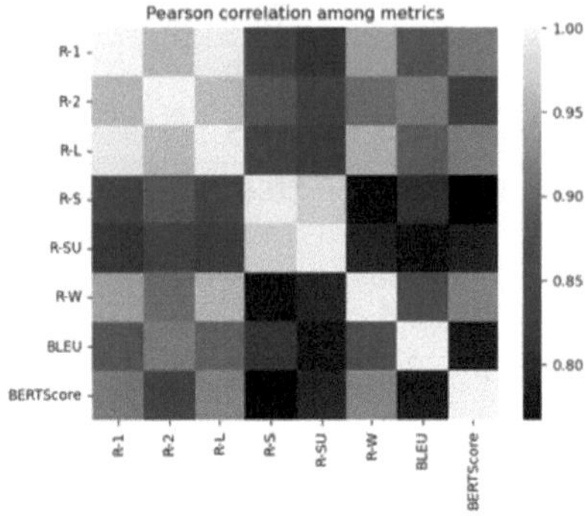

Fig. 1. Metrics clustering with Pearson correlation

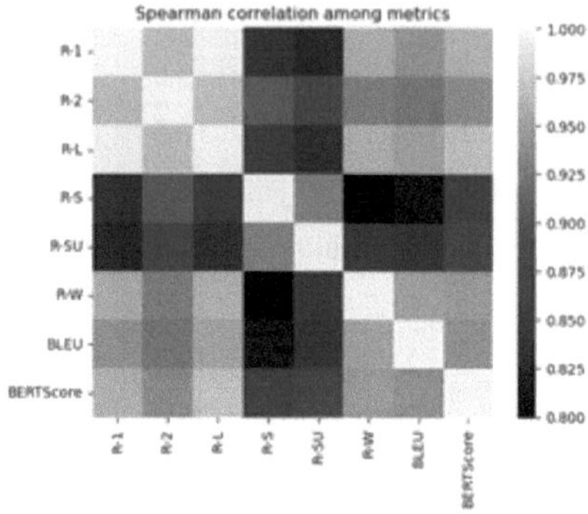

Fig. 2. Metrics clustering with Spearman correlation

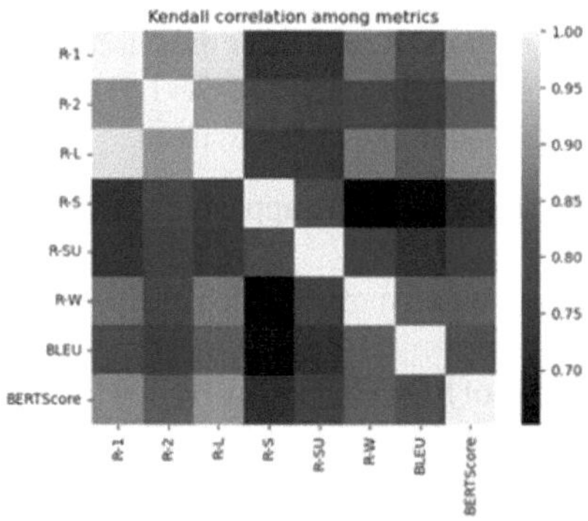

Fig. 3. Metrics clustering with Kendall correlation

6 Results and Evaluation

The primary task of this work was to analyze how models behave in different languages. Most useful in this case will be T5 model fine-tuned on XLSum dataset – this model is available for a number of languages. We could evaluate both FLAN-T5 and BART only on four languages (three of them in each case are Indo-European languages), so analyzing their results may not be so helpful as T5. We will focus on analyzing the results from T5 model.

6.1 Comparison Among Language Families

In this section we discuss how summarization models tackle languages from different families. From the point of view accepted in comparative linguistics and language typology, languages, like Hindi or English, belong to Indo-European family. The languages of one family have similar features: in most cases they can be found in vocabulary. E.g., English and Hindi have a lot of genetically similar words (e.g., English ‘mead’, meaning an alcoholic drink made of honey, is somewhat similar to Hindi ‘medhu’, which basically means ‘honey’). In NLP this problem is crucial when we discuss two languages of one family with the same script. E.g., both English and French use a Latin script, so that some words in both languages are written similarly. In our research we have 8 Indo-European languages; other families are represented with only one language (cf. Table 1). This is due to the fact that language families beyond Indo-European family are either unfairly poorly presented in NLP, or they have only one relatively big language (e.g., Koreanic family includes only Korean). Nonetheless, we hope this study will give a least understanding of the influence of language families on multilingual summarization. As shown on Fig. 4, the best results are obtained on Austronesian languages. This is because the single language, represented in this group, is Indonesian – the one that has the best scores on T5 model among all other languages, including English.

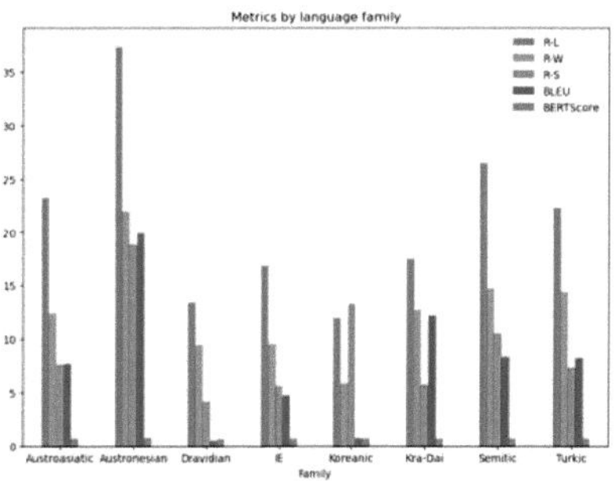

Fig. 4. Average metric scores by language family on T5 model

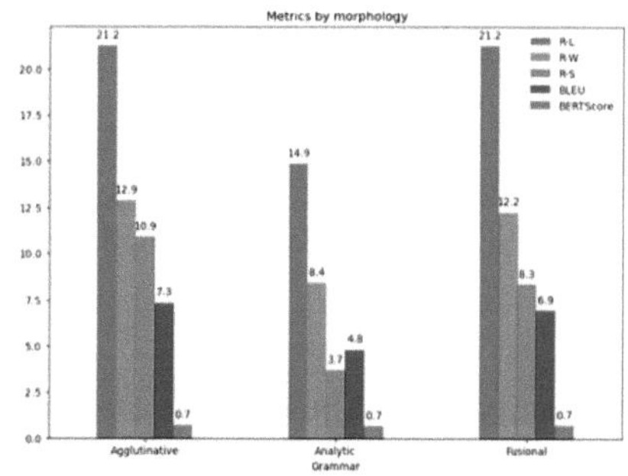

Fig. 5. Average metric scores by morphological types on T5 model

6.2 Comparison Among Morphological Types of Languages

There are two main morphological types of languages: synthetic and analytic. In brief, the difference between them is that synthetic languages use inflection or agglutination to express the values of grammatical categories and relations while analytic languages rely less on affixes and more on function words. Synthetic languages can be fusional and agglutinative. In agglutinative languages a morpheme is expected to express a single meaning (e.g., only case, or number, etc.), while fusional languages use forms potentially expressing more than one meaning. A set of suffixes may be added to a root word in agglutinative languages.

Our initial hypothesis was that metrics would be higher for analytic languages, since they have less number of unique tokens, thus making it easier to generate a coherent text. It is worth noting that analytic languages are generally easier to process in NLP: e.g., it is easier to train a lemmatizer for English than for Finnish or Kazakh. Surprisingly, our study reveals that analytic languages perform the worst among all metrics. The best results are shown by agglutinative languages (their average score is just a little higher than for fusional ones). This means that summarization model works better on synthetic languages, cf. Fig. 5. A possible explanation of this behaviour could be the fact that both T5 and BART are context-sensitive language models, while synthetic languages offer more context inside one token. In analytic languages tokens often present a little context. E.g., in English (which is an analytic language) a phrase 'I will go' contains a token 'go' which does not imply a future tense, while in French (which is fusional) a token 'irai' expresses the meaning of 'go' and grammatical features of a future tense and of the 1st person. This fact possibly helps natural language understanding, e.g., in text encoding and decoding when we know more precisely the possibility of the exact token appearing in the specific context (contextual prediction).

Additionally, T5 Tokenizer is based on Google's Sentencepiece tokenizer, which uses Byte-Pair Encoding (BPE) Dropout. In BPE the token is divided into sub-word sequences, thus making it possible to analyze a word on morphemic level. For fusional languages BPE is able to encode both lexical meaning and grammatical information (and context), for analytic languages BPE is more focused on meaning, while grammatical information is only slightly affected. BPE-Dropout is good at analyzing affixes which is relevant for agglutinative languages. BPE shows a little worse results on fusional languages, as multifunctional affixes may complicate the process of encoding. It is also worth to mention that while our comparison among language families was unbalanced since the vast majority of languages were Indo-European, as regards morphological type the data is balanced: four languages are agglutinative, five are analytic and six are fusional.

6.3 Comparison Among Syntactic Structures

We have also compared different syntactic structures and their dependence on metrics. Generally, there are the following types of syntactic structures: SOV, SVO, VSO, and FREE. These patterns reflect the sentence word order: 'S' – Subject, 'O' – Object, 'V' – Verb. So, 'SOV' sentence type basically means Subject-Object-Verb syntactic structure. We compared different syntactic structures in order to specify if there is any difference for Transformers which is the word order in the language we study. We found out that there is no big difference between SOV and SVO, though SOV works a little bit better on all the set of evaluation metrics. According to Fig. 6, VSO demonstrates higher results than both SOV and SVO. However, VSO is represented only by Arabic, while SOV and SVO are represented with six and seven languages respectively. The free word order illustrated by Russian has the lowest score on the whole set of metrics as it is presumably harder for the model to understand the language when the word order changes from text to text. When a language uses a fixed word order it is easier for the model to understand the overall sentence structure and then generate a new text following strict syntactic patterns.

6.4 Comparison Among Models

As can be checked in Table 1, all three language models discussed in our study include English, French and Russian data. All other languages are available only in one or two mentioned models: e.g., Indonesian and Italian are available in T5 and FLAN-T5,

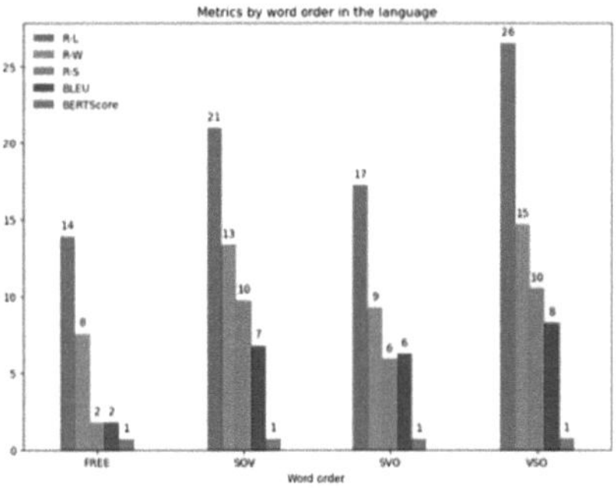

Fig. 6. Average metric scores by word order on T5 model

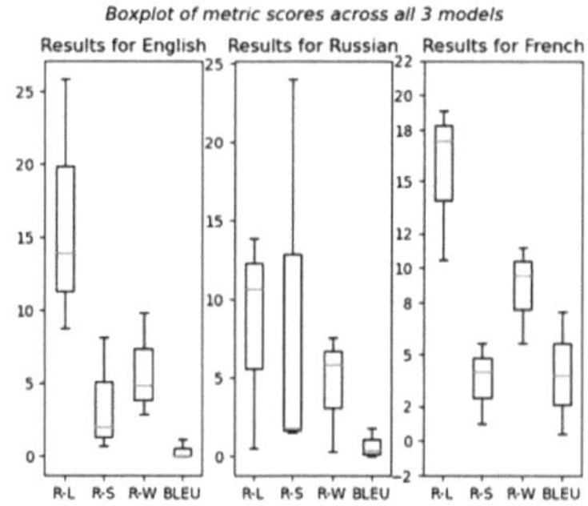

Fig. 7. Average ROUGE and BLEU scores across models for English, Russian and French

Turkish is available in T5 and BART, Thai – only in T5, etc. Figure 7 shows that summarization models perform better for Russian and French texts according to ROUGE-L and ROUGE-S. ROUGE-W and BLEU show approximately same results both for Russian and English texts. It is notable that XLSum dataset, on which multilingual T5 was fine-tuned, has 6 times more samples in English than in Russian (300k+ vs. 52k respectively). Our results slightly differ from those obtained by the developers of multilingual T5 model: ROUGE evaluation on XLSum test set revealed that model performs slightly better in English.

7 Conclusion

In this work we have proved that multilingual summarization models based on Transformers perform in various ways, depending on typological features of the target language. We found out that the most remarkable feature influencing summarization quality is the morphological type of languages: agglutinative languages get the highest scores, while analytic ones, surprisingly, get the lowest ones. We could not find any specific dependency between language families. We explored that there is no correlation between the amount of samples for specific language in the training dataset and the model performance. We have also made an assumption that languages with free word order may be harder to analyze for language models – this hypothesis, though, should be proven on a more extensive analysis. We evaluated not just with N-gram ROUGE metrics, but also with skip-gram and weighted ROUGE metrics – these metrics that are usually unfairly omitted. We have also performed summarization metrics clustering which showed that there are two groups of similar ROUGE metrics: (1) ROUGE-1, ROUGE-2, ROUGE-L and (2) ROUGE-S, ROUGE-SU.

Our work leads to strong understanding that linguistic typology is very important in NLP. The most important discovery in this paper is the fact that encoder-decoder Transformers are best for agglutinative languages, while for analytic ones some adjustments might be helpful (a much larger training set as a possible solution). Future research can be focused on scoring modern LLMs for summarization. There is also a need for a more extensive research on multilingual vs. monolingual summarization models, analyzing a large number of world languages. Experimental results are of great significance for summarization of domain-specific texts, in particular, for Legal NLP and BioNLP tasks. In future this research can be extended to a larger number of languages as we hope datasets for minor languages will emerge too.

Acknowledgements. The authors acknowledge Saint-Petersburg State University for a research project 123042000068-8.

References

1. Pires, T., Schlinger, E., Garrette, D.: How multilingual is multilingual BERT? arXiv https://arxiv.org/abs/1906.01502 (2019). https://doi.org/10.48550/arXiv.1906.01502. Accessed 30 Mar 2025
2. Cotterell, R., Mielke, S.J., Jason Eisner, J., Roark, B.: Are all languages equally hard to language-model? arXiv https://arxiv.org/abs/1806.03743 (2018). https://doi.org/10.48550/arXiv.1806.03743. Accessed 30 Mar 2025
3. Torres-Moreno, J.-M.: Automatic Text Summarization, p. 376. Wiley, Hoboken (2014)
4. Blinova, S., Zhou, X., Jaggi, M., Eickhoff, C., Bahrainian, S.A.: SIMSUM: document-level text simplification via simultaneous summarization. In: Proceedings of the 61st Annual Meeting of the Association for Computational Linguistics, vol. 1 (Long Papers), pp. 9927–9944. Association for Computational Linguistics (2023). https://doi.org/10.18653/v1/2023.acl-long.552
5. Lin, D., Jing, L., Song, X., Liu, M., Sun, T., Nie, L.: Adapting generative pretrained language model for opendomain multimodal sentence summarization. In: Proceedings of the 46th International ACM SIGIR Conference on Research and Development in Information Retrieval, pp. 195–204 (2023)
6. Adams, G., Fabbri, A., Ladhak, F., Lehman, E., Elhadad, N.: From sparse to dense: GPT-4 summarization with chain of density prompting. arXiv https://arxiv.org/abs/2309.04269 (2023). https://doi.org/10.48550/arXiv.2309.04269. Accessed 30 Mar 2025
7. de Vries, W., Bartelds, M., Nissim, M., Wieling, M.: Adapting monolingual models: data can be scarce when language similarity is high. arXiv https://arxiv.org/abs/2105.02855 (2021). https://doi.org/10.48550/arXiv.2105.02855. Accessed 30 Mar 2025
8. Schrader, S.R., Gultepe, E.: Analyzing Indo-European language similarities using document vectors. Informatics **10**, 76 (2023). https://doi.org/10.3390/informatics10040076
9. Saggion, H., Torres-Moreno, J.-M., da Cunha, I., Eric San Juan, E., Velázquez-Morales, P.: Multilingual summarization evaluation without human models. In: The Proceedings of the 23rd International Conference on Computational Linguistics, COLING 2010, Posters Volume, 23–27 August 2010, Beijing, China, pp. 1059–1067 (2010)
10. Jia, Q., Ren, S., Liu, Y., Zhu, K.Q.: Zero-shot faithfulness evaluation for text summarization with foundation language model. arXiv https://arxiv.org/abs/2310.11648 (2023). https://doi.org/10.48550/arXiv.2310.11648. Accessed 30 Mar 2025
11. Hasan, T., et al.: XL-sum: large-scale multilingual abstractive summarization for 44 languages. arXiv https://arxiv.org/abs/2106.13822 (2021). https://doi.org/10.48550/arXiv.2106.13822. Accessed 30 Mar 2025
12. Aumiller, D., Chouhan, A., Gertz, M.: EUR-lex-sum: a multi- and cross-lingual dataset for long-form summarization in the legal domain. arXiv https://arxiv.org/abs/2210.13448 (2022). https://doi.org/10.48550/arXiv.2210.13448. Accessed 30 Mar 2025

13. Keung, Ph., Lu, Y., Szarvas, G., Smith, N.A.: The multilingual Amazon reviews corpus. In: The Proceedings of the 2020 Conference on Empirical Methods in Natural Language Processing (EMNLP2020) (2020). https://doi.org/10.18653/v1/2020.emnlp-main.369
14. See, A., Liu, P.J., Manning, Ch.D.: Get to the point: summarization with pointer-generator networks. In: Proceedings of the 55th Annual Meeting of the Association for Computational Linguistics, volume 1: Long Papers, pp. 1073–1083. Association for Computational Linguistics, Vancouver, Canada (2017). https://doi.org/10.18653/v1/P17-1099
15. Scialom, Th., Dray, P.-A., Lamprier, S., Piwowarski, B., Staiano, J.: MLSUM: the multilingual summarization corpus. arXiv https://arxiv.org/abs/2004.14900 (2020). https://doi.org/10.48550/arXiv.2004.14900. Accessed 30 Mar 2025
16. Greene, D., Cunningham, P.: Practical solutions to the problem of diagonal dominance in kernel document clustering. In: The Proceedings of the 23rd International Conference on Machine learning (ICML 2006), pp. 377–384. ACM Press, Pittsburgh, Pennsylvania, USA (2006). https://doi.org/10.1145/1143844.1143892
17. Gusev, I.: Dataset for automatic summarization of Russian news. In: The Proceedings of the 9th Conference on Artificial Intelligence and Natural Language, AINL 2020, Helsinki, Finland, 7–9 October 2020, pp. 122–134. Springer, Cham (2020). https://doi.org/10.1007/978-3-030-59082-6_9
18. Kamal Eddine, M., Tixier, A., Vazirgiannis, M.: BARThez: a skilled pretrained French sequence-to-sequence model. In: The Proceedings of the 2021 Conference on Empirical Methods in Natural Language Processing, Online and Punta Cana, Dominican Republic: Association for Computational Linguistics, pp. 9369–9390 (2021). https://doi.org/10.48550/arXiv.2010.12321
19. Landro, N., Gallo, I., La Grassa, R., Federici, E.: Two new datasets for Italian-language abstractive text summarization. Information **13**(5), 1–12 (2022). https://doi.org/10.3390/info13050228
20. Navjord, J.J., Korsvik, J.-M.R.: Beyond extractive: advancing abstractive automatic text summarization in Norwegian with transformers. Master's thesis, Norwegian University of Life Sciences. https://nmbu.brage.unit.no/nmbu-xmlui/handle/11250/3079868 (2023). Accessed 30 Mar 2025
21. https://huggingface.co/datasets/Someman/hindi-summarization. Accessed 30 Mar 2025
22. Bhattacharjee, P., Mallick, A., Islam, M.S.: Bengali abstractive news summarization (BANS): a neural attention approach. In: Proceedings of International Conference on Trends in Computational and Cognitive Engineering: Proceedings of TCCE 2020, pp. 41–51. Springer, Cham (2020). https://doi.org/10.1007/978-981-33-4673-4_4
23. https://www.kaggle.com/datasets/malekzadeharman/farsnews1399. Accessed 30 Mar 2025
24. Kurniawan, K., Louvan, S.: Indosum: a new benchmark dataset for Indonesian text summarization. In: International Conference on Asian Language Processing (IALP), Bandung, Indonesia, pp. 215–220 (2018). https://doi.org/10.1109/IALP.2018.8629109
25. https://www.kaggle.com/datasets/abdalrahmanshahrour/arabicsummarization. Accessed 30 Mar 2025
26. Baykara, B., Güngör, T.: Abstractive text summarization and new large-scale datasets for agglutinative languages Turkish and Hungarian. In: Language Resources and Evaluation, vol. 56, pp. 1–35 (2022). https://doi.org/10.1007/s10579-021-09568-y
27. Chumpolsathien, N.: Using knowledge distillation from keyword extraction to improve the informativeness of neural cross-lingual summarization. Master's thesis, Beijing Institute of Technology (2020)
28. https://www.kaggle.com/datasets/aswin037/tamil-wiki-summarization. Accessed 30 Mar 2025
29. https://www.kaggle.com/datasets/dungtuan/1700-vietnam-news. Accessed 30 Mar 2025

30. https://huggingface.co/datasets/daekeun-ml/naver-news-summarization-ko. Accessed 30 Mar 2025
31. https://huggingface.co/csebuetnlp/mT5_multilingual_XLSum. Accessed 30 Mar 2025
32. https://huggingface.co/docs/transformers/main/model_doc/flan-t5. Accessed 30 Mar 2025
33. https://huggingface.co/ctu-aic/mbart25-multilingual-summarization-multilarge-cs. Accessed 30 Mar 2025

Word Sense Disambiguation in Russian: A Generative LLM Approach

Polina Gousyatskaya(✉) and Natalia Loukachevitch

Lomonosov Moscow State University, Moscow, Russia
polinagousyatskaya@gmail.com

Abstract. Various statistical and neural approaches to Word Sense Disambiguation (WSD) for the Russian language have been extensively studied, yet little attention has been given to leveraging generative LLMs for this task. The ability of generative LLMs to draw insightful conclusions due to their black-box nature and the possibility of interacting with them in natural language make them a promising tool for linguistic research. The aim of this study is to test the ability of generative models, particularly those adapted for Russian language, to distinguish the senses of ambiguous Russian words. The experimental setup we employ involves prompting the model to select the correct sense of an ambiguous word from a predefined list. We conduct the experiment on a range of Russian-language decoder-based LLMs, from state-of-the-art models to smaller ones. The objective of this study is twofold: first, to establish a baseline for generative LLM performance in Russian WSD; second, to conduct a linguistic analysis examining how different models handle various types of lexical ambiguity, namely homonymy and polysemy, as well as their ability to process sparse data. As a result, we outline the performance range across various models, with F1 scores spanning from 0.45 to over 0.9. We also identify linguistic factors influencing disambiguation difficulty, namely the semantic relatedness and representation of the senses. The largest average F1 score of 0.75 is achieved on homonyms with well-represented senses. These findings highlight key areas for future improvement in generative LLMs' handling of lexical ambiguity in Russian.

Keywords: Word Sense Disambiguation · generative LLM · classification · lexical ambiguity · decoder-based models · homonymy · polysemic words

1 Introduction

Word Sense Disambiguation (WSD) is an indispensable problem in natural language processing (NLP), forming the foundation for the analysis of all other linguistic levels: WSD is not considered an end goal but rather a component of other natural language processing tasks, such as machine translation, information retrieval, or named entity extraction and linking [1].

This paper focuses on generative, or decoder-based, large language models. The encoder-based models, vividly represented by the BERT family, are capable of analyzing text with high precision and depth and have been successfully applied across various NLP

M. Bakaev et al. (Eds.): IMS 2025, CCIS 2671, pp. 145–156, 2026.
https://doi.org/10.1007/978-3-032-04958-2_11

tasks, achieving notable results in all its subfields. Decoder-based models, which generate text based on a natural language prompt, have been explored less frequently in NLP research. Being able to interpret user's instructions in natural language is one of the most prominent features of generative LLMs; in comparison, encoder-based models, while being extremely effective, require a classic machine learning experimental setup, which makes them much less accessible to the general user. In modern research generative LLMs are widely regarded as a disruptive innovation, driving advancements across multiple domains, including NLP. Their rapid development has significantly expanded LLM-based research, with computational linguistics being no exception.

This study aims to integrate generative LLM-based methodologies with Word Sense Disambiguation as a key challenge in NLP. Given that this research direction remains relatively unexplored, particularly for Russian-language data, our objective is to establish a baseline through a foundational experiment, as well as to investigate how Russian-adapted models generally respond to the WSD task: how the models handle different types of lexical ambiguity, namely polysemy and homonymy, and to what extent the known influential factors in automated WSD affect the performance of decoder-based models on this task.

2 Related Work

Word Sense Disambiguation (WSD) is traditionally framed as a classification problem, in contrast to Word Sense Induction, which is approached through clustering. One of the most well-established approaches in the field is the knowledge-based approach that utilizes structured, machine-readable lexical resources, such as WordNet and its Russian counterparts, RussNet [3] and RuWordNet [13]. Resources of this kind prove to be highly effective in disambiguation tasks, as the structure of ontologies and thesauri reflects paradigmatic and syntagmatic relationships between concepts, their corresponding lexical representations, and their meanings [1, 16]. Nevertheless, the time and labor required to develop structured lexical resources hinder the active development of knowledge-based approaches in the modern WSD.

The most widely-used setting for WSD is supervised machine learning encompassing classic machine learning algorithms that typically demand complex feature representations of natural language data, and neural approaches with encoder-based LLMs methods as their subset: the latter managed to notably relax the strict requirements for the complexity of feature representations, making it possible to embed individual tokens without the need for additional text annotation. The latest evolution in this approach involves relying not on human-constructed feature representations, but on the reasoning capabilities of the models themselves, a shift exemplified by the emergence of generative, or decoder-based, LLMs.

Disambiguation experiments on generative LLMs have not been extensively conducted due to the relative novelty of generative LLMs as a phenomenon. Such studies are relatively scarce even on the English-language material, though they have progressed further than those conducted on Russian-language material: in English-language research the foundational experiments have been carried out, providing reference points for further studies, while the more nuanced and innovative approaches are already in active exploration [4, 22].

A significant shift in modern LLM-based Word Sense Disambiguation (WSD) research is marked by the increasing use of such models as primary disambiguation tools. Previously, generative models were employed in WSD tasks as supplementary tools to support supervised machine learning methods, such as for generating and labeling synthetic datasets, augmenting data [5], among other tasks.

Using generative LLMs as a main disambiguation tool has several notable advantages, the most prominent of which being the opportunity to perform inference without any training or fine-tuning with the high probability of achieving noteworthy results. Among the other advantages of this approach are the capabilities of such models to use advanced reasoning to draw meaningful conclusions, the relative easiness of interaction, due to the possibility to communicate with models in natural language via prompts.

Among the trailblazing English-language WSD studies it is crucial to name [22] and [20], introducing the basic experimental setup implemented in the present paper, as well as outlining baseline model performance, providing reference values for comparison.

Further studies basing on English models are focusing on implementing the known techniques of improving the LLM performance from the side of the user: prompt optimization, human in the loop approaches, Chain-of-Thought reasoning, etc. Additionally, the studies combine the LLM setting with some of the disambiguation methods known since the pioneering works on WSD: disambiguation through translation, leveraging wide and narrow context, etc. [11]. Some studies, following the tendency of allowing the LLM to self-regulate and perform the entire pipeline independently, with the minimum of human-made constraints, resort to more basic tests: for instance, prompting generative LLMs to first detect ambiguity in a sentence and then proceed with disambiguation [17].

3 Experimental Setup

The analysis of contemporary research on LLM-based WSD methods led us to develop the following experimental setup:

Basic zero-shot LLM-based classification: given that our primary goal is to conduct foundational research and establish a baseline for Russian-language WSD, selecting the simplest setup was a logical choice.

Structured output and batch evaluation: most LLM-based experiments have involved human-evaluated, long-form responses. However, for the purposes of our study, we deemed structured output as a crucial condition for the experiment: to facilitate the calculation of metrics, we required the models to produce output in JSON format, i.e. a dictionary where keys correspond to context indices and values represent the sense indices predicted by the model. Precisely this requirement led us to reject Chain-of-Thought prompt enhancement methods, as instructions for reasoning are known to hinder the model's ability to generate structured output, the latter being prioritized in this study.

Data handling: in the present experiment, involving the simultaneous disambiguation of multiple contexts, we do not aim to observe the relationship of the number of contexts presented in the single prompt and the quality of disambiguation. In other words, we do not test if it is easier for the models to disambiguate 10 contexts at once versus 50. Instead, batch construction followed a straightforward approach: preliminary trials indicated that providing the model with more than 40 contexts in a single prompt often led to hallucinations and increased error rates. Consequently, we structured the dataset such that the contexts for each ambiguous word were divided into multiple balanced groups, ensuring that no batch contained more than 40 contexts.

4 Data

In this section we describe the experiment material and outline the principles underlying its selection. For the experiment we selected nine ambiguous words from the three datasets created for RUSSE'18 shared task [18]. The datasets differed in sense structure and the number of available contexts for each sense: the wiki-wiki dataset contained only homonyms with exactly two senses, the bts-rnc dataset comprised words with the average ambiguity of 3.2, and the active-dict dataset manifested even higher average ambiguity scores, along with the broader range of senses.

Below we provide a table with all the target ambiguous words, the extensive description of the senses they have in the Russian language, as well as the number of contexts representing each sense in the corresponding dataset (Table 1).

Table 1. Experiment material with metadata

Word	Senses	Contexts per sense	Word	Senses	Contexts per sense
бор	1. chemical element	14	винт	1. screw	39
	2. pine forest	42		2. propeller	67
лук	1. weapon	65		3. card game	16
	2. vegetable	45	жаба	1. amphibia	79
замок	1. building	100		2. ugly person	6
	2. device for closing the doors	38		3. greed	9
клетка	1. cage	38		4. illness	27
	2. pattern	7	дар	1. present	13
	3. biological cell	96		2. divine blessing	8
	4. staircase	4		3. innate talent	15
	5. chest	4	девятка	1. number	11
крыло	1. body part of a bird	50		2. group of nine people	7
	2. part of a plane	19		3. card	5
	3. part of a car	4		4. type of billiard	9

(*continued*)

Table 1. *(continued)*

Word	Senses	Contexts per sense	Word	Senses	Contexts per sense
	4. part of a building	3		5. car	6
	5. flank of an army	5		6. corner of a football goal	4
	6. group within a political party	7		7. place on a target	5

5 Models

In the experiment we used a range of generative LLMs adapted for Russian language: GigaChat-2-Max (closed-source flagship model of Sber released in 2025), T-Lite-it-1.0 and T-Pro-it-1.0 (open-source models, 7B and 32B parameters respectively, released in 2024), YandexGPT-5-Pro (closed-source model of Yandex released in 2025) and RefalMachine/RuadaptQwen2.5-32B-Pro-Beta (Ruadapt further: open-source model developed by the Research Computing Center of Lomonosov Moscow State University in 2024 [21]). The range of models taken into account varied from flagship models to smaller ones, more typically used for improving inference speed or for less challenging tasks. All chosen models, except YandexGPT-5-Pro, that has not been evaluated, are among the leaders on the MERA-benchmark for Russian-language model evaluation: even the smaller ones rank within the top 30 positions on the leaderboard [7].

GigaChat-2-Max was accessed through its official GUI, in other cases we resorted to using the LLM Arena, the benchmark for Russian-language LLMs, that offers a wide selection of models for testing and evaluation. The links to both GUIs are available in the references section.

Additionally, the aforementioned requirements to structured output led us to discarding some of the models from the initial list of test subjects: their inference capabilities did not prove advanced enough to abide by this rule. Any reasoning and comments the models outputted was not taken into account: the evaluation was carried out automatically basing only on the predictions in machine-readable format.

6 Experiment: Selecting the Correct Sense from a Predefined List

The experiment consisted in prompting a model to determine in which sense from a predefined list the target word is used in the provided list of contexts. The sense inventories we used for each ambiguous word exactly corresponded to the sense inventories present in the respective datasets.

Below we provide a prompt used for all the models:

```
You are a specialist in word sense disambiguation. You are given a list
of contexts containing an ambiguous word. Your task is to determine in
which meaning the target word is used in each context.
Target word: {word}
Senses of the target word with INDICES: 1.(...)\n2. (...)\n3. (...)
Provide the answer in a JSON format with the following fields:
{
  "context number in the analyzed list": sense index (int)
}
```

6.1 Metrics Overview

Models' performance was evaluated by the accuracy and macro-averaged F1 scores, the latter being chosen to better deal with class imbalance, as some of the senses of the ambiguous words, especially from bts-rnc and active-dict datasets are represented by significantly fewer contexts than the others.

Table 2. F1 and accuracy scores on the first experiment

	Yandex GPT 5 Pro		T-pro		Ruadapt		Giga-2-Max		T-Lite	
	acc	f1	acc	f1	acc	f1	acc	f1	acc	f1
бор	1.00	1.00	0.95	0.93	0.91	0.88	0.86	0.81	0.46	0.44
лук	0.98	0.98	0.90	0.90	0.81	0.80	0.66	0.60	0.56	0.56
замок	0.99	0.98	0.84	0.80	0.82	0.76	0.74	0.59	0.73	0.67
девятка	0.93	0.93	0.74	0.73	0.72	0.73	0.15	0.07	0.72	0.72
клетка	0.91	0.82	0.81	0.76	0.72	0.58	0.74	0.55	0.53	0.18
крыло	0.75	0.61	0.61	0.4	0.73	0.63	0.55	0.36	0.61	0.38
винт	0.65	0.39	0.6	0.27	0.67	0.29	0.55	0.24	0.53	0.15
жаба	0.6	0.54	0.65	0.6	0.64	0.54	0.54	0.43	0.54	0.34
дар	0.53	0.53	0.47	0.46	0.52	0.53	0.58	0.52	0.33	0.32
AVG	0.83	0.79	0.73	0.72	0.70	0.66	0.57	0.46	0.57	0.42

6.2 Models' Response to the Experiment

The experiment proved to be manageable for the selected models. The top results produced by the leading models align with the outcomes obtained by [22] on GPT-4o in a similar basic test using English data. As shown in the table, the flagship models – YandexGPT-5-Pro and T-Pro – occupy the leadership positions in this task based on average scores, although their performance, along with that of the other models, is not entirely stable across the entire dataset. Other models performed worse and in some cases appeared disoriented, behaving almost at random. Despite the nature of the experiment being a one-class classification, where the model must choose from multiple senses, allowing for some error tolerance, less powerful models experienced issues with confidence, particularly in cases of greater ambiguity.

Overall, the models exhibited consistent performance, with each model's results not varying significantly, except in two instances of unusually low metric values – *бор* on T-Lite and *девятка* on GigaChat-2-Max. These outliers, which deviate from the average results both in terms of the word and the model, can likely be attributed to model hallucinations and are considered anomalous. LLMs, especially those of the mid-tier, are known to occasionally produce hallucinations due to the black-box nature of the models and the inability to fully explain their reasoning processes. As such, these two results were excluded from the metric calculations.

While the models' performance was not entirely stable, the obtained metrics allowed us to divide the dataset into two groups. One group demonstrated consistent accuracy and F1 scores, indicating relative stability in precision and recall. The other group showed notable drops in F1 scores, suggesting that for certain words, the models struggled to correctly identify positive cases – either defaulting to the majority class or failing to generalize across the dataset. In general, the drops in F1 were attributed to low recall, which seems justifiable given the poorly represented senses for certain words. YandexGPT was the only model that occasionally exhibited significant drops in precision, misclassifying too many negative cases.

6.3 Models' Performance: Linguistic Interpretation

In this section a closer look is taken on some linguistic patterns found in the received results. The highest and the most stable results was achieved on *бор, лук, замок* taken from the wiki-wiki dataset, and on *девятка* from active-dict. On these four words the models achieve the average accuracy of 0,78 and the average f1 of 0,75 and manifest no severe discrepancy between accuracy and f1 scores. Linguistically, *бор, лук, замок* are textbook homonyms, i.e. the ambiguous words the senses of which are not connected diachronically not through metaphor or metonymy (refer to Table 2 for the detailed sense description); therefore, the coincidence of their exponents is accidental. Moreover, their sense structure is binary, and the numbers of contexts representing each sense, although being imbalanced, never differ by an order of magnitude. The word *девятка* possesses a more complex sense structure: with seven senses represented by 11, 7, 5, 9, 6, 4 and 5 contexts respectively, it would have been close to impossible to disambiguate in a supervised WSD framework: generative LLMs, on the other hand, do not seem to struggle with data sparsity, which prompts us to suggest that the class balance in this case results more useful than the absolute numbers of contexts representing each one. What is more, by its nature *девятка* is not a homonym, which apparently does not hamper the disambiguation as much as it could have been expected; we will provide a more extended commentary on this phenomenon further.

The next group, represented by polysemous words *крыло, клетка, винт, жаба* showed middle-range performance across all LLMs: drops on recall become more apparent, and the average metrics decrease to 0,64 on accuracy and 0,44 on f1. All words from this group share similar sense structures, with central and marginal senses, the latter being represented by 1–7 contexts, which often entails the number of contexts varying by an order of magnitude. Zero-shot LLM-based experiments prove more suitable for processing such underrepresented senses, as there is no need to split the dataset into training and testing subsets. Nevertheless, given that the presence of rare senses in such setups do not always result in total failure in recognizing the class, it is obvious that some LLMs do not manage to extract sufficient contextual information from too few contexts to successfully disambiguate the word. In this case the models tend to behave conservatively or shift towards more frequent senses, which produces notable drops in recall.

Lastly, the polysemous word *дар* proved to be the most challenging for all the LLMs, achieving average accuracy of 0,49 and f1 of 0,47, the maximum values on both metrics grouping around 0,5. This word stands out among all the others, being both contextually underrepresented and possessing three quite semantically similar senses. It is safe to say that in some cases the sense distinction was not entirely clear even to the human annotator.

7 Discussion

Following the basic principles of distributional semantics and the related works on WSD, the results obtained in this study can be explained through two primary factors: quantitative and qualitative. The quantitative factor refers to the number of contexts representing each sense in relation to other senses – even if LLM-based setting does not imply traditional model training, the model makes its decisions basing on the patterns recognized in the provided data: therefore, the sufficiency of this data remains a critical consideration. The qualitative factor concerns the semantic properties of senses and contexts: during the inference process, the model transforms the texts in natural language into vector embeddings, which must be counted and weighted in a manner that conserves as much semantic and syntactic information about a target word as possible. These two factors happen to be the only parameters of computational semantics that can be tracked without resorting to more complex feature representations involving more extensive tagging. Their interdependence, reflecting the particularities of the disambiguation process at least to some extent, appears to be a very complex phenomenon, the precise and coherent description of which is hampered by the natural language material itself.

It is essential to acknowledge several key limitations in this analysis. First, the differences in word and sense frequency, as well as the availability of data make it impossible to conduct any experiments on exactly the same quantities of data. Second, even if two senses are represented by the same number of contexts, evaluating the quality of these contexts or determining how informative they are for an LLM is inherently challenging, as the semantic fields to which words and senses pertain vary in size and frequency, often correspond to different registers of the language, etc. As a result, the most we can do at this stage is to outline general patterns and tendencies observed in the data.

7.1 Qualitative Factor: Semantics and Ambiguity Types

The hypothesis that homonyms tend to be easier for automatic disambiguation than polysemous words has been occasionally acknowledged by NLP studies [18], not to mention that it aligns well with the classic semantic theory that deals primarily with prototypical examples of language categories. In fact, the exponents of the senses of a homonym coincide either coincidentally or through borrowing, sometimes followed by the modification of the uncommonly sounding foreign word by associating it with a phonetically similar word from the target language. As a result, the homonym senses are totally distinct and frequently pertain to different domains, rarely appearing in the same contexts. On the contrary, the senses of the polysemous word, being metaphorically or metonymically connected by definition, are likely to appear in similar collocations, as well as form part of closer semantic fields. Semantic distinction between contexts plays a major role in Word Sense Disambiguation: as it essentially reflects the difference between "close" and "distant" senses. In the context of NLP, this is what directly influences the distribution of the context embeddings on a vector space, provided the model itself is able to construct embeddings that adequately reflect the semantic and syntactic features of the words.

The results of the models' inference support the hypothesis to some extent models indeed demonstrate higher and more stable metric values when disambiguating textbook homonyms compared to other types of ambiguous words. The example of *девятка*, nevertheless, implies that the proposed homonym/polysemous word distinction is not entirely suitable for explaining the phenomena at hand. *Девятка* constitutes a prototypical example of a polysemous word: the concept of nine as a number or value serves as a point of derivation of all its senses – the number nine, the group of nine people, the playing card with the respective value, the variation of billiard played with nine balls, the Soviet car colloquially named by its model (VAZ-2109), the upper corner of a football goal (due to a specific zoning principle), and a target in darts that corresponds to nine points. Although the senses are diachronically related, they appear distinct in actual usage, with little to no overlap in their semantic fields. This shows that the diachronic connection between the senses does not necessarily imply the similarity of the contexts where each sense is used. Sense origins and evolution, provided they have no manifestation at the context level, are imperceptible to the embedding model. Additionally, numerals typically do not form their own semantic fields, as their meanings are ubiquitous and not confined to a specific domain.

The example of *девятка* suggests that considering polysemous words as a uniform class is an apparent mistake: the presence of metonymical connection between the senses of a word does not correlate with the semantic proximity of its senses whatsoever. This conclusion could be enforced by an example from the other extremity of the spectrum: the polysemous word *дар*, manifesting the senses of a present, a divine blessing and an innate talent. These contexts manifest a notable contextual similarity, especially on the level of collocations, which results in the fact that in some cases only the author's intent determines the precise meaning of the word.

To demonstrate the arbitrariness of the homonym/polysemous word distinction in NLP terms, we measured the pairwise cosine similarity between sense embeddings of each ambiguous word in order to observe if semantic proximity of the contexts correlate with the target word being homonymic or polysemic. The received cosine similarity values suggest that there is no statistically significant correlation between observed phenomena.

The sense embeddings were produced by the paraphrase-multilingual-MiniLM-L12-v2 model, available at HuggingFace. We provide the table with the results below (Table 3).

Table 3. Context similarity in relation to homonymic/polysemous status

Word	Category	Average cosine similarity	Range	Word	Category	Average cosine similarity	Range
бор	H	0.3225	-	жаба	P	0.78	0.1699
лук	H	0.57	-	клетка	P	0.42	0.5473
замок	H	0.78	-	крыло	P	0.52	0.5536
винт	P	0.51	0.3917	дар	P	0.8	0.0324
				девятка	P	0.63	0.46

The obtained data suggests that in the context of polysemous words with more than two senses, the average context similarity does not impact the successful disambiguation as much as the range between each pairwise similarity values, i.e. the spread of sense embeddings in the vector space. The range parameter helps us define the semantic structure of the word in more detail, specifically, whether the senses are evenly spaced or, conversely, whether some form clusters while others are more isolated. This distinction could provide insight into how easily the senses can be disambiguated: for instance, a smaller similarity range in our data correlates with lower disambiguation quality.

Finally, the cosine similarity values produced on the three binary homonyms – *бор*, *лук*, *замок*, highlight the sheer importance of the correct interpretation of cosine similarity as a metric. The data shows that, despite the relatively high metric scores in disambiguation, two of the homonyms exhibit unexpectedly high cosine similarity between sense embeddings. Apparently, cosine similarity alone does not always capture the contextual markers crucial for disambiguation. Sense vectors may appear close in the vector space while still forming distinct clusters that the model can easily differentiate. These conclusions are consistent with findings from domain-labeling experiments as a WSD approach [19]. This study demonstrated that mapping a sense to a domain—generally aligning with the One Sense Per Discourse (OSPD) approach [8], which relies on measuring embedding similarity within a broad context window—does not necessarily guarantee high-quality disambiguation. While we adopt a more optimistic perspective and recognize OSPD's continued relevance in WSD, these discoveries underscore the necessity of considering multiple parameters rather than relying on a single factor.

7.2 Quantitative Factor: The Number of Senses and Contexts

The discussion of the impact of quantitative factors in the present experiment should begin with the acknowledgment that our data is highly sparse. Regarding the number of contexts, previous research [3, 12] suggests that a minimum of 80 to 200 contexts per sense of an ambiguous word is necessary for effective supervised word sense disambiguation (WSD). As mentioned earlier, zero-shot large language model (LLM)-based experimental setups significantly mitigate this issue, as the absence of sufficient contexts no longer results in a technical failure of the experiment. Nevertheless, the negative impact of data sparsity on any natural language processing (NLP) setup, including WSD, cannot be overlooked.

While the absolute number of contexts is generally considered a positive factor in WSD, the results of the first experiment suggest that this may not hold in LLM-based settings. First, LLMs can infer meaning from much sparser data than traditional machine learning algorithms. Second, rather than the sheer number of contexts, a more critical factor for successful disambiguation appears to be the evenness of sense representation. It is possible that the most frequent sense disproportionately attracts the LLM's attention, leading it to favor this sense while neglecting less common ones. This phenomenon explains the relatively high performance on words like *девятка*, where senses are represented in a balanced manner, in contrast to words with a more pronounced distinction between dominant and marginal senses.

The multiple-choice sense disambiguation experiment suggests that while the well-established factors influencing WSD remain relevant in LLM-based settings, they may operate differently than in supervised WSD. These differences primarily stem from the nature of generative LLMs in a zero-shot experimental setup. While semantic factors remain largely consistent, the advanced reasoning capabilities of generative models mitigate the traditionally critical issue of requiring sufficient data, making it less of a limiting factor.

8 Conclusion

In the present study we conducted a foundational experiment on generative LLM-based WSD using a set of common ambiguous Russian-language words. The experimental setup – a general multiple-choice sense classification task – allowed us to test a range of Russian-language LLMs and establish a baseline. The leading models performed similarly to OpenAI GPT on the same task in English [22].

We also made several linguistic observations regarding the WSD problem, focusing on the impact of two measurable linguistic factors – quantitative (the number of contexts representing each sense) and qualitative (the semantic proximity of senses) – on the quality of disambiguation. The results suggested that, while the general interdependency of these factors remains foundational in computational semantics, they behave differently in a generative LLM setting. This difference is largely attributed to the black-box nature of the model and the specific characteristics of its reasoning capabilities. It is clear that the tendencies and best practices for interacting with generative LLMs differ from those in supervised machine learning, and will need to be further elaborated in future research.

Acknowledgements. The work is supported by the RSF grant 24-18-00988.

References

1. Agirre, E., Edmonds, P. (eds.): Word Sense Disambiguation: Algorithms and Applications, vol. 33. Springer, Cham (2007)

2. Azarova, I.V., et al.: Razrabotka komp'yuternogo tezaurusa russkogo yazy'ka tipa WordNet (Development of a Russian-language computer thesaurus of the WordNet type). Doklady' nauch. konf. «Korpusnaya lingvistika i lingvisticheskie bazy' danny'x» /pod red. A. C. Gerda. SPb.: Izd-vo Sankt-Peterburgskogo universiteta, pp. 6–18 (2002)
3. Azarova, I.V., Marina, A.S.: Avtomatizirovannaya klassifikaciya kontekstov pri podgotovke danny'x dlya komp'yuternogo tezaurusa RussNet. Komp'yuternaya lingvistika i intellektual'ny'e texnologii: Trudy' mezhdunarodnoj konferencii «Dialog» (Automated Context Classification for Data Preparation in the RussNet Computational Thesaurus, pp. 13–17 (2006)
4. Basile, P., et al.: Exploring the word sense disambiguation capabilities of large language models. arXiv preprint arXiv:2503.08662 (2025)
5. Ding, B., et al.: Data augmentation using LLMs: data perspectives, learning paradigms, and challenges. In: Findings of the Association for Computational Linguistics (ACL 2024), pp. 1679–1705 (2024)
6. Fenogenova, A., et al.: Mera: a comprehensive LLM evaluation in Russian. arXiv preprint arXiv:2401.04531 (2024)
7. Gale, W.A., Church, K., Yarowsky, D.: One sense per discourse. In: Speech and Natural Language: Proceedings of a Workshop Held at Harriman, New York (1992)
8. Ide, N., Véronis, J.: Introduction to the special issue on word sense disambiguation: the state of the art. Comput. Linguist. **24**(1), 1–40 (1998)
9. Kang, H., Blevins, T., Zettlemoyer, L.: Translate to disambiguate: zero-shot multilingual word sense disambiguation with pretrained language models. arXiv preprint arXiv:2304.13803 (2023)
10. Kashkin, E.V., Lyashevskaya, O.N.: Tipy' informacii o leksicheskix konstrukciyax v sisteme FrejmBank (Types of Information About Lexical Constructions in the FrameBank System). Trudy' instituta russkogo yazy'ka im. VV Vinogradova **6**, 464–556 (2015)
11. Loukachevitch, N.V., Lashevich, G., Gerasimova, A.A., Ivanov, V.V., Dobrov, B.V.: Creating Russian WordNet by conversion. In: Proceedings of Conference on Computational Linguistics and Intellectual Technologies Dialog-2016, pp. 405–415 (2016)
12. Moro, A., Raganato, A., Navigli, R.: Entity linking meets word sense disambiguation: a unified approach. Trans. Assoc. Comput. Linguist. **2**, 231–244 (2014)
13. Navigli, R.: A quick tour of word sense disambiguation, induction and related approaches. In: Bieliková, M., Friedrich, G., Gottlob, G., Katzenbeisser, S., Turán, G. (eds.) Theory and Practice of Computer Science, SOFSEM 2012. LNCS, vol. 147. Springer, Heidelberg (2012). https://doi.org/10.1007/978-3-642-27660-6_10
14. Ortega-Martín, M., et al.: Linguistic ambiguity analysis in ChatGPT. arXiv preprint arXiv:2302.06426 (2023)
15. Panchenko, A., et al.: RUSSE'2018: a shared task on word sense induction for the Russian language. arXiv preprint arXiv:1803.05795 (2018)
16. Sainz, O., et al.: What do language models know about word senses? Zero-shot WSD with language models and domain inventories. arXiv preprint arXiv:2302.03353 (2023)
17. Sumanathilaka, T., Micallef, N., Hough, J.: Can LLMs assist with Ambiguity? A quantitative evaluation of various large language models on word sense disambiguation. arXiv preprint arXiv:2411.18337 (2024)
18. Tikhomirov, M., Chernyshov, D.: Facilitating large language model Russian adaptation with learned embedding propagation. J. Lang. Educ. **10**(4), 130–145 (2024)
19. Yae, J.H., et al.: Leveraging large language models for word sense disambiguation. Neural Comput. Appl. **37**(6), 4093–4110 (2025)

Russian Neural Morpheme Segmentation: From Lemmata to Wordforms

Dmitry Morozov[1,3(✉)], Olga Shcherbakova[1], and Anna Glazkova[2,3]

[1] Novosibirsk State University, 1 Pirogova str., Novosibirsk 630090, Russia
morozowdm@gmail.com, o.sherbakova@g.nsu.ru
[2] University of Tyumen, 6 Volodarskogo str., Tyumen 625003, Russia
[3] Russian National Corpus, Moscow, Russia

Abstract. Among the algorithms for automated morpheme segmentation for the Russian language, the best-performing ones are based on machine learning. The quality of these algorithms is currently close to expert-level. However, most research focuses on the analysis of lemmata rather than word forms. In this study, we compare state-of-the-art methods for morpheme segmentation using a prepared dataset of word forms. We evaluate three approaches: an ensemble of convolutional neural networks, a subword Transformer model DeepSPIN-3, and RuRoberta-based Morphberta models. To assess the robustness of these models, we employed multiple strategies for splitting the dataset into training and test sets, specifically to examine how performance degrades when handling out-of-vocabulary lemmata and roots. The best results were achieved using Morphberta models (over 99.5% completely accurate segmentations). However, our findings also demonstrate that random dataset splitting does not provide a comprehensive understanding of quality of the algorithm. Specifically, when dealing without-of-vocabulary morphemes, segmentation accuracy significantly declines, with the extent and nature of the decline varying across algorithms.

Keywords: Morpheme Segmentation · Russian Language · Deep Learning

1 Introduction

Morpheme segmentation is the process of mapping words to lists of morphemes, which are the smallest meaningful units of a word, such as roots, prefixes, suffixes. In languages with rich derivational morphology, such as Russian, morpheme segmentation is important not only for linguists studying the language but also for native speakers, as it is often tied to spelling rules [19]. Morpheme segmentation also shows promise as a subword tokenizer for language models. Matthews et al. [11] suggest that morpheme-based tokenization can outperform traditional methods like Byte-Pair Encoding (BPE). Additionally, morpheme annotation is applied in large linguistic corpora [16] to improve search functionality, supporting both research and practical applications.

Since morpheme segmentation for Russian words is far from trivial [8], non-experts often require assistance in this task. The most common solution is the use of morpheme dictionaries. However, existing morpheme dictionaries are incomplete: the largest

M. Bakaev et al. (Eds.): IMS 2025, CCIS 2671, pp. 157–167, 2026.
https://doi.org/10.1007/978-3-032-04958-2_12

ones contain 100,000 to 150,000 segmentations, while the Main Corpus of the Russian National Corpus [16] includes over 250,000 unique lemmata. Automatic expansion of such dictionaries is possible through machine learning-based algorithms. Research shows that the average quality of automatic morpheme segmentation is now close to expert-level performance [12]. Nevertheless, these algorithms face challenges with out-of-vocabulary (OOV) roots and incorporating word semantics.

Most research for Russian in this domain has been conducted using lemma dictionaries. This is primarily due to the lack of large datasets of morpheme segmentations for word forms: nearly all morpheme dictionaries provide information only for lemmata. However, for certain practical tasks, such as developing morpheme tokenizers for language models, algorithms capable of segmenting word forms are required. Several studies have addressed the segmentation of Russian word forms [2, 4, 14], but these were conducted on different datasets, and the task formulations varied significantly, making it difficult to compare the results. For instance, Morozov et al. [12] demonstrated that the DeepSPIN-3 algorithm [14], which achieved the best performance for Russian in the SIGMORPHON 2022 shared task [1], significantly underperformed compared to other approaches when dealing with OOV roots in a lemma-based training scenario.

Thus, this work focuses on comparing several state-of-the-art approaches to automatic morpheme segmentation for Russian word forms. Our main contributions are as follows:

1. **Morphodict-K-Wordform Dataset Creation:** We prepared a morpheme segmentation dataset for Russian word forms, containing a total of 1,392,789 segmentations.
2. **Model Comparison:** Using the prepared dataset, we compared three state-of-the-art approaches (an ensemble of convolutional neural networks (CNN), a subword Transformer model DeepSPIN-3, and RuRoberta-based Morphberta models) under different evaluation scenarios:
   a. Random split of the dataset into training and test sets;
   b. Split by lemmata (i.e., word forms sharing a lemma were assigned exclusively to either the training or test set);
   c. Split by roots (i.e., word forms sharing a root were assigned exclusively to either the training or test set).

   The Morphberta-lex model achieved the highest performance in most scenarios.
3. **Evaluation Insights:** The results varied significantly across evaluation scenarios. While all algorithms achieved 98–99% completely correct segmentations in the random split scenario, in the root-based split scenario the proportion of completely correct segmentations dropped below 80% for all algorithms. This indicates that random splitting, which is most commonly used to evaluate performance in this problem, cannot provide a comprehensive assessment of model quality and may overestimate a model's generalization ability.

2 Related Work

One of the earliest and most studied approaches in the field of automatic morpheme segmentation is the Morfessor family of algorithms [6], which includes both unsupervised and semi-supervised methods. The advancement of neural network techniques in natural language processing has led to significant improvements in this task. State-of-the-art algorithms were showcased in the SIGMORPHON 2022 shared task [1], which featured nine languages including Russian. The DeepSPIN team [14] achieved the best results in this competition with solutions based on LSTM networks featuring specialized loss functions and Transformer architectures.

With the widespread adoption of large language models, researchers have begun exploring their applicability to the morpheme segmentation task. While recent work [15] demonstrated improved segmentation quality for several low-resource languages, the slow inference speed and relatively modest performance on major languages like English currently limit the practical utility of this approach.

The most effective and well-studied approaches for the Russian language include CNN ensembles [18] and LSTM networks [3]. Comparative studies across multiple morpheme dictionaries revealed that CNN ensembles achieve near-human performance [12], though recent work by Morozov et al. [13] demonstrated that fine-tuned BERT-like models can surpass this, achieving 92.5–93.5% completely accurate segmentations.

Despite these strong average-case results, current algorithms exhibit notable limitations. A series of studies [7, 12, 13] have shown significant performance degradation with out-of-vocabulary (OOV) roots, where word-level accuracy drops to 77% or lower. This issue particularly affects algorithms that do not incorporate word semantics, though pretrained embedding models can partially mitigate the problem [12, 13, 17].

Research specifically targeting Russian word form segmentation remains limited, primarily due to the lack of comprehensive morpheme dictionaries. Notable exceptions include the SIGMORPHON competition [1] and the works by E. Bolshakova and A. Sapin [2, 4], though these studies employed substantially different task formulations: SIGMORPHON focused on segmentation without morpheme typing but with canonical morpheme forms restoration, while E. Bolshakova and A. Sapin examined surface segmentation with morpheme classification. Neither study adequately addressed the OOV root performance degradation issue. Furthermore, the applicability of BERT-like models when moving from lemmata to word forms remains an open research question worthy of investigation.

3 Data

3.1 Morphodict-K

As a reference dataset, we utilized the Morphodict-K dataset of morpheme segmentations, which is used in the Russian National Corpus [16]. This dataset is based on the Dictionary of Morphemes of the Russian Language [10]. It contains 75,649 morpheme segmentations: each lemma is associated with a list of morphemes, and each morpheme is assigned one of seven types: ROOT, PREF (prefix), SUFF (suffix), END (ending), POST (postfix), LINK (linking vowel), HYPH (hyphen). A brief description of the Morphodict-K dataset is provided in Table 1. This dataset has previously been used in a number of studies to evaluate the quality of automatic morpheme segmentation [7, 12].

Table 1. Brief characteristics of the datasets

	Morphodict-K	Morphodict-K-Wordform
Unique words	75,649	1,392,789
Unique morphemes	8,079	8,761
Unique roots	7,125	7,720
Average morphemes per word	4.12	4.76
Average morpheme occurrence	38.56	756.79
Average root occurrence	12.24	197.33
Average root length in symbols	4.62	4.67

3.2 Morphodict-K-Wordform

Based on the Morphodict-K dataset, we created an extended Morphodict-K-Wordform dataset containing segmentations for word forms. It contains a total of 1,392,789 unique morpheme segmentations, and as before, each of its word forms is associated with a list of morphemes belonging to seven different types.

For automatic expansion of the dataset, we first divided it into three parts. The first part contained nouns and adjectives, the second one contained verbs, and the third one contained adverbs and other parts of speech. We then utilized the inflection engine of the morphological analyzer PyMorphy2, which is specifically designed for Russian and Ukrainian languages [9], to create all possible inflections of each lemma. After obtaining an expanded set of word forms, we focused on the task of automatically segmenting word forms into morphemes based on the segmentation of the corresponding lemmata.

Morpheme segmentation for inflected nouns and adjectives was performed as follows. First, we extracted the word stem from the segmentation of the lemma and compared it with the word form. If the stem matched the beginning of the word form, the remaining part was identified as an ending, and the segmentation was updated accordingly. The word forms that did not match the stem of the lemma had to be segmented manually. This was mainly due to the presence of alternations in some word forms, as well as suffixes or prefixes that were absent in the lemma, such as the superlative suffix *-ейш-* and the comparative prefix *по-*. A separate script was written for each word form containing such morphemes or alternations.

The segmentation approach for verbs followed a similar principle: we compared the stem to the word form to identify verb endings in the present tense, and then separately processed past and future tense verbs, participles and forms with alternations. After completing the segmentation process, we manually reviewed and corrected any incorrectly segmented word endings. Additionally, the acquired segmentations were compared to the inflected forms to ensure that they did not contain any redundant morphemes.

A brief description of the Morphodict-K-Wordform dataset is provided in Table 1. It should be noted that the increased number of roots in the Morphodict-K-Wordform dataset compared to Morphodict-K is associated precisely with the presence of alternations in the roots.

4 Models

We examined three high-performing approaches for Russian morpheme segmentation: a convolutional neural network ensemble (hereinafter **CNN**) [18], the subword Transformer model **DeepSPIN-3** [14], and RuRoberta-based Morphberta models [13].

The CNN and Morphberta approaches employ character-level labeling of lemmata. Each character receives a two-part tag where the first component indicates position within the morpheme (B [beginning], M [middle], E [end], S [single-character morpheme]); and the second specifies morpheme type (ROOT, PREF, SUFF, END, POST, LINK, HYPH). This represents a *surface* segmentation approach [5].

The CNN ensemble consisted of 3 models, with each network comprising three layers featuring a window size of 5 and 192 filters. Training proceeded for 25 epochs with early stopping after 10 epochs of no improvement.

For Morphberta approach, we implemented two variants based on RuRoberta-large[1] [20] following the paper [13], differing in input sequence construction: a) character-separated lemma as input (hereinafter **Morphberta-char**); b) whole lemma prefixed to the character sequence with special class '0' as target (hereinafter **Morphberta-lex**). The models were fine-tuned for 10 epochs, using a learning rate of 5e-6 and batch size of 16. The values of the remaining parameters were set to default.

Unlike these approaches, DeepSPIN-3 was designed for *canonical* segmentation – simultaneously splitting words into morphemes while restoring their underlying forms [5]. DeepSPIN-3 model also does not provide morpheme classification. This is a Transformer-based model trained with the inverse square root learning schedule up to 400,000 parameter updates. The model consists of 6 layers in the encoder and decoder, with 8 attention heads per layer. All hyperparameters were kept as specified in the original paper. DeepSPIN-3 performs sequence-to-sequence generation, taking a lemma as input and producing morpheme substrings separated by `"@@"`.

5 Experimental Setup

5.1 Train-Test Split Scenarios

We conducted three series of experiments, each differing in how the dataset was split into training and test sets. In all cases, we performed 5-fold cross-validation:

1. **Split-by-form.** In this scenario, we randomly divided the entire dataset into five folds without any additional constraints.
2. **Split-by-lemma.** Here, we first grouped all word forms by their lemmata and then evenly distributed the lemmata into five groups. All word forms associated with lemmata in group *k* were assigned to fold *k*.
3. **Split-by-roots.** For this setup, we first excluded words with multiple roots from consideration. Next, we grouped the remaining words by their roots and evenly distributed the roots into five groups. All word forms associated with roots in group *k* were assigned to fold *k*.

[1] https://huggingface.co/ai-forever/ruRoberta-large.

5.2 Evaluation Metrics

To evaluate the performance of the CNN, Morphberta-char, and Morphberta-lex models, we employed the metrics proposed in [18]: Precision, Recall, and F-score for morpheme boundaries, as well as character-level accuracy (Accuracy) and word-level accuracy (WordAccuracy). For the DeepSPIN-3 model, we used the metrics introduced in [1]: Levenshtein distance between the generated segmentation and the reference one, along with Precision, the ratio of correctly predicted morphemes over all predicted morphemes, Recall, the ratio of correctly predicted morphemes over all gold-label morpheme, and F-score. Additionally, we calculated word-level accuracy for DeepSPIN-3, as prior research [12] has shown that labeling morpheme types for an existing segmentation can achieve near-perfect accuracy. This allowed us to compare all models on a common metric.

5.3 Implementation Details

1. **CNN Ensemble**. We employed an implementation by A. Sorokin[2]. All experiments were conducted on an AMD Ryzen 5 5600X CPU without GPU acceleration, with each epoch requiring approximately 90 s of computation time.
2. **DeepSPIN-3**. We utilized the implementation by J. Stephenson[3] without modifications. The models were trained on an Nvidia RTX 3060 GPU. Training of one model took up to 150 min.
3. **Morphberta models**. We utilized the `simpletransformers`[4] framework. The models were trained on an Nvidia RTX 4090 GPU. Each training epoch took up to 100 min.

6 Result and Discussion

Tables 2 and 3 present the obtained results. Each model was evaluated using six scenarios: for each of the three train-test split scenarios (by-form, by-lemma, by-roots), we computed metrics both for all word forms and exclusively for lemmata in the test set. All results are reported as mean $\pm$ std.

As expected, performance degrades progressively from split-by-form to split-by-lemma and finally split-by-roots scenarios. This is most pronounced for the DeepSPIN-3 model—for instance, Levenshtein distance increases by an order of magnitude with each transition, while WordAccuracy drops from 99% (split-by-form) to just 20% (split-by-roots). The CNN ensemble and Morphberta models show less dramatic but still significant declines, with word forms metrics falling from 98.5–99.5% (split-by-form) to 77–82% (split-by-roots).

Notably, word forms metrics, including word-level accuracy, consistently outperform lemmata metrics across all split scenarios. This suggests that highly inflected words with OOV stems/roots are generally segmented more accurately than uninflected parts of speech.

[2] https://github.com/AlexeySorokin/NeuralMorphemeSegmentation.

[3] https://github.com/joshstephenson/MorphemeSegmentation.

[4] https://simpletransformers.ai/

Comparing the CNN ensemble and Morphberta models reveals that the Morphberta-lex model achieves superior performance in all cases except word forms metrics under split-by-form. The advantage is marginal for split-by-form and split-by-lemma scenarios (particularly for word form metrics), but becomes substantial in split-by-roots scenario, outperforming other approaches by 4.5 percentage points (word forms) and 5.5 points (lemmata). Remarkably, these lemmata metric results surpass those achieved by a structurally similar model on the Morphodict-K dataset, with WordAccuracy reaching 0.7814 ± 0.0151 compared to 0.7717 ± 0.0196 [13]. This indicates that expanding the training data with word forms enhanced the model's generalization capability.

Table 2. Results for DeepSPIN-3

Metric	DeepSPIN-3	
split-by-form		
	word forms	lemmata
Precision	0.9968 ± 0.0010	0.9816 ± 0.0027
Recall	0.9970 ± 0.0009	0.9846 ± 0.0021
F-score	0.9969 ± 0.0010	0.9831 ± 0.0024
Levenshtein	0.01 ± 0.01	0.08 ± 0.01
WordAccuracy	0.9922 ± 0.0014	0.9598 ± 0.0033
split-by-lemma		
	word forms	lemmata
Precision	0.9700 ± 0.0016	0.9489 ± 0.0027
Recall	0.9728 ± 0.0016	0.9558 ± 0.0033
F-score	0.9714 ± 0.0016	0.9523 ± 0.0030
Levenshtein	0.17 ± 0.01	0.25 ± 0.02
WordAccuracy	0.9148 ± 0.0029	0.8805 ± 0.0043
split-by-roots		
	word forms	lemmata
Precision	0.7625 ± 0.0068	0.7083 ± 0.0070
Recall	0.7728 ± 0.0025	0.7219 ± 0.0063
F-score	0.7676 ± 0.0044	0.7151 ± 0.0064
Levenshtein	1.49 ± 0.03	1.54 ± 0.04
WordAccuracy	0.2145 ± 0.0176	0.2088 ± 0.0138

Error analysis reveals patterns consistent with prior research [2, 4, 12, 13]. The CNN ensemble and Morphberta models primarily err in root boundary identification—either oversegmenting roots into prefixes/suffixes or undersegmenting them. Another common error type involves suffix splitting, which may reflect inconsistencies in the

Table 3. Results for CNN Ensemble and Morphberta models

Metric	CNN	Morphberta-char	Morphberta-lex
split-by-form, word form metrics			
Precision	0.9985 ± 0	0.9996 ± 0	0.9994 ± 0
Recall	0.9986 ± 0.0001	0.9996 ± 0	0.9995 ± 0
F-score	0.9986 ± 0	0.9996 ± 0	0.9995 ± 0
Accuracy	0.9968 ± 0	0.9990 ± 0	0.9989 ± 0
WordAccuracy	0.9848 ± 0.0002	0.9955 ± 0.0001	0.9947 ± 0.0001
split-by-form, lemmata metrics			
Precision	0.9927 ± 0.0003	0.9960 ± 0.0003	0.9966 ± 0.0004
Recall	0.9956 ± 0.0003	0.9972 ± 0.0003	0.9978 ± 0.0002
F-score	0.9941 ± 0.0003	0.9966 ± 0.0002	0.9972 ± 0.0001
Accuracy	0.9880 ± 0.0005	0.9922 ± 0.0002	0.9936 ± 0.0003
WordAccuracy	0.9550 ± 0.0018	0.9686 ± 0.0009	0.9739 ± 0.0008
split-by- lemma, word form metrics			
Precision	0.9925 ± 0.0005	0.9943 ± 0.0003	0.9948 ± 0.0005
Recall	0.9934 ± 0.0004	0.9946 ± 0.0003	0.9952 ± 0.0003
F-score	0.9929 ± 0.0003	0.9945 ± 0.0003	0.9950 ± 0.0004
Accuracy	0.9865 ± 0.0006	0.9891 ± 0.0005	0.9902 ± 0.0007
WordAccuracy	0.9450 ± 0.0026	0.9558 ± 0.0023	0.9591 ± 0.0026
split-by-lemma, lemmata metrics			
Precision	0.9843 ± 0.0007	0.9889 ± 0.0001	0.9908 ± 0.0003
Recall	0.9892 ± 0.0007	0.9907 ± 0.0004	0.9926 ± 0.0004
F-score	0.9867 ± 0.0005	0.9898 ± 0.0002	0.9917 ± 0.0003
Accuracy	0.9744 ± 0.0011	0.9788 ± 0.0006	0.9825 ± 0.0008
WordAccuracy	0.9106 ± 0.0038	0.9232 ± 0.0026	0.9344 ± 0.0029
split-by-roots, word form metrics			
Precision	0.9687 ± 0.0012	0.9696 ± 0.0027	0.9779 ± 0.0020
Recall	0.9637 ± 0.0046	0.9602 ± 0.0041	0.9715 ± 0.0036
F-score	0.9662 ± 0.0028	0.9648 ± 0.0029	0.9747 ± 0.0015
Accuracy	0.9410 ± 0.0044	0.9383 ± 0.0046	0.9548 ± 0.0028
WordAccuracy	0.7795 ± 0.0156	0.7717 ± 0.0145	0.8243 ± 0.0097
split-by- roots, lemmata metrics			
Precision	0.9510 ± 0.0012	0.9562 ± 0.0027	0.9677 ± 0.0021

(*continued*)

Table 3. (*continued*)

Metric	CNN	Morphberta-char	Morphberta-lex
Recall	0.9501 ± 0.0052	0.9438 ± 0.0049	0.9609 ± 0.0047
F-score	0.9505 ± 0.0032	0.9499 ± 0.0036	0.9641 ± 0.0026
Accuracy	0.9119 ± 0.0058	0.9090 ± 0.0068	0.9341 ± 0.0050
WordAccuracy	0.7247 ± 0.0143	0.7160 ± 0.0180	0.7814 ± 0.0151

Morphodict-K dataset annotation [12]. We also examined 100 randomly selected incorrect segmentations by DeepSPIN-3, finding that while this model does exhibit instances of over- and undersegmenting roots (approximately 20% of errors), these constitute a significantly smaller proportion compared to other models. The most prevalent error category (66 out of 100 cases) involved the model generating roots that exhibited minimal Levenshtein distance to roots present in the training data. Several examples of this phenomenon are presented in Table 4 (incorrect root is underlined). This finding suggests an important direction for improving the DeepSPIN-3 handling of OOV roots: shifting the learning objective to focus on generating all non-root morphemes (since these appear in the training data with near-certainty probability) while deriving the root as the residual substring after removing all other identified morphemes.

Table 4. Examples of DeepSPIN-3 incorrect segmentations in split-by-roots scenario

Word form	DeepSPIN-3 segmentation	Examples from training set
раскусываются	рас-кос-ыва-ют-ся	под-кос-ишь-ся, у-кос-ин-а
перешлифовывались	пере-лиш-ов-ыва-л-и-сь	из-лиш-еств-о, из-лиш-н-им
отплатишь	от-лат-ишь	под-лат-а-вш-его, под-лат-а-нн-ому
палящая	пакл-ящ-ая	про-пакл-и-ть, про-пакл-и-в
взыскательной	вз-рыск-а-тель-н-ой	рыск-а-л-и, об-рыск-а-вш-их

7 Conclusion

Automatic morpheme segmentation algorithms hold potential for two key applications: expanding existing morpheme dictionaries and developing enhanced tokenizers for language models. The latter application particularly requires robust performance on word forms rather than just lemmata—an underexplored area for Russian due to the lack of comprehensive word-form morpheme dictionaries. A critical outstanding challenge involves the algorithms' generalization capability, particularly their ability to produce correct analyses for words containing OOV stems and roots.

In this study, we evaluated three state-of-the-art approaches for Russian morpheme segmentation on word-form data: a CNN ensemble, a subword Transformer model

DeepSPIN-3, and RuRoberta-based Morphberta models. To perform this evaluation, we created the Morphodict-K-Wordform dataset by algorithmically extending the lemma-based Morphodict-K dataset with word forms segmentations. Our experimental design incorporated three dataset train-test splitting strategies: random split, lemma-based split (all forms of a lemma assigned to the same set), and root-based split (all forms containing a given root assigned to the same set).

The results demonstrate superior performance of the Morphberta approach, achieving over 99.5% completely correct segmentations in random split scenario. However, all approaches showed significant challenges with OOV roots, with word-level accuracy dropping by at least 17 percentage points. This demonstrates that random splitting fails to provide a comprehensive assessment of algorithm performance. DeepSPIN-3 exhibited particularly problematic behavior, frequently substituting OOV roots with orthographically similar roots from the training data. At the same time, Morphberta models showed the best result due to the implicit semantics consideration. Moreover, this model outperformed its own previous Morphodict-K results by 1 percentage point, suggesting that word forms augmentation of lemmata dataset may improve OOV root handling in this problem. Thus, Morphberta-lex model currently emerges as the most effective and robust algorithm for Russian word form morpheme segmentation.

References

1. Batsuren, K., et al.: The SIGMORPHON 2022 shared task on morpheme segmentation. In: Nicolai, G., Chodroff, E. (eds.) Proceedings of the 19th SIGMORPHON Workshop on Computational Research in Phonetics, Phonology, and Morphology, pp. 103–116. Association for Computational Linguistics, Seattle, Washington (2022). https://doi.org/10.18653/v1/2022.sigmorphon-1.11. https://aclanthology.org/2022.sigmorphon-1.11/
2. Bolshakova, E., Sapin, A.: An experimental study of neural morpheme segmentation models for Russian word forms. In: Proceedings of the Computational Models in Language and Speech Workshop (CMLS 2020), vol. 2780, pp. 79–89 (2020)
3. Bolshakova, E., Sapin, A.: Bi-LSTM model for morpheme segmentation of Russian words. In: Ustalov, D., Filchenkov, A., Pivovarova, L. (eds.) Artificial Intelligence and Natural Language, pp. 151–160. Springer, Cham (2019). https://doi.org/10.1007/978-3-030-34518-1_11
4. Bolshakova, E.I., Sapin, A.S.: Building a combined morphological model for Russian word forms. In: Burnaev, E., et al. (eds.) Analysis of Images, Social Networks and Texts, pp. 45–55. Springer, Cham (2022)
5. Cotterell, R., Vieira, T., Schutze, H.: A joint model of orthography and morphological segmentation. In: Knight, K., Nenkova, A., Rambow, O. (eds.) Proceedings of the 2016 Conference of the North American Chapter of the Association for Computational Linguistics: Human Language Technologies, pp. 664–669. Association for Computational Linguistics, San Diego, California (2016). https://doi.org/10.18653/v1/N16-1080. https://aclanthology.org/N16-1080/
6. Creutz, M., Lagus, K.: Unsupervised discovery of morphemes. In: Proceedings of the ACL-02 Workshop on Morphological and Phonological Learning, pp. 21–30. Association for Computational Linguistics (2002). https://doi.org/10.3115/1118647.1118650. https://aclanthology.org/W02-0603/
7. Garipov, T., Morozov, D., Glazkova, A.: Generalization ability of CNN-based Morpheme Segmentation. In: 2023 Ivannikov Ispras Open Conference (ISPRAS), pp. 58–62 (2024)

8. Iomdin, B.L.: How to define words with the same root? Russian Speech = Russkaya Rech' (1), 109–115 (2019). https://doi.org/10.31857/S013161170003980-7
9. Korobov, M.: Morphological analyzer and generator for Russian and Ukrainian languages. In: Analysis of Images, Social Networks and Texts: 4th International Conference, AIST 2015, Yekaterinburg, Russia, 9–11 April 2015, Revised Selected Papers 4, pp. 320–332. Springer, Cham (2015). https://doi.org/10.1007/978-3-319-26123-2_31
10. Kuznetsova, A.I., Efremova, T.F.: Dictionary of Morphemes of the Russian Language. Russkii yazyk, Moscow (1986)
11. Matthews, A., Neubig, G., Dyer C.: Using morphological knowledge in open-vocabulary neural language models. In: Proceedings of the 2018 Conference of the North American Chapter of the Association for Computational Linguistics: Human Language Technologies, Volume 1 (Long Papers), pp. 1435–1445, New Orleans, Louisiana. Association for Computational Linguistics (2018)
12. Morozov, D., Garipov, T., Lyashevskaya, O., Savchuk, S., Iomdin, B., Glazkova, A.: Automatic morpheme segmentation for Russian: can an algorithm replace experts? J. Lang. Educ. **10**(4), 71–84 (2024). https://doi.org/10.17323/jle.2024.22237. https://jle.hse.ru/article/view/22237
13. Morozov, D., Glazkova, A., Garipov, T.: BERT-like models for automatic morpheme segmentation of the Russian language. In: Computational Linguistics and Intellectual Technologies: Proceedings of the International Conference "Dialogue 2025". https://doi.org/10.28995/2075-7182-2025-23-257-266
14. Peters, B., Martins, A.F.T.: Beyond characters: subword-level morpheme segmentation. In: Nicolai, G., Chodroff, E. (eds.) Proceedings of the 19th SIGMORPHON Workshop on Computational Research in Phonetics, Phonology, and Morphology, pp. 131–138. Association for Computational Linguistics, Seattle, Washington (2022). https://doi.org/10.18653/v1/2022.sigmorphon-1.14. https://aclanthology.org/2022.sigmorphon-1.14/
15. Pranji'c, M., Robnik-Sikonja, M., Pollak, S.: LLMSegm: surface-level morphological segmentation using large language model. In: Calzolari, N., Kan, M.Y., Hoste, V., Lenci, A., Sakti, S., Xue, N. (eds.) Proceedings of the 2024 Joint International Conference on Computational Linguistics, Language Resources and Evaluation (LREC-COLING 2024), pp. 10665–10674. ELRA and ICCL, Torino, Italia (2024). https://aclanthology.org/2024.lrec-main.933/
16. Savchuk, S.O., et al.: Russian National Corpus 2.0: new opportunities and development prospects. Voprosy Jazykoznanija (2), 7–34 (2024). https://doi.org/10.31857/0373-658x.2024.2.7-34
17. Sorokin, A.: Improving morpheme segmentation using BERT embeddings. In: Burnaev, E., et al. (eds.) Analysis of Images, Social Networks and Texts, pp. 148–161. Springer, Cham (2022)
18. Sorokin, A., Kravtsova, A.: Deep convolutional networks for supervised morpheme segmentation of Russian language. In: Ustalov, D., Filchenkov, A., Pivovarova, L., Zizka, J. (eds.) Artificial Intelligence and Natural Language, pp. 3–10. Springer, Cham (2018). https://doi.org/10.1007/978-3-030-01204-5_1
19. Volskaya, A.S., Korneyeva, T.A., Markova, T.D.: Word-formation, morphemic, etymological analysis in school. Amazonia Investiga **7**(15), 190–195 (2018). https://www.amazoniainvestiga.info/index.php/amazonia/article/view/440
20. Zmitrovich, D., et al.: A family of pretrained transformer language models for Russian. In: Calzolari, N., Kan, M.Y., Hoste, V., Lenci, A., Sakti, S., Xue, N. (eds.) Proceedings of the 2024 Joint International Conference on Computational Linguistics, Language Resources and Evaluation (LREC-COLING 2024), pp. 507–524. ELRA and ICCL, Torino, Italia (2024). https://aclanthology.org/2024.lrec-main.45/

TL; DR: Text Normalization for Social Media Corpus

Grigorii Feoktistov[1] and Dmitry Morozov[1,2(✉)]

[1] Novosibirsk State University, 1 Pirogova str., Novosibirsk 630090, Russia
g.feoktistov@g.nsu.ru, morozowdm@gmail.com
[2] Russian National Corpus, Moscow, Russia

Abstract. Text annotation is the process of enriching text with metalinguistic information. The most common types of annotation include morphological annotation, which involves assigning grammatical tags to words; syntactic annotation, which identifies syntactic relationships within sentences; and lemmatization, which determines the base form (lemma) of each word. Text annotation is a fundamental task in computational linguistics and plays a crucial role in both linguistic research and practical applications of natural language processing (NLP). Given the scale of modern text corpora (exceeding 1 billion words), manual annotation is virtually unfeasible, making automated annotation tools the only viable solution. However, most of these tools have been developed, trained, and tested on texts with standard orthography. As a result, their performance can significantly degrade when applied to non-standard texts, such as those from social media. This issue can be mitigated through automated text normalization prior to annotation. This task is related to automated spelling correction but is not equivalent to it, and remains significantly less studied. For instance, text normalization requires not only correcting mistyping and spelling errors but also restoring abbreviations commonly used in online communication. To explore approaches to text normalization, we compiled a corpus of social media sentences and manually paired them with their normalized versions. Using this corpus, we compared various text normalization methods, leveraging pre-trained language models. We examined both fine-tuning and prompt-based approaches. Our study has identified the most effective strategies in this domain, providing valuable insights for future research and applications.

Keywords: Russian Language · Social Networks · Corpus Linguistics · Text Normalization

1 Introduction

Variability and freedom from normative restrictions in the language of social networks are of considerable interest for the research of new language phenomena. Unlike normative language of news, fiction and non-fiction texts, social media discourse evolves rapidly due to cultural exchange and uncontrolled influence from foreign languages. Language phenomena such as slang, jargon, non-standard abbreviations and grammatical

M. Bakaev et al. (Eds.): IMS 2025, CCIS 2671, pp. 168–176, 2026.
https://doi.org/10.1007/978-3-032-04958-2_13

constructions, typical misspellings and others make social media an invaluable source for studying real-time language change. To systematically analyze these phenomena, researchers must rely on annotated corpora – structured collections of texts enriched with linguistic metadata.

The most widespread and demanded types of metadata are morphological annotations, such as part of speech and grammatical categories. Another common metadata for linguistic research purposes as well as for practical applications of natural language processing are lemmas. To annotate high volume collections of text language models are used due to impracticality of manual annotation. Nevertheless, such models are usually trained on a standardized language, which leads to many annotating errors, such as incorrect lemma definition of abbreviations or misspelled words in corpora with a lot of non-standard spelling, such as social media corpora.

This issue can be addressed in two ways: adapting the annotation model to the unnormalized texts or normalizing the texts. The first option will require a large amount of texts with manual annotations. On the contrary, the second option will require only manual spelling correction and correction of distorted and modified spellings found in Internet for which it is often possible to involve not expert linguists (as in the case of annotating grammatical categories), but ordinary native speakers. In this case, for further annotating of social network corpora, it will be possible to use analyzers that show high quality of annotating on other, more classic domains. Such analyzers for the Russian language can be considered, for example, Stanza [7] models trained on various Russian-language datasets or qbic [1] and Rubic [4] algorithms.

At the same time, there is no generally recognized leader among the language standardization algorithms. It is important to note that although the task of language normalization at first glance is very similar to the task of spelling correction, for which there are prepared datasets, we believe the difference between these tasks is fundamental: the task of text normalization is much broader and includes not only the correction of spelling errors, but also, for example, the restoration of original word forms from slang variants (e.g. *разраб* → *разработчик* 'developer', *заблочили* → *заблокировали* 'blocked') and decoding of abbreviations (e.g. *тп* → *тому подобное* 'so on', *шт* → *штук* 'pieces'). In such cases, attributing normalized word forms is necessary to improve the quality of automated annotation and simplify further linguistic analysis of the corpus under consideration.

In this paper, we present an experimental dataset of normalized Russian-language sentences. To prepare the dataset, we developed an annotation protocol formalizing the concept of "text normalization" and manually prepared annotation of normalized variants for two thousand sentences selected from the Social Networks corpus of the Russian National Corpus [8]. We selected sentences that were expected to have an increased number of distorted spellings using a heuristic approach. We analyzed the collected dataset and tested several simple baseline approaches to text normalization on its basis.

The paper is structured as follows: Sect. 2 reviews related work in the field of text normalization and spelling correction. Section 3 detail the corpus assembly and annotation protocol, as well as the features of the corpus. Section 4 describes testing several baselines on the material of the prepared corpus. Finally, Sect. 5 summarizes the results of the study.

2 Related Work

Text normalization has received significantly less attention than spelling correction. Among the existing studies on text normalization, key contributions include works by [2, 3, 6]. Most approaches rely on multi-stage processing pipelines that combine heuristic rules with machine learning techniques. For instance, the MoNoise algorithm [3] generates replacement candidates for each word using an Aspell dictionary, a word2vec model, heuristics for missing spaces, etc. Each candidate is then scored using a set of features (e.g., Levenshtein distance from the original word and cosine similarity between word2vec embeddings), with the final replacement decision made by a trained Random Forest model. The authors of [2] explored normalization via BERT-like masked token prediction. Their approach is a hybrid step-by-step system: dictionary lookup to identify unnormalized tokens, decoding acronyms/constructions using predefined tables + named entity detection, and masking remaining unnormalized tokens for BERT to predict. Sequence-to-sequence generation (e.g., using BERT or BART, as in [6]) has also been investigated. However, for the Russian language, it is impossible to conduct a representative comparison of different approaches due to the lack of a suitable dataset.

The field of Russian spelling correction has seen significant progress, particularly through the SpellRuEval competition [9]. Analysis of the top-performing systems reveals several critical insights:

1. **Candidate selection proves more challenging than generation.** The primary difficulty lies not in generating potential corrections but in accurately selecting the right candidate.
2. **Real-word errors present the greatest challenge.** Misspellings that result in valid dictionary words (along with misplaced hyphens and spaces) were the most difficult to detect.
3. **Consistent methodology among top systems.** All three leading teams employed similar approaches combining edit distance metrics with trigram language models.

In [10] an improved method was introduced that surpassed the best SpellRuEval results, particularly in handling hyphenation and spacing errors. However, with approximately 30% of remaining errors classified as real-word errors, the study highlights the need for incorporating neural language models to address this persistent challenge.

Recent comprehensive benchmarking [5] evaluated multiple LLMs including M2M100, FredT5, OpenAI models, and open-source solutions across diverse test sets (RUSpellRU, MultidomainGold, MedSpellChecker, and GitHubTypeCorpusRu). The study examined four configurations for M2M100 and FredT5: base models with zero-shot learning, pretrained models with zero-shot, base models fine-tuned on task-specific data, pretrained models fine-tuned on task-specific data. Key findings demonstrate, that pretrained models consistently outperformed their non-pretrained counterparts. The optimally configured M2M100 model exceeded both OpenAI's solutions and other open-source alternatives. In our opinion, this indicates that in the future, better results in text normalization can be achieved using LLM.

3 Corpus Preparation

Our dataset was formed based on the sentences from the Social Networks corpus of the Russian National Corpus [8]. Firstly, we collected ten thousand randomly selected sentences from Telegram public channels and chats and discussion from VK social network (vk.com) subcorpora. We filtered these sentences to select those that were likely to contain more examples of non-normalized spelling. For this filtering, we used the Aspell dictionary for Russian, excluding from consideration words containing non-Cyrillic characters (numbers, Latin, etc.). The final number of unnormalized sentences is 2000.

Before normalization all sentences were tokenized: all punctuation was deleted and tokens are separated by spaces. Normalization of the dataset was splitted into 3 steps. Firstly, we described the raw version of a protocol for first normalization. Secondly, using this protocol we normalized the whole dataset, discussing ambiguous cases and adjusting the protocol accordingly to dataset examples. Finally, we formulated the protocol and checked the dataset to standardize and correct the normalization. During the normalization process we tended to preserve original writing in case of ambiguity and lack of a context. The final protocol can be described as follows:

1. **Correction.** We included in this group of rules those cases in which the token was replaced with its normalized version.
   a. **Clipped and modified spelling.** Under clipped and modified spelling we understand the spelling of a word with one-to-one correspondence to the original word: *уши* → *наушники* ‘headphones’, *прошка* → *про-версия* ‘pro version’, *50к* → *50 тысяч* ‘50 thousand’.
   b. **Colloquial and distorted spelling.** Examples of correction: *чё* → *что* ‘what’, *гамно* → *говно* ‘shit’, *тыща* → *тысяча* ‘thousand’, *бачи* → *баксы* ‘dollars’. It should be noted that we do not correct colloquial spelling formed using affixes within rules of Russian language, e.g. diminutives *ясненько* ← *ясно* ‘clear’, *скучновато* ← *скучно* ‘boring’.
   c. **Open, closed and hyphenated spelling.** Due to the token alignment between source and normalized sentence split words are replaced using sign “|” instead of space, e.g. *коллцентры* → *кол-центры* ‘call centers’, *по больше* → *побольше* ‘more’, *шьююбки* → *шью|юбки* ‘(I) sew skirts’.
   d. **Agreement and prepositions.** Examples of correction: *(спасибо чудесной) моделе* → *(спасибо чудесной) модели* ‘thanks to a wonderful model’, *на голову приходит* → *в голову приходит* ‘comes to mind’, *с старой* → *со старой* ‘with old’.
   e. **Spelling errors and typos.** Examples of correction: *типо* → *типа* ‘like’, *пачему* → *почему* ‘why’, *учпеть* → *успеть* ‘to be in time’.
   f. **Redundant word or syllable repetitions.** Examples of correction: *ноно там ещё* → *но там ещё* ‘but there is more’.
   g. **Words without letter “ё”.** Examples of correction: *причем* → *причём* ‘moreover’.
   h. **Ordinal suffixes.** Examples of correction: *16тый* → *16-й* ‘16th’.

i. **A combination of previous cases.** For example, *обращаи тесь* → *обращайтесь* 'contact (us)' which combines closed spelling and typo or spelling error, *штт* → *штук* 'pieces' which combines typo and clipped spelling.
2. **Preservation.** We included in this group of rules those cases in which the token remained unchanged.
   a. **Original spelling of profanity** due to lack of regulations in Russian language, though we correct clipped spelling and typos.
   b. **Wordplays.** Examples of preservation: *вымираты* ← *вымирать* 'to extinct' + *эмираты* 'emirates'.
   c. **Nonce words.** Example of preservation: *вкдилдодрон.*
   d. **Neologisms.** Examples of preservation: *дистрибутив* 'distribution', *фейк* 'fake'.
   e. **Foreignisms and barbarisms.** Examples of preservation: *диджтл* 'digital', *комьюнити* 'community'.
   f. **Jargon.** Examples of preservation: *бабки* 'money', *жопошник* 'cheapskate'.
   g. **Clipped compound words.** For example, *голосовое* 'voice' ← *голосовое сообщение* 'voice message'.
3. **Word-to-tag cases.** In some cases, we replaced the word with special tags. These tokens were not taken into account when evaluating metrics in further experiments.
   a. Non-Cyrillic words are replaced with the tag `<foreign>`.
   b. From two parts put together the left is replaced with the correct closed spelling of a word and the right is replaced with the tag `<conjoint>` to preserve the token alignment. For example, *обращаи тесь* → *обращайтесь <conjoint>* 'contact (us)'.
   c. From two parts put together with a hyphen the left is replaced with the correct hyphenated spelling of a word and the right is replaced with the tag `<hyphen>` to preserve the token alignment. For example, *что то* → *что-то <hyphen>* 'something'.
   d. Interjections are replaced with the tag `<interjection>`. For example, *Вауууу* → *<interjection>* 'wow'.
4. **Complex cases.** Following cases allow for different correction options and required discussion during normalization.
   a. **Spelling errors and typos in words not presented in dictionaries** (new words, except for the named entities). We tend to choose the most spread option of spelling. For example, *павербанк* → *повербанк* 'power bank', *коммьюнити* → *комьюнити* 'community', *скил* → *скилл* 'skill'.
   b. **Capitalized writing.** We tend to correct capitalization for the first words sentences, for the proper nouns, such as *Лимасол* 'Limassol' and in caps spelling. Though, due to deleted punctuation marks and variation in spelling of names, this case is not coherent.
   c. **Abbreviations and acronyms.** In cases of names of countries, organizations, etc. we tend to preserve abbreviation spelling, for example *ОАЭ* 'UAE, United Arab Emirates', *ТТ* 'TT, TikTok'. The same can be applied to terminology, for example *ОЗУ* 'RAM, random access memory', non-Russian abbreviations, for instance *ВПН* 'VPN, virtual private network' and to the abbreviations that are usually not deciphered, namely *ФИО* 'surname, first name and patronymic'. Though we decipher abbreviations common for the internet, such as *мб* → *может быть*

'may be', *лс* → *личные сообщения* 'private messages', *НГ* → *Новый год* 'New Year' or are not obvious like *КЗ* → *Казахстан* 'Kazakhstan'.

The final dataset is available for download at: https://huggingface.co/datasets/ruscorpora/normalization. A few examples from the dataset are presented in the Table 1. We store data in CSV format, but for ease of reading, the lines in the table are written without commas.

Table 1. Examples from the dataset

<table>
<tr><th>Original sentence</th><th>Target sentence</th></tr>
<tr><td>Еще есть твинк с 5к</td><td>Ещё есть твинк с 5|тысячами</td></tr>
<tr><td>чо там как приложение для apple tv не подвезли юзаем easy tv пока</td><td>Что там как приложение для <foreign> <foreign> не подвезли юзаем <foreign> <foreign> пока</td></tr>
<tr><td>авчом прикол то</td><td>А|в|чём прикол-то <hyphen></td></tr>
<tr><td>На голову приходит только Samsung galaxy S9 или iPhone 8</td><td>В голову приходит только <foreign> <foreign> <foreign> или <foreign> 8</td></tr>
<tr><td>ну хз мне норм</td><td>Ну хрен|знает мне нормально</td></tr>
<tr><td>у кавото робит у кавото нет</td><td>У кого-то работает у кого-то нет</td></tr>
<tr><td>Вауууу 20 забагованных кусков говна с бесконечными данжонами крутаааа</td><td><interjection> 20 забагованных кусков говна с бесконечными данжонами круто</td></tr>
<tr><td>впринципи класна но вообще та гавно</td><td>В|принципе классно но вообще-то <hyphen> говно</td></tr>
</table>

4 Experiments with Baselines

4.1 Baselines and Metrics

To evaluate the complexity of normalizing the constructed dataset, we conducted experiments with several simple baseline approaches. Generation quality was assessed using the following metrics:

1. ROUGE-1 for full sentences;
2. F1-score for tokens requiring correction only;
3. average Levenshtein distance between target and predicted sentences (both raw and length-normalized by word count);
4. average Levenshtein distance between target and predicted tokens (both raw and length-normalized by character count).

We examined multiple approaches, adapting them for Russian where necessary:

1. **MoNoise** [3]. We adapted a two-step algorithm for Russian: 1) candidate generation – producing potential replacement candidates, 2) candidate ranking – selecting the most probable candidate. Modifications from the original implementation included using

a Russian Aspell dictionary and employing an embedding model trained on unnormalized data from social network corpus and one trained on the Russian Wikipedia. The system was implemented in Python.

2. **BERT-Based Replacements**. We adapted an approach from [2], combining heuristic dictionary-based substitutions with replacements from a pretrained BERT-like model (ruBert-base [12] in our case). Enhancements included extending the heuristic rule set. We evaluated two BERT interaction strategies:
   a. masking and restoring all tokens not processed by heuristics (hereinafter, ALL),
   b. excluding Aspell dictionary tokens from replacement (hereinafter, OOV).

   We also explored fine-tuning RuBERT-base-cased on the target task (standard parameters, three epochs).
3. **Sequence-to-Sequence Generation**. We investigated fine-tuning pretrained models on our dataset, testing both full-sentence and token-level generation (feeding the model the target word's context: ± 2 words, with the target marked by _SEP_). For full-sentence generation, we evaluated ruT5-base [12] and mbart-large-50-many-to-many-mmt [11] models; for token-level, MBart only. Models were fine-tuned with standard parameters for three epochs.

Finally, we computed metrics comparing source tokens against their target references.

It is extremely important to note that our results with the baselines are only preliminary and do not claim to be a comprehensive study of approaches to text normalization. Our task here was to test simple, intuitive solutions. In our opinion, models pre-trained on the spelling correction task, or LLMs, will be able to cope with the task much better, but this requires a separate study, which is made possible by the dataset we created.

4.2 Results

The experimental results are presented in Table 2. MLD-s (MLD-t) and NMLD-s (NMLD-t) stand for mean Levenshtein distance and normalized mean Levenshtein distance at the sentence (token) level, respectively. FT stands for finetuned ruBert-base.

It is obvious from the table that the considered baselines cope with the task quite poorly. To analyze the results, we analyzed a few representative sentences from the test part of the dataset containing abbreviations, acronyms, colloquial variants, hyphenated and separate spelling, spelling errors, jargon/neologisms, tags, prepositions, and compared how some of the models handled these cases of normalization.

We found that MoNoise has a tendency to preserve the original spelling, perhaps due to the fact that the relative number of tokens that were corrected was insufficient for the model to choose the correction rather than preserve the original spelling. At the same time, most algorithms that use token generation quite often predict a word that is completely different from the target. Thus, the finetuned ruBert-base model (OOV replacement only) generates for the sentence *у кавото робит у кавото нет* 'It works for some, it doesn't for others' for the sentence *у тебя работает у гугла нет* 'It works for you, but not for Google'. Sequence-to-sequence models cope with frequent abbreviations (for example, they translate *хз* into *хрен знает* 'who the hell knows'), but do not correct spelling errors. We associate this primarily with the size of the dataset.

Table 2. Baselines results

Metric	Source	MoNoise	RuBERT-based model				MBart-t	MBart-s	ruT5
			OOV	ALL	FT+OOV	FT+ALL			
ROUGE-1	0.11	0.19	0.15	0.09	0.15	0.14	0.20	0.18	0.11
MLD-s	4.3	3.0	5.0	28.7	5.1	26.0	2.5	2.6	10.9
NMLD-s	0.10	0.09	0.15	0.77	0.14	0.67	0.06	0.06	0.21
F1	0.00	0.18	0.40	0.17	0.40	0.18	0.71	0.66	0.69
MLD-t	0.28	0.45	0.77	4.55	0.77	4.09	0.36	0.32	10.94
NMLD-t	0.05	0.13	0.12	0.84	0.12	0.76	0.04	0.04	0.21

5 Conclusion

Text normalization algorithms are relevant when processing texts with frequent non-standard spelling, in particular, when processing social networks. Today, the vast majority of algorithms for lemmatization and tagging of morphological and other linguistic features are designed to work with normalized texts, which is why the quality of automatic tagging drops sharply when working with such domains. At the same time, the task of text normalization is related, but not identical to the task of spelling correction: we understand text normalization more broadly.

In this paper, we present a dataset of 2 thousand pairs of source and normalized Russian language sentences with various types of normalization cases. This dataset can be further used as a benchmark for assessing the quality of text normalization. In addition, we described in detail the developed tagging protocol, which will allow us to further expand the dataset.

We compared a few baselines using the collected dataset. The results have shown that the simple approaches are insufficient to address the task of normalization. Our further research will be aimed at creating an advanced model to cover the peculiarities of normalization of social networks for the Russian language and apply the model to the high volume social networks corpus such as the Social Networks corpus of the Russian National Corpus.

References

1. Anastasyev, D.: Exploring pretrained models for joint morpho-syntactic parsing of Russian. In: Computational Linguistics and Intellectual Technologies, Moscow, Russia, pp. 1–12 (2020). https://doi.org/10.28995/2075-7182-2020-19-1-12
2. Doshi, F., Gandhi, J., Gosalia, D., Bagul, S.: Normalizing text using language modelling based on phonetics and string similarity (2020). https://arxiv.org/abs/2006.14116
3. van der Goot, R., van Noord, G.: Monoise: modeling noise using a modular normalization system (2017). https://arxiv.org/abs/1710.03476

4. Lyashevskaya, O., et al.: Disambiguation in context in the Russian National Corpus: 20 years later. In: Proceedings of International Conference "Dialogue", Moscow, Russia, pp. 1–12 (2023). https://doi.org/10.28995/2075-7182-2023-22-307-318
5. Martynov, N., Baushenko, M., Kozlova, A., Kolomeytseva, K., Abramov, A., Fenogenova, A.: A methodology for generative spelling correction via natural spelling errors emulation across multiple domains and languages. In: Graham, Y., Purver, M. (eds.) Findings of the Association for Computational Linguistics: EACL 2024, pp. 138–155. Association for Computational Linguistics, St. Julian's, Malta (2024). https://aclanthology.org/2024.findings-eacl.10/
6. Nguyen, D.H., Nguyen, A.T.H., Van Nguyen, K.: A weakly supervised data labeling framework for machine lexical normalization in Vietnamese social media. Cogn. Comput. **17** (2025). https://doi.org/10.1007/s12559-024-10356-3
7. Qi, P., Zhang, Y., Zhang, Y., Bolton, J., Manning, C.D.: Stanza: a Python natural language processing toolkit for many human languages. In: Proceedings of the 58th Annual Meeting of the Association for Computational Linguistics: System Demonstrations, pp. 101–108. Association for Computational Linguistics, Online (2020). https://doi.org/10.18653/v1/2020.acl-demos.14
8. Savchuk, S.O., et al.: Russian national corpus 2.0: new opportunities and development prospects. Voprosy Jazykoznanija (2), 7–34 (2024). https://doi.org/10.31857/0373-658x.2024.2.7-34
9. Sorokin, A., Shavrina, T., Baytin, A., Galinskaya, I., Rykunova, E.: SpellRuEval: the first competition on automatic spelling correction for Russian. In: Komp'juternaja Lingvistika I Intellektual'nye Tehnologii, vol. 15, pp. 660–673 (2016)
10. Sorokin, A.: Spelling correction for morphologically rich language: a case study of Russian. In: Erjavec, T., Piskorski, J., Pivovarova, L., Snajder, J., Steinberger, J., Yangarber, R. (eds.) Proceedings of the 6th Workshop on Balto-Slavic Natural Language Processing, pp. 45–53. Association for Computational Linguistics, Valencia, Spain (2017). https://doi.org/10.18653/v1/W17-1408. https://aclanthology.org/W17-1408/
11. Tang, Y., et al.: Multilingual translation with extensible multilingual pretraining and finetuning (2020). https://arxiv.org/abs/2008.00401
12. Zmitrovich, D., et al.: A family of pretrained transformer language models for Russian. In: Calzolari, N., Kan, M.Y., Hoste, V., Lenci, A., Sakti, S., Xue, N. (eds.) Proceedings of the 2024 Joint International Conference on Computational Linguistics, Language Resources and Evaluation (LREC-COLING 2024), pp. 507–524. ELRA and ICCL, Torino, Italia (2024). https://aclanthology.org/2024.lrec-main.45/

Creating a Dataset for Automatic Detection of Vague Expressions in Russian Legal Texts

Olga Blinova[1,2(✉)] and Alyona Berlin[1]

[1] St. Petersburg State University, 7/9 Universitetskaya nab., 199034 St. Petersburg, Russia
o.blinova@spbu.ru, ovblinova@hse.ru, st133294@student.spbu.ru
[2] National Research University Higher School of Economics, 16 Soyuza Pechatnikov Street, 190121 St. Petersburg, Russia

Abstract. This paper deals with adjectival vagueness, introduced by a gradable adjective. In a legal domain presence of vague expressions is undesirable or explicitly forbidden. Our goal is to create a classifier for vagueness detection in Russian legal texts. A Russian dataset of vague expressions (words or sentences) did not exist, so we created one. We describe (1) previous experience in forming annotated datasets; (2) our experience in collecting and manually annotating sentences based on the presence/absence of vagueness criterion; and (3) the structure of the resulting dataset. Initially, we used multiple independent labeling by three lawyers. However, the legal team demonstrated a significantly different approaches to vagueness annotation (with inter-annotator agreement being less than the expected by chance), so we selected the most competent expert. Our resulting dataset is of 6,000 sentences. It contains contexts from the "CorCodex" corpus of laws. Each sentence is accompanied by lemmas with vagueness tags.

Keywords: Russian legal texts · Legal vagueness · Linguistic vagueness · Classifier · Vagueness detection · Manual annotation

1 Introduction

There is an extensive academic literature on linguistic vagueness, including from the fields of philosophy of language, fuzzy logic and semantics, see for example the bibliography [1]. Filip Devos [8, p. 124] defines semantic vagueness as "intrinsic uncertainty with regard to the application of a word to a denotatum". This definition can also be extrapolated to linguistic expressions larger than words.

As [27] points out, "vagueness is a pervasive feature of natural language". Meanwhile, there are classes of natural language texts (these are **legal documents**, especially legislative ones), that are subject to special requirements concerning vague expressions, see [4]. On the one hand, the presence of vague expressions can lead to different interpretations of the same provisions, resulting in judicial conflicts and arbitrariness in law enforcement. On the other hand, vagueness has been assessed as an inevitable and, moreover, a useful feature of a legal text, providing the necessary space for interpretation, see, e.g. [10].

M. Bakaev et al. (Eds.): IMS 2025, CCIS 2671, pp. 177–195, 2026.
https://doi.org/10.1007/978-3-032-04958-2_14

Thus, special requirements are imposed on the language of law, which allow legal texts to be contrasted with other types of texts in natural language. Legal texts are intended to accurately convey the intentions of their authors, without allowing for multiple interpretations, see [9] and many others. Lawyers point out that in contexts that allow for multiple interpretations, there is "legal vagueness". At the same time, "legal vagueness" is rooted in language, growing out of linguistic one.

F. Devos [8] distinguishes two types of vagueness: vagueness in criteria, or categorical vagueness, and vagueness in degree, or gradual vagueness. Vagueness in criteria is uncertainty about which criterion or set of criteria are necessary or sufficient for the application of a certain word (e.g., whether *chess* can be called "a sport"). Vagueness in degree is uncertainty about the degree to which some clear criterion can be applied (e.g., what height of person can be called "tall"). Vagueness in criteria and vagueness in degree are linked to part-of-speech classes of words: the former is more characteristic of nouns, the latter of adjectives. In this paper, we are interested in one of the varieties of vagueness in degree, namely, **adjectival vagueness**.

Adjectival vagueness is a phenomenon in which the locus of vagueness is an adjective, primarily a qualitative one. It denotes the features of objects, more specifically, gradable features. Such adjectives in Russian can generally have degree forms and short forms. In addition, they can be combined with modifiers such as *very, quite, extremely* and with the so-called hedges such as *obviously, seemingly* [16].

2 Approaches to Collecting and Annotating Data for Vagueness Classification

The task of vagueness classification has not yet been comprehensively addressed. Some studies are field-specific [6], while others are more academic but focus on vagueness subclasses, such as gradable adjectives [26] or vague time expressions [21] or noun phrases [24]. The datasets vary accordingly.

When exploring approaches to collecting and annotating texts, the following parameters should be noted.

- Type of classification: binary or multiclass. It determines the complexity of the problem.
- Source of data, its chronological boundaries. Models trained on outdated data can impact efficiency of classification.
- Annotation on the level of a word, a phrase or a sentence. The choice of an- notation level effects the granularity and usability of the annotated dataset.
- The overall size of the dataset, it's structure and balance. A larger dataset and more balanced data are preferable for machine learning tasks.
- Inter-annotator agreement in case of several annotators. High inter-annotator agreement indicates clear annotation guidelines.
- Whether a dataset was annotated by experts in a specific domain. Non-expert annotation can lead to misinterpretation.

Manually annotated datasets for vagueness identification are mostly in English. Russian texts have not yet been annotated for the task of vagueness classification, however, there is a corresponding task, namely word-sense disambiguation (WSD). Such datasets as the Sense-Annotated Corpus for Russian [13] and Labeled Russian Context for WSD [23] contain annotated sets of contexts for individual words. Such data could be suitable for our task if the annotation accounted for context vagueness. Although word-sense disambiguation appears similar, it differs from the task of identifying vagueness, because resolving ambiguity (including lexical one) involves choosing one of the interpretations, instead of vagueness being unresolvable with reliance on language context. Vague expression can be partly clarified or discarded [4].

Existing datasets can be grouped based on **type of classification** (binary and multiclass), and **annotation level** (word, phrase, sentence or multilevel annotation). Below, we analyze datasets examples of different types and discuss their implications.

2.1 Binary Annotation

Alexopoulos & colleagues [2] dealt with the identification of vague expressions in ontologies. The dataset was carefully collected, annotated by experts and balanced. First of all, adjective definitions were collected from WordNet [22] and labelled as shown in Table 1.

Table 1. Vague and non-vague adjective senses.

Vague adjectives	Non-vague adjectives
Impenitent: impervious to moral persuasion	Biweekly: occurring every two weeks

Chronological boundaries are not explicitly mentioned, but since WordNet is continuously updating its lexical database, the dataset was likely based on a contemporary to the research version.

The dataset consisted of 2,000 pairs (1,000 vague and 1,000 non-vague), and annotated by an ontology expert. Two additional experts annotated a subset (100 definitions), and inter-annotator agreement was measured: Joint Probability of Agreement (JPA) = 0.81, Cohen's Kappa = 0.64. These scores represent high and average inter-annotator agreement and highlight the fact that vagueness is inherently subjective but can still be reliably identified.

Phrase-level annotation for vague time expressions in German is presented in [21]. The dataset was derived from two sources: the KRAUTS corpus and the Short News corpus, which covered a range of recent and past news articles. The combined dataset comprised 96,721 tokens, making it a substantial resource for the analysis of temporal expressions (TE). Approximately 29.74% of the time expressions were classified as vague (VTE), with certain categories such as "anchorType" having a particularly low number of instances, slightly contributing to class imbalance (see Table 2).

The annotation was performed by an ontology expert. Time expressions were tagged with such attributes as **value**, **meaning**, and **modifiers**. If an expression was too vague to be normalized into an exact timestamp, it was assigned a placeholder or a relative

Table 2. Dataset structure in [21]

Source of data	TE tokens	% TE of tokens	VTE tokens	% VTE of tokens	% VTE of TE
KRAUTS	854	1.7	7.5	0.75	44.15
Short News	1056	2.27	2.8	0.41	18.09
Both	1910	1.97	5.2	0.59	29.74

reference (e.g., future_ref, past_ref, or values containing X to indicate uncertainty). The following sentence[1] (exampled from the paper) contains a vague temporal expression:

```
Wir haben uns zuletzt bei unserer Abschlussfeier getroffen.
<Timex3 type="date" anchorType="dct" value="past_ref" mean-
ing="dct - 000X &lt; Z &lt; dct" vague="true">
Inzwischen </Timex3> habe ich mir ein Auto gekauft
```

An example of the interpretation of the vague temporal expression *Inzwischen* ‘in the meantime’ is given in Table 3.

Table 3. Interpretation scheme

Attribute	Value	Explanation
TIMEX3	–	The standard TimeML tag for temporal expressions.
type	date	The phrase refers to a point in time rather than a duration or a set.
anchorType	dct	The time expression is anchored to the document’s creation date rather than an explicit reference within the text.
value	Past_ref	The expression refers to an unspecified point in the past but does not indicate an exact date.
meaning	dct - 000X < Z < dct	The exact period is unknown, but the event occurred sometime before the document’s creation date (dct).
vague	true	The expression is classified as vague due to its inherent lack of specificity.

The use of “000X” within the meaning attribute indicates that the precise temporal boundaries of the event remain unknown. Moreover, there are three different types of VTEs that were reflected in the annotation:

- **Modified Value** (e.g., “about 10 days” → mod = “approx” value = “P10D”);
- **Imprecise Value** (e.g., “a few days ago” → meaning = “dct – 0000-00-0X”);

[1] ‘We last met at our graduation. In the meantime, I bought a car’.

- **Range of Values** (e.g., "between August 13 and 15" $\rightarrow$ meaning = "2021–08- 13 $\leq$ Z $\leq$ 2021–08-15")

The dataset created by [21] is an important contribution to the analysis of vague time expressions. Although the annotation was performed by only one expert, its findings enhance an annotation framework, based on TimeML [25].

2.2 Multiclass Annotation

In [17] instances of vagueness in privacy policies are classified at multiple levels. In this study, the dataset was developed through a structured process that included text selection, filtering, annotation, and validation.

Basically, it was constructed by first selecting 100 privacy policies from various commercial websites. It was done by random sampling. Since privacy policies are typically lengthy documents, averaging around 2,300 words each, the researchers implemented a filtering step to ensure that a meaningful proportion of the dataset contained vague language. This step was made using a list of 40 predefined "vague cue words" such as *may, certain, generally, reasonable*. Only sentences containing at least one of these predefined words were retained for annotation. This step helped to balance data, but lead to exclusion of potential vague terms, which occurred in sentences without "vague cue words".

Annotation was performed by Amazon Mechanical Turk (MTurk) workers. Unlike lawyers or linguists, MTurk workers were chosen for their scalability and cost-effectiveness, although they had to fulfil certain criteria: be US residents (to ensure familiarity with English privacy policy terminology) and have an approval rating of 90% or higher on previous assignments. They were provided with clear annotation guidelines, including examples of vague and non-vague expressions.

The procedure involved two levels of annotation.

- **Word-Level Annotation:** the annotators identified vague words or short phrases ($\leq$5 words) within a sentence. Each word was labeled as vague ("1") or non-vague ("0"), and a word was considered vague if two or more annotators agreed on it.
- **Sentence-Level Annotation:** the annotators rated entire sentences on a 1–5 vagueness scale, with the following categories:

  - *1–2: Extremely Clear,*
  - *2–3: Somewhat Clear,*
  - *3–4: Vague,*
  - *4–5: Extremely Vague.*

The following examples show vague sentences with intensity 3.8 and 3.2 out of 5 and expressions, marked as vague:

We ***may*** *use the* ***information*** *automatically collected from your computer or* ***other devices*** *for the following uses* (Vagueness: 3.8).

Our Sites and Services ***may, from time to time****, provide links to sites operated by* ***third parties*** (Vagueness: 3.2).

After filtering, the final dataset contained 133,000 annotated words and 4,500 labeled sentences. The majority of sentences fell into the "somewhat clear" category (50.8%), while only 1.8% were labeled as "extremely vague", indicating a potential data imbalance (see Table 4).

Table 4. Dataset structure in [16].

Category	% of Sentences
Clear (1–2)	26.9%
Somewhat Clear (2–3)	50.8%
Vague (3–4)	20.5%
Extremely Vague (4–5)	1.8%

Speaking about inter-annotator agreement, at the word level, 46.1% of words were labeled vague by at least three annotators, while 18.5% of words had agreement from four or more annotators. At the sentence level, 47.2% of sentences had three or more annotators agreeing on their vagueness score, and 12.5% of sentences had four or more annotators agreeing. These rates suggest a moderate level of agreement, though the subjectivity of vagueness naturally led to some disagreement among annotators, consequently some examples with low agreement were removed.

This dataset is one of the largest publicly available English datasets specifically targeting vagueness in privacy policies. The multi-level annotations (word and sentence) allow for both fine-grained analysis of vague terms and broader classification of entire sentences.

The dataset in the study [19] does not differ from the previously discussed except that ratings were aggregated using different methods: arithmetic, geometric and harmonic means. Moreover, annotation included only the sentence level.

Another research introduces the first large-scale annotated resource dedicated to **vague noun phrases** [24]. The study chose Wikipedia's featured articles, representing the highest quality writing on the website, as its primary resource. To ensure diversity, the researchers extracted an abstract from each Wikipedia's main topic as history, science, and culture.

To focus on vagueness in noun phrases (NPs) rather than full sentences, the study used the Natural Language Toolkit (NLTK) [18] to extract NPs and then researchers manually verified them to ensure accuracy.

Once the noun phrases were extracted, they underwent manual annotation to determine, whether they exhibited vagueness and, if so, which type of vagueness they contained:

- **Scalar Vagueness**: a phrase where truth depends on a numerical threshold (e.g., *"long-running debate"* → How long?).
- **Quantitative Vagueness**: a phrase referring to an unspecified number of entities (e.g., *"many scientists"*, *"several projects"*).

- **Subjective Vagueness**: a phrase that is opinion-based or lacks clear evaluation criteria (e.g., *"high ethical standards"*, *"significant impact"*).

Some noun phrases were marked with multiple labels (e.g., *"talented statesmen"* contains both quantitative and subjective vagueness).

Each phrase was annotated independently by two annotators, and cases of disagreement were discussed and resolved. The Cohen's Kappa inter-annotator agreement score was 0.91, indicating high reliability in the annotation process.

After manual annotation, the final dataset was of 2,457 noun phrases, distributed across different vagueness categories. The results showed that 26% of noun phrases exhibited some form of vagueness (see Table 5).

Table 5. Dataset structure in [24].

Category	% of NPs
No Vagueness	73.99%
Scalar Vagueness	6.03%
Quantitative Vagueness	13.84%
Subjective Vagueness	9.37%

These findings indicate that quantitative vagueness (13.84%) was the most common form, while scalar vagueness (6.03%) was the least frequent.

The researchers also analyzed vagueness across different semantic classes of noun phrases (e.g., persons, places, abstract concepts). The main findings of the research were as follows:

- Intangible concepts were the vaguest (39.38%); these include phrases like *"fame"*, *"reputation"*, and *"efforts"*, which are inherently difficult to quantify or define precisely.
- Creative works (26.26%) had a high vagueness rate due to descriptive modifiers (e.g., *"realistic portrayal"*, *"fantastic elements"*).
- People and organizations showed the least vagueness ($\approx$17%), as proper nouns and specific entities are typically well-defined.

A total of 79 noun phrases (3.22% of all NPs, or 12.37% of vague NPs) had multiple vagueness types.

This dataset provides a valuable linguistic resource for studying vagueness in English noun phrases. High inter-annotator agreement, extended annotation, that include semantic features, make it useful for machine learning tasks.

2.3 Other Approaches to Detecting Vagueness

There are number of studies aimed at vagueness detection, that use linguistic features of vague expressions instead of manual annotation. These features include comparative forms, modifiers and determiners as well as semantic representations of words [12, 20].

For instance, assuming that revised sentences on wikiHowToImprove are always less vague than originals, the researches collected a corpus of sentence pairs, that included POS tagging and FrameNet annotation [7].

Another approach is to create manually generated black- and whitelists of words and phrases considered (in case of a blacklist) vague or ambiguous, that will work as a filter for classification [6]. Finally, some datasets, that are made for understanding borderlines of vague phrases, include annotation on how humans and machines detect these borderlines [12, 29].

Although most studies focus on specific tasks and do not develop a systematic approach to the problem, a common pattern emerges. Some datasets are not manually annotated. Instead, they represent a result of a rule-based algorithms. Manually annotated datasets typically consist of sentences annotated at various levels, including word, phrase, and sentence levels, with tags that either indicate binary classification or represent varying degrees of vagueness. These context-specific texts are frequently annotated by industry experts, and the inter-annotator agreement scores range from reasonable to high. Most of these datasets exhibit imbalance, with the vague elements being underrepresented compared to the non-vague ones. In terms of size, the datasets generally contain between 2,000 and 4,500 sentences. The texts within these datasets are sourced either from public repositories, such as Wikipedia, or from private databases.

3 Dataset Annotated by One Linguist and Three Lawyers

Our goal is to create a binary classifier capable of detecting, whether a Russian sentence contains or does not contain vagueness. Accordingly, we used annotation scheme where each sentence was manually assigned tags like 'no' ("non-vague") or 'yes' ("vague").

3.1 Obtaining a Set of Sentences

We used the **"CorCodex"** corpus as the source of sentences for annotation. This corpus is of 282 **normative documents** (a total of 3 million 227 thousand tokens). Corpus statistics by document type are shown in Table 6.

Table 6. Structure of the corpus of laws.

Document type	Document count
Federal laws	200
Government Resolutions	37
Codes of the Russian Federation	21
Laws of the Russian Federation	17
Fundamentals of Legislation of the Russian Federation	5
Resolutions of the Supreme Soviet	2

We obtained all sentences containing **any adjectives with the tone labels "PSTV" or "NGTV"** from the KartaSlovSent dictionary [15]. In selecting such sentences, we proceeded from the premise that at least some words labelled in terms of tonality contain vagueness (in particular, adjectival vagueness, cf. rus. *spravedlivyj* 'fair', *pravil'nyj* 'correct', *razumnyj* 'reasonable', *neblagoprijatnyj* 'unfavourable'). These sentences were then examined by a linguist. All sentences with vague adjectives were selected to be presented to the lawyers.

The results of the linguist's examination of the set of sentences are summarised as follows. The sentences labelled as containing vagueness include 226 types (in terms of lemmas); the most frequent ones are presented in Table 7.

Table 7. The most frequent vague adjectives.

Rank	Lemma	Freq	Rank	Lemma	Freq
1	*neobhodimyj* 'necessary'	1896	11	*motivirovannyj* 'motivated'	125
2	*nenadlezhashhij* 'improper'	376	12	*nesvoevremennyj* 'untimely'	124
3	*tjazhkij* 'grave'	251	13	*opasnyj* 'dangerous'	115
4	*uvazhitel'nyj* 'honourable'	202	14	*osobyj* 'special'	112
5	*razumnyj* 'reasonable'	189	15	*novyj* 'new'	108
6	*nedostovernyj* 'unreliable'	182	16	*dostatochnyj* 'sufficient'	105
7	*negativnyj* 'negative'	177	17	*obosnovannyj* 'reasonable'	99
8	*lozhnyj* 'false'	142	18	*dostovernyj* 'credible'	96
9	*svoevremennyj* 'timely'	133	19	*vazhnyj* 'important'	92
10	*nepravomernyj* 'wrongful'	127	20	*vrednyj* 'harmful'	88

3.2 Legal Expert Team and Annotation Procedure

The experts were **three lawyers**, one PhD candidate (A1) and two postgraduate students (A2, A3). A1 has extensive expertise of monitoring Russian legislation and a good understanding of which linguistic expressions are capable of introducing legal vagueness into the text of a law.

The legal team received 6,153 sentences for manual tagging. They conducted annotation independently of each other. We discussed the annotation process in several seminars, so detailed written instructions were not developed.

The annotation procedure was as follows: the annotator filled in the Google table and wrote "yes" (if vagueness was detected), "no" (if no vagueness was detected), or "unclear". The experts saw not only sentences but also lemmas that in the opinion of the linguist introduce vagueness. If there were two potentially vague lemmas in the sentence, the expert made a judgement about each of them, see Table 8 for an example of interpreting the sentence *'The application may contain other information, including telephone numbers, fax numbers, e-mail addresses, if they are necessary for the* ***correct*** < Lemma1 > *and* ***timely*** < Lemma2 > *consideration of the case, may contain motions, including motions to demand evidence from the defendant or other persons'.*

Table 8. Example of labelling.

Sentence	Lemma1	Lemma2	Vagueness1	Vagueness2
V zajavlenii mogut byt' ukazany i inye svedenija, v tom chisle nomera telefonov, faksov, adresa elekt- ronnoj pochty, esli oni neobhodimy dlja pravil'nogo i svoevremennogo rassmotrenija dela, mogut soder- zhat'sja hodatajstva, v tom chisle hodatajstva ob istrebovanii dokazatel'stv ot otvetchika ili drugih lic.	*pravil'nyj*	*svoevre-mennyj*	yes	yes

3.3 Annotation Results

Thus, each lawyer considered **6,153 sentences with 7,207 lemmas**, in the opinion of the linguist introducing vagueness. The distribution of lawyers' answers is shown in Table 9.

Table 9. Labelling results in terms of lemmas.

Annotator	Responses	Vagueness	No vagueness	Unclear	No tag	Total
A1	Number	2,113	4,952	0	142	7,207
A1	Percentage	29.32%	68.71%	0%	1.97%	100
A2	Number	3,755	29	3,420	3	7,207
A2	Percentage	52.1%	0.4%	47.45%	0.04%	100
A3	Number	5,916	1,142	0	149	7,207
A3	Percentage	82.09%	15.85%	0%	2.07%	100

It can be clearly seen how differently annotators labelled our set of sentences. A1 and A3 never chose the answer "unclear", while A2 did so half of the time. A1 considered a third of the sentences to contain vagueness, while A3 labelled about 80% of the sentences in this way. We add that the absence of the tag "No tag" (NA) is not coincidental. According to comments from A1 and A3, the lawyers considered the size of some of the contexts presented to be insufficient to make a decision. Note also that during the annotation, A1 gave the most comments both on the quality of the presented contexts (their interpretability) and on his solutions.

The computing of **inter-rater agreement measures** is based on a dataset with the answers of three annotators (A1, A2, A3), see Table 10 as an example. We calculated five coefficients of agreement. The inter-annotator agreement coefficients values, estimated using the R package [11], are shown in Table 11.[2]

Table 10. Dataset example

A1	A2	A3	Lemma
yes	unclear	yes	*uvazhitel'nyj* 'respectful'
no	unclear	yes	*osobyj* 'special'
NA	yes	yes	*nepravomernyj* 'wrongful'

Table 11. Agreement coefficients

coeff.name	pa	pe	coeff.val	coeff.se	conf.int	p-value
Percent Agreement	0.33	0	0.33	0.004	(0.327, 0.34)	$p < 0.0005$
AC1	0.33	0.29	0.06	0.006	(0.044, 0.067)	$p < 0.0005$
Fleiss' Kappa	0.33	0.41	−0.13	0.004	(−0.141, −0.125)	$p < 0.0005$
Krippendorff's Alpha	0.33	0.41	−0.14	0.004	(−0.145, −0.13)	$p < 0.0005$
Conger's Kappa	0.33	0.32	0.02	0.003	(0.014, 0.025)	$p < 0.0005$

As can be seen, the percentage agreement is 33%; Fleiss' Kappa and Krippendorff's Alpha take negative values; this means that **the inter-annotator agreement is less than expected by chance**. It appears that the challenge of interpreting a limited context within single-sentence scope combined with the substantial workload (exceeding 6,000 sentences) rendered the annotation task extremely arduous and potentially overwhelming for inexperienced annotators.

Given the level of expertise and the thoroughness of analysing the language examples (including the number of insightful comments and the overall ability to discuss examples in detail in our seminars), we decided to use only the responses of annotator A1.[3]

3.4 Results of Expert A1

A1 labelled occurrences of 150 unique lemmas as containing vagueness (see Table 12 showing the most frequent ones). Next, A1 marked occurrences of 171 unique lemmas as containing no vagueness (see Table 13 for the most frequent ones).

[2] Table 11 shows: pa (the percent agreement), pe (the percent chance agreement), coeff.val (the estimated value of an agreement coefficient), coeff.se (the agreement coefficient standard error), and conf.int (the confidence interval), see [14] for details.

[3] The authors would like to thank the first annotator (Mikhail Arkadievich Revazov, Project Administrator of the Centre of Expertise of St. Petersburg State University) for his careful attention to the linguistic examples and their thoughtful discussion.

Table 12. The most frequent adjectives that inject vagueness: lawyer's judgement

Rank	Lemma	Freq	Rank	Lemma	Freq
1	*neobhodimyj* 'necessary'	394	11	*grubyj* 'harsh'	50
2	*uvazhitel'nyj* 'respectful'	193	12	*novyj* 'new'	48
3	*razumnyj* 'reasonable'"	179	13	*racional'nyj* 'rational'	45
4	*dostatochnyj* 'sufficient'	81	14	*vazhnyj* 'important'	42
5	*effektivnyj* 'effective'	71	15	*blagoprijatnyj* 'favourable'	41
6	*motivirovannyj* 'motivated'	70	16	*ustojchivyj* 'sustainable'	41
7	*tjazhkij* 'grave'	60	17	*osobyj* 'special'	37
8	*obshhepriznannyj* 'recognised'	57	18	*udobnyj* 'convenient'	30
9	*znachitel'nyj* 'significant'	56	19	*neobosnovannyj* 'unreasonable'	22
10	*svoevremennyj* 'timely'	55	20	*zdorovyj* 'healthy'	21

Table 13. The most frequent adjectives that did not inject vagueness: lawyer's judgement.

Rank	Lemma	Freq	Rank	Lemma	Freq
1	*neobhodimyj* 'necessary'	1,461	11	*obosnovannyj* 'justified'	85
2	*nenadlezhashhij* 'improper'	353	12	*vrednyj* 'harmful'	83
3	*tjazhkij* 'grave'	189	13	*nepravil'nyj* 'wrong'	81
4	*nedostovernyj* 'untrustworthy'	181	14	*nevozmozhnyj* 'impossible'	80
5	*negativnyj* 'negative'	159	15	*svoevremennyj* 'timely'	76
6	*lozhnyj* 'false'	141	16	*osobyj* 'special'	75
7	*nepravomernyj* 'wrongful'	124	17	*primernyj* 'approximate'	75
8	*nesvoevremennyj* 'untimely'	121	18	*tochnyj* 'exact'	72
9	*opasnyj* 'dangerous'	110	19	*pravil'nyj* 'correct'	71
10	*dostovernyj* 'credible'	96	20	*neobosnovannyj* 'unreasonable'	62

As can be seen in Tables 12 and 13, **the same lemmas appear both as injecting and non-injecting vagueness**. This is the most important result for our study: the same words (or words with the same linguistic properties) do or do not introduce legal vagueness. This means that it is not enough to use a list of words or a set of rules to diagnose legal vagueness.

Now let us analyze which lemmas made it to both lists. Consider the 100 most frequent lemmas in the "yes list" (vague) and "no list" (non-vague). There is a total of 53 such lemmas in the labelled dataset. For our purposes, we are most interested in vague/non-vague lemmas that have approximately the same ranks in both frequency lists. Therefore, we arrange the list of lemmas by decreasing modulus of the value of the difference between ranks, see the table in the appendix to this paper. The lemmas at the top of this list are likely to pose the most significant difficulties in analyzing legal texts from the point of view of legal vagueness.

Of separate interest are the features of sentences labelled by A1 as containing no vagueness. In interpreting a particular sentence, a lawyer relies not only on the narrow linguistic context, but also on the presence in a particular statutory provision of a reference to another provision of the same statute (or other statutes) that clarify the vagueness. Thus, legal interpretation differs significantly from linguistic one.

For example, the linguist sees vagueness in the sentence *Pobeditelem konkursa priznaetsja uchastnik konkursa, predlozhivshij* ***nailuchshie uslovija****, opredel- jaemye v porjadke, predusmotrennom chastjami 5 i 6 stat'i 32 nastojashhego Federal'nogo zakona* 'The winner of the tender is the bidder who offered **the best conditions** determined in accordance with the procedure stipulated by parts 5 and 6 of Article 32 of this Federal Law', the locus of which is the adjective 'good' in superlative form. A1 marks this sentence as containing no vagueness because 'the best conditions' are somehow described in another part of the same legislative document.

This means that, when considering a particular sentence, we may take into account references to other provisions of the regulations (such as '*in the cases provided for in paragraphs 2 and 3 of Part 6 of this Article*' or '*in the cases provided for in Article 382 of this Code*'). The presence of such references can indicate the absence of legal vagueness.

Finally, there are such cases of interpretation, when the expert relies not on a specific provision of the law, but on the body of laws as a whole. In this regard, we will achieve greater success in the analysis of vagueness if we introduce the level of noun phrases into the dataset. This will allow us to take into account multi-word terms such as *tjazhkoe predstuplenie* 'grave crime' (non-vague) or *tjazhkie posledstvija* 'grave consequences' (vague).

3.5 Dataset Structure

Thus, we obtained a dataset with labeling performed by expert A1. We consider it to be of high quality. It consists of 6037 sentences. Each sentence is assigned lemmas that can introduce vagueness. Each lemma is provided with a label like "(yes)_vague" or "(no)_non-vague".

4 Conclusion and Future Work

Thus, this paper describes the method of constructing an annotated dataset, which we plan to use for automatic detection of legal vagueness. As a result of the work of a linguist, a set of sentences was obtained from a corpus of laws of size 3,200 thousand tokens. About 6,000 sentences were given to three lawyers with different qualifications for independent annotation. During the annotation, the lawyers showed fundamentally different strategies and significantly different levels of confidence. As a result, we chose A1's expert annotation based on his experience and the actual quality of the labelling. Thus, we obtained 6,037 sentences with labelled lemmas.

Apart from the dataset itself, the results of our study are findings such as:

- Linguists and lawyers use **fundamentally different interpretation algorithms** when analyzing linguistic contexts. The linguist relies on semantics and explicit indicators of adjective gradability. Lawyers take linguistic features into account, but rely on knowledge of the law or on the presence of a reference to another article of the law (another normative document) in the sentence being interpreted.
- This means that further **involvement of legal experts** is also necessary to successfully complete a dataset suitable for automatic detection of legal vagueness.
- An additional insight can be drawn: when annotations necessitate specialized expertise, the overall quality hinges predominantly upon the proficiency and domain-specific knowledge of individual experts rather than their sheer quantity.
- We find that **the same lemmas do or do not introduce legal vagueness**. Consequently, rule-based classification methods will be completely unsuitable for us.
- Moreover, it seems that introducing **the level of noun phrases** into the labelled dataset can improve the quality of the classification.

Further work involves taking into account the different types of vagueness described in [5]. At the time of this writing, we have assembled a dataset with gradable adverbs and intend to present it to lawyers for annotation. We add that we took into account the experience of tagging sentences with gradable adjectives; accordingly, the new expert team will include A1 and two new annotators with high competence and experience in detecting vagueness.

Finally, we conducted a series of experiments with binary classification of Russian sentences based on the presence/absence of vagueness, using classical machine learning algorithms and our annotated data. The experiments have shown the applicability of the approach; see [3]. By using Transformer family models for classification tasks in the future, we hope to account in more detail for contextual features that can predict vagueness.

Acknowledgments. This paper was prepared with the support of SPbU under the project "Legal and linguistic vagueness in the texts of legal acts taking into account their communicative features and legal functions", project ID 123042000068-8.

A Appendix

Lemma	Translation	Rank (vague)	Freq (vague)	Rank(non-vague)	Freq(non-vague)	Rank difference
neblagoprijatnyj	unfavourable	23	15	23	51	0
neobhodimyj	necessary	1	394	1	1461	0
unikal'nyj	unique	30	12	30	34	0
neobosnovannyj	unreasonable	19	22	20	62	1
osobyj	special	17	37	16	75	1
horoshij	good	30	12	29	41	1
vygodnyj	favourable	60	4	58	8	2
ekstrennyj	urgent	60	4	63	7	3
otricatel'nyj	negative	60	4	56	9	4
tjazhkij	grave	7	60	3	189	4
svoevremennyj	timely	10	55	15	76	5
aktual'nyj	relevant	69	3	76	4	7
dobrosovestnyj	conscientious	39	8	46	13	7
nedostatochnyj	inadequate	39	8	46	13	7
operativnyj	prompt	47	6	54	10	7
poleznyj	useful	34	10	41	17	7
gumannyj	humane	78	2	87	3	9
novyj	new	12	48	21	60	9
vazhnyj	important	14	42	24	50	10
polozhitel'nyj	positive	60	4	49	12	11

(*continued*)

(*continued*)

Lemma	Translation	Rank (vague)	Freq (vague)	Rank(non-vague)	Freq(non-vague)	Rank difference
sposobnyj	capable	39	8	28	45	11
blizkij	close	47	6	35	26	12
obosnovannyj	reasonable	26	14	11	85	15
blagoprijatnyj	favourable	15	41	31	32	16
motivirovannyj	motivated	6	70	22	54	16
negativnyj	negative	21	18	5	159	16
tochnyj	accurate	34	10	18	72	16
dostojnyj	honourable	69	3	87	3	18
trudnodostupnyj	inaccessible	60	4	40	18	20
zdorovyj	healthy	20	21	41	17	21
bezvrednyj	harmless	98	1	76	4	22
nepredvidennyj	unforeseen	78	2	56	9	22
grubyj	rough	11	50	34	28	23
nebrezhnyj	careless	45	7	70	6	25
znachimyj	significant	28	13	54	10	26
nedobrosovestnyj	dishonest	78	2	49	12	29
optimal'nyj	optimal	45	7	76	4	31
pravil'nyj	correct	51	5	19	71	32
cennyj	valuable	26	14	58	8	32
dostatochnyj	sufficient	4	81	37	23	33
spravedlivyj	fair	30	12	63	7	33
ustojchivyj	sustainable	15	41	51	11	36
vrednyj	harmful	51	5	12	83	39
dostupnyj	accessible	21	18	63	7	42
opasnyj	dangerous	51	5	9	110	42
prigodnyj	suitable	69	3	26	49	43
jeffektivnyj	effective	5	71	51	11	46
znachitel'nyj	significant	9	56	58	8	49
nenadlezhashhij	inappropriate	60	4	2	353	58
zablagovremennyj	early	28	13	87	3	59
bezopasnyj	safe	98	1	27	47	71
uvazhitel'nyj	respectful	2	193	76	4	74
razumnyj	reasonable	3	179	87	3	84

References

1. Theories of Vagueness (2021). https://philpapers.org/browse/theories-of-vagueness. Accessed 24 May 2025
2. Alexopoulos, P., Pavlopoulos, J.: A vague sense classifier for detecting vague definitions in ontologies. In: Wintner, S., Riezler, S., Goldwater, S. (eds.) Proceedings of the 14th Conference of the European Chapter of the Association for Computational Linguistics, Vol. 2: Short Paper, pp. 33–37. Association for Computational Linguistics (2014). https://doi.org/10.3115/v1/E14-4007
3. Berlin, A., Blinova, O., Mitrofanova, O.: Classification models for the detection of vague sentences in Russian legal texts. In: Proceedings of the International Conference Corpus Linguistics-2025. SPbU (in print). (in Russian)
4. Blinova, O., Belov, S.: Linguistic ambiguity and vagueness in Russian legal texts. Vest. Saint Petersburg Univ. Law **11**(4), 774–812 (2020). https://doi.org/10.21638/spbu14.2020.401. (in Russian)
5. Cruz, B.D., Jayaraman, B., Dwarakanath, A., McMillan, C.: Detecting vague words & phrases in requirements documents in a multilingual environment. In: 2017 IEEE 25th International Requirements Engineering Conference (RE), pp. 233–242 (2017). https://doi.org/10.1109/RE.2017.24
6. Debnath, A., Roth, M.: A computational analysis of vagueness in revisions of instructional texts (2023). http://arxiv.org/abs/2309.12107. Accessed 24 May 2025
7. Devos, F.: Semantic vagueness and lexical polyvalence. Stud. Linguist. **57**(3), 121–141 (2003). https://doi.org/10.1111/j.0039-3193.2003.00101.x
8. Durant, A., Leung, J.H.: Pragmatics and legal interpretation. In: Language and Law. A Resource Book for Students, pp. 79–85. Routledge (2017)
9. Engberg, J., Heller, D.: Vagueness and Indeterminacy in Law. In: Bhatia, V.K., Candlin, C.N., Engberg, J. (eds.) Legal Discourse across Cultures and Systems, pp. 144–168. Hong Kong University Press (2008). https://doi.org/10.5790/hongkong/9789622098510.003.0007
10. Gwet, K.L.: irrCAC: computing chance-corrected agreement coefficients (CAC) (2019). https://CRAN.R-project.org/package=irrCAC. Accessed 24 May 2025
11. Icard, B., Claveau, V., Atemezing, G., Égré, P.: Measuring vagueness and subjectivity in texts: from symbolic to neural VAGO (2023). https://doi.org/10.48550/ARXIV.2309.06132, https://arxiv.org/abs/2309.06132. Accessed 24 May 2025, Number: 2
12. Kirillovich, A., Loukachevitch, N., Kulaev, M., Bolshina, A., Ilvovsky, D.: Sense-annotated corpus for Russian. In: Proceedings of the Fifth International Conference on Computational Linguistics in Bulgaria (CLIB 2022), pp. 130–136. Department of Computational Linguistics, IBL – BAS (2022). https://aclanthology.org/2022.clib-1.15/. Accessed 24 May 2025
13. Klein, D.: Implementing a general framework for assessing interrater agreement in stata. **18**(4), 871–901 (2018). https://doi.org/10.1177/1536867X1801800408, https://journals.sagepub.com/doi/10.1177/1536867X1801800408. Accessed 24 may 2025

14. Kulagin, D.: Publicly available sentiment dictionary for the Russian language KartaSlovSent. In: Computational Linguistics and Intellectual Technologies: Proceedings of the International Conference "Dialog" [Komp'yuternaia Lingvistika i Intellektual'nye Tekhnologii: Trudy Mezhdunarodnoj Konferentsii "Dialog"], vol. 20, pp. 1106–1119 (2021)
15. Lakoff, G.: Hedges: a study in meaning criteria and the logic of fuzzy concepts **2**(4) (1973). https://doi.org/10.1007/BF00262952. Accessed 2025/05/24
16. Lebanoff, L., Liu, F.: Automatic detection of vague words and sentences in privacy policies. In: Proceedings of the 2018 Conference on Empirical Methods in Natural Language Processing. pp. 3508–3517. Association for Computational Linguistics, Brussels (2018)
17. Loper, E., Bird, S.: NLTK: the natural language toolkit. In: Proceedings of the ACL-02 Workshop on Effective Tools and Methodologies for Teaching Natural Language Processing and Computational Linguistics, vol. 1, pp. 63–70. Association for Computational Linguistics (2002). https://doi.org/10.3115/1118108.1118117, http://portal.acm.org/citation.cfm?d=1118108.1118117. Accessed 24 May 2025
18. Malik, G., Yildirim, S., Cevik, M., Bener, A.: An empirical study on vagueness detection in privacy policy texts (2023). https://doi.org/10.21428/594757db.2728303d, https://caiac.pubpub.org/pub/t7g1t33y. Accessed 24 May 2025
19. de Marneffe, M.C., Manning, C.D., Potts, C.: "Was it good? It was provocative". Learning the meaning of scalar adjectives. In: Hajič, J., Carberry, S., Clark, S., Nivre, J. (eds.) Proceedings of the 48th Annual Meeting of the Association for Computational Linguistics, pp. 167–176. Association for Computational Linguistics (2010). https://aclanthology.org/P10-1018/. Accessed 24 May 2025
20. May, U., Zaczynska, K., Moreno-Schneider, J., Rehm, G.: Extraction and normalization of vague time expressions in German. In: Proceedings of the 17th Conference on Natural Language Processing/Konferenz zur Verarbeitung natürlicher Sprache (KONVENS), pp. 114–126 (2021)
21. Miller, G.A.: WordNet: a lexical database for English. In: Human Language Technology: Proceedings of a Workshop held at Plainsboro, New Jersey (1994). https://aclanthology.org/H94-1111/. Accessed 24 May 2025
22. Panchenko, A., et al.: RUSSE'2018: a shared task on word sense induction for the Russian language (2018). https://doi.org/10.48550/ARXIV.1803.05795, https://arxiv.org/abs/1803.05795. Accessed 24 May 2025
23. Paris, P.H., Aoud, S.E., Suchanek, F.M.: The vagueness of vagueness in noun phrases. In: Conference on Automated Knowledge Base Construction (2021). https://imt.hal.science/hal-03344675v1/document. Accessed 24 May 2025
24. Saurí, R., Moszkowicz, J., Knippen, B., Gaizauskas, R., Setzer, A., Pustejovsky, J.: TimeML annotation guidelines version 1.2.1 (2006). https://nilsreiter.de/assets/2017-10-01-howto-annotation/timeml-1.2.1.pdf. Accessed 24 May 2025
25. Shivade, C., De Marneffe, M.C., Fosler-Lussier, E., Lai, A.M.: Identification, characterization, and grounding of gradable terms in clinical text. In: Proceedings of the 15th Workshop on Biomedical Natural Language Processing, pp. 17–26. Association for Computational Linguistics (2016). https://doi.org/10.18653/v1/W16-2903

26. Solt, S.: Vagueness and imprecision: empirical foundations. Annu. Rev. Linguist. **1**(1), 107–127 (2015). https://doi.org/10.1146/annurev-linguist-030514-125150
27. Stengel-Eskin, E., Guallar-Blasco, J., Van Durme, B.: Human-model divergence in the handling of vagueness. In: Proceedings of the 1st Workshop on Understanding Implicit and Underspecified Language, pp. 43–57. Association for Computational Linguistics (2021). https://doi.org/10.18653/v1/2021.unimplicit-1.6, https://aclanthology.org/2021.unimplicit-1.6. Accessed 24 May 2025

Cyberpsychology and Post-AI Education

Digital Pedagogy: Current State, Development Patterns, Prospects

Pavel Konyukhovskiy(✉) and Anna Yakovleva

Herzen State Pedagogical University, 48 Moika Embankment, St. Petersburg 191186, Russia
kon_pv@mail.ru, yeif@mail.ru

Abstract. Over the last decade, the concept of "digital pedagogy" has successfully entered the scientific discourse. It should be recognized that at the moment there is no unambiguous, consensus interpretation of it. This is largely due to the evolution of meanings put by different authors into the concept of "digital pedagogy". Initially, digital pedagogy was associated with the forced application of computer technologies in the educational process - automated learning systems, specialized software and hardware tools, etc. It was at this time that the conditions for radical changes and the emergence of the phenomenon that can be identified as "digital pedagogy" in the modern educational environment were formed. The most important properties of this environment are the digital transformation of the economy and society, permanent changeability (hypervolatility). At present, the subject of digital pedagogy incorporates the problems of analyzing the effectiveness of digital and non-digital (traditional) methods in the educational process, searching for their optimal combination. Of particular importance are the models of predicting the consequences for future states of society, a significant part of which will be people educated with the help of digital pedagogy methods. The models and methods of evolutionary game theory, dating back to the ideas of J. Maynard Smith, can become a constructive tool for studying the regularities of the development of digital pedagogy and its incorporation into the educational system of modern society. These models can describe and study the strategic interaction between universities of different types (digital, traditional, hybrid, blended learning etc.), on the one hand, and students with different systems of individual target attitudes, on the other. The proposed model can be directly applied in solving the problems of overcoming the conflict of expectations and goals. This conflict is caused by the contradiction between what universities can teach and what students want and can learn.

Keywords: Digital Pedagogy · Cyberpsychology · Hypervolatility · Evolutionary Model of Education

M. Bakaev et al. (Eds.): IMS 2025, CCIS 2671, pp. 199–214, 2026.
https://doi.org/10.1007/978-3-032-04958-2_15

1 Introduction

1.1 A Subsection Sample

The aim of this study is to develop and conduct a primary analysis of models and methods that allow describing the processes of digital pedagogy development, as well as their impact on the evolution of the education sector in general and educational institutions in particular.

An important specific feature of the approaches developed in this article is their relevance to the state of the modern world, its political and socio-economic characteristics. To describe this state, we deliberately use the not quite standard term "hypervolatility". It is intended to reflect not just a situation of instability and variability, but permanent, self-reproducing variability, in which shocks and upheavals of previous periods have a high level of aftereffects on the future.

The starting point of the research is the answer to the question "what meanings are currently attached to the concept of digital pedagogy?".

This issue is related to such questions as:

- How does digital pedagogy transform the goals of the educational process?
- How does digital pedagogy change the social roles of educational institutions and contribute to their repositioning?
- What is the place of AI technologies in the system of digital pedagogy methods?
- What are the patterns of relationship between the methods (tools) of traditional and digital pedagogy?
- How to assess the prospects for competition between natural (anthropogenic) and artificial intelligence and the role of digital pedagogy methods in these processes?

The present study focuses on the search for methods that could provide adequate, rational solutions to the listed problems.

2 Previous Research

A significant number of studies devoted to digital pedagogy, to one degree or another, touch upon the problems of its identification and positioning among related scientific disciplines. In the article (Guangbin, Kexun) [4], digital pedagogy is characterized as an interdisciplinary practical science integrating the spheres of education, computer science, information and communication science. It is aimed at studying the phenomena, problems and laws of digital education, the development of humanity in the digital era. In the spirit of Chinese stylistic traditions, the authors formulate the "four principles", "three stages", "four forces" of digital pedagogy. Particular attention is paid to the theoretical analysis of the modernization and transformation of digital education and the methods of managing these processes.

In accordance with the author's position, digital pedagogy seeks an answer to the question "how and: what kind of people to educate and how to educate them in the digital era?". In the digital era, education harmoniously moves into the digital world, data becomes an indispensable element of education, the digital space becomes a new space for education. At the same time, people and digital technologies move towards deep integration in interactive experience, jointly opening up new forms and new areas for the development of digital education, creating a new impetus and new advantages for the development of digital education and contributing to the modernization of traditional pedagogy into digital pedagogy.

The article (Tan and oth.) [15] notes the controversial nature of the integration of digital technologies into teaching and learning processes. The authors provide a comparative analysis of the pros and cons. Supporters of new technologies rely on the new opportunities they open up. This includes both a simple improvement in the level of solving standard educational problems and optimizing information exchange, as well as qualitatively new epistemic means of presenting new knowledge structures and ways of learning. At the same time, supporters of the opposite position express skepticism regarding the positive properties of digital technologies.

The JISC Digital Pedagogy Toolkit [8] defines digital pedagogy as the discipline that studies how digital technologies can be used to best effect in teaching and learning. This can be seen in part as an extension of the more concise formulation "digital pedagogy is the study of how to teach using digital technologies" (Howell) [6].

According to Istrate [7], digital pedagogy is a scientific field that studies the creation, implementation and evaluation of educational situations that are largely based on digital technology components. Its focus also includes synchronous and asynchronous interactions in virtual and blended learning environments, platforms and learning management tools, digital educational resources, the use of various digital applications and tools in education, virtual assistants for learning and teaching, digital competencies of teachers, educational policies and special programs. From the point of view of this author, the specificity of digital pedagogy is determined by those features that add digital components to teaching methods, content, conditions and assessment of learning outcomes. Digital pedagogy is primarily associated with situations where teaching cannot be transferred to a traditional non-digital ("analog") environment without changing its essence, goals and didactic strategies.

As a further illustration of the points discussed above, it is useful to refer to the definition of digital pedagogy on the University of Toronto Library website. According to it, digital pedagogy is not so much the use of digital technologies for learning, but rather an approach to these tools from a critical pedagogical point of view. This implies that it is about both the thoughtful use of digital tools and the decision-making when not to use them, as well as the impact of digital tools on learning [20].

Another important area of research and publication in digital pedagogy is related to the relevance of the problems it solves. The work (Waddell, Clariza) [19] emphasizes the role of digital pedagogy as a tool for empowerment, through which students are motivated to explore the world and themselves. The article (Fyfe) [3] raises the problem of rethinking analog learning from the perspective of digital technologies.

Research into the development patterns of digital pedagogy is closely and organically linked to research into the processes of digital transformation of the economy and society. In particular, it is necessary to note the points of contact between these scientific fields in terms of information security and cybersecurity issues.

The article (Yakovleva, Konyukhovskiy) [23] provides a fairly comprehensive analysis of the factors influencing the level of cybercrime. Among the most significant are the indicators characterizing the level of education of the population and digital literacy. On the other hand, there is no doubt that these indicators depend on the education system in the society in question and the role that digital pedagogy plays in it.

The influence of digital pedagogy methods on the general atmosphere in society cannot be ignored either. These methods, under certain conditions, can become a source of serious risks and threats. In particular, they can be used as channels of external influence on the domestic political situation, the mood of certain social strata, the political and moral atmosphere.

The principled position of the authors of this article suggests the need to shift the emphasis in defining the subject of digital pedagogy. It is not enough to consider digital pedagogy as a discipline dealing with new (digital) teaching methods. Its subject in modern conditions also becomes education in the conditions of digital transformation. It should deal not only with the problems of new educational tools, but also with the problems of changes in the goals and objectives of the educational process in the post-transformation environment characterized by a radical change in the competition between human and software technologies.

3 Methodological Aspects of the Study

One of the main consequences of the global digital transformation has been the change in the attitude of "new generations" to education, reassessing its place and influence on subsequent life. The thesis about the erasure of boundaries in the minds of modern youth between real and digital life has become quite popular.

In these conditions, the role of such a scientific discipline as cyberpsychology has radically increased, focusing on the problems and patterns of interaction between people and the virtual information and software environment. A separate subject area of cyberpsychology is the relationship between people mediated by the virtual information environment.

It seems entirely expected that in the near future the development of cyberpsychological directions related to the interaction of natural (anthropogenic) and artificial intelligence, and the tasks of identifying (separating) types of intelligence, will occur.

A relevant and promising project seems to be the study of the interaction of digital teachers with digital students. It is necessary to emphasize the importance and fruitfulness of cyberpsychology as a tool for studying new types of relationships in a society that has experienced a digital transformation. To a large extent, the attitude towards neural networks at the current moment is determined by the effect of novelty and unfamiliarity against the background of previous experience. However, it is quite reasonable to expect that this perception will change quite quickly, and society will begin to perceive neural networks, large language models as something natural and ordinary. Among the significant Russian studies in the field of cyberpsychology, one can note the works (Voiskounsky) [17, 18]. Of particular interest are the articles (Demareva) [1, 2], which, in particular, raise the issue of university training of specialists in cyberpsychology.

A separate important topic, closely related to both cyberpsychology and digital pedagogy, is the study of new personal properties and characteristics of representatives of the "new generations". Understanding the patterns of formation and evolution of these typical personality traits of young people is extremely important for organizing an effective educational process. For example, articles [21, 22] analyze the patterns of personal dependence on digital electronic devices, which has acquired the stable name phubbing.

A possible alternative to traditional, well-developed cyberpsychological approaches may be research into the ideas of modern society subjects about the long-term development prospects of their life path based on the so-called concept of "life trajectory". Within the framework of this method, respondents are asked to construct a graphical representation of the "ideal" trajectory of their life path (career): the abscissa axis represents the life span, and the ordinate axis represents the level of life success (in conventionally abstract units). The collected information may be subject to quantitative analysis methods that involve approximating life trajectories using curves of the beta distribution density function family. The parameters of the obtained distributions may subsequently be used in the formal typification of subjects of the society under study. Changes in the parameters may be used as indicators of structural changes in society. For example, regarding shifts in ideas about "ideal" (standard) life path configurations, see [9].

An effective and constructive tool for analyzing the processes of incorporating digital pedagogy into the activities of higher education institutions, from the authors' point of view, can be models based on the mathematical apparatus of the theory of evolutionary games. This choice is largely determined by the content adequacy between the nature of the proposed methods and the evolutionary nature of the processes under study.

Let us recall that the fundamental ideas for evolutionary games were those of the prominent British scientist Maynard Smith [10–12], who worked at the intersection of mathematics and evolutionary biology. Subsequently, the development of the theory of evolutionary games was contributed to by the works of Samuelson, Zhang [13], Schaffer [14], Hofbauer [5], and Vasin [16].

4 Evolutionary Models of Competition of Forms of Education

In this section of the work, we will focus on the possibilities of applying the apparatus of evolutionary game theory to modeling the processes of development of digital pedagogy.

The evolutionary concept of decision-making (as opposed to the optimization one) is based on the hypothesis that subjects in successive situations requiring management actions do not choose the strategies that are optimal for these situations, often because the necessary information is simply not available, but those that were optimal in previous games. As you can easily see, this assumption looks quite realistic and adequate in the context of the tasks of studying digital pedagogy and cyberpsychology.

Let us consider the simplest evolutionary model of competition between types of education: traditional and digital. This model formalizes a certain conditional society (population). Within its framework, agents (players) with different types of education operate. At the initial (qualitative) stage of the study, two types can be considered: traditional (classical) education ($\boldsymbol{T}$) and digital education ($\boldsymbol{D}$). The competition of education carriers is modeled as a paired confrontation between two players, randomly extracted from the general population (society). It is necessary to recognize the conventionality and abstractness of such an approach. Undoubtedly, the specifics of competition between subjects in the realities of the modern labor market are much more complex.

Table 1. Basic model of evolutionary competition of types of education.

Player I \ Player II	*T*	*D*	
T	α, α	γ, 0	ε
D	0, γ	β, β	$1-\varepsilon$

The proposed evolutionary model is based on a bimatrix game defined by the Table 1.

The players' utilities in the game under consideration are specified by the parameters α, β, γ:

- α – the result of competing participants in the labor market in the "clash" of traditionally educated people;
- β – the result of competition between participants who received digital education;
- γ – the result of a traditional education carrier when confronted with a digital education carrier, while the result of the player, without limiting the generality with digital education, we can set equal to 0, considering it as a "base" relative to which the relationships of the remaining parameters are determined.

It is easy to see that the logic of the proposed game model is identical to the classic game of "hawks and doves".

When implementing the scenario of suppression of elite traditional education by more accessible, cheaper, mass digital education, at the fundamental level, the relationship of the parameters of the model of evolutionary competition of types of education will take the form

$$\alpha < 0 < \beta < \gamma. \tag{1}$$

The negative value of α in (1) can be interpreted as the "disappointment" of the traditionally educated player regarding the invested costs due to the lack of competitive advantages when facing an "equal strength" opponent. On the other hand, when facing a weaker ("digital") opponent, he gains a significant advantage γ. The value of β represents a "peaceful" compromise variant of competition between "weak" players with a non-elite education.

The fundamental conclusion that can be made on the basis of the evolutionary model is quite obvious. When the number of carriers of one or another form of education becomes "sufficient" (excessively many), it is advisable to switch to an alternative form of education.

The threshold value ε at which switching becomes advisable is determined from the condition of equality of utilities.

$$\varepsilon \cdot \alpha + (1 - \varepsilon) \cdot \gamma \tag{2}$$

the utility of a player who has a traditional education.

$$\varepsilon \cdot 0 + (1 - \varepsilon) \cdot \beta \tag{3}$$

the utility of a player who has a digital education.

As a result, we find that it is more profitable to be a «owner» of traditional education if (2) is not less than (3)

$$\varepsilon \cdot \alpha + (1 - \varepsilon) \cdot \gamma \geq \varepsilon \cdot 0 + (1 - \varepsilon) \cdot \beta. \tag{4}$$

Thus, the threshold value is given by

$$\varepsilon = \frac{\gamma - \beta}{\gamma - \beta - \alpha}. \tag{5}$$

The value of ε can be interpreted as the probability of encountering an opponent with a traditional type of education. Accordingly, $(1 - \varepsilon)$ is the probability of encountering an opponent with a digital type of education.

If the share of players of the traditional type is less than the threshold $\frac{\gamma-\beta}{\gamma-\beta-\alpha}$, this type of education becomes attractive, and, consequently, objective conditions arise for the growth of the number of players of this type. When their number exceeds the specified limit, a switch to the opposite trend occurs.

A graphical illustration reflecting the logic of the formation of the threshold value ε is shown in Fig. 1. The envelope line corresponding to the maximum value of utility is highlighted in bold. The value $\varepsilon = \frac{\gamma-\beta}{\gamma-\beta-\alpha}$ corresponds to the state of indifference when choosing types of education. In both cases, utility will be equal to the value $\frac{-\alpha\beta}{\gamma-\beta-\alpha}$.

The methods for determining specific values of the parameters α, β, γ are a weak point of the proposed approach. The subject of doubt and discussion, in particular, is the assumption that they are constants. In all likelihood, this premise can be somewhat acceptable on relatively short time intervals.

At the same time, an argument in their defense can be the fact that they quite adequately reflect the potential oscillatory ("pendulum") nature of the expected evolutionary dynamics between traditional and digital types of education. Such models, subject to modification, can be used to describe the cyclical processes of transformation of the educational sphere.

An important positive aspect of the evolutionary approach is that it allows us to get away from direct, naive, simplistic oppositions between traditional and digital education, where one is perceived as high-quality and elite, and the other, on the contrary, as cheap and mass. Evolutionary modeling allows us to interpret the relationship between forms of education from the perspective of their competitive opposition and successive iterations of achieving equilibrium. In this case, the levels of attractiveness of one or another version of education change alternately.

5 Econometric Research

As can be easily seen, the substantive testing of the model presented above is a very labor-intensive and time-consuming process. Due to the fact that at the moment the processes of incorporating digital pedagogy into the activities of universities are at the initial stages,

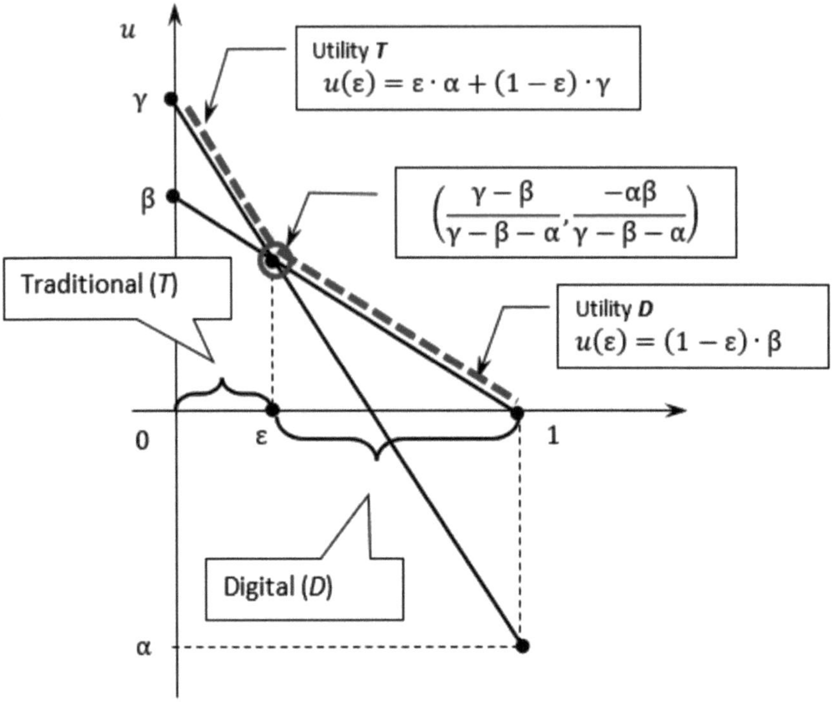

Fig. 1. Determination of the level ε in the evolutionary model of competition of types of education

we can judge their subsequent impacts and fundamental consequences exclusively at a hypothetical level, focusing on ambiguously interpreted indirect signals.

Expert assessments and analytics from surveys of subjects of the educational process can act as such indirect signals. As part of this study, a survey of junior students of the Herzen State Pedagogical University and the St. Petersburg branch of the National Research University Higher School of Economics was conducted. The survey was of an exclusively optional preliminary nature. Nevertheless, its results provide certain grounds for significant qualitative conclusions and generalizations. Separately, it should be noted that the results of this survey reflect the position of the generation that is destined to take leading positions in the post-transformational digital society.

General information about the structure and main results of the survey is presented in Table 2. For each of the proposed questions, the respondent was asked to give an assessment on a 10-point scale (0 – absolute disagreement, 10 – complete support).

The overall distribution ratio of the survey scores is given by the box-and-whisker diagram shown in Fig. 2.

Quite interesting information is provided by bar charts comparing empirical distribution densities of assessments for mutually related questions.

Figure 3 compares the distribution densities of the assessments given by respondents to the theses “AI in education is EVIL” and “AI in education is inevitable”. As can be seen, the antisymmetry in the diagram configurations is quite clearly visible, including

Table 2. Results of the survey "Attitude of modern students to AI technologies and digital pedagogy"

Question	Brief designation (code) of the question	Mean	Median	Sd
I am very familiar with digital pedagogy	Digital Pedagogy	5,05	5	2,62
I'm interested in cyberpsychology	Cyberpsychology	5,65	6	3,04
AI in education is EVIL	AI-Evil	2,84	2	2,59
AI in education is inevitable	AI-Inevitability	7,69	8	2,21
Ideally, exams should be taken by AI	AI-examinator	3,18	3	2,59
Ideally, exams should be taken by a "live teacher" and AI, with the average score as the assessment	NI-AI- assessment (mean)	6,42	7	2,70
Ideally, exams should be taken by a "live teacher" and AI, with the maximum score as the assessment	NI-AI- assessment (max)	5,90	6	2,99
In a few years, tutors will be teaching classes together with AI assistants	AI as assistant	6,32	7	2,88
In the future, students should be given the right to choose between an anthropogenic and an AI teacher	AI choosing	5,32	5	3,14
An anthropogenic teacher is easier to deceive	Deception	5,14	5	2,91
It is necessary to actively use virtual reality tools in the educational process	VR instruments	6,60	7	2,31
AI is the author of this survey	AI author	5,75	6	2,81

in the median values (2 for the first thesis and 8 for the second). The fact of symmetry of opinions in the area of assessment 5 is noteworthy.

Figure 4 shows the results of comparing the scores given to the thesis "Ideally, exams should be taken by AI" and "Ideally, exams should be taken by a 'live teacher' and AI, with the average score used as the grade". It shows a high degree of distrust in 'digital methods' and AI. At the same time, there is a clear interest in involving it in assessment procedures as a co-expert (alternative arbiter). It would probably be

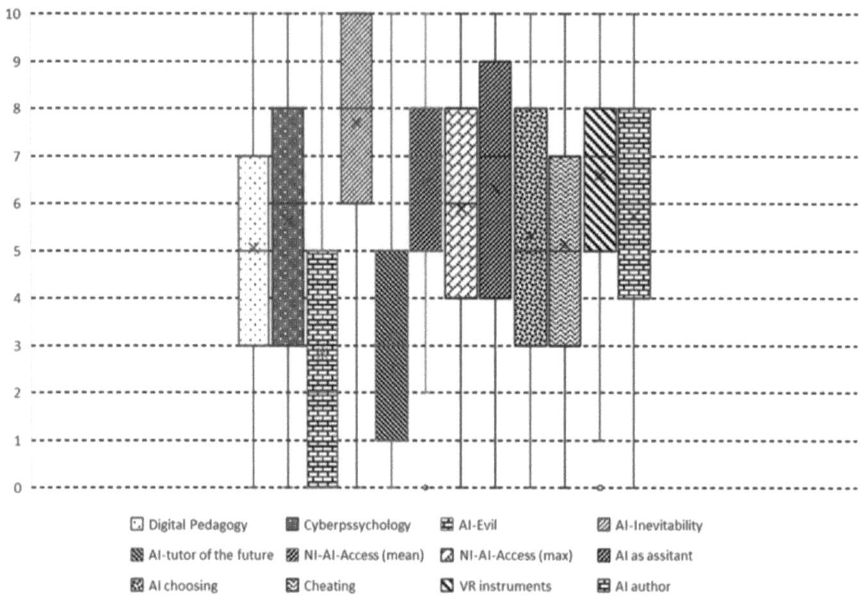

Fig. 2. Overall distribution of ratings received in the survey

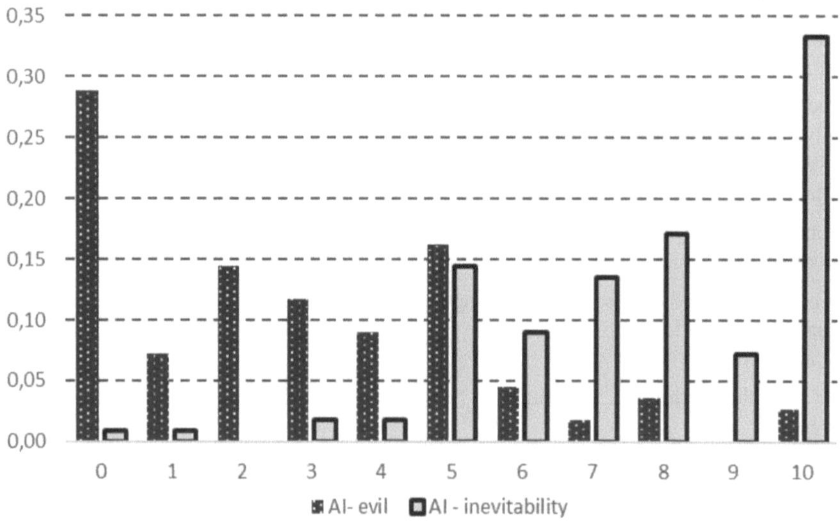

Fig. 3. Comparison of rating distributions

premature to interpret these responses as students' expectations that the AI tutor would be more objective and fairer to them. Rather, they reflect an expectation that the AI tutor's grades will be different from those of the "humanized" tutor. This, subject to averaging, may yield additional "bonuses". This observation is valuable in that it anticipates to some extent one of the mechanisms for the spread of digital pedagogy in the educational sphere.

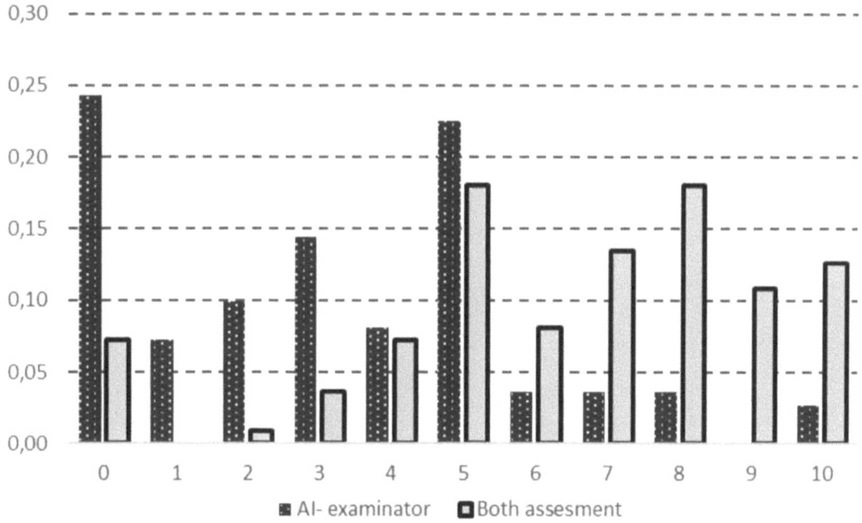

Fig. 4. Comparison of rating distributions

The distributions of the ratings for the statements "in the future, students should be given the right to choose between an anthropogenic and an AI teacher" and "an anthropogenic teacher is easier to deceive", presented in Fig. 5, are in complete agreement with this conclusion.

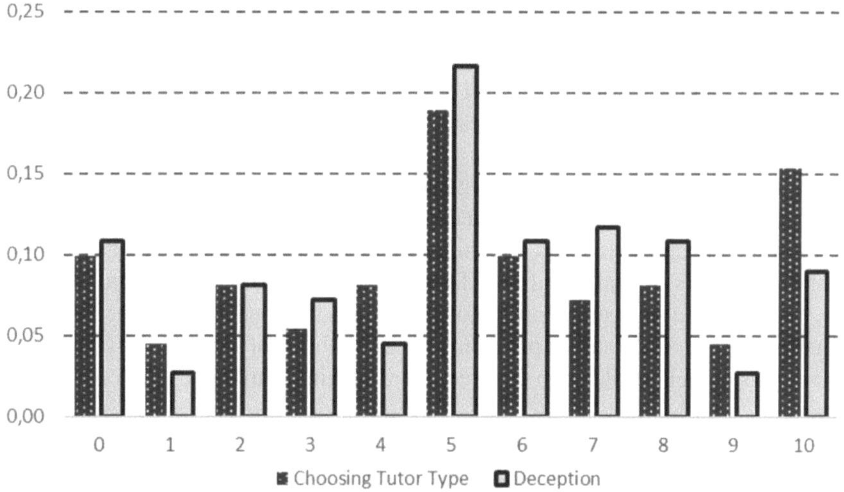

Fig. 5. Comparison of rating distributions

A convincing characteristic of respondents' indirect recognition of artificial intelligence capabilities is the distribution of evaluations of the thesis "AI is the author of this survey", presented in Fig. 6. As can be seen, the share of those who believe in the authorship of AI is quite significant - the median value is 6. At the same time, the share of "doubters" is high, the mode of the distribution is reached at a score of 5. In fact, the questions were compiled exclusively by the authors of the article without the help of any software tools.

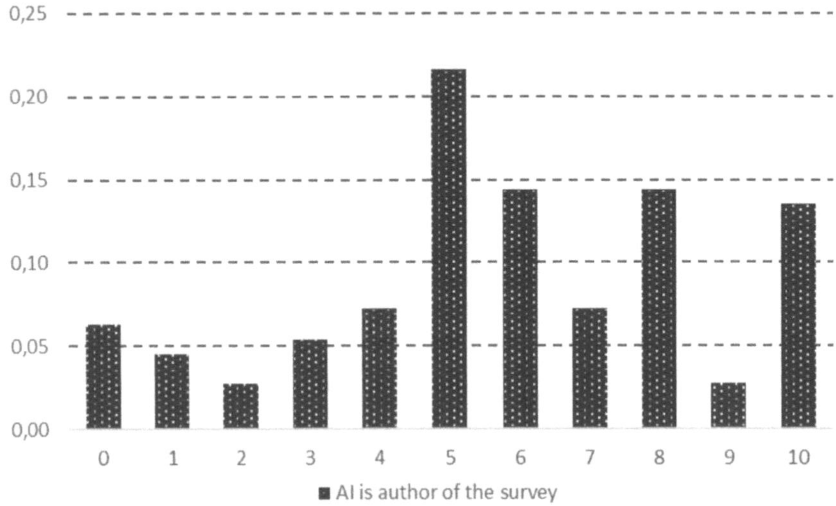

Fig. 6. Distribution of ratings for the statement "AI is the author of this survey"

At a general level, the results of the conducted empirical study of opinions can be characterized as an expectation of active development of digital pedagogy methods with a very cautious attitude towards possible negative consequences associated with them. It is quite symptomatic that the standard deviation for the assessments of the thesis "AI in education is inevitable" is the smallest compared to the standard deviations of other assessments (2.21).

Based on the results of such econometric procedures, simulation experiments with the evolutionary game models discussed above can be organized. Based on the results of generalization of survey statistics, the initial value of parameters (ε, $1 - \varepsilon$) determining the ratio of carriers of traditional and digital education can be established. From this value, studies of the subsequent oscillatory dynamics are conducted.

In the case of repeated survey procedures, the possibility of studies involving comparative analysis of their results with the predictions obtained through evolutionary models arises.

6 Results and Discussion

The theoretical and empirical analysis of the incorporation and infiltration of digital pedagogy into the educational sphere allows us to draw the following qualitative conclusions at the present time.

In the foreseeable future, the processes of dissemination of methods and technologies of digital pedagogy in the educational sphere will be of an evolutionary and oscillatory nature with periods of strengthening and recoil against the background of an overall growing trend.

The rate of spread of new information and digital technologies, primarily artificial intelligence technologies, will have a radical impact on the spread of digital pedagogy.

Artificial intelligence technologies (perhaps it would be more correct to use the term pre-intelligence or para-intelligence) inevitably change the structure of the labor market. It is quite expected that in the foreseeable future, professional competencies previously associated with the need for higher education will lose this "privileged" status.

It should be recognized that already at the present moment the higher education of a significant part of university graduates is "higher" solely by formal criteria. As a consequence, the differentiation of "higher education" with its gradation into levels is quite expected.

Predictably, there will be an intensive spread of digital pedagogy methods in educational institutions specializing in preparing students with "less than the highest education" and a concentration of "person-teaching-person" methods in "elite higher education".

At the same time, we should not absolutize the dichotomy of "cheap, accessible, but not very high-quality digital education versus expensive, elite traditional teaching methods." It is quite possible that in a number of situations, digital education will be more accessible, more effective, and of higher quality.

An important element of the study of the processes of dissemination and evolution of digital pedagogy is the problem of assessing the results of educational activities. In turn, its most important component is the assessment systems.

It should be noted that the 5-point (in fact, three-point) assessment system, which is still practiced by many educational institutions, is archaic and inadequate to the real existing system of differentiation of students. The real number of significantly different strata, into which the contingent of schools and universities is divided, significantly exceeds the number three. Merging them into three groups distorts the actual picture and becomes the most important demotivating factor, reducing the effectiveness and efficiency of the educational process.

An important area of research in modern digital pedagogy is related to its relationship with the problem of technological singularity. As is known, technological singularity is understood as a hypothetical situation in which technical progress becomes irreversible, uncontrollable and incomprehensible to humanity. In the pedagogical context, the manifestation of technological singularity can be expressed in the substitution of the goals of the educational process. In particular, in the substitution of the system of fundamental goals with the priorities of fulfilling formal procedures and complying with regulations.

Correct, balanced approaches to the problems of transforming modern pedagogy are, in a certain sense, a guarantee against both a frivolous attitude towards potential threats posed by new technologies and against unfounded, exaggerated alarmist expectations.

Taking into account the evolutionary oscillatory nature of the development processes of the educational sphere and digital pedagogy as its essential element, we should expect an increase in demand for methods and instruments based on the theory of evolutionary games. A promising direction for improving the basic evolutionary model considered in this article is the transition from a binary system of education types to a multiple one. Namely, to versions of models that are not limited to the dichotomy of traditional education vs digital, but provide for combined (mixed) options. Accordingly, the coefficients of the most stable combinations and the patterns of phase transitions between these states become an additional subject of study.

Another promising direction for the development of evolutionary models may be their extension to the processes of interaction (competition) between humans (i.e. the bearer of anthropogenic intelligence) and artificial intelligence in the labor market.

One of the medium-term tasks of digital pedagogy is the transformation of the educational process taking into account the new competitive environment in the labor market. The new competitive environment implies a refusal to form competencies in which a person will be obviously dominated by software and hardware systems and, conversely, priority in developing competencies in which natural intelligence is superior to artificial intelligence.

One of the accompanying effects of competition between natural and artificial intelligence may be a rethinking of society's attitude to mental and physical labor. The consequence of this may be shifts in the proportional ratios of their value assessments. The evolutionary game models considered in this article can be used to describe such processes.

7 Conclusion

Successful research into the problems of digital pedagogy is possible only with an integrated approach that involves the systematic use of methods and apparatus of quantitative (mathematical) methods with cyberpsychological approaches, the interrelation of the system of research goals with the tasks of the sphere of innovative digital technologies, cybersecurity, socio-political development, and state building.

The processes of incorporation and infiltration of digital pedagogy in the field of education are only at the initial stage, which does not allow for serious, objective, scientifically based conclusions. At this point, it is reasonable and constructive to limit ourselves to primary hypotheses and conclusions. In this regard, it is quite natural to conclude that it is extremely important to restructure the activities of universities in the direction of flexibility and adaptability to the methods of digital pedagogy, the ability to quickly abandon outdated traditional methods.

References

1. Demareva, V.A.: Magisterskaya Programma Kiberpsihologiya v NNGU im. N.I. Lobachevskogo (37.04.01 Psihologiya) [Master's Program Cyberpsychology at N.I. Lobachevsky State University (37.04.01 Psychology)]. Vestnik psihofiziologii [Psychophysiology news], vol. 2, pp. 27–32 (2023)
2. Demareva, V.A., Pleshakov, V.A.: Trendy i perspektivy kiberpsihologii [Trends and prospects of cyberpsychology]. Psihologicheskoe konsul'tirovanie Onlajn [Psychol. Counsel. Online]. **1**, 12–16 (2024)
3. Fyfe, P.: Digital pedagogy unplugged. Digit. Humanit. Q. **5**(3) (2011). https://www.digitalhumanities.org/dhq/vol/5/3/000106/000106.html
4. Zhang, G., Xue, K.: The underlying logic and construction path of digital pedagogy: on the construction of Chinese digital pedagogy. J. East China Norm. Univ. Educ. Sci. **11**, 67–84 (2023). https://doi.org/10.16382/j.cnki.1000-5560.2023.11.006
5. Hofbauer, J., Sigmund, K.: Evolutionary Games and Population Dynamics. University Press, Cambridge (1998)
6. Howell, J. Teaching with ICT. Digital Pedagogies for Collaboraon and Creavity. Oxford University Press, South Melbourne (2013)
7. Istrate, O.: Digital pedagogy. Definition and conceptual area. J. Digit. Pedag. **1**(1) 3–10 (2022). https://doi.org/10.61071/JDP.0313
8. JISC Digital Pedagogy Toolkit. Helping academics to make informed choices when embedding digital into the curriculum (2020/2021). https://www.jisc.ac.uk/guides/digital-pedagogy-toolkit
9. Konyukhovskiy, P.V., Yakovleva, A.V.: Kolichestvennye metody ocenivaniya dolgovremennyh kar'ernyh ustanovok sub"ektov sovremennogo obshchestva (Model 'Traektorii zhizni') [Quantitative methods for evaluating long-term career attitudes of the subjects of modern society ("model of the life trajectory")]. Upravlencheskoe konsul'tirovanie [Adm. Consul.] **1**(181), 53–73 (2024)
10. Maynard Smith, J.: The theory of games and evolution in animal conflicts. J. Theor. Biol. **47**, 209–221 (1974)
11. Maynard Smith, J.: Evolution and the Theory of Games. Cambridge University Press (1982)
12. Maynard Smith, J., Price, G.R.: The logic of animal conflict. Nature **246**, 15–18 (1973)
13. Samuelson, L., Zhang, J.: Evolutionary stability in asymmetric games. J. Econ. Theory **57** (1992)
14. Schaffer, M.: Evolutionary stable strategies for a finite population and a variable contest size. J. Theor. Biol. **132**, 469–478 (1988)
15. Tan, S.C., Voogt Joke, T.: Lynde Introduction to digital pedagogy: a proposed framework for design and enactment. Pedag.: Int. J. **19**(3), 327–336 (2024). https://doi.org/10.1080/1554480X.2024.2396944
16. Vasin, A.A.: Human reproduction and utility functions: an evolutionary approach. Psychol. Rational. Econ. Behav. **142**, 106–124 (2005)
17. Voiskounsky, A.E.: Kiberpsihologicheskie perspektivy izucheniya gruppovyh form tvorcheskoj deyatel'nosti [Cyberpsychological Perspectives of Studying Group Forms of Creative Activity]. V sbornike: Tvorchestvo v sovremennom mire: chelovek, obshchestvo, tekhnologii. Materialy Vserossijskoj nauchnoj konferencii, posvyashchennoj 100-letiyu so dnya rozhdeniya Ya.A. Ponomareva, Moscow, pp. 22–23 (2020)
18. Voiskounsky, A.E.: Kiberpsihologiya v psihologii [Cyberpsychology in psychology]. V sbornike: Cifrovoe obshchestvo kak kul'turno-istoricheskij kontekst razvitiya cheloveka. Sbornik nauchnyh statej i materialov III mezhdunarodnoj konferencii. Kolomna, pp. 68–74 (2020)

19. Waddell, M., Clariza, E.: Critical digital pedagogy and cultural sensitivity in the library classroom. Coll. Res. Libr. News **79**(5), 228–233 (2018). https://doi.org/10.5860/crln.79.5.228
20. What is Digital Pedagogy? University of Toronto Scarborough Library. https://guides.library.utoronto.ca/digitalpedagogy
21. Yakovleva, A.V.: Fabbing kak social'no-psihologicheskij fenomen sovremennogo obshchestva [Phubbing as a social-psychological phenomenon of modern digital society]. Saratov (2022)
22. Yakovleva, A.V., Konyukhovskiy, P.V.: Fabbing kak social'no-psihologicheskij fenomen sovremennogo obshchestva [Pubbing as a social and psychological phenomenon of modern society]. Sociopolit. Sci. **12**(6), 150–161 (2022). https://doi.org/10.33693/2223-0092
23. Yakovleva, A.V., Konyukhovskiy, P.V.: Problems of cybercrime in the era of hypervolatility: legal aspect. Econ. Probl. Legal Pract. **20**(6), 14–34 (2024). https://doi.org/10.33693/2541-8025

Understanding Player Experience: Eye-Tracking Insights into Cognitive Behaviour in Video Games

Valeriia Viakhireva(✉)

Lobachevsky State University, Nizhny Novgorod 603022, Russia
vvv@fsn.unn.ru

Abstract. Statistics indicate that over 80% of individuals aged 16 to 44 engage in video games across various genres. Video games are closely linked to players' cognitive abilities and decision-making skills, which, in turn, are associated with their fundamental personality traits. This study aimed to examine the relationship between players' psychological profiles and their cognitive characteristics during video game sessions. The experiment involved 10 participants (3 women and 7 men) aged 18 to 39. The psychological profile was assessed using the Five-Factor Personality Inventory (FFPI). Participants completed a custom-designed gaming experience questionnaire and the FFPI before engaging in a 15-min gaming session in Doom (ID Software, 2016) while wearing Pupil Labs eye-tracking glasses. Based on duration, fixations were categorized into four types: very short, express, cognitive, and long. The results revealed that personality traits and oculomotor behavior are interrelated. This, a significant positive correlation was found between the "Extraversion" score and the count of cognitive ($p < 0.05$) fixations and minimal duration of fixations ($p < 0.05$), suggesting a tendency toward quick decision-making and a dynamic playing style. It is also supported by negative correlation with the count of long ($p < 0.01$) fixations. The "Agreeableness" score showed a significant negative correlation with the maximum fixation duration ($p < 0.01$), indicating a preference for rapid scanning of information to facilitate prompt decision-making and flexible adaptation to changing conditions. These findings align with our previous research on the correlation between personality traits, heart rate variability, and in-game avatar states. This study provides useful insights for the development of personalized gaming experiences and training programs for professional eSports athletes.

Keywords: Gaming Experience · Eye Tracking · Eye Movements · Psychological Profile · Fixations

1 Introduction

According to statistics, more than 80% of individuals aged 16 to 44 engage in video gaming daily, ranging from large-scale AAA projects to simple mobile puzzles [1]. Video games represent a triumph of creativity and technology, offering immersive worlds that evoke emotions, facilitate learning, and provide entertainment. The enjoyment derived

M. Bakaev et al. (Eds.): IMS 2025, CCIS 2671, pp. 215–221, 2026.
https://doi.org/10.1007/978-3-032-04958-2_16

from gameplay is crafted by its elements, including an engaging virtual environment, immersive soundscapes, and a compelling narrative structure. These components interact with key cognitive processes, including emotions, motivation, memory, and attention.

Gameplay often requires players to seek information, develop strategies, devise approaches, and make decisions. Notably, video games significantly influence eye movement strategies and information processing. For instance, the authors in [2] demonstrated that action video game players may develop cognitive profiles characterized by enhanced processing speed and task-switching abilities, albeit with a potentially higher error rate. Similarly, the research [3] highlighted that active video game players outperform non-players in multiple cognitive domains, particularly those related to spatial perception and attention mechanisms. Also, it was demonstrated that the direct measurement of players' fixation behaviors can provide designers with more precise insights into visual attention patterns, leading to improvements in gameplay experience and the selective enhancement of visual fidelity [4]. Differences in fixation patterns between active players and non-players were also confirmed in [5], which identified variations in the frequency and duration of fixations on specific screen areas within the virtual environment. These findings suggest that professional players allocate their visual attention differently, potentially contributing to enhanced in-game performance.

Players do not form a homogeneous group; rather, they enter the gaming environment with distinct personalities, background and experience [6, 7]. These personality characteristics influence how individuals interpret and respond to presented challenges, particularly within virtual contexts. At the same time, cognitive processes are closely intertwined with personality dimensions, and recent research has increasingly focused on this aspect. Numerous studies have attempted to establish links between personality traits and eye movement behavior in various contexts. According to the research of [8] eye-tracking technology has a growing potential in psychological assessment within computer-mediated communication. Authors highlight that certain metrics such as fixation count and duration can be predictors of particular behavioral patterns commonly found in specific psychological types. Given the increasing digitalization of the environment, researchers have explored interaction patterns with websites, virtual environments, video games, and other digital interfaces. For instance, it was found that different personality types exhibit distinct eye-gazing behavior in terms of perceiving different design patterns and elements [9]. The authors of [10] discuss the consistency of gaze-based personality features across different contexts. Thus, individuals with higher openness scores tended to exhibit broader visual exploration, while those with higher conscientiousness scores demonstrated more focused and systematic gaze patterns. Authors highlight that personality types affect visual behavior regardless of content type. In [11] the authors investigate the relationship between personality type and information-seeking behavior, concluding that during information search tasks, personality type can be determined based on fixation count, fixation duration, and pupil size, in accordance with the Five-Factor Personality Inventory. Specifically, individuals with high levels of extraversion exhibited the greatest tendency for rapid information scanning, characterized by fewer fixations. The role of personality in cognitive processes was also examined in [12], where researchers assessed performance across five key domains, including memory tasks and speed-attention-executive tasks. The findings indicated that the highest success in cognitive tasks was associated with the "Agreeableness" personality type, while tasks requiring rapid information scanning and precise execution were best performed by individuals with the "Extraversion" personality type. In [13] authors present a systematic review of connections between personality and cognitive constructs. Among their key findings we can highlight the link of extraversion-related traits to active behavior, dominance and enthusiasm. They also note positive correlation of "Extraversion" with tasks related to fluency and speed ability. The other important insight is related to "Agreeableness", which was found to have positive correlations with general mental abilities. To add to this, we should mention the recognition of the Five-Factor Personality Inventory as relevant to gaming experience by game development community [14].

The present study aimed to find connections between players' psychological profile and particular cognitive patterns based on eye-gazing behavior. It can be further applicable to enhanced video game usability and experience personalization given the growing integration of eye-tracking methods in gaming controls.

2 Methods

The study was conducted at the Cyberpsychology Laboratory of the Faculty of Social Sciences at the National Research Lobachevsky State University of Nizhny Novgorod. The study was conducted according to the guidelines of the Declaration of Helsinki and approved by the Institutional Review Board of Faculty of Social Sciences of Lobachevsky State University. Informed consent was obtained from all subjects involved in the study.

The study involved 10 participants (7 men and 3 women) aged 18 to 39. Before the experiment, participants were provided with comprehensive information regarding the study's procedure, the methods used, the game and its virtual environment, control mechanisms, and data usage policies.

Each participant completed a custom questionnaire on gaming experience, detailing their prior gaming background, preferred genre, and gaming platform. Following this, they took the Five-Factor Personality Inventory, using the adaptation developed by A.B. Khromov at Kurgan State University [15]. This questionnaire assesses personality structure based on five fundamental traits: neuroticism (emotionality-restraint), extraversion (extraversion-introversion), openness to experience (playfulness-practicality), agreeableness (attachment-detachment), and conscientiousness (control-spontaneity).

For this study, we used the PC version of Doom (2016), developed by id Software. The game's protagonist is stationed at a scientific research facility on Mars, which has been overrun by hordes of demons following the failure of a secret project investigating demonic entities and artifacts from Hell. As a result, the demons have taken control of the complex and are preparing to invade Earth. The player's objective is to repel the attack and save the humankind.

This game is a first-person shooter (FPS), a genre characterized by a direct yet simplified connection between the player and their avatar. A key feature of this connection is the minimization of environmental complexity. Gameplay mechanics and interactive elements are relatively limited, with objects in the game world possessing predefined functions.

As typical FPS game, Doom includes the following elements [16]:

- A central player-controlled avatar, with whom the player closely identifies by experiencing the game world through their perspective.
- Exploration and movement through a hazardous, unfamiliar environment.
- The presence of hostile entities, whose elimination is the primary objective within short gameplay cycles.
- A predominantly linear narrative structure that requires the player to resolve a central conflict.
- Fundamental mechanics such as movement, camera control, jumping, running, crouching, stealth, and shooting.
- A diverse range of methods for neutralizing enemies.

The additional value of this game is its quick and efficient introduction of its mechanics and rules. This accessibility benefits both experienced players and newcomers. Every moment is meticulously designed—for example, at the very beginning, the protagonist is already holding a pistol aimed at an enemy, prompting the player to shoot intuitively, even without explicit instructions.

Another key advantage is the game's dynamic gameplay, which encourages active engagement rather than defensive play. Instead of allowing players to take cover and wait, the mechanics promote an aggressive combat style and immersion in high-intensity action. This pacing is further reinforced by level design, which provides ample space for movement and exploration without unnecessary clutter. At the same time, environmental obstacles introduce variety into combat encounters. These features were crucial in selecting Doom for this study, as they make the game suitable for both experienced players and individuals with no prior gaming experience.

Eye-gaze data were recorded using the portable eye tracker Pupil Invisible. Statistical analysis was conducted using the 'scipy.stats' module in a Jupyter Notebook environment with Python. For statistical evaluation, fixation-related metrics were calculated. Additionally, following the approach outlined in [17] all fixations were categorized into four distinct types. A comprehensive list of metrics is presented in Table 1. To analyze correlations between fixation metrics and personality traits, Spearman's rank correlation coefficient was used (r).

3 Results and Discussion

The analysis revealed statistically significant correlations between specific fixation metrics and personality trait scores. A comprehensive list of the identified correlations between personality types and fixation metrics is presented in Table 2.

Based on the presented data, a positive correlation was found between the "Extraversion" personality type and cognitive fixations ($r = 0.71^*$, $p < 0.05$), indicating a tendency for this personality type to focus on processing and analyzing information during tasks. Additionally, the "Extraversion" type showed a positive correlation with the minimal fixation duration ($r = 0.69^*$, $p < 0.05$) and a negative correlation with longer fixations ($r = -0.71^{**}$, $p < 0.01$), suggesting that extraverts are inclined towards rapid information processing, attention shifting, and avoiding prolonged focus on a single object.

It is likely that extraverts are more prone to making quick and potentially riskier decisions compared to introverts. Comparing this with our previous findings [18] where

Table 1. The description fixation metrics.

Metrics	Description
very_short	with a duration of 0–90 ms
express	with a duration of 90–150 ms
cognitive	with a duration of 150–900 ms
long	with a duration of more than 900 ms
sum_count	fixation duration count
mean_dur	mean fixation duration
count	fixation count
median_dur	median fixation duration
std_dur	standard deviation of fixation duration
min_dur	minimal fixation duration
max_dur	maximal fixation duration

Table 2. List of identified correlations between personality types and fixation metrics (E – extraversion, A – agreeableness, C – conscientiousness, N – neuroticism, O – openness to experience).

	E	A	C	N	O
very_short	−0.49	−0.15	0.5	−0.25	0.16
express	−0.34	0.0	0.44	−0.1	0.1
cognitive	0.71*	0.15	−0.53	0.16	−0.07
long	−0.71*	0.34	0.44	0.1	−0.13
sum_count	−0.49	−0.15	0.5	−0.25	0.16
mean_dur	0.55	0.11	−0.49	0.09	−0.11
count	−0.47	−0.05	0.59	−0.27	0.19
median_dur	0.52	0.12	−0.43	0.13	−0.15
std_dur	0.47	0.13	−0.44	0.19	−0.15
min_dur	0.69*	−0.11	−0.3	0.09	−0.14
max_dur	0.14	−0.83**	−0.19	−0.22	0.24

introverts were shown to experience significant discomfort with changes occurring to their character, it can be concluded that introverts are less inclined to make fast and risky decisions. Furthermore, these findings align with other research indicating that extraverts tend to perform more effectively in tasks involving rapid information scanning.

For the "Agreeableness" personality type, a negative correlation was found with maximum fixation duration ($r = -0.83^{**}$, $p < 0.01$). Individuals with this personality type, oriented toward flexible social interaction, tend to quickly scan their surroundings in order to respond promptly to any changes. This aligns with the results from our previous study, where the "Agreeableness" type was associated with a dynamic activation of the sympathetic nervous system, responsible for active behavior, in response to variability in the character's health points. Essentially, this suggests that individuals of this type, who are inclined toward cooperation and focused on the values and interests of others, become more engaged during active gameplay, solving survival challenges for the character in difficult circumstances. Their fixations are shorter, indicating rapid scanning of the surrounding environment for quicker decision-making. People of this type avoid prolonged gaze, which reflects flexibility in their decision-making processes. This also goes in line with findings from other studies, which suggest that individuals of this personality type perform better in factual tasks—those involving the search for a specific move, solution, or piece of information.

A limitation of the study was the small sample size; however, the study will be scaled up in future research. Additionally, it is planned to expand the study by analyzing behavioral and gaming patterns in relation to gaming experience.

4 Conclusions

The research presents connections between the personality type and cognitive features. Individuals with higher "Extraversion" score showed more active and fluent eye-gaze behavior, confirming the tendency of better performance in tasks that require prompt reactions and information processing – as ones exposed by FPS games. As for participants with higher "Agreeableness" score, they engaged less in deep information processing and expose fewer durable fixations, allowing them to adopt a more flexible and agile behavioral approach. Considering the fact that first-person shooters are characterized by fast-paced and dynamic gameplay, it can be assumed that players with higher scores on "Agreeableness" and "Extraversion" are more likely to show better performance in such games.

Given that players may experience identical game content in fundamentally ways, we could possibly suggest that games could be customized or dynamically adapted to accommodate individual player profiles. Such personalization has the potential to increase enjoyment, foster engagement, and enhance accessibility across diverse user groups. The data on cognitive information processing could be valuable for integrating into the development and testing of video games to create personalized gaming experiences, especially in the context of incorporating eye-tracking technologies as controls in videogames.

References

1. Digital 2024: Global Overview Report. https://datareportal.com/reports/digital-2024-global-overview-report. Accessed 28 Mar 2025
2. Kowal, M., Toth, A.J., Exton, C., Campbell, M.J.: Different cognitive abilities displayed by action video gamers and non-gamers. Comput. Hum. Behav. **88**, 255–262 (2018). https://doi.org/10.1016/j.chb.2018.07.010
3. Bediou, B., Adams, D.M., Mayer, R.E., Tipton, E., Green, C.S., Bavelier, D.: Meta-analysis of action video game impact on perceptual, attentional, and cognitive skills. Psychol. Bull. **144**, 77–110 (2018). https://doi.org/10.1037/bul0000130

4. Sundstedt, V., Stavrakis, E., Wimmer, M., Reinhard, E.: A psychophysical study of fixation behavior in a computer game. In: Proceedings of the 5th symposium on Applied perception in graphics and visualization, pp. 43–50. ACM, Los Angeles (2008). https://doi.org/10.1145/1394281.1394288
5. Wang, H., Yang, J., Hu, M., Tang, J., Yu, W.: A comparative analysis for eye movement characteristics between professional and non-professional players in FIFA eSports game. Displays **81**, 102599 (2024). https://doi.org/10.1016/j.displa.2023.102599
6. Fooken, J., Schaffner, M.: The role of psychological and physiological factors in decision making under risk and in a dilemma. Front. Behav. Neurosci. **10** (2016). https://doi.org/10.3389/fnbeh.2016.00002
7. Dam, L.: Primary social emotions toward a non-player character: an examination of moral decision-making in video games. Health New Media Res. **6**, 189–201 (2022). https://doi.org/10.22720/hnmr.2022.6.2.222
8. Berkovsky, S., et al.: Detecting personality traits using eye-tracking data. In: Proceedings of the 2019 CHI Conference on Human Factors in Computing Systems, pp. 1–12. ACM, Glasgow (2019). https://doi.org/10.1145/3290605.3300451
9. Al-Samarraie, H., Sarsam, S.M., Alzahrani, A.I., Alalwan, N., Masood, M.: The role of personality characteristics in informing our preference for visual presentation: an eye movement study. AIS. **8**, 709–719 (2016). https://doi.org/10.3233/AIS-160399
10. Le Bras, T., Allibe, B., Doré-Mazars, K.: The way we look at an image or a webpage can reveal personality traits. Sci. Rep. **14**, 15488 (2024). https://doi.org/10.1038/s41598-024-62210-z
11. Al-Samarraie, H., Eldenfria, A., Dawoud, H.: The impact of personality traits on users' information-seeking behavior. Inf. Process. Manage. **53**, 237–247 (2017). https://doi.org/10.1016/j.ipm.2016.08.004
12. Sutin, A.R., Stephan, Y., Luchetti, M., Terracciano, A.: Five-factor model personality traits and cognitive function in five domains in older adulthood. BMC Geriatr. **19**, 343 (2019). https://doi.org/10.1186/s12877-019-1362-1
13. Stanek, K.C., Ones, D.S.: Meta-analytic relations between personality and cognitive ability. Proc. Natl. Acad. Sci. **120**, e2212794120 (2023). https://doi.org/10.1073/pnas.2212794120
14. Hodent, C., Brathwaite, B.: The Gamer's Brain: How Neuroscience and UX Can Impact Video Game Design. CRC Press, Taylor & Francis Group, Boca Raton/London/New York (2018)
15. Khromov, A.B.: Five-factor personality questionnaire: guidelines [Pyatifactorny oprosnik lichnosty: uchebno-metodicheskoe posobie], 24 p. Kurgan State University Publishing House, Kurgan (2010). (in Russian)
16. Pinchbeck, D.: Doom: Scarydarkfast. University of Michigan Press, Ann Arbor (2013). https://doi.org/10.3998/lvg.11878639.0001.001
17. Samsonovich Alexei V.: Toward a unified catalog of implemented cognitive architectures. In: Frontiers in Artificial Intelligence and Applications. IOS Press (2010). https://doi.org/10.3233/978-1-60750-661-4-195
18. Viakhireva, V., Brueva, A., Zaladina, A., Kuznetsova, N., Demareva, V.: Understanding player experience: the role of psychological profile in gaming. In: Samsonovich, A.V., Liu, T. (eds.) BICA 2024. SCI, vol. 477, pp. 416–425. Springer, Cham (2024). https://doi.org/10.1007/978-3-031-76516-2_42

Cognitive Complexity of User Inquiries in Digital Environments: Impact on Operator Response Quality

Valeriia Demareva[1](✉), Sergei Repjev[2], and Dmitry Scherbakov[2]

[1] Lobachevsky State University, Nizhny Novgorod 603022, Russia
valeriia.demareva@fsn.unn.ru
[2] Deeray, Nizhny Novgorod 603003, Russia

Abstract. This study explores the relationship between the cognitive complexity of user inquiries and the quality of operator responses in social media. The research is based on an analysis of 2,498 user inquiries related to housing and utility issues, published on vk.com and ok.ru. Cognitive complexity of inquires was assessed using linguistic metrics, including the Gunning Fog Index, average word length, lexical and part-of-speech diversity coefficients. Based on these metrics, the texts were classified according to complexity levels. Regression analysis revealed significant associations between cognitive complexity of inquiries and operator response quality. ANOVA and post-hoc analysis demonstrated that inquiries with short words but complex grammatical structures were more likely to result in low-quality responses. These findings contribute to a better understanding of how inquiry complexity affects communication efficiency in digital environments and can inform the development of automation strategies and user service improvements.

Keywords: Cognitive Complexity · Cognitive Load · Inquires · Customer · Operator · Response Quality · Digital Environment

1 Introduction

In the digital age, users of online environments encounter textual materials of varying complexity daily. From news articles to technical documentation, the cognitive load imposed by texts affects comprehension, memory retention, and decision-making [1, 2]. This issue is particularly relevant in digital services, where operators must process and respond to user inquiries that often serve a functional and practical purpose. The quality of operator responses plays a crucial role in shaping users' perceptions of the organization or institution they represent.

Research in cognitive psychology and linguistics suggests that text characteristics such as sentence length, lexical diversity, and syntactic complexity influence the cognitive effort required for information processing [3, 4]. Higher text complexity can lead to comprehension difficulties, increased cognitive load, and reduced trust in the information provided [5]. In digital communication, this implies that the complexity of a

M. Bakaev et al. (Eds.): IMS 2025, CCIS 2671, pp. 222–232, 2026.
https://doi.org/10.1007/978-3-032-04958-2_17

user's inquiry may impact an operator's ability to interpret it correctly and formulate an adequate response. However, the extent of this influence remains insufficiently explored.

This study aims to examine the relationship between the cognitive complexity of user inquiries and the quality of operator responses. Various linguistic complexity metrics are analyzed to assess their impact on response quality. Based on previous research and the study's objectives, the following hypothesis was proposed: higher cognitive complexity of user inquiries negatively affects the quality of operator responses.

The following sections provide a review of existing research, describe the methodology of analysis, present the results, and discuss their implications.

2 Related Work

Research on cognitive load in textual communication has been gaining increasing attention, particularly in the context of user experience, digital interaction, and human information processing. Previous studies have established that linguistic complexity influences cognitive load, making it more difficult to comprehend and evaluate textual content [6]. Furthermore, the cognitive complexity of an individual's contextual environment can increase the complexity of their speech [7] and affect cognitive load during task performance [8].

In digital communication, content readability plays a crucial role in user engagement and information retention. Readability metrics such as the Gunning Fog Index [9] and Flesch-Kincaid Readability Scores are widely used to assess text complexity [10]. Research suggests that texts with higher readability demand less cognitive effort and enhance comprehension [11]. However, traditional readability measures may not fully capture the cognitive demands of digital texts [12].

A particularly challenging area is the analysis of user-generated content on social media, where messages vary significantly in lexical complexity, sentence structure, and syntactic diversity. In a study [13], it was found that the characteristics of social media posts influence engagement and awareness. Analyzing 135 fashion retail posts on Facebook, the study showed that longer texts, a higher number of hashtags, and increased readability (as measured by the Gunning Fog Index) positively correlated with user engagement and awareness. Posts containing more than 31 words or 321 characters, along with multiple hashtags, tended to perform better. Additionally, research in this area suggests that information richness strengthens the connections between retrospective and prospective information processing and the breadth of public engagement [14]. Moreover, emotional tone in social media posts has been shown to increase user engagement [15].

Cognitive load plays a significant role in text processing within digital environments. Modern digital services are not only platforms for communication, entertainment, and commerce but also serve as channels for citizen-institution interactions, including public inquiries directed at regional authorities. A key aspect of this research is the analysis of government responses to user inquiries on social media. Among all citizen appeals to authorities and state institutions, housing and public utilities consistently rank among the most frequent topics [16].

On digital platforms, there is a growing interest in predictive models assessing the relationship between linguistic complexity and response characteristics. Machine learning and deep learning techniques are increasingly being applied to analyze cognitive load in texts [17]. Identifying which aspects of textual complexity serve as predictors of high-quality responses is crucial.

Despite the significance and extensive study of cognitive load in digital textual materials, most research focuses on user perception of cognitive load in digital environments. This study expands the existing literature by examining how different linguistic complexity metrics of citizen inquiries to regional authorities relate to the quality of operator responses in social media. Unlike studies centered on user satisfaction with operator responses, this research evaluates the objective quality of responses provided by operators. Special attention is given to the relationship between the cognitive complexity of inquiries and the quality of responses given by operators.

3 Materials and Methods

3.1 Data and Sample

This study utilized textual data comprising posts and comments from the social media platforms vk.com and ok.ru, focusing on issues related to housing and communal services (HCS) in the Nizhny Novgorod region. The procedure for selecting user inquiries followed the steps outlined in Fig. 1.

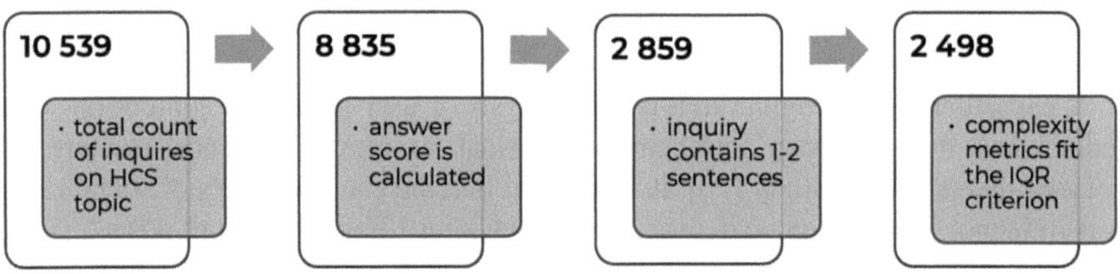

Fig. 1. Flow chat of data selection

The IQR criterion ensured that all computed cognitive complexity metrics of an inquiry fell within:

$$(Q1 - 1.5 * IQR) - (Q3 + 1.5 * IQR),$$

where:

- $Q1$ – first quartile boundary of the distribution,
- $Q3$ – third quartile boundary of the distribution,
- IQR – interquartile range.

As a result, the final dataset consisted of 2,498 inquiries published between 2024-05-01 and 2024-12-18. Cognitive complexity metrics were computed for each text.

3.2 Preprocessing and Calculation of Cognitive Complexity Metrics

Various linguistic metrics were employed to assess the cognitive complexity of user inquiries. Data processing was performed in the Jupyter Notebook environment using the libraries 'nltk', 'pymorphy3', 'textstat,' and 're'. The preprocessing pipeline included the following steps:

1. Removal of special characters, emojis, and extra spaces using regular expressions (re).
2. Tokenization of texts into words and sentences using nltk.tokenize.
3. Stop-word removal based on the Russian stop-word list (https://raw.githubusercontent.com/stopwords-iso/stopwords-ru/master/stopwords-ru.txt).
4. Lemmatization using the pymorphy3 morphological analyzer to bring words to their base forms.

The following cognitive complexity metrics were calculated:

1. Gunning Fog Index (GFI) was calculated using 'textstat' library as (1) where complex words are defined as those containing three or more syllables (excluding proper nouns and short suffix-based forms).

$$GFI = 0.4 * \left(\frac{Words\ count}{Sentences\ count} + 100 * \frac{Complex\ words\ count}{Words\ count}\right) \tag{1}$$

2. Average Word Length (AWL) was calculated using formula (2):

$$AWL = \frac{\sum_{i=1}^{Words\ count} Word_i length}{Words\ count} \tag{2}$$

3. Type-Token Ratio (TTR) measures lexical diversity as (3) where unique words were identified based on their lemmatized forms.

$$TTR = \frac{Unique\ words\ count}{Words\ count} \tag{3}$$

4. Part-of-Speech Diversity (PoSD) was evaluated by analyzing text with 'pymorphy3' to determine the variety of parts of speech (PoS), calculated as (4).

$$PoSD = \frac{Unique\ PoS\ count}{PoS\ count} \tag{4}$$

Each metric was computed separately for every user inquiry. All complexity metrics (GFI, AWL, TTR, and PoSD) were standardized using z-scores and categorized into three levels:

- Low level: $z < -0.5$
- Medium level: $-0.5 < z < 0.5$
- High level: $z > 0.5$

This classification allowed for comparative analysis of texts with varying degrees of complexity. The computed values were used in subsequent analyses to examine the relationship between cognitive complexity and response quality.

3.3 Analysis Methodology

To investigate the relationship between textual cognitive load and response perception, regression modeling and ANOVA were performed in RStudio (v. 2024.04.2 + 764). The dependent variable was the automated evaluation of operator answer quality (AS) to user inquiries. The scoring algorithm assigned an initial score of 10 points per response, deducting points based on identified error categories:

- Minor flaws (1–2 points deduction): lack of greeting, politeness, use of template phrases.
- Moderate errors (4 points deduction): redirection, insufficient information, use of abbreviations or complex terms.
- Severe errors (6 points deduction): lack of specificity, inappropriate clarifications, formal or indirect responses.
- No response (10 points deduction): failure to address the issue, lack of solution proposals, or missing final response.

The regression model used the following predictors:

$$AS \sim AWL\_level * GFI\_level * TTR\_level * PoSD\_level$$

ANOVA was conducted to assess the significance of predictors and their interactions. Post-hoc analysis using Tukey's Honest Significant Difference (HSD) test was performed to identify significant differences between categorical predictor levels.

4 Results

Table 1 presents the significant predictors of the regression model.

Table 1. Significant predictors of the regression model.

Predictors	Estimate	Standard Error	t	p-value
(Intercept)	8.46	0.55	15.32	<0.001
GFI_level[Medium]:TTR_level:PoSD_level	5.03	2.53	1.99	0.047

The regression analysis demonstrated that the most significant predictor is the interaction GFI_level[Medium]:TTR_level:PoSD_level, with a coefficient $\beta = 5.03$ ($SE = 2.53$, $t = 1.99$, $p = 0.047$).

Table 2 summarizes the results of the ANOVA.

The ANOVA results indicated that answer evaluation depends on TTR_level ($F = 3.24$, $p = 0.032$). Additionally, the interactions AWL_level:GFI_level ($F = 2.52$, $p = 0.039$) and AWL_level:PoSD_level ($F = 3.50$, $p = 0.007$) were also found to be significant.

Post-hoc analysis results are shown in Fig. 2.

Table 2. ANOVA: Significant factors.

Factor	Df	Sum Sq	Mean Sq	F	p-value
TTR_level	2	27.21	13.60	3.43	0.032
AWL_level:GFI_level	4	39.92	9.98	2.52	0.039
AWL_level:PoSD_level	4	55.55	13.89	3.50	0.007

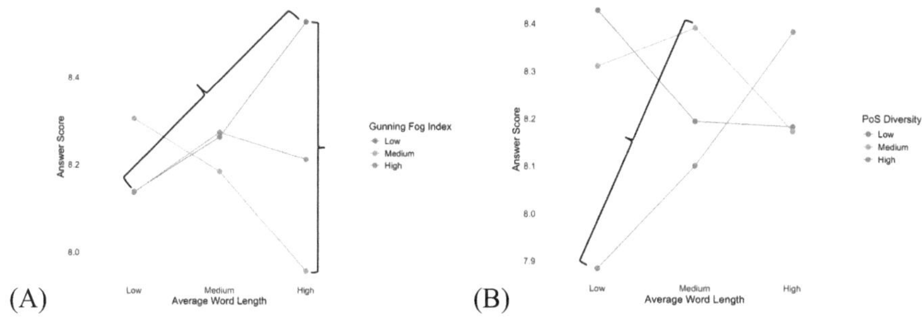

Fig. 2. Mean values of Answer Score. (A) In relation to AWL_level (Average Word Length) and GFI_level (Gunning Fox Index). (B) In relation to AWL_level and PoSD_level (PoS Diversity). Curly brackets identify significant differences ($p < 0.05$).

The post-hoc pairwise analysis revealed that answer quality scores were higher for messages with long words and high GFI_level than for those with short words and low GFI_level ($p = 0.047$) and for messages with long words and medium GFI_level ($p = 0.034$). Additionally, the answer quality score was found to be higher for messages with medium word length and medium PoSD_level compared to messages with short words and high PoSD_level ($p = 0.021$).

Based on the conducted analysis, an algorithm was developed to automatically identify messages that are likely to receive low-quality responses. The algorithm relies on the significant predictors identified in the regression model and post-hoc analysis (see Tables 1 and 2, Fig. 2). The following unfavorable combinations were identified:

- Short words (Low AWL) combined with low GFI (Low GFI_level).
- Short words (Low AWL) combined with high part-of-speech diversity (High PoSD_level).

To determine whether a new message belongs to a risk group, threshold values of cognitive complexity metrics are checked. If a message satisfies one of the following conditions:

- Low AWL + Low GFI_level,
- Low AWL + High PoSD_level,

it is assigned the label "Risk of Low-Quality Response".

For ranking messages based on their likelihood of receiving a poor response, a Risk Score index was introduced, calculated as the sum of points for unfavorable characteristics:

- Low AWL – 1 point
- Low GFI_level – 1 point
- High PoSD_level – 1 point

If the total Risk Score ≥ 2, the message requires special attention.

Thus, the proposed algorithm enables the automatic classification of messages that require increased attention. This can be used to improve response quality and optimize the interaction system between users and operators.

5 Discussion

The obtained results confirm that the characteristics of the inquiry texts significantly influence the quality assessment of the operator's response, supporting the hypothesis proposed in this study. In particular, the interaction between the Gunning Fog index, lexical diversity, and syntactic diversity had the greatest impact on the quality assessment. This finding emphasizes the importance of text complexity features in the perception of information content and clarity, aligning with previous research in cognitive linguistics.

Analysis of the factors revealed that lexical diversity (TTR_level) has a significant impact on the evaluation of the response. This finding aligns with previous studies, which suggest that a more diverse vocabulary can increase the perceived complexity of a text, while simultaneously making it more expressive and content-rich [3, 4]. These results echo findings from cognitive psychology and linguistics, which emphasize the role of lexical variety in cognitive processing [5].

Moreover, the interaction between average word length (AWL_level) and the Gunning Fog index (GFI_level) proved statistically significant. This suggests that not only word length, but also the overall level of text complexity, plays a crucial role in response evaluation. Long words, when combined with a high Gunning Fog index, were associated with higher ratings, while short words coupled with a low Gunning Fog index resulted in lower ratings. These findings resonate with research indicating that higher text complexity can lead to comprehension difficulties and increased cognitive load [6, 7].

The interaction between average word length and syntactic diversity also proved significant. Post hoc analysis showed that inquiries with short words and high syntactic diversity received lower ratings, likely due to the high cognitive load associated with processing diverse syntactic structures. This is consistent with the idea that increased linguistic complexity requires greater cognitive effort for processing, which may hinder comprehension and response formulation [8, 9].

The findings of this study have important practical implications. Firstly, they highlight the need to optimize the complexity of user inquiries:

- Short words combined with a low Gunning Fog index may lead to a poor-quality response from the operator.

- High syntactic variability with short words may also lead to a poor-quality response, likely due to the difficulty the operator faces in understanding the inquiry.

These insights were used to develop an algorithm for automatically identifying inquiries at high risk of receiving low-quality responses. The implementation of such an algorithm in user support systems and chatbots will enable the early identification of "complex" inquiries, allowing operators to allocate more resources or adjust their approach to these more challenging requests.

By addressing the cognitive load imposed by linguistic complexity, this research expands on existing studies, offering new insights into how digital communication can be optimized for better interaction and engagement. The relationship between linguistic complexity and response quality in digital environments has been underexplored, and this study contributes to filling this gap, particularly in the context of governmental responses to user inquiries on social media platforms [10, 11].

In addition to its theoretical contributions, the study offers practical value for designing responsive and intelligent communication systems in both public and commercial sectors. The findings can be used to enhance human-in-the-loop moderation systems and automated message triage tools by enabling early detection of cognitively complex user inquiries. For instance, in service platforms that rely on chatbot-operator handover mechanisms, the proposed algorithm can serve as a trigger to route inquiries with high complexity to human specialists instead of automated systems, thus minimizing miscommunication and improving user satisfaction.

Moreover, the approach can be adapted for different domains, such as healthcare, education, and transportation, where user queries often contain specialized terminology and vary greatly in tone, urgency, and structure. Customizing the classification algorithm to detect contextual difficulty (e.g., emotionally charged messages, vague formulations) could further enhance its accuracy. This highlights the flexibility of the method in addressing a broad range of real-world communication challenges.

6 Study Limitations

Despite the significant results obtained, the study has several limitations.

First, the analysis was conducted on a sample of inquiries collected from only two social networks (vk.com and ok.ru) and focused on a limited topic—housing and utilities problems in one region, containing 1–2 sentences. This reduces the generalizability of the findings to other platforms, regions, and topics of user inquiries.

Second, a set of linguistic metrics (GFI, AWL, TTR, PoSD) was used to assess the cognitive complexity of texts. While these metrics are well-established and offer insights into surface-level textual features, they do not account for deeper semantic or pragmatic aspects of communication. For instance, inquiries containing emotional language, sarcasm, or implicit assumptions may present a high cognitive load despite being syntactically simple. Likewise, domain-specific vocabulary or urgency markers may affect how an operator interprets and responds to a message.

Third, the categorization of text complexity levels (low, medium, high) was based on the z-transformation of individual metrics, which is statistically justified but may not always fully reflect real differences in perceived difficulty across users and contexts. These classifications may overlook messages that combine moderate values across multiple indicators but still impose high cognitive demands when interpreted holistically.

Given these limitations, future work should explore the integration of semantic features into complexity assessment. This may include affective computing (e.g., sentiment polarity, emotion detection), contextual embeddings from large language models (e.g., BERT), and pragmatic cues such as politeness, intent, and formality. Multimodal approaches incorporating non-textual elements (e.g., images, attached documents, formatting) should also be considered.

Further research is planned to expand the study by incorporating data from other platforms, analyzing a broader range of factors, and conducting experiments to refine the relationship between the cognitive complexity of inquiries and the effectiveness of responses.

7 Future Research Directions

Building on the findings of this study, future research may focus on expanding and refining the model to account for a wider range of factors influencing response quality. One direction involves incorporating psycholinguistic variables such as emotional valence, subjectivity, and politeness markers, which are known to affect both the perceived complexity of a message and the quality of interpersonal communication. Sentiment analysis and affective computing approaches may be integrated with structural linguistic metrics to provide a more comprehensive evaluation.

Another area of exploration is the application of transformer-based language models (e.g., BERT, RoBERTa) to better capture nuanced semantic structures in user inquiries. These models could be used to augment the classification of cognitive load by identifying implicit cues in syntax and discourse, potentially surpassing traditional readability metrics. Incorporating such models would also allow for more accurate prediction of response relevance and tone.

Furthermore, extending the study to multilingual datasets and diverse service domains will help assess the generalizability of the findings. Evaluating how language-specific syntactic and morphological features influence operator response patterns can provide valuable insights for localization and platform-specific design. Finally, experimental testing of the model's implementation in live digital support systems—particularly its integration into chatbot interfaces—can yield critical evidence for its real-time effectiveness and operational scalability.

8 Conclusion

The study demonstrated that the cognitive complexity of inquiry texts significantly influences the perceived quality of operators' responses. We found that factors such as the complexity of the inquiry, lexical diversity, and syntactic structure can either enhance or diminish response quality. In particular, inquiries characterized by short words and complex grammatical structures tend to elicit lower-quality responses from operators.

These findings underscore the importance of clarity and structural coherence in texts for effective communication in digital environments. They can inform the development of guidelines for optimizing inquiry phrasing, thereby improving the quality of interactions on digital platforms. Future research will examine additional factors, such as the context in which inquiries are made and individual differences in text perception.

The study's results have several practical applications. First, they can support the creation of systems that flag high cognitive load inquiries, using the developed model for identifying complex texts, thereby ensuring that operators give these messages special attention. Second, they can inform the design of supplementary modules for auto-response systems, enabling more accurate replies or rerouting particularly complex inquiries for manual handling.

These insights also open up new possibilities for advancing the integration of cognitive science and natural language processing in digital interaction frameworks. By providing a scalable, language-aware, and user-sensitive approach, the proposed methodology can contribute to the design of adaptive communication platforms that optimize resource allocation and improve citizen experience across digital channels. Such integration is particularly timely as digital service environments increasingly rely on hybrid human-AI systems to deliver consistent, contextually appropriate responses.

Beyond the current application, the model developed in this study holds potential for broader implementation in hybrid communication systems that combine automated and human responses. With minimal adaptation, the risk classification algorithm can be embedded into customer service platforms, allowing for dynamic rerouting of inquiries or automatic suggestion of response templates based on complexity. This would not only improve user satisfaction but also reduce operator cognitive overload and burnout in high-volume communication environments.

From a policy perspective, the findings support the need for communication guidelines and staff training programs tailored to the processing of cognitively complex content. In government and municipal services, where prompt and accurate responses are essential for citizen trust, such optimization can directly contribute to institutional transparency and accountability.

Lastly, the integration of complexity-aware tools into conversational agents and smart interfaces opens new avenues for personalized and context-sensitive digital services. By using data-driven insights into language structure and cognitive effort, digital systems can become more attuned to users' needs, ultimately creating a more equitable and effective information environment.

References

1. Sweller, J.: Cognitive load during problem solving: effects on learning. Cogn. Sci. **12**(2), 257–285 (1988). https://doi.org/10.1207/s15516709cog1202_4
2. Paas, F., van Merriënboer, J.J.G.: Variability of worked examples and transfer of geometrical problem-solving skills: a cognitive-load approach. J. Educ. Psychol. **86**(1), 122–133 (1994). https://doi.org/10.1037/0022-0663.86.1.122
3. Kintsch, W.: Comprehension: A Paradigm for Cognition, 2nd edn. Cambridge University Press, Cambridge (1998)

4. Graesser, A.C., McNamara, D.S., Louwerse, M.M., Cai, Z.: Coh-Metrix: analysis of text on cohesion and language. Behav. Res. Methods Instrum. Comput. **36**, 193–202 (2004). https://doi.org/10.3758/BF03195564
5. Platonov, K., Svetlov, K.: Readability of posts and user engagement in online communities of government executive bodies. In: Meiselwitz, G. (eds.) HCII 2021. LNCS, vol. 12774, pp. 323–340. Springer, Cham (2021). https://doi.org/10.1007/978-3-030-77626-8_22
6. Lee, J.: Task complexity, cognitive load, and L1 speech. Appl. Linguis. **40**(3), 506–539 (2019). https://doi.org/10.1093/applin/amx054
7. Khwaja, M.A., Chen, F., Marcus, N.: Using language complexity to measure cognitive load for adaptive interaction design. In: Proceedings of the 15th International Conference on Intelligent User Interfaces, pp. 333–336. Association for Computing Machinery, New York (2010)
8. Tremblay, M.L., Rethans, J.J., Dolmans, D.: Task complexity and cognitive load in simulation-based education: a randomised trial. Med. Educ. **57**(2), 161–169 (2023). https://doi.org/10.1111/medu.14941
9. Gunning, R.: The Technique of Clear Writing. McGraw-Hill, New York (1952)
10. Kincaid, J.P., Fishburne, R.P., Rogers, R.L., Chissom, B.S.: Derivation of new readability formulas (automated readability index, fog count, and flesch reading ease formula) for Navy enlisted personnel. Research Branch Report 8–75. Chief of Naval Technical Training, Naval Air Station Memphis (1975). Accessed 15 Oct 2024
11. Singh, S., Jamal, A., Qureshi, F.: Readability metrics in patient education: where do we innovate? Clin. Pract. **14**(6), 2341–2349 (2024). https://doi.org/10.3390/clinpract14060183
12. Sheppard, S.M., et al.: One font doesn't fit all: the influence of digital text personalization on comprehension in child and adolescent readers. Educ. Sci. **13**(9), 864 (2023). https://doi.org/10.3390/educsci13090864
13. Gkikas, D.C., Tzafilkou, K., Theodoridis, P.K., Garmpis, A., Gkikas, M.C.: How do text characteristics impact user engagement in social media posts: Modeling content readability, length, and hashtags number in Facebook. Int. J. Inf. Manag. Data Insights **2**, 100067 (2022)
14. Li, K., Zhou, C., Luo, X.R., Benitez, J., Liao, Q.: Impact of information timeliness and richness on public engagement on social media during COVID-19 pandemic: an empirical investigation based on NLP and machine learning. Decis. Support. Syst. **162**, 113752 (2022). https://doi.org/10.1016/j.dss.2022.113752
15. Kite, J., Foley, B.C., Grunseit, A.C., Freeman, B.: Please like me: Facebook and public health communication. PLoS ONE **11**(9), e0162765 (2016). https://doi.org/10.1371/journal.pone.0162765
16. Citizens' appeals to the Government of the Russian Federation received in May 2024. http://services.government.ru/overviews/51834/. Accessed May 2024
17. Santucci, V., Santarelli, F., Forti, L., Spina, S.: Automatic classification of text complexity. Appl. Sci. **10**(20), 7285 (2020). https://doi.org/10.3390/app10207285

Using Self-created Video Tutorials to Enhance Self-regulated Learning Strategies for Adaptive Digital Language Learning

Julia Edeleva[1(✉)], Svetlana Leonova[2], Anastasiia Brueva[3], Elena Kostyleva[4], and Aleksandra Meshcheriakova[3]

[1] Martin-Luther-University Halle-Wittenberg, 06108 Halle, Germany
yulia.edeleva@germanistik.uni-halle.de
[2] Higher School of Economics, Nizhny Novgorod 603155, Russia
[3] Lobachevsky State University, Nizhny Novgorod 603022, Russia
{brueva,ameshcheryakova}@unn.ru
[4] Nizhny Novgorod State University of Engineering and Economics, Knyaginino 606340, Russia

Abstract. The utility of self-regulated learning strategies (e.g., whether the learners prefer to use tables, formulate rules, or develop working examples) is essential for grammar acquisition in a second or foreign language (L2). In the current study, we consider the potential of *SimpleShow* as a digital tool to enhance self-regulated learning strategies (SRL; specifically, cognitive and metacognitive strategies) via self-generated video tutorials that feature selected grammatical phenomena. 26 student L2 learners of German were requested to generate *SimpleShow* video tutorials explaining the use of adjective inflection in a German noun phrase. Their mastery of adjective declension was screened in a grammar test before and after they created video tutorials in the pre-/post design. We analyzed both the knowledge growth experienced by the students and the error patterns that they exhibited. Additionally, the SRL strategies that the students used in their self-explanations were annotated. The results generally confirm the effectiveness of *SimpleShow* as a tool to enhance metacognitive reflection leading to significant knowledge growth, particularly with less well-achieving students. We discuss the implications of our results for generating adaptive learning pathways in a digital environment.

Keywords: Metacognitive Strategies · L2 Learning · German as an Additional Language · Self-Explanations · Video Tutorials

1 Introduction

Language pedagogy, like any other pedagogy, follows major foundational principles in education. With technological advances, the field constantly demands innovative and adaptive approaches both for classroom and for extracurricular learning. A prominent global trend in language teaching involves the development of intelligent language tutoring systems (ILTs) leveraging the capabilities of artificial intelligence [1]. The widespread adoption of AI technologies brings about a growing awareness of societal [2], ethical [3], psychological [4], and cognitive [5, 6] threats and potential opportunities.

M. Bakaev et al. (Eds.): IMS 2025, CCIS 2671, pp. 233–244, 2026.
https://doi.org/10.1007/978-3-032-04958-2_18

The cognitive dimension plays an important role in designing intelligent language tutoring systems as a personalized adaptable solution. Due to the salient role of cognitive and metacognitive strategies in learning, numerous attempts have been made within the framework of Intelligent Language Tutoring Systems (ILTS) to foster and enhance their acquisition [7, 8]. For example, intentional development of metacognitive strategies represents a well-established and traditionally recognized approach in critical thinking education [9–11]. Besides the learning experience tailored to the needs of specific learners, learners can develop interdisciplinary critical thinking skills through a conscious reflection on their learning process, which would enhance their general learning abilities [6]. Yet not so many attempts to promote metacognitive reflection have been implemented in the field of second language education despite the obvious benefits documented in empirical studies. In the current study, we attempt to estimate the viability of self-generated video tutorials as a digital solution to promote metacognitive reflection through and for second language learning.

The differentiation between cognitive and metacognitive strategies in learning and specifically in language learning remains a contentious issue. Numerous scholarly works do not separate between the two [12]. This ambiguity stems from the inherent difficulty to isolate their discrete effects on the learning progress [13]. Conventionally, cognitive strategies are defined as those directly involved in processing learning materials, i.e., in activities such as classification, rote memorization, and identification of key concepts in a specific discipline. Conversely, metacognitive strategies are understood as processes regulating one's own learning, including planning, monitoring, correction, and evaluation [14]. This distinction suggests a hierarchical relationship between the two: cognitive strategies represent lower-order functions and metacognitive strategies represent higher-order functions. Empirical evidence suggests that optimal learning outcomes are achieved through the concurrent application of both cognitive and metacognitive strategies [15]. In the context of second language learning, metacognitive and cognitive strategies are subsumed under self-regulated learning strategies (SRL, 16) on a par with behavioral, motivational, emotional, and contextual factors. It has been confirmed that learners who received instruction in SRL-based strategies indeed outperformed their peers in selected language outputs such as essay writing [17]. They also felt more confident in their skills and were adept at monitoring their learning progress [17]. Previous research also observed a noticeable difference between high- and low-achieving language learners regarding their metacognitive regulatory behavior. High achievers set more demanding metacognitive goals and adapted their metacognition to develop their listening skills in short- and long-term [17].

One method for activating SRL strategies in language learning is offered by the Focus-on-Form (FoF) approach. This pedagogical strategy directs learners' attention to selected features of a linguistic system (e.g., phonology, lexis, sentence structure) within authentic communicative contexts and meaningful tasks, rather than presenting them as isolated rules for rote memorization. Existing research documents potential learning benefits associated with integrating FoF on a par with developing communicative competence [18].

Therefore, the need to create environments that facilitate the application of linguistic knowledge in authentic interactional settings is increasingly recognized, particularly in conjunction with established advantages of FoF. We hypothesize that FoF, in general, promotes the utilization of SRL strategies in language learning, as it fosters a richer experiential landscape for linguistic engagement and encourages learners to reflect on their language experience within a communicative situation. FoF techniques infuse language activities with pragmatic significance and promote a deeper internalization of knowledge in students [19].

Self-explanation represents a promising technique to effectively promote the awareness of SRL strategies during FoF. The self-explanation effect, i.e. the idea that the learners receive a specific educational benefit when explaining worked examples to themselves, has been widely documented in psychological literature [20]. This approach implies that students put themselves into the role of an educator during the self-explanation process. This role-playing exercise is believed to elevate internal comprehension standards and to increase subjective responsibility during task preparation. In its digital implementation, this task might stimulate students' interest as it is novel and can be complemented by multi-modal materials (e.g., voice recordings, graphic illustrations, extended information research, and exemplification). It might also increase learners' awareness of their learning habits to make them transferable onto other educational contexts.

2 Current Study

In the current study, we report the results of an investigation of SRL strategies developed by L2 learners of German for the correct use of adjective inflection in a noun phrase. The learners were asked to deliver self-explanations of one or several adjective declension types in short video tutorials using an online software with a free license for education. Their level of prior knowledge and the knowledge growth regarding German adjective declension were assessed via a fill-in-the-blank test in a pre-/post-design. We hypothesize that an explicit focus on one or several preferred SRL strategies in student-made video tutorials will contribute to a greater adaptability of learning and enhance the acquisition of the grammatical phenomenon in question. Thus, the learners will show an improved performance on the post-test compared to the pre-test.

2.1 Adjective Declension in German

German adjectives can bear an attributive (*kaltes Wetter*/Eng. *cold weather*) or a predicative (*Das Wetter ist kalt.*/Eng. *The weather is cold*) relation to the element that they semantically modify[1]. Used attributively, they precede the respective noun and agree with it morphologically in case, gender and number. Among existing word classes, adjectives in German are characterized by an alternating declension paradigm and can take on a 'strong' or a 'weak' inflection. The strong or the weak inflection is determined by the presence or the absence of a determiner within a noun phrase and the type of this determiner (definite or indefinite). With a definite determiner (e.g., the definite, the demonstrative or the interrogative article *der/Eng. the, dieser/Eng. this, welcher/Eng.*

[1] Cases of the adverbial use of adjectives are disregarded in the current contribution.

which), the adjective takes on a weak inflection *-e* or *-en.* With an indefinite determiner (e.g., the indefinite, the negative or the possessive article *ein*/Eng. *a, kein*/Eng. *no, mein*/Eng. *my*) in certain case forms or absence thereof, the adjective takes on a strong inflection that corresponds to the inflection of the definite article for a particular gender, number, and case. In a noun phrase *ein kalter Abend*/Eng. *a cold evening*, the indefinite determiner *ein*/Eng. *a* is not informative regarding the gender, number, and case of the head noun *Abend*/Eng. *Evening.* The strong inflection on the adjective becomes informative as it conveys the relevant gender, number, and case attributes (masculine, singular, nominative in this case). By contrast, in a noun phrase like *der kalte Abend*/Eng. *the cold evening*, the adjective receives a weak inflection *-e* since the definite determiner *der*/Eng. *the* signposts the gender, number, and case for the adjective *kalt*/Eng. *cold* to agree with the noun *Abend*/Eng. *evening.* Thus, the choice of an inflection follows a compensatory pattern where a noun with an informative determiner is modified by an adjective with a weak inflection. Conversely, a noun with an uninformative determiner is modified by an adjective with a strong inflection.

Adjective declension is a grammar topic which is taught at basic language proficiency levels, i.e., A1-A2 of the Common European Framework of Reference [21], as it is crucial for grammatically correct agreement between the noun and the adjective. In textbooks and grammar reference works in German as an additional language, individual forms are pulled together into inventories of forms (i.e., inflection paradigms). A paradigm for each declension type is usually presented as a summary table. In addition to the strong and the weak declension paradigms, a mixed declension paradigm is also introduced. In the strong declension paradigm, all the case forms receive a strong inflection (e.g., without a determiner). In the weak declension paradigm, all the case forms receive a weak inflection (e.g., in combination with a definite determiner). Mixed declension is characterized by a mixture of strong and weak forms that occur within the paradigm. An overview of paradigms is provided in Table 1.

Table 1. German Adjective Declension Paradigms by Declension Type. The example is provided only for the masculine gender in the singular. In the plural, gender is indistinguishable.

Singular	**Strong** *kalt-er Hund* (name of a German dessert)	**Weak** *der schwarz-e Anzug* (Eng. *The black suit)*	**Mixed** *ein schwarz-er Anzug* (Eng. *a black suit)*
Nominative	kalt-***er*** Hund	der schwarz-***e*** Anzug	ein schwarz-***er*** Anzug
Accusative	kalt-***en*** Hund	den schwarz-***en*** Anzug	einen schwarz-***en*** Anzug
Dative	kalt-***em*** Hund	dem schwarz-***en*** Anzug	einem schwarz-***en*** Anzug
Genitive	kalt-***en*** Hundes	des schwarz-***en*** Anzugs	eines schwarz-***en*** Anzugs
Plural	**Strong** *kalt-e Füße* (Eng. *Cold feet)*	**Weak** *die kalten Füße* (Eng. *The cold feet)*	**Mixed**[2] *keine kalten Füße* (Eng. *no cold feet*)
Nominative	kalt-***e*** Füße	die kalt-***en*** Füße	keine kalt-***en*** Füße

(*continued*)

[2] There is no proper mixed declension in the plural paradigm.

Table 1. (*continued*)

Singular	**Strong** *kalt-er Hund* (name of a German dessert)	**Weak** *der schwarz-e Anzug* (Eng. *The black suit*)	**Mixed** *ein schwarz-er Anzug* (Eng. *a black suit*)
Accusative	kalt-***e*** Füße	die kalt-***en*** Füße	keine kalt-***en*** Füßen
Dative	kalt-***en*** Füßen	den kalt-***en*** Füßen	keinen kalt-***en*** Füßen
Genitive	kalt-***er*** Füße	der kalt-***en*** Füße	keiner kalt-***en*** Füße

3 Participants

26 fourth-year university students (20 females and 6 males with the age range between 19 and 21 years) took part in the study. All of them were native speakers of Russian with no known history of language disorders. At the time of the investigation, the participants were enrolled in an A2-level German-as-an-additional-language course which was delivered as a part of their curriculum. The sessions took place regularly two times a week. The study was administered by the course instructor and integrated smoothly into the course structure. The students completed all the experimental stages subsequently over a period of one month as part of a course credit. Prior to the experiment, they were asked to sign an informed consent form and polled for their demographics. The study was administered in compliance with the Declaration of Helsinki for the investigation of human participants [22].

4 Materials and Methods

To surface the SRL strategies that L2 learners use to master the correct use of German adjective inflection, they were prompted to use *SimpleShow*[3] to create short video tutorials where they explain the grammatical phenomenon. *SimpleShow* is an online software with a free user plan for education. It has an intuitive easy-to-follow interface which allows to create animated videos based on pre-defined scenarios. An advantage of *SimpleShow* compared to similar software types is that it guides the user through individual steps of video production and, thus, enhances their digital literacy skills through video creation.

The materials for the pre- and post-test were customized versions of journal articles adapted from *Deutsch Perfekt*[4], a journal for L2 learners of German. The test was subdivided into three sections. In the first and in the second section, the learners had to fill in the blanks using the correct adjective inflection. The number and type of blanks were not explicitly manipulated; however, care was taken to ensure that the blanks are maximally diverse regarding different inflected forms conditioned by specific constellations

[3] https://simpleshow.com/.

[4] https://shop.zeit-sprachen.de/de_DE/deutsch-perfekt/deutsch-perfekt-abo/deutsch-perfekt-magazin/2123486.html.

of gender, number, and case. In the third section, the participants had to describe a visual image using different adjective declension types. The students had to write 5 sentences for each declension type and use 10 additional inflected forms of their choice.

5 Procedure

The study was broken down into three stages that were administered sequentially in three sessions within one month: a pre-test, a phase of video creation, and a post-test. Prior to the pre-test, the students revised adjective declension as a grammatical phenomenon in German and were made aware of possible strategies that could help to select the correct inflection in each case. Those strategies were: 1) the search for the inflection with the necessary paradigmatic characteristics in a summary table (e.g., inflection *-e* for a masculine, nominative, singular adjective with a definite determiner); 2) cross-paradigm generalizations such as 'the dative case always receives the *-en*-inflection'; 3) logical analysis prompting the learners to consider which of the constituents in a noun phrase becomes informative regarding the number, gender, and case of the corresponding noun.

The learners practiced the use of strategies in a series of activities where they had to either select/reproduce a specific inflection or use different inflected forms of adjectives in a controlled speaking practice activity. The learners found it relatively easy to locate the correct inflection in a summary table containing an overview of forms. The analytical strategy where the learners would trace the 'division of labor' between the determiner and the adjective in a noun phrase was the most difficult to implement.

Then, the pre-test was administered. Pre-tests were graded by the course instructor. They were given out to students so that the students could make notice of their individual errors. Additional practice activities targeting common errors (e.g., the use of adjective inflection in the genitive case) were offered. Subsequently, video creation was administered to the study participants as an out-of-class assignment. The learners were asked to choose one or several declension types and create their own explanation in a video using *SimpleShow*. After the students submitted their videos, the post-test was administered in an in-class session to find out to what extent the grammatical phenomenon had been mastered.

6 Results

6.1 Scoring

The students' responses for each gap were scored as 0 ('incorrect') and 1 ('correct'). The maximum number of points that could be scored was 141 on the pre-test and 133 on the post-test. The difference in the number of points was due to task constraints and the difficulty to create fully identical versions of the test without significant changes to the content of the texts which would compromise their authenticity. Incorrect responses were further classified as to the following four error types[5]: 1) weak declension (e.g.,

[5] Incorrect inflections are marked in bold.

*bei der *jung-**e** Firma*/Eng. *at a young company*; *Sprache des *ander-**er** Menschen/Eng. the language of another person*); 2) strong declension (*trotz *groß-**e** Misserfolges/*Eng. *despite a great failure; *mit groß-**en** Erfolg/* Eng. *with great success)*; 3) mixed declension (*eine *toll-**es** Stadt*/Eng. *a wonderful city; einen magisch-**e** Effekt/*Eng. *a magical effect*). The fourth error type subsumed contextual errors, i.e., those errors that were related to the misassignment of the grammatical gender of the noun. Thus, incorrect adjective inflection in *ein *lecker-**er** Dessert nehmen/*Eng. *to take a tasty dessert* can be explained by the learners' misconception regarding the grammatical gender of *Dessert* (neuter, but not masculine). The contextual error type was also assigned in cases where the learners exchanged the singular for the plural and vice versa. Consider, for example, the error in *jüng-**er** Sportler würden /* Eng. *young sportsmen would.* Though the verb inflection disambiguates '*the sportsmen'* towards the plural form, the learner still selects the adjective in the singular. The points that the learners scored on all the three tasks were added up and the proportion of correct responses was calculated.

6.2 Accuracy Data on the Pre- and the Post-test

Descriptive statistics regarding the participants' accuracy on the pre- and post-test are provided in Table 2. The distribution of target and non-target response patterns is additionally visualized in Fig. 1.

Table 2. Descriptive Statistics for the Proportions of Different Response Types in the Pre- and the Post-Tests.

Pre-Test			Post-Test	
Response Type	Mean	SD	Mean	SD
Correct	0.79	0.15	0.86	0.08
Strong	0.067	0.06	0.043	0.033
Weak	0.058	0.05	0.034	0.037
Mixed	0.033	0.04	0.017	0.025
Contextual	0.032	0.02	0.019	0.017

As can be seen from the table, the learners performed above chance both in the pre- and in the post-test. However, the proportions of correct responses numerically increased from the pre- to the post-test, with a parallel decrease in non-target responses for specific declension types. Non-target responses were most common in the strong followed by the weak declension type. Barely any errors could be observed in the mixed declension and in the contextual category, especially in the post-test.

To statistically evaluate the knowledge growth from the pre- to the post-test, we fitted a Bayesian beta regression model for repeated measures using the brms-package [24] in the R programming environment [25]. Proportions of correct responses were fitted as the dependent variable and the pre-/post-test parameter as a predictor. The random-effects structure was specified as (1 + pre/post-test|participant) incorporating both random intercepts and random slopes. The *adapt_delta* parameter was adjusted to

0.99 to improve sampling efficiency. This adjustment resulted in no observed divergent transitions, and model convergence was confirmed.

The analysis revealed a statistically significant effect of the pre-/post-test on the log-odds of response accuracy (Estimate = 0.18, 95% Credible Interval [0.01, 0.34]). This suggests that the participants showed an improved performance in the post-test, although the credible interval indicates some uncertainty in the magnitude of this effect. The model also indicated substantial variability in both the baseline proportion of response accuracy across participants (SD = 0.83) and in the pre-/post-test effect (SD = 0.27). The correlation between these random effects was estimated to be −0.62, suggesting a tendency for participants with lower baseline accuracy to show a stronger pre-/post-test effect. The precision parameter (phi) was estimated to be 54.75, indicating relatively low variability in the proportions. Convergence diagnostics (Rhat and effective sample sizes) suggested good convergence of the MCMC chains despite a relatively small sample size.

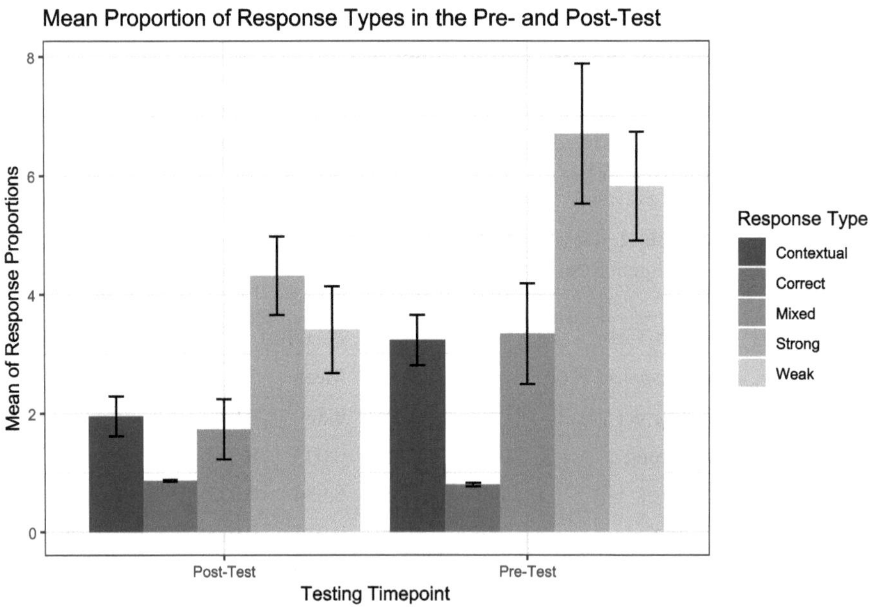

Fig. 1. Mean Proportions of Response Types in the Pre- and the Post-Test. The proportions for non-target responses were multiplied by 100.

6.3 Analysis of Videos

To assess the quality of self-explanations, we attempted to identify the strategies that were reported to distinguish successful students. Specifically, successful learners 1) 'assign meaning to operators by identifying the underlying domain principles (principle-based explanations)', 2) 'assign meaning to operators by identifying the (sub)goals achieved by those operators (explication of goal-operator combinations)', 3) 'anticipate the next solution step (anticipative reasoning)' [23]. An analysis of student-produced videos revealed that the learners exhibited three different types of strategies: 1) strategies related to information structuring (e.g., the ordering of information from general to specific); 2) domain-specific strategies guiding the selection of adjective inflection (the use of a summary table, cross-paradigm generalizations, or the role of a determiner); 3) strategies related to the use of examples (contextual or functional examples). Overall, it could be noticed that the learners first named a general rule which puts an adjective into a specific declension type, followed by the inflection forms that occur in its declension paradigm. Those general principles were later illustrated by concrete examples. The examples were selected to primarily illustrate general principles rather than for the principles to be deduced from examples. Thus, the main selection criterion for the examples was its functional utility to illustrate different declension types or individual inflection forms. Only in two videos across the entire data sample, examples were embedded into a story and connected in a meaningful way.

To give a concrete example, one of the student videos distinguishes between the two adjective declension types (strong, weak) and foregrounds the analysis of inflected forms rather than the determiner type. For the weak declension, the learner reasons: "*Once all the grammatical categories of a word are in place, we use the so-called weak declension. In this case, only two inflections are possible:* ***-e*** *and* ***-en****.*" In case of the strong declension, the student explains that the inflected forms correspond to those of the definite article in the relevant case and gender. The learner further illustrates with an example *ein gutes Beispiel* (Eng. *a good example*) and explains: "*For example, if you say 'ein gutes Beispiel,' the indefinite article here does not indicate gender, case, or number because it lacks a specific inflection. Therefore, the adjective takes on the inflection of the definite article 'das'.*" The example makes evident that the student applies a functional explanation and grounds the choice of an inflection in the presence or absence of a determiner which spells out the grammatical properties of the noun. Such a strategy can be considered more complex compared to a summary table, as it requires the participant to engage in metacognitive reflection.

7 Discussion

In the current study, we tested the effectiveness of self-explanations to foster SRL strategies in L2 learners of German promoting metacognitive reflection under the FoF approach. We estimated the learners' prior knowledge and their knowledge growth after the intervention in two independent tests where students were asked to fill in the blanks with correct adjective inflections. Despite a relatively small data sample (N = 26), our study revealed a significant knowledge growth in the mastery of adjective declension which became evident in accuracy scores on the pre-/post-tests. Generally, the learners performed above chance both in the pre-and in the post-test which might be due to their familiarity with the topic. However, knowledge growth could be observed not only in the proportions of correct responses, but also in the reduction of non-target responses for specific declension types. Thus, it can be concluded that an explicit focus on SRL strategies through self-generated video explanations generally has a positive effect on language learning. It may be particularly beneficial for students who exhibit a low degree of prior knowledge.

In one of the original studies by Chi et al. [20], successful learners differed from the unsuccessful ones not only as to the time that they devoted to learning, but also as to the quality of self-explanations. The quality of self-explanations was significantly related to the learning outcomes even when the study time was kept constant [26]. To trace how the quality of self-explanations might affect our results, we analyzed student-generated videos qualitatively and determined which type of strategy they used to generate self-explanations. In our study, the learners heavily relied on table summaries presenting adjective inflections or explicating the need to check adjective inflection forms against a summary table. Only two videos demonstrated a more functional explanation leveraging the informativity of the determiner. This strategy differentiates between two types of adjective inflection forms (strong vs. weak) rather than three adjective declension types (strong, weak, mixed), which is the way of reasoning in current German linguistics research. This strategy also correlates with the highest accuracy on the test. Overall, analytical strategies lead to better test performance compared to explicit references to summary tables.

The current study offers great potential for optimizing intelligent language tutoring systems towards greater personalization through the enhancement of SRL strategies. It also opens up new perspectives regarding the use of digital tools such as *SimpleShow* in language education demonstrating its efficiency to promote metacognitive reflection under the FoF approach through self-explanations. Expanding our understanding of the nature of SRL strategies is crucial for cultivating students' critical thinking skills, enhancing their overall intellectual adaptability, and, most importantly, promoting the quality and transferability of the knowledge acquired during instruction. Additionally, AI-based language tutoring systems could be trained to promote SRL strategies through tailored FoF exercises.

Further research should focus on developing more systematic ad-hoc criteria to categorize the SRL strategies employed by the students in self-explanations of specific grammatic phenomena. A more fine-grained distinction can be obtained between the cognitive and the metacognitive strategies, revealing the most efficient strategies for L2 learning. It should also be noted that SRL strategies may vary significantly between individuals. Thus, it could also be interesting to survey them in relation to specific learner profiles. Finally, a relatively small sample size restricts the generalizability of our findings. A greater robustness can be achieved through examining a larger participant sample and applying more robust statistical methods provided that the number of responses in the pre- and the post-test is kept constant.

References

1. Nwana, H.S.: Intelligent tutoring systems: an overview. Artif. Intell. Rev. **4**(4), 251–277 (1990)
2. Huertas-Abril, C.A., Palacios-Hidalgo, F.J.: Artificial intelligence–assisted language learning for all in the new global context: threats and opportunities. In: The Routledge Handbook of Endangered and Minority Languages, pp. 355–376. Routledge (2025)
3. Javed, F.: The evolution of artificial intelligence in teaching and learning of english language in higher education: challenges, risks, and ethical considerations. In: The Evolution of Artificial Intelligence in Higher Education: Challenges, Risks, and Ethical Considerations, pp. 249–276 (2024)

4. Zhang, L., Hu, X., Andrasik, F., Feng, S.: Benefits and potential issues for intelligent tutoring systems and pedagogical agents. In: The Frontlines of Artificial Intelligence Ethics, pp. 84–101. Routledge (2022)
5. Luburić, N., et al.: An intelligent tutoring system to support code maintainability skill development. IEEE Trans. Learn. Technol. (2025)
6. Humble, N., Mozelius, P.: Artificial intelligence in education—a promise, a threat or a hype. In: Proceedings of the European Conference on the Impact of Artificial Intelligence and Robotics, pp. 149–156 (2019)
7. Caro Piñeres, M.F.: Metamodel for personalized adaptation of pedagogical strategies using metacognition in Intelligent Tutoring Systems (Doctoral dissertation) (2015)
8. Mudrick, N.V.: Designing adaptive intelligent tutoring systems: fostering cognitive, affective, and metacognitive self-regulated learning processes using multimodal, multichannel process data. North Carolina State University (2018)
9. Ku, K.Y., Ho, I.T.: Metacognitive strategies that enhance critical thinking. Metacogn. Learn. **5**, 251–267 (2010)
10. Magno, C.: The role of metacognitive skills in developing critical thinking. Metacogn. Learn. **5**, 137–156 (2010)
11. Rivas, S.F., Saiz, C., Ossa, C.: Metacognitive strategies and development of critical thinking in higher education. Front. Psychol. **13**, 913219 (2022)
12. Fooladvand, M., Yarmohammadian, M.H., Zirakbash, A.: The effect of cognitive and metacognitive strategies in academic achievement: a systematic review. New Trends Issues Proc. Humanit. Soc. Sci. **3**(1), 313–322 (2017)
13. Phakiti, A.: Melbourne papers in language testing. modeling cognitive and metacognitive strategies and their relationships to EFL reading test performance (2006)
14. Khezrlou, S.: The relationship between cognitive and metacognitive strategies, age, and level of education. Read. Matrix **12**(1) (2012)
15. Berthold, K., Nückles, M., Renkl, A.: Do learning protocols support learning strategies and outcomes? The role of cognitive and metacognitive prompts. Learn. Instr. **17**(5), 564–577 (2007)
16. Teng, L.S., Zhang, L.J.: A questionnaire-based validation of multidimensional models of self-regulated learning strategies. Mod. Lang. J. **100**(3), 674–701 (2016)
17. Teng, L.S., Zhang, L.J.: Empowering learners in the second/foreign language classroom: can self-regulated learning strategies-based writing instruction make a difference? J. Second. Lang. Writ. **48**, 100701 (2020)
18. Ellis, R.: The importance of focus on form in communicative language teaching. Eur. J. Appl. Linguist. **1**(2), 1–12 (2015)
19. Vygotsky, L.S.: On psychological systems, vol. 1, pp. 109–131 (1982)
20. Chi, M.T., Bassok, M., Lewis, M.W., Reimann, P., Glaser, R.: Self-explanations: how students study and use examples in learning to solve problems. Cogn. Sci. **13**(2), 145–182 (1989)
21. Council of Europe: Common European Framework of Reference for Languages: Learning, Teaching, Assessment – Companion Volume. Council of Europe Publishing (2020)
22. World Medical Association: World Medical Association Declaration of Helsinki. Ethical Principles for Medical Research Involving Human Subjects. Bull. World Health Organ. **79**(4), 373–374 (2001)
23. Schworm, S., Renkl, A.: Learning argumentation skills through the use of prompts for self-explaining examples. J. Educ. Psychol. **99**(2), 285–296 (2007)

24. Bürkner, P.: Brms: an R package for bayesian multilevel models using stan. J. Stat. Softw. **80**(1), 1–28 (2017)
25. R Core Team: R: A Language and Environment for Statistical Computing. R Foundation for Statistical Computing, Vienna, Austria (2024)
26. Renkl, A.: Learning from worked-out examples: a study on individual differences. Cogn. Sci. **21**(1), 1–29 (1997)

AI-Enhanced Psychopedagogy for Esports Athletes: A Global Approach to Education, Well-Being, and Competitive Success

Emanuele Isidori(✉)

University of Rome Foro Italico, 00135 Rome, Italy
emanuele.isidori@uniroma4.it

Abstract. Esports has rapidly evolved into a global phenomenon, generating new demands for innovative and evidence-based training frameworks that integrate psycho-pedagogical principles with emerging artificial intelligence (AI) technologies. This paper proposes a holistic approach to the education and development of esports athletes by combining human-centred learning theories with intelligent, adaptive training systems. Psychopedagogical models offer valuable insights into motivation, cognitive development, self-regulation, and inclusive learning processes, while AI-powered tools provide personalized feedback, real-time performance monitoring, and cognitive load adaptation. These two domains foster technical mastery and long-term personal growth in esports athletes. Drawing on recent interdisciplinary research and international case studies, the article highlights how AI-enhanced pedagogical strategies can improve engagement, optimize skill acquisition, and promote sustainable career pathways—including dual academic-athletic trajectories and support for players with disabilities. In order to ensure practical relevance, the paper concludes with a structured implementation framework designed for coaches, educators, and esports organizations. This practical schema guides designing, delivering, and evaluating AI-integrated training programs that align with psycho-pedagogical best practices. It aims to facilitate the development of inclusive, personalized, and ethically grounded learning environments within the dynamic context of competitive gaming.

Keywords: Psychopedagogy · Esports · Artificial Intelligence

1 Introduction

The emergence of esports as a legitimate global sporting and cultural practice has fundamentally reshaped how we conceptualize athlete development. With over 640 million viewers projected by 2025 and rapidly expanding institutional support in education, entertainment, and industry, esports demand novel pedagogical and technological frameworks that move beyond informal or ad hoc training models.

Traditional coaching methods often fail to address the complex cognitive, emotional, and social demands placed on esports athletes. These athletes must develop

M. Bakaev et al. (Eds.): IMS 2025, CCIS 2671, pp. 245–256, 2026.
https://doi.org/10.1007/978-3-032-04958-2_19

acute decision-making skills, strategic thinking, and emotional resilience under intense pressure in digital environments.

Psychopedagogy understood as applying psychological insights to educational practice, offers a theoretical lens for interpreting and guiding esports athlete development. Esports players must internalize complex decision trees, develop high-speed motor and cognitive responses, and function in team-based environments—all within constant digital stimulation. Within this context, motivation plays a key role. Studies show that intrinsic motivators—such as mastery, personal growth, and the experience of "flow"—drive sustained engagement in gaming environments.

Psychopedagogy supports athletes by addressing the interplay of cognitive development, emotional regulation, and motivation in high-performance learning environments. Unlike traditional models focused on content delivery, it promotes a holistic, learner-centred approach that fosters self-regulation, stress management, and reflective learning. In esports, psycho-pedagogical guidance helps student-athletes enhance academic and in-game performance, develop metacognitive skills, and build resilience. By promoting identity formation and long-term well-being, psychopedagogy emerges as a key element in training autonomous, emotionally balanced, and ethically aware competitors.

Furthermore, esports offer unique opportunities to cultivate cognitive and metacognitive skills. Participation can enhance visual attention, working memory, spatial reasoning, and strategic thinking. However, these benefits only emerge when structured training systems support self-regulation and reflective learning practices. For instance, metacognitive strategies such as self-assessment of performance and error recognition can be systematically taught and practised, elevating esports training from reactive play to conscious learning.

The psycho-pedagogical model also emphasizes inclusive learning environments, especially for players with physical, cognitive, or emotional disabilities. As a non-contact, digitally mediated activity, esports hold significant social integration and empowerment potential. However, these potentials are often unrealized due to the lack of adapted pedagogical frameworks and access tools.

2 Artificial Intelligence in Esports Tutorship and the Dual Career of University Cyber-Athletes

Artificial Intelligence (AI) is increasingly transforming a wide range of sectors, with education emerging as one of its most dynamic application areas. Within educational contexts, AI is fundamentally reshaping instructional methodologies and learning experiences. Adaptive learning systems, for example, enable the customization of content delivery based on individual learner profiles, thereby promoting more efficient and targeted educational engagement. These technologies assess student comprehension in real time, detect specific learning gaps, and modify instructional strategies to enhance effectiveness.

Beyond personalized instruction, AI contributes significantly to institutional efficiency by automating routine administrative tasks such as grading and scheduling. That allows educators to devote more time to meaningful pedagogical interactions with their students. Furthermore, AI-driven chatbots and virtual tutors are becoming widespread.

These tools provide on-demand academic support, answering student queries, explaining complex concepts, and continuously improving their responses through iterative learning processes [1]. AI's predictive capabilities also support the early identification of students at academic risk. By analyzing large datasets, machine learning models can detect patterns associated with potential underperformance, enabling instructors to intervene promptly and proactively.

As AI becomes more embedded in academic institutions, it is essential to balance innovation with ethical and pedagogical responsibility, ensuring that the human dimension of education is preserved even as technological tools evolve [2].

This issue is particularly relevant for university student-athletes, a unique population navigating the dual demands of academic achievement and athletic performance. These individuals often require flexible, customized educational support to manage their time-intensive training and competition schedules [3]. AI-powered tutoring systems offer a valuable solution by providing adaptive, individualized academic assistance. These systems adjust content and pacing according to each learner's cognitive profile based on specific algorithms, offering round-the-clock guidance tailored to fluctuating athletic commitments [4].

Such AI tutors deliver immediate feedback, assist in concept clarification, and track student progress over time. That helps athletes maintain academic performance despite competing demands. Beyond educational benefits, AI also supports the athletic dimension of their development. It can analyze biometric and performance data, suggest individualized training programs, and even detect early indicators of injury risk through predictive modelling.

Also, AI can play a critical role in career planning. For student-athletes approaching the transition from competitive sport to post-academic life, AI systems can generate personalized guidance by mapping performance data, academic strengths, and labour market trends to potential career trajectories—be it in professional athletics or alternative fields.

AI-based tutoring systems can deliver personalized content, monitor progress, and adapt real-time instruction. These platforms analyze in-game behaviour—such as reaction time, decision latency, and pattern recognition—and generate customized training regimens for esports athletes. For example, systems like DreamBox and Knewton, widely used in education, can be adapted to esports to offer micro-learning sessions tailored to a player's performance and preferred learning pace.

Moreover, neuro-pedagogical applications of AI are emerging as a frontier in athlete training. By integrating biometric data (e.g., EEG, heart rate variability), AI can monitor cognitive load and emotional stress during gameplay, providing coaches and educators with actionable insights into a player's mental state. That allows training to be adjusted for cognitive fatigue, attentional decline, or emotional dysregulation—particularly acute challenges in high-stakes competitive gaming.

AI also contributes to inclusive training through adaptive interfaces and assistive technologies. For players with disabilities, AI can adjust screen resolution, response times, or even the nature of visual cues to support motor coordination or perceptual challenges. Furthermore, it enables the design of universally accessible esports curricula that respond to individual cognitive profiles rather than assuming normative performance baselines.

3 Managing the Dual Career in Esports: Educational Challenges and the Role of AI

Student-athletes involved in competitive esports face a distinctive set of challenges as they strive to maintain a balance between academic responsibilities and high-performance gaming. Unlike traditional athletes, esports players engage in cognitively demanding, screen-intensive training environments, often characterized by irregular hours, global online competitions, and high emotional and psychological strain. Successfully managing this dual-career pathway—where education and esports performance must progress simultaneously—requires exceptional adaptability, time management, and resilience [5].

One of the core challenges lies in esports athletes' unpredictable and demanding schedules. Tournaments, live-streamed games, international events across time zones, and recovery from mental fatigue can conflict directly with fixed academic schedules, making attendance and timely assignment completion difficult. This conflict is intensified by the mental and emotional toll associated with competitive gaming, which includes stress, fatigue, performance anxiety, and, in some cases, burnout [6].

Cultural and institutional barriers continue to shape the educational experience of esports student-athletes significantly. While traditional sports are increasingly recognized and supported within university systems—often through scholarships, dedicated tutoring services, and flexible learning accommodations—esports still struggle to achieve equivalent institutional legitimacy. This disparity often results in the academic dimension of the esports journey being overlooked or undervalued. Consequently, student-athletes engaged in esports may find it more challenging to access the structured academic guidance, psychological support, and curricular flexibility commonly extended to their counterparts in conventional sports.

Among the key challenges that esports athletes face, time management emerges as a particularly pressing concern. The intense demands of training, including prolonged gaming sessions, strategic planning meetings, and live competitions, often conflict with fixed academic schedules, leaving students with limited opportunities to attend lectures, study effectively, or complete assignments on time. These scheduling conflicts are further compounded by cognitive and mental fatigue. The sustained screen exposure, high cognitive load, and competitive pressure inherent in esports can lead to burnout and diminished concentration, impeding academic performance and knowledge retention.

Moreover, participation in online tournaments and international competitions frequently requires travel or real-time engagement across time zones, which may cause students to miss key classes or deadlines, resulting in persistent academic gaps. In parallel, student-athletes often experience heightened academic stress, as they are expected to meet rigorous standards in their sporting and scholarly pursuits. This dual expectation can create compounded psychological pressure, undermining motivation and increasing the risk of academic disengagement.

The social dimension of university life may also be affected. Because esports training tends to be solitary and time-consuming, athletes may have limited opportunities for social interaction outside their gaming communities, restricting their access to peer networks and informal learning experiences. Financial constraints can also present a significant obstacle. Esports student-athletes frequently bear the cost of specialized equipment, high-speed internet, travel to competitions, and general educational expenses, often without the financial aid mechanisms available to traditional athletes.

Finally, a critical gap exists in academic support tailored to esports. Many institutions lack tutors, mentors, or instructional models adapted to esports players' digital rhythms, cognitive demands, and learning preferences. This absence of targeted pedagogical infrastructure further exacerbates the academic vulnerability of esports student-athletes and calls for the urgent development of integrated support systems that recognize the unique challenges of this emerging discipline.

Given these intersecting pressures, educational systems must adopt flexible and personalized learning models that can accommodate the specific demands of esports careers. That is where Artificial Intelligence (AI) offers transformative possibilities. AI-powered learning platforms are particularly well-suited to support the esports student-athlete. These systems allow asynchronous access, enabling students to learn at their own pace, from any location, and anytime—after late-night competitions or during short breaks between training sessions. Platforms can be configured to generate adaptive learning paths, automatically adjusting content difficulty, format, and pace based on real-time performance and cognitive load. Such personalized systems offer several advantages:

a) Efficiency. AI can prioritize learning modules based on the student's strengths and weaknesses, helping optimize study time—an essential asset for esports athletes with tightly packed schedules.
b) Immediate feedback. AI tutors can deliver real-time feedback on quizzes, assignments, or exercises, reinforcing learning without waiting for instructor responses.
c) Academic monitoring. Predictive analytics can identify when a player's academic performance might be at risk and alert faculty or support services, enabling timely intervention.
d) Athletic optimization. In parallel, AI can monitor player metrics—reaction speed, fatigue patterns, or cognitive overload—to design rest protocols, identify risk factors, and propose adaptive training routines.
e) Career support. AI can also assist in career planning, offering data-informed projections on post-competitive paths aligned with a student's academic strengths and performance analytics.

The unique educational challenges esports student-athletes face demand a systematic reevaluation of support structures. By combining AI-driven educational tools with adaptable pedagogical frameworks, institutions can create learning environments that effectively accommodate these students' dual pursuits, fostering success in their digital and academic endeavours.

4 From Classroom to Arena: AI Tools for Academic and Competitive Success

Artificial Intelligence (AI) revolutionizes how esports student-athletes balance academic and competitive demands. Adaptive learning systems and data-driven training platforms are now essential to personalizing education, optimizing performance, and supporting well-being.

Platforms like DreamBox Learning and Knewton dynamically adjust educational content based on real-time performance, helping students address learning gaps without cognitive overload. ALEKS further enhances this by offering granular control over pacing and curriculum sequencing, which is ideal for STEM subjects.

Flexibility is key for athletes managing irregular schedules. Coursera and Khan Academy provide 24/7 access to diverse academic resources, while Turnitin offers immediate feedback on writing quality, not just plagiarism. Predictive analytics tools such as BrightBytes monitor engagement and performance to flag academic risks early, allowing timely intervention to ensure academic eligibility and progress.

AI tools are equally impactful in the competitive sphere. Platforms like STRIVR use VR to simulate high-pressure game environments, helping players rehearse strategic decisions and improve cognitive performance under load. Physiological analytics tools—Zone7 and CoachNow—track metrics like sleep, stress, and focus, offering personalized feedback and flagging early signs of burnout or overexertion. Initially designed for traditional sports, these systems are now tailored to esports-specific challenges.

At the team level, platforms such as Catapult Sports offer sophisticated performance analytics that assists coaches and managers in optimizing player roles, refining strategic planning, and enhancing intra-team synergy within esports squads. More broadly, combining AI-based tutoring systems with advanced performance-tracking technologies creates a comprehensive and intelligent support ecosystem tailored for esports student-athletes. These integrated tools enable learners to progress academically at their own pace, guided by personalized instruction that adapts to individual needs and learning styles. They also provide immediate and formative feedback, reinforcing understanding and fostering continuous improvement. Furthermore, AI systems facilitate real-time monitoring of cognitive and physical well-being, allowing for timely identification of issues such as fatigue, stress, or disengagement. Simulation technologies enhance the training experience by allowing athletes to rehearse complex in-game scenarios in immersive environments, supporting decision-making under pressure. Finally, predictive analytics serve as an early warning system, identifying potential academic setbacks or physiological risks before they escalate—thus enabling proactive and targeted interventions that safeguard academic and athletic performance.

By leveraging these innovations, universities and training institutions can ensure that esports athletes are prepared to compete at the highest levels and equipped with the cognitive, academic, and strategic skills to thrive beyond the arena.

5 Integrating AI, Psychopedagogy, and Counseling in Esports Tutorship

Integrating Artificial Intelligence (AI), psychopedagogy, and counseling within university esports programs constitutes a comprehensive and ethically grounded framework designed to support the academic achievement, psychological well-being, and competitive development of student-athletes [7]. When coherently aligned, these three dimensions form a multidimensional support system capable of addressing the complexity of dual careers in the evolving landscape of esports. Each component contributes unique and complementary value: AI provides adaptive and data-driven educational tools; psychopedagogy fosters deep learning, motivation, and self-regulation; and counselling ensures emotional resilience, identity development, and interpersonal balance, all essential in the high-pressure, cognitively demanding environment of competitive gaming.

However, learning is not solely a cognitive process but inherently emotional and motivational. Psycho-pedagogical frameworks enrich AI-based systems by cultivating self-regulated learning, intrinsic motivation, metacognition, and inclusive educational practices, particularly for neurodiverse students or those facing learning challenges. These models emphasize the developmental nature of learning, integrating personal identity, social context, and reflective inquiry as essential elements in fostering autonomy and purpose-driven engagement. Psychopedagogy reframes learning as a holistic process that aligns with each student's evolving needs and aspirations.

Counseling can sustain the mental and emotional health of esports athletes, who are frequently exposed to high-stress levels due to performance expectations, intense focus, online scrutiny, and the solitary nature of digital training. These students often face challenges such as anxiety, identity conflict between academic and gamer roles, emotional burnout, and social isolation. University counseling services offer targeted interventions to manage these stressors through individual psychological support, relational counselling to improve team communication, career counselling to navigate the uncertain future of professional esports, and group workshops focused on emotional resilience, digital well-being, and life balance.

Within this intelligent infrastructure, psycho-pedagogical counseling becomes essential. Unlike AI, which processes behavioural and biometric data, psycho-pedagogical counselling interprets the learner's internal narrative, focusing on motivation, self-regulation, identity formation, and emotional resilience.

Counselors can help student-athletes process competitive stress, manage frustration after a poor performance, and reconnect academic goals with personal meaning, especially when motivation declines. Moreover, they serve as human mediators between the insights generated by AI systems and students' lived experiences, facilitating reflective decision-making and preventing the over-mechanization of learning processes.

In this way, counseling does not merely supplement the technological ecosystem—it grounds it ethically and developmentally, ensuring that AI-based interventions are aligned with the learner's holistic growth. This human-centred integration is crucial in esports, where high-performance expectations, screen-related isolation, and identity tensions are common. By combining AI's precision with psycho-pedagogical depth, institutions can foster educational environments that are efficient, emotionally intelligent, inclusive, and sustainable.

The integration of AI with counseling is particularly innovative; emotion-aware chatbots, for example, can detect linguistic indicators of distress and prompt timely referrals to human professionals. Mental health platforms enhanced by AI can track mood trends, deliver mindfulness exercises, and coordinate personalized therapeutic support.

The synergy between AI, psychopedagogy, and counseling creates a dynamic and responsive ecosystem that supports student-athletes academic and athletic development. When AI systems detect a decline in academic performance or engagement—such as irregular logins or a drop in task completion—a psycho-pedagogical tutor might explore adaptive strategies, goal-setting, or motivational barriers. At the same time, a counselor can simultaneously address underlying emotional or interpersonal issues. This triadic interaction ensures that students are not reduced to mere data points or performance metrics but acknowledged as whole persons navigating complex and interdependent learning, growth, and identity formation [8].

At the institutional level, embedding this integrated model within esports education enhances individual student outcomes and broader strategic goals such as student retention, academic persistence, and well-being. Counseling services, in particular, contribute to building communities of care and trust, offering safe spaces for reflection, identity consolidation, and critical dialogue [9; 10]. These actions demonstrate a university's commitment to values such as dignity, inclusion, and long-term student success—beyond mere academic or competitive achievement.

6 The AI-Psychopedagogical Esports Training Scheme (AIPETS)

Based on what we have said and researched, we propose an interdisciplinary model for esports training based on integrating psycho-pedagogical theory and artificial intelligence technologies. The convergence of these fields offers improvements in individual performance and cognitive development and addresses broader educational goals such as inclusivity, accessibility, and ethical responsibility.

Here, we introduce a structured practical framework—the AI-Psychopedagogical Esports Training Scheme (AIPETS)- to translate theoretical insights and deepen them into actionable practices. The scope of this scheme is to provide (see Fig. 1):

- Assessment protocols for identifying motivational profiles, cognitive styles, and learning challenges.
- Instructional design templates that integrate AI tutors, reflection modules, and collaborative tasks.
- Monitoring systems use behavioural data and biometric inputs to adapt real-time training.
- Inclusion checklists to ensure accessibility for learners with diverse needs and abilities.
- Ethical oversight guidelines to safeguard transparency, consent, and human engagement in AI use.

Educators, coaches, and policymakers can use this framework to design training environments that foster technical excellence, psychological resilience, and ethical inclusivity. As esports continues to evolve, such integrative approaches will be essential for shaping a sustainable and human-centred competitive culture.

The AIPETS framework is designed for educators, coaches, and esports organizations. This model is a practical guide for developing, delivering, and evaluating training programs that are not only technologically advanced but also pedagogically meaningful, ethically sound, and inclusively designed.

The AIPETS outlines five core dimensions that reflect a holistic approach to student-athlete development, combining AI-driven personalization with the reflective depth of psychopedagogy and the emotional support of counseling. It aims to empower institutions to create learning ecosystems where student-athletes can thrive—academically, competitively, and personally—within the dynamic context of esports.

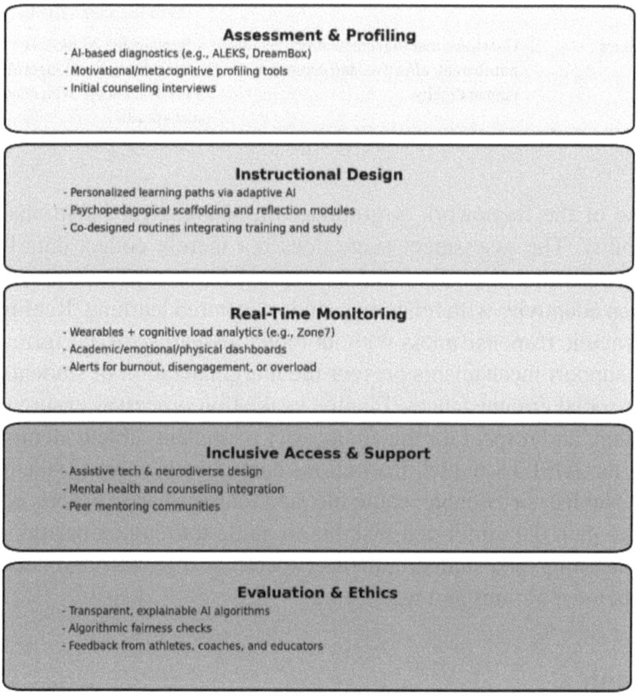

Fig. 1. AI-Psychopedagogical Esports Training Schema (AIPETS)

Each of the five core dimensions corresponds to a phase of an educational intervention designed to harmonize artificial intelligence, psycho-pedagogical principles and counseling practices (Table 1).

Table 1. A structured framework for AI-integrated psychopedagogical support in esports training

Dimension	Function	Tools/Methods
1. Assessment & Profiling	Diagnose learner needs, motivations, stressors, and cognitive styles.	- AI-based diagnostics - Motivational and metacognitive questionnaires - Initial counseling intake sessions
2. Instructional Design	Co-create learning paths and training routines personalized for esports athletes.	- AI-adaptive platforms - Psycho-pedagogical scaffolding strategies - Reflective journaling tools
3. Real-Time Monitoring	Continuously assess academic, emotional, and athletic performance for timely adjustment.	- Wearables + AI dashboards - Cognitive load trackers - Self-regulation and emotional tracking apps
4. Inclusive Access & Support	Ensure that content and interactions are accessible to neurodiverse learners and athletes with disabilities.	- Assistive AI tools (e.g., screen readers, custom UIs) - Counseling services - Peer mentoring systems
5. Evaluation & Ethics	Guarantee that implementation remains transparent, effective, and centred on human dignity.	- Explainable AI models - Periodic audits of algorithmic fairness - Feedback loops with educators, coaches, and athletes

Each phase of the framework is grounded in pedagogical intentionality and ethical accountability. The assessment stage does not merely collect data but interprets it considering motivational profiles and contextual realities. The instructional design aligns AI-driven adaptivity with reflective, student-centred learning. Real-time monitoring enables dynamic responsiveness without reducing learners to performance metrics. Inclusion and support mechanisms prevent the marginalization of students with different abilities or social circumstances. Finally, evaluation processes ensure transparency, informed consent, and respect for the complexity of student-athlete identities.

Following the AIPETS model, institutions can move beyond ad hoc technological adoption and establish sustainable, equitable, and transformative esports education programs. Coaches gain data-informed insights to guide training, educators receive tools to foster deep learning, and student-athletes experience a growth-oriented environment that respects their aspirations and well-being.

7 Conclusion

Integrating Artificial Intelligence into tutoring and training systems for university esports student-athletes is a technological innovation and a pedagogical necessity. As institutions face the growing complexity of supporting dual careers in sports and education, AI offers scalable and personalized solutions that can adapt to the evolving needs of this population. Soon, AI will increasingly enable the creation of individualized learning pathways aligned with students' cognitive profiles and athletic commitments, allowing for greater engagement and time efficiency. Adaptive content delivery will enhance understanding by presenting materials in the most effective formats for each learner.

At the same time, real-time monitoring and feedback will make it possible to detect fatigue, overload, or disengagement, prompting timely interventions. AI systems will also promote integrated skill development, connecting academic progress with performance improvement through targeted exercises and tasks. Immersive learning environments like simulations and virtual scenarios will provide realistic and risk-free spaces for developing tactical and strategic abilities. Most importantly, AI will be part of a holistic and inclusive educational ecosystem, working in synergy with psycho-pedagogical approaches and counselling services to support emotional well-being, motivation, and ethical development.

To harness this potential, universities must implement AI responsibly, ensuring data protection, transparency, algorithmic fairness, and preserving human relationships at the heart of the learning experience. AI should augment human expertise rather than replace educators, coaches, or counselors, enabling more efficient, responsive, and meaningful support.

The future of esports education lies in the intelligent integration of artificial and human intelligence. When guided by ethical principles and embedded within a human-centred pedagogical model, AI tutorship can empower student-athletes to excel academically, compete at high levels, and grow as reflective, resilient individuals prepared for life on and off the digital stage.

Beyond the specific domain of esports, the implications of this work are far-reaching for the landscape of higher education at large. As universities worldwide grapple with the dual challenges of massification and personalization, AI emerges as a critical tool for reimagining educational delivery in more adaptable, inclusive, and learner-centered ways. The structured, ethically aware, and psychopedagogically-informed model outlined in this study can serve as a blueprint for AI integration in various disciplines, particularly in contexts where students pursue complex developmental trajectories—such as working professionals, hybrid learners, or students with disabilities.

In conclusion, this work invites institutions, researchers, and policymakers to envision AI not merely as an efficient tool but as a catalyst for renewing the mission of higher education itself, grounded in the formation of autonomous, critical, and socially responsible individuals. The model proposed here is not limited to esports; it opens a path for rethinking how emerging technologies can be ethically harnessed to build inclusive, flexible, and humanizing educational futures.

References

1. Saqib, H., Al-Hashmi, S.H., Mazhar, H.M., Syed Imran, A.K.: Chatbot in E-learning. In: SHS Web Conference, vol. 156, pp. 1–6 (2023)
2. Zhu, C., Sun, M., Luo, J., Li, T., Wang, M.: How to harness the potential of ChatGPT in education? Knowl. Manag. E-Learn. **15**(2), 133–152 (2023)
3. Isidori, E.: The dual career of student-athletes: a pedagogical challenge. Cult. Cienc. Deporte **10**(29), 99–101 (2015)
4. Dilekci, A., Karatay, H.: The effects of the 21st-century skills curriculum on the development of student's creative thinking skills. Think. Skills Creat. **47**, 101229 (2023)
5. Conde, E., et al.: Perception of the influence of the Esports model in the dual career of student-athletes in universities in Spain and Italy. Cult. Cienc. Deporte **16**(47), 31–37 (2021)

6. Conde, E., Martínez-Aranda, L.M., Leiva-Arcas, A., García-Roca, J.A., Sánchez-Pato, A.: Efficacy of European sport tutorship model (ESTPORT) in the dual career of athletes in Spain. J. Hum. Sport Exerc. **18**(1), 59–70 (2023)
7. Cao, Y., Fan, J., Yang, Q.: ChatGPT in education: ethical predicaments of generative AI. Trans. Soc. Sci. Educ. Humanit. Res. (2024)
8. Ashikullah, M.: Investigating the pros and cons of artificial intelligence (AI)-based systems: a case study on the use of ChatGPT in higher education in the northern region of Bangladesh. Int. J. Stud. Engl. Lang. Lit. **12**(6), (2024)
9. Virvou, M., Tsihrintzis, G.: Is ChatGPT beneficial to education? A holistic evaluation framework based on intelligent tutoring systems. In: Proceedings of International Conference Information Intelligence System and Application (IISA), pp. 1–8 (2023)
10. Ahmed, Z., et al.: The generative AI landscape in education: mapping the terrain of opportunities, challenges, and student perception. IEEE Access **12**, 147023–147050 (2024)

Digital Transformation in Governance and Society

From "Disabilities" to "Additional Needs": Digital Transformation and the Changing Disability Paradigm

Olga Ignatjeva[1(✉)], Konstantin Kondratenko[1], Irina Tolstikova[2], Alexander Pletnev[3], and Iuliia Platonova[4]

[1] St Petersburg State University, St Petersburg, Russia
olga7919@mail.ru
[2] ITMO University, St Petersburg, Russia
[3] St Petersburg University of Internal Affairs Ministry, St Petersburg, Russia
[4] St Petersburg State Institute of Psychology and Social Work, St Petersburg, Russia

Abstract. The article is devoted to the impact of digitalization of modern society on people with disabilities, identifying various aspects of this process. The purpose of this study is to examine the readiness of people with disabilities to be involved in the new digital reality, their use of digital public services, social networks and various applications for mobile devices. The research methodology includes a review of the literature on disability and social inclusion, as well as an empirical analysis of data obtained from a survey of people with disabilities conducted at the St. Petersburg Institution "Professional Rehabilitation Center". The results of the study show that digitalization helps to strengthen the transition from the traditional model of understanding disability to a social one based on a comprehensive health model. However, strengthening digital transformation not only strengthen known forms of inequality, stigmatization and exclusion, but also give rise to new ones, such as relative digital deprivation and "crip-dissonance". The study revealed insufficient use of and trust in regional digital services, as well as weak implementation of the network potential of social networks for people with disabilities. The study also showed the presence of technical barriers to the use of digital services, their non-compliance with accessibility standards. The results obtained allow us to formulate recommendations for improving digital accessibility and social integration of people with disabilities.

Keywords: digitalization · disabled · inclusion · crip-dissonance · digital isolation · Professional Rehabilitation Center

1 Introduction

The global trend of "turning to the disabled" and including them in full-fledged public life is certainly a fair and human-oriented approach. This trend also penetrates the digital reality, creating additional means for persons with disabilities to meet their needs.

The main objective of this study is precisely to study the readiness of disabled people to be involved in the new digital reality. It must be assumed that, despite the

M. Bakaev et al. (Eds.): IMS 2025, CCIS 2671, pp. 259–273, 2026.
https://doi.org/10.1007/978-3-032-04958-2_20

positive effect of digital inclusivity, there are risks of not only the transfer of studied and understandable forms of discrimination to the digital world, but also the emergence of new forms associated with the intersection of discriminatory characteristics - disability, digital illiteracy and falling out of the target audience of publics and communities. This also leads to a new form of social isolation - digital isolation of disabled people.

The study of readiness for digital inclusion fits into the logic of "values, needs, activities", i.e. the study of the values and advantages of digital transformation for people with disabilities, the analysis of their needs and the degree to which these needs are met through digital platforms and solutions, as well as the study of the specific behavior of people with disabilities in the digital environment. In other words, the interest of the study is attracted not only by the actors, but also by the digital context of the respondents.

The article presents a review of modern literature on disability and social inclusion, research methodology, results of an empirical study conducted using the questionnaire method, as well as analysis and interpretation of the data obtained in the context of existing theoretical approaches. In conclusion, the main findings and recommendations for improving digital accessibility and social integration of people with disabilities, minimizing and overcoming new forms of social discrimination will be formulated. The empirical study was conducted on the basis of the St. Petersburg State Budgetary Institution "Professional Rehabilitation Center".

2 Literature Review

Research on the problems of disability, rehabilitation and factors of social adaptation and activity of people with disabilities in modern life form a significant layer of literature in science. At present, Russia is transitioning from the traditional (medical) model of understanding disability to a social one based on a comprehensive biopsychosocial model of health [1].

The medical model of disability has had a significant impact on both the formation of legislation in the field of social protection and rehabilitation, and on the practices of including disabled people in social relations. The role of the "sick" is based on a person's inability to perform other social roles, and, therefore, threatens the normal functioning of the social system and requires the introduction of the roles of "doctor" and "disabled person" to stabilize relations (Parsons) [2]. I. Goffman introduced the term "stigma" to denote the exclusion of a disabled person from social relations with an accompanying negative assessment of this social status by the dominant value system [3]. The flip side of this approach is the perception of disabled people as helpless, pathetic, incapable of a full independent life. Attempts by a disabled person to go beyond the prescribed models of behavior are perceived as inadequate and antisocial actions [4].

Until recently, social policy in the Russian Federation was primarily focused on the implementation of social protection programs for disabled people, social exclusion, while the ratified UN convention emphasizes increasing the possibility of independent and self-sufficient life for disabled people [1], social inclusion.

The theories of social action by M. Weber and structural functionalism by T. Parsons, the theories of social stratification and social mobility by P. Sorokin, S. Lipset, R. Bendix, social constructivism by P. Berger and T. Luckmann are productive for studying the social citizenship of people with disabilities. Modern social models of disability are based on the theories of constructivism, stigmatization and social exclusion, in which "a person creates reality and thereby creates himself" [2]. In the 1980s, the term "social exclusion" appeared in scientific literature and was actively used in the context of studying poverty and marginalization [5]. According to P. Abrahamson, social exclusion implies a condition when a minority is marginalized, and the level of participation of the excluded group in the life of society decreases. Social exclusion emphasizes the limitations of material, educational, professional resources and access to social institutions and lifts, which narrows the possibilities of rehabilitation, social choice, freedom and activity of people with disabilities [6, 7]. Thus, foreign researchers (E. Barnes et al.) consider disability as a way of being a minority, which requires certain models of resistance to social oppression [8].

Of fundamental importance is a new reading of the socio-cultural meaning of disability as the basis for the emergence of discrimination and oppression, as well as the interpretation of disability enshrined in the UN Convention. The movement for the rights of persons with disabilities is based on the restoration of a sense of pride and the rejection of the idea of disability as something inherently bad or abnormal. The inability of a disabled person to leave his own home, attend educational institutions, culture, social services, etc. becomes a "social trap". Ghettoization of persons with disabilities occurs - the concentration of this group in a certain place of residence, namely, in boarding schools, specialized housing for the disabled, isolation in apartments in houses that are not equipped in accordance with the requirements of a barrier-free environment [9]. Supporters of this approach are E.R. Yarskaya-Smirnova and I.A. Grigorieva, whose research confirms the inaccessibility of people with disabilities to join prestigious social groups, the existence of barriers to the realization of the right to work [10, 11].

The study of social models of disability is based on Bourdieu's structuralist-constructivist theory. The special type of reflexivity that is characteristic of disabled people is, in fact, a form of cultural capital. [12, 13]. An important conclusion from Bourdieu's concept of cultural capital is that cultural capital is extremely dependent on education and the introduction of innovations in society requires an impact on the individual's habitus. Bourdieu noted that cultural capital stems from habitus [14], which, in turn, is extremely dependent on the external social environment [13].

In the course of solving the problems of normalizing the lives of disabled people and implementing the rights of disabled people to access resources and benefits the term "social citizenship" was introduced. Studies of social citizenship of disabled people in the works of E. Yarskaya-Smirnova and P. Romanov [6], E. Naberushkina [15, 16] showed that many people are almost completely excluded from society or their rights as citizens are violated, i.e. we are talking about social inequality. The beginning of the theorization of citizenship in the aspect of social inequality and the ideology of justice was laid in the works of T. Marshall [17], and in domestic science – in the works of B. Kapustin [18], I. Kuznetsova-Morenko [19], N. Osipova [20]. Mobile citizenship, developed in the research of E.K. Naberushkina, is one of the forms of social citizenship, combining the themes of social mobility, construction of spatial justice and the right to the environment [15, 16].

The solution to the problem of becoming a viable individual who transforms the environment in his/her interests is within the framework of W. Bronfenbrenner's concept [21]. W. Bronfenbrenner's sociocultural ecological approach is a dynamic process that goes in two directions. A person is constantly affected by various elements of the environment around him/her and at the same time actively restructures his/her multi-level living environment.

The development of mobile citizenship in the context of socially oriented urbanism in line with the socio-cultural ecological approach of W. Bronfenbrenner was undertaken by A. Makhnach, who introduced the term "human resilience" into domestic psychological research [22, 23]. He noted the empirical, ideological and theoretical shift in the research paradigm from illness to health, from vulnerability to coping, from deficiency to resourcefulness, which became decisive in the research of human resilience. This issue was developed in the works of foreign and domestic researchers: "the phenomenon of sustainability" (Ungar M., Clark S.E., 2009) [24], "a sense of coherence" (Antonovsky, 1974) [25], "invulnerability" (Garmezy, 1976) [26], "hardiness" (Leontiev, 2002) [27, 28].

An analysis of the existing literature on the subject area of the research allows us to draw a conclusion about the main trend in scientific research on inclusion issues – considering citizens with physical disabilities as a social task of becoming a viable individual who transforms the environment in their interests.

3 Methodology

This article presents the results of a research conducted on the basis of a survey of students of the Professional Rehabilitation Center in October 2024. Technical School for the Disabled "Professional Rehabilitation Center" (hereinafter referred to as the Professional Rehabilitation Center) is the only educational institution of secondary professional education for people with disabilities. Currently, more than 420 students with disabilities and limited health opportunities are studying in the center under the main programs of secondary professional education.

The project used a sample of students of this specialized educational institution, which included 54.6% men and 44.7% women. The sample size was 152 respondents. In terms of age composition, the group under 20 years old included 39.6% of respondents; from 21 to 30 years old - 29.9%; from 31 to 40 years old 12.5%; from 41 to 50 years old - 8.3%; from 51 to 60 years old - 7.6%; after 61 years - 2.10%. The students of the center are people with disabilities, both congenital and acquired. All students have undergone training in working with digital services with different levels of results based on the results of certification. That is, according to the concept of Hoffman, they have already gone beyond the prescribed models of behavior [4]. This sample is a simple random sample. The survey results were processed using frequency analysis, which allowed us to identify consistent patterns for this population group.

4 Research Results

During the study of the adaptation of people with disabilities to digitalization processes, a survey was conducted, the results of which demonstrate the main trends and vectors of the integration of people with disabilities into the digital communication space.

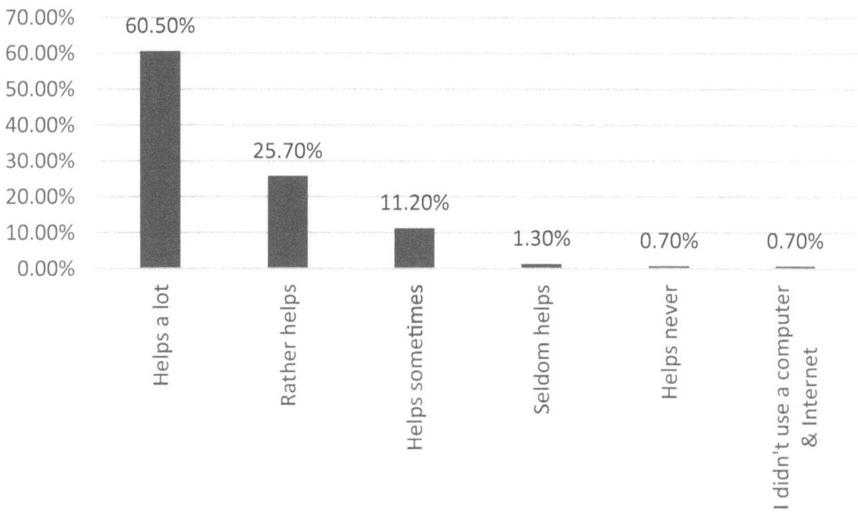

Fig. 1. The answer to the question: "Do you think digitalization helps you?"

To assess the overall impact of digitalization on people with disabilities, they were asked whether digitalization helps them (Fig. 1), and the vast majority rated the impact of digitalization positively. The empirical results obtained during the questionnaire survey allow us to get a fairly detailed picture of the impact of digitalization processes on various aspects of the lives of people with disabilities. More than half of the respondents (60.5%) said that digitalization helps them a lot. A quarter of the respondents (25.7%) say that digitalization rather helps them. Only 1.4% of respondents said that digitalization does not help them. These are extremely positive results that indicate a high level of integration of people with disabilities in the digital space. To improve the lives of people with disabilities, society must move from the paradigm of people with disabilities to the paradigm of people with additional needs. This will require changing the perceptions of both people with disabilities and all other members of society. The theoretical basis for this transition is the constructivist paradigm in the social sciences. This problem is referred to in the social sciences as "crip-dissonance" - "lack of mutual understanding of disability and disabled lives between disabled and non-disabled people" [29, p. 15]. Overcoming this gap between the worlds can be achieved through the activities of social services, volunteers and activists, and by stimulating the development of various types of activity for disabled people in the digital space.

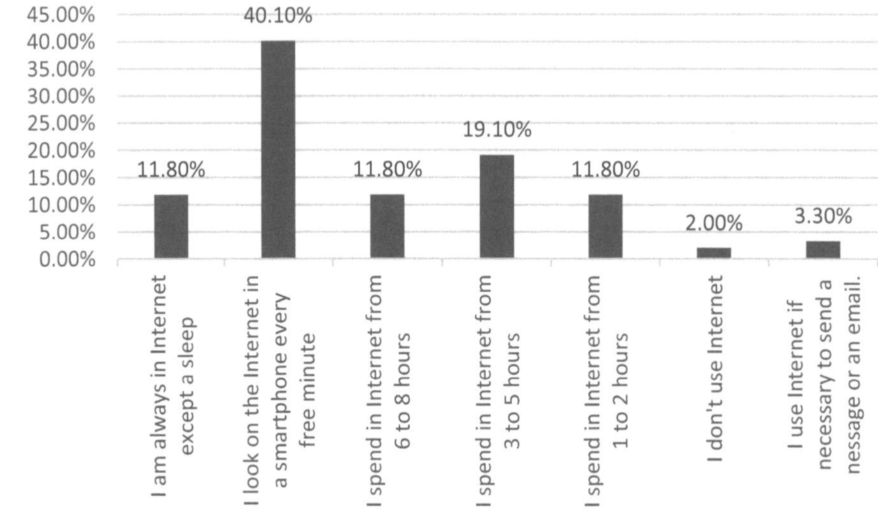

Fig. 2. The answer to the question: "How many hours a day do you spend on the Internet?"

Another important indicator of the impact of digitalization on people with disabilities is the amount of time spent on the Internet. The respondents were also asked about this (Fig. 2). A significant portion of respondents (40.1%) surf the Internet on a smartphone or computer whenever they have free time. 19.1% of respondents spend three to five hours a day on the Internet. The same number of respondents (11.8%) are those who spend all their time on the Internet, except for sleep, spend 6 to 8 h on the Internet and spend 1 to 2 h on the Internet. And only 2% of people with special needs do not use the Internet at all. The results indicate a significant integration of the community and people with disabilities into virtual communication processes. Since the study of social models of disability is based on Bourdieu's structuralist-constructivist theory and Putnam's concept of social capital, the construction of social connections and inclusion in network interactions, which presuppose relationships of reciprocity and trust, contribute to digital inclusion and, through innovations introduced into society, influence the habitus of the individual.

Respondents were also asked how they subjectively assess their level of proficiency in Internet-related technologies (Fig. 3). The largest share of respondents (32.3%) stated that they can work with individual programs. 28.9% consider themselves experienced Internet and computer users. 27.6% of respondents called themselves people who easily master new programs, applications and network services on the Internet. 7.9% prefer to use a telephone instead of the Internet (to make an appointment with a doctor, file a complaint or perform other actions). 0.7% prefer, if possible, not to use either a computer or a telephone. The results reviewed indicate that the share of respondents who do not have basic digital literacy is only slightly more than 8% of students. At the same time, against the backdrop of the construction of the urban environment based on technological innovations and various digital everyday practices, the result of 8% with limited access reflects the transformation of the system of social inequality.

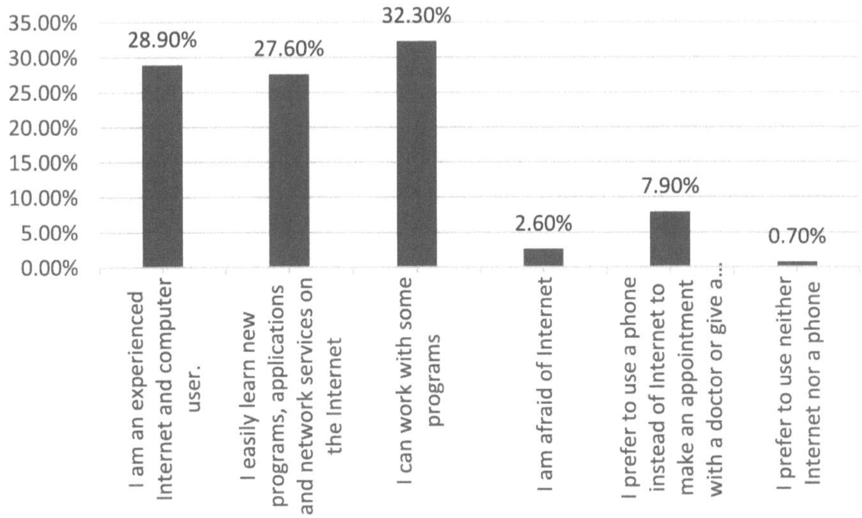

Fig. 3. The answer to the question: "What level of Internet user do you consider yourself to be?"

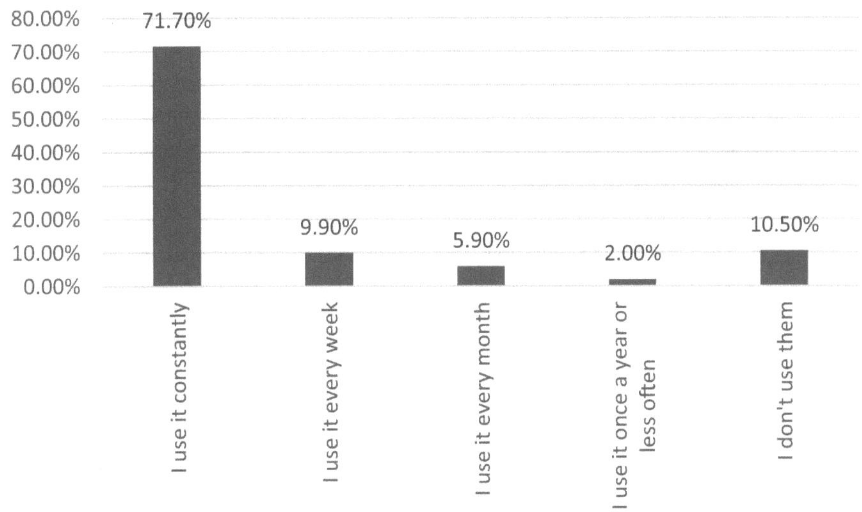

Fig. 4. The answer to the question: "Do you use social networks?"

Understanding of the benefits of digitalization by persons with disabilities is closely related to their needs in using digital technologies in everyday life. To study this aspect, respondents were asked how often they use social networks (Fig. 4). The largest proportion of respondents (71.7%) answered that they constantly use social networks. 10.5% of respondents do not use social networks at all. 9.9% of respondents use social networks every week. 5.9% of respondents visit social networks once a month. 2% of respondents use social networks only once a year. The presented results clearly indicate the significant involvement of people with special needs in digital communication through social networks. At the same time, in addition to the additional communication opportunities that digital technologies create for persons with disabilities, they can also create additional barriers. In sociological science, this problem has received understanding thanks to the conceptualization of the concept of "access", which reflects the transformation of the system of social inequality. For example, "Many older people and people with disabilities lack the visual acuity, manual dexterity, and cognitive ability successfully to operate much modern technology."[30, p. 285]. New digital devices and programs inevitably create new barriers for people with disabilities. In order to develop mechanisms to overcome social exclusion, it is necessary to more actively involve people with disabilities in digital projects of society and government as subjects of social activity.

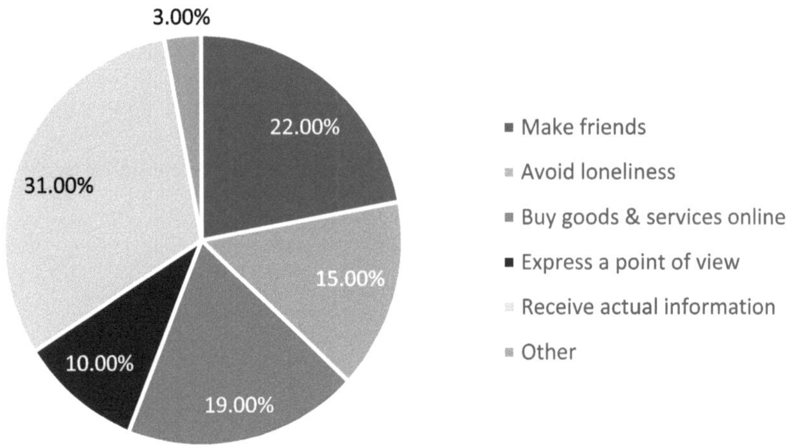

Fig. 5. The answer to the question: "What help does social networks provide?"

Next, respondents were asked whether social networks help them (Fig. 5). Most respondents (31%) use social networks to receive up-to-date information. 22% of respondents try to make friends on social networks. 19% of respondents receive goods and services through social networks. 15% of respondents try to avoid loneliness with the help of social networks. 10% of respondents express their point of view through social networks. Discussing the role of human viability from the standpoint of W. Bronfenbrenner's ecological theory, we can say that digital activity (activity as the basis for human development, Makhnach A.V.) turns into a person's ability to overcome unfavorable life circumstances with the ability to recover and use all internal and external resources for this. Social activity in the form of interaction with other people helps to maintain a sense of self-importance, as well as to claim one or another social role beyond employment.

The obtained results on the respondents' level of proficiency in digital technologies are extremely interesting to compare with the share of those respondents whose work is directly related to the use of information and communication technologies (Fig. 6). More than half of the respondents (54.6%) have work related to a computer in some situations. 30.9% of respondents are engaged in work directly related to digital technologies. 7.9% of respondents have work that is almost not related to digital technologies. 6.6% of

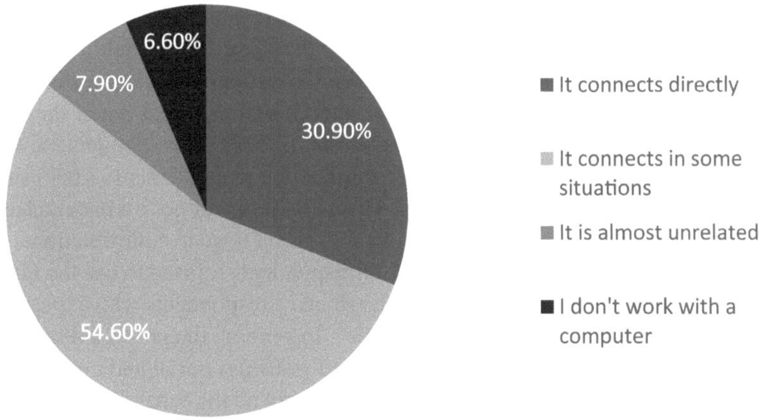

Fig. 6. The answer to the question: "What help does social networks provide?"

respondents do not work with a computer due to the nature of their professional activities. These results can be characterized as weak involvement of people with disabilities in activities related to digital technologies.

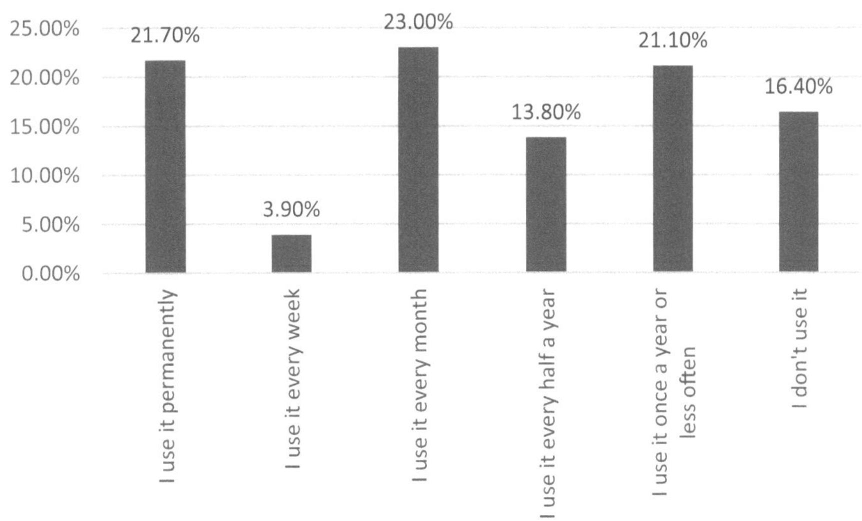

Fig. 7. The answer to the question: "Do you use the public services portal Gosuslugi?"

The answers to the question about the frequency of using the public services portal "Gosuslugi" show that almost half of people with disabilities (48.6%) use this portal at least once a month (Fig. 7). At the same time, every fifth respondent (21.7%) said that they use Gosuslugi constantly. The given figures testify to the popularity of this portal, its sufficient convenience of use and its ability to simplify interaction with government agencies for people with disabilities. Only 16.4% of respondents said that they never use the Gosuslugi portal. 16.4% would rather use the Gosuslugi portal.

Next, we compare the presented results with the answers to the question about the probability with which respondents will use the Gosusligi portal when they need to receive public services (certificates, passports, etc.). 27.6% of respondents always use the Gosuslugi portal for these purposes. A third of the respondents (33.6%) said that, depending on the situation, they can use the Gosusligi portal or go to a personal appointment. A significant portion of respondents (17.1%) prefer to go to multifunctional centers instead of using the Gosuslugi portal. 5.3% of respondents refused to use the Gosuslugi portal. This number almost coincides with the share of respondents who experience difficulties in using information technology (3.9%). In general, the presented results allow us to conclude that although respondents use the Gosuslugi portal and consider it quite convenient, they do not have sufficient knowledge about all the capabilities of this portal.

The survey results show that the majority of respondents do not use the Digital Petersburg digital services ecosystem (83.2%). See Fig. 8. A significant portion of respondents do not even know about the existence of this ecosystem (44.4%). These results indicate the need to develop digital services for people with disabilities at the regional level. St. Petersburg as a region has enormous intellectual and technological resources for the successful implementation of this task. The reason for this state of affairs is the insufficient convenience of the Digital Petersburg ecosystem and the poor familiarity of ordinary citizens of St. Petersburg with it. The introduction of digital services at the regional level is increasingly becoming a global trend [31, p. 247–258], within the framework of which both digital opportunities for helping people with disabilities and the activities of activists protecting the interests of people with disabilities are developing.

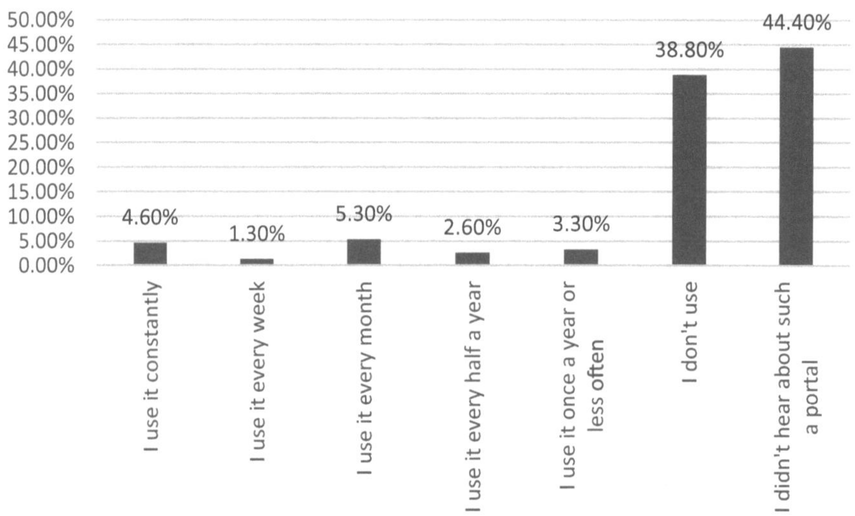

Fig. 8. The answer to the question: “Do you use the Digital Petersburg ecosystem of city services?”

An important part of the study was the question about the ergonomics of government websites. People with disabilities were asked whether they thought that government websites used accessibility standards sufficiently. Most respondents (34.2%) said that government websites rather used accessibility standards. 31.6% of respondents found it difficult to answer this question. 17.1% of respondents thought that government websites rather did not use accessibility standards. 12.5% of respondents thought that government websites fully used accessibility standards. Respondents who thought that government websites did not use accessibility standards accounted for 4.6% of respondents. The presented results clearly indicate the need to improve government websites and conduct relevant research in this area "specialized software, assistive technologies are needed, digitalization creates additional social barriers associated with the impossibility or difficulty of using ICT." [32, p. 50]. The described phenomenon can be defined as the second digital divide, characteristic only of people with disabilities. To overcome the second digital development, it is necessary to provide people with disabilities with the necessary technical means. But the main efforts should be directed at overcoming the "crip-dissonance" in society.

5 Discussion

The conducted research was able to shed light on several important topics, the most significant of which is the recognition of the problem of inclusion and integration of persons with disabilities as a complex problem, including cognitive, political, organizational, technical and other aspects, which are quite difficult to separate from each other in practice. In this sense, identifying the mutual influence of these aspects seems to be an even more difficult task for future research.

Another important topic that deserves attention is the rethinking of classical sociological concepts of disability in the context of digital transformation. Thus, in the theory of T. Parsons, disability is interpreted as a disfunction, an inability to bear a significant functional social burden, but the Internet and digital technologies are able to reduce this disfunction to a minimum. For example, the results of the study indicate that more than 85% of respondents use a computer to one degree or another for work, and for 30.9%, work is directly related to digital technologies. This result confirms the ideas of the philosophy of science about the equalizing role of technology in society.

On the one hand, such a situation can be interpreted as the first phase or serious prerequisites for the implementation of social citizenship, which was mentioned by researchers B. Kapustin [18], I. Kuznetsova-Morenko [19], N. Osipova [20] and others, but, on the other hand, this immersion in the digital world can also be interpreted as an escape from the real world as a result of the "crip-dissonance" discussed in the study.

In addition to social barriers, the study also revealed technical obstacles for people with disabilities. Thus, the survey showed that only a third of respondents believe that government websites comply with accessibility standards, a quarter of respondents expressed direct distrust of government websites. Almost half of respondents have not even heard of the "Digital Petersburg" digital services ecosystem, within the framework of which some projects are directly aimed at solving the problems of people with disabilities. If this does not refute A. Makhnach's thesis about the transition from deficiency to resourcefulness [22], then in any case it raises doubts about the success of the implementation of the digital inclusion policy in St. Petersburg.

The initial thesis about the complexity and comprehensiveness of the problem is most evident in the assessment of the impact of social networks on the level of social capital of people with disabilities. On the one hand, a large percentage of respondents (71.7%) noted the fact of constant use of social networks, but only a third indicated the social focus of using these digital resources. In other words, social networks do not fully realize their network potential, which is probably due to the lack of attention of communities to disability issues or stigmatization. On the other hand, it is difficult in principle to link the classical concepts of habitus and social capital with the world of virtual networks: social networks can be perceived as an extension of real networks when it comes to communicating with friends, but they can also be perceived as a tool for finding networks and social involvement, and in this case act as a tool for "social intelligence".

6 Conclusion

This article analyzes the impact of digitalization on the lives of people with disabilities based on a literature review and the results of an empirical study. It was shown that the adaptation and integration of people with disabilities is a complex, comprehensive process that includes work not only with people with disabilities themselves, but also with public opinion, city authorities and technologies, i.e. the work presents an ecosystem approach to solving this problem. An important link in this ecosystem is digital technologies that can have a positive impact on various aspects of the lives of people with disabilities, facilitating communication, access to information and services. However, each element of the inclusive ecosystem has risks and barriers, both social (stigmatization, exclusion, inequality) and technical (discrimination, non-compliance with accessibility standards, mistrust of technology).

The conducted empirical study showed the complexity, contradiction and dialectic nature of the process of digital transformation and inclusivity. Thus, on the one hand, the overwhelming majority of respondents noted the positive impact of digitalization on various social aspects, but, on the other hand, a considerable number of respondents noted the presence of "crip-dissonance" and "relative digital deprivation", which indicates the non-linearity of the transition from the medical to the biopsychosocial paradigm of inclusivity, and also expands the understanding of social citizenship in the context of the digital environment. The study also revealed a discrepancy between the social and technical components in the use of social networks - almost three quarters of respondents constantly use social networks, but only a quarter use them to expand social connections. This significantly corrects Bourdieu's theory, showing the limitations of cultural (and sociotechnical capital) without the transformation of social habitus, and emphasizes the need for an ecosystem approach to the problems of inclusiveness, in which technologies act not as a self-sufficient, significant phenomenon in itself, but as an element of the complex interaction of the state, society and technologies.

In view of this, it is worth noting the significance of the results obtained for the development and implementation of state policy in the field of social protection and support for people with disabilities. It is necessary to take into account not only the specific needs of people with disabilities, but also the entire ecosystem of inclusiveness, including the dissemination of information, work with public opinion, transformation of urban space, and improvement of digital technologies.

As areas for further research, we can propose studying other aspects of the inclusiveness ecosystem, in particular, studying public opinion on digital accessibility policy, developing and evaluating the effectiveness of digital literacy and hygiene programs, and the impact of digitalization on certain categories of people with disabilities. An important area of research seems to be studying the depth of "crip-dissonance" and relative digital deprivation for a deeper understanding of the features of social construction of reality by people with disabilities, the rejection by all members of society of the paradigm of "people with disabilities" and the adoption of the paradigm of "people with additional needs".

References

1. Konvencija o pravah invalidov (prinjata rezoljuciej 61/106 General'noj Assamblei OON ot 13 dekabrja 2006 g., podpisana ot imeni Rossijskoj Federacii 24 sentjabrja 2008 g., ratificirovana Federal'nym zakonom №46-FZ ot 03.05.2012) [Convention on the Rights of Persons with Disabilities (adopted by resolution 61/106 of the UN General Assembly on 13 December 2006, signed on behalf of the Russian Federation on 24 September 2008, ratified by Federal Law No. 46-FZ of 03.05.2012)]. http://base.garant.ru/2565085/ https://www.un.org/ru/documents/decl_conv/conventions/disability.shtml
2. Parsons, T.: O social'nyh sistemah [About social systems]. Academic Project, Moscow (2002)
3. Goffman, E.: Stigma: Zametki ob upravlenii isporchennoj identichnost'ju [Stigma: Notes on the Management of Spoiled Identity], trans. by M.S. Dobryakova. https://www.hse.ru/data/2011/11/15/1272895702/Goffman_stigma.pdf
4. Krasuckaja, O.V.: Kategorii invalidnosti i reabilitacii v razlichnyh sociologicheskih koncepcijah [Categories of disability and rehabilitation in various sociological concepts]. In: Vestnik Permskogo nacional'nogo issledovatel'skogo politehnicheskogo universiteta. Social'no-jekonomicheskie nauki [Bulletin of Perm National Research Polytechnic University. Social and economic sciences] 3, 132–141 (2017)
5. Abrahamson, P.: Social'naja jekskljuzija i bednost' [Social exclusion and poverty]. In: Obshhestvennye nauki i sovremennost' [Social Sciences and Modernity] **2**, 158–166 (2001)
6. Romanov, P.V., Yarskaya-Smirnova, E.R.: Politika invalidnosti: social'noe grazhdanstvo invalidov v sovremennoj Rossii [Disability policy: social citizenship of disabled people in modern Russia]. Scientific book, Saratov (2006)
7. Voevodina, E.V.: «Invalid» kak social'naja stigma i prostranstvo dlja diskussij ["Disabled" as a social stigma and a space for discussion]. In: Chelovek. Obshhestvo. Inkljuzija [Man. Society. Inclusion] **4**(20), 10–15 (2014)
8. Barnes, C.: Disabling Imagery and the Media: An Exploration of the Principles for Media Representations of Disabled People. Ryburn, Halifax (1992)
9. Naberushkina, Je.K.: Gorod dlja vseh: sociologicheskij analiz dostupnosti gorodskogo prostranstva dlja invalidov [City for All: Sociological Analysis of Accessibility of Urban Space for Disabled People]. In: Zhurnal sociologii i social'noj antropologii [Journal of Sociology and Social Anthropology] 3 (56), Vol. XIV, 119–139 (2011)
10. Grigorieva, M. I.: Issledovanie problemy invalidnosti v sociologii [Research of the problem of disability in sociology]. In: Vestnik Permskogo nacional'nogo issledovatel'skogo politehnicheskogo universiteta. Social'no-jekonomicheskie nauki [Bulletin of Perm National Research Polytechnic University. Social and economic sciences] 2 (2021). https://cyberleninka.ru/article/n/issledovanie-problemy-invalidnosti-v-sotsiologii

11. Bourdieu, P.: The forms of capital. In: Richardson, J. (ed.) Handbook of Theory and Research for the Sociology of Education, pp. 241–258. Greenwood, New York (1986)
12. Bagnasco, A.: Trust and Social Capital. In: Nash, K., Scott, A. (eds.) The Blackwell Companion to Political Sociology, pp. 230–239. Blackwell Publishing, Oxford (2004)
13. Bourdieu, P., Passeron, J.C.: Reproduction in Education, Society and Culture Beverly Hills. Sage Publications, London (1977)
14. Bourdieu, P., Wacquant, L.D.: An Invitation to Reflexive Sociology. University of Chicago Press, Chicago (1992)
15. Naberushkina, Je.K.: Invalidy v bol'shom gorode: problemy social'nogo grazhdanstva [Disabled People in the Big City: Problems of Social Citizenship]. Variant, Moscow (2012)
16. Naberushkina, Je.K.: Social'noe grazhdanstvo invalidov v logike prostranstvennoj spravedlivosti [Social citizenship of people with disabilities in the logic of spatial justice]. In: Social'naja rabota v sovremennom mire: vzaimodejstvie nauki, obrazovanija i praktiki : materialy VI Mezhdunarod. nauch.-prakt. konf. [Social work in the modern world: interaction of science, education and practice: Proc. of the VI International scientific and practical conf.], eds. M.S. Zhirova, O.A. Volkovoj, E.I. Mozgovoj. NRU «BelGU», Belgorod (2014)
17. Mjurberg, I.I. T.H.: Marshall i konceptual'naja istorija rezhimov grazhdanstva [T.H. Marshall and the Conceptual History of Citizenship Regimes]. In: Zhurnal'nyj klub Intelros, Politiko-filosofskij ezhegodnik [Intelros Magazine Club, Political and Philosophical Yearbook] 3 (2010). http://www.intelros.ru/readroom/politiko-filosofskij-ezhegodnik/vyp-3/13458-th-marshall-i-konceptualnaya-istoriya-rezhimov-grazhdanstva.html
18. Kapustin, B. G.: Grazhdanstvo i grazhdanskoe obshhestvo [Citizenship and civil society]. Higher School of Economics, Moscow (2011). https://publications.hse.ru/pubs/share/folder/v2bydyig3d/54924806.pdf
19. Kuznecova-Morenko, I.B.: Teorija social'noj spravedlivosti: universalizm i partikuljarizm [Theory of Social Justice: Universalism and Particularism]. In: Zhurnal "Kollegium" [Journal "Collegium"] 8–14 (2008)
20. Osipova, N.G., Vershinina, I.A., Martynenko, T.S.: Neravenstvo i neopredelennost': sovremennye vyzovy dlja gorodov [Inequality and Uncertainty: Contemporary Challenges for Cities]. In: Sociologicheskie issledovanija [Sociological research] 1, 153–155 (2019)
21. Bronfenbrenner, U.: Ecology of the family as a context for human development: Research perspectives. Dev. Psychol. **6**(22), 723–742 (1986)
22. Mahnach, A.V.: Zhiznesposobnost' cheloveka i sem'i: social'no-psihologicheskaja paradigma [Viability of an individual and family: a socio-psychological paradigm]. Institute of Psychology RAS, Moscow (2016)
23. Mahnach, A.V., Laktionova, A.I.: Zhiznesposobnost' sem'i s pozicii organizacionnoj teorii A.A. Bogdanova [Family Viability from the Position of A.A. Bogdanov's Organizational Theory]. In: Social'naja psihologija i obshhestvo [Social Psychology and Society] 2, Vol. 12, 41–55 (2021). https://doi.org/10.17759/sps.2021120203
24. Ungar, M., Clark, S.E., Kwong, W-m., Makhnach, A., Cameron, C.A.: Studying resilience across cultures. J. Ethnic Cult. Diversity Soc. Work 3/4, 14, 1–19 (2005). https://www.researchgate.net/publication/254362327_Studying_Resilience_Across_Cultures
25. Antonovsky, A.: Conceptual and methodological problems in the study of resistance resources and stressful life events. In B. S. Dohrenwend & B. P. Dohrenwend (Eds.), Stressful life events: Their nature and effects. John Wiley & Sons, Hoboken, New Jersey (1974)
26. Garmezy, N.: Vulnerable and invulnerable children: theory, research, and intervention catalog of selected documents in psychology. Am. Psychol. Assoc. **6** (1976). https://openlibrary.org/books/OL50454153M/Vulnerable_and_invulnerable_children
27. Leont'ev, D.A., Rasskazova, E.I.: Zhiznestojkost' kak sostavljajushhaja lichnostnogo potenciala / Lichnostnyj potencial: struktura i diagnostika [Resilience as a component of personal potential / Personal potential: structure and diagnostics]. Smysl, Moscow (2011)

28. Leont'ev, D.A., Rasskazova, E.I.: Test zhiznestojkosti [Vitality test]. Smysl, Moscow (2006)
29. Olsen, J., Pilson, A.: Developing understandings of disability through a constructivist paradigm: identifying, overcoming (and embedding) crip-dissonance. Scand. J. Disabil. Res. 24(1), 15–28 (2022). https://doi.org/10.16993/sjdr.843
30. Gregor, P., Sloan, D., Newell, A.F.: Disability and technology: building barriers or creating opportunities? Adv. Comput. **64**, 283–346 (2005). https://doi.org/10.1016/s0065-2458(04)64007-1
31. Berghs, M., Chataika, T., El-Lahib, Y., Dube, K.: The Routledge Handbook of Disability Activism. Routledge (2019)
32. Meshcheryakova, N.N., Rogotneva, E.N.: Digitalization: new risks for people with disabilities. Problem statement. Digital Sociol. **4**(3), 44–52 (2021). https://doi.org/10.26425/2658-347X-2021-4-3-44-52

Digital Infrastructure for Psychological Counseling Services in Higher Education: Opportunities and Prospects

Zulfiya Khayrova[1,2](✉), Alexander Plotnikov[1], Irina Kelareva[1], and Svetlana Gani[2]

[1] Peoples' Friendship, University of Russia named after Patrice Lumumba, Moscow 117198, Russia
khayrova-zr@rudn.ru
[2] The Russian Academy of Education, Moscow 119121, Russia

Abstract. Digital technologies have become an integral part of modern society. They are widely used not only for communication, entertainment, and education but also in addressing professional challenges. Increasingly, digital tools are being employed by educators and psychologists in the field of education to provide psychological support to students. To explore the specifics of digital platform usage by psychologists in higher education, a study was conducted examining their experience with various digital tools (platforms and services). To achieve the research objectives, a questionnaire was developed, covering aspects such as the experience of using platforms and services in professional practice, their advantages, drawbacks, and technical limitations. The study sample included 14 universities participating in the pilot testing of a psychological service model within the higher education system of the Russian Federation. The findings revealed the prevalence of digital platforms and services as tools in psychologists' professional work, along with the most commonly used forms of implementation, key benefits, and limitations. The results of the study will contribute to more effective integration of digital technologies into the professional practice of psychologists.

Keywords: psychological counseling service · education system · psychological support · distance counseling tools · digital transformation · digital platforms · digital infrastructure · digital services

1 Introduction

In the modern world, digital transformation is permeating all spheres of public life. The use of digital tools accelerates and automates professional tasks, reduces the risk of critical errors, simplifies communication processes, and enhances their accessibility and efficiency. The Internet also offers vast opportunities for information retrieval and facilitates interaction among various participants in communication processes. Digital platforms and services are increasingly being utilized in business operations, manufacturing, healthcare, social services, and education. Moreover, digital tools are now frequently employed by mental health professionals for counseling, psychological assessment, and

M. Bakaev et al. (Eds.): IMS 2025, CCIS 2671, pp. 274–287, 2026.
https://doi.org/10.1007/978-3-032-04958-2_21

the provision of psychological support. Their integration into psychological practice demonstrates the growing role of technology in improving service delivery and expanding access to mental health care [1]. In order to examine the extent to which this issue has been explored in foreign research, an analysis was conducted of international studies focusing on the use of digital technologies in the provision of psychological support to participants in educational relations.

2 Literature Review

Psychological support using digital technologies refers to the interaction between a counselor and a client through video conferencing, real-time chat communication, or delayed exchanges via email. This type of interaction presents several challenges, such as: the occasional inability to conduct diagnostic assessments to the necessary extent,

difficulties in exchanging nonverbal cues; the need to maintain contact during crisis situations while adhering to the dynamics of therapeutic relationships (e.g., chat responses must be delivered in real time, regardless of the hour, if stipulated by the communication guidelines); the frequently raised question of how supervision for online counselors should be conducted—whether remotely or requiring in-person contact with the supervisor [2, 3]. Counselors may not always possess the necessary knowledge about how to work with the platform and may insufficiently understand the specifics of counseling using remote technologies [4, 5].

Despite this, digital platforms help overcome barriers that clients might face: geographical distance and logistical inaccessibility [6], excessive travel expenses, inability to make long trips due to health conditions and ongoing treatment. On the other hand, electronic devices, the Internet, social networks, and messengers have become an integral part of modern life [7]. Professional communities dealing with mental health issues actively use social media tools to educate adolescents and young adults: they provide opportunities to discuss psychological health maintenance with professionals, conduct surveys aimed at disseminating information about available help options, and organize online events allowing teenagers to discuss relevant issues with peers [8, 9].

Among the advantages of using information and communication technologies in psychological support is not only the elimination of these barriers but also the ability to adapt tools easily and flexibly according to client needs, monitor progress using automated and gamified methods [10]. Remote consultations can be anonymous since parties don't meet in person, while also making help more accessible through reduced costs per session. However, digital technologies also face certain limitations. While remote access may provide anonymity, it can also identify users through phone numbers or email addresses; system failures or targeted attacks may compromise confidentiality. Other limitations include clients' negative attitudes toward Internet-based information, lack of technical capability to access digital platforms, and insufficient digital literacy [11].

Foreign researchers identify several types of digital platforms for psychological support. The first type includes applications primarily based on self-help principles, offering simulated individual consultations with specialists when needed [12]. However, not all clients could equally and effectively use the application's features, and consultations weren't integrated into the public healthcare system. When seeking in-person help, application users might encounter contradictions between online counselor recommendations and face-to-face consultations.

The second type comprises applications designed for autonomous mental health maintenance - all necessary tools are integrated into the interface, with no option for human consultation. The number of such applications grows annually, most commonly offering stress management tools and promoting psychologically healthy habits, while fewer focus on specific mental disorders [13]. However, many such applications fail to track their effectiveness for users and are developed without scientific validation. Only some are theoretically grounded in published research. Primary developers are commercial companies that often exclude clinical practitioners from the development process, consequently creating products disconnected from established healthcare-based psychological support systems. Exceptions exist for applications supplementing in-person counseling - while lacking online support, their functionality is supervised by the treating therapist.

Another application type involves online support groups. Participants experience a sense of belonging among like-minded individuals with fewer barriers to group participation. Groups may serve both those needing help and their relatives [14]. However, the crucial factor determining the group's therapeutic effectiveness is moderation. Unmoderated communities risk conflicts, emotional contagion, and participant collusion. When moderated by professional counselors, groups are perceived as safe and supportive, demonstrating positive emotional impacts.

The final category consists of real-time online consultation platforms. Clients select specialists for sessions where therapeutic mechanisms mirror in-person consultations, except for physical separation, potentially across different regions. The primary limitation involves maintaining sufficient counselor staffing for around the clock operation with associated costs.

Some digital platforms combine multiple service types. For instance, the «Social Therapy (Majority +)» platform allows clients to choose interaction methods based on needs: using interactive platform features; social media-style communication (posting, newsfeed); participating in peer-moderated or professionally moderated support groups; or video sessions with psychotherapists [15, 16].

Digital psychological support systems are also being developed for university students [17, 18]. Typically serving either as comprehensive support tools or additional crisis intervention channels [19]. In 2018, Madrid University established a psychological service offering hotline calls plus optional email or chat communication. Its primary functions included emergency psychological support and mental health prevention/early detection. Consultant operators were coordinated by experienced clinicians, with all staff receiving specialized training in remote methodologies. Standardized protocols enabled express diagnostics, counseling, and referrals to specialists or medical institutions when necessary [20].

The application system proposed by University of Chicago specialists represented a mood management tool incorporating cognitive-behavioral therapy techniques [21]. During development, the creators deliberately excluded real-time specialist consultation features to enhance scalability within the limited budgets typically allocated by universities for psychological support systems [22, 23]. The application system allows customization, addition or removal of components based on users' specific needs [24].

During COVID-19 lockdowns, Indiana University School of Medicine administration encountered insufficient capacity of campus psychological services to meet all students' needs. Students who relocated to other regions sometimes faced geographical and logistical barriers to accessing psychological support. This created demand for digital services providing psychological assistance. The primary application focused on resilience building, positive self-perception, sleep hygiene, stress management, and mindfulness development. However, these platforms had limitations: they were inaccessible to students without appropriate devices or stable internet connection. Challenges remained in engaging students with visual and hearing impairments or language barriers. Additionally, pandemic-related technology fatigue emerged - with restrictions forcing online education, socializing and services, excessive technology use caused irritation and stress [25].

Educational institutions frequently employ digital platforms for student psychological support. In Australia, a digital service assisting school counselors enabled at-risk student identification, preventive psychological work, and mental health education. Parents reported easier access to school counseling systems and psychological health screenings. Limitations included insufficient high school student support features and mandatory parental consent requirements. The application process involves four stages: student screening, analysis of results to determine the necessary level of support, participation in assistance programs—which include counselor involvement for cases of high anxiety, depression, or suicide risk—and monitoring of mood post-intervention through periodic express diagnostics coupled with program reminders [26].

Digital services also implement health-preserving technologies for adolescents. Australia and New Zealand developed a text-message application reminding users about physical activity, healthy sleep [27], providing behavior modification recommendations, and maintaining motivation for healthy habits. The text message system adapted individually to user profiles (considering dietary restrictions and health conditions), with message content dynamically adjusting based on recorded progress. Students could consult medical professionals when needed, discussing implementation barriers, setting behavioral goals, and analyzing program progress [28].

In India, gaming applications were employed to reach vulnerable adolescent populations, targeting anxiety reduction, depression identification, and behavioral difficulties. The proposed gamification model facilitates behavioral skill development through interactive, engaging, and visually compelling formats. The program's methodology involves students identifying target «Problems» requiring resolution via the application, system-generated «Solution Options», and creation of personalized «to-do lists» for goal achievement. The program incorporates comic-style illustrations depicting adolescent characters modeling constructive behavioral strategies in various situations, including both dialogue and thought representations. Another module reinforces acquired knowledge through experiential reflection on problem-solving. Subsequent updates introduced an interactive «Solution Bank» featuring common scenarios in educational, domestic, and public settings related to emotional experiences and communication processes.

The application additionally provides muscle relaxation techniques, self-regulation exercises, and breathing practices. Navigation utilizes an anthropomorphic guide character fulfilling informational, motivational, and educational functions, including personalized encouragement based on user responses [29]. Similar graphic information delivery methods are applied in other psychological support domains, such as social anxiety intervention [30].

2.1 Methodology, Materials and Methods

Digital tools are actively employed by specialists of psychological services within the education system of the Russian Federation. This study was conducted to examine the prevalence of digital platforms and services in the professional practice of educational psychologists (psychologists working in education), as well as to analyze their potential benefits and limitations. The research aimed to collect data on the use of digital platforms and services by psychologists in higher education institutions for professional purposes. These findings will serve as a foundation for planning and implementing measures to enhance the digital infrastructure of psychological services within the education system.

Research objectives:

1. Assessment of the current state of digital infrastructure supporting psychologists' professional activities;
2. Identification of opportunities and limitations in psychologists' use of digital platforms and services;
3. Determination of key directions and necessary measures for developing psychological services in education with regard to psychologists' utilization of digital platforms and services.

The study involved 14 universities from 8 federal districts of the Russian Federation, which are pilot participants in testing the model of psychological services in the system of higher education. Specialists (heads, teacher-psychologists, psychologists) of psychological services took part in the survey. The questionnaire consists of questions that allowed to study the experience of using digital platforms and services by specialists; the tasks of professional activity solved with the help of these platforms and services; difficulties arising in connection with their use.

2.2 Results of the Study

Let us consider the use of digital platforms and services in the professional activities of psychologists. The figure shows that 78.53% of psychological services use digital platforms and services, as well as have access to electronic databases of the university (92.86%) (Fig. 1).

Next, let us consider what software is used by specializations for psychological support (according to the directions of professional activity) by subdivisions (Fig. 2). Digital platforms and services are used by 64.29% of the studied psychological services of universities for electronic documentation. Respondents indicate the use of such platforms as 1C "Medicine", Google Tables, Yandex Documents, Google Disk, Microsoft Excel (electronic journal), OneDrive.

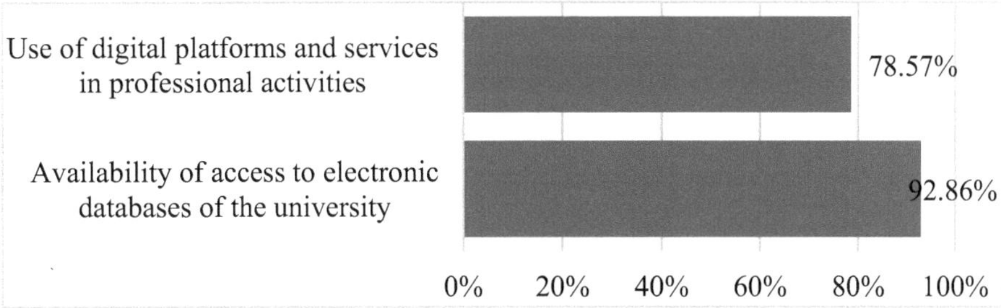

Fig. 1. The use of digital infrastructure by units that provide psychological support at the university.

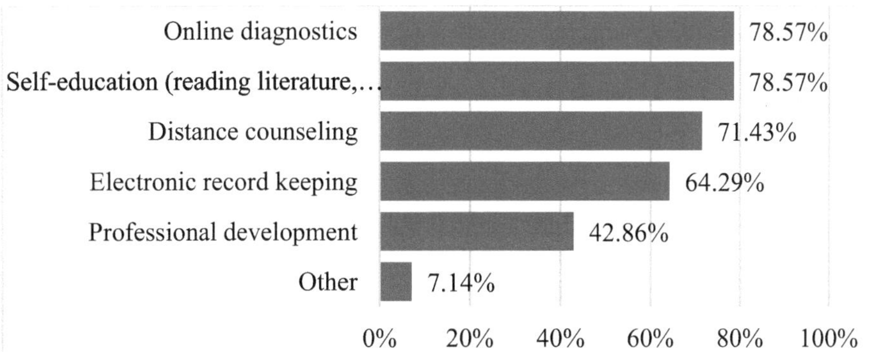

Fig. 2. Use of software for psychological support (by areas of professional activity) by subdivisions.

The platforms used for remote counseling are presented in Fig. 3. The most common are Google Meet (21.43%), WhatsApp (21.43%) and Telegram (21.43%). Zoom (14.29%), Yandex Telebridge (14.29%). The least used platforms are BigBlueButton (7.14%), Microsoft Teams (7.14%), VKontakte (7.14%) and other online messengers (7.14%).

Let's consider the forms used by employees of psychological services for online diagnostics (Fig. 4). Employees of psychological services of higher education institutions use Google Forms (28,57%) to conduct social-psychological testing of students in educational organizations of higher education, 21,43% - platforms SPT, Moodle. Yandex Forms - 14.29%, Botman.on, Google-tables, Maintest, Microsoft Forms, Psy-chometric Expert - 7.14% of respondents.

Zoom (14.29%) was the most common platform for online training, in which employees of psychological services of higher education institutions participated (Fig. 5). Professional development was conducted by specialists on digital platforms BigBlueButton, Webinar, Imaton, MTS Link - 7.14%. Let's analyze the published digital content of psychological services, the results are presented in Fig. 5.

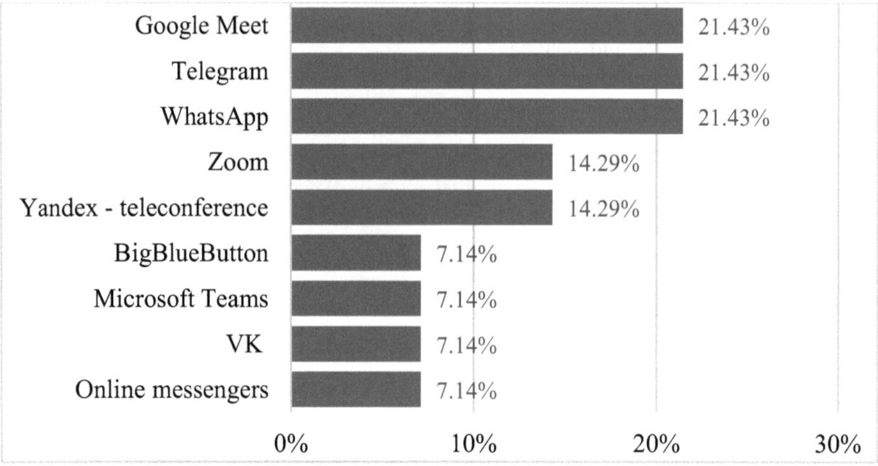

Fig. 3. Digital platforms/services for remote counseling.

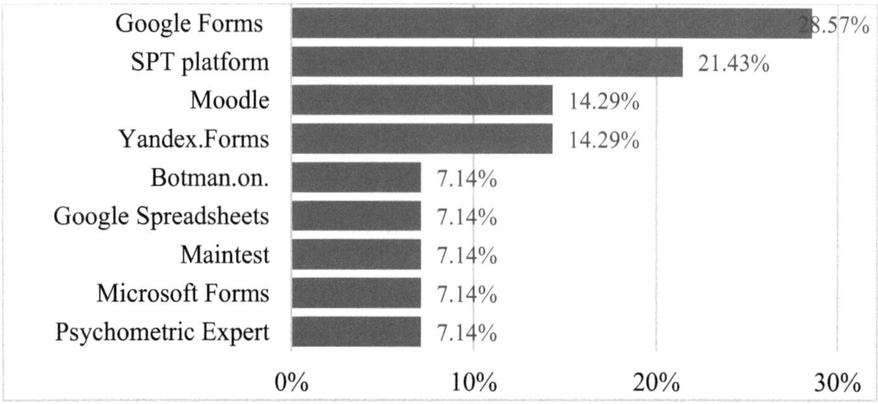

Fig. 4. Digital platforms/services of online diagnostics

We see that among the digital content used by psychological services of higher education institutions, the most popular are video content posted on video hosting sites (21.43% of the sample), radio broadcasts (21.43%), video podcasts (21.43%), audio podcasts are used less frequently (7.14%). In addition, psychological services use a variety of forms of digital content (64.29%), namely topic posts, webinars, surveys and media projects.

In the course of the study, professionals selected areas of their professional activities, in the realization of which digital platforms and services are applied (Fig. 6). Based on the obtained data, it was revealed that most often digital products are used for psychological diagnostics (preparation of materials, processing of results), psychlogical education (preparation of visual handouts and information materials, scenarios of events), and self-education of specialists.

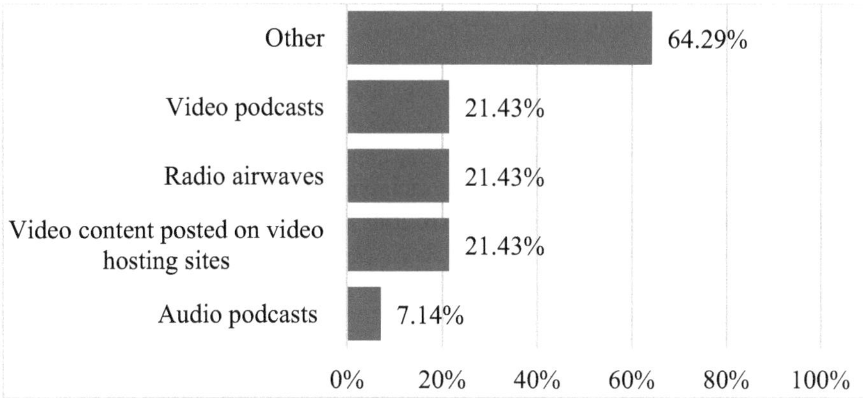

Fig. 5. Publication of digital content by units that provide psychological support in higher education institutions.

The next selected group of work directions included organizational and methodological activities (filling in databases, plans and reporting documents in electronic form), professional development (taking distance courses, watching webinars), preventive work, psychological counseling using the capabilities of messengers and videoconferencing services.

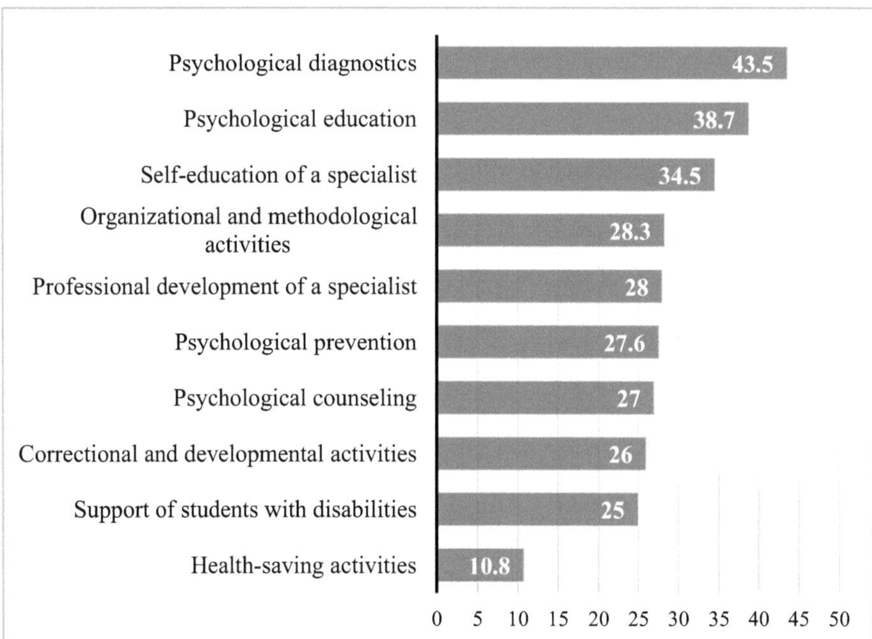

Fig. 6. Distribution of areas of psychologist's activity in the realization of which digital platforms and services are applied.

Various digital platforms and services can also be used for remedial work (from searching for tested scenarios to interactive progress tracking) and for supporting students with disabilities (maintaining databases, using adapted and distance technologies).

The least frequent choice was health-preserving activities, which indicates less attention to preserving physical resources when it comes to digital platforms and services.

The next indicator of the questionnaire demonstrates the most frequently solved professional tasks with the help of digital platforms and services, these data indicate the level of flexibility and functionality in the labor activity of a psychologist (Fig. 7).

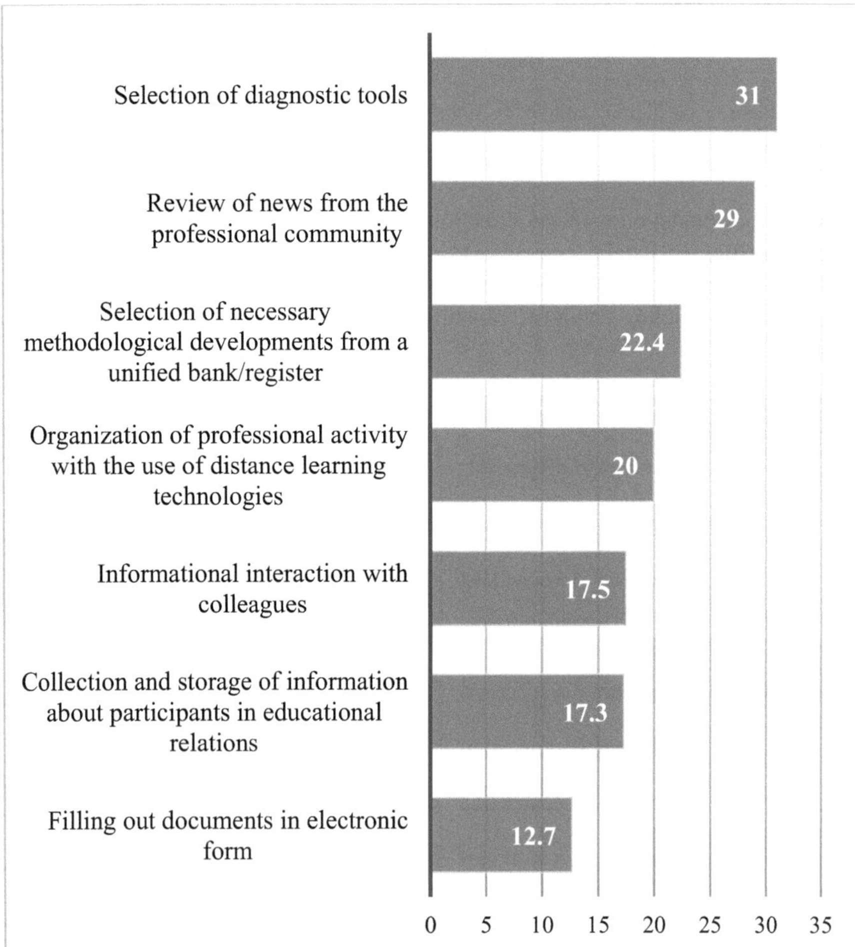

Fig. 7. Number of mentions of professional tasks of psychologist, in which digital platforms and services are applied.

The main advantages of using digital platforms and services by specialists of psychological service in the system of higher education are simplification of the process of solving professional tasks related to the convenience and reliability of processing the results of psychological diagnostics, storage and systematization of data, search for methodological developments of psychological and pedagogical orientation. One of the most important indicators for the participants of the study was the reduction of paperwork time (Fig. 8).

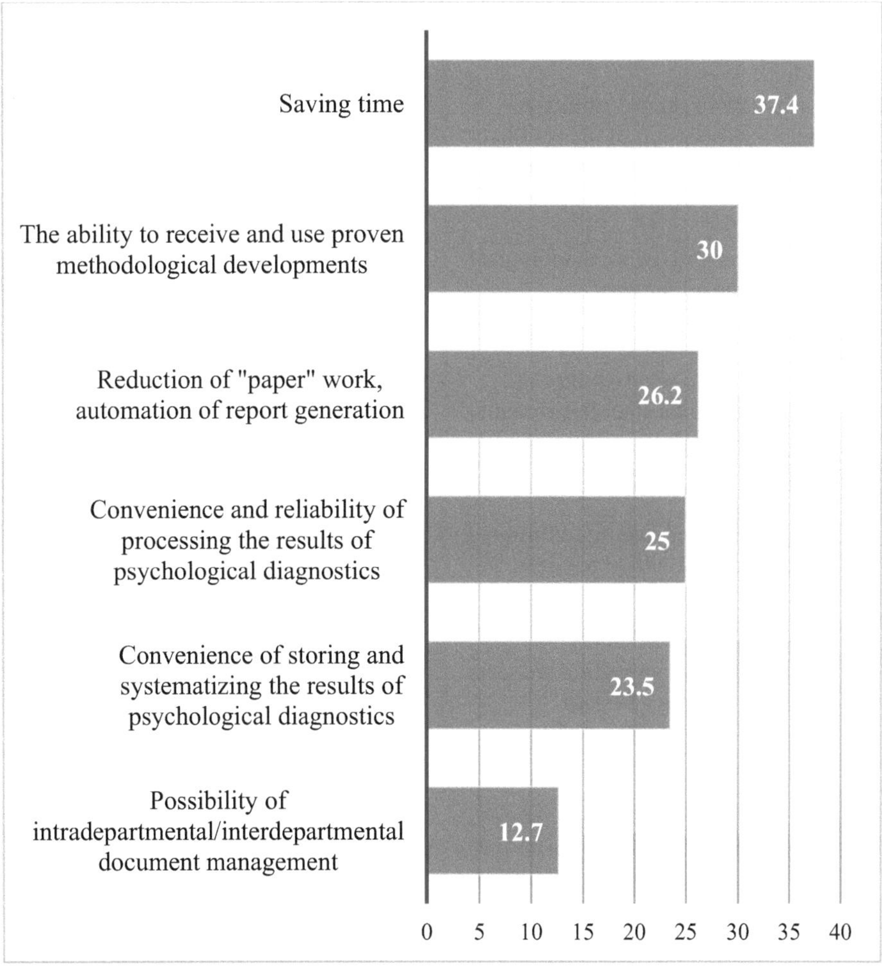

Fig. 8. Frequency of selection of the main factors indicating the usefulness of using digital platforms and services.

Based on the results obtained, the disadvantages of psychologists' use of digital platforms and services in their professional activities were also identified. The main ones are related to the allocation of additional time to work in platforms and services, as well as the lack of the possibility of automatic data processing and uploading, which would speed up the work of specialists. One of the problems that psychologists often face is the availability of unproven methodological developments that require additional time to verify their proven effectiveness (Fig. 9).

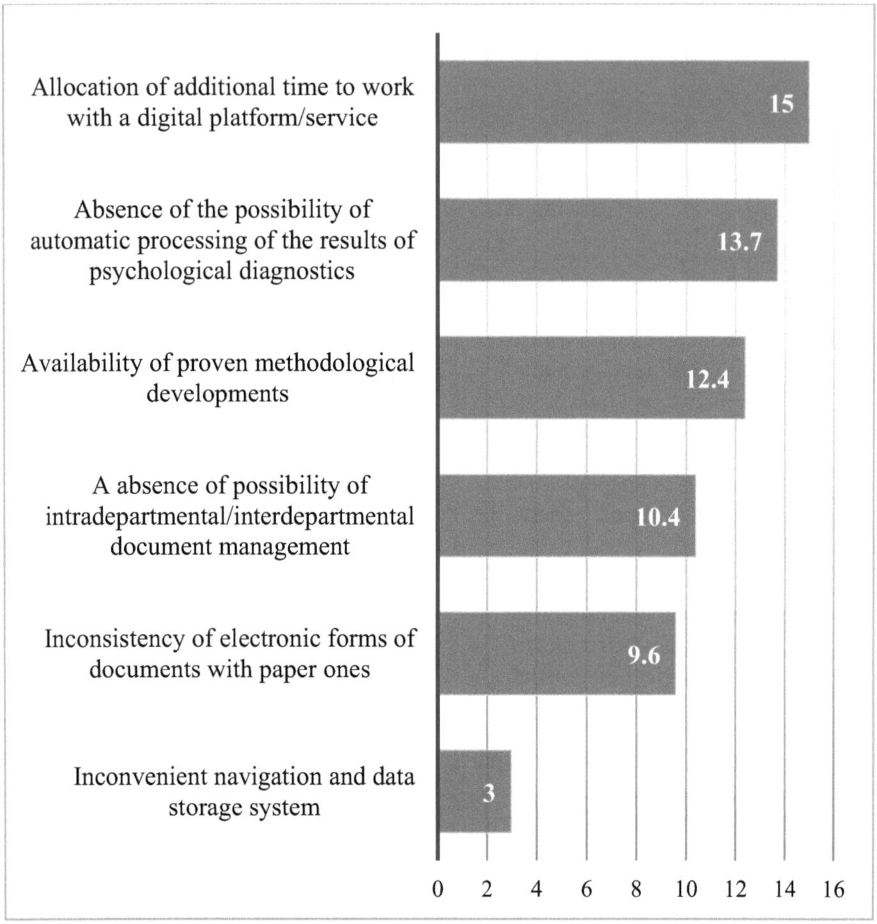

Fig. 9. Frequency of deficiencies in the use of digital platforms and services by psychologists.

3 Discussion of Results

The presented study was conducted to obtain information about the current state of the psychological service in the educational system in terms of the use of digital platforms and services by psychologists in their professional activities. The results obtained allow us to draw several conclusions. First, slightly less than half of the respondents in the study sample use digital services in their psychological practice. Secondly, the use of digital platforms and services occurs primarily for the purpose of expanding diagnostic capabilities and sharing experience within the professional community, as well as self-improvement and self-education of the specialist. Thirdly, the most frequently mentioned difficulties include slow downloading/uploading of the data obtained during diagnostics, inconsistency of electronic forms with paper forms and documents, inability to automatically process empirical data and quickly obtain the necessary results, insufficient availability of tested methodological developments and lack of interagency cooperation. Based on the presented results and conclusions, the following suggestions are offered for discussion:

1. Raising awareness among psychologists in the system of higher education about the possibilities of using digital platforms and services in solving professional problems, holding thematic seminars to exchange experience among specialists, training meetings to master the functionality of digital platforms and services.
2. Development of a navigator of digital platforms and services that can be used to solve a wide range of problems in the professional activity of a psychologist in compliance with the rules of information security and the law on the preservation of personal data.
3. Conducting a study of the degree of satisfaction with the use of digital platforms and services by psychologists, as well as assessing the formation of digital competencies of psychological service specialists in the system of higher education.

This publication has been supported by the RUDN University Scientific Projects Grant System, project № 051331-2-000.

References

1. Glueckauf, R.L., et al.: Survey of psychologists' telebehavioral health practices: technology use, ethical issues, and training needs. Prof. Psychol. Res. Pract. **49**, 205–219 (2018)
2. Giotakos, O., Papadomarkaki, E. Online counselling: the prospect of a therapeutic connection. Psychiatriki: Q. J. Hellenic Psychiatr. Assoc. **27**(2), 127–135 (2016)
3. Mohr, D.C., Riper, H., Schueller, S.M.: A solution-focused research approach to achieve an implementable revolution in digital mental health. JAMA Psychiat. **75**(2), 113–114 (2018)
4. Mendes-Santos, C., Weiderpass, E., Santana, R., Andersson. G.: Portuguese psychologists' attitudes towards internet interventions: An exploratory cross-sectional study. JMIR Mental Health **7**, 1–17 (2020)
5. Cipolletta, S., Mocellin, D.: Online counseling: an exploratory survey of Italian psychologists' attitudes towards new ways of interaction. Psychother. Res. **28**, 909–924 (2018)
6. Pierce, B.S., Perrin, P.B., Tyler, C.M., McKee, G.B., Watson, J.D.: The COVID-19 telepsychology revolution: a national study of pandemic-based changes in U.S. mental health delivery. Am. Psychol. **76**(1), 14–25 (2021)
7. Feijt, M.A., de Kort, Y.A., Bongers, I.M., IJsselsteijn, W.A.: Perceived drivers and barriers to the adoption of eMental health by psychologists: the construction of the levels of adoption of eMental health model. J. Med. Internet Res. **20**, 1–13 (2018)
8. Pretorius, C., Chambers, D., Coyle, D.: Young people's online help-seeking and mental health difficulties: systematic narrative review. J. Med. Internet Res. **1**(11), 1–17 (2019)
9. Rice, S., O'Bree, B., Wilson, M., McEnery, C., Lim, M.H., Hamilton, M., et al.: Leveraging the social network for treatment of social anxiety: pilot study of a youth-specific digital intervention with a focus on engagement of young men. Internet Interv. **20**, 1–10 (2020)
10. Borghouts, J., Eikey, E., Mark, G., et al.: Barriers to and Facilitators of user engagement with digital mental health interventions: systematic review. J. Med. Internet Res. **23**, 1–29 (2021)

11. Dores, A.R., Geraldo, A., Carvalho, I.P., Barbosa, F.: The use of new digital information and communication technologies in psychological counseling during the COVID-19 pandemic. Int. J. Environ. Res. Public Health **17**(20), 1–24 (2020)
12. Rice, S., Gleeson, J., Davey, C., Hetrick, S., Parker, A., Lederman, R., et al.: Moderated online social therapy for depression relapse prevention in young people: pilot study of a "next generation" online intervention. Early Interv. Psychiatry **12**(4), 613–625 (2018)
13. Baumel, A., Muench, F., Edan, S., Kane, J.M.: Objective user engagement with mental health apps: systematic search and panel-based usage analysis. J. Med. Internet Res. **21**(9), 1–15 (2019)
14. Lederman, R., Gleeson, J., Wadley, G., D'alfonso, S., Rice, S., Santesteban-Echarri, O., et al.: Support for carers of young people with mental illness. ACM Trans. Comput. Hum. Interact. **26**(1), 1–33 (2019)
15. Rice, S., Gleeson, J., Leicester, S., Bendall, S., D'Alfonso, S., Gilbertson, T., et al.: Implementation of the enhanced moderated online social therapy (MOST+) model within a national youth e-mental health service (eHeadSpace): protocol for a single group pilot study for help-seeking young people. JMIR Res. Protocols **7**(2), 1–14 (2018)
16. Alvarez-Jimenez, M., et al.: A novel multimodal digital service (moderated online social therapy+) for help-seeking young people experiencing mental ill-health: pilot evaluation within a national youth e-mental health service. J. Med. Internet Res. **22**(8), 1–18 (2020)
17. Lattie, E.G., Adkins, E.C., Winquist, N., Stiles-Shields, C., Wafford, Q.E., Graham, A.K.: Digital mental health interventions for depression, anxiety, and enhancement of psychological well-being among college students: systematic review. J. Med. Internet Res. **21**(7), 1–19 (2019)
18. Rackoff, G.N., Fitsimmons-Craft, E.E., Tyalor, C.B., et al.: A randomized controlled Tiral of internet-based self-help for stress during the COVID-19 pandemic. J. Adolesc. Health. **71**, 157–163 (2022)
19. Kern, A., Hong, V., Song, J., Lipson, S.K., Eisenberg, D.: Mental health apps in a college setting: openness, usage, and attitudes. Mhealth **4**, 1–12 (2018)
20. Martos Torrecilla, L., et al.: PciCALL, emergency psychological assistance. BMJ Open **9**, 9–10 (2019)
21. Mohr, D.C., Schueller, S.M., Tomasino, K.N., Kaiser, S.M., Alam, N., Karr, C., et al.: Comparison of the effects of coaching and receipt of app recommendations on depression, anxiety, and engagement in the IntelliCare platform: factorial randomized controlled trial. J. Med. Internet Res. **21**(8), 1–20 (2019)
22. Lattie, E., Cohen, K.A., Winquist, N., Mohr, D.C.: Examining an app-based mental health self-care program, IntelliCare for college students: single-arm pilot study. JMIR Mental Health **7**(10), 1–9 (2020)
23. Cohen, K.A., Graham, A.K., Lattie, E.G.: Aligning students and counseling centers on student mental health needs and treatment resources. J. Am. Coll. Health **70**(3), 724–732 (2022)
24. Graham, A.K., Greene, C.J., Kwasny, M.J., Kaiser, S.M., Lieponis, P., Powell, T., et al.: Coached mobile app platform for the treatment of depression and anxiety among primary care patients: a randomized clinical trial. JAMA Psychiat. **77**(9), 906–914 (2020)
25. Hensel, D.J.: Digital interventions to improve college and university student mental health. J. Adolesc. Health. **71**(2), 141–142 (2022)
26. O'Dea, B., et al.: Delivering a digital mental health service in Australian secondary schools: understanding school counsellors' and parents' experiences. Health Serv. Insights **14**, 1–9 (2021)
27. Van Vuuren, C.L., Wachter, G.G., Veenstra, R., Rijnhart, J.J.M., van der Wal, M.F., Chinapaw, M.J.M., et al.: Associations between overweight and mental health problems among adolescents, and the mediating role of victimization. BMC Public Health **19**(1), 1–10 (2019)

28. Raeside, R., et al.: A healthy lifestyle text message intervention for adolescents: protocol for the Health4Me randomized controlled trial. BMC Public Health **22**, 1–9 (2022)
29. Gonsalves, P.P., et al.: Design and development of the "POD adventures" smartphone game: a blended problem-solving intervention for adolescent mental health in India. Front. Public Health **7**, 1–12 (2019)
30. Rice, S., O'Bree, B., Wilson, M., McEnery, C., Lim, M.H., Hamilton, M., et al.: Development of a graphic medicine-enabled social media-based intervention for youth social anxiety. Clin. Psychol. **25**(2), 140–152 (2021)

Determinants of Attitudes Toward COVID-19 Vaccination: A Survey-Based Analysis

Elena Artemenko and Anna Probst(✉)

Laboratory for Social and Cognitive Informatics, National Research University Higher School of Economics (HSE University, Saint Petersburg 192148, Russia
an.probst2004@gmail.com

Abstract. Despite the high mortality from COVID-19, the severity of symptoms, evidence of vaccine effectiveness, and its free availability, the adoption rate of COVID-19 vaccination in Russia was slow. Attitude is suggested to be one of the major factors associated with health-related decisions, particularly vaccine refusal. However, less attention is paid to the factors underlying the attitude itself. The current study systematizes the question of exploring factors related to COVID-19 vaccine attitudes and examines predictors of attitudes toward the vaccine. As part of this study, we analyze the results of a survey (N = 170) conducted at the end of 2023, assessing COVID-19 vaccination experience, general perceptions of vaccines, and attitudes toward the COVID-19 vaccine. The results identified a group of factors influencing the formation of a positive attitude toward COVID-19 vaccination. These factors include being female, perceiving the COVID-19 vaccine as similar to other vaccines, having a more positive attitude toward vaccines in general, and getting vaccinated voluntarily.

Keywords: Attitude · COVID-19 · Survey-based approach · Vaccination

1 Introduction

The first identified case of COVID-19 in Russia was reported by the Federal Service for Surveillance on Consumer Rights Protection and Human Wellbeing on 31 January 2020 [1]. By 2022, there were 4 vaccines developed (Gam-COVID-Vac, Gam-COVID-Vac-Lio (Gam-COVID-Vac booster), EpiVacCorona, CoviVac, Sputnik Light) [2]. The effectiveness of developed vaccines is the subject of research now; however, most conclusions are concerned with its effectiveness rather than non effectiveness. One of the most prevalent vaccines mentioned is Sputnik V or Gam-COVID-Vac, the effectiveness of which is estimated to be 71% and 87% with 2 and 3 vaccination doses respectively [3]. By January 2024 the cumulative number of deaths from COVID-19 in Russia has exceeded 670 000 [4]. The number of death highlights the critical need for public health measures. Vaccination cannot only be a tool to prevent disease transmission and the combat of mortality, but also to reduce the severity of COVID-19, especially when containment is not closely followed or absent. Even though, early adoption rate of vaccination in Russia was slow [5]. Moreover, the vaccine is free and widely available with

M. Bakaev et al. (Eds.): IMS 2025, CCIS 2671, pp. 288–303, 2026.
https://doi.org/10.1007/978-3-032-04958-2_22

many vaccination points opened, even offering the possibility to get vaccination at home [6]. Indeed, in November 2024 nearly 60% of the Russian population was vaccinated with at least one dose of vaccine and 54.5% were fully vaccinated [5].

Refusal for vaccination is one of the problems faced when addressing the issue of non-achieving desirable vaccination rates required for collective immunity obtaining [7]. Despite the fact that vaccination was mandatory for certain groups of population in most regions of Russia, vaccination rates were lower than required for future morbidity prevention [6]. Researches show that while mandatory vaccination increased vaccine uptake, it still does not cover particular groups of people [8]. This evidence can suggest that obligatory measures solely are not sufficient to increase immunization of population. Thus, it raises the question of importance to study other factors which can shape vaccination-related decisions.

Under discussions about increasing voluntary vaccination rates, researchers often come to a question of understanding hesitancy, the origins of it and ways to change them [9]. One of major concepts discussed is attitude. In turn, attitude comprises individual's beliefs, safety and effectiveness perceptions and is also often associated with age, gender, education and other socio-economic features as modifying factors [6]. Understanding what is associated with attitude to vaccination and which factors can predict the attitude can be helpful for designing interventions aimed at encouraging voluntary vaccination.

2 Literature Review and Hypotheses

2.1 Theoretical Model

As it was introduced, the vaccination uptake in Russia was not high. Coming to the question of what else could make people willing to vaccinate, we turn to Health Beliefs Model (HBM). HBM proposes the idea of personal perceptions, attitudes and beliefs for behavioral practices in shaping health-related behaviors of people. Thus, components of the model can serve as predictors of people taking or not taking actions to prevent some kind of illness [10]. As it is harder to explore the vaccination uptake in Russia by vaccination status from the point of people's opinions and desires. Applying it to Russian context, it can be used for understanding people's opinions for increasing the rate of people's own decisions to get vaccinated. The current study, therefore, is interest in predicting of personal attitudes towards COVID-19 vaccine. In vaccine context preventive behavior for HBM is mostly operationalized as vaccination intention, which is not yet completed action [11–13], or hesitancy, which is vaccine refusal or delayed acceptance [14].

The current paper systematizes the question of exploring factors, related to attitude on COVID-19 vaccine.

The objectives of the study are to examine (1) what is associated with the attitude to COVID-19 vaccine, and (2) what are the predictors of attitude towards COVID-19 vaccine.

2.2 Socio-demographics

Researches show that people of older ages are more willing to take vaccine than younger ages [15–17]. The potential explanation is devoted to higher risk of symptom severity

[18]. Gender is sometimes associated with vaccine hesitancy: some studies reveal that men show higher vaccine acceptance than women [15, 16, 19, 20]. However, other findings support that there is no difference between genders [6, 21, 22]. With no significant difference between genders it is discussed that men are not concerned about having COVID but women are concerned, however, they require providing more information about vaccine [23]. The difference in attitudes among males and females was also seen as women are concerned with fertility-related outcomes after receiving the vaccine which results even in more negative attitude among younger women [24].

Studies also show that a worse self-rated health level (either 'bad' or 'fair') is found to have significant positive association with annual vaccination [25]. Additionally, women with 'good' self-rated health are associated with getting vaccine over not getting it. Researches show that lower self-reported health is associated with more technical reasons for non-vaccination (e.g. transportation problems, long waiting time) and higher self-reported health is associated with perceptual reasons of non-vaccination (e.g. considering no need for vaccination) [26].

Medical education is suggested to be associated with vaccination attitudes and willingness to be vaccinated. Studies prove that among medical students and healthcare professionals vaccination attitudes are more positive [27]. It is often explained by the idea of knowledge and awareness: medical background suggest higher chance for individual to obtain more trustworthy information about vaccination, and additionally it provides more skills in working with health-related information allowing to have better vaccine knowledge and increase their attitude and willingness to receive vaccination [27].Therefore, mentioned variables can result in creating cofounding effects and should be controlled for in the model.

2.3 Interest in Medicine

Interest in medicine can be treated as another source of obtaining deeper knowledge of health-related topics. The study where interest in alternative medicine was investigated in relation to attitude towards it [28] found no difference between medical and nursing students. Authors mention high interest in alternative medicine among most students regardless of specialization which highlights that it may well be that presence of medical/nursing background serves as an interactive term. Thus, it may be proper to compare interest among people with and without any medical background (either education or occupation). In addition, Vasileva et al. [20] suggest that high variability among healthcare professionals in their attitudes towards vaccination reviewed in Sallam et al. [29] may be explained by individual ways of information processing based on some deeper beliefs. Taking it into consideration may also suggest the idea to investigate how for people with and without medical background interest in medicine shape the attitude to vaccination against covid.

H1(1) Individuals with interest in medicine have a more positive attitude towards COVID-19 vaccine than those not interested in medicine.

H2(2) Among people with education/occupation in medicine those with interest in medicine have a more positive attitude towards COVID-19 vaccine and among people without education or occupation in medicine those with interest in medicine have a more positive attitude towards COVID-19 vaccine with greater difference in attitudes among people without education or occupation.

2.4 General Vaccines Perception

Some research aimed at examining willingness to COVID-19 vaccination and COVID-19 vaccine acceptance examine general vaccine perceptions as possible predictor. Such perception is seen as a complex variable which consists of such dimensions as safety, importance, effectiveness perceptions etc. [30–32]. Attitudes to vaccination in general are shown to be significant in prediction of intention to get vaccinated. Russia is found to demonstrate low acceptance rate [29]. Among the main reasons are perception of general vaccines effectiveness and perception of general vaccines safety. The combination of similar constructs may be used as general perception of vaccines in Russian context.

Also, the popularity of anti-vax movements can suggest to researchers that vaccines rejection in general may also be a reason for non-vaccination or negative attitude towards vaccine. Thus, it can go beyond mere effectiveness and/or safety related reasons and should be treated as a separate variable similarly to what research of Neumann-Böhme et al. [33] shows and it is interesting to see the relationship with attitude of both mentioned measures.

H2(1) Individuals with more positive attitude towards vaccines in general have more positive attitude towards COVID-19 vaccine.

Another part of associated with vaccine perception factors can be vaccination background. Studies show that previous experience of vaccination against influenza [34–36]. This study is aimed to utilize measure of person's vaccination history, asking whether they continue to vaccinate after 18 years. Firstly, it covers not only actions committed in the past, but may be understood as grasping current or future behavior as well. Secondly, it asks more about personal decision rather than happened action, so it can provide additional meaning to examining the relationship with attitude towards COVID-19 vaccine.

H2(2) Individuals who continue to vaccinate have a more positive attitude towards COVID-19 vaccine.

2.5 Vaccine COVID-19 Perception

Vaccine attitude can be studied in different ways. Some researchers refer to vaccine attitude as levels of hesitancy to vaccinate [30]; or willingness to vaccinate [37]; or intention to receive vaccination [31]. Often the scale is presented as categories of willing, doubtful, hesitant [38]. Also, attitude to vaccine can be derived from various questions aimed to grasp different specific vaccination sides such as perceptual benefits, risks, usefulness, importance, trust etc. or implementing known scales e.g. Vaccine Attitudes Examination Scale (VAX) [39] Another aspect of measurement is vaccination uptake which can be binary and presented as status of whether the person was vaccinated or not [40]. Some studies do not differentiate measurements of attitude and acceptance, measuring acceptance through action [41], while others try to differentiate between intention, action, behavior, and attitudes [36]. Intention-action gap is among potential reasons when addressing low vaccination uptake [42]. Therefore, it can be useful to examine already committed action in relation to attitudes. Chambon et al. [43] also indicate that intention and attitude often co-occur. Hence, there is a potential redundancy problem when using both variables in research, since they can be related to the same concept in the understanding of such questions. Therefore, it may be appropriate to use a more general variable of the overall attitude towards vaccination to reduce the possibility of measuring the same concept.

It can be important to investigate reasons of vaccination as it gives different perception of vaccine [23]. It should be noted that vaccination in Russia was obligatory for specific groups of population and the implementation of it varied by decision of regional authorities. There was no region where vaccination was completely obligatory for every person, however, there were still many criteria for inclusion into the obligatory vaccination group list. Thus, it suggests some variety of vaccination reason. Moreover, obligation can create different perception in relation to the rest of vaccines which are mostly not obligatory.

H3(1) Attitudes towards COVID-19 vaccine differ between (1) people who were needed (forced) to vaccinate; (2) those whose decision to be vaccinated was their own decision; (3) people who decided not to receive vaccination at all.

Personal past experiences [34–36] with vaccines and attitude to vaccines in general [30–32] can be associated with attitude towards particular vaccine, it may be useful to see if treating vaccines similarly or differently can predict attitude towards COVID-19 vaccine. It may derive from the fact that people can unintentionally compare COVID-19 vaccines to the rest of vaccines and evaluate their opinion based on it.

H3(2) Attitudes towards COVID-19 vaccine differ between people who think that COVID-19 vaccine is similar to the rest of vaccines and those who perceive it differently.

3 Methodology

3.1 Data Collection

The data was collected with Yandex Toloka platform through Google form. Data collection was organised by Laboratory for Social and Cognitive Informatics. The participation was paid. 179 respondents were recruited.

3.2 Measures

Socio-demographics

Gender and *age* were reported by respondents. *Health* was measured with 7-point likert scale asking respondents to rate own health level where 1 is Very low and 7 is Very high. *Medical education/occupation* was measured with binary questions asking respondents if their education or field of current work is related to medicine and if they are interested in medicine respectively. *Interest in medicine* was measured with binary questions asking respondents if they are interested in medicine.

General Vaccines Measures

General vaccines attitude was measured with 7-point likert scale through statement for respondents ‘I could evaluate my attitude towards vaccines as’ where 1 is Negative and 7 is Positive. *General vaccines perception* was received as a rounded mean of vaccines safety and vaccines helpfulness evaluation with 1 as most Negative and 7 as most Positive attitude. In turn, vaccine safety and vaccine helpfulness variables were measured with questions ‘I think that vaccines are safe for the organism’ and ‘I think that vaccines are helpful for preventing diseases in the future’ respectively.

Continue vaccinating was measured with binary question asking if person continues getting vaccinated after the age of 18 (e.g. flu vaccination).

COVID-19 Specific Measures

Vaccination decision variable was received from question which asked respondents to select their reason for vaccination from the following: ‘It was my decision to avoid illness/get over it easier/not infect relatives/reduce the burden on hospitals’ and.

‘I was forced to study/work/relatives/other circumstances’, then the former was coded as My decision to vaccinate and the latter as Was forced to vaccinate. It was possible not to select reason or leave free answer, then answers where checked on vaccination status of individual (measured with the same questionnaire) and coded as Not vaccinated. *Vaccine similarity* was obtained through binary question asking if COVID-19 vaccine is the same as the rest of vaccines.

4 Results

4.1 Characteristics of Participants

A total of 178 respondents participated in the study, with half identifying as female. The participants ranged in age from 18 to 77 years (M = 38.97, SD = 11.13). Among the respondents, 53.4% reported an interest in medicine, and 11.2% indicated having medical education or working in a medical occupation.

The mean self-assessed health level was 4.98 with 1 meaning “Very low”. The mean score for attitude toward vaccines in general was 4.83 (SD = 1.55), while the mean score for attitude toward the COVID-19 vaccine was slightly lower at 4.25 (SD = 1.91). Notably, 56.7% of respondents perceived the COVID-19 vaccine as distinct from other vaccines. Additionally, the mean score for perceptions of vaccine safety and helpfulness was 4.85 (SD = 1.56), with all scores measured on a scale from 1 (“Very negative”) to 7 (“Very positive”) (See Fig. 1).

In terms of vaccination, 36% of participants reported being vaccinated by own incentive, 16.9% reported the external obligations to do so and the remainder decided not to get vaccination. Furthermore, 65.7% of respondents indicated that they continue to receive vaccinations after 18. The results with mean attitude on COVID-19 vaccine can be found in Table 1.

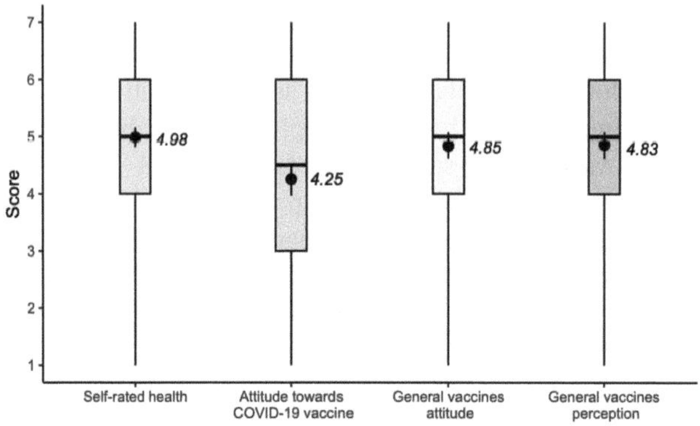

Fig. 1. Distribution of numeric variables responses, with mean scores

Table 1. Descriptive statistics

Variable	Category	Number of people	Proportion, %	Mean attitude
Gender	Female	89	50	4.4
	Male	89	50	4.1
Medical education/occupation	Yes	20	11.2	4.2
	No	158	88.8	4.3
Interest in medicine	Yes	95	53.4	4.5
	No	83	46.6	3.9
Vaccination decision	Vaccinated, my decision	64	36	5.7
	Vaccinated, was forced	30	16.9	3.8
	Not vaccinated	84	47.1	3.3
Continue vaccinationg	Yes	61	34.3	5.6
	No	117	65.7	3.5
Vaccines similarity	COVID-19 vaccine is the same as all vaccines	77	43.3	4.5
	COVID-19 vaccine is different	101	56.7	4.0

4.2 Interest in Medicine

Interest in medicine was not found to be significant in predicting attitude towards COVID-19 vaccine. The association between interest in medicine and medical education/occupation is significant (*p = 0.006*). However, people of medical education/occupation having no interest in medicine included 3 people only, so medical education/occupation was not included to the model as either interaction or separate predictor. Results of linear regression are presented in Table 2.

Table 2. Linear regression on attitude towards COVID-19 vaccine

Predictors	Estimates	CI	p	Estimates	CI	p
(Intercept)	3.74	–0.15–7.62	0.059	4.54	0.58–8.50	**0.025**
Age	–0.76	–1.76 – 0.25	0.138	0.95	–1.98 – 0.08	0.070
Gender [Male]	–4.76	–9.44 – –0.09	**0.046**	5.10	–9.89 – –0.31	**0.037**
Self–rated health	0.14	–0.02 – 0.30	0.085	0.11	– 0.05 – 0.28	0.165
Interest in medicine [No]	–0.14	–0.51 – 0.24	0.477	0.04	–0.43 – 0.34	0.829
Continue vaccinating	–0.44	–0.92 – 0.04	0.071	0.43	–0.92 – 0.06	0.083
Vaccines similarity [Similar]	0.47	0.12 – 0.83	0.009	0.48	0.11 – 0.85	**0.010**
General vaccines perception	2.27	1.83 – 2.71	**< 0.001**			
Not vaccinated	–1.20	–1.68 – –0.72	**< 0.001**	–1.22	–1.71 – –0.73	**< 0.001**
Vaccinated [Was forced]	–1.03	–1.60 – –0.45	**0.001**	0.90	–1.49– –0.30	**0.003**
Age × Gender [Male]	1.31	0.02 – 2.60	**0.046**	1.43	0.11 – 2.76	**0.034**
General vaccines attitude				2.21	1.76 – 2.67	**< 0.001**
Observations	178			178		
R^2 / R^2 adjusted	0.648 / 0.626			0.630 / 0.608		

4.3 General Vaccines Perception

Both correlation between general vaccines perception and general vaccines attitude were found to be strongly positively correlated with attitude towards COVID–19 vaccine (*p* < *0.001* and *rho* = *0.73, rho* = *0.77* respectively). Both variables of general measures were shown to be significant predictors for attitude towards COVID-19 vaccine: with increasing of general attitude/perception, attitude to COVID-19 vaccine also increases. The model, that included general vaccine perception, performed slightly better than the one that included general vaccine attitude, explaining 62.6% of variance in the first case and 60.8% in second.

People who continue to vaccinate after 18 years differ significantly from those who do not in attitude to COVID-19 vaccine ($p < 0.001$), the magnitude is large (*effsize* = *0.53*). Most people of this category have positive opinion about vaccines in general with very few cases of negative opinion towards COVID-19 vaccine. In examining relationship between general vaccines perception and attitude towards COVID-19 vaccine the correlation is stronger among those who continue to vaccinate (*rho* = *0.76* vs *rho* = *0.67*). The situation is similar for general vaccines attitude and attitude towards COVID-19 vaccine: 0.74 among people continuing vaccination after 18 and 0.67 among the opposed category. The difference in answers is more present in opposed category as well: those who do not continue vaccinating after 18 with negative attitudes to COVID-19 vaccine have different levels of general attitude (Fig. 2a). In examining general perception of vaccines, this same category has more cases of undefined opinion, but still the attitude towards COVID-19 vaccine is negative (Fig. 2b).

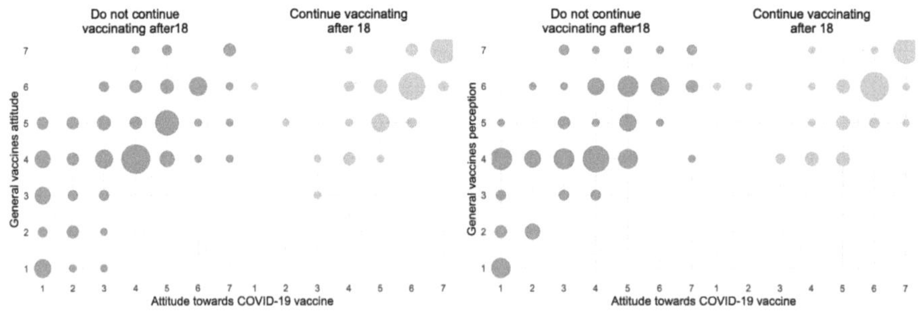

(a) (b)

Fig. 2. Relationship between general vaccines attitude, perception and COVID-19 vaccine attitude by levels of continuing vaccination

As predictor of attitude towards COVID-19 vaccine, it was not found to be significant – the effect disappears after controlling for health. It is possible that these variables share some variance, because the relationship between them is significant, however, effect size is 0.3.

4.4 Vaccine COVID-19 Perception

People who were vaccinated due to own decision have a more positive attitude towards the COVID-19 vaccine (*median* = *6.0*) than those who were vaccinated because they were needed to (*median* = *4.0*) and those who were not vaccinated (*median* = *4.0*). There is no difference found between later two groups ($p = 0.45$) (Fig. 3).

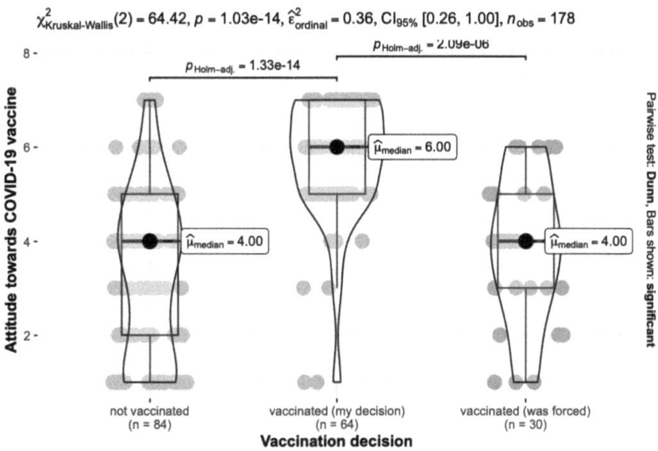

Fig. 3. Attitude towards COVID-19 vaccine by vaccination decision

When predicting attitude towards COVID-19 vaccine with linear regression the result remains: people who made their own decision to get vaccination differ significantly from those not vaccinated and forced ($p < 0.001$). People who think that COVID-19 vaccine is similar to the rest of existing vaccines were not shown to significantly differ from those of the opposite opinion ($p = 0.122$). However, including opinion on vaccines similarity was found to be significant predictor for attitude towards COVID-19 vaccine ($p = 0.013$). For people thinking that COVID-19 vaccine is similar to other vaccines attitude towards COVID-19 vaccine is more positive. Additionally, among people who think vaccines are similar, the correlation between attitude towards COVID-19 vaccine and general vaccines attitude (rho = 0.81), general vaccines perception (*rho* = *0.75*) was higher than among the opposite group (*rho* = *0.75* and *rho* = *0.73* respectively). People thinking of COVID-19 vaccine as similar with the rest of vaccines have more linear relationship between general vaccines perception and attitude with COVID-19 vaccine attitude and larger part of the opinion is neutral or positive. People who think vaccines are different have more cases when they exhibit negative attitude to COVID-19 vaccine, but have different levels of attitude to vaccines generally (Fig. 4a). Most people of the same group when evaluating helpfulness and safety of vaccines remained neutral in general vaccines attitude (Fig. 4b).

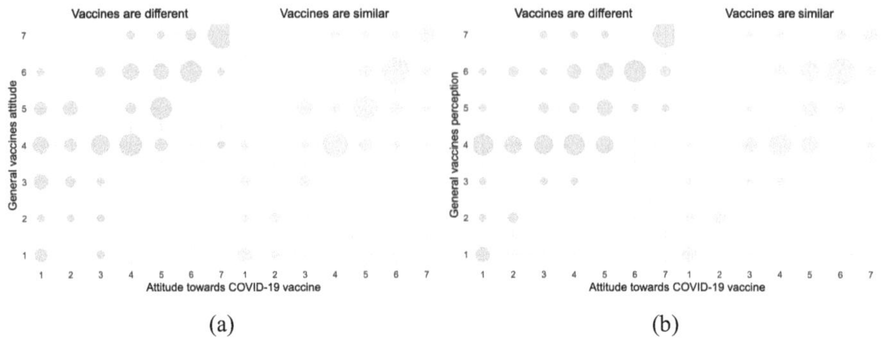

Fig. 4. Relationship between general vaccines attitude, perception and COVID-19 vaccine attitude by levels of continuing vaccination

5 Discussion

For prediction of attitude towards COVID-19 vaccine, being female of younger age or being older for males, seeing COVID-19 vaccine as similar to the rest vaccines, having more positive attitude to vaccines in general, being vaccinated for own will increases the attitude.

The variables of main interest in the study are interest in medicine, vaccines related variables (continuing vaccination after 18; general vaccines perception; general vaccines attitude) and COVID-19 specific variables (similarity of COVID-19 vaccine; COVID-19 vaccination decision).

5.1 Interest in Medicine

Interest in medicine was not significant for predicting attitude towards COVID-19 vaccine, however, was associated with it. Probably, the variables included can be moderators or mediators in the relationship between interest and attitude, so that we do not see significance. For example, interest can be among factors related to openness to information, intellectuals humility or conspiracy beliefs [44], which create complex relationships and cannot be examined only through interest.

5.2 General Vaccines Perception

General vaccines perception showed to be significant for predicting attitude towards COVID-19 vaccine. The variable was utilised as combination of two other measures: vaccines safety and helpfulness. Thus, the coefficient may be explained by the fact that people tend to have more favourable attitude if they are sure in its helpfulness and safety. Researches found that distrust to vaccines effectiveness and safety are of main reasons for vaccination refusal [45, 46]. Also – as a reason for decreased safety and/or helpfulness of vaccine - people may be concerned with side effects and more unwilling to get vaccinated for this reason. It goes alongside with evidences suggested in reviews [47, 48], who show that people's belief in presence of side effects or health interventions is often associated with more negative attitudes. Side effects are cited as reason for hesitance and refusal, for example, as popular myth about autism as a vaccination cause [9]. Important notion here is devoted to healthcare professionals as sources of providing guidelines, recommendation and knowledge about vaccination to their patients. As study of Lin et al. [49] reveals, better knowledge of vaccine provided by healthcare professionals is associated with its acceptance. Professionals refer to scientific knowledge for explaining the need of vaccination, therefore, patients better understand safety and helpfulness of vaccines. This can be a reason of a more positive vaccine perception among patients.

The second measure about general vaccination does not account for safety ad helpfulness directly asking about opinion generally. Models with first and second variable differ slightly, suggesting similar results for perception and attitudes. As perception measure is more clear and specific (comprised from safety and helpfulness variables) we could be expecting rarer cases of neutral opinions (score 4 on 7-point scale), however, answers distribution does not prove it. Maybe it can be attributed to the fact that respondents do not have sufficient knowledge on safety and helpfulness, thus, they are not confident in their evaluations. This goes alongside with the research of [50], where lack of knowledge is found to be associated with higher vaccine hesitancy. Those people who continue to vaccinate after 18 have mostly both positive attitudes to general vaccines and COVID-19 vaccine. The reason for that may well be that these people continue to communicate with doctors or healthcare professionals more frequently, thus they are told about vaccines from scientific point of view. It creates a situation when such people, possessing deeper and correct knowledge, positively think about vaccines because of understanding the vaccination process more clear.

It should be added that experience of vaccination after 18 became insignificant after controlling for health. It goes alongside with Braimah et al. [51], who hypothesized that people are less acceptant to vaccination if they had no experience with vaccines previously and the result was significant unless accounting for covarities including socio-demographics, economic status and knowledge in vaccines. It is suggest then that their is some moderation underlying between health level and vaccination experience.

5.3 Vaccines COVID-19 Perception

Following the ideas of healthcare professionals and scientific knowledge, we can turn to our evidence that people who think COVID-19 vaccine are different to the rest of vaccines and people who do not continue vaccinate mostly remained neutral in evaluating vaccines helpfulness and safety in general, while their attitude to COVID-19 vaccines was negative and in some cases hardly positive. The difference is probably related to some specificity of COVID-19: since the topic is quite recent and surrounded by many conspiracy theories, especially those who do not have a definite opinion about vaccination yet, can be more prone to supporting conspiracy theories. As discussed [44], people who are more open to information and beliefs differing from existing ones are more often prone to conspiracy theories for explaining vaccination. We can suggest that maybe people expressed neutral opinion can stick easier to conspiracy theories as they care less about confirming the positivity or negativity of attitude and it is easier to them to accept new beliefs. Or, as Pišl [52] claim, people experiencing dissonance about the topic are associated with accepting first met information solving their dissonance. Therefore, such people are more prone to myths and conspiracy theories that suggest fast ad easy explanation of the phenomena.

No people think negatively of vaccines in general and at the same time positively about COVID-19 vaccine even among people who think that COVID-19 vaccine is different from the rest. At the same time, the opposite situation is met quite often. It can happen because of COVID-19 vaccine quite recent introduction and relatively long period of existence for the rest of vaccines. Miskulin et al. [53] show in their study on the experience of healthcare professionals, even though they are supportive for immunization in general, they have many doubts in COVID-19 vaccine as it is not yet sufficiently tested, however, already stated to be an obligatory measure. Earlier study of Lutringer-Magnin et al. [54] also shows that it is not only a problem of COVID-19 vaccine, but rather of recently introduced vaccines: recent introduction, side effects and early targeted age cited most often as reasons of vaccine hesitancy and doubtful opinions. We can also note here that people who told that some circumstances forced them to be vaccinated think of COVID-19 vaccine more negatively than those who have taken this decision on own desire. Before, we should refer to the sample: the distribution of age was skewed, so that the category of people over 60 is not large. Since workplaces required vaccination and most of the participants are of working age, we can suggest that mandatory aspect of vaccination could decrease people's initial attitude on vaccination. As the median answer was the middle of the scale, it is possible that individuals became more hesitant because of recent vaccine introduction followed by obligation. This goes alongside with researches [53, 54] that showed that participants expressed their fears regarding recent vaccine introduction with fast implementation of it as mandatory procedure.

6 Conclusion

The study shows that interest in medicine, continuing vaccination after the age of 18, treating COVID-19 vaccine similarly to other vaccines, reasoning of vaccination and general attitude to vaccines are associated with attitude towards COVID-19 vaccine. With the exception of medicine interest and continuing vaccination, the rest variables are found to be significant predictors for attitude towards COVID-19 vaccine. Female gender, treating vaccines similarly, being vaccinated voluntarily and having more positive attitude towards vaccines generally predict more positive attitude towards COVID-19 vaccine. Gender moderates the relationship of attitude and age: the attitude is getting more positive with age increasing for females, however, the opposite relationship is found among males. Notably, similarity of vaccines is insignificant if general perception is assessed through safety and helpfulness estimations. The study suggests that different assessments of general attitude to vaccines can show different results. It can be further examined if the attitude predicts vaccination status, taking into consideration the vaccination reason.

References

1. Rospotrebnadzor: Information on cases of pneumonia caused by 2019-nCoV. https://rospotrebnadzor.ru/files/news/31.01%20(8.00%20мск)%20Информация%20о%20случаях%20пневмонии,%20вызванной%202019-nCoV.docx. Accessed 17 Nov 2024
2. Rospotrebnadzor, South-Western Branch of the Federal Budget Institution of Public Health "Center for Hygiene and Epidemiology in the City of St. Petersburg": COVID-19 Vaccination: Presentation, Truths, and Myths about Vaccination [Вакцинация от COVID-19: презентация, правда и мифы о вакцинации]. https://do.nios.ru/sites/do.nios.ru/files/.1new_files/vakcinaciya_ot_covid_19_prezentaciya_pravda_i_mify_o_vakcinacii.pdf. Accessed 7 Dec 2024
3. Barchuk, A., et al.: Gam-COVID-Vac, EpiVacCorona, and CoviVac effectiveness against lung injury during Delta and Omicron variant surges in St. Petersburg, Russia: a test-negative case–control study. Respir. Res. **23**(1), 276 (2022)
4. GOGOV: COVID-19 Fatality Statistics in Russia [Смертность от коронавируса в России на сегодня]. https://gogov.ru/covid-fatality/russia. Accessed 17 Dec 2024
5. GOGOV: Statistics on Coronavirus Vaccination in Russia [Статистика вакцинации от коронавируса в России]. https://gogov.ru/articles/covid-v-stats. Accessed 17 Dec 2024
6. Maleva, T.M., Kartseva, M.A., Korzhuk, S.V.: Socio-demographic determinants of COVID-19 vaccine uptake in Russia in the context of mandatory vaccination of employees. Population Econ. **5**(4), 30–49 (2021)
7. Abenova, M., Shaltynov, A., Jamedinova, U., Ospanov, E., Semenova, Y.: The association between parental child vaccination refusal rate and the impact of mass vaccination against COVID-19 in Kazakhstan: an interrupted time series analysis with predictive modelling of nationwide data sources from 2013 to 2022. Vaccines **12**(4), 429 (2024)
8. Horodovenko, V., Udovyka, L., Shekhovtsova, T.: Vaccination in the system of human rights and obligations: impact of the COVID-19 pandemic. Wiadomości Lekarskie **74**(11/2), 2983–2991 (2021)
9. Yaqub, O., Castle-Clarke, S., Sevdalis, N., Chataway, J.: Attitudes to vaccination: a critical review. Soc Sci Med **112**, 1–11 (2014)
10. Champion, V., Skinner, C.: The Health Belief Model. In: Glanz, K., Rimer, B.K., Viswanath, K. (eds.) Health Behavior and Health Education: Theory, Research, and Practice, 4th edn., pp. 45–65. Jossey-Bass, San Francisco (2008)
11. Mercadante, A., Law, A.: Will they, or Won't they? Examining patients' vaccine intention for flu and COVID-19 using the health belief model. Res. Social Adm. Pharm. **17**(9), 1596–1605 (2021)
12. Alshagrawi, S.: Determinants of intention to uptake COVID-19 vaccination among Saudi adults: application of the health belief model. Risk Manage. Healthc. Policy **17**, 1803–1814 (2024)
13. Seangpraw, K., et al.: Using the Health Belief Model to predict vaccination intention among COVID-19 unvaccinated people in Thai communities. Front. Med. **9**, 890503 (2022)
14. Limbu, Y., Gautam, R., Pham, L.: The health belief model applied to COVID-19 vaccine hesitancy: a systematic review. Vaccines **10**(6), 973 (2022)
15. Latkin, C., Dayton, L., Yi, G., Colon, B., Kong, X.: Mask usage, social distancing, racial, and gender correlates of COVID-19 vaccine intentions among adults in the US. PLoS ONE **16**(2), e0246970 (2021)
16. Kini, A., et al.: Differences and disparities in seasonal influenza vaccine, acceptance, adverse reactions, and coverage by age, sex, gender, and race. Vaccine **40**(11), 1643–1654 (2022)
17. Hajure, M., et al.: Attitude towards COVID-19 vaccination among healthcare workers: a systematic review. Infect. Drug Resist. **14**, 3883–3897 (2021)

18. Lindholt, M.F., Jørgensen, F., Bor, A., Petersen, M.B.: Public acceptance of COVID-19 vaccines: cross-national evidence on levels and individual-level predictors using observational data. BMJ Open **11**(6), e048172 (2021)
19. Zintel, S., Flock, C., Arbogast, A.L., Forster, A., von Wagner, C., Sieverding, M.: Gender differences in the intention to get vaccinated against COVID-19: a systematic review and meta-analysis. J. Public Health **31**(8), 1303–1327 (2023)
20. Vasileva, A.V., Karavaeva, T.A., Radionov, D.S., Yakovlev, A.V.: The relationship between socio-demographic characteristics and individual experience of the COVID-19 pandemic with attitudes toward vaccination: Identifying targets for psychosocial interventions. Rev. Psychiatry Med. Psychol. named after V.M. Bekhterev **55**(2), 27–36 (2021)
21. Ulbrichtova, R., Svihrova, V., Svihra, J.: Prevalence of COVID-19 vaccination among medical students: a systematic review and meta-analysis. Int. J. Environ. Res. Public Health **19**(7), 4072 (2022). https://doi.org/10.3390/ijerph19074072
22. Espejo, B., Martín-Carbonell, M., Romero-Acosta, K.C., Fernández-Daza, M., Paternina, Y.: Evidence of validity and measurement invariance by gender of the vaccination attitudes examination (VAX) scale in Colombian university students. J. Clin. Med. **11**(16), 4682 (2022)
23. Afifi, T., Salmon, S., Taillieu, T., Stewart-Tufescu, A., Fortier, J., Driedger, S.: Older adolescents and young adults willingness to receive the COVID-19 vaccine: Implications for informing public health strategies. Vaccine **39**(26), 3473–3479 (2021)
24. Bartosiewicz, A., Łuszczki, E., Bartosiewicz, A., Dereń, K., Oleksy, Ł, Stolarczyk, A.: COVID-19-related predictors of fear and attitude to vaccination displayed by Polish students. Vaccines **10**(9), 1524 (2022)
25. Watson, I., Oancea, S.C.: Does self-rated health status influence receipt of an annual flu vaccination? Prev. Med. **131**, 105949 (2020)
26. Guthrie, J., Fisman, D., Gardy, J.: Self-rated health and reasons for non-vaccination against seasonal influenza in Canadian adults with asthma. PLoS ONE **12**(2), e0172117 (2017)
27. Vranic, S., et al.: Knowledge, attitudes, and practices among medical and non-medical students about immunization during the COVID-19 pandemic: a cross-sectional study. Population Med. **5**(July), 1–9 (2023)
28. James, P., Bah, A., Kondorvoh, I.: Exploring self-use, attitude and interest to study complementary and alternative medicine (CAM) among final year undergraduate medical, pharmacy and nursing students in Sierra Leone: a comparative study. BMC Complement. Altern. Med. **16**, 1–8 (2016)
29. Sallam, M.: COVID-19 vaccine hesitancy worldwide: a systematic review of vaccine acceptance rates. Vaccines **9**(2), 160 (2021)
30. Jing, R., Fang, H., Wang, H., Wang, J.: The role of general attitudes and perceptions towards vaccination on the newly-developed vaccine: results from a survey on COVID-19 vaccine acceptance in China. Front. Psychol. **13**, 841189 (2022)
31. Boyle, J., Nowak, G., Kinder, R., Iachan, R., Dayton, J.: Understanding the impact of general vaccine attitudes on the intent for early COVID-19 vaccination. Vaccines **11**(2), 235 (2023)
32. El-Sokkary, R.H., et al.: Predictors of COVID-19 vaccine hesitancy among Egyptian healthcare workers: a cross-sectional study. BMC Infect. Dis. **21**, 1–9 (2021)
33. Neumann-Böhme, S., et al.: Once we have it, will we use it? A European survey on willingness to be vaccinated against COVID-19. Eur. J. Health Econ. **21**, 977–982 (2020)
34. Wang, J., et al.: Acceptance of COVID-19 vaccination during the COVID-19 pandemic in China. Vaccines **8**(3), 482 (2020)
35. Ştefănuţ, A.M., Vintilă, M., Tomiţă, M., Treglia, E., Lungu, M.A., Tomassoni, R.: The influence of health beliefs, of resources, of vaccination history, and of health anxiety on intention to accept COVID-19 vaccination. Front. Psychol. **12**, 729803 (2021)

36. Mahameed, H., et al.: Previous vaccination history and psychological factors as significant predictors of willingness to receive Mpox vaccination and a favorable attitude towards compulsory vaccination. Vaccines **11**(5), 897 (2023)
37. Guidry, J.P., et al.: Willingness to get the COVID-19 vaccine with and without emergency use authorization. Am. J. Infect. Control **49**(2), 137–142 (2021)
38. Freeman, D., et al.: Effects of different types of written vaccination information on COVID-19 vaccine hesitancy in the UK (OCEANS-III): a single-blind, parallel-group, randomised controlled trial. Lancet Public Health **6**(6), e416–e427 (2021)
39. Alabdulla, M., Reagu, S.M., Al-Khal, A., Elzain, M., Jones, R.M.: COVID-19 vaccine hesitancy and attitudes in Qatar: a national cross-sectional survey of a migrant-majority population. Influenza Other Respir. Viruses **15**(3), 361–370 (2021)
40. Ndasauka, Y., Twabi, H.S., Kainja, J., Gunde, A.M., Makhumula-Mtimuni, C.: Knowledge, attitudes and demographic drivers for COVID-19 vaccine hesitancy in Malawi. Sci. Rep. **14**(1), 9578 (2024)
41. Talukdar, D., Stojkovski, K., Suarez, D.B., Gupta, M.M., Suarez, D.: Role of information technology in COVID-19 vaccination drive: an analysis of the COVID-19 global beliefs, behaviors, and norms survey. Cureus, **13**(6) (2021)
42. Muldoon, O.T., et al.: Vaccination roll-out: a time to develop and maintain trust in science and health care. Br. J. Gen. Pract. **71**(712), 518–519 (2021)
43. Chambon, M., Kammeraad, W.G., van Harreveld, F., Dalege, J., Elberse, J.E., van der Maas, H.L.J.: Understanding change in COVID-19 vaccination intention with network analysis of longitudinal data from Dutch adults. NPJ Vaccines **7**(1), 114 (2022)
44. Bossert, A., Jongman-Sereno, K.: Misinformation beliefs, intellectual humility, and vaccine attitudes and status. Psi Chi J. Psychol. Res. **29**(2), 158 (2024)
45. Kues, J.R., et al.: COVID-19 vaccine hesitancy: a critical time period analysis. Int. J. Environ. Res. Public Health **19**(13), 8098 (2022)
46. Troiano, G., Nardi, A.: Vaccine hesitancy in the era of COVID-19. Public Health **194**, 245–251 (2021)
47. Konstantinou, P., et al.: Barriers, facilitators, and interventions for medication adherence across chronic conditions with the highest non-adherence rates: a scoping review with recommendations for intervention development. Transl. Behav. Med. **10**(6), 1390–1398 (2020)
48. Dubé, E., Laberge, C., Guay, M., Bramadat, P., Roy, R., Bettinger, J.A.: Vaccine hesitancy: an overview. Hum. Vaccin. Immunother. **9**(8), 1763–1773 (2013)
49. Lin, C., Mullen, J., Smith, D., Kotarba, M., Kaplan, S.J., Tu, P.: Healthcare providers' vaccine perceptions, hesitancy, and recommendation to patients: a systematic review. Vaccines **9**(7), 713 (2021)
50. Sallam, M., et al.: High rates of COVID-19 vaccine hesitancy and its association with conspiracy beliefs: a study in Jordan and Kuwait among other Arab countries. Vaccines **9**(1), 42 (2021)
51. Braimah, J.A., Achore, M., Dery, F., Ayanore, M.A., Bisung, E., Kuuire, V.: Do self-rated health and previous vaccine uptake influence the willingness to accept MPOX vaccine during a public health emergency of concern? A cross-sectional study. PLOS Global Public Health **4**(8), e0003564 (2024)
52. Pišl, V.: Conspiracy theories as a natural part of pandemics. Casopis Lekaru Ceskych **160**(1), 37–39 (2021)
53. Miskulin, M., et al.: Vaccination attitudes and experiences of medical doctors in Croatia amid the COVID-19 pandemic: a social roles conflict? Vaccines **10**(3), 399 (2022)
54. Lutringer-Magnin, D., et al.: Human papillomavirus (HPV) vaccination: perception and practice among French general practitioners in the year since licensing. Vaccine **29**(32), 5322–5328 (2011)

Accepting Artificial Intelligence at the Individual Level: Empirical Evidence from Russian Market

Maria Smirnova and Anastasiia Shiryaeva(✉)

Graduate School of Management, St. Petersburg State University, St. Petersburg, Russia
smirnova@gsom.spbu.ru, st033084@student.spbu.ru

Abstract. This study aims to examine a combination of drivers of acceptance of AI-based solutions by individuals – as citizens and consumers, combining socio-psychological foundations, theory of the diffusion of innovations and the cognitive responses triggered by AI innovations and their impact on individual's behavior, offering a deeper understanding of how technology is reshaping the digital market landscape. Based on a quantitative survey at the level of individual behavior, the study offers new insights into AI-acceptance and expands our understanding of how to integrate technology into the solutions offered to individuals by organizations in digital governance, commercial solutions and other contexts. The findings offer insights on the level of behavioral attitudes and beliefs and their contribution to the intention to use the AI solutions. The empirical tools used to collect the data offer a contribution to adapting empirical methodology for future research, and the model contributes by a combination of classic and established theoretical approaches in a new combination to suggest a holistic picture of AI-based individual behavior.

Keywords: Artificial Intelligence · Trust · Consumer Behavior

1 Introduction

Over the past few decades, technology has dramatically reshaped the way we live, interact, and make decisions. One of the most profound changes has been the rise of digital technologies, which now permeate almost every aspect of our lives. Among these, Artificial Intelligence (AI) stands out as a defining innovation, revolutionizing the way people are involved in traditional functions, consumption, interaction with organizations of commerce, e-government, other consumers and society in general.

To fully understand the effects of AI on individual's behavior, it is crucial to evaluate how people make individual decisions in digital environments and how they perceive AI-generated content. Prior research demonstrates that consumer trust and acceptance of AI technologies are shaped by their interactions and experiences with digital services [1]. Moreover, the perception of AI-driven content significantly influences consumers' intentions to engage and transact, as shown in service delivery contexts [2]. The digital transformation of marketing further underscores the importance of understanding how digital content, including AI-generated information, affects decision-making processes

M. Bakaev et al. (Eds.): IMS 2025, CCIS 2671, pp. 304–321, 2026.
https://doi.org/10.1007/978-3-032-04958-2_23

[3]. These studies collectively highlight that consumer behavior in digital environments cannot be fully understood without considering their perceptions and cognitive responses to AI-generated content.

Despite the growing body of research, there is still a lack of empirical studies focusing on holistic, person-centered experiences in emerging markets such as Russia. Most existing studies are concentrated on Western contexts, leaving a gap in understanding how cultural and regulatory factors shape AI acceptance in other regions. The focus of this research is to explore how AI influences individual decisions and how organizations in Russia can leverage AI-driven insights to better align with individual's needs. Moreover, this study aims to examine a combination of drivers of acceptance of AI-based solutions, combining socio-psychological foundations, theory of the diffusion of innovations and the cognitive responses triggered by AI innovations and their impact on individual's behavior, offering a deeper understanding of how technology is reshaping the digital market landscape. Based on a quantitative survey at the level of individual behavior, the study offers new insights into AI-acceptance and expands our understanding of how to integrate technology into the solutions offered to individuals by organizations in digital governance, commercial solutions and other contexts. Ultimately, this study aims to expand both theoretical and practical understanding of AI acceptance in digital marketing, offering evidence-based recommendations to responsible integration of AI into consumer-facing solutions.

2 Review of Theoretical Foundations

As AI technologies become increasingly integrated into everyday life and industry, the determinants of user acceptance have come to the forefront of both academic and practical interest. Understanding what drives individual acceptance of AI is essential for the successful integration of these technologies across industries and daily life [4]. Despite the predicted economic and social impact of AI, research on user acceptance remains fragmented, in part due to inconsistent definitions of AI and the diversity of contexts in which it is applied.

The Technology Acceptance Model (TAM) is the most widely used framework for analyzing user acceptance of AI. TAM centers on two core constructs: perceived usefulness (PU) - the belief that a technology will enhance one's life or performance, and perceived ease of use (PEOU) - the perceived effort required to use the technology. PU is consistently identified as the strongest predictor of behavioral intention to use AI, while the influence of PEOU may be less pronounced for familiar or frequently used technologies [5–7]. To improve explanatory power, TAM is often extended with constructs like trust and knowledge [8, 9]. Trust is a critical antecedent of acceptance: Choung et al. found that trust enhances perceived usefulness and showed that trust can even outweigh usefulness in predicting intention to use AI for biometric identification.

Recognizing the limits of generic models for AI, Gursoy et al. developed the AI Device Use Acceptance Model (AIDUA), which incorporates unique AI features such as anthropomorphism and hedonic motivation. In AIDUA, users first appraise AI devices based on social and emotional factors, then evaluate performance and effort, leading to either acceptance or objection [2]. This approach acknowledges that users may accept some aspects of AI while rejecting others, especially for ethical reasons. Finally, the literature highlights the importance of social, cultural, and ethical factors. For example, in some contexts, the need for human contact cannot be replaced by AI, regardless of its perceived usefulness. Ethical considerations such as transparency, accountability, and privacy are increasingly recognized as crucial for acceptance, particularly as AI becomes more autonomous and embedded in sensitive domains [10].

The next section provides a more detailed explanation of how the theory of planned behavior can be used to understand the relationship between intention and attitude - a summary of a single individuals´ evaluations of a given behavior in a positive or negative light, and factual behavior. Individual attitudes towards technology and products and solutions, based on it, can vary significantly and are formed based on a variety of factors, including intended use, reputation, personal prior experience, public perception, and an individual's evaluation of alternative options.

Our approach combines a class approach of the theory of planned behavior, that represents a universal social psychology perspective, and an innovative angle through the lens of the innovation diffusion theory, thus combining both approach to the perception and intended use of AI.

2.1 Core Elements of Social Psychology Approach

Theory of planned behavior (TPB) [11], rooted in the field of social psychology, aims to explain an individual's behavior based on their attitudes and personal characteristics. This theory is used in various fields, such as business, medicine, management, and accounting, to predict human behavior due to base on an individual's intention to engage in a specific behavior, considering their level of preparedness to act, which depends on their efforts to carry out that behavior. As Ajzen, "individuals themselves are the only ones who can control whether they will engage in each behavior, based on their abilities and resources to do so" [12]. A systematic review by Rozenkowska [13] synthesizes a decade of TPB applications in consumer behavior research, emphasizing its adaptability across contexts such as sustainable consumption, online shopping, and halal product adoption. For instance, studies integrating TPB with the Technology Acceptance Model (TAM) reveal that perceived ease of use and perceived usefulness significantly amplify purchase intentions in digital environments. Azad et al. achieved 91% accuracy in predicting purchases by operationalizing TPB variables (attitude, social norms, perceived control) alongside machine learning, underscoring the model's relevance in AI-driven markets [14]. Their findings align with Ajzen's assertion that behavioral control mediates intention-action gaps, particularly when consumers perceive AI tools as compatible with their lifestyles.

In this context, it can be concluded that behavioral beliefs play a role in shaping both positive and negative attitudes [11] as "an individual's evaluation of a given behavior in a positive or negative light". Subjective norms, on the other hand, are related to the social pressures individuals feel regarding whether they should engage in a particular behavior. A key factor in the theory of planned behavior is the role of behavioral beliefs, which can be defined as the individual's internal perceptions of the consequences of engaging in each behavior that influence their attitude [11]. According to Prodanova, the elements of attitude, which represent subjective norms, are believed to have a positive impact on an individual's behavioral intentions and actual behavior [15]. Researcher further validate that subjective norm—rooted in social media influence—are now pivotal in shaping attitudes toward AI-generated content, especially among younger demographics. This is echoed by Hsu and Lin [16], who found that social influence significantly affects online shopping behaviors among millennials. The interplay between social media dynamics and TPB suggests that marketers can leverage these insights to craft targeted campaigns that resonate with consumers' values and perceived norms. Additionally, Lim and An suggest that people are more likely to engage in certain behaviors if they believe such actions will lead to outcomes consistent with their values [17]. Researchers also argue for the applicability of a theory concerning an individual's intention to purchase in an online setting, in conjunction with their personal beliefs, norms, and values [17]. A study by Wang and Zhang [18] also emphasizes the impact of cultural background on consumer behavior, suggesting that cultural values can moderate the effect of subjective norms on purchase decisions.

Behavior intention to use a product or a solution has become an integral part of an individual's behavior, enabling sellers to understand their customers' unique buying patterns. Market researchers believe that a positive attitude towards and perception of a product enhances the likelihood that a customer intends to purchase and consequently increases the probability of an actual purchase. Referring to Murat, it can be stated that individuals' identity and lifestyle have an impact on their purchasing behavior in relation to the perceived values of products and brands [19]. Researchers also emphasize the extent to which attitudes and behaviors are correlated with individuals' intention to make a purchase; thus, it can be argued that individual's purchasing decisions are significantly influenced by social, psychological, cultural, and personal characteristics that are difficult for marketers to influence. While external factors influencing behavior include demographic, situational, technological, social, and economic factors that each have their unique characteristics, the same can be said for internal factors such as beliefs, training, motives, attitudes, personality, needs, values, and perceptions that influence consumer behavior. A positive mindset can lead to an individual's intention to make action and influence their attitude towards a particular goal in a specific situation. Thus, we assume that:

H3: Positive attitudes towards Gen AI usage in marketing has a favorable effect on consumers purchasing intention of a product that has been offered/advertised using Gen AI.

Next, the theories of cognitive traps that influence an individual's attitude to innovation were considered. The most relevant ones, due to their direct impact on the relationship with innovation, are the following three: conformity bias, anchoring bias, and fear of missing out. The main result of the literature review is a conceptual model, which linked all the assumptions. Thus, we believe that factors of perception of AI as innovation as well as internal behavioral factors influence the formation of a positive or negative attitude towards AI content, which in turn affects the intention to make a purchase (See Fig. 1).

2.2 Innovation Lens and Diffusion Analysis

Evolving from a mathematical tool for solving problems to the algorithm that defeated the chess grandmaster in 1997, to a self-learning technology used in business, society and between the individuals in wide context of everyday life reflects the merging area of technology and human interaction, aiming for increasing personalization [19]. Diffusion of AI-based solutions in society can be addressed using the theory of the diffusion of innovations [20] (DOI). Within this theory, Rogers identifies several critical factors that influence an individual's acceptance of new technologies, including AI-based solutions. These factors encompass a broad spectrum of classic determinants of innovation adoption, which have been further refined to address contemporary risks and potential barriers to acceptance. Among the fundamental factors identified by Rogers, two stand out as particularly significant in the context of AI: compatibility and observability. Compatibility refers to the degree to which an innovation aligns with the existing values, past experiences, and needs of potential adopters. In the realm of AI, a strong sense of compatibility can foster a more favorable attitude towards its acceptance. Observability, on the other hand, pertains to the extent to which the benefits and results of an innovation are visible to others. In the case of generative AI, a high level of observability can significantly enhance positive perceptions and attitudes toward technology, as individuals witness their practical applications and successes. A systematic review by Vieira et al. [21] identifies compatibility and observability as dominant factors in technological uptake, particularly for AI solutions requiring behavioral change. At the same time Vieira [21] critique traditional DOI for underestimating cultural barriers, noting that collectivist societies exhibit slower AI adoption due to stronger conformity biases - a gap addressed by integrating TPB's subjective norms into diffusion frameworks. Additionally, research by Moore and Benbasat [22] emphasizes the importance of compatibility with existing values and practices for successful innovation adoption. They argue that innovations perceived as compatible are more readily accepted by users. This is particularly relevant for AI technologies designed to enhance user experience without requiring significant changes to existing behaviors. Moreover, research conducted by Rogers et al. [20] explores how communication strategies influence the diffusion process across different demographic groups. Their findings indicate that tailored messaging can significantly enhance adoption rates among specific segments of the population. In addition, recent work by Azad et al. [14] examines how social media platforms serve as accelerators for innovation diffusion through user-generated content and peer recommendations. Their study reveals that innovations introduced through influencers or trusted figures tend to diffuse faster than those promoted through traditional advertising channels.

The factors of innovation acceptance suggested by Rogers [20] provide an additional lens to determine both the attitude and behavioral intentions of an individual towards AI-based solutions and offerings. These factors include a range of classic factors, which were later extended by addressing more risks and potential barriers (see Fig. 1).

Compatibility refers to the degree to which an innovation aligns with the existing values, past experiences, and needs of potential adopters. This alignment is crucial, as it can greatly influence an individual's willingness to embrace AI technologies. This dependency has been explored in several scientific studies before. H. F. Lin's study on mobile banking found that compatibility has a significant impact on attitudes, which, in turn, leads to behavioral intentions to adopt and continue using mobile banking services. Similarly, it has been found that compatibility has a statistically significant impact on attitudes towards the use of anti-spyware programs [16]. These studies confirm the existence of a positive correlation between the variables under consideration. We propose a significant relationship between the acceptance of artificial intelligence and the concept of compatibility:

H1: The high level of Compatibility in Gen AI technology has a positive impact on people's perception of the use of AI in marketing.

Furthermore, we argue that a high level of observability - meaning the benefits and functionalities of generative AI are clearly visible and demonstrable - will positively shape users' attitudes towards these technological advancements. This aspect is more social and therefore more controversial. Y. Park found that a high level of observability positively influences users' attitudes towards innovation [23]. Although data on the impact of visibility on attitudes is mixed, numerous previous studies have demonstrated that visibility has a significant and positive influence on attitudes towards innovation.

Based on this, we can assume that a high level of visibility in generative AI will also have a significant and positive impact on attitudes towards the technology. When individuals can easily observe the advantages and practical applications of generative AI, they are more likely to develop a favorable disposition towards its adoption, ultimately enhancing their behavioral intentions to integrate such solutions into their daily practices:

H2: The high level of Observability in Gen AI technology has a positive impact on people's perception of the use of Gen AI in marketing.

2.3 Cognitive Biases

The integration of artificial intelligence (AI) into diverse aspects of contemporary existence has been profoundly influenced by cognitive biases, which often result in systematic departures from rational decision-making processes. This in-depth analysis explores three critical cognitive biases - conformity bias, anchoring bias, and the fear of missing out (FOMO) - and examines their substantial effects on public perceptions and attitudes toward AI technologies. Through this comprehensive exploration of these biases, we can gain deeper insights into how they shape societal attitudes toward AI, informing both the development of these technologies and the strategies for their effective implementation in our lives.

According to the psychological theory of conformity, conformity bias is characterized by the propensity of individuals to align their choices with those of the majority, often driven by implicit social pressures and the desire for acceptance. Within the realm of AI, this bias can catalyze the adoption of new technologies through a phenomenon known as the "bandwagon effect." Essentially, when individuals observe widespread acceptance of AI tools among their peers, they become more inclined to adopt these technologies themselves, even if they initially hold reservations. Research by Kowalczuk [24] highlights the interplay between conformity bias and cognitive dissonance in technology adoption, illustrating that users often choose AI-powered tools when they see others embracing them, despite any prior skepticism. This dynamic is particularly salient for generative AI tools, such as ChatGPT, which have surged in popularity and visibility, as evidenced by their positioning on the Gartner hype cycle.

We hypothesized that this cognitive process could serve as a catalyst for the widespread adoption of AI, particularly among individuals who are inclined to mimic trends. In this context, we are referring to imitators and followers, as generative AI has reached the peak of popularity according to the Gartner hype cycle [25]:

H4: High amount of «trend imitators» qualities have a positive effect on the individuals 'attitudes towards Gen AI usage in marketing.

The second cognitive bias that is being discussed, known as the anchoring effect, refers to the tendency for people to place excessive importance on the first piece of information they encounter when deciding. This initial information influences individuals' judgments and choices because it acts as a reference point or anchor for the evaluation and processing of subsequent information. In the context of AI, first impressions can significantly influence long-term trust and usage behaviors. Research conducted by Huang and Rust [26] underscores the importance of initial interactions with AI chatbots, revealing that these early experiences can profoundly shape user trust. This finding suggests that developers should prioritize optimizing user onboarding experiences to create positive anchors that foster trust and engagement. However, anchoring bias can lead consumers to become overly reliant on potentially flawed initial perceptions, complicating their ability to objectively assess subsequent information or alternative options. We assume that a customer faced with a high level of personalization would consider this level to be minimally acceptable. Therefore, their general expectations for future interactions with products and brands would be based on this experience. However, it is important to note that a high level of personalization requires a significant amount of data from customers. Concerns about digital security may negatively affect attitudes toward AI.

H5: High degree of personalization given by Gen AI instruments in marketing has a positive effect on the individuals' attitudes towards AI usage in marketing.

Another cognitive bias is the fear of missing out as a psychological phenomenon that describes people's anxiety about missing out on social events, experiences, investments, or activities that they perceive as desirable. FOMO is a common form of anxiety that can influence people's decision-making and behavior, particularly in relation to consumer behavior and marketing. Researchers have identified FOMO as an important factor in understanding consumer behavior and the impact of marketing messages. This bias is particularly pertinent in the marketing of AI technologies, where a sense of urgency is frequently emphasized to drive consumer behavior. However, while FOMO can effectively stimulate consumer interest, it also poses risks by potentially exploiting consumer anxieties, leading to impulsive purchasing decisions that lack thorough evaluation and consideration. A study by Liu et al. [18] examined the relationship between FOMO and generative AI adoption in China. The findings revealed that personal FOMO (fear of losing individual benefits like productivity) and social FOMO (anxiety about falling behind peers or competitors) significantly influence behavioral intentions to adopt generative AI tools such as ChatGPT and Ernie Bot. Interestingly, while utilitarian attitudes (e.g., efficiency and productivity) were positively correlated with adoption, social-adjustive attitudes were found to have no significant impact.

In the context of Gen AI and its increasing presence in society, it is possible that consumers may experience FOMO regarding the potential benefits of AI, leading them to become more engaged with AI-powered products and services.

H6: High amount of exultation around Gen AI has a positive effect on the individuals´attitudes towards AI usage in marketing.

These cognitive biases often intersect, collectively shaping consumer attitudes toward AI adoption. For instance, conformity bias can exacerbate FOMO, as individuals are more likely to feel anxious about missing out when they observe peers adopting AI tools in large numbers. Simultaneously, anchoring effects can entrap consumers in their initial perceptions, complicating their ability to make informed evaluations of alternative technologies later. As the landscape of AI continues to evolve, future research must prioritize the development of ethical frameworks aimed at mitigating these biases. Such frameworks will be essential in fostering an environment where AI adoption is not only informed but also equitable, ensuring that consumers can make decisions based on a comprehensive understanding of the technologies at hand.

2.4 Ethical Considerations

Generative AI technologies have revolutionized marketing by enabling the creation of tailored content, personalized experiences, and efficient consumer engagement. However, as these technologies gain traction, ethical considerations surrounding their use may have emerged as critical factors influencing consumer perception. Ethical practices directly influence consumer trust in generative AI technologies. According to Roberts, transparency initiatives significantly enhance trust, with consumers preferring brands that prioritize ethical AI use over those focused solely on innovation [27]. Trust is further reinforced when companies demonstrate accountability by addressing errors and ensuring fair treatment of all stakeholders. Ethical considerations also affect willingness to adopt generative AI-powered services. Consumers are more likely to embrace AI technologies when they perceive them as ethically governed and aligned with societal norms. Ethical lapses in generative AI can damage brand reputation. For instance, controversies surrounding biased or inappropriate chatbot responses have highlighted the risks of deploying generative AI without robust ethical safeguards [27]. Conversely, companies that proactively address ethical challenges are perceived as socially responsible leaders in innovation.

The hypothesis that ethical considerations significantly influence consumer perception of generative AI technologies in marketing is strongly supported by existing research. Martínez-López et al. [28] identify bias in AI-generated marketing content as a significant ethical concern that negatively impacts consumer attitudes. Their research underlines the necessity of bias detection and mitigation tools to prevent discrimination and maintain fairness in AI applications, which directly influences consumers' willingness to accept AI-generated marketing messages. Liu et al. [29] further argue that transparency about AI processes and accountability for AI-driven decisions are key to mitigating consumer skepticism. Their qualitative study, based on interviews with healthcare professionals, reveals that insufficient adherence to these principles often leads to ethical issues like privacy violations and algorithmic bias, which in turn reduce user trust and satisfaction. This erosion of trust negatively impacts the effectiveness of

AI-enabled marketing initiatives. Transparency, accountability, bias prevention, and privacy safeguards emerge as critical factors shaping attitudes toward these technologies. Consumers are more likely to trust and adopt generative AI-powered services when they perceive them as ethically governed.

H7: Ethical considerations negatively affect purchasing intention of a product that has been advertised/offered using Gen AI.

Figure 1 suggests an overview of a conceptual framework that is based on the combination of selected theoretical approaches and represents a foundation for the empirical phase of the study.

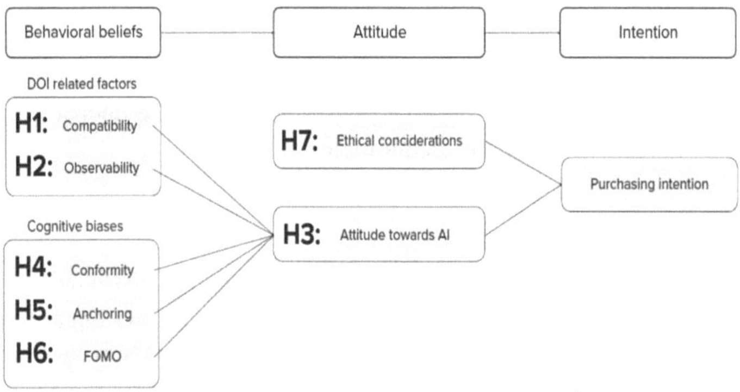

Fig. 1. Conceptual model

3 Methodology

Given the limited empirical information available about AI perception and acceptance, this research is developed in strict adherence to a deductive approach, which begins by considering the development of AI as a technology, followed by the intersection of AI and individual behavior. We also aim at providing insight into holistic, person-centered experiences and for these purposes we use descriptive and inferential statistics, as well as content analysis. Empirical methodology is based on adaptation of existing theory and methods to measure the constructs, required to evaluate the factors, driving the perception of AI and resulting intended behavior.

3.1 Research Design

This research employs a deductive, quantitative research design to systematically examine the drivers of consumer perception and acceptance of generative AI technologies in marketing. The choice of a quantitative methodology is grounded in the need for generalizable, statistically robust insights and the ability to rigorously test theoretically derived hypotheses. [30] Quantitative research is particularly suited for studies exploring relationships among multiple constructs and for validating conceptual models in emerging fields such as AI in marketing, where empirical evidence remains limited. Given the complexity of the research model and the need to simultaneously assess multiple latent constructs and their interrelationships, the Partial Least Squares SEM (PLS-SEM) was chosen as the primary analytical technique for its suitability in exploratory contexts, its ability to handle complex models with relatively small to medium sample sizes, and its relaxed requirements regarding data normality.

3.2 Data Collection

Data was collected via a structured online questionnaire, designed to quantitatively capture consumer awareness, attitudes, personal values, and behavioral intentions related to the use of AI in marketing. The survey instrument was developed based on a comprehensive literature review and incorporated validated scales for all key constructs, including perceived ethicality, observability, compatibility, FOMO, conformity, anchoring, and purchase intention. Items were adapted from prior studies [31–36] to ensure both content validity and contextual relevance.

Three types of questions were utilized: binary (yes/no), 5-point Likert scale (from 1 – «strongly disagree» to 5 – «strongly agree»), and open-ended questions. Filtering questions were included to assess respondents' ability to distinguish between AI-generated and human-created content, thereby enhancing the validity of the data. The survey was preceded by clear instructions to minimize respondent misinterpretation.

The target population comprised Russian residents exposed to digital marketing and AI-generated content. The only inclusion criterion was current residence in Russia; there were no restrictions on age, gender, or occupation.

A total of 197 responses were collected, with 191 complete and valid cases used for analysis (53% female, 47% male). The age distribution was broad, with the largest group (41.8%) aged 18–25, followed by 25–30 (22.5%), 31–43 (16.2%), 44–59 (13.1%), and smaller proportions under 18 and above 60. Education and occupation were similarly diverse.

3.3 Scale Validation and Reliability

To ensure the reliability and validity of the measurement instruments, a confirmatory factor analysis (CFA) was conducted for all constructs in the conceptual model. Table 1 presents statistical data on Cronbach's Alpha coefficient for all the constructs under study: the test was conducted using a 95% confidence interval (p-value < 0.05) and shows that each construct has an acceptable level of internal consistency, since Cronbach's Alpha values exceed 0.7. Moreover, CR for all constructs was above 0.70, supporting the internal consistency of the scales, AVE for each construct exceeded the recommended minimum of 0.50 indicating strong convergent validity.

Table 1. Reliability and validity of measures

Items	Standardized factor loading	Cronbach' s Alpha > 0.7	CR > 0.7	AVE > 0.5
AI		0,71	0,735	0,52
I think AI technology is positive for humanity	0,732			
I believe AI technology is a threat to humans	0,604			
Artificial Intelligence is exciting	0,723			
I shiver with discomfort when I think about future uses of Artificial Intelligence	0,839			
I keep track of the achievements of AI	0,505			
Observability		0,845	0,871	0,576
Many people around me talk about AI generated content in marketing	0,636			
I often see generated by AI content in marketing	0,846			
I feel that AI in marketing is used largely	0,768			
I am sure AI is not widely applied in marketing	0,864			
Compatibility		0,908	0,92	0,753
Using AI in marketing goes against my values	0,725			
Using AI in marketing does fit into my life paradigm	0,812			

(continued)

Table 1. (*continued*)

Items	Standardized factor loading	Cronbach' s Alpha > 0.7	CR > 0.7	AVE > 0.5
I think it's appropriate to use AI for marketing purposes	0,958			
FOMO		0,717	0,721	0,512
It bothers me when I miss an opportunity to catch up a trend	0,783			
I get anxious when I don't know the current trends in social networks	0,667			
Ethic concerns		0,842	0,87	0,567
Artificial Intelligence is used to spy on people	0,701			
The rise of AI poses a threat to people's job security	0,647			
Organizations use AI unethically	0,831			
I worry when I read about art stolen through AI	0,867			
Conformity		0,705	0,763	0,53
I will buy something because of product recommendations and reviews	0,875			
How likely are you to change your opinion based on the recommendations of others	0,728			
I feel uncomfortable deviating from popular trends	0,631			
Anchoring		0,717	0,817	0,678

(*continued*)

Table 1. (*continued*)

Items	Standardized factor loading	Cronbach' s Alpha > 0.7	CR > 0.7	AVE > 0.5
I am delighted that the personalization of content has reached an individual level	0,832			
It annoys me when I see notifications with unpersonalized newsletter	0,542			
I am ready to provide more information about myself if it means getting a personalized approach	0,839			
Attitude		0,929	0,954	0,743
I find seeing the generated content appealing	0,683			
I find seeing the generated content unappealing	0,95			
How pleased are you to see generated content from companies?	0,893			
I am inspired by looking at advertising campaigns that break down the boundaries of what is possible	0,945			
I dislike that content creation is done by a machine, not a person	0,854			

Discriminant validity (see Table 2) was assessed by comparing the square root of the AVE for each construct with the inter-construct correlations; in all cases, the square root of the AVE exceeded the corresponding correlations, supporting the distinctiveness of each construct. All factor loadings were statistically significant at the 0.05 level ($p < 0.05$).

Table 2. Discriminant validity testing

	AI	O	C	PI	FOMO	EC	CF	An	At	AVE
AI	0,72									0,524
O	0,14	0,75								0,576
C	0,20	0,13	0,87							0,753
PI	0,14	0,16	0,18	0,76						0,584
FOMO	0,10	0,04	0,07	0,16	0,75					0,512
EC	0,12	0,11	0,2	0,09	0,05	0,75				0,567
CF	0,03	0,003	0,03	0,05	0,07	0,13	0,73			0,53
An	0,07	0,12	0,03	0,13	0,12	0,15	0,02	0,82		0,678
At	0,15	0,12	0,05	0,19	0,12	0,17	0,04	0,11	0,86	0,743

Note: AI – Artificial Intelligence, O – Observability, C- Compatibility, PI – Purchase Intention, EC – Ethical Concerns, CF – Conformity, An – Anchoring, At - Attitude

These results provide strong evidence for the reliability and validity of the measurement model, supporting the use of these constructs in subsequent analyses.

4 Research Findings and Discussion

The research findings presented herein are grounded in the application of structural equation modeling (SEM), which has been identified as the most suitable methodological framework for examining the intricacies of the decision-making process. This approach allows for a nuanced analysis of the hypothesized relationships between various constructs within the model, leveraging previously established reliability and validity of the measurement instruments employed. The comprehensive results of the analysis, detailed in Table 2, provide partial support for the study's hypotheses. Notably, the overarching chain of effects that influences individual behavior has been substantiated, albeit with certain exceptions where specific factors did not achieve statistical significance. This chain illustrates a clear pathway from beliefs to behavior, mediated by attitude.

Among the significant findings, we can emphasize the factors derived from the literature on innovation acceptance. Specifically, compatibility emerges as a crucial determinant, exerting a positive and statistically significant influence on attitude. This suggests that individuals who perceive a strong alignment between their existing values and the functionalities of AI technologies are more likely to develop favorable attitudes towards these innovations. This finding is consistent with Mariani & Borghi, who highlight compatibility as a critical determinant of technology acceptance [37]. Moreover, the positive impact of compatibility reinforces the notion that individuals who are predisposed to embrace technology are more likely to actualize their attitudes towards AI applications. This predisposition is further enhanced by a clear understanding of how to effectively utilize these AI-based tools. Furthermore, the cognitive dimensions of the study reveal that social influences, particularly conformity and the fear of missing out (FOMO), act as significant drivers in the acceptance and utilization of artificial intelligence. This underscores the pivotal role of social mechanisms in shaping individuals' interactions with technology and fostering a constructive mindset towards its adoption. Interestingly, the analysis indicates that observability - traditionally considered a key factor in the adoption of technology - may not be as critical in this context. This aligns with the findings of Dwivedi et al., who note that while visibility of AI applications is increasing, consumers often lack sufficient understanding to translate observability into positive attitudes or trust. Instead, the mere discourse surrounding the scale of adoption appears to be a positive influence, suggesting that discussions and perceptions around AI can enhance its acceptance. Lastly, the findings confirm a significant positive relationship between the actualized attitude towards AI and the intention to engage in behavior that reflects this attitude. This highlights the importance of fostering a positive attitude as a precursor to behavioral intention, ultimately driving the adoption of AI technologies (Table 3).

Table 3. SEM for conceptual model results

Hypothesized Path	Coef.	t-value	p-value	Hypothesis testing
Compatibility - > Attitude	0,41	7,15	***	Supported
Observability - > Attitude	0,09	1,12	0.177	Not supported
Conformity - > Attitude	0,38	4,82	***	Supported
Anchoring- > Attitude	0,05	1,70	0.218	Not supported
FOMO- > Attitude	0,35	2,36	***	Supported
Ethical considerations - > Behavioral intention	-0,11	0,85	0.112	Not supported
Attitude - > Behavioral intention	0,62	11,36	***	Supported

Note: ***: $p < 0.001$

The influence of ethical considerations as an additional factor was not substantiated by our empirical data. We propose several potential explanations for this finding. Firstly, the current landscape surrounding artificial intelligence is characterized by a surge of novelty and hype, which tends to overshadow more reflective ethical considerations. This phenomenon may stem from a general lack of experience among individuals when confronted with genuine ethical dilemmas related to AI. As a result, we find ourselves in a phase of exploration, where curiosity and excitement about AI's capabilities dominate the discourse rather than a critical examination of its ethical implications. However, this situation presents a significant opportunity for future initiatives aimed at educating citizens on the responsible use of AI in their daily lives. As academic institutions begin to formulate regulations and guidelines surrounding AI, there is potential for these efforts to proactively cultivate a deeper understanding of ethical frameworks associated with AI technologies. By integrating ethical discourse into educational curricula and public awareness campaigns, we can foster a more nuanced comprehension of the ethical frontiers in AI, preparing individuals to navigate the complex moral landscapes that may arise as AI continues to evolve and permeate various aspects of society.

5 Conclusions and Limitations

In this study we aimed to develop a more holistic approach to understand how individuals – as consumers – perceive the AI-based opportunities and solutions, and how their attitudes and behavioral intentions are shaped. We combined three theoretical approaches and developed a conceptual model that is both comprehensive and parsimonious. Empirical results provide empirical evidence for a chain of effects, connecting individual beliefs, attitude and behavioral intention. While not all the effects were proven to be significant, we assessed several strong results from this empirical study. Firstly, we witness adequate results of applying and adapting the measures from existing studies to this new context. The quality of measures is adequate and suggests good quality of measurement model and reliability of testing the hypothesized relationships. Secondly, despite not all the effects being significant, we see the positive side of proving the whole chain of effects from beliefs to intention over the attitude. These results confirm the role of shaping the beliefs and attitudes of consumers in the area of technology innovations, including AI and AI-based solutions.

Still, there are some limitations to this study. Firstly, in the theoretical part, we limited the research to generative AI narrowed the studied phenomena to generated images, video materials and message texts. A different approach to methodology might also lead to different results. Secondly, the novelty of the research area suggests there is room for multiple alternative or nested models to be explored. We hope our effort suggests another perspective and will contribute to the field and future research attempts. Another notable limitation of this study concerns the conceptual treatment of technology acceptance and adoption. In the present research, these terms were used interchangeably within the conceptual model and empirical analysis. However, recent literature highlights that these constructs, while closely related, are not synonymous and represent distinct stages in the process of technological diffusion. Acceptance generally refers to an individual's positive attitude or intention to use a technology, reflecting psychological readiness or willingness to engage with an innovation. Adoption, in contrast, denotes the actual, observable implementation and sustained use of the technology in practice. Contemporary studies emphasize that acceptance (as measured by intention or attitude) does not always translate into adoption (actual use), as various contextual, organizational, and personal factors can intervene and prevent the realization of intended behavior. By treating acceptance and adoption as a single construct, this study may not fully capture the potential gap between intention and actual behavior. As a result, the findings should be interpreted with caution, and future research is encouraged to distinguish more clearly between these two stages - measuring both behavioral intention (acceptance) and actual technology use (adoption) - to provide a more nuanced understanding of the factors influencing the diffusion of AI-driven solutions.

References

1. Lankton, N.K., McKnight, D.H., Tripp, J.: Technology, humanness, and trust: rethinking trust in technology. J. Assoc. Inf. Syst. **16**(10), 880–918 (2015)
2. Gursoy, D., Chi, O.H., Lu, L., Nunkoo, R.: Consumers accept the application of artificially intelligent (AI) device use in service delivery. Int. J. Inf. Manage. **49**, 157–169 (2019)

3. Zhou, T.: Understanding the determinants of mobile payment continuance usage. Ind. Manag. Data Syst. **120**(3), 533–549 (2020)
4. Kelly, S., Kaye, S.-A., Oviedo-Trespalacios, O.: What factors contribute to the acceptance of artificial intelligence? A systematic review. Telematics Inform. **77**, 101925 (2023)
5. Rafique, H., Almagrabi, A.O., Shamim, A., Anwar, F., Bashir, A.K.: Investigating the acceptance of mobile library applications with an extended technology acceptance model (TAM). Comput. Educ. **145**, 103732 (2020)
6. Liu, Z., Shan, J., Pigneur, Y.: The role of personalized services and control: an empirical evaluation of privacy calculus and technology acceptance model in the mobile context. J. Inf. Priv. Secur. **12**(3), 123–144 (2016)
7. Mun, Y.Y., Jackson, J.D., Park, J.S., Probst, J.C.: Understanding information technology acceptance by individual professionals: toward an integrative view. Inf. Manag. **43**(3), 350–363 (2006)
8. Lin, C.-Y., Xu, N.: Extended TAM model to explore the factors that affect intention to use AI robotic architects for architectural design. Tech. Strat. Manag. 1–14 2021
9. Kashive, N., Powale, L., Kashive, K.: Understanding user perception toward artificial intelligence (AI) enabled e-learning. Int. J. Inf. Learn. Technol. **38**(1), 1–19 (2021)
10. Taddeo, M., Floridi, L.: How AI can be a force for good. Science **361**(6404), 751–752 (2018)
11. Ajzen, I.: The theory of planned behavior. Organizational behavior and human decision processes (1991)
12. Bosnjak, M., Ajzen, I., & Schmidt, P.: The Theory of Planned Behavior: Selected Recent Advances and Applications (2020)
13. Rozenkowska, K.: Theory of planned behavior in consumer behavior research: a systematic literature review. Int. J. Consum. Stud. **47** (2023)
14. Azad, M.S., Khan, S.S., Hossain, R., Rahman, R., Momen, S.: Predictive modeling of consumer purchase behavior on social media: Integrating theory of planned behavior and machine learning for actionable insights. PLoS ONE **18**(12), e0296336 (2023)
15. Prodanova, J., San-Martín, S., Jimenez, N.: Are you technologically prepared for mobile shopping? (2021)
16. Hsu, C.L., Lin, J.C.C.: What drives purchase intention for paid mobile apps?–An expectation confirmation model with perceived value. Electron. Commer. Res. Appl. **14**(1), 46–57 (2015)
17. Lim, H.-R., & An, S.: Intention to purchase wellbeing food among Korean consumers: An application of the Theory of Planned Behavior (2021)
18. Liu, Y., Zhang, X., Wang, T.: Bonus or Burden? The Impact of Attitudes and Fear of Missing Out (FOMO) on Generative AI Adoption. SSRN (2023)
19. Murat, A.: Understanding the impacts of lifestyle segmentation & perceived value on brand purchase intention: an empirical study in different product categories. Eur. Res. Manag. Bus. Econ. **27**(3), 100155 (2021)
20. Rogers E.M.: Diffusion of innovations, New York (1995)
21. Vieira, K.C., Pinto, G.A., Sugano, J.Y.: Consumer behavior towards technological innovations: a systematic review. J. Inf. Syst. Technol. Manage. **19** (2022)
22. Moore, G.C., Benbasat, I.: Development of an instrument to measure the perceptions of adopting an information technology innovation. Inf. Syst. Res. **2**(3), 192–222 (1991)
23. Park, Y., Chen, J.V.: Acceptance and adoption of the innovative use of smartphone. Ind. Manag. Data Syst. **107**(9), 1349–1365 (2007)
24. Kowalczuk, P.: Consumer acceptance of smart speakers: a mixed methods approach. J. Res. Interact. Market. **12** (2018)
25. O'Leary, D.E.: Gartner's hype cycle and information system research issues. Int. J. Account. Inf. Syst. **9**(4), 240–252 (2008)
26. Huang, M.-H., Rust, R.T.: Engaged to a robot? The role of AI in service relationships. J. Serv. Res. **24**(1), 30–41 (2021)

27. Roberts, M., MetLife CMO Insights Team.: Transparency in Generative AI: Building Trust Through Ethical Practices. Forbes (2023)
28. Martínez-López, F.J., et al.: Generative AI adoption in retail: balancing innovation and consumer skepticism. Span. J. Market. – ESIC (2023)
29. Liu, R., Gupta, S., Patel, P.: The application of the principles of responsible AI on social media marketing for digital health. Inf. Syst. Front. **25**, 2275–2299 (2023)
30. Podsakoff, P., MacKenzie, S., Podsakoff, N.: Recommendations for creating better concept definitions in the organizational, behavioral, and social sciences. Organ. Res. Methods (2016)
31. Schepman, A., Rodway, P.: Initial validation of the general attitudes towards artificial intelligence scale. Comput. Hum. Behav. Rep.
32. Barrett, A.M., Baum, S.D.: A model of pathways to artificial superintelligence catastrophe for risk and decision analysis. J. Exp. Theor. Artif. Intell. **29**, 397–414 (2017)
33. Scott, I.A., Carter, S.M., Coiera, E.: Exploring stakeholder attitudes towards AI in clinical practice. BMJ Health Care Inform. **28** (2021)
34. Sohn, K., Kwon, O.: Technology acceptance theories and factors influencing artificial intelligence-based intelligent products. Telematics Inform (2020)
35. Venkatesh, V.: Adoption and use of AI tools: a research agenda grounded in UTAUT. Annals Oper. Res. 1–12 (2022)
36. Wijayati, D.T., Rahman, Z., Rahman, M.F.W., Arifah, I.D.C., Kautsar, A.: A study of artificial intelligence on employee performance and work engagement: the moderating role of change leadership. Int. J. Manpow. **43**, 486–512 (2022)
37. Borghi, M., Mariani, M.M., Vega, R.P., Wirtz, J.: The impact of service robots on customer satisfaction online ratings: the moderating effects of rapport and contextual review factors. Psychol. Mark. **40**, 2355–2369 (2023)

Russian Portals of E-Participation on the Example of Solving the Ecological Problem of Invasive Plants in St. Petersburg and Leningrad Region

Natalia Kovalenko[1] and Georgiy Panfilov[2](✉)

[1] Saint-Petersburg State Agrarian University, Petersburg Highway 2, 196601 Saint Petersburg, Russia

[2] ITMO University, Birzhevaya Line 14, 199034 Saint Petersburg, Russia

panfilowgeorg@gmail.com

Abstract. The reader is presented with a paper conducted at the intersection of the study of e-participation and the environmental problem of invasive plants and the legal aspects of its solution. In order to collect data on the extent to which existing e-participation channels allow solving real problems of citizens, the authors used a participant observation method («test purchase»): they registered on portals and sent appeals to government agencies on real social problems. The topic of the appeals was an environmental problem relevant to Russia - overgrowing of territories with invasive plant - Sosnowsky's hogweed (SH). A total of 136 appeals were generated and sent about overgrowing in two regions of Russia - St. Petersburg and Leningrad region. The obtained results allowed us to draw conclusions about the factors influencing the quality of problem solving in the regions under study. The legal status of the e-participation channel (official letter or message through the portal) through which the appeals were submitted influenced the completeness of the responses, but did not always lead to a solution to the problem. The authors note the category of the territory where the overgrowing occurred as a significant factor. Thus, on lands located in cities, the fight was more effective due to greater civic activity around. At the same time, state-owned suburban areas, about which complaints are rarely written, were cleared of invasive plants rather poorly, and there was a long bureaucratic redirection of appeals. The presence of a regional law on the fight against invasive plants in one of the two studied regions had a significant impact on the quality of problem solving only in cases where the lands were privately owned. In the region where there is a law, officials were more active in issuing warnings and fines, but the final solution to the problem depended on the activity of the owner himself.

Keywords: E-Participation · E-Portals · Appeals to Authorities · participant observation method · Ecology · Invasive Plants · Sosnowsky's Hogweed

M. Bakaev et al. (Eds.): IMS 2025, CCIS 2671, pp. 322–337, 2026.
https://doi.org/10.1007/978-3-032-04958-2_24

1 Introduction

The topic of citizen participation in public policy has been and remains relevant. Currently, against the backdrop of digitalization of various sectors of life, many types of communication between government bodies and citizens are moving to an online format. At the international level, the issue of e-participation has been intensified at the level of the UN [32], the International Telecommunication Union (ITU) and other structures. E-participation channels that allow citizens to express their opinions on various issues exist today and are becoming an integral part of public policy in many countries [1]. Russia is no exception in these matters and has been implementing citizen participation practices since the 2010s [9].

At the same time, the multi-level structure of public administration in Russia, the specifics of the political system and the different political, economic and socio-cultural status of the regions in some cases lead to institutional crises in terms of the ability to quickly and efficiently implement public policy and respond to existing challenges. The structure of e-Government is one of the tools for overcoming these crises, reducing bureaucratic costs and optimizing the work of government bodies. In those industries where the level of civic activity affects the solution of current problems, e-participation services are used. Channels that allow citizens to express their opinions help in monitoring and solving existing problems.

However, the creation of a well-established system of e-participation channels is still in its formation and is developing unevenly. The creation of electronic resources by civil activists, which began in the early 2010s, was continued by the authorities of some of the most active regions [5]. In 2020, unified federal channels were created throughout Russia at the initiative of the President [35]. As a result, there is currently a variety of channels with different capabilities and legal status through which citizens can contact authorities and municipalities. Channels have different functional capabilities and different legal status. On the one hand, this activates the problem of assessing the effectiveness of the formed model, identifying its effective and ineffective components and possible duplication. On the other hand, the practical relevance of studying the effectiveness of channels is obvious for citizens to understand which of them and when solving which problems it is advisable to use.

This paper aims to fill these gaps in the research of the phenomenon of e-participation in terms of the possibilities of citizens to actually solve their problems through existing channels. To do this, the authors tried on the role of active citizens and submitted 136 appeals to government bodies, and analyzed their effectiveness.

2 Portals of E-Participation in the Russian Federation: Theoretical and Methodological Foundations of the Study

This study uses a combination of a number of theoretical concepts that define the nature of the phenomenon of e-participation and the specific features of its functioning. The theoretical basis of the study is the neo-institutional approach in political science. Based on the provisions of neo-institutionalism of rational choice, the authors consider the subjects of public policy as actors making a rational choice based on achieving the greatest efficiency [30]. The institutions available in the state - both formal (regulatory and legal acts) and informal (established features of communication between actors) are considered as "restrictions" (established "rules of the game"), within which actors carry out their activities and make rational choices [22]. The channels of e-participation available in the country or region are also considered as institutions. The authors draw on the achievements of the interdisciplinary scientific direction specializing in the study of e-participation. The phenomenon is studied by representatives of both social sciences - primarily political science and public and municipal administration, and technical sciences - primarily applied areas of computer science. In this paper, e-participation is understood as «A set of methods and tools that ensure interaction between citizens and government bodies through digital channels in order to take into account public opinion when making political and managerial decisions» (definition by A. Chugunov) [6]. In political science, e-participation is associated, first of all, with such concepts as political participation, public participation, democracy and civil society - in terms of the nature and characteristics of citizen activity, and such concepts as e-Government, e-Governance, e-Democracy in terms of formalizing the terminology related to the introduction of technologies in public policy and management.

Quite a lot of research has been devoted to e-participation in Russia, including the study of the functional capabilities of electronic services [25], analysis of the regulatory framework governing their work [12], analysis of the results of the services [15], demand for the offered services among users (both citizens and civil servants) [28] and others. Assessing the general level of opportunities provided by existing channels of e-participation, most researchers agree that in the existing channels offered by the authorities, the degree of the actual powers of citizens in making management decisions is relatively low. Most existing e-portals are focused on the practice of informing citizens about the activities of government bodies and municipalities, as well as citizen complaints about existing problems [13]. Researchers of e-participation associate this, among other things, with the peculiarities of the political system of Russia, which has a high centralization of power. A number of researchers note that the creation of electronic channels for civic participation in a number of countries is due to such factors as the desire to control lower levels of government officials, manipulating the political agenda, increasing the country's investment attractiveness, the desire to take leading positions in international rankings, etc. [7, 20]. A number of studies are devoted to the implementation of such feedback channels in China [4, 18]. A similar model is currently being established in Russia, with the active use of information technologies, but the leading role of central government bodies [27].

It is worth noting that the overwhelming majority of studies devoted to e-participation channels are focused on studying rather "external" aspects of portal functioning. The data for analysis are mostly quantitative characteristics of portal performance, such as the number of users and subscribers, the number of responses, the frequency of topics raised by citizens in their appeals, etc. At the same time, almost no attention is paid to the actual effectiveness of portals, their ability to solve public problems. Such an attempt is made by the authors in this study.

Today, a large number of electronic services have been implemented in Russia that can be classified as e-participation channels (including the sending of problem reports, electronic initiatives and petitions, voting and surveys). Regions of the country vary in the number of e-participation channels provided and their quality. At the same time, there are also centralized channels created by the federal government, available for use throughout the country. Many channels are classified as informative types of participation [2, 13], purely informing citizens without their active involvement, some are closer to «facade» forms [14, 27], but some still allow citizens to express their opinions in limited forms. The most significant form of e-participation in Russia today is the submission of electronic appeals to government agencies about existing problems [13]. Today, citizens can contact authorities and report problems when using the following four types of electronic channels.

2.1 E-Receptions (Official Letters)

This channel of communication with government bodies and municipalities has the highest legal status. In Russia, there is a separate federal law "On Appeals" [33]. According to this law all government bodies and municipalities must have electronic forms for receiving letters from citizens on their websites. The period for reviewing official letters is up to 30 days. Failure by officials to comply with the provisions of the law provides for administrative liability. To send appeals through forms, citizens are required to undergo official registration and verification through the Portal of State Services of the Russian Federation.

2.2 Feedback Platform (FP)

This federal channel was created in 2020 based on the instruction of the President of Russia [32]. It is a mobile application with a map, through which a citizen can report any problem in a simplified form from anywhere in Russia and attach a photo/video. Messages on operational issues (accidents, medicine, etc.) submitted through FP are not considered an official letter and are considered in a simplified manner within 10 days. More global issues are considered in accordance with the same federal law as official letters through the e-reception.

2.3 Portals for Reporting Problems of Regions and Municipalities

These portals operate in parallel with the FP in some regions and municipalities. For example, in the city of St. Petersburg, there is a portal called "Our St. Petersburg", which was created 7 years earlier than the FP [38]. Such portals have a lower legal status than official letters and the FP. The federal law on appeals does not apply to these portals, and the responsibility of officials for violations is not administrative, but only disciplinary. Messages submitted through them are governed by separate regulations adopted at the regional/municipality level (including response times for different categories of appeals). Some studies show that such channels were retained by regional officials so that citizens would contact the FP less often, and the federal government would not see the problems existing in the region [24].

2.4 Messages to Authorities via Social Networks

Social networks, primarily Vk.com, are also used by authorities to receive messages from citizens in Russia. Many officials, including governors, have been actively using social networks since the 2010s to monitor problems in the region that citizens write about [10]. Starting in 2022, amendments were made to federal laws requiring all government agencies to have official accounts on social networks and to collect messages from citizens about problems [34]. As a result, social networks have become a full-fledged channel of communication with the authorities, mandatory for officials to process. However, social networks have the lowest legal status among e-channels for appeals. Messages submitted through them are not considered official letters, but are processed by officials as a regular "request for information".

Thus, currently in Russia there is a diversity of e-participation channels for appeals, operating in different territories and having different legal status, which determines the social and scientific relevance of analyzing their work, identifying advantages and disadvantages and forming recommendations for the existing model.

3 Purpose and Research Design of the Study

The purpose of this study is to determine the effectiveness of e-participation portals in the Russian Federation in solving citizens' problems, as well as possible factors influencing this effectiveness.

When forming the research subject, the authors chose a specific environmental problem relevant to Russia - the uncontrolled spread of invasive plants and their overgrowing of green spaces (city parks and squares, as well as suburban areas). One of the most serious problems of invasive species in Russia is the spread of Sosnowsky's hogweed (hereinafter - SH) [16]. This plant was grown in the Soviet Union as an agricultural crop, as a result of which it successfully naturalized, began to displace local biological species and transform ecosystems. The problem is most serious for the northern, eastern and central parts of Russia, where SH covers areas of tens of square kilometers [19]. Federal laws require that SH be combated only in agricultural areas. However, the regions of Russia that suffer most from SH have adopted their own local laws making it mandatory to combat it throughout the entire territory. In addition, there are civil associations in Russia that are concerned about the problem and are combating SH as volunteers. One way to combat it is to file complaints with authorities, including through e-participation channels. This problem was chosen by the authors because they are members of the public environmental organization "Anti-hogweed," which fights BS [31]. The authors write appeals to government bodies, including through e-participation channels as part of the public activities, and therefore have in-depth expert knowledge on the topic of combating this invasive plant and the legal regulation of its control.

In order to collect data on the effectiveness of e-participation channels for solving the SH problem, the authors used the participant observation method. Participant observation refers to qualitative methods and involves the researcher conducting field observations of social processes in everyday life as a participant in them [29]. The method is most widely used in socio-anthropological studies, but in some cases it is used to study public policy, including various aspects of the behavior of state and municipal employees, the quality of their services to the population, etc. [3, 8, 11]. There have also been attempts to use the method to study the level of openness of government bodies and the readiness of civil servants to respond constructively to citizens' re-quests [17, 21].

It is worth noting the advantages and disadvantages of using the participant observation method to study the effectiveness of the channels of interaction between citizens and government bodies. The disadvantages of the method include its high cost in terms of time resources, requiring the full involvement of the researcher throughout the entire process of contacting government bodies and collecting feedback. This does not allow collecting a large amount of data and determines the low representativeness of the study. At the same time, the method has a significant advantage, which is that when submitting requests independently, the researcher gets the opportunity to study the communication process in detail from the inside. Researchers can monitor problem solving, check the quality of execution, write follow-up requests, draw conclusions about the work of performers based on the responses received, and promptly respond to changes. It is also important to note that in the case of studying electronic participation channels, the use of the participant observation method is additionally conditioned by the fact that data on citizens' requests on many electronic resources (for example, POS or electronic reception rooms) are closed, which excludes the possibility of gaining access to them. These reasons determine the relevance of using the method of participant observation and "transformation" of the researcher into a user.

In this study, the participant observation method (working title is «test purchase») was applied according to the following principle. The authors selected electronic portals intended for writing messages about problems at the federal and regional levels and registered on them. Actual areas of overgrowing SH green areas were identified, photographs were taken and requests for solutions were sent. A total of 136 appeals were sent. Based on the submitted appeals, the authors received responses from the responsible authorities and municipalities. Previously, this method was used by one of the authors to study e-participation portals and showed its effectiveness [23]. The results obtained were analyzed using a comparative analysis and are presented in Sect. 4.

3.1 Territorial Scope of the Study

Data collection was carried out in two neighboring regions of Russia: (1) the city of St. Petersburg and (2) the Leningrad region.

The choice of these cases was due to the fact that the two regions have different legal regulations governing the fight against invasive plants. Saint Petersburg is a city of federal significance. There is no separate law on combating SH here, and the rules for combating SH are regulated by only one point of the city improvement rules. The lack of combating SH is not separately highlighted in the city's code of offenses, so it is impossible to track the punishments applied to violators. Leningrad region is a separate subject of the Russian Federation, neighboring Saint Petersburg. In 2023, a separate regional law "On the organization of activities to combat Sosnowsky's hogweed…" [37]. The law defines the procedure and list of control methods (digging, cutting, chemical treatment, etc.) and introduces penalties for violations.

The number of applications submitted in the context of the two regions under consideration is presented in Table 1.

Table 1. Number of appeals by region

Region of Russia	City Saint Petersburg	Leningrad Region	Total
Number of appeals	65	71	136

3.2 List of the Studied Channels of E-Participation

When writing the appeals, the authors used the following channels of e-participation, available in the territory of the two studied regions.

1. Official letter through the website of the regional governments.
2. Feedback platform (federal channel for quick submission of appeals).
3. Portal "Our Saint Petersburg" (regional portal of the city of Saint Petersburg).

Through the first channel, 18 appeals (official letters) were submitted, through FP - 76 appeals, through the regional portal - 42 appeals (submitted only in Saint Petersburg, since the Leningrad Region does not have its own portal). The fourth channel described in the previous section – social networks – was not considered in the study, since this channel has the lowest legal status, and the authors of the study do not use it to submit requests.

3.3 Time Frame of the Study

The study used data on appeals submitted by the authors from 2021 to 2024. The frequency of writing appeals was arbitrary and was determined by the facts of the authors identifying problems with overgrowth of SH in urban and suburban areas.

3.4 Research Hypotheses

At the stage of forming the research methodology, the authors put forward three hypotheses. The first hypothesis is related to the different legal status of the three studied channels of e-participation. The work of the first is regulated by federal law, and appeals submitted through them are equivalent to official letters. The second channel is also regulated in some cases by federal law, but responses through it are provided in a simplified form. The third channel has the lowest status - it is purely regional, and its work is regulated by service regulations.

H1: The higher the legal significance of the e-participation portal, the higher the effectiveness of solving problems submitted by citizens through it.

The second and third hypotheses are related to the differences in the legislation of the two regions under consideration. The second hypothesis appeals to the fact that in St. Petersburg there is no separate law on combating SH, while in the Leningrad Region there is one. In this regard, we assumed that in the second case the solution to the problems would be more effective.

H2: If the region has well-developed industry legislation that provides for problem solving and responsibility, the effectiveness of applications submitted by citizens through e-participation portals will be higher.

The third hypothesis is related to the fact that at the beginning of 2022, due to the consequences of sanctions imposed by foreign states, the federal authorities of the Russian Federation introduced a moratorium on unscheduled inspections of businesses and compliance with land legislation [36]. In this regard, in regions where the SH problem was not legislatively enshrined (St. Petersburg), the moratorium became an obstacle to inspections on private territories.

H3: In the region where the SH problem is legally enshrined (Leningrad region), the solution to the SH problem on private territories after the introduction of the moratorium (since 2022) was more effective.

4 Findings of the Study

4.1 Overall Results

As a result of using the participant observation method, we obtained the following results. For each of the 136 sent appeals, responses were received from the responsible executors - government bodies, municipalities, subordinate institutions and contractors. The responses received can be classified into seven categories according to the degree of problem solving, presented in Table 2.

Table 2. Overall results for directed appeals

№	Result	Number and % of appeals
1	Problem completely resolved	26 (19,4%)
2	Problem completely resolved after appeals was returned for revision	4 (3%)
3	Problem partially resolved	28 (20,9%)
4	Problem partially resolved after appeals was returned for revision	5 (3,7%)
5	Interim response provided	38 (28,4%)
6	Meaningless response ("formal reply") provided, problem not resolved	25 (18,7%)
7	Refusal to resolve problem / sabotage	8 (6%)

Category 1 included situations where the SH was completely removed from the area using excavation, chemicals or other methods. Category 2 included situations where the problem was also solved, but after a repeated appeal. Category 3 is situations where the problem was only partially solved - most often the SH was mechanically cut but not completely removed. Category 4 is the same situation, but when this was done after the appeal was returned for reconsideration. Category 5 included situations where the problem was not solved, but the contractor justified the reason for this (for example, no budget for SH control now, but work is planned for the next period). Category 6 included requests for which the authorities avoided solving the problem and gave a vague, formalized response. Finally, category 7 is appeals that received the most negative result - a direct refusal of the contractor to perform the work or a lie that the work was completed.

According to Table 2, about a quarter (22.4%) of SH problems for which appeals were written were fully resolved. Another 24.6% of problems were partially resolved. Interim responses were given in 28%. And in 24.7%, the performers gave formal replies or a direct refusal to resolve the problem. The average response time to appeals was 22 days. In some cases, the response was provided very quickly, while in others it took a long time.

4.2 Results by E-Participation Channels

The results obtained by three e-participation channels are presented in Table 3.

Table 3. Overall results for directed appeals

e-participation channel	Official letter via the E-Receptions	Federal portal	Regional portal
Number of appeals	18	76	42
Number of resolved issues (fully or partially)	7 (37,5%)	36 (47,3%)	17 (40,7%)
Average response time (days)	25	21	31

The obtained results showed that the first hypothesis about the influence of different legal status of the channels was partially confirmed. However, it is worth noting the following identified patterns. In the case of official letters, the authors sent appeals with more detailed requests for information, sometimes for several territories at once. In the case of this channel, fewer problems were solved than for the other two. At the same time, there were many results of category 5 (intermediate responses). It is worth noting that, unlike the portals, a full-fledged official letter in the form of a document was provided in response, many of which included statistical data and work plans for combating SH for the next year. The average response time to official letters was 25 days (with a maximum permissible period of 30 days). The greatest number of problems were solved through the FP-portal, also regulated by federal law, but operating in a simplified form of shorter messages. The shortest average response time was also for appeals submitted through FP (21 days). In the case of the regional portal, the number of resolved problems was slightly lower, but not significantly, and the average response time was slightly higher - 31 days, which is considered acceptable for this channel.

4.3 Results by Region

Figure 1 shows the data obtained as a result of reviewing appeals by the two regions of Russia we are considering - St. Petersburg and the Leningrad Region.

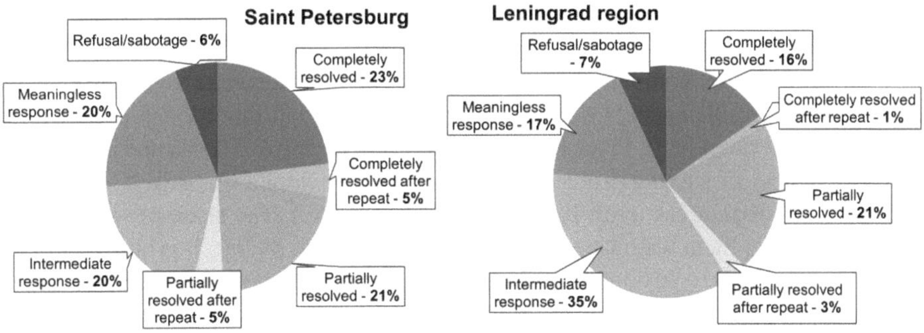

Fig. 1. Results for St. Petersburg and the Leningrad Region

Contrary to expectations about the impact of the separate law on combating SH in the Leningrad Region, very close results were obtained for the two regions. At the same time, problems were completely solved in more cases in St. Petersburg (27.7%) than in the Leningrad Region (16.9%). The number of partially solved problems was also higher in the city (26.1% in St. Petersburg versus 23.9% in the Leningrad Region). At the same time, there were more problems that could not be solved at all (26.2% versus 23.9%). The main difference is that in the Leningrad Region a much larger number of responses were intermediate (35.2% versus 24.6 in St. Petersburg). The average response time in St. Petersburg was also shorter and amounted to 19 days, while in the Leningrad Region it was 24 days. Thus, the second hypothesis about the impact of the level of an industry regulatory act on the effectiveness of solving the SH problem through e-participation channels was not confirmed.

4.4 Results by Territory Type

An important criterion for differentiating the submitted appeals is the different status of the green spaces where SH was spreading. In total, appeals were submitted for territories that can be divided into the following five categories:

1. City parks and squares.
2. Street lawns.
3. Territory along roads and highways.
4. Suburban territories, state and municipal
5. Suburban territories, privately owned or leased.

The positive response of government bodies and effective problem solving were achieved most in those territories that were located in cities. In category 1 territories, it was possible to achieve a solution to the problem (completely or partially) in 65% of cases, and in category 2 territories (street lawns) - in 66.7% of cases. Moreover, all parks and squares for which appeals were written were located in St. Petersburg. Of the 33 appeals written for the second category territories, 27 objects were located in St. Petersburg and 6 in the Leningrad Region, but in both cases the solutions were quite effective. The average response times for objects located in the city were quite fast and amounted to 17 days for parks and 22 days for street lawns.

The most difficult areas to resolve were those in category 3 - areas located along highways and roads - the share of refusals and formal replies for them was 58.4%. In most cases, the federal subordinate agencies for road management were responsible for them. Most of the appeals were written in the Leningrad Region, but even for the few that were written in St. Petersburg, the result was negative. The second area where the effectiveness of solving problems was low in both regions was area 4 - state and municipal suburban areas (river banks, forests, fields, etc.). The share of refusals and formal replies for them was also very high and amounted to 40.9%. It is also important to note that these two types of objects had the longest average response times (25 days).

Resolving problems in category 5 (privately owned lands) is the most specific. For these areas, the authorities provided the fewest refusals and formal replies (12.3%). This is due to the fact that the authorities and municipalities are not directly responsible for these territories, but can only try to oblige the owners to combat SH. At the same time, the final result depends on the activity and responsibility of the owner. The problem was fully or partially solved in 32.6% of cases. Another 55.1% of the results were intermediate responses (notification that the authorities sent the owner an order, but the problem has not yet been solved).

These results once again rejected hypothesis 2 and allowed us to conclude that the administrative affiliation of the territory does not play a decisive role in solving the problem. Rather, the type of territory itself, in which the problem occurred, plays a significant role. In the case of territories located in urbanized parts of the city, problems were solved faster and more effectively. In the case of more remote territories, problems were solved worse and slower, regardless of the region in which they occurred.

5 Discussion

When conducting a comparative analysis of the data, the authors formulated the following provisions for testing hypotheses that deserve discussion.

Both the data collection process and subsequent processing confirmed that the territories of the two regions under study are very diverse and include green zones that differ in size, urbanization, legal status, and areas of responsibility of the performers. For most appeals, the effectiveness of the problem solution was determined by the complexity of the subject of the appeal itself and the type of territory subject to SH overgrowth. For example, solving the problem of SH overgrowth on a small lawn in the city and a large remote suburban area requires completely different amounts of work and preparation. At the same time, in the case of sending official letter via e-Reception, officials provided more detailed information, including plans to combat SH for the coming years, a planned list of events, etc. In the case of appeals through the FP and the regional portal, more abbreviated responses were provided, most often a short message that the problem was solved or an explanation of why it was not solved. At the same time, the channel level did not significantly affect the quality of the solution to the problem and the decision taken on it. In this regard, hypothesis 1 about the influence of the level of the e-participation channel through which the appeal is submitted on the solution of the problem was confirmed only partially.

The presence in one of the regions (Leningrad region) of a separate regional law on combating SH also did not play a decisive role in the effectiveness of problem solving.

The share of solved problems in St. Petersburg, which does not have a separate law, was even slightly higher than in Leningrad region. At the same time, a positive relationship was established between the type of territory and the level of its urbanization with the number of solved problems. For parks, squares and lawns located within the city limits (both in St. Petersburg and in small towns of Leningrad region), the share of solved problems was significantly higher than for territories of other categories. In our opinion, the fact that these territories are visible to a large number of people, more appeals are written about them, and in the case of inaction or refusal to solve the problem, there is a higher probability of publicity and responsibility of officials, contributes to the fact that in cities the authorities are more active in combating SH. It can be assumed that this concerns not only SH, but also other urban problems for which citizens contact the authorities. In areas located far outside the city, on the contrary, the number of resolved problems was low (both in the case of the Leningrad Region and in the case of the suburbs of St. Petersburg). In many cases, appeals were sent multiple times between departments, response times were longer, and many responses were incorrect, contained inaccurate information or an outright refusal to resolve the problem. Most of these cases occurred in the Leningrad Region. Thus, the second hypothesis about a positive relationship between the level of a regulatory act and the effectiveness of solving the problem was not confirmed. The results obtained for areas in private ownership deserve special attention. The authors of the study believe that not only the direct removal of SH from such areas is a positive result, but also the holding of owners of areas liable for violating the law. The cases with private owners under consideration are interesting because during the study, a moratorium on inspections was introduced in the country (hypothesis 3). Therefore, the owners could only be held liable in one of the two regions studied (Leningrad region), which had its own law on combating SH.

In St. Petersburg in 2021, the Executors sent demands to owners to bring the territories into proper condition, and also reported that if the owners failed to act, they would be brought to administrative responsibility. However, since 2022, the Executors refused to bring violators of the law to justice in connection with the adoption of the moratorium, and could only send letters to owners demanding that the territory be brought into proper condition, but there were no consequences for violating mandatory requirements.

In the Leningrad Region in 2021, it was not possible to bring landowners to administrative responsibility in the Leningrad Region. In 2022, amendments were adopted to the improvement rules concerning private territories, and in 2023, a separate law was adopted to combat SH. As a result, owners began to be fined for violating the law under the moratorium on inspections, because there was a regional law allowing inspections based on citizens' appeals for violations of the law. Thus, none of the responses to appeals from private owners' territories mentioned the moratorium and the impossibility of carrying out inspections and holding violating owners accountable. On the contrary, several cases were recorded when owners were brought to administrative responsibility in 2023, and in 2024 these owners began to combat SH in order to avoid repeated fines. Thus, hypothesis 3 that under the moratorium, the presence of a separate regional law had a positive effect on the effectiveness of solving the problem was confirmed.

The authors will continue their research. It seems promising to continue the analysis of the dynamics of data on the research topic, expanding the geography to other regions with different legal regulation of the problem. It is possible to expand the list of studied forms of citizen participation and add such channels as social networks and personal receptions with officials. The methodology of data collection and analysis proposed by the authors, based on the method of participant observation, can be applied to study other social problems.

6 Conclusion

The conducted research allowed to achieve a number of both substantive and methodological results. Firstly, the topic of e-participation in Russia was considered by the authors from an unusual angle - from the point of view of the actual effectiveness of existing government portals in solving citizens' problems. For the analysis, the form of e-participation was chosen that assumes the greatest initiative on the part of citizens - filing appeals to government bodies with complaints about problems in electronic form. The electronic channels that exist today that allow sending appeals are distinguished by their diversity in their legal status (from official letters via e-Receptions to comments on social networks). As part of the study, the hypothesis about the influence of this legal status on the effectiveness in solving problems was tested (hypothesis №1), which was partially confirmed.

Secondly, the authors used a participant observation method in the logic of "test purchase" to collect data. Registration was carried out on the portals of e-participation, 136 appeals were submitted to the authorities and municipalities, the responses to them and the response of the performers to the problems were analyzed. For the purity of the data and the possibility of comparison, the authors selected one specific problem related to ecology - the overgrowing of urban and suburban areas with invasive plants. Within the framework of the problem under consideration, two hypotheses were tested on the influence of the regional regulatory framework (the presence of a regional law) on the solution of the problem (hypothesis №2 and hypothesis №3). The results demonstrated that the presence of a separate regional law obliging to combat SH in the region does not have a clear connection with the number of problems solved. For many submitted appeals, the effectiveness of the solution was determined by other factors, including the category of lands that were subject to overgrowing with invasive plants, their urbanization. In areas located within the boundaries of cities, with a much higher degree of probability, problems were solved qualitatively, regardless of the presence of a law in the region. The solution to the problem was also determined by the subjective complexity of the subject of the appeal itself (the scale of the problem and the availability of resources for its solution by the performers). At the same time, the presence of the law in the region influenced the solution of problems in those territories that were in private hands, allowing for control checks and holding owners accountable for violations.

Thirdly, the methodological conclusions should include the fact that the applied participant observation method ("test purchase") demonstrated its effectiveness in terms of the possibility of collecting relevant data for the study. According to the authors, the use of data on real problems, verified by the direct involvement of the researcher in their identification and writing appeals on them, ensures greater accuracy of conclusions than the use of statistical data or data on other people's appeals collected from open sources. Data collection in the "test purchase" format ensures greater involvement of the researcher in the problems of the phenomena under study, forms a more in-depth understanding of the subject of the study, allowing you to pay attention to those patterns that remain invisible when using data from external sources. Another positive aspect is the fact that the use of the "test purchase" method allows you to achieve a practical solution to some social problems for which data is collected. In the case of this study, the authors completely or partially solved 63 problems of overgrowing green areas with invasive plants.

References

1. Aichholzer, G., Rose, G.: Experience with digital tools in different types of e-participation. In: Hennen, L., van Keulen, I., Korthagen, I., Aichholzer, G., Lindner, R., Nielsen, R. (eds.) European E-Democracy in Practice. Studies in Digital Politics and Governance, pp. 93–140. Springer, Cham (2020).https://doi.org/10.1007/978-3-030-27184-8
2. Arnstein, S.: A ladder of citizen participation. J. Am. Inst. Plan. **35**(4), 216–224 (1969). https://doi.org/10.1080/01944366908977225
3. Berda, Y.: Colonial Bureaucracy and Contemporary Citizenship: Legacies of Race and Emergency in the Former British Empire. Cambridge University Press, Cambridge (2022)
4. Chen, J., Pan, J., Xu, Y.: Sources of authoritarian responsiveness: a field experiment in China. Am. J. Polit. Sci. **60**(2), 383–400 (2016). https://doi.org/10.1111/ajps.12207
5. Chugunov, A.: Digital interaction of citizens and authorities in the Russian Federation: a trend towards centralization. In: Sokolov, A., Frolov, A. (eds.) Opportunities and Threats of the Digital Society. Proceedings of the All-Russian Scientific and Practical Conference, 2022, pp. 10–17, Yaroslavl (2022). (In Russian)
6. Chugunov, A.: E-participation in the context of the transformation of the concept of democracy. Manag. Consult. **8**, 14–20 (2017). (In Russian). https://doi.org/10.22394/1726-1139-2017-8-14-20
7. Cooley, A.: The emerging politics of international rankings and ratings: a framework for analysis. In: Cooley A., Snyder J. (eds.) Ranking the World (2015)
8. Douglas, M.: How Institutions Think. Elementary Forms, Moscow (2020). (In Russian)
9. Filatova, O., Chugunov, A., Bolgov, R.: Transformation of the e-participation system in Russia in the early 2020s: centralization trends. In: Bolgov, R., et al. (eds.) Proceedings of Topical Issues in International Political Geography. TIPG 2021, pp. 309–319. Springer Geography. Springer, Cham (2023). https://doi.org/10.1007/978-3-031-20620-7_27
10. Filatova, O.: State communications in the digital public sphere of Russia: 2011–2020. Contours of global transformations: politics, economics. Law **13**(2), 72–91 (2020). https://doi.org/10.23932/2542-0240-2020-13-2-4 (In Russian)
11. Galindabaeva, V.V.: Moral economy, local community and social service in rural areas. Professions of the social state/edited by by P. V. Romanov, E. R. Yarskaya-Smirnova. Moscow: Variant; TsSPGI, 250–270 (2013). (In Russian)
12. Isaeva, E., Sokolov, A., Frolov, A. Digital Ecosystems: How Are They Defined and Regu-lated in Russia? In: Springer (2024). https://doi.org/10.1007/978-3-031-67762-5_32
13. Kabanov, Y., Chugunov, A., Panfilov, G.: Drivers of e-participation performance from a supply-side perspective: the case of the Russian regions. In: ICEGOV 2023: 16th International Conference on Theory and Practice of Electronic Governance Belo Horizonte Brazil September, 2023, pp. 191–196. ACM, Brazil (2023). https://doi.org/10.1145/3614321.3614347

14. Kabanov, Y.: E-participation and hybrid regime: the case of the "Russian public initiative". In: V International Scientific and Practical Conference "Social Computing: Funda-mentals, Development Technologies, Social and Humanitarian Effects", Moscow, RANEPA, 2016, pp. 129–130 (2016). (In Russian)
15. Kaisarov, A., Kaisarova, V., Vasilyeva, E.: Electronic government and citizens: an empiri-cal study of interaction on the official portal in St. Petersburg. Manag. Consult. **12**, 48–69 (2021). https://doi.org/10.22394/1726-1139-2021-12-48-69 (In Russian)
16. Kirichenko, N., et al.: Economic costs of biological invasions in terres-trial ecosystems in Russia. In: Zenni, R.D., McDermott, S., García-Berthou, E., Essl, F. (eds.) Economic Costs of Biological Invasions Around the World. NeoBiota 67. pp. 103–130 (2021). https://doi.org/10.3897/neobiota.67.58529
17. Kononenko, P.: Information openness of parliaments of the constituent entities of the Russian Federation: experimental analysis. Bull. Volgograd State Univ. **1**(31), 99–110 (2015). (In Russian)
18. Kornreich, Y.: Authoritarian responsiveness: online consultation with "issue publics" in China. Governance **32**(3), 547–564 (2019). https://doi.org/10.1111/gove.12393
19. Koldasbayeva, D., Tregubova, P., Shadrin, D. Gasanov, M.: Large-scale forecasting of Heracleum Sosnowskyi habitat suitability under the climate change on publicly available data. Sci. Rep. **12**(11) (2022). https://doi.org/10.1038/s41598-022-09953-9
20. Linde, J., Karlsson, M.: The dictator's new clothes: the relationship between E-participation and quality of government in non-democratic regimes. Int. J. Public Adm. **36**(4), 269–281 (2013)
21. Nikulin, A.M.: Between the state and citizens: features of the worldview of municipal employees of the Arkhangelsk region, Russian official: sociological analysis of the life world of state and municipal employees/edited by D. M. Rogozin Moscow: Institute of Sociology of the Russian Academy of Sciences, pp. 228–250 (2015). (In Russian)
22. North, D.: Institutions, Institutional Change and Economic Performance. Cambridge University Press, Cambridge (1990)
23. Panfilov, G.: Electronic portals for reporting problems in the context of centralization of digital development policy (on the example of St. Petersburg). Soc. Polit. Stud. **3**(24), 48–70 (2024). (In Russian). https://doi.org/10.20323/2658-428X-2024-3-24-48
24. Panfilov, G.: Goals and factors of institutional transformations of the electronic civil participation system in Russia: data from expert interviews. In: State and citizens in the electronic environment. Issue 8 (Proceedings of the XXVII International United Scientific Conference "Internet and Modern Society", IMS-2024, St. Petersburg, 24–26 June 2024. Collection of scientific articles), pp. 13–25 (2024). https://doi.org/10.17586/2541-979X-2024-8-00-00
25. Panfilov, G., Volkova, O., Chugunov, A.: Monitoring of E-participation channels in the Russian federation: research results 2020–2023. In: State and Citizens in the Electronic Environment. Issue 7 (Proceedings of the XXVI International Joint Scientific Conference "Internet and Modern Society", IMS-2023, St. Petersburg, 26–28 June 2023. Collection of Scientific Articles), pp. 34–46 (2023). (In Russian). https://doi.org/10.17586/2541-979X-2023-7-34-46
26. Salem, F.: Open governance is authoritarian states: a framework for assessing digital participation in the age of mass surveillance. In E-participation: 8th IFIP WG 8.5 Inter-national conference, ePart-2016, Guimaraes, Portugal, 5–8 September 2016, Proceedins 8, pp. 94–105 (2016). https://doi.org/10.1007/978-3-319-45074-2_8
27. Schlaufer, C.: Why do nondemocratic regimes promote e-participation? The case of Moscow's active citizen online voting platform. Governance **34**(3), 821–836 (2020). https://doi.org/10.1111/gove.12531
28. Smorgunov, L., Popova, O., Tropinova, E.: Citizens' attitudes to eGovernment: a study across ten Russian regions. In: International Conference on Digital Transformation and

Global Society. pp. 250–262. Cham, Springer (2020). https://doi.org/10.1007/978-3-030-65218-0_19
29. Spradley, J.P.: Participant Observation. Holt, Rinehart and Winston, New York, 1980
30. Weingast, B.R.: Political institutions: rational choice perspectives: a new handbook of political science. Chapter: Rational Choice Perspectives on Institutions. In: Goodin, R.E.H.D. (eds.) Klingemann. Oxford University Press (1996). https://doi.org/10.1093/0198294719.003.0005
31. Anti-hogweed. Community for combating Sosnowsky's hogweed. https://antiborschevik.info
32. UN E-Government Knowldgebase. E-participation Index. https://publicadministration.un.org/egovkb/en-us/About/Overview/E-participation-Index
33. Federal Law of the Russian Federation of 02.05.2006 No. 59 "On the procedure for considering appeals from citizens of the Russian Federation". Office of the President of the Russian Federation for work with appeals. http://letters.kremlin.ru/info-service/acts/2
34. Federal Law of 14.07.2022 No. 270 "On Amendments to the Federal Law "On Ensuring Access to Information on the Activities of State Bodies and Local Self-Government Bodies" and Article 10 of the Federal Law "On Ensuring Access to Information on the Activities of Courts in the Russian Federation". Official Internet Portal of Legal Infor-mation, http://publication.pravo.gov.ru/Document/View/0001202207140024
35. List of instructions (approved by the President of the Russian Federation on 01.03.2020 No. 354) following the meeting of the Council for the Development of Local Self-Government. President of Russia. http://kremlin.ru/acts/assignments/orders/62919
36. Resolution of the Government of the Russian Federation of 10.03.2022 No. 336 "On the specifics of organizing and implementing state control (supervision), municipal control". http://publication.pravo.gov.ru/Document/View/0001202203100013
37. Law of the Leningrad Region of 06.27.2023 No. 76 "On the organization of activities to combat Sosnowsky's hogweed in the Leningrad Region and on amendments to the re-gional law "On administrative offenses". http://publication.pravo.gov.ru/document/4700202306270001
38. Regional portal for reporting problems "Our Saint Petersburg". https://gorod.gov.spb.ru/

Network Strategies of Tuareg Separatists: Media Communications of the Azawad Liberation Front on X

Denis Degterev[1(✉)], Daria Draganova[2], Iaroslav Sychev[3], Mariia Bazlutckaia[4], and Anna Sytnik[2]

[1] Institute for African Studies, Russian Academy of Sciences, Moscow 119991, Russia
ddegterev@inafr.ru
[2] Saint-Petersburg State University, Saint-Petersburg 199034, Russia
[3] Telegram Channel Departamente, Moscow, Russia
[4] Autonomous Non-Commercial Research Organisation "Coordination Lab" (ANO Colaboratoria), Saint-Petersburg 194064, Russia

Abstract. This article examines the digital activity and informal communication networks of the Tuareg separatist movement, the Azawad Liberation Front, on the platform X. By analyzing a dataset comprising 18,335 posts through methods of hashtag and mention network analysis, as well as engagement metrics, the authors identify key characteristics of the movement's media strategies from May 1, 2021, to March 10, 2024. Special attention is given to periods of heightened digital activity closely corresponding to significant conflict events, including terrorist offensives in Menaka in 2022–2023, clashes in Ber and Kidal in 2023, and battles near Tinzawatene in 2024. The study highlights that central themes include military actions involving Malian armed forces (FAMA), regional terrorist groups, and Russian military instructors. Although there are occasional references to Ukrainian events and European media, the group's communication predominantly focuses on internal regional dynamics. Network analysis further reveals informal structures and patron-client relationships within the Azawad Liberation Front's Politburo, a Tuareg separatist entity established in late 2024 through the restructuring of the Strategic Framework for the Defense of the People of Azawad (CSP-DPA). Investigating media communications of Tuareg separatist movements sheds light on how informal digital networks influence conflict trajectories and political dynamics in unstable regions. The authors conclude that separatists use information strategies and social media to build relationships with international actors and organizations, seeking attention for the crisis in northern Mali and forging alliances that could shape the conflict's dynamics and escalation. Analysis of these communication patterns reveals internal operational mechanisms of such movements and serves as an essential tool for anticipating crisis developments and designing effective stabilization measures.

Keywords: Sahel · FLA · Azawad Liberation Front · network-analysis · Twitter · X · social media · communication

M. Bakaev et al. (Eds.): IMS 2025, CCIS 2671, pp. 338–350, 2026.
https://doi.org/10.1007/978-3-032-04958-2_25

1 Introduction

In the digital age, social media has evolved beyond a mere communication tool into a weapon of information warfare [1]. In 2012, a conflict erupted in northern Mali [2], serving as a striking example of how social networks have become an additional dimension of real-world confrontations. Tuareg separatists, advocating for the independence of Azawad, actively utilized Twitter and other platforms from the outset of the conflict to disseminate news of their successes, circumventing traditional government-controlled media. Today, more than a decade later [3], their media resources not only capture the attention of international outlets but also shape a political narrative that unites independence supporters in the vein of Benedict Anderson's concept of socially constructed communities [10]. In contexts where traditional methods of gauging public opinion in closed societies are often inaccessible or unreliable, social media offers a unique window into the dynamics of conflict. It sheds light on how sentiments take shape, how national identity is forged, and how information transforms into a weapon.

The aim of our research is to explore how separatists from the Azawad Liberation Front (FLA) leverage Twitter (now known as X) to craft a political narrative and shape public opinion. We seek to examine how their posts contribute to constructing an image of the enemy, rallying supporters, and influencing the international agenda. To this end, we have outlined the following objectives:

1. To investigate how separatists use Twitter to disseminate information about combat operations and events on the territories under their control.
2. To identify connections between social media activity of FLA representatives and significant political developments.
3. To explore how informal relationships within the FLA are formed and how they influence the movement's media strategy.
4. To evaluate the impact of separatist publications on public opinion and perceptions of the FLA movement, both within Mali and beyond its borders.

2 Literature Review

First and foremost, it is worth noting that the role of media in the Sahel region extends beyond merely informing the population; it serves as a powerful force in shaping public opinion, which can either contribute to stabilizing the situation or exacerbate conflicts. Specifically, the securitization (or "weaponization") of media [4], the concept of "conflict-sensitive journalism" [6], and analyses of information campaigns in the Sahel [9] highlight the dual nature of media influence, where key actors actively leverage social platforms to shape the sentiments of local communities.

Studies of political activity in social media are inherently interdisciplinary, spanning areas like digital sociology, communication research, and political science. Of particular importance is the investigation of digital authoritarianism, well summarized in a recent article by Roberts, T., & Oosterom, M. [25].

The historical context—particularly the legacy of colonial policies and the imposition of artificial borders [14]—remains a critical factor shaping contemporary tensions in the Sahel, especially in the case of Azawad and Tuareg separatists [16]. This is compounded by the actions of local actors, such as the National Movement for the Liberation of Azawad (MNLA) [2], which acts as a catalyst for regional instability, and jihadist groups driven by both ideological and pragmatic motives [13]. Meanwhile, transnational social movements [1] and digital culture—exemplified by Berber websites [12]—illustrate the potential of new media resources to forge collective identities and resist the erosion of cultural distinctiveness. Analyzing the data through the lens of political opportunity structures, a framework often used to examine political opposition movements against state authorities, offers a promising approach for this paper [26].

Geopolitical rivalry between Western and non-Western powers [19] further complicates conflict dynamics [18]. The waning influence of traditional actors like France is paralleled by the growing presence of Russia, China, Turkey, and the UAE—a trend particularly evident in the Sahel [17]. Here, interactions between external players, local communities, and terrorist groups give rise to new security and stability challenges [8]. Concepts such as "positive peace" [3], "collective self-reliance" [20], and "geopolitical structures of recognition" [19], proposed within the framework of the Alliance of Sahel States—a sort of "laboratory of minilateralism" [11]—reflect the region's search for alternative development paths amid a multipolar world and an increasingly complex political landscape.

Insurgent communications in the Global South, including Afghanistan [27], have been analyzed in numerous studies. The conceptual connection between Afghanistan and the Sahel, sometimes framed through the "Africanistan" discourse, is also explored [28].

In conclusion, all these studies underscore the need for an interdisciplinary approach to understanding conflicts in the Sahel, one that integrates media, historical, social, and geopolitical dimensions. Further exploration of this topic is thus highly relevant. Employing network analysis of social media—particularly the X platform—offers a deeper understanding of the dynamics of informational influence and real-time actor interactions. This is especially significant given the rising digital presence of external actors and the media activity of local communities, positioning X as a unique data source for studying contemporary Sahel crises.

M. Castells's work on the Theory of network society [29] provides a framework for understanding power dynamics in the global network society. In his analysis, Castells identifies four major types of power, including "network-making power," which involves managing mass communication and elaborating identity, as seen in the Touregs community's use of Twitter [30].

Research on the role of social media in conflicts is not new. For instance, Pathé Duarte's article [9] provides a detailed examination of how Russia utilized Twitter for information campaigns to bolster its influence in Mali and Burkina Faso, demonstrating how social networks became tools for undermining trust in the West. However, this study does not explore the internal workings of armed groups themselves.

Social media has become an integral part of social movements in the Global South, shaping their strategies and impact. As Zibran Choudhury compellingly argues, «I just can't imagine writing about a social movement that doesn't have a technology, digital media, social media component partly because it's so integrated into it. It's not – here's a social movement there and here's this technology there – because it's not just that they're using it, it affects how they do things, how they think about it, how they get attention and how they try to shape the narrative» [31].

Another example is S. Vicari's work [1], which investigates how transnational social movements harness the internet to construct collective identities, analyzing hyperlinks between websites to map networks of solidarity. Yet, this approach has not been tailored to examine armed groups like the Azawad Liberation Front (FLA) or their media strategies. Similar limitations apply to other related studies [5, 6].

Many scholars have written about web activism, but the edited volume by J. Earl and K. Kimport is a particularly important contribution [32].

While these works are undoubtedly valuable, they overlook a critical question: how do social media function within movements to foster informal relationships and shape public opinion? This is the gap our research aims to address. We hypothesize that Twitter has evolved beyond a mere platform for disseminating information for the FLA, becoming a tool for crafting a cohesive political narrative. Additionally, we propose that informal relationships within the movement—such as patron-client ties [23]—play a pivotal role in shaping its media strategy. Our study focuses on the separatists' posts and communication networks on Twitter as its object, with the subject being how these posts influence the formation of political narratives, public opinion, and informal structures within the FLA.

By focusing on open source data (publicly available posts on network X), this research avoids potential ethical complications in analyzing communications related to international conflicts. The analysis is limited to the communications that actors themselves have deemed appropriate for public dissemination on the internet.

Our research offers a fresh perspective on the role of social media in conflicts. Unlike prior studies that are centered on the influence of external actors or state structures, we concentrate on the internal dynamics of armed groups. Through network analysis, we have identified informal relationships within the FLA and demonstrated their impact on the movement's media strategy.

3 Method

Our research focuses on examining the communication networks and activity patterns of separatist formations within the social network X. Building on prior studies that employ engagement analysis of social media [21], we utilized data on publication dates from separatist-affiliated channels to trace correlations between periods of heightened account activity and significant political events (see the Results section for a detailed breakdown) [22].

Beyond capturing the reflection of political upheavals in online behavior, this approach also facilitates the identification of potential patron-client dynamics through network analysis [23]. To this end, the software Gephi was selected as an effective tool, offering a comprehensive visualization and analytical framework to map interactions and uncover how these channels strategically leverage digital platforms to advance their agendas on the global stage.

3.1 Data Sample

The dataset consisted of metadata extracted from tweets posted by selected X accounts. The latter were specifically chosen according to predefined criteria relevant to the scope of the study: a) affiliation (direct or indirect) with the Azawad Liberation Front; b) audience bigger than 8,000 Followers. All in all, 12 X accounts were identified (see Table 1). To answer the research question, a computer program written in Python using the Selenium library was employed to systematically collect and analyze data retrieved from X Advanced Search [24]. Data collection covered the period from May 1, 2021, to March 10, 2025, and included all accessible tweets published by these accounts, enabling comprehensive analysis and robust insights into their communication patterns. As a result, 18,335 posts, including information about the data of publication, the hashtags and mentions used by the author, were retrieved.

May 2021 was chosen as a starting point of the analysis as it was marked by two significant events: the rise to power of Assimi Goïta, reshaping Mali's political landscape, and the establishment of the Strategic Framework for the Defense of the People of Azawad, which sought to unify separatist groups under a coordinated strategy. These developments likely influenced both the structure and intensity of separatist online activity, making this period a critical starting point for analysis. The end date of analysis corresponds to the date of data retrieval and the last post published by the channels in question.

Data Pre-cleaning. Before proceeding to network-analysis the dataset has undergone the pre-cleaning process. The date of publication was adjusted to the unique format used in Excel tables. Hashtags and mentions, some of which were delimited by a comma, were sorted into separate rows in a table to ensure ease of follow-up in Gephi. Multiple repetitions on each channel have been removed to avoid confusion. Arabic characters and single letters of the French alphabet (e.g., "é") were transliterated and/or reduced to a common denominator in Latin (e.g. "e"). All characters have been converted to lower case. Only after that the authors could proceed with the Gephi-graph.

Network Analysis. The network graph was constructed using the ForceAtlas 2 algorithm, which simulates a physical system where nodes repel each other while edges act as springs, drawing connected nodes together. This layout effectively reveals clusters, indicating tightly interconnected groups and their peripheral counterparts. To enhance readability and interpretability, label adjustments and node customizations were applied: the channels were distinctly colored, while the hashtags and mentions used in common placed in the center of the web. The bigger the node on the graph, the more of common hashtags or mentions it applies.

Table 1. X accounts chosen for the study

№	Channel ID	Channel Affiliation
1	@BilalAgAcherif	*Bilal Ag Acherif*, FLA General Secretary
2	@MohmedRAMADANE	*Mohamed Elmaouloud Ramadane*, FLA Press Secretary
3	@Agintalla1	*Alghabas Ag Intalla*, FLA Reconciliation and Social Cohesion Officer
4	@Idarfa	*Fahad Ag Almahmoud*, Secretary General of GATIA (until December 1, 2024)
5	@ attaye_ag	*Attaye Ag Mohamed*, FLA member, media activist
6	@Inkinane1	*Inkinane Ag Attaher*, FLA field commander, history teacher
7	@BenBenbella	*Said Ben Bella*, FLA member, scientist
8	@kalakal2012	Association Kal Akal
9	@Walid_Leberbere	*Walid Le Berbère*, Tuareg journalist, closely associated with FLA
10	@oumaragg	FLA combatant
11	@akli_sh	*Akli Sh'kka*, British activist, connected with FLA
12	@SouleymaneAnara	*Souleymane Ag Anara*, Tuareg journalist

4 Results

4.1 Periods of Media Activity of Separatist Groups

Analyzing the social media activity of separatist groups reveals several key periods, each tied to significant events in the conflict in northern Mali. These periods not only reflect shifts in the tactics and strategies of armed factions but also highlight their efforts to shape public opinion, both domestically and on the international stage.

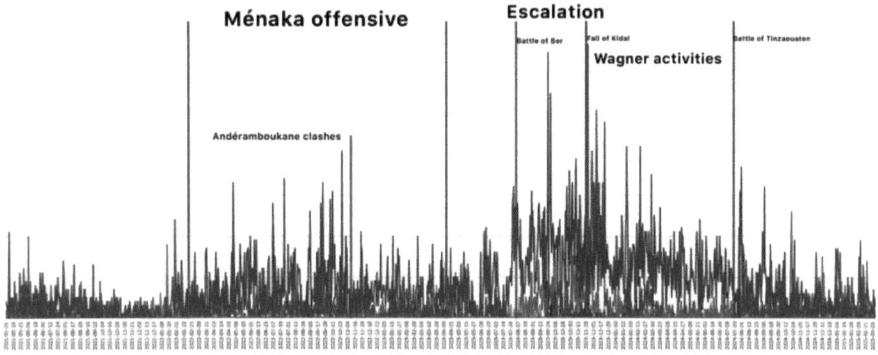

Fig. 1. Activity of separatist groups in social media based on X publications of all channels analyzed.

Establishment of CSP-PSD and the Start of Dialogue with the Government (2021). The first period of media activity (see Fig. 1) coincided with the founding of the Permanent Strategic Framework for Peace, Security, and Development (CSP- PSD) [7] and the creation of a unified political platform representing the interests of both pro-government groups, such as GATIA (Imghad Tuareg Self-Defense Group and Allies) and MSA-D (Movement for the Salvation of Azawad), and separatist factions, including MNLA (National Movement for the Liberation of Azawad), HCUA (High Council for the Unity of Azawad), and MAA (Arab Movement of Azawad), united under the Coordination of Azawad Movements (CMA). During this time, separatist-affiliated accounts actively covered the consolidation process, stressing the need for dialogue to foster mutual understanding among diverse Tuareg ethnic groups.

Social media emerged as a platform for facilitating dialogue between separatists and pro-government forces. Posts on Twitter aimed to portray separatists as legitimate representatives of Tuareg interests, emphasizing the shared destiny of these movements—a theme evident in hashtags like #gatia, #csp_psd, #csp, and #msa (see Fig. 2).

Offensive by Terrorist Groups in the Menaka Region (March 2022). The second period of media activity (see Fig. 1) began with intense clashes between pro-government forces and radical Islamists near the town of Anderamboukane. Starting on March 8, 2022, the conflict escalated sharply, triggering a mass exodus of civilians and acts of violence against non-combatants. Hashtags such as #EI, #EIGS, and #DAESH emerged, referencing the forbidden terrorist organisation Islamic State.

The events in Tamalat and Telataye—marked by mass killings of civilians—gained particular notoriety, sparking widespread discussion among Tuareg communities under threat. Separatists leveraged social media to highlight these incidents, accusing the government of inaction and urging international intervention. However, after terrorist groups seized Anderamboukane, the region's information space became largely inaccessible, leading to a temporary decline in separatist account activity, though it did not cease entirely.

Coverage of Russian Military Instructors' Activities (2022–2023). During this period, a trend emerged focusing on the activities of Russian military instructors, whom separatists accused of perpetrating violence against civilians. References to the nationality of foreign specialists (#russe and derivatives) and the #wagner organization, often paired with #fama (Malian Armed Forces), became prevalent (see Fig. 2).

These accusations intensified following heightened hostilities between separatists and government forces in August 2023. Separatists used social media to disseminate reports of government reconnaissance operations in Tuareg-populated areas, sharing photos and videos purportedly documenting military violence. From this point, mentions of international human rights organizations surfaced, with separatists demanding condemnation of the Malian government. Location-specific hashtags like #ber, #tessalit, and #tessit also proliferated across various accounts.

This period saw increased separatist activity aimed at garnering international attention for their cause. They engaged actively with foreign journalists and human rights advocates to amplify their narrative globally. Notably, references to Ukraine (#ukraine) emerged, framed as part of a shared struggle against so-called mercenaries.

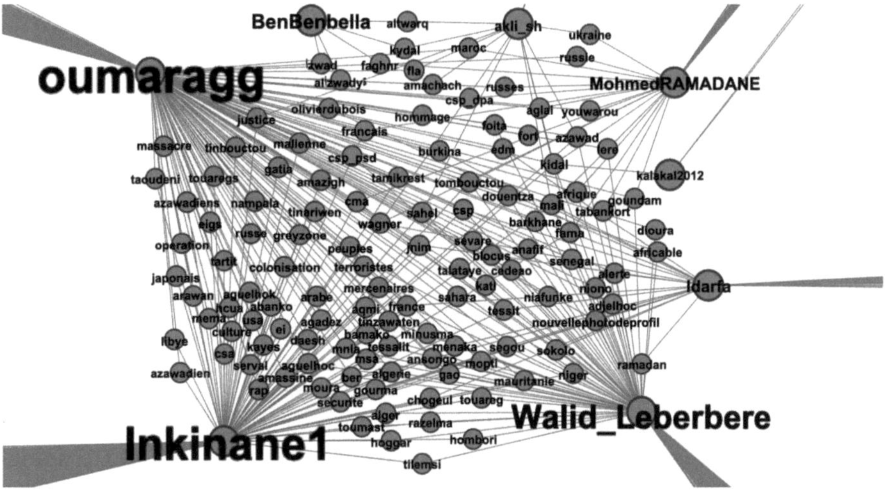

Fig. 2. Common hashtags used by FLA affiliated accounts analyzed.

Sporadic Activity Following the Capture of Kidal (2023–Present). After government forces captured Kidal, separatist account activity became more sporadic, though it surged in response to high-profile incidents, such as allegations of violence by the armed forces. While separatists continued using social media to spotlight their struggle, their posts grew more strategic.

A narrative of historical continuity in Tuareg uprisings took shape, alongside emphasis on a shared Tuareg fate under French colonization. This messaging sought to rally previously uninvolved community members. Beyond Tuaregs, the emerging political concept of the "Azawad people" began incorporating Songhai, Fulani, Arabs, and other ethnic groups in northern Mali.

This period also featured increased references to international human rights organizations and the establishment of groups like Kal Akal, which wove incidents into a cohesive narrative.

Battle of Tinzawatene and International Outreach (July 25–27, 2024). Separatist account activity spiked significantly after the Battle of Tinzawatene (July 25–27, 2024), which ended in a government defeat. This event marked a turning point in their media strategy.

They provided extensive coverage of the fighting, posting updates on enemy losses and touting their victories. Following the Tinzawatene triumph, the separatist media campaign reached new heights, particularly after Ukrainian officials claimed responsibility for the incident, prompting efforts to forge ties.

This period also saw greater involvement of international actors. Separatists engaged with foreign media, human rights organizations, and political figures to bolster their global standing. The Saudi media outlet Al-Hadath emerged as a key supporter and mouthpiece, frequently cited by separatists.

4.2 Hashtag Analysis

Despite their international outreach, separatist accounts primarily focus on reporting internal developments within the region (see Fig. 2). Mentions of external actors, such as #Ukraine and #Morocco, are extremely rare and not dominant. In contrast, #Algeria and #Mauritania are referenced more frequently due to the significant presence of Tuareg refugee communities linked to the separatists in these countries.

There is a concerted effort to construct a national identity, engaging other Berber groups in this process. In this context, #Libya is mentioned, where many Tuareg generals have fought [15]. Hashtags like #culture, #Azawadians, #Tuaregs, and #Arabs are actively used, reflecting an attempt to create a unified narrative for all peoples inhabiting northern Mali. Tuareg music bands such as #Tamikrest and #Tinariwen are also highlighted, promoting the region's culture on a global stage.

References to specific localities underscore the "Azawad-centric" nature of the discourse. Events outside the region are given far less attention compared to the territories claimed by the separatists. This is because their media campaign targets a domestic audience, aiming to foster sympathy for the separatists among the Tuaregs and other northern Mali communities. This is further reinforced through frequent mentions of acts of violence against civilians, which they attribute to government forces and Russian PMCs. This framing establishes a clear "us-versus-them" narrative, with the Malian government in Bamako positioned as the "other" (Fig. 3).

4.3 Analysis of Mentions

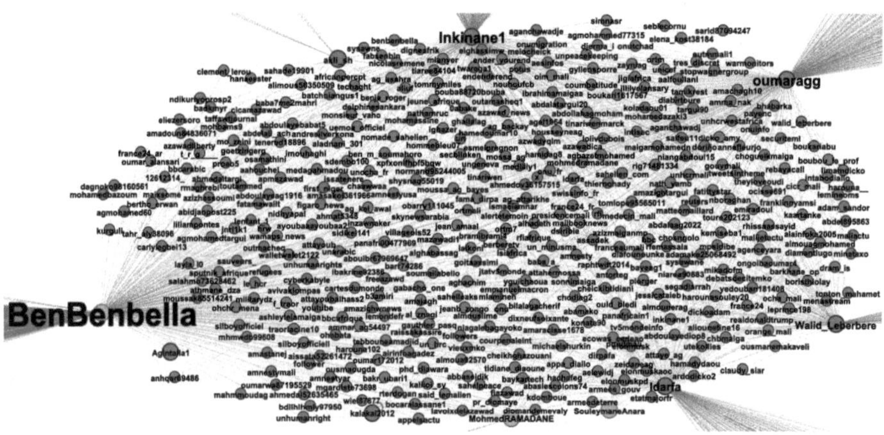

Fig. 3. Common mentions used by FLA affiliated accounts analyzed.

Mentions offer a broader insight into the relationships among FLA supporters on social media and reveal the audiences the separatists target to promote their ideas. A significant portion of mentions centers on the @BenBenBella account, which frequently highlights regional residents, drawing attention to key events in northern Mali and the plight of displaced persons in Mauritania.

Connections are often observed with @dirpafa (Information Bureau of the Malian Armed Forces) and @AssimiGoita (the official X account of Mali's transitional president). These accounts are frequently tagged in relation to allegations of violence against civilians, linking them to the accusations. Malian state media outlets are also regularly mentioned, criticized for their perceived failure to adequately represent the pro-separatist perspective.

On the international front, the Saudi-based outlet Al-Hadath stands out, often basing its articles on separatist social media statements. The French jihadologist Wassim Nasr (@SimNasr), who has ties to the FLA, is also held in high regard among them. Additionally, numerous human rights organizations are tagged, as separatists seek to gain their attention. More recently, mentions of @realDonaldTrump (the official account of U.S. President Donald Trump) and @elonmusk (senior adviser to the U.S: President D. Trump) have appeared, indicating attempts to appeal to U.S. representatives as well.

Internally, mentions often focus on Inkinane Ag Attaher (@inkinane1), the FLA's most prominent media-savvy field commander. This reflects his significant authority among the separatists. It is likely that he plays a key role in shaping the broader political narrative by channeling much of the news flow. He could be considered the informal leader of the FLA's media wing. In contrast, mentions of official political bureau members are limited, likely due to their minimal social media presence.

5 Conclusion

An analysis of the media activity of separatist groups in northern Mali, particularly the Azawad Liberation Front (FLA), enables us to derive several key conclusions regarding the role of social media in modern conflicts. Social media platforms, such as X, have evolved beyond mere tools for disseminating information, becoming a cornerstone of the separatists' strategy designed to shape political narratives, forge national identity, and influence public opinion both within Mali and on the international stage.

5.1 Evolution of Media Strategy

The separatists' media activity evolved through several stages, each tied to pivotal events in the conflict. From the initial unification of groups under the CSP-PSD and efforts to engage in dialogue with the government, to the active coverage of combat operations and expansion to the global stage, social media have served as a platform for legitimizing their struggle. This became particularly evident following the Battle of Tinzavaten in July 2024, when the separatists successfully garnered the attention of international media and human rights organizations.

5.2 Formation of National Identity

The separatists leveraged social media to craft a cohesive narrative that binds the Tuareg and other ethnic groups of northern Mali. Hashtags like #azawadien, #touaregs, and #culture, alongside references to historical events such as the colonial legacy and Tuareg uprisings, have served as instruments for forging a shared identity. This allowed them not only to consolidate their supporters but also to draw international attention to their struggle.

5.3 The Role of International Actors

The separatists engaged actively with foreign media outlets, such as Saudi Arabia's Al-Hadath, and human rights organizations to communicate their perspective to a global audience. Mentions of actors such as Ukraine, Russia (in the context of instructors' activities), and international human rights advocates reflect their desire to transcend the local conflict and highlight their struggle on a global level. However, this does not appear to be their primary focus.

5.4 Internal Dynamics and Informal Leaders

An analysis of mentions and network interactions highlighted key figures within the FLA, such as Inkinan Ag Attaher, who emerged as the informal leader of the movement's media wing. His activity on social media and frequent mentions by other accounts underscore his significant role in shaping the separatists' media strategy.

Meanwhile, official FLA politburo members remain less visible on social media, emphasizing the importance of informal structures within the movement.

5.5 The Azawado-Centricity of Discourse

The primary focus of the separatists' media activity remains centered on events occurring in northern Mali. References to settlements like Kidal, Tinzavaten, and Tessalit, as well as acts of violence against civilians, establish a distinct "friend-or-foe" dichotomy, portraying the central government in Bamako and its allies as adversaries. This approach enables the separatists to reinforce their position among the local population and attract new supporters.

6 Limitations

Several limitations should be acknowledged when interpreting the findings of this study. One key constraint lies in the inconsistent use of hashtags and mentions across the analyzed channels. While some separatist-affiliated accounts actively employed these tools to amplify their messages and engage with broader audiences, others refrained from doing so. As a result, the final network graphs reflect communication patterns without incorporating these missing data points, potentially underestimating the extent of connections for less interactive or more insular channels.

Another notable limitation stems from the linguistic diversity present in the dataset. A number of hashtags appeared in Arabic, complicating the decoding process and, consequently, the accuracy of visualization and analysis. This challenge highlights the potential for information loss or misinterpretation when working with multilingual content in network analysis. Future studies could benefit from integrating advanced natural language processing (NLP) techniques or collaborating with regional experts to ensure a more comprehensive capture of such data.

Acknowledgements. The authors received no funding for their research.

Conflict of Interest. The authors declare no conflict of interests.

References

1. Vicari, S.: Networks of contention: the shape of online transnationalism in early twenty-first century social movement coalitions. Soc. Mov. Stud. **13**(1), 92–109 (2014). https://doi.org/10.1080/14742837.2013.832621
2. Zounmenou, D.: The national movement for the liberation of Azawad factor in the Mali crisis. Afr. Secur. Rev. **22**(3), 167–174 (2013). https://doi.org/10.1080/10246029.2013.823794
3. Degterev, D.: The Sahel belt: in search of a 'positive peace' formula. Russia Glob. Affairs **23**(1), 104–122 (2024). https://doi.org/10.31278/1810-6374-2025-23-1-104-122. Accessed 20 Mar 2025
4. Andrews, N., Obi, C.: Security threats, african agency, and the role (and Weaponization) of the media. Afr. Secur. **17**(3–4), 141–147 (2024). https://doi.org/10.1080/19392206.2024.2446103
5. Issaev, L.M., Shishkina, A.R., Liokumovich, Y.B.: Russian policy of securitization in Africa: features of perception. Vestnik RUDN. Int. Relat. **23**(2), 322–338 (2023). https://doi.org/10.22363/2313-0660-2023-23-2-322-338
6. Danso, S., Adjin-Tettey, T.D., Serwornoo, M.Y.W., Azanu, B.: African broadcast media participation in conflict resolution and peacebuilding: an examination of practices across nine countries. Afr. Secur. **17**(3–4), 177–204 (2024). https://doi.org/10.1080/19392206.2024.2420544
7. Degterev, D.A., Davidchuk, A.S., Sidibe, O.: Malian Crisis Actors Mosaic, 2021. https://dataverse.harvard.edu/dataset.xhtml?persistentId=doi:10.7910/DVN/8HMZ7G
8. Ponomarev, I.V.: Ethno-social aspects of conflict in Northern Mali. Asia Africa Today **5**, 56–65 (2024). (In Russian). https://doi.org/10.31857/S032150750030862-0
9. Duarte, P.: Information disorder and civil unrest: Russian Weaponization of Social Media Platforms in Mali and Burkina Faso – 2020–2022. Afr. Secur. **17**(3–4), 205–223 (2024). https://doi.org/10.1080/19392206.2024.2423139
10. Anderson, B.: Imagined Communities: Reflections on the Origin and Spread of Nationalism. Verso, London (1991)
11. Loshkariov, I.D.: The Alliance of Sahel States as a "Laboratory" of Minilateralism. Vostok. Afro-Aziatskie obshchestva: istoriia i sovremennost **5**, 108–119 (2024). (In Russian). https://doi.org/10.31696/S086919080030925-4
12. Merolla, D.: Cultural heritage, artistic innovation, and activism on Amazigh Berber websites. J. Afr. Cult. Stud. **33**(2), 42–59 (2021). https://doi.org/10.1080/13696815.2019.1624153
13. Skretting, V.B.: Pragmatism and purism in jihadist governance: the Islamic emirate of Azawad revisited. Stud. Conflict Terror. **7**, 725–749 (2024). https://doi.org/10.1080/1057610X.2021.2007562
14. Boilley, P.: Nord-Mali: les frontières coloniales de l'Azawad. Can. J. Afr. Stud./Revue canadienne des études africaines. **53**(3), 469–484 (2019). https://doi.org/10.1080/00083968.2019.1667840
15. Filippov, V.R.: Azawad as a self-proclaimed Tuareg state. Outlines Glob. Transform. Polit. Econ. Law **14**(1), 214–227 (2021). (in Russian). https://doi.org/10.23932/2542-0240-2021-14-1-11
16. Keita, K.: Conflict and conflict resolution in the Sahel: the Tuareg Insurgency in Mali. Small Wars Insurgencies **9**(3), 102–128 (1998). https://doi.org/10.1080/09592319808423221
17. Davidchuk, A.S., Degterev, D.A., Sidibe, O.: Crisis in Mali: interrelationship of major actors. Asia Afr. Today. **12**, 47–56 (2021). (In Russian). https://doi.org/10.31857/S032150750017789-9
18. African Pressure Points: Sahel (situation review and future prospects). RIAC and ICRC Report No. 77 / 2022. https://russiancouncil.ru/en/activity/publications/african-pressure-points-sahel-situation-review-and-future-prospects/. Accessed 24 Mar 2025

19. Western and non-Western actors in the provision of security in Africa. RIAC and RUDN Report №89 / 2023 (In Russian). https://russiancouncil.ru/activity/publications/zapadnye-i-nezapadnye-aktory-v-obespechenii-bezopasnosti-v-afrike/. Accessed 24 Mar 2025
20. Degterev, D.A.: Re-Sovereignising Africa in the context of the new world order formation. J. Inst. Afr. Stud. **4**, 29–48 (2024). https://doi.org/10.31132/2412-5717-2024-69-4-29-48
21. Degterev, D.A.: Collective self-reliance: restarting the concept in the Sahel in the context of a multipolarizing world order. J. Inst. Afr. Stud. **2**, 60–81 (2024). https://doi.org/10.31132/2412-5717-2024-67-2-60-81
22. Bazlutckaia, M.M., Sytnik, A.N., Tsvetkova, N.A.: Evaluating audience engagement as a measure of digital diplomacy effectiveness. MGIMO Rev. Int. Relat. **17**(4), 48–82 (2024). (In Russian). https://doi.org/10.24833/2071-8160-2024-4-97-48-82
23. RAND. Using Social Media to Gauge Iranian Public Opinion and Mood After the 2009 Election. RAND Technical Reports. 2012. https://www.rand.org/pubs/technical_reports/TR1161.html. Accessed 24 Mar 2025
24. Ivanov, Y.A., Melnikov, K.V., Petrov, N.V.: Informal structure of the elite space in Russia. Evidence from network analysis. Politia **1**, 72–91 (2022). (In Russian). https://doi.org/10.30570/2078-5089-2022-104-1-72-91
25. García B., Munoz-Organero M., Alario-Hoyos C., Kloos C.D.: Automated driver management for selenium webdriver. Empir. Softw. Eng. **26**(107) (2021). https://doi.org/10.1007/s10664-021-09975-3
26. Roberts, T., Oosterom, M.: Digital authoritarianism: a systematic literature review. Inf. Technol. Dev. 1–25 (2024). https://doi.org/10.1080/02681102.2024.2425352
27. Bloom, J.M.: Political opportunity structure, contentious social movements, and state-based organizations: the fight against solidarity inside the Polish United workers party. Soc. Sci. Hist. **38**(3–4), 359–88 (2014)
28. Michailof, S.: Africanistan. Development or Jihad, p. 360. Oxford University Press, Oxford, 2018
29. Drissel, D.: Reframing the Taliban insurgency in Afghanistan: new communication and mobilization strategies for the Twitter generation. Behav. Sci. Terror. Polit. Aggress. **7**(2), 97–128 (2014). https://doi.org/10.1080/19434472.2014.986496
30. Castells, M.: Communication Power, p. 590. Oxford University Press, Oxford, 2009
31. Castells, M.: Network theory: a network theory of power. Int. J. Commun. **5**, 773–787 (2011)
32. Choudhury, Z.: Global South muffled by #TechBros in pursuit of healthy digital societies. Alliance, 4 March 2024. https://www.alliancemagazine.org/blog/voices-of-global-south-muffled-by-techbros-pursuing-healthy-digital-societies/
33. Earl, J., Kimport, K.: Digitally Enabled Social Change: Activism in the Internet Age, p. 258. MIT Press, Cambridge (2011)

How to Evaluate the Social Impact of Digital Urban Services? Testing the Methodology (Evidence from St. Petersburg)

Olga Filatova[1,2(✉)], Radomir Bolgov[1,3], Dmitry Arkatov[1,2,4], and Daniil Volkovskii[5]

[1] ITMO University, 49 Kronverksky Pr., 197101 St. Petersburg, Russia
ogfilatova@itmo.ru
[2] HSE University, 16 Soyuza Pechatnikov Street, 190121 St Petersburg, Russia
[3] St. Petersburg State University, Universitetskaya Emb., 7, 199004 St. Petersburg, Russia
[4] European University, 6/1A Gagarinskaya Street, 191187 St. Petersburg, Russia
[5] Université Paris 1 Panthéon-Sorbonne, Paris, France

Abstract. The article presents the materials of one of studies conducted within the framework of a research project supported by the Russian Science Foundation and the St. Petersburg Science Foundation. The project is devoted to identification of effectiveness of the urban services' ecosystem developed in St. Petersburg. We test the following hypothesis: an active use of urban digital services leads to formation of social capital among citizens through active involvement in the activities of authorities and local government as well as contributes to the growth of trust in public authorities. To identify factors and indicators of social performance, a special methodology based on the use of various research methods is proposed. A representative survey of citizens, the results of which are presented in this report, is a part of this methodology. The survey allowed us to test the methodology and draw preliminary conclusions about social performance of different types of urban digital ecosystems.

Keywords: Digital Governmental Communications · Social Efficiency · Digital Services · Social Capital · Political Trust · Saint-Petersburg

1 Introduction

Today, research on the quality of online communication and digital interaction between Russian authorities and citizens on socio-political issues through digital urban services, state and non-state Internet platforms, and social media is becoming increasingly in demand in political science, as indicated by the growth of domestic research in the field of e-participation and political communication (Kabanov & Sungurov, 2016; Rodriquez et al., 2021, Pedrosa et al. 2020; Szalkowski & Johansen, 2023). Government agencies are increasingly realizing that digital communications are crucial for citizen engagement and are focusing on increasing public interaction with government online. Through digital communications, authorities can provide information and services to citizens anytime,

M. Bakaev et al. (Eds.): IMS 2025, CCIS 2671, pp. 351–365, 2026.
https://doi.org/10.1007/978-3-032-04958-2_26

anywhere, and on any platform or device, which contributes to increasing transparency in the activities of authorities and strengthening citizens' trust in government, as well as legitimizing public policies.

Russian researchers from the Center for e-Government Technologies point out several key trends in the institutional evolution of online participation in Russia. One of them is correlated with an increasing usage of social networks and digital services as a tool for interaction between society and government both at the federal level and at the regional and municipal levels (Filatova & Bolgov, 2020). An important issue is not only the number of platforms and services of digital interaction, their accessibility and usability, but also the ways of their use by citizens, assessment of the quality of interaction between authorities and citizens through them, including social effectiveness of such services.

The purpose of the following study is to test a methodology for assessing social effectiveness of digital services from the point of view of the region's residents as Internet users. The research is conducted within the framework of a scientific project devoted to formation of an optimal model of the ecosystem of urban services of communication and interaction with the residents of St. Petersburg to increase institutionalized trust, social efficiency and administrative and managerial effectiveness, contributing to the growth of social capital in the region. *Social capital* is understood as a set of real and potential resources arising in the process of electronic (network) interactions between citizens and authorities on the basis of common social norms, mutual recognition and trust. *Urban digital service* is understood as a provider of digital services that promote the optimal use of the urban digital environment for realization of citizens' needs and establishment of a dialogue with government structures.

The project considers three types of digital services being developed by the St. Petersburg government. The first type of services are the basic elements of the Digital Petersburg ecosystem of urban services, which are updated data sets coming from city's information systems. The flagship project of urban services' ecosystem is a mini-application "I live here" on the VKontakte platform. The second type of services actually consists of one service – the portal "Our St. Petersburg", created on the initiative of the Governor of St. Petersburg for prompt interaction between city residents and authorities. On the "Our St. Petersburg" portal users can receive information about progress of consideration and processing of sent messages, as well as evaluate received responses. The third type includes the "Your Budget" project, dedicated to urban services, which realizes communicative practices of interaction between citizens and authorities. The "Your Budget" project gives the residents of St. Petersburg an opportunity to directly participate in improving the city's life and in distribution of city budget, to take part in (co)management of the city.

To analyze the emerging ecosystem of urban services in 2023–2024, a number of studies were conducted, including surveys, focus groups, expert interviews, and automated methods of service monitoring. The conducted studies and discussions of their results made it possible to develop a test version of the methodology for assessing social performance of urban digital services. The developed methodology involves the study on social performance of use of three identified types of digital services by surveying users from the point of view of social capital formation and assessing the quality of services themselves.

The main research question in this paper (**RQ1**): Is it possible to use the social capital measurement methodology to assess performance of digital services? The need to develop another version of the methodology will also be assessed (**RQ2**).

The remainder of the paper is structured as follows: Section "Theoretical Background" provides a review of theoretical works. Section "Empirical Data and Methodology" describes sampling, methods of data collection and their analysis. Section "Results" provides the findings according to the RQs. Section "Discussion and Conclusion" summarizes the paper by discussing the results, limitations of research, and potential venues of future research.

2 Theoretical Background

Since urban digital services are provided to citizens by government, the process of using services can be considered as network interactions ranked according to the principle of satisfying citizens' needs for a specific service. That is, digital interactions in the process of using services can be considered as a process of providing and accumulating resources where the government provides a digital resource for satisfying citizens' needs, and citizens receive new opportunities (resources) for implementing personal economic and social strategies. The formation of these resources occurs on the basis of sustainable social norms and certain level of trust. Thus, these digital interactions can be considered as a process of forming (accumulating) social capital. Consequently, the task of determining the social impact of urban digital services implies an assessment of social capital. But since network interactions occur through digital services, an assessment of the quality of these services as a platform where interactions take place is also required.

The criteria for selecting literature for this review were: 1) studies devoted to the concept of social capital; 2) studies of strategies for implementing digital services in the digital ecosystems; 3) studies of the methods for assessing digital interactions and social impact of digital services.

The analysis of the concept of "social capital" is presented in the classic works of Bourdieu (Bourdieu, 2002). The approach that involves specifying the structural components of social capital, and, therefore, its possible measurement, belongs to Nahapiet & Ghoshal (1998). Since social capital is determined by interactions between people, the latter may depend on both norms of group behaviour and mental attitudes that determine readiness for interaction, as well as self-identification.

The development of a methodology for assessing the social impact of digital services required a careful study of works devoted to tools for measuring social capital. A work of experts at the World Bank (Grootaert et al., 2004) can be considered as an important study on this topic, since it includes a set of empirical tools for measuring social capital. In essence, this is an integrated questionnaire for measuring social capital (SC-IQ). It is designed to obtain quantitative data on various aspects of social capital. In particular, six aspects are considered: groups and networks; trust and solidarity; collective action and cooperation; information and communication; social cohesion and inclusion; empowerment and political action. In the future, for more than twenty years, this study, published in 2004, has been the starting point in building methods for studying social capital of various communities.

Among studies that applied this methodology, one can highlight the work of Campos et al. (2015). Here, social capital was measured in groups of working adolescents in Brazil. The IQ-CS methodology focused on three dimensions (groups and networks, trust and solidarity, collective action and cooperation). These three dimensions were used simultaneously to identify the most important factors in constructing an individual social capital indicator for population studied. For purposes of studying the social impact of digital services through application of social capital methodology, the presented case is an important model for constructing our own methodology for analysing services.

It was important to understand what effects of social capital could be expected from digital interactions within urban services, the use of which does not imply economic benefit in some cases. In this regard, the review study on social capital conducted by the HSE University (Anikin et al., 2022) is especially valuable. Researchers drew attention to the complexity of quantitative measurement of social capital and proposed to distinguish micro-effects and macro-effects of social capital. The presence of micro-effects does not yet indicate the full acquisition of social capital, including economic benefits, but since the structure of social capital involves the availability, provision and accumulation of resources, such micro-effects can be considered as elements of the effectiveness of social interactions. "Satisfaction" as a complex indicator consists of both effects and technical components related to the convenience of services (usability). Thus, satisfaction is the very micro-effect that marks presence of social capital in interactions (including digital ones) where it is difficult to determine presence of economic benefits, and / or this benefit is deferred.

An international framework for methodological approaches to assessing digital governance and service delivery has been developed by the World Bank and presented as sub-indices in the GovTech Maturity Index. National criteria for assessing digital services are developed based on the criteria included in the Public Service Delivery Index (quality of online government service portals with an emphasis on citizen-centric design and universal accessibility) and the Digital Citizen Engagement Index (public participation platforms, citizen feedback mechanisms, open data, and open government portals) (GovTech Maturity Index). Citizen satisfaction with digital services is measured through surveys.

It was also important to analyse the experience of the European Union (E-government Benchmark 2023). Progress in promoting digital services in the EU countries is assessed by four key dimensions, which include many basic indicators: 1. User Centricity (online availability, mobile friendliness, user support). 2. Transparency (service provision, personal data, service design). 3. Key identification factors (ability to use a digital signature and use key documents in digital format). 4. Provision of cross-border digital services (for EU citizens in different countries) (E-government Benchmark 2023). The eGovernment Benchmark 2024 Factsheets analyse each of the countries participating in the Digital Decade program using these indicators. It is worth paying special attention to the User Centricity and Transparency indicators. In our opinion, they reflect the main aspects of satisfaction (with the service): focus on people and their needs, i.e. client- and human-centricity, as well as accessibility, convenience, design and user support. That is, these aspects, even within the framework of European approach, can be considered as intangible benefits of digital interactions (micro-effects that mark social capital). This is also supported by the experience of assessing digital public services, presented in the article by Rodriguez Müller et al. (2021). One of the important points in promoting and improving public digital services noted by the authors was personalization of services.

It is impossible to ignore the research on what specific channels users choose to interact with government agencies. Thus, in e-government studies, the concept of "media richness" (Ebbers et al., 2016; Madsen & Kræmmergaard, 2015), based on the theory of "information richness" by Daft & Lengel (1984), is widely used to understand the paradox associated with continued use of traditional channels of interaction by citizens (such as face-to-face visits to government offices, phone calls, etc.) rather than less labour-intensive digital communication channels. According to the theory of media richness, communication channels with a high degree of saturation, high bandwidth for transmitting several types of information and providing a high level of expressiveness are required to solve communication tasks that require transmission of ambiguous, uncertain and complex messages (Daft & Lengel, 1984). A 2015 study (Madsen & Kræmmergaard, 2015) well demonstrated that some of the citizen interactions with government are the simplest interactions, mainly related to searching for information or carrying out other transactions of low complexity, ambiguity and uncertainty. For such transactions, citizens tend to use digital channels (e.g. searching for the information on government websites), which have a lower information capacity than traditional channels and allow to use low levels of expressiveness (e.g. a citizen can only enter some keywords to search). However, another significant part of citizen interactions with government agencies is characterized by increased complexity, ambiguity and uncertainty, so citizens prefer to use the "high richness" of traditional channels – mainly personal visits or phone calls to authorities, which allow them to convey more information about their specific situation, problem or need, to explain the details, with higher levels of expressiveness (Androutsopoulou et al., 2019).

It is important to highlight that mobile messaging apps and news aggregators are becoming increasingly important to people (Kalogeropoulos et al., 2019). There is a shift towards a distributed media environment that is reconfiguring communication channels for information retrieval and opening up new ways of digital interaction and participation due to the rapid growth of groups in messaging apps (Newman et al., 2019). There are studies showing that mobile messaging apps are dominating the digital media environment, making it a place for significant socio-cultural transformations across the board (Park et al., 2013), as well as studies demonstrating the increasing use of chatbots in government communication (Androutsopoulou et al., 2019).

It worth noting the previous literature reviews on social impact of digital public services. Desmal et al. (2022) focus on the mobile services. The authors note that the research on e-government users' satisfaction is lacking, leading to difficulties in understanding users' expectations. They propose six quality constructs: usability, interaction, consistency, information, accessibility, privacy and security. Kim et al. (2015) argue that a mobile application is considered as a main channel that conducting interactivity between service provider and end-users. It means that mobile interactivity is requested from user to machine to perform a service. Pedrosa et al. (2020) published a systematic review on indicators for measuring the impact (not only social) of digital services. The authors found two groups of indicators: technical factors based on service quality and usefulness of the service. The review by Szalkowski and Johansen (2023) focuses on evaluating the social sustainability effects of digital technologies. The analysis identified four categories, namely "Area of Impact," "Approach to technology," "Measured/Measurable Effect," and "Measuring Methods", accumulating 30 labels, which they use to classify the papers at study. The authors revealed such social implications as employment, security and privacy. They revealed five research gaps: (1) lack of empirical data on the impact of digital technologies on social sustainability, (2–3) lack of mathematical models and simulations, (4–5) few studies on crime and safety effects, etc. They state that negative impacts of digital technologies are often given less importance, especially when it comes to health. Bendebka et al. (2022) studied the impact of digital services on social stability with a specific focus on Muslim cultures. The authors found the key implications of digital services for social stability: quality of information accessibility, equality, social trust, social cohesion, and community engagement.

In order to measure the social impact of digital agendas, Katz et al. (2014) developed a digitization index with a specific focus on Europe's performance. The index was based on six components: affordability, infrastructure investment, network access, capacity, usage, and human capital. Tassabehji et al. (2019) developed a contingency value approach for evaluating digital public services with a focus on countries of sub-Saharan Africa. The authors conducted a substantive survey of citizens. The researchers note that if digital services are of no benefit, even if they are more convenient and lower cost, they are unlikely to be used. Accessing digital public services directly addresses the needs of economically active citizens and can also facilitate the steps towards an improved quality of government and interaction with civil society (Tassabehji et al., 2019). The understanding of citizen needs could drive decisions related to what public services need to be prioritised.

Hodson et al. (2023) examine the social impact of smart city services. The study focuses on eight smart city projects. The authors outline different levels of social impact, from individual to household, organization, specific community or society. The social change can be evident in direct impacts, such as how design improves health or increases inequalities. The social impacts can take place outside of the scope of a project", and they can be unintended and difficult to quantify (Hodson et al., 2023). The authors identified four common approaches with projects that: focus on human- and/or eco-centred work; prioritize inclusion, participation and empowerment; identify new roles for citizens and their data; and make connections between impact, social and environmental sustainability (Hodson et al., 2023).

Several studies (Alawneh et al., 2013; Kitsios et al., 2019; Horan & Abhichandani, 2006) developed the frameworks for evaluating citizen satisfaction with digital services. The studies focus on specific fields (for instance, health) and countries (for instance, Jordan and Greece). Kitsios et al. (2019) applied the MUSA (MUlticriteria Satisfaction Analysis) method to assess the users' satisfaction with an e-appointment system in Greece. Alawneh et al. (2013) conducted a survey of 400 employees in four universities of Jordan and identified five factors (security and privacy, trust, accessibility, awareness of public services, and quality of public services) that may affect the Jordanians' satisfaction with e-government. Novak, Hoffman & Yung (2003) used usability/ease of use to measure electronic customer satisfaction. Thus, we found out that in order to conceptualize the social impact it is necessary to distinguish some changes that occurred as a result of some activity from social. Social impact is not the product or service itself produced as a result of enterprise/organization/institution's activity, but the consequences of use of this product by clients-beneficiaries.

To summarize, it can be noted that the social impact of digital services (online interaction between citizens and authorities) is an indicator of satisfaction with services provided, in the form of a social resource of citizens (time, energy, new communication opportunities, etc.) and a social resource of authorities (trust). This digital social resource can be considered as a mini-effect of social capital.

An important point that should be emphasized in analyzing the scientific literature is the principles that guide governance institutions, expecting non-material benefits from digitalization: growth of trust, maintenance of social balance. In this regard, the main principles of digital public administration are client-centeredness and human-centeredness, i.e. focus on the individual as a consumer of services and the individual as the center of multilevel interactions with society. In this regard, the task of studying social effectiveness of digital interactions between citizens and authorities in St. Petersburg on the example of the urban digital services is very timely and promising.

3 Empirical Data and Methodology

Three services being developed by the government of St. Petersburg, listed in the introduction, are presented as objects of research: (1) VK application "I live here" as a component of the Ecosystem of city services "Digital Petersburg"; (2) e-participation portal "Our St. Petersburg"; (3) project "Your Budget". To assess the social performance of digital services, an online survey among the population of St. Petersburg was developed and conducted in August-October 2024 using the professional service "Anketolog". 500 respondents answered the questionnaire. The sample is randomized, stratified by sex, age and area of residence in St. Petersburg based on the population correspondence data of Rosstat. Data were also collected on the gender, income level of the interviewed respondents, their age and the sector in which they are employed.

In general, the distribution by age cohort is normal, with the highest number of respondents in the 36 to 45 years category. Within each age cohort, the proportions by gender are almost identical.

In the questionnaire, respondents were asked questions regarding:

1. their assessment of their use of digital services in St. Petersburg: the platform "Our St. Petersburg", participatory budgeting "Your Budget", and the mini-application "I live here" promoted in VKontakte by the Information and Analytical Center;
2. their assessment of effectiveness level of state and local government bodies;
3. their level of institutional, group, personal and generalized trust; various aspects of social capital: involvement in groups, willingness to help strangers, participation in volunteer activities.

It should be emphasized that the questionnaire for user survey includes all measurable characteristics of social capital for all its structural elements: a) group characteristics; b) shared norms; c) cooperativeness: how well people make connections and act together; d) everyday socialization; e) connections with local community; f) volunteering; g) trust.

Since the objects of evaluation are not offline groups or organizations, but digital services, the second component of performance evaluation should be an assessment of their quality. It is determined by the following criteria: a) interface, UX/UI; b) usability; c) relevance and completeness of information; d) satisfaction with the speed and quality of the digital product provided; e) degree of improvement of e-interaction compared to analog ones.

In this text, only the first part, the questionnaire survey, will be discussed further.

All questions have a scale from 1 to 5, with 1 indicating complete disagreement and 5 indicating complete agreement. In the questions on the use of digital services, respondents were asked to choose from 3 options: a) don't know and don't use, b) know but don't use, and c) know and use.

The data were processed and analyzed through the construction of descriptive statistics and data visualization.

4 Results

4.1 Usage of Services Among Citizens in St. Petersburg

Let us consider how widespread the use of St. Petersburg's digital services is among different age categories. As follows from respondents' answers, very few people use the portal "Our St. Petersburg", which allows reporting problems with roads, lighting, heating and other things that require a quick response from competent services. Despite the fact that the portal has existed for almost 10 years, its popularity remains low, and proportionally equally low among all age cohorts of citizens (see Fig. 1).

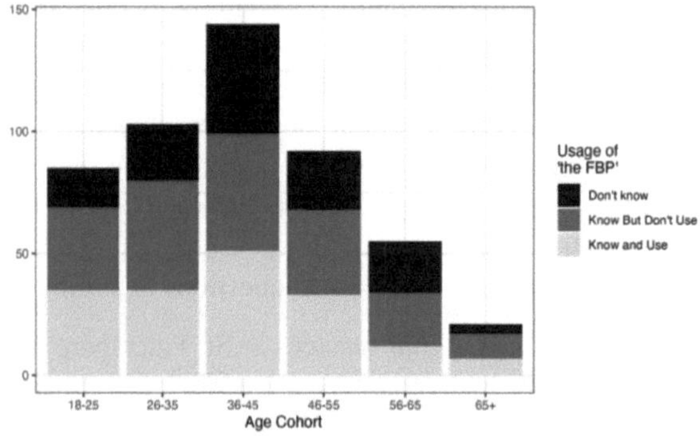

Fig. 1. Participation in I Live Here in different age cohorts

Even fewer citizens use the mini-application "I live here". According to the results of focus groups conducted before the survey on experience of using the mini-application, citizens are skeptical about its functionality, usefulness, convenience and security. This thesis is confirmed by survey results, which show very low involvement in the use of application and low awareness of its existence. At the same time, the application is quite actively promoted through the use of outdoor and Internet advertising (see Fig. 2).

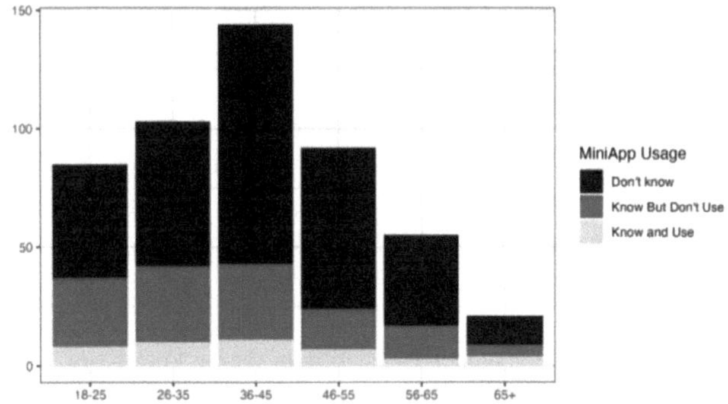

Fig. 2. Participation in I Live Here in different age cohorts

It is noticeable that involvement in Your Budget projects among citizens is even lower as it requires effort: either to create a project and draw attention to it, or to carefully examine project proposals and thoughtful voting. Nevertheless, as in the case of other digital services, there is low awareness and extremely low levels of involvement (see Fig. 3).

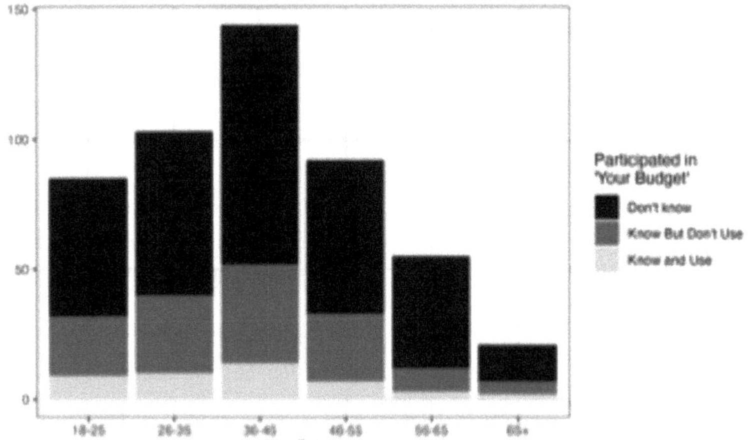

Fig. 3. Participation in Your Budget in different age cohorts

4.2 Citizens' Trust to the Government of St. Petersburg and Evaluation of Its Activity

Before linking the use of digital services with certain effects, it is necessary to look at how the activity of state and local authorities in St. Petersburg is assessed in general. Respondents were asked questions: how they assess the competence of St. Petersburg authorities, their transparency and openness, and whether they believe that authorities do everything possible for citizens of St. Petersburg. The answer was given on a scale from 1 to 5, where 1 – completely disagree and 5 – completely agree. First, it can be noted that the levels of institutional trust in age cohorts are generally stable and do not change with age, contrary to the standard trend where the youngest citizens most often have a negative attitude to the activity of officials, while older generations have a more positive attitude to their work. In this case, fluctuations in trust are not observed and it remains at a rather insignificant level (see Table 1).

Table 1. Competence Evaluation of the St. Petersburg Government by age cohorts.

18–25	26–35	36–45	46–55	56–65	65 +
3.15	3.07	2.98	3.11	3.21	3.23

A similar trend is observed in the assessment of transparency and openness of authorities. Importantly, a slightly higher level of transparency assessment is observed among the youngest cohort (see Table 2).

Table 2. Evaluation of transparency of the St. Petersburg Government by age cohorts.

18–25	26–35	36–45	46–55	56–65	65 +
3.15	3.02	2.82	2.97	3.05	3.00

When assessing government effort, results differ between cohorts, with noticeably lower results in the 36–45 and 46–55 age cohorts. However, in general, all components that are related to institutional trust in the questionnaire show approximately the same results – the average level at all ages (see Table 3).

Table 3. Evaluation of efforts of the St. Petersburg Government by age cohorts.

18–25	26–35	36–45	46–55	56–65	65 +
3.00	2.91	2.62	2.77	3.03	2.85

4.3 Impact of the Use of Digital Platforms on Citizens' Trust in Public Authorities in St. Petersburg

Let us consider how assessment of responsiveness, transparency and accountability, competence and efforts of the government authorities in St. Petersburg by citizens differs in different groups of digital services use - those "who know and use", those "who know but do not use", those "who do not know".

Our St. Petersburg. Analysis of the data showed that the average values in the different usage groups do not differ practically. Among those who know and use the "Our St. Petersburg" site the assessment of responsiveness of the government authorities is slightly higher than among those who have never heard of the site. The same situation is observed when assessing transparency and openness of public authorities, and difference between groups is even smaller. A slightly opposite situation is observed in the case of assessing the competence of public bodies – the average assessment of competence is lower in group of those who use the Our St. Petersburg portal. In terms of efforts (answering the question whether the St. Petersburg government does everything possible for citizens of St. Petersburg?) the assessment is almost identical. Thus, we can say that digitalization of complaints about public policy issues has no effect on the institutional trust of citizens. The answer to the question "why?" requires additional research, but it is possible to assume problems with resolution of complaints, speed of responses or their quality as factors of the lack of effect.

Your Budget. A similar situation is observed in the case of Your Budget. There are no significant differences between groups. However, in the case of assessing transparency and openness we get a statistically significant result. The analysis of variance demonstrates that the averages are significantly different from each other - among citizens who use or are familiar with Your Budget the level of assessment of transparency and openness is higher than among those who are not familiar with participatory budgeting. This may indicate that creation of a procedure in which people themselves can propose projects, vote for them and distribute budget allocations allows to increase the level of trust and assessment of openness of public authorities. There is also a statistically significant difference in the assessment of competence of authorities depending on the group of using Your Budget, which also partially confirms our hypothesis presented above. However, no significant result is observed for the assessment of effort. Thus, we can tentatively conclude that participatory budgeting is a more effective digital tool in terms of increasing institutional trust. However, this does not apply to all its components.

I Live Here. Quite intriguing is the result of responsiveness assessment based on the use of the mini-application "I Live Here". There is a statistically significant difference between those who do not know about the application and those who know and use it. Moreover, a statistically significant positive effect from the use of the mini-application "I Live Here" is observed for all four indicators of institutional trust (responsiveness, openness, competence, effort). In spite of above-mentioned criticism in focus groups, people are noticeably more positive about the work of the St. Petersburg Government in the group of those who use this application. In order to avoid endogeneity problems and holistically assess the impact of using St. Petersburg digital services, we built 4 full regression models with clustered robust standard errors where all 4 dimensions of institutional trust were tested as the dependent variable. The constructed models also demonstrated that in comparison with people who are not familiar with and do not use digital services, citizens who know and use mini-apps significantly better evaluate the work of St. Petersburg authorities and trust them to a greater extent. This result demonstrates the "social effectiveness" of this innovation, despite skepticism of some citizens and experts.

5 Discussion and Conclusion

Thus, the conducted survey on all types of urban services allowed to give a positive answer to the main research question (RQ1) and confirmed the possibility of using the survey methodology to assess social performance of digital services in terms of identifying trust in authorities. The obtained data of research demonstrate that the social performance, one part of which is trust in the authorities of St. Petersburg, has a positive relationship with the use of digital services at the city level, in particular, "I Live Here". However, this requires further verification using a case study strategy to establish causal mechanisms between the use of digital services and trust. Potentially, social performance may be associated with greater awareness of the activities of the government authorities, as well as a more detailed understanding of urban problems and labor-intensive nature of solving them. It is also possible that manifestation of trust to government authorities when using the mini-application "I live here" is due to the fact that the services provided are tied to the location of the user. This indicates the personalization of service, the client-centered approach of authorities and suggests that the further process of personalization (addressing personally to each person) can be regarded by consumers as a manifestation of care and attention of authorities to each citizen personally, which can help to increase trust in authorities. This hypothesis should be tested in future surveys and focus groups.

Some increase in institutional trust was also recorded in the third type of services ("Your Budget 2.0"), which allows not only to receive information, but also to interact directly with authorities. But the result of social capital fixation within the framework of the "I Live Here" also suggests that pre-trust in authorities can arise not only in services with communication opportunities, but it can also be formed for other reasons, within the framework of other indicators. In particular, such an indicator of emergence and increase of trust can be the personalization of services, which, in turn, can influence satisfaction with service. As we found out in the framework of the theoretical study, user satisfaction is a micro-effect that marks the presence of social capital in interactions (including digital ones), where it is difficult to determine the presence of economic benefits, and/or these benefits are deferred. Aspects of satisfaction are: focus on the person and his/her needs, i.e. client- and person-centeredness, as well as accessibility, convenience, design and user support. Since the issues of personalization of services and client-centeredness are related to the study of needs, they can be studied both by surveys and focus groups. And if surveys (on the demand of users and trust formation) register a general trend in a representative sample of urban population, the methodology of focus groups is especially suitable for researching the needs of target audiences, where it is important to obtain an informal assessment of both the existing services and to identify proposals for their improvement. Interviews also contribute to the crystallization of qualitative indicators of service evaluation.

Accordingly, the answer to RQ2 is that the survey methodology can be used in the future as one of the parts of a comprehensive, combined quantitative-qualitative methodology for assessing the social performance of digital services.

The social efficiency of urban digital services should be considered as a set of indicators of satisfaction with the use of the provided services, which is expressed in the form of emergence of the digital social resource of citizen (time, energy, new communication opportunities) and the social resource of power (trust). Since social performance is not a product or service, but the consequences of using this product, assessment of social performance is a system of measuring the consequences (results) of using the service by its users. Thus, assessment of social performance of digital services is a set of consistent and regularly recurring activities, including: indicators of audience coverage; regular surveys of satisfaction with services, social and group trust; conducting focus groups with representatives of target audiences; monitoring of new needs, etc.

As a limitation of the study, it should be noted that the methodology testing left out another ecosystem of digital services actively developed by the local government – the smart card "Unified Card of St. Petersburg resident". The authors plan to fill this gap at the next stage of research.

However, research on social performance of digital services should not stop here. Future works should be devoted to such a component of the issue of citizens' use of digital services as fears, concerns and problems they face. This topic becomes particularly relevant, especially in the context of cybersecurity as most citizens face cyber-terrorism and digital threats, which affects their motivation to use and get satisfied with various urban online services. Touching on the topic of satisfaction, it is necessary to conduct research on factors affecting its level. These factors may include interface, usability, relevance and completeness of information; satisfaction with speed and quality of the digital product provided; degree of improvement of electronic interaction compared to analog ones. In addition, research should focus on studying factors contributing to the increase/decrease in demand for digital services (expansion of the target audience of certain categories of digital services) and increase in social impact of urban digital services within the framework of an in-depth study of generational (age) digital needs of the population, including the level of trust in digital services and government in general.

Acknowledgements. The research was supported by the Russian Science Foundation & St. Petersburg Science Foundation grant No. 23-18-20079 «The Social Efficacy of Electronic Interaction between Citizens and the Government: The Case of Urban Digital Services in St.Petersburg» (https://rscf.ru/en/project/23-18-20079/).

References

1. Alawneh, A., Al-Refai, H., Batiha, K.: Measuring user satisfaction from e-Government services: lessons from Jordan. Gov. Inf. Q. **30**(3), 277–288 (2013)
2. Androutsopoulou, A., Karacapilidis, N., Loukis, E., Charalabidis, Y.: Transforming the communication between citizens and government through AI-guided chatbots. Gov. Inf. Q. **36**, 358–367 (2019)

3. Anikin, V.A., et al. (eds.).: A review study of social capital in the context of human enhancement. HSE University (2022)
4. Bendebka, R., Fettane, A., Shogar, I.: Digital services and social stability: evaluating the impact from a maqasidic approach. KnE Soc. Sci. **7**(10), 198–209 (2022). https://doi.org/10.18502/kss.v7i10.11357
5. Bourdieu, P.: Forms of capital. Econ. Sociol. **3**(5), 60–74 (2002)
6. Campos, A.C.V., Borges, C.M., Vargas, A.M.D., et al.: Measuring social capital through multivariate analyses for the IQ-SC. BMC Res. Notes **8**, Article 11 (2015). https://doi.org/10.1186/s13104-015-0978-2
7. Daft, R.L., Lengel, R.H.: Information richness – a new approach to managerial behavior and organizational design. Res. Organ. Behav. **6**, 191–233 (1984)
8. Desmal, A.J., Hamid, S., Othman, M.K., Zolait, A.: A user satisfaction model for mobile government services: a literature review. PeerJ Comput. Sci. e1074 (2022). https://doi.org/10.7717/peerj-cs.1074
9. Ebbers, W., Jansen, M., Pieterson, W., van de Wijngaert, L.: Facts and feelings: the role of rational and irrational factors in citizens' channel choices. Gov. Inf. Q. **33**(3), 506–515 (2016)
10. Egovernment Benchmark 2023: Insight Report. Connecting Digital Government. https://prod.ucwe.capgemini.com/wp-content/uploads/2023/08/Capgemini_Public-Sector_eGovernment-Benchmark-2023-report.pdf
11. eGovernment Benchmark 2024 Factsheets. https://digital-strategy.ec.europa.eu/en/library/digital-decade-2024-egovernment-benchmark
12. Filatova, O., Bolgov, R.: Digital transformation of government communications in Russia: from 2011 to 2020. In: Proceedings of the International Conference "Internet and Modern Society" IMS-2020. CEUR Proceedings. 2020, pp.169–180 (2020)
13. Filippova, O.: "I Live Here": How Digital Services for Citizens are Being Launched in St. Petersburg (2023). (In Russian). https://vc.ru/services/943735-ya-zdes-zhivu-kak-v-peterburge-zapuskayut-cifrovye-servisy-dlya-gorozhan
14. GovTech Maturity Index. https://www.worldbank.org/en/programs/govtech/gtmi
15. Grootaert, G., Narayan, D., Nyhan Jones, V., Woolcock, M.: Measuring Social Capital: An Integrated Questionnaire. World Bank Working Paper, 18. World Bank (2004). http://hdl.handle.net/10986/15033
16. Hodson, E., Vainio, T., Sayún, M.N., Tomitsch, M., et al.: Evaluating social impact of smart city technologies and services: methods, challenges, future directions. Multimodal Technol. Interact. **7**(3), 33 (2023). https://doi.org/10.3390/mti7030033
17. Horan, T.A., Abhichandani, T.: Evaluating user satisfaction in an e-government initiative: results of structural equation modeling and focus group discussions. J. Inf. Technol. Manag. **17**(4), 187–198 (2006)
18. Kabanov, Y., Sungurov, A.: E-Government development factors: evidence from the Russian regions. In: Chugunov A.V. (ed.). Digital Transformation and Global Society Communications in Computer and Information Science, pp. 85–95. Springer, Cham (2016)
19. Kalogeropoulos, A., Fletcher, R., Nielsen, K.: News brand attribution in distributed environments: do people know where they get their news? New Media Soc. **21**(3), 583–601 (2019)
20. Katz, R., Koutroumpis, P., Martin Callorda, F.: Using a digitization index to measure the economic and social impact of digital agendas. Info **16**(1), 32–44 (2014). https://doi.org/10.1108/info-10-2013-0051
21. Kim, M., et al.: The effects of service interactivity on the satisfaction and the loyalty of smartphone users. Telematics Inform. **32**(4), 949–960 (2015)
22. Kitsios, F., Stefanakakis, S., Kamariotou, M., Dermentzoglou, L.: E-service evaluation: user satisfaction measurement and implications in health sector. Comput. Stand. Interfaces **63**, 16–26 (2019). https://doi.org/10.1016/j.csi.2018.11.002

23. Madsen, C.Ø., Kræmmergaard, P.: Channel choice: a literature review. In: Tambouris, E., et al. (eds.), Electronic Government. EGOV 2015. LNCS, vol. 9248, pp. 3–18. Springer, Cham (2015). https://doi.org/10.1007/978-3-319-22479-4_1
24. Nahapiet, J., Ghoshal, S.: Social capital, intellectual capital, and the organizational advantage. Acad. Manag. Rev. **23**(2), 242–266 (1998)
25. Newman, N., Fletcher, R., Nielsen, K., Kalogeropoulos, A.: Reuters Institute Digital News Report 2019. Reuters Institute for the Study of Journalism, Oxford University (2019)
26. Novak, T.P., Hoffman, D.L., Yung, Y.-F.: Measuring the customer experience in online environments: a structural modeling approach. Mark. Sci. **19**(1), 22–42 (2003)
27. Park, K.-G., Han, S., Kaid, L.L.: Does social networking service usage mediate the association between smartphone usage and social capital? New Media Soc. **15**(7), 1077–1093 (2013)
28. Pedrosa, G.V., Kosloski, R.A.D., Menezes, V.G.D., Iwama, G.Y., et al.: A systematic review of indicators for evaluating the effectiveness of digital public services. Information **11**(10), 472 (2020). https://doi.org/10.3390/info11100472
29. Rodriguez Müller, A.P., Casiano Flores, C., Albrecht, V., Steen, T., Crompvoets, J.: A scoping review of empirical evidence on (Digital) public services co-creation. Adm. Sci. **11**(4), 130 (2021). https://doi.org/10.3390/admsci11040130
30. Szalkowski, G.A., Johansen, C.: Defining and measuring the effects of digital technologies on social sustainability: a systematic literature review. Sustain. Dev. **32**, 1678–1699 (2023)
31. Tassabehji, R., Hackney, R., Maruyama, T.: Evaluating digital public services: a contingency value approach within three exemplar developing countries. Inf. Technol. People **32**(4), 1021–1043 (2019). https://doi.org/10.1108/ITP-08-2017-0260

User Dysfunctionality and Its Conditions in Online Completion of Typical Tasks

Alexander Yakunin and Svetlana Bodrunova(✉)

St. Petersburg State University, 7-9 Universitetskaya Nab., St. Petersburg 199004, Russia
{a.yakunin,s.bodrunova}@spbu.ru

Abstract. In the process of digital transformation of society, various fields of social and industrial practice move towards the use of semi-automated interactive systems that imply a high cognitive load on the operators who manage them, as well as the users who utilize them. Usability studies lack a conceptual step towards seeing results of task performance as complex cognitive-emotional user states where cognitive load may be diminished or enhanced by the surrounding factors, to the extent that a given user loses functionality. We employ the concept of (dys)functional worker states to explain users' resulting states after they perform two typical real-world tasks of information search and/or assessing online content. Moreover, formation of complex user states is cumulatively conditioned by four 'contextual fidelity' factors, including user traits, task nature, experiment conditions, and interface quality. Thus, we develop a research design that integrates navigation vs. analytical tasks, group vs. individual performance, and monotony- vs. anxiety-inducing conditions. The results provided by 40 assessors and received via measuring five cognitive and emotional metrics show that the navigational task evokes anxiety, while the analytical task induces fatigue and a drop of intellectual lability, both results being simultaneously conditioned by all the three control factors. Partly contradicting previous knowledge on group vs. individual task completion, our results call for multiple-group usability tests for all interfaces, including multi-modal, chatbot, genAI, and industrial ones.

Keywords: Usability · Interface · Quantitative Usability Studies · Dysfunctional User States · Contextual Fidelity Model · User Performance

1 Introduction

In the process of digital transformation of society, various fields of social and industrial practice move towards the use of semi-automated interactive systems that imply a high cognitive load on the operators who manage them. The growth of cognitive load naturally leads to an increase in errors in the management of such systems [1, 2], with the price of each error being significant economic losses, social crises or lost lives. This is especially relevant for industries critical to society (medical, educational, or logistic services, including transport interfaces, as well as decision support systems and industrial complexes). No less is it of high importance for social (personal, interpersonal, and public) communication, a significant part of which operates on interactive digital platforms.

M. Bakaev et al. (Eds.): IMS 2025, CCIS 2671, pp. 366–379, 2026.
https://doi.org/10.1007/978-3-032-04958-2_27

Therefore, the study of the usability of graphical web-interfaces and its psychological impact on the user (and user groups) is to be seen as a priority area within today's digital transformation research.

Today's quantitative usability studies have gathered evidence on myriad individual effects in subjective user perception of interfaces as well as in objective user efficiency. There is also understanding that, during task performance, just as during other types of human working activity, users' functionality may drop, as both cognitive and emotional conditions of a user may change to the worse (e.g., a person may get tired, distracted, or irritated). However, quantitative usability studies still lack a conceptual step forward towards understanding the resulting user states that emerge, e.g., after information search or long enough analytical work with online texts as complex, multi-faceted user states that signal of dropping functionality.

As a response to this conceptual gap, we employ the concepts from cognitive research and psychology of professions which help seeing the resulting user states in a more complex way. Thus, in works [3–5] one may find the concept of workers' functional states. In these works, the authors also foster the concept of dysfunctional states as complexes of cognitive and emotional features of a worker that prevent efficient task performance.

In previous research [6–8], the concept of dysfunctional states was already applied to task performance in usability studies. This has led to formulating and testing dysfunctional user states in user experience, with a particular focus on the states of monotony and anxiety. The first one characterizes by growth of fatigue, slowing down of operations, and loss of concentration and intellectual lability due to that. Anxiety as a complex user state also leads to concentration loss but due to emotional stress and growth of anxious behavior. In previous experiments, the specially created tasks were expected to induce either monotony or anxiety. Experiments proved that the states, indeed, formed in the expected directions: Thus, monotony-inducing tasks led to drops in intellectual lability and growth of fatigue, while anxiety-inducing tasks clearly rose anxiety and also led to intellectual lability drops, which, in both cases, demonstrated the complex nature of post-performance user states and the impact of task completion to users' emotions and cognition.

However, the effects discovered were conditioned by several important factors. In this research, it is also taken into account that usability testing is always subjected to four major factors. The 'contextual fidelity' model suggested in 2011 [9] and elaborated later [7, 10] summarizes a long history of quantitative usability studies and unites under one conceptual umbrella the four influential factors that may alter testing results and thus need controlling. These factors are:

- user traits (including age, gender, group belonging, and cultural identity);
- interface features, including its functional elements and aesthetic quality;
- testing environment (including testing in groups vs. individual testing, online vs. offline testing etc.);
- task features, which, in our earlier works, were represented by monotony- or anxiety-inducing nature.

The previous tests that took into consideration these contextual factors have shown that, e.g., the resulting states of monotony and anxiety differ substantially under the cumulative impact of the 'contextual fidelity' factors. The authors even come to a conclusion that there cannot be 'objective' (unconditioned) results of usability testing, and they need to be perceived as inevitably conditioned by one or more 'contextual fidelity' factors, which demands usability testing for new interfaces to be always performed via complex research designs, with control for such factors. Although, the growth of dysfunctionality has been proven only for the tasks (and instruments for performance assessments, like website interfaces) artificially created to induce dysfunctional states. In this paper, though, we test two typical real-world tasks to learn what types of dysfunctionalities they evoke, without previously assuming which tasks create certain user states. In our experiment, following the logic of previous studies, we still control for several 'contextual fidelity' factors, such as individual vs. group task completion, limited vs. unlimited time of testing, and the nature of tasks (one navigational and one analytical). We expect that performance on real-world tasks shows signs of dysfunctionality discovered previously, and we expect them to be conditioned in certain ways.

2 Dysfunctional User States and Their Conditioned Formation

2.1 Dysfunctionality in Task Performance

As stated above, we have employed several concepts from psychology of professions to explain how users' functionality drops as a result of performance of everyday tasks. In it, we combine the findings of the Russian school of psychology of work as a part of the international human activity theory with works on applied assessment of user performance.

Thus, according to Leonova [3, 4], functional states of workers (in our case, assessors/users) are integral and simultaneous complexes of mental and bodily functions that determine professional performance. Such user states are assessed for both working efficiency, on one hand, and the state of individual mind, mood, and behavior, on the other. Psychologists claim that such user states may be either functional (that is, leading to the rise of measured objective performance and/or higher subjective satisfaction) or dysfunctional (that is, leading to dropping performance quality and lower subjective satisfaction) [11]. Due to the changes in sensitivity thresholds and in the sympathetic nervous system [9], observable changes may be fixed in mental functions crucial to online performance, such as the ability to memorize information, longer-term memory, reactions to stimuli, or intellectual lability and dynamics [12]. These features of a worker's mental state form especially intensely when (s)he undergoes growth of mental fatigue or subjective anxiety [13].

As the research within the activity theory and human work studies shows, four factors have been identified that may shape the functional states. These are the content of an activity under scrutiny, its implementation conditions, the working person's functions, and his/her personal traits, including the psychological profile [14, 15]. These factors clearly correspond to the 'contextual fidelity' factors that have been studied in usability research but are still unrelated to psychology of work and professions.

Online, extreme working conditions are very rarely found; however, users, just as other workers, may frequently experience boredom, or tiredness of monotonous work, or anxiety (or even despair) due to compressed timing of task completion. This is why, in previous research, the focus was on two of the dysfunctional states well described by Leonova and her school, namely monotony and anxiety. Monotony is induced by a repeated task of monotonous nature, e.g., copying text from a range of documents into another document, and reveals itself via drops in intellectual lability (the efficiency of switching from one type of reaction to another), increased fatigue, lowered attention to the task, and overall decrease of pace of task solving [5, 7]. The state of anxiety, on the contrary, shows up via speeding up the pace of task solving accompanied by the growing number of errors, due to which the increase in unproductive information processing is observed. Attention switching between activities tends to rise but to the hyper level leading to distraction and loss of self-control [16, 17]. The two states oppose each other psychologically, but both of them mark the loss of functionality.

As said above, monotony and anxiety were proved to be detectable via combinations of mental (drops of lability) and emotional (growth of the respective emotions, that is, fatigue or anxiety) features with the help of specially created state-inducing tasks [7, 8]. Here, though, we test whether the typical real-world tasks performed online by millions of users are also capable of inducing such dysfunctional states, or at least their elements. If so, this would have many implications for office workers, students, schoolchildren, freelancers who crucially depend on computer-based work, and other people with similar computer-based occupations. Subsequent paragraphs, however, are indented.

2.2 Conditioning Usability Tests: The 'Contextual Fidelity' Model

The concept of dysfunctional user states may be seen as consistent with the 'contextual fidelity' model of the factors that condition the results of usability tests. The model, as stated above, describes four groups of factors including user traits, interface quality, testing environment, and task features. They all affects the results of usability testing, making them relative to the context in which testing is conducted.

Previous research demonstrates that these four factors, taken cumulatively, create patterns in how exactly dysfunctionality forms. Among the rest, combinations of factors condition the intensity of the rising monotony/anxiety, as well as drops in particular cognitive/emotional elements of functionality. We call these patterns of functionality loss dysfunctional state patterns. Such patterns describe stable linkages between combinations of 'contextual fidelity' factors, the cognitive/emotional configuration of user's dysfunctionality, and intensity of dysfunctionality. The patterns are actually a sort of cumulative effects that persist and affect user performance. Previously, three such patterns were detected, playing both for and against higher quality of user performance [7, 8]. The varying task complexity highly affects the patterns, with effects getting full-scale only after a certain complexity threshold [18].

To test the real-world tasks against the 'contextual fidelity' factors, we set them the following way. First, we expect that the type of task matters (see 2.3 on setting the conceptual framework for task selection). Second, as earlier studies showed group vs. individual testing formats to highly affect testing results, we have introduced this element of the research design to the current study. Third, usually, users either have strict enough time frames for task completion or browse Internet in a more relaxed and non-constraint mode; thus, we test the formation of user dysfunctionality in the conditions of limited and unlimited time for task performance; in this respect, the time factor use had not been tested previously.

2.3 Regimes of Cognitive Activity and Cognitively Different Tasks

When selecting tasks, we relied on the knowledge on two fundamental modes of cognitive activity presented in the research by Velichkovsky [19, 20]. According to these works, the two fundamental modes of cognitive activity upon which most of the everyday tasks of a computer user are based are the search for target content (navigation-based behavior) and its detailed studying (examining content on the screen). However, based on the two modes, specific patterns of interaction experience evolve, which may be detected via two groups of objective indicators reflecting the relationship between the nature of the task (search vs. examination) and the cognitive activity caused by it. In particular, in Velichkovsky's research, considerable attention is paid to patterns of oculomotor activity. According to his theory, a certain task execution mode activates the cognitive processes that correspond to it, which is reflected in the metrics of eye movement on a web page.

The first cognitive process is associated with an increase in concentration of attention - it develops when performing the task of analyzing an object and studying it in detail. It is characterized, first of all, by prolonged fixation and a progressive reduction in the amplitude of saccades, in some cases accompanied by an increase in the frequency of blinks per minute and a tendency to increase the average pupil diameter during an interactive session. According to some studies of Velichkovsky's school [21], growth of these indicators also indicates an increase in the level of cognitive load, which does not necessarily indicate less efficient strategies of mental activity used by assessors; in particular, longer fixations (about 300 ms or more) are usually associated with an increase in pupil diameter, as well as they are preceded and completed by relatively small saccades in amplitude.

The second cognitive process accompanies the search for an object on a web page and is associated with deconcentration of attention. I It is characterized by the quantitative dominance of short-term fixations, by slight narrowing of the field of view during task solution, and by the absence of an explicit strategy in the distribution of saccades, indicating the random nature of the search.

Thus, the main criterion for distinguishing between the two modes of cognitive activity is the ordering of information processing during visual perception. When the processes of focal processing are activated, a directional selection of zones in the visual field is carried out for subsequent cognitive processing of the fragment. On the contrary, in the search mode, the energy of perception is dissipated due to the constant switching of attention to distracting stimuli within the visual field, which excludes the implementation of any search strategy. In accordance with this, we have assumed that, during the execution of tasks, the two cognitive regimes will be activated via two corresponding behavioral modes, namely orientation on the web page and examination of the proposed textual content.

Two more ideas from Velichkovsky's theory were of particular importance for the design of the proposed study. Firstly, the patterns of the two fundamental cognitive modes are strictly differentiated. A user cannot employ them simultaneously. Therefore, we have assumed that the two modes of cognitive activity may correspond to specific patterns of functional states that would be detectable in our experiment. Secondly, according to Velichkovsky, the level of concentration of attention is crucial for differentiating the two cognitive modes. During a search task, concentration decreases; when performing a viewing task, it increases. The nature of attention distribution is, therefore, one of the key factors in the formation of the users' psychophysiological states. This suggests a connection between the cognitive mode and the functional state patterns; this is why, in our experiment, we measure intellectual lability as one of the indicators of ability to concentrate. High enough probability of such a connection shows up as well in the studies that explore dependence of user productivity upon the nature of cognitive load, conditioned by the type of tasks being solved [22–25].

In accordance with what is said above, we have set two types of tasks for our experiment. The tasks would be navigational (the search mode) and analytical (the focal attention mode). Both types of tasks are universal as to user activity all over the world and across topics, including business communications, documentation practices, learning activities etc.

2.4 Research Hypotheses

In designing the experiment, we have taken into account all the described above. We have proceeded from the following guiding question: How does solution of cognitively different tasks in varying testing conditions (group/individual environment and varying time constraints) affect the formation of user dysfunctionality? Are there patterns of dysfunctionality?

In accordance with this question, we have put forward three hypotheses:

H1: We expect that the decrease in intellectual lability and increase in anxiety would be greater for time-limited tasks than for similar tasks with unlimited time.
H2: Unrestricted timing for task completion ('long reading') will have a greater impact on the formation of dysfunctionalities associated with monotony. That is, a drop in intellectual lability and an increase of fatigue will be more significant than with a time limit.
H3: In accordance with the cumulative effects of testing factors discovered earlier [7, 8], we expect smaller saliency of dysfunctional effects for H1 and H2 during group testing. Thus, the drop in intellectual lability and the increase in the corresponding emotional parameters (either anxiety or fatigue) will be less intense for group testing, given that the interface for task completion is of high quality (for low-quality interfaces, a reverse effect would be expected [7]).

3 Method

3.1 The Research Design

To test our hypotheses, we have developed a '2 $\times$ 4' study design. The test tasks were performed in eight subgroups, each of which worked with a specific type of task (navigation or analytical) in one of the two testing formats (group or individual) and in one of the two timing modes (under strict or unrestricted time limits). Thus, our experiment included 40 assessors and had the following design (see Table 1).

The students selected as assessors were within the age range of 20–22 years. The choice of this age group was justified by the following considerations:

1) homeostatic and adaptive self-regulation mechanisms are most natural at this age;
2) reactions to stimuli at this age are the most adequate and are not altered by professional experience and age-related changes.

Table 1. Assessor groups based on the research design, 5 assessors per group

Test mode	Test format			
	Group test		Individual test	
	navigation task	analytical task	navigation task	analytical task
limited time	subgroup1	subgroup3	subgroup5	subgroup7
unlimited time	subgroup2	subgroup4	subgroup6	subgroup8

The total sample of assessors was formed taking into account that each of the eight subgroups had a minimum of five people. The small sample size in subgroups in this case was compensated for by a large number of experiments, which is largely acceptable in the practice of usability testing.

In accordance with the research questions and Table 1, we have developed the structure of the experiment with the following stages.

(1) Input (pre-experiment) testing for fixing the initial indicators of cognitive efficiency and emotional stress for the state of 'operational comfort' of each user:
   - assessment of intellectual lability (via 'Schulte – Gorbov tables' [26] – see below in detail);
   - assessment of the current level of emotional tension (via 'self-assessment of emotional states' questionnaires by Wessman and Ricks [27] – see below in detail).

(2) Performing the experiment tasks.
(3) Post-experiment testing in the same order as in (1) to record changes in the indicators of cognitive efficiency and emotional stress of each user, to compare the received values to those of (1) and to discover the change in functionality.

3.2 The Experimental Tasks

As stated above, we have offered to the assessors two types of tasks, namely a navigational and an analytical one.

The navigation task implies searching for target content within the architecture of a website. Via solving this task, a user's capacity to organize the search strategy, distribution of his/her attention, and availability of sufficient time resources to complete the task shape the efficiency of available navigation tools.

The analytical task implies reading a text piece from the screen with simultaneous analysis of its content according to a list of pre-proposed questions. This type of task is based on 'screen reading' which may result into 'deep reading'; the latter implies actualization of attention in the conditions of intense cognitive load. The essence of such tasks is evaluating content according to a range of certain criteria.

For both tasks, the renewed web portal of University of Iowa was used.

3.3 Dysfunctionality Metrics

As stated above, we have offered to the assessors two types of tasks, namely a navigational and an analytical one.

As dysfunctional user states are seen as complex ones in which cognitive and emotional elements co-exist, we have employed cognitive performance and emotional stress assessment measures.

For cognitive performance, intellectual lability was chosen as an indicator. Intellectual lability has mostly been researched upon in the 'practical thinking' studies within education research. We measured intellectual lability using the test for switching attention known as the 'Schulte – Gorbov table' [26], We applied it before and after the experiment. The method implies that the participants pronounce figures from 1 to 25 (shown on grey squares of the table where grey and red squares are mixed) and from 24 to 1 (shown on red squares of the table), switching from grey to red and back. The duration of task solution and the number of errors both are fixed and then rendered into two respective scales proposed by Schulte and (later) Gorbov. The overall lability is measured for each participant individually and calculated as $A = T - C$, where T is the scaled metric for the longevity of the test, and C is the scaled metric for the number of errors. The smaller A, the worse the performance. We calculated A for each participant before and after task completion, thus detecting the drops and rises (if any) of intellectual lability. Then, we have calculated A_{mean} for all the assessors in each subgroup.

To assess emotional stress, we have chosen the so-called indicators of self-esteem. In accordance with the method of self-assessment of emotional states proposed in [27], we measured, by the 1–10 Likert scales, the level of:

- anxiety (the 'anxiety/calmness' scale);
- fatigue (the 'fatigue/energy' scale);
- arousal (the 'depression/excitement' scale);
- confidence (the 'helplessness/self-confidence' scale).

The scales consist of statements that describe emotional states and are assigned discreet values of 1 to 10. Therefore, the scales might be imperfect and provide for answers more similar than expected and more leaning towards the center of the scale; however, this method is more elaborated than simpler Likert scales and is capable of mirroring the nature of our tasks. The four scales are also structured in the way that higher values mean lesser emotional stress. That is, from 1 to 10, calmness, energy, excitement, and self-confidence grow, while anxiety, fatigue, depression, and helplessness fade. E.g., moving from 7 to 5 (the – 2 'delta') means growth of emotional stress.

We have also calculated the deltas (Δ) between the mean values before and after the experiment for each subgroup, as well as standard - for each metric (before the test, after the test, and the delta between them) for each subgroup, to detect the shifts in assessors' states.

The results of our study are presented below.

4 Results

The overall results of our experiment are presented in Table 2 (a,b); significant values are highlighted.

As the results of the empirical study show, the development of dysfunctional states in general reveals a relationship between the experimental conditions and the content features of the tasks.

H1. Time constraints do affect cognitive results. In particular, time limitation contributes to the formation of dysfunctional states associated with anxiety and reduced intellectual lability.

In general, for both types of tasks there is a decrease in intellectual lability under conditions of limited time compared to similar tasks under conditions of uncertain time. The intensity of this decrease depends on the test format and differs for each type of task.

Thus, in the group test for the navigation task, we observe a significant decrease in intellectual lability: Δ-2.4 for the search under time-limited conditions versus Δ-0.9 for the task without a time limit. The same task in the individual performance format causes a decrease in intellectual lability, although not as significant: $\Delta = -1.74$ for the time-limited search vs. $\Delta = -1.48$ for the no time limit task.

In the case of the analytic task in the individual test condition, the difference is $\Delta = -1$ for the time-limited search vs. $\Delta = -0.68$ for the no time limit task. However, in the group version of the same task, intellectual lability decreases more, on the contrary, in the case of the task without a time limit ($\Delta = -1.4$ for the non-limited task vs. $\Delta = -1.3$ for the task under time-limited conditions). This combination of conditions is the only exception to the general trend that time scarcity reduces mental lability and the ability to switch between tasks.

In line with this observation, we can argue that in-depth analytical work upon content within a limited amount of time, which implies intense attention, is more efficient in the presence of other people engaged in similar activities. The increased importance of the social context in this case can compensate for deficiencies in the aesthetic quality and usability of a website designed for research purposes.

However, in the results of emotional self-assessment, we do not see an effect of time deficit on the increase of anxiety for both types of tasks. This is especially true for the results confirmed by the standard deviation.

Thus, H1 is confirmed only partially; it is only valid for intellectual lability, and only in three cases out of four. We cannot speak about pronounced patterns of dysfunction, but we can state the relationship between the factors of the 'contextual fidelity' model: the content of the task, the time limit for its fulfillment and the presence of social environment.

The reasons for such unpredictable behavior of intellectual lability, undoubtedly, deserve deeper further study. At this stage, we can confidently speak about the manifestation of the specific impact of the 'contextual fidelity' model factors both individually and in their various combinations. Thus, for task properties, the interaction between content specificity and time limit is evident - navigation tasks are characterized by a decrease in intellectual lability to a greater extent than analytical ones, but the absence of time limits can cancel this tendency. On the other hand, performing a navigation task in a group as a whole causes a greater decrease in intellectual lability than in an individual mode, but only under time-limit conditions. This may indicate that solving navigation tasks without time constraints in the presence of other people contributes to the preservation of the ability to switch tasks for longer periods of time.

This observation is of practical importance for the de-sign of online services intended for use without time con-straints and in particular social contexts, like library e-catalogs, interactive reference systems of shopping malls, or exposition spaces. In the interface design of such prod-ucts, high cognitive and visual complexity of the layout with its low aesthetic quality is acceptable. In this case, the users' cognitive abilities are less dependent upon these factors.

Table 2. The results of the experiment

a) for group testing

Stat		**Indicator**	**Navigation task**			**Analytical task**		
			before task	after task	*delta (Δ)*	before task	after task	*delta (Δ)*
Monotony		Intellectual lability (A_{mean})	194,2 (2,77)	191,8 (2,387)	-2,4 (3,286)	188,6 (2,30)	187,3 (2,22)	-1,3 (4,46)
	Emotional stress	Calmness/ anxiety	7 (0,707)	5 (0,707)	**-2 (1,224)**	6,8 (1,303)	6,6 (1,140)	-0,2 (0,447)
		Energy/ fatigue	7 (0,707)	7 (0,707)	0 (0)	7 (0,707)	7 (0,707)	0 (0)
		Excitement/ depression	7,8 (0,447)	7,8 (0,447)	0 (0)	7,2 (0,447)	7,4 (0,547)	-0,2 (0,447)
		Self-conf./ helplessness	7,2 (0,447)	7,2 (0,447)	0 (0,707)	6,8 (0,447)	6,8 (0,447)	0 (0)
Anxiety		Intellectual lability (A_{mean})	188,3 (0,836)	187,4 (1,557)	-0,9 (1,387)	186,44 (2,732)	185 (2,549)	-1,44 (3,669)
	Emotional stress	Calmness/ anxiety	7 (0)	6 (0,707)	**-1 (0,707)**	6,8 (0,836)	6,8 (0,836)	0 (0)
		Energy/ fatigue	6,4 (0,547)	6,4 (0,547)	0 (0,707)	6 (0,707)	4 (0,707)	**-2 (0)**
		Excitement/ depression	7,4 (0,547)	7,4 (0,547)	0 (0)	7,6 (0,547)	7,6 (0,547)	0 (0)
		Self-conf./ helplessness	7,2 (0,447)	7,2 (0,447)	0 (0)	7,2 (0,447)	7,2 (0,447)	0 (0)

(continued)

Table 2. (*continued*)

b) for individual testing

Stat	Indicator		Navigation task			Analytical task		
			before task	after task	*delta (Δ)*	before task	after task	*delta (Δ)*
Monotony	Intellectual lability (A_{mean})		192,74 (1,427)	191 (2,549)	-1,74 (1,880)	189,2 (1,303)	188,2 (1,303)	-1 (0)
	Emotional stress	Calmness/ anxiety	8,2 (0,836)	7 (0,707)	**-1,2** **(0,447)**	7 (0)	7 (0,707)	0 (0,707)
		Energy/ fatigue	5,9 (0,741)	5,9 (0,894)	0 (0,353)	6,8 (0,447)	6,8 (0,447)	0 (0)
		Excitement/ depression	7,2 (0,447)	7,2 (0,447)	0 (0)	7,6 (0,547)	7,6 (0,547)	0 (0)
		Self-conf./ helplessness	6,6 (0,894)	6,6 (1,140)	0 (0,707)	7 (0,707)	7 (0,707)	0 (0,707)
Anxiety	Intellectual lability (A_{mean})		188,52 (0,825)	187,04 (3,036)	-1,48 (3,210)	186,7 (1,095)	186,02 (1,669)	-0,68 (2,587)
	Emotional stress	Calmness/ anxiety	6,8 (0,447)	6,8 (0,447)	0 (0)	6,2 (1,095)	6,2 (1,095)	0 (0)
		Energy/ fatigue	5,4 (0,547)	5,4 (0,547)	0 (0)	6 (0,707)	5 (0,707)	**-1** **(0)**
		Excitement/ depression	7 (0)	7 (0)	0 (0)	7,2 (0,447)	7,2 (0,447)	0 (0)
		Self-conf./ helplessness	7 (0,707)	7 (1)	0 (0,707)	6,8 (1,095)	6,8 (1,095)	0 (0)

H2. The combined effect of testing conditions and the task mode upon formation of the dysfunctional states is visible, especially in the case of analytical tasks performed within indefinite timing: Thus, in this case, the growth of fatigue is clear in both testing formats, namely individual and group, with $\Delta = -1$ and–2, respectively), confirming H2.

This observation has implications for design practice. When developing interfaces of projects designed for long-lasting reading and study of detailed information, more visual expression and visual diversity of content is required. Of particular importance for the prevention of monotony is the temporal rhythm in working with information, where regulation of the alternation of activities (e.g., switching between text and video) must occur. The use of means of active attention control, like color highlighting or sharp contrast, is also of crucial importance.

H3. The results clearly show a tendency to a greater decrease in intellectual lability in the conditions of a group test for all types of tasks. The obvious regularity in the results, despite the anomaly in the case of a forced navigation task, nevertheless allows us to talk about partial confirmation of the H3 hypothesis. However, the results for anxiety contradict to the previously received results where we saw group testing to compensate for lability drops and growth of fatigue. This may be explained by either the small enough number of assessors in our subgroups or by low quality of the interface employed for the experiment, which needs additional testing.

The increase of negative effects in collaborative group work is significant for the development of projects used in socialized work environments (e.g., e-learning, reference systems of libraries and social institutions, or online terminals in airports and at railway stations). The interface design of such services should be adapted to possible attention dysfunctions. In particular, the control of distractions in the layout, aimed at reducing visual noise, plays here a significant role. In terms of aesthetics, minimalism can be a solution to this problem.

5 Conclusion

In this paper, we have presented the research that allows for seeing typical tasks performed online as, first, capable of fast enough inducing of dysfunctionality and, second, conditioned by the circumstances of task performance.

We have shown that navigational practices can cause a decline in cognitive performance in any information retrieval mode other than individual reading under conditions of unlimited time. Our results are almost all in line with our previous research and expand its results, except for the compensatory effect for anxiety in individual testing format which we did not observe in the previous studies. More assessors need to pass the test to get clearer results on this effect.

Acknowledgments. This research has been supported in full by the project 'Cumulative public opinion and deliberation: Theorizing, research methods, and assessment of the quality of today's deliberative process' of St. Petersburg State University, Russia (ID Pure 128786104), year 1.

Disclosure of Interests. The authors declare no conflict of interest.

References

1. Bannert, M.: Managing cognitive load, recent trends in cognitive load theory. Learn. Instr. **12**, 139–146 (2002)
2. Hancock, P.A., Desmond, P.A.: Stress, Workload and Fatigue. Lawrence Erlbaum Associates, London (2001)
3. Leonova, A.B.: The concept of human functional state in Russian applied psychology. Psychol. Russia: State Art **2**, 517–538 (2009)
4. Leonova, A.B., Medvedev, V.I.: Functional states of a person in labor activity: A textbook [Funktsional'nye sostoyaniya cheloveka v trudovoy deyatel'nosti]. Lomonosov Moscow State University Publishing House, Moscow (1981)
5. Leonova, A.B.: Functional status and regulatory processes in stress management. In: Hockey, G.R.J., Gaillard, A.W.K., Burov, O. (eds.), Operator Functional State: The Assessment and Prediction of Human Performance Degradation in Complex Tasks, pp. 36–52. Ios Pr Inc., Amsterdam, The Netherlands (2003)
6. Yakunin, A.V., Bodrunova, S.S.: Cumulative distortions in usability testing: combined impact of web design, experiment conditions, and type of task and upon user states during internet use. In: Design, User Experience, and Usability: UX Research, Design, and Assessment - 11th International Conference, DUXU 2022, Held as Part of the 24th HCI International Conference, HCII 2022, Proceedings, pp. 526–535 (2022)

7. Yakunin, A.V., Bodrunova, S.S.: Cumulative impact of testing factors in usability tests for human-centered web design. Future Internet **14**(12), 359 (2022)
8. Yakunin, A.V., Bodrunova, S.S.: Dysfunctional user states in interface use and their dependency on work environment and task complexity. In: Social Computing and Social Media 15th International Conference, SCSM 2023, Held as Part of the 25th HCI International Conference, HCII 2023, Copenhagen, Denmark, 23–28 July, Proceedings, Part I (2023)
9. Sauer, J., Sonderegger, A.: The influence of product aesthetics and user state in usability testing. Behav. Inf. Technol. **30**(6), 787–796 (2011)
10. Sauer, J., Sonderegger, A., Heyden, K., Biller, J., Klotz, J., Uebelbacher, A: Extra-laboratorial usability tests: an empirical comparison of remote and classical field testing with lab testing. Appl. Ergon. **74**, 85–96 (2019)
11. Ushakov, I.B., Bogomolov, A.V., Kukushkin, Y.A.: Patterns of operator functional states [Patterny funktsional'nyh sostoyaniy operatora]. Nauka, Moscow (2010)
12. Chuprikova, N.I.: Human reaction time: Physiological mechanisms, verbal-semantic regulation, connection with intelligence and properties of the nervous system [Vremya reaktsiy cheloveka: Fiziologicheskie mehanizmy, verbal'no-smyslovaya regulyatsiya, svyaz' s intellektom i svoystvami nervnoy systemy]. Yask Publishing House, Moscow (2019)
13. Ushakov, I.B., Bogomolov, A.V., Kukushkin, Y.A.: Psychophysiological mechanisms of formation and development of functional states. Russian J. Physiol. (Formerly I. M. Sechenov Physiological Journal) **100**(10), 1130–1137 (2014)
14. Suvorova, G.A.: Psychology of activity [Psihologiya deyatelnosti]. PER SE Publishing House, Moscow (2003)
15. Kaptelinin, V., Nardi, B.: Activity Theory in HCI: Fundamentals and Reflections. Morgan & Claypool Publishers, San Rafael (2012)
16. Russ, A.L., Saleem, J.J.: Ten factors to consider when developing usability scenarios and tasks for health information technology. J. Biomed. Inf. **78**, 123–133 (2018)
17. Kuutti, K., Bannon, L.J.: The turn to practice in HCI: towards a research agenda. In: Proceedings of the SIGCHI Conference on Human Factors in Computing Systems, pp. 3543–3552 (2014)
18. Yakunin, A.V., Bodrunova, S.S.: The influence of usability on user cognitive activity: a differential intelligence perspective. in: social computing and social Media:16th International Conference, SCSM 2024, Held as Part of the 26th HCI International Conference, HCII 2024, Washington, DC, USA, June 29–July 4 2024, Proceedings, Part I, pp. 285–297 (2024)
19. Velichkovskii, B.M.: Novel technologies in cognitive functions research. Her. Russ. Acad. Sci. **80**(3), 223–228 (2010)
20. Velichkovsky, B.M., Zlokazova, T.A., Kapiza, M.S.: The efficiency of interruption handling in free and forced switching tasks [Effektivnost' obrabotki preryvaniy v usloviyah svobodnyh i vynuzhdennyh pereklyucheniy]. Eksperimental'naya psikhologiya [Experimental psychology] **3**(2), 45–57 (2010)
21. Blinnikova, I.V., Velichkovsky, B.B., Kapiza, M.S., Leonova, A.B.: Interruptions in computerized activity: strategies of switching between the main and the secondary tasks [Preryvaniya v komp'yuterizovannoy deyatel'nosti: strategii pereklyucheniya mezhdu osnovnoy i dopolnitel'noy zadachami]. Eksperimental'naya psikhologiya [Experimental psychology] **1**, 35–51 (2009)
22. Campbell, D.J.: Task complexity: a review and analysis. Acad. Manag. Rev. **13**(1), 40–52 (1988)
23. Byström, K.: Information and information sources in tasks of varying complexity. J. Am. Soc. Inform. Sci. Technol. **53**(7), 581–591 (2002)
24. Gwizdka, J., Spence, I.: What can searching behavior tell us about the difficulty of information tasks? A study of web navigation. Proc. Am. Soc. Inf. Sci. Technol. (ASIS&T) **43**(1), 1–22 (2006)

25. Holden, R.J., et al.: Human factors engineering and human-computer interaction: supporting user performance and experience. Clin. Inf. Study Guide 119–132 (2022)
26. Mashin, V.A.: Analysis of heart rate variability based on the graph method. Hum. Physiol. **28**, 437–447 (2002)
27. Wessman, A.E., Ricks, D.F.: Mood and Personality. Holt, Rinehart and Winston, New York (1966)

Metaverses and Public Policy: Prospects for Virtual Civic Participation

Andrey Nosikov(✉)

Saint Petersburg State University, 7/9 Universitetskaya Nab., St. Petersburg 199034, Russia
a.nosikov@spbu.ru

Abstract. The rise of metaverses as dynamic digital environments presents new opportunities and challenges for civic participation and public policy. This study examines the potential of metaverses as platforms for digital activism, decentralized governance, and electoral experimentation. By enabling virtual protests, transnational advocacy, and immersive political simulations, metaverses redefine traditional mechanisms of political engagement, offering alternative public spheres beyond the constraints of state- controlled media and physical space. Despite their transformative potential, metaverses face structural barriers, including algorithmic content moderation, platform-based governance, and digital inequality. Corporate control over virtual spaces raises concerns about censorship, data privacy, and the instrumentalization of digital activism for political or commercial interests. Furthermore, the accessibility gap in virtual reality infrastructure and the need for advanced digital literacy limit broad -based participation in metaverse-based political processes. This study highlights the necessity of regulatory frameworks that ensure democratic accountability, transparency, and inclusivity in virtual civic ecosystems. The integration of blockchain technology, decentralized autonomous organizations (DAOs), and immersive educational platforms may enhance political engagement, but their institutionalization requires careful policy interventions. The findings suggest that metaverses have the potential to function as laboratories for digital democracy, testing new governance models that could influence offline political institutions. The article contributes to the theory of public policy by offering a conceptual deconstruction of traditional frameworks of the public sphere in favor of incorporating virtual spaces of the metaverse as autonomous arena-forming structures of digital publicity. Within the context of this study, virtual worlds are examined not merely as technological platforms, but as socio-political ecosystems in which a new network-mediated agency emerges – an agency of actors capable of collectively shaping norms and values. This study is aimed at a comprehensive analysis of the potential of metaverses as an environment for political civic engagement in the context of the digital transformation of the public sphere. The research focuses on identifying key «windows of opportunity» for the institutionalization and legitimation of political activity within virtual environments, as well as on developing potential scenarios for the use of metaverses as platforms for the enactment of political action.

Keywords: Metaverse · Virtual Civic Participation · Virtual Policy

M. Bakaev et al. (Eds.): IMS 2025, CCIS 2671, pp. 380–393, 2026.
https://doi.org/10.1007/978-3-032-04958-2_28

1 Relevance of the Research Problem

The rapid advancement of digital technologies and the evolution of virtual communication environments are transforming traditional forms of civic participation, fostering new mechanisms of political interaction. Metaverses, as a dynamically developing phenomenon, represent not only a technological construct but also a socio-political framework capable of modifying the structures of public policy. In the context of platform-mediated social life, virtual spaces emerge as alternative arenas for political mobilization, civic initiatives, and the formation of networked communities engaged in decision-making processes. However, despite the potential of metaverses as an environment for digital democracy, their degree of institutionalization, regulatory frameworks, and the sustainability of political participation mechanisms remain subjects of debate.

Existing research on digital civic participation highlights the ambiguous impact of virtual platforms on democratic processes. On the one hand, metaverses can contribute to the inclusivity of political discussions, reduce the transaction costs of collective action, and expand horizontal communication networks [48]. On the other hand, they generate new challenges, including issues of digital inequality, algorithmic governance, and platform censorship, which complicate the realization of genuinely democratic practices in virtual environments [25]. An additional factor requiring analysis is the extent of metaverses autonomy from traditional institutions of power and economic structures, which directly influences the feasibility of self-governance and political co-governance within digital ecosystems.

Current studies on metaverses in the context of public policy remain fragmented and are predominantly focused on technological, economic, and cultural dimensions, while their political implications necessitate a comprehensive interdisciplinary examination. Specifically, the mechanisms of political subjectivation within metaverses, the potential of virtual environments for generating civic initiatives, and the impact of platform regulation on political articulation and mobilization remain underexplored. Given the global expansion of digital civic society, the deepening platformization of public policy, and the growing interest of states in regulating virtual spaces, investigating the prospects for virtual civic participation in metaverses becomes particularly relevant. This study is aimed at a comprehensive analysis of the potential of metaverses as an environment for political civic engagement in the context of the digital transformation of the public sphere. The research focuses on identifying key "windows of opportunity" for the institutionalization and legitimation of political activity within virtual environments, as well as on developing potential scenarios for the use of metaverses as platforms for the enactment of political action. In addition, the study seeks to provide a theoretical conceptualization of the metaverse phenomenon through the lens of contemporary political theory.

2 Theoretical and Methodological Framework

This study is based on an interdisciplinary approach that integrates concepts of the public sphere, digital civic participation, and platform regulation. The theoretical foundation encompasses both classical and contemporary approaches to the study of public policy in digital environments, enabling an analysis of metaverses as potential spaces for political articulation and mobilization.

A key theoretical basis is J. Habermas's concept of the public sphere [19], reconsidered in the context of digital communication. Virtual environments within metaverses can be understood as digital public spheres where political discourse can develop; however, their functioning is influenced by platform architecture and algorithmic moderation. The study also draws upon theories of digital citizenship (Mossberger et al. [32]), the network society (M. Castells [8]), and platform capitalism (N. Srnicek [43]), which facilitate an examination of how digital ecosystems establish new regimes of political interaction and contribute to the structuring of virtual public institutions.

To analyze the specific characteristics of political mobilization in metaverses, the study employs approaches from digital activism research (Tufekci [46]; Earl & Kimport [14]), including the concept of "collective action without collectivity," which highlights new forms of horizontal engagement in political processes. Another essential aspect is the theory of platform regulation (Gillespie [16]; Suzor [44]), which explains how corporate structures define the boundaries of permissible political interaction within digital environments.

Methodologically, the research relies on digital ethnography [37], which enables an in-depth examination of the dynamics of civic participation in metaverses through immersive observation and an analysis of user behavioral practices in virtual political spaces [29], as well as the user-driven architecture of interactions [20]. An integrative literature review [45] facilitates the systematization of existing studies, the identification of key areas of scholarly debate, and the development of an analytical framework [42]. A set of criteria was applied to the selection of scientific sources. First, the study includes sources published between 2021 and 2025, as the topic remains highly relevant and rapidly evolving, with scholarly and expert discussions on metaverses intensifying only after 2021. This shift was catalyzed by Facebook's rebranding to «Meta» («Meta Platforms», like its «Facebook» product, are recognized in the Russian Federation with extremist organizations and prohibited) in 2021, signaling its strategic commitment to metaverse development and stimulating broader academic interest in the field. Exceptions to this timeframe include foundational theoretical contributions (e.g., platform capitalism, platform regulation, the public sphere, and the network society), which are primarily considered in the context of integrating the metaverse concept into existing theoretical paradigms. Second, the selection process prioritized scientific articles and monographs indexed in Scopus and Web of Science to enhance the relevance of the synthesized theoretical insights.

The case analysis includes an examination of protest movements, self-governance initiatives, and experiments with digital voting in metaverses, allowing for an empirical assessment of these environments' potential for civic participation. This analysis draws upon both secondary data from academic research and information published in socio-political, business, and technology-focused media outlets.

This comprehensive approach enables the identification of factors influencing political interaction in metaverses, as well as an assessment of their role in shaping new models of democratic practices and digital civic society.

3 Integration of the Metaverse Concept into Existing Theoretical Frameworks

The concept of the metaverse, positioned at the intersection of technological, social, and political discourses, necessitates integration into existing theoretical frameworks that describe digital forms of civic participation, political communication, and platform regulation. Metaverses can be conceptualized as digital public spheres, networked political ecosystems, and platform-based infrastructures within which new models of interaction between citizens, the state, and technology corporations emerge [26].

From the perspective of the public sphere concept, metaverses can be analyzed as potential spaces for democratic discourse; however, their structure is shaped by the logic of platform capitalism. Unlike the traditional public sphere, which is institutionalized within media and civic organizations, metaverses are created by private corporations and operate under algorithmic governance, raising questions about their autonomy as spaces for free political exchange. Theoretical developments in platform regulation [44] provide insight into how corporate content moderation policies, platform economic interests, and the technological architecture of metaverses influence the conditions for civic participation and the possibilities for political mobilization. Research in this area also highlights the importance of evaluating algorithmic mechanisms of digital platform governance, as they can shape the political landscape by either restricting or facilitating digital democracy [39].

In the context of digital citizenship theories [32], metaverses can be seen as environments for expanding digital rights and political participation practices. However, they also reproduce structural forms of digital inequality and political alienation. Metaverses enable new forms of collective action, including protest movements, digital strikes, and decentralized self- governance initiatives; however, the extent of their institutionalization and their stability as political entities remain subject to debate.

The network society concept [8] provides a foundation for interpreting metaverses as nodal points of global political interaction, where civic initiatives can transcend national boundaries and form transnational political movements. At the same time, when applying digital democracy models (J. Coleman [10], P. Dahlgren [11]) to metaverses, it becomes evident that institutional mechanisms of participation in these environments require further conceptualization, as their architecture does not always facilitate democratic principles, and decision-making processes are often concentrated in the hands of platform operators.

Thus, integrating the concept of the metaverse into existing theoretical frameworks reveals its multidimensional and complex nature: metaverses function simultaneously as technological platforms, arenas of networked politics, and subjects of platform regulation. Their political potential depends on a combination of factors, including digital rights architectures, self-governance mechanisms, and platform regulatory policies.

4 Virtual Civic Participation Practices in the Metaverse

Virtual civic participation in the metaverse represents an emerging phenomenon that reshapes traditional political engagement and self-expression within digital ecosystems. These virtual environments serve as arenas for citizen interaction with governmental and private institutions and platforms for new forms of political activism and collective action. The practices of virtual civic participation in the metaverse encompass various aspects, including protest actions, self-governance initiatives, experiments with digital elections, and forms of civic mobilization and political organization.

A key practice of virtual civic participation is **digital political activism**, which, similar to traditional digital platforms, can take the form of online campaigns, virtual rallies, petitions, and initiatives on social and political issues [1]. Metaverses, by offering users immersive spaces for interaction through avatars and other digital identities, create unique conditions for deeper political engagement. Users can participate in mass protests, flash mobs, or other forms of digital demonstrations without leaving the virtual world. Examples of such practices include protests against censorship in metaverses, demands for algorithmic transparency, or actions aimed at protecting user rights from unfair platform regulation [13].

One prominent example of digital activism in the metaverse is a protest held in «Decentraland» -- a popular blockchain-based virtual platform. In 2021, a virtual protest against platform censorship was organized by a group of activists advocating for freedom of expression. Participants used avatars to stage mass virtual rallies and demonstrations, expressing their dissatisfaction with content moderation policies in virtual worlds [33]. These protests resemble similar actions in the physical world but occur in digital spaces, allowing participants from across the globe to engage without geographical limitations. Research suggests that Decentraland is evolving into a platform for social interaction and political mobilization, enabled by its decentralized structure and the opportunities for collective digital expression [18].

Cases described in the article "Second Life Users Are Protesting With Their Avatars" [9] examines the phenomenon of virtual political activism within the «Second Life» community. Special attention is given to the «Avatars Against Trump» initiative, in which users of massive multiplayer online (MMO) games united to protest against the policies of former U.S. President Donald Trump. This initiative was launched in collaboration with active Second Life participants. They created a Flickr group to collect images of protest avatars and machinima content. This group remains open to users from various MMO games or VR platforms with user-generated content.

Another significant practice of virtual civic participation is **governance initiatives**. In some metaverses, forms of self-governance are emerging, where participants, organized into communities, collectively decide on the internal structuring of the space, behavioral norms, content regulation, and resource management [15]. These initiatives often take the form of decentralized autonomous organizations (DAOs), which operate within the metaverse [5]. Participants may vote on changes to economic or political practices, modifications of platform algorithms, the management of virtual assets, or the establishment of rules for user interactions [30]. The absence of centralized authority in these initiatives allows metaverses to be viewed as experimental arenas for decentralized self-governance [49].

In «Somnium Space», a decentralized governance model enables participants who own virtual real estate to vote on projects aimed at platform development and improvement. Users can make decisions regarding the creation of new territorial units, land allocation, and content moderation policies. This self-governance practice is implemented through a DAO system, where every participant has the opportunity to contribute to key decision-making processes within the virtual world. In 2022, «Somnium Space» conducted an experiment utilizing DAO mechanisms for voting on issues related to enhancing the infrastructure of its virtual economy. The article "Lessons from Second Life? Democracy in the Metaverse" [51] explores the experience of democratic structures within the virtual world of Second Life, focusing on the activities of the Confederation of Democratic Simulators (CDS). Second Life, launched in 2003 by Linden Lab, is a 3D virtual platform that allows users to create and interact within an open-ended digital environment. Users can generate and trade virtual objects, such as clothing, furniture, and buildings, on an internal marketplace with a currency convertible to real-world USD. Founded in 2004, CDS is the longest-running democratic community in Second Life, operating on democratic self-governance principles. Citizens participate in elections, nominate candidates, and vote, mirroring real-world democratic processes. Elected leader within CDS, emphasizes that in this context, virtual identity holds more significance than real-world identification. The experience of CDS demonstrates that virtual platforms can sustain complex political structures that reflect and simulate real democratic processes. This underscores the potential of metaverses as spaces for experimenting with new forms of civic engagement and political organization.

Digital voting and electoral experiments within the metaverse represent another significant practice of virtual civic participation. Some virtual environments conduct experimental elections that simulate real-world political processes, including the election of representatives and voting on key governance issues, such as user behavior regulations or infrastructural changes. These experiments offer insights into voting mechanisms and political democracy within virtual spaces, allowing for an evaluation of different voting methods (e.g., blockchain- based voting) and their potential integration into real-world democratic practices.

One prominent example is the multiple instances of digital voting and elections within «Decentraland» [17], where governance is facilitated through a decentralized autonomous organization (DAO). Owners of digital assets, such as «MANA» tokens, virtual land parcels, and unique usernames, have the right to vote on proposals shaping the development and governance of the metaverse. Key areas of voting include banning specific usernames, adding new servers, allocating grants from the DAO treasury, modifying points of interest on the metaverse map, and integrating wearable NFT accessories. All voting processes are conducted on the Ethereum blockchain, ensuring full transparency and public accountability. This case exemplifies how electoral processes and voting mechanisms are already operational within the metaverse, enabling collective governance of digital spaces. The integration of blockchain technology further enhances the legitimacy and security of these processes, providing a potential model for future experiments in digital democracy beyond virtual environments.

Moreover, a crucial dimension of virtual civic participation in the metaverse is **inclusivity and equality in engagement**. Metaverses have the potential to enhance opportunities for diverse social groups to participate in political processes. Virtual spaces, unbounded by physical location, enable individuals from different regions of the world to interact and exchange ideas, fostering the formation of global networked movements

[2]. This aspect is particularly significant for marginalized groups which often face structural barriers to participation in traditional political systems - whether ethnic minorities, migrants, individuals with disabilities, or other underrepresented populations. The metaverse offers an environment that mitigates some of these constraints by providing greater accessibility, anonymity, and avenues for political expression [35]. Examples of such engagement include transnational advocacy campaigns for minority rights, environmental awareness initiatives, and human rights activism, all of which become increasingly viable through metaverse platforms that facilitate global civic mobilization and collective action.

Algorithmic regulation and moderation in metaverses play a critical role in defining the boundaries of virtual civic participation. Platforms hosting metaverses implement mechanisms to control content and user interactions, which, on the one hand, protect against harmful information and violations but, on the other hand, may impose restrictions on freedom of expression and political activity [41].

Research indicates that AI-driven algorithmic content moderation is essential for combating disinformation and harmful speech. However, it also raises concerns regarding transparency and the potential for unjustified censorship [38]. The practices of content censorship and filtering in metaverses require particular scrutiny, as they can influence the dynamics of political engagement and the freedom of civic participation. Studies suggest that user perceptions of transparency in blockchain-based regulatory mechanisms impact trust in metaverse platforms and willingness to engage in digital political participation [21]. The challenge for metaverse developers is to strike a balance between content control and the autonomy of virtual communities while upholding the principles of free speech and user protection [24]. One of the most prominent cases of algorithmic regulation in the metaverse is Roblox, a widely used gaming platform that has faced significant challenges in content moderation and censorship. Following incidents of sexualized content and hate speech proliferating through user-generated games, Roblox was compelled to enhance its moderation algorithms and implement stricter content control policies in response to public criticism [28]. This case exemplifies how metaverse platforms address potentially harmful content while simultaneously raising critical questions about freedom of expression and the limits of censorship in virtual environments.

Thus, practices of virtual civic participation in metaverses encompass a wide range of political engagement forms, including protest movements, self-governance, electoral procedures, and activism, reflecting the evolving nature of digital political involvement in immersive environments.

5 Challenges and Prospects of Digital Democracy in Metaverses

However, civic political participation in metaverses encounters challenges of platform regulation, algorithmic control, and digital inequality, warranting further investigation. Four key tracks can be delineated.

The first track involves **institutional constraints**. Despite individual initiatives and notable successes, unified mechanisms for legitimizing political activity in metaverses are absent. Virtual spaces enable novel digital civil institutions, but their development is hampered by unclear regulatory norms and interaction standards [47]. Platforms act as quasi-state regulators, setting discourse boundaries that curtail self- governance and collective action. Unlike traditional democracy - which relies on electoral procedures and representation—metaverses are governed by corporations and algorithmic moderation systems, limiting users influence over rules and governance [22]. The opaque institutionalization of virtual civil society raises doubts about its capacity to affect real-world politics. Platforms may restrict public discourse, block sensitive content, or limit digital protests, engendering new digital inequalities. Legal uncertainty persists: users often cannot defend their speech rights, as platform accountability remains undefined [34].

In the absence of harmonized legal norms, platforms independently regulate political initiatives, fragmenting civic participation mechanisms. Experimental models, such as decentralized autonomous organizations (DAOs) - offer users enhanced community management, yet they do not fully replace traditional civil institutions. Thus, metaverses remain trial grounds for civic participation without clear regulatory frameworks.

The second track considers **algorithmic mediation** in political communication. Algorithms govern information dissemination, content management, and interactions, facilitating but also restricting participation [50]. Personalized recommendation systems generate information bubbles that reinforce cognitive biases and polarize public opinion. Content moderation algorithms prevent misinformation and extremism [52] but may also suppress significant political initiatives, raising transparency and accountability concerns [31]. Platforms shape discursive environments to serve economic or political interests. Moreover, AI integrated into metaverses can perpetuate bias by training on historically imbalanced data, diminishing some topics' visibility while amplifying others [53]. Algorithmic mediation thus offers scalability and protection, yet threatens opinion pluralism and equitable participation. Addressing algorithmic transparency, platform accountability, and digital rights protection is vital for the future of digital democracy.

The third track addresses **digital inequality**, both technological and socioeconomic. Participation requires high-speed internet, powerful hardware, and VR equipment, creating barriers for vulnerable groups [48]. Insufficient digital literacy further excludes users from engaging with blockchain, cryptocurrencies, and DAO's [21], intensifying the third level of digital inequality: the ability not only to consume but to utilize digital technologies for political ends. High equipment and connectivity costs preclude mass involvement in digital governance [54], resulting in a «metaverse oligarchy» of financially privileged users. Economic limitations reduce political representativeness: users from developed countries enjoy more opportunities, while those from underdeveloped regions remain observers. Ensuring accessibility, digital literacy, and economic inclusion demands technical, political, and legal initiatives to guarantee equal access to virtual civic spaces.

The fourth track concerns **legal regulation** and user rights in metaverses. Transnational platforms lack unified mechanisms for free speech, data protection, and accountability in digital political activities [7]. Virtual spaces transcend jurisdictions, creating conflicts over speech regulation, identity, and legal enforcement [23]. Establishing electronic jurisdiction with algorithmic law enforcement is theoretically possible but requires major technological and regulatory changes. Data protection is another challenge: platforms extensive data processing capabilities heighten cyber risks, and fragmented internal norms complicate rights protection. Adapting GDPR- like international data standards to virtual environments could address this.

Criminal liability for metaverse offenses - fraud, cyberbullying, illegal data collection, identity manipulation - necessitates specialized legal norms, potentially a «meta-criminal law» [41]. Intellectual property in virtual assets and user-generated content also lacks clear legal standards [55]. Proposals include hybrid legal frameworks for metaverse dispute resolution, combining traditional norms with algorithmic selfregulation [3].

Overall, civic participation in metaverses depends on overcoming these institutional, technological, and legal challenges to foster sustainable democratic practices. Integrating virtual formats into real political processes will shape the future of digital democracy, as virtual participation has the potential to transform traditional political interaction models.

Now, let's examine the most promising scenarios for the development of metaverses as public spaces for civil participation. One significant prospect is the **institutionalization of virtual citizenship**. Research highlights metaverses potential to form digital communities with autonomous self-governance and collective decision-making [4]. Virtual public organizations, DAOs and digital parliaments could represent citizens, establish internal regulations, and govern interactions via smart contracts and blockchain [15]. Built on blockchain, DAOs enable autonomous ecosystem management, allowing collective voting and algorithmic consensus; they might function as digital legislatures, regulating metaverse economies and societies [30].

Virtual citizenship in metaverses emerges as a form of digital identity with accompanying rights and obligations within virtual jurisdictions. Yet legal uncertainty persists: unified international norms and enforcement mechanisms for digital conflicts are lacking. Integrating metaverses into real-world politics by deploying digital parliaments in virtual environments could test novel democratic governance and participation models [39]. Thus, metaverses may serve as experimental grounds for decentralized governance adaptable to traditional institutions. Successful institutionalization of virtual citizenship demands enhanced regulatory frameworks, robust digital identification, and integration of virtual jurisdictions into global law.

A second prospect lies in **digital activism** and virtual political mobilization. VR/AR technologies open new horizons for activism, transforming traditional protest and participation [1]. Metaverses can act as alternative public spheres where citizens express dissent, organize campaigns, and coordinate actions beyond state media control [31]. Virtual rallies and demonstrations, leveraging immersive technologies, amplify symbolic impact and attract global audiences. Transnational activist networks can form across regions, collaborating on social initiatives, unlike state-regulated media, metaverses could enable autonomous digital civil societies. However, algorithmic moderation and platform regulation may suppress protest content [12], and corporate or state control risks instrumentalizing metaverses for political ends.

Third, **electoral processes** could evolve within digital environments. Metaverses offer experimental platforms for digital voting mechanisms, political program discussions, and modeling electoral democracy. Decentralized identification and blockchain registries could reduce fraud and enhance transparency, potentially integrating with national e- voting systems to expand secure, inclusive participation. Virtual formats like pre-election debates, public forums, electoral simulations might educate and engage youth, fostering informed electorates. Yet cybersecurity, data protection, digital literacy, and technological accessibility remain critical challenges [27].

Additional prospects concern **digital political education and socialization**. Metaverses' immersive learning environments enable simulations of negotiations and democratic institutions, fostering civic consciousness and digital skills [6]. Interactive simulations of elections, parliamentary debates, and virtual conferences support critical thinking essential for democratic engagement [56]. Virtual educational platforms contribute to new forms of digital citizenship, granting access to global political discourse and promoting transnational activism [57].

In sum, metaverses have the potential to redefine civic participation by creating novel forms of political communication, self- governance, and activism. Realizing these prospects requires development of institutional, technological, and legal mechanisms to sustain digital civil society within virtual environments.

6 Discussion and Conclusions

Metaverses represent an emerging digital environment with the potential to reshape traditional mechanisms of civic engagement and public policy. This study has identified key trends and challenges that define the prospects of political mobilization, public discourse, and collective action in virtual spaces. The findings indicate that metaverses can function as alternative public spheres, providing platforms for digital activism, decentralized governance, and electoral experimentation. Virtual protests, decentralized initiatives, and simulations of democratic processes demonstrate the possibility of establishing new forms of political communication within these environments. However, institutionalizing these practices requires the development of regulatory frameworks that ensure the legitimacy of virtual citizenship and the autonomy of digital self-governance.

Despite their potential, civic participation in metaverses faces structural limitations, including platform regulation, algorithmic mediation, and digital inequality. The control exerted by platform providers - through proprietary content moderation algorithms and censorship mechanisms - may restrict political expression and shape civic participation agendas. Additionally, the high cost of access to VR infrastructure and the necessity of digital literacy create barriers to inclusive engagement in virtual political processes. These constraints underscore the need for policies aimed at ensuring equal access, technological transparency, and the protection of digital rights in virtual environments.

The future of civic participation in metaverses is closely linked to the institutionalization of digital democracy, the implementation of innovative electoral practices, and the expansion of transnational activism. Blockchain technology, decentralized autonomous organizations (DAOs), and immersive educational platforms hold promise for enhancing the transparency and efficiency of political processes while equipping citizens with new tools for expressing political will. In the long term, metaverses may evolve beyond alternative political mobilization spaces into experimental laboratories for testing new models of digital self-governance, which could influence offline political institutions and practices.

Moreover, metaverses open new frontiers for political education and socialization, fostering interactive and immersive learning experiences that cultivate civic awareness and democratic engagement among younger generations. By enabling users to participate in virtual electoral simulations, parliamentary debates, and global policy discussions, these environments can contribute to the formation of politically informed and digitally competent citizens. The development of transnational activist networks within metaverses also highlights their potential to facilitate crossborder political cooperation and grassroots initiatives beyond the constraints of national jurisdictions.

Furthermore, the integration of metaverses into public policy raises critical ethical and governance questions regarding privacy, security, and digital autonomy. The potential for data exploitation, algorithmic biases, and state or corporate surveillance necessitates the implementation of robust oversight mechanisms to prevent the monopolization of virtual civic spaces. Addressing these risks requires collaboration between policymakers, technology developers, and civil society actors to establish regulatory frameworks that uphold democratic values and digital sovereignty within metaverses.

Thus, metaverses represent a rapidly evolving field of political communication, demanding further interdisciplinary research. Issues such as digital rights, platform governance, algorithmic biases, and technological inequality remain critical challenges shaping the scope and limitations of virtual civic participation. It is important to underscore that alongside the democratizing potential of political participation in metaverses, countervailing dynamics are emerging, driven by corporate platform regulation, algorithmic control and censorship mechanisms, and initiatives to impose comprehensive regulatory regimes on digital infrastructure within authoritarian contexts. These areas demonstrate the risk that virtual environments may be transformed into closed «control shells», wherein political discourse is vulnerable not only to overt content removal but also to covert visibility constraints (shadow banning). The intensification of efforts to develop multi-layered legal and technical protocols in non-democratic political regimes further elevates the likelihood of institutionalizing authoritarian models of public-sphere administration within metaverse platforms. In this light, there is a pressing need for expanded empirical and theoretical inquiry aimed at unmasking the "black boxes" of algorithmic moderation, assessing threats to digital sovereignty, and formulating strategies to safeguard civil liberties in hybrid digital ecosystems. The future of metaverses as a domain of public policy depends on the ability of developers, researchers, and policymakers to balance digital freedom of expression, democratic accountability, and the institutional sustainability of virtual civic ecosystems. Addressing these challenges will determine whether metaverses become a space for meaningful democratic participation or a domain subject to corporate and governmental control. Ensuring the responsible development and regulation of metaverses will be essential in realizing their potential as legitimate arenas for civic engagement and political innovation in the digital age.

Acknowledgments. The author acknowledges Saint-Petersburg State University for a research project 116471555.

References

1. Achkasova, V.A., Nosikov, A., Zhuravleva, N.N.: The phenomenon of networked media activism: bifurcation point. In: Proceedings of the 2023 Communication Strategies in Digital Society Seminar (ComSDS), pp. 155–158 (2023). https://doi.org/10.1109/ComSDS58064.2023.10130353
2. Al-kfairy, M., Ahmed, S., Khalil, A.: Factors impacting users' willingness to adopt and utilize the metaverse in education: a systematic review. Comput. Hum. Behav. Rep. 100459 (2024)
3. Allouzi, A., Alomari, K.: Adequate legal rules in settling metaverse disputes: Hybrid legal framework for metaverse dispute resolution (HLFMDR). Int. J. Data Netw. Sci. **7**(4) (2023). https://doi.org/10.5267/j.ijdns.2023.8.001
4. Alsamhi, S., Hawbani, A., Kumar, S., Porwol, L., Curry, E.: Decentralized metaverse: towards a secure, autonomous, and inclusive virtual world. In: Proceedings of the 2023 International Conference on Electrical, Computer and Energy Technologies (ICECET), pp. 1–7 (2023). https://doi.org/10.1109/ICECET58911.2023.10389478
5. Altaleb, H., Zoltán, R.: Decentralized autonomous organizations review, importance, and applications. In: Proceedings of the 2022 IEEE 26th International Conference on Intelligent Engineering Systems (INES), pp. 000121–000126 (2022)
6. Amemiya, T.: The potential of the metaverse to transform education and training. Brain Nerve **75**(10), 1107–1113 (2023)
7. Bronnikov, I., Bedenkova, A.S.: Metauniverses and states: together and apart. Ars Administrandi (The Art of Management) **15**(2), 224–250 (2023)
8. Castells, M.: The Rise of the Network Society. John Wiley & Sons, Hoboken (2011)
9. Cole, S.: Second Life users are protesting with their avatars. Vice (2024). https://www.vice.com/en/article/second-life-users-are-protesting-with-their-avatars/. Accessed 22 Mar 2025
10. Coleman, S., Blumler, J.G.: The Internet and Democratic Citizenship: Theory, Practice and Policy. Cambridge University Press, Cambridge (2009)
11. Dahlgren, P.: The Internet, public spheres, and political communication: dispersion and deliberation. Polit. Commun. **22**(2), 147–162 (2005)
12. Deseriis, M., Vittori, D.: Platform politics in Europe: the impact of online participation platforms on the internal democracy of two southern European parties: podemos and the five star movement. Int. J. Commun. **13**, 19 (2019)
13. Distor, C., Dhaou, S.B., Nielsen, M.M.: Metaverse vs. metacurse: the role of governments and public sector use cases. In: Proceedings of CEUR Workshop (2023). https://doi.org/10.1016/j.techfore.2024.123346
14. Earl, J., Kimport, K.: Digitally Enabled Social Change: Activism in the Internet Age. MIT Press, Cambridge (2011)
15. Ghosh, A., et al.: A survey on decentralized metaverse using blockchain and web 3.0 technologies, applications, and more. IEEE Access **12**, 146915–146948 (2024). https://doi.org/10.1109/ACCESS.2024.3469193
16. Gillespie, T.: The politics of 'platforms.' New Media Soc. **12**(3), 347–364 (2010)
17. Goldberg, M., Schär, F.: Metaverse governance: an empirical analysis of voting within decentralized autonomous organizations. J. Bus. Res. **160**, 113764 (2023). https://doi.org/10.1016/j.jbusres.2023.113764
18. Guidi, B., et al.: Social games and blockchain: exploring the metaverse of Decentraland. In: Proceedings of the 2022 IEEE 42nd International Conference on Distributed Computing Systems Workshops (ICDCSW), pp. 199–204 (2022). https://doi.org/10.1109/ICDCSW56584.2022.00045
19. Habermas, J.: The public sphere: an encyclopedia article. Crit. Theory Soc. 136–142 (2020)

20. Howard, A., Mawyer, A.: Ethnography in the digital age. Emerging Trends in the Social and Behavioral Sciences, pp. 1–15 (2015). https://doi.org/10.1002/9781118900772.ETRDS0119
21. Jin, S.: "In the metaverse we (mis)trust?" Third-level digital (in)equality, social phobia, neo-luddism, and blockchain/cryptocurrency transparency in the artificial intelligence-powered metaverse. Cyberpsychol. Behav. Soc. Netw. **27**(1), 64–75 (2024). https://doi.org/10.1089/cyber.2022.0376
22. Karadayı, Z., et al.: Establishing the future of work and collaboration through institutional metaverse. In: Proceedings of the 2024 International Wireless Communications and Mobile Computing (IWCMC), pp. 1400–1403 (2024)
23. Kholodnaya, E.: On the legal concept of metaverses. Lex Russica **77**(3), 116–128 (2024). https://doi.org/10.17803/1729-5920.2024.208.3.116-128
24. Kovaleva, N., Izotova, V., Chaikovsky, D., Shakhnovskaya, I., Solovjov, P.: Metaverse: problems of legal regulation. Vestnik of Polotsk State University. Part D: Econ. Legal Sci. **69**(4), 119–123 (2024). https://doi.org/10.52928/2070-1632-2024-69-4-119-123
25. Li, L., Jia, H.: Analysis of metaverse development in the context of digital economy. In: Proceedings of the 2023 2nd International Conference on Artificial Intelligence, Internet and Digital Economy (ICAID 2023), pp. 481–490 (2023)
26. Lnenicka, M., et al.: Government in the metaverse: requirements and suitability for providing digital public services. Technol. Forecast. Soc. Change **203**, 123346 (2024)
27. Lohakare, P.: Online voting system. Gurukul Int. Multidiscip. Res. J. (2024). https://doi.org/10.69758/scel2919
28. MacDonald, K.: Pushing buttons: with the safety of Roblox under scrutiny, how worried should parents be? The Guardian (2024). https://www.theguardian.com/games/2024/oct/16/pushing-buttons-roblox-games-for-children. Accessed 22 Mar 2025
29. Markham, A.: Doing digital ethnography in the digital age. Emerg. Trends Soc. Behav. Sci. (2020). https://doi.org/10.31235/osf.io/hqm4g
30. Martha, G., Gaol, F., Supangkat, S., Ranti, B.: Utilization of decentralized autonomous organization (DAO) for virtual property transaction governance in metaverse: a conceptual framework. In: Proceedings of the 2023 3rd International Conference on Intelligent Cybernetics Technology & Applications (ICICyTA), pp. 306–311 (2023). https://doi.org/10.1109/ICICyTA60173.2023.10429035
31. Mascitti, M.: The metaverse impact on the politics means. Comput. Law Secur. Rev. **55**, 106037 (2024). https://doi.org/10.1016/j.clsr.2024.106037
32. Mossberger, K., Tolbert, C.J., McNeal, R. S.: Digital Citizenship: The Internet, Society, and Participation. MIT Press, Cambridge (2007)
33. Ozkochill, E., Sarabil, S.Y.: Models for positioning public spaces in the metaverse. J. Technol. Archit. Des. Plan. **2**(2), 64–76 (2024)
34. Perez-Seijo, S., et al.: Journalism and the metaverse: opportunities and challenges for news production and consumption. Journal. Digit. Media Fourth Ind. Revolut. 85–97 (2024)
35. Radanliev, P., Roure, D., Novitzky, P., Sluganovic, I.: Accessibility and inclusiveness of new information and communication technologies for disabled users and content creators in the metaverse. Disabil. Rehabil. Assist. Technol. **19**, 1849–1863 (2023). https://doi.org/10.1080/17483107.2023.2241882
36. Rahman, K.R., et al.: Use of metaverse technology in education domain. J. Metaverse **3**(1), 79–86 (2023)
37. Russo, V.: Digital ethnography theories, models and case studies. In: Hošková-Mayerová, Š., Maturo, F., Kacprzyk, J. (eds.) Mathematical-Statistical Models and Qualitative Theories for Economic and Social Sciences. Studies in Systems, Decision and Control, LNCS, vol. 104, pp. 41–53. Springer, Cham (2017). https://doi.org/10.1007/978-3-319-54819-7_4
38. Sanghvi, H., et al.: MetaHate: ai-based hate speech detection for secured online gaming in metaverse using blockchain. Secur. Priv. **7**(2), e343 (2024)

39. Shin, J., et al.: Evaluating metaverse platforms: status, direction, and challenges. IEEE Consum. Electron. Mag. **13**, 46–52 (2024). https://doi.org/10.1109/MCE.2024.3350898
40. Singh, C., Patil, A., Mahajan, S.: Meta land: redefining virtual communities through centralized governance, inclusivity and innovation. Int. J. Innov. Sci. Res. Technol. (IJISRT) (2024). https://doi.org/10.38124/ijisrt/ijisrt24may109
41. Sitnikov, M.: How and why should we regulate the metaverse?. *Digital Law Journal*, 5(1) (2024). https://doi.org/10.38044/2686-9136-2024-5-1-4
42. Snyder, H.: Literature review as a research methodology: an overview and guidelines. J. Bus. Res. **104**, 333–339 (2019)
43. Srnicek, N.: Platform Capitalism. John Wiley & Sons, Hoboken (2017)
44. Suzor, N., Van Geelen, T., Myers West, S.: Evaluating the legitimacy of platform governance: a review of research and a shared research agenda. Int. Commun. Gaz. **80**(4), 385–400 (2018)
45. Torraco, R.J.: Writing integrative literature reviews: guidelines and examples. Hum. Resour. Dev. Rev. **4**(3), 356–367 (2005)
46. Tufekci, Z.: Twitter and tear gas: the power and fragility of networked protest. Yale University Press (2017)
47. Xu, X.: Meta-universe empowers the innovative development mechanism of the ideological education in colleges and universities. J. Educ. Educ. Res. (2024). https://doi.org/10.54097/y3ek9q73
48. Zhang, C.Y., Chemnad, K.: Is the metaverse accessible? An expert opinion. Nafath **9**(25) (2024). https://doi.org/10.54455/mcn2507
49. Zhang, J., Xie, X.: A study of community-based ecological governance model of DAO organizations. In: Proceedings of the 2nd International Conference on Public Management, Digital Economy and Internet Technology (ICPDI 2023) (2023). https://doi.org/10.4108/eai.1-9-2023.2338812
50. Zhang, Y.: Fusion application of new media communication and intelligent AI algorithms in the metaverse ecology. In: Proceedings of the 2023 IEEE 15th International Conference on Computational Intelligence and Communication Networks (CICN), pp. 704–710 (2023). https://doi.org/10.1109/CICN59264.2023.10402161
51. Hill G.: Democracy in the metaverse: What can we learn from Second Life? Whyy (2024). https://whyy.org/segments/lessons-from-second-life-democracy-in-the-metaverse/. Accessed 22 Mar 2025
52. Li, C., Zeng, L., Huang, X., Miao, X., Wang, S.: Secure semantic communication model for black-box attack challenge under metaverse. IEEE Wirel. Commun. **30**, 56–62 (2023). https://doi.org/10.1109/MWC.005.2200622
53. Khalid, U., Ulum, M., Farooq, A., Duong, T., Dobre, O., Shin, H.: Quantum semantic communications for metaverse: principles and challenges. IEEE Wirel. Commun. **30**, 26–36 (2023). https://doi.org/10.1109/MWC.002.2200613
54. Jin, S., Ryu, E.: Unraveling the dynamics of digital equality and trust in AI-empowered metaverses and AI-VR-convergence. Technol. Forecast. Soc. Change **210** (2025). https://doi.org/10.1016/j.techfore.2024.123877
55. Karimov, E.: Meta-morphosis of copyright and user-generated content: can East Asia's emerging policies navigate through the metaverse? Asian J. Law Soc. 1–22 (2024). https://doi.org/10.1017/als.2024.32
56. Lin, H., Wan, S., Gan, W., Chen, J., Chao, H.: Metaverse in education: vision, opportunities, and challenges. In: 2022 IEEE International Conference on Big Data (Big Data), 2857–2866 (2022). https://doi.org/10.1109/BigData55660.2022.10021004
57. Wang, J., et al.: Logical innovation of metaverse empowerment ideological and political education: reconstruction based on people, things and scenes. Acad. J. Humanit. Soc. Sci. **5**(18), 92–99 (2022)

Peculiarities of Regulation and Functioning of Social Rating Systems of Russian Companies

Alexander Sokolov(✉), Elena Isaeva, and Egor Grebenko

P. G. Demidov Yaroslavl State University, 150003 Yaroslavl, Russian Federation
alex8119@mail.ru

Abstract. The digital transformation of modern society has given rise to many new forms and mechanisms of control over human activities. Today, the issues of evaluating the "effectiveness" of both modern organizations and enterprises, as well as individuals, are becoming increasingly relevant. Digitalization not only allows for a detailed assessment of various people and organizations based on constantly collecting data about users from the global network, but also makes it possible to introduce incentive and restrictive control mechanisms based on their trustworthiness. This process became known as social rating. The most active rating creators are commercial enterprises that want to optimize their work by introducing mechanisms for evaluating the effectiveness and trustworthiness of individual citizens. The purpose of this study is to identify the specifics of the regulation and functioning of rating systems of modern Russian companies. A comprehensive analysis of the internal documents of Russian companies that have implemented rating in the framework of their public activities was carried out. To identify the specifics of the functioning of the rating systems of these companies, a case study (with elements of comparative analysis) of assessment and ranking systems was conducted. The paper includes the results of 2 series of in-depth interviews with experts, which made it possible to identify the need for state regulation of rating systems. The study showed that modern rating systems are actively used in commercial digital services, regulating users' access to services and influencing their privileges. Even the internal regulation of these systems remains underdeveloped, which creates risks for users. All systems have similar rating principles, but they differ in details, such as the impact of rating on access to services, rehabilitation mechanisms, and the degree of publicity.

Keywords: social rating · rating · digitalization · evaluation · regulation

1 Introduction

In the context of the rapid development of digital technologies and global informatization of society, the mechanisms of personality assessment and ranking are becoming increasingly important. Social rating processes are becoming an integral part of modern social, economic, and political systems, influencing access to resources, opportunities, and public trust.

M. Bakaev et al. (Eds.): IMS 2025, CCIS 2671, pp. 394–407, 2026.
https://doi.org/10.1007/978-3-032-04958-2_29

The relevance of social rating research is due to its increasingly widespread application in various spheres of life: from the commercial sector to social platforms and government programs. Today, social rating systems are used to assess citizens' trustworthiness, form credit histories, select job candidates, and manage public order. At the same time, the proliferation of such mechanisms generates discussions about the limits of privacy interference, the need to protect personal data, and the threat of digital discrimination. The main factor determining the relevance of this topic is the contradiction between the advantages and risks of social rating. On the one hand, such systems can enhance social responsibility, transparency, and security, and on the other, generate new forms of control, inequality, and social pressure. The issues of the ethics of algorithms, data bias, and citizens' rights to anonymity are becoming central to discussions about the future of digital social interaction.

In this regard, it is possible to identify an existing scientific problem: the lack of information about the applied rating procedures and the consequences of this rating for its objects.

Therefore, attention in this study is paid to the functioning of rating systems in Russian digital services of large domestic companies. In recent years, services such as marketplaces, taxi aggregators, and online trading systems have been actively implementing evaluation mechanisms for users and service providers. These rating systems have a direct impact on users' access to certain services, special terms of service, and even on the reputation of companies and private performers. Therefore, this work is aimed at a comprehensive study of social rating processes in Russian digital ecosystems, an analysis of their mechanisms, consequences and possible ways of regulation.

2 The Theoretical Framework

Evaluation and ranking issues play a significant role in modern society, especially in the context of the development of digital technologies. Thus, consumers are increasingly turning to reviews and ratings when choosing goods and services, which makes these mechanisms an important factor influencing their decisions [1]. Research confirms that rating systems, such as star-based classification, are able to shape consumers' perceptions and stimulate changes in their behavior. At the same time, Abell, Morgan and Romero emphasize that not only the rating itself, but also the format of its presentation on digital platforms can significantly influence consumer choice [2]. In the service industry, quality assessment is often associated with the ability to leave a tip. Chen, Xu, Rodas, and Liu have found that the sequence of offers of appreciation and tips can affect the amount of remuneration, which is of practical importance for the design of digital interfaces [3]. The so-called phenomenon of "rating bubbles" is also interesting, when there is an excess of extremely positive ratings. Based on the interpretation of this phenomenon, Cicognani, Figini, and Magnani investigated, pointing to the influence of the social factor and the need to adjust rating systems to reduce bias [4].

A significant amount of research is devoted to studying the experience of social rating in China. In particular, it is noted that the Chinese social credit system is a unique and almost poorly researched phenomenon [5]. Y.Zhu analyzed the impact of mandatory geolocation disclosure on social media and noted its limited impact on expression of opinions, as well as described the development of tracking systems in the country, including registration under real names [6]. The author also highlights the expansion of surveillance systems in both the public and private sectors. At the same time, the Chinese government considers the social credit system as a tool to combat social problems and increase the level of trust in society [7]. In the Western context, trust regulation is traditionally carried out in the context of state regulation. R. Hou and D. Fu draw attention to the discrepancy between reputational losses in social rating systems and the capabilities of the legal system, as well as the risks of abuse in the absence of centralized regulation [8]. In contrast, E.Szwajnoch believes that the Chinese social credit system is mainly aimed at ensuring compliance with existing laws, although it allows the introduction of additional sanctions through various agreements [9]. R. Hou and D. Fu also analyze the goals and components of the Chinese social rating system, emphasizing that it includes not only political, but also financial, credit, administrative and moral aspects. In turn, Von Blomberg and Haixu Yu analyze the use of the "shaming" strategy in the Chinese social credit system, noting the lack of its legal basis and the problems faced by the courts when considering related disputes [10]. The authors also point to the irreversibility of reputational damage and the complexity of its compensation. A.Trauth-Goik and L. Chuncheng consider the impact of social rating on interpersonal relationships, drawing historical parallels and noting the problem of the legitimacy of collective punishment [11]. At the same time, Russian researchers also pay attention to social rating as a form of state control over society, considering the prospects for its implementation and development, as well as potential threats [12].

Thus, the review of modern research demonstrates a wide range of studies devoted to the study of various aspects of social rating, from its impact on consumer behavior to the specifics of implementation and regulation in different countries. Despite a fairly broad overview of rating as a process, most authors still focus on considering social rating as a mechanism for monitoring human activities. The apparent concentration in modern literature on the interpretation of the Chinese experience reveals only a partial understanding of the existing possibilities for evaluating and ranking individuals. Therefore, the purpose of this article is to identify the specifics of the regulation and functioning of social rating systems in Russia through the prism of the experience of commercial companies.

3 Research Methods

The empirical basis of the study was formed through a comprehensive analysis of internal documents regulating the functioning of rating systems used in the public activities of Russian commercial companies. To achieve the purpose of the study, the case-study method was applied, which includes elements of comparative analysis. The objects of the study were the rating systems of four leading Russian digital services: Ozon, Wildberries, YandexGo and Avito. The choice of these companies is due to their wide popularity among Russian users, the active use of rating mechanisms to regulate interaction between platform participants and differences in their business models and fields of activity.

The case study examined user agreements, offers, privacy policies, and help sections posted on the official websites and mobile applications of the companies under study.

The main focus of the analysis was on identifying the declared goals of the implementation of rating systems, the specifics of the assessment and ranking of users (sellers, buyers, passengers, drivers), the mechanisms of rating influence on access to services and privileges, as well as procedures for correcting and challenging ratings. The comparative analysis revealed the general principles and specific differences in the functioning and regulation of social rating systems in the Russian commercial sector.

To expand and refine the results, the results of 2 series of in-depth interviews with experts were also included in this work. The experts assessed the current state of the digital space, ecosystems (the study was conducted in 2023 by a sample of 34 experts) and the need to regulate social rating systems (the study was conducted in 2024 by a sample of 32 experts). The interviews were conducted using a formalized questionnaire, where all questions were open-ended. This study includes only a number of questions that help to support the results of the study with new interpretations. Here are examples of questions included in the study from expert guides: "What are the trends of digitalization (introduction of digital services)?" Do you see?", "What differences do you see between digital services/platforms and digital ecosystems? What is their key difference?", "Do you consider it necessary to restrict and regulate the formation and functioning of digital ecosystems?", "What regulates the creation and introduction of social ratings (law, ethics,….)?", " In your opinion, who is more successful in forming social ratings, the state or business?", "What prospects do you see for the introduction of social rating? What political consequences can there be from the introduction of social rating?".

Thus, it was possible to collect data on both the specific rating systems used in modern Russia and the articulated needs for regulating their operation.

4 The Results of the Study

4.1 Features of Regulation of Social Rating Systems in Russian Companies

The issue of regulating social rating systems, actively implemented by commercial companies, is becoming increasingly relevant in scientific discourse. This is due to certain risks of personal ratings influencing citizens' access to various services. This section provides a more detailed review of each of the cases studied, with an emphasis on the specifics of internal and external regulation of rating processes in our selected services.

One of the illustrative examples of 2024 was the statement by the taxi aggregator YandexGo that the rating of a passenger will affect the speed of processing his order and the possibility of ordering several cars at the same time. At the same time, the personal rating system for drivers has been functioning for a long time and is available to passengers through a mobile application. For a more detailed analysis, we will consider this case, highlighting the key aspects concerning both the user of the service (passenger) and its supplier (driver). The terms of use of the YandexGo service provide for the possibility of evaluating taxi services and posting comments/reviews both on the part of the user and in relation to him.

The passenger rating, introduced in test mode in February 2020, was initially visible only to passengers and had no consequences until 2024. It is formed on the basis of driver ratings on a five-point scale, where new ratings have more weight. Yandex explained to users the principles of rating formation and ways to increase it, calling for compliance with generally accepted standards of behavior. However, in March 2024, the negative consequences of low ratings were introduced, including slowing down the search for a car and blocking the simultaneous ordering of several cars for passengers who often cancel trips. This innovation is aimed at reducing unjustified cancellations that cause losses for drivers and the company. The passenger rating now has several statuses that affect the pickup speed of the vehicle. At the same time, questions remain about the transparency of the criteria for "forced" cancellation of an order, which does not affect the rating. The new rules could potentially reduce the number of discriminatory cancellations. There is a risk of subjective ratings and unfair downgrade due to the actions of an unregistered user. At the same time, representatives of the drivers' unions generally supported the innovation.

YandexGo drivers also have a rating calculated as a weighted average of the last 150 ratings. A decrease in the driver's rating below 4.5 points automatically blocks access to the service for at least six months and restricts the ability to fulfill orders in higher tariff categories. To protect against unfair ratings, a special algorithm has been developed that automatically detects unreasonably low ratings. Yandex emphasizes that the support service cannot influence the rating. Due to YandexGo's dominant position in the market, the innovations aroused the interest of the Federal Antimonopoly Service, which requested clarification on the practice of blocking users. The YandexGo Terms of Use provide for the possibility of temporary or permanent restriction of access to the service for systematic cancellation of orders, non-payment, misuse, misconduct towards drivers and other violations.

In general, the YandexGo case demonstrates a tendency to use rating systems not only to evaluate the quality of services, but also as a tool for managing user behavior with potential legal and ethical consequences.

Next, let's look at the regulatory features of the Avito ad placement service. Since 2023, KEH Ecommerce LLC, the owner of the Avito service, has started implementing a social rating system for sellers. The rating influences the position of the seller's ad in the search results, encouraging sellers to maintain a high quality of interaction with customers. The platform provides detailed information about the rating conditions on a separate page, indicating that the rating is the average of the ratings given by customers after in-person meetings or delivery orders. The rating of private sellers becomes visible after the first review, and for stores and professional sellers – after the third review with an assessment. The rating is displayed in all ads, with the exception of the "Resume" and "Real Estate" categories (except for daily rent).

The rating is formed by calculating the arithmetic mean of all ratings received by the seller on a scale from 1 to 5. All reviews left are checked by Avito and can be edited or deleted. All reviews are taken into account, including situations where contact between the seller and the buyer has not taken place. Avito reserves the right to delete suspicious reviews without the possibility of recovery, and sellers have the opportunity to challenge the received review within three months.

Since 2021, Avito has been operating a "Trusted Partner" status system, which, according to the service's research, significantly increases the attractiveness of ads. Sellers who have provided an INN and are registered on the platform as a company with at least 10 reviews and a rating above four stars can receive this status. Avito itself provides sellers with recommendations for improving their rating, including detailed communication with customers, providing complete information about the product, timely closing of ads after the sale, filling out a high-quality profile and asking customers to evaluate their work. For this purpose, a special technical function is provided for sending an assessment request. The platform also provides a detailed methodological base for working with reviews.

Avito's Terms of Use initially inform users of the right to leave feedback and responses to them, expressing their subjective opinion about the interaction or transaction. It is prohibited to knowingly post false information in reviews, leave reviews without the intention of making a deal, as well as any form of "cheating" reviews. In 2024, Avito introduced a color ranking of sellers in a test mode, providing for the assignment of one of three color markers: green (priority issue), yellow (neutral position) and red (lower priority issue). At the moment, buyers still do not see the sellers' color designations, the rating is carried out inside the Avito system, and sellers can see their service level (from 41% to 100% and below 40%) in their personal account. Despite this, according to Avito, buyers have become 5% more likely to interact with sellers who have a high rating in terms of color markings. The color ranking system is based on such factors as the relevance and reliability of ads, their compliance with Avito rules, profile confirmation, courtesy of communication, speed of responses, and the speed of sending goods.

The Avito Terms of Use do not directly regulate the terms of the rating, but they consolidate the right of users to leave reviews, while prohibiting the abuse of this right. Since May 2024, Avito has introduced a social rating system for buyers in the "Goods" category, giving sellers the opportunity to leave feedback based on the results of interaction with counterparties. Since September 2023, this system has been operating in a test mode in the categories of "Short-term rentals" and "Goods" and has collected a significant number of reviews.

The popular Wildberries marketplace uses a seller rating system based on customer reviews and ratings of purchased goods. The Wildberries User Agreement provides for the possibility of leaving feedback for publication on the platform. The platform displays the sellers' public rating, which is directly regulated by the Wildberries Seller Agreement. According to the Offer, the seller's rating depends on the average rating of his goods given by the buyers. If there are fewer than 1,000 estimates, all estimates are taken into account, and if there are more, estimates for the last two years are taken into account, while older estimates (beyond the last thousand and left more than 90 days before the calculation) are used with a decreasing coefficient.

The offer excludes ratings that are considered spam (unrelated to the product, offensive, or violating the rules of the platform) from the rating calculation. Such estimates may be considered spam based on Wildberries' automated algorithms, information from open sources, or other circumstances indicating their unreliability. Subparagraph 9.9.7 of the Offer provides for the blocking of part of the seller's functionality in the event of a decrease in the delivery rating (calculated separately for various delivery methods) below the established thresholds (70% or 80%). The lock is applied for 5 calendar days for the first violation and increases by 5 days for each subsequent rating decrease. Access to the blocked functionality is restored automatically after the expiration of the blocking period or prematurely when the delivery rating is increased to the set level.

Wildberries customers have access to information about the percentage of purchase of goods and a personal discount in their personal account. However, a request to the Wildberries support service did not confirm a direct link between the buyback percentage and the discount amount, indicating that the buyback percentage is currently a technical indicator. Nevertheless, Wildberries applies a differentiated cost for the return of goods of good quality depending on the percentage of the buyer's purchase, which raises questions from the point of view of compliance with the Law of the Russian Federation "On Consumer Rights Protection", which does not provide for the possibility of differentiating consumer rights based on their purchase history. The rules for using the Wildberries trading platform indicate that the cost of return transportation of goods of proper quality is determined in advance and communicated to the consumer when placing an order, to which the consumer agrees by confirming the order. The criteria for determining the cost of a refund and its dependence on any circumstances are not indicated.

The Ozon trading platform also uses a seller rating system based on customer reviews and ratings. Ozon identifies a number of key service indicators that affect the seller's rating: products and prices, shipment and delivery, complaints from customers. In addition to the public rating, Ozon calculates additional indicators for evaluating the seller's work, available only in the seller's personal account. The platform provides detailed instructions on the principles of evaluation and the impact of rating on the seller's work.

In fact, Ozon builds a clear algorithm for sellers, aimed at ensuring a high level of service and quality of goods, which is a key factor in attracting and retaining customers on the site. In the context of competition between marketplaces, the requirements for the quality of sellers' work are likely to only increase, and rating systems will evolve and include new metrics that help optimize turnover. At the moment, Ozon has not introduced a customer rating system, and the percentage of purchase of goods is not publicly available, although, by analogy with Wildberries, it can be assumed that this indicator is monitored. The seller's rating affects a number of parameters, in particular, the possibility of participating in the Premium program. Sellers with a rating of 4.5 or higher receive a "Premium Seller" badge, which increases customer confidence and sets them apart from competitors. A decrease in the rating below 4.5 leads to the loss of the badge and the exclusion of the seller's goods from the "Premium sellers' goods" filter. The badge is restored when the rating is increased to 4.5 or higher. A Premium-Plus subscription, which also depends on the rating, provides additional benefits.

The rating systems implemented by YandexGo, Avito, Wildberries, and Ozon demonstrate not only a general tendency to use reputation as a regulator, but also specific approaches to their state regulation, reflecting the specifics of each service's business models and fields of activity.

At YandexGo, the focus is shifting to operational management of user behavior in real time, affecting the speed and availability of taxi services. Avito, as an ad platform, relies on the long-term formation of sellers' reputation, affecting the visibility of their offers. Regulation focuses on moderating reviews and providing tools to improve ratings, as well as introducing color differentiation that is not yet fully transparent to buyers. It is noteworthy to introduce a customer assessment system that expands the scope of rating.

Wildberries and Ozon, as marketplaces, use seller ratings to control the quality of goods and services, which is directly reflected in their offers. Wildberries is notable for using a buyer's buyback percentage to determine return terms, raising questions about legal compliance. Ozon, in turn, actively uses the rating to provide additional advantages to sellers, striving to increase the overall level of service on the platform.

Thus, two conclusions can be drawn:

- the general conclusion underlines the systemic importance of ratings in regulating the activities of the services described above;
- an additional conclusion allows us to focus on differences in approaches to their regulation: from operational management in YandexGo to an emphasis on moderation of reviews in Avito and consolidation in the offers of Wildberries and Ozon marketplaces. These differences confirm the different goal-setting of companies when using and implementing rating systems and, consequently, the different mechanisms of their internal regulatory support.

4.2 Features of the Implementation of Rating Systems in Russian Companies

A visual representation of the existing rating systems in domestic commercial companies can be obtained from existing systems implemented in the operation of large digital services. In this study, we managed to obtain a fairly broad description of the existing rating systems of four Russian companies: Ozon, Wildberries, Yandex and Avito.

Before proceeding to a direct interpretation of the comparison of these rating systems, it is necessary to note the objectives of the rating implementation declared by the companies themselves. It is noteworthy that during the initial search for cases for analyzing rating systems, we came across an interesting pattern, which is expressed in the fact that rating systems are actively used by those companies and organizations where it is important to optimize the work between the service provider and their direct recipient. Therefore, the most common rating systems turned out to be among the so-called marketplace services, where the interaction of users and sellers is evaluated by rating suppliers of goods and services. Digital taxi aggregators have become the second most common commercial example of the introduction of rating systems. Following a similar pattern to digital marketplaces, companies try to optimize interactions between passengers and drivers. And this is where an interesting feature of the declared rating goals is revealed. It is typical for Ozon, Wildberries and Avito companies to evaluate sellers, when, as in the YandexGo service, the assessment is carried out for all participants in the interaction (drivers and passengers). In the first case, this situation creates the dependence of sellers on the ratings of buyers and users, and in the second case, the situation tries to appear more fair regarding compliance with the two-way assessment of the overall interaction (trip). At the same time, users of ratings of these services themselves find themselves in a situation where, wishing to use or already actively using the service for their needs, they are forced to join the rating system without a choice to participate in the evaluation or not. Joining the rating is mandatory for everyone, but in the case of Ozon and Wildberries marketplaces and Avito ad platforms, buyers are free not to participate in the evaluation and do not risk being evaluated by sellers. In the YandexGo taxi aggregator, both drivers (service providers) have the option to opt out of evaluation so do the passengers. This situation actually creates an inequality of initial engagement and evaluation opportunities for participants representing different sides of the provision of services (supplier and consumer). The service acts as an intermediary, which only creates the conditions for making an assessment and subsequent rating. Thus, the objectives of rating each of the analyzed services are based on who is the subject of evaluation. For Ozon, Wildberries, and Avito, it is sellers who become the objects of evaluation, so the purpose of rating for them is to determine the reliability of sellers providing services on a digital platform (since sellers act as independent platforms within the marketplace). For YandexGo, the goal is defined by a broader range based on the fact that two subjects of the relationship are evaluated at once, so the purpose of rating here can be defined as ensuring the effectiveness of interaction between passengers and drivers based on a mutual assessment of the service provider and its consumer.

Speaking about the more detailed features of the analyzed rating systems, we can say that all services have both significant differences and similarities that allow us to formulate conclusions about the state of the rating implementation process in domestic commercial companies. The analysis reveals key differences in the mechanisms of the rating impact, the severity of the applied sanctions, the possibilities of correcting ratings, the level of transparency of algorithms, the likelihood of unfair restrictions, the degree of interaction with the support service, the psychological impact on users and the overall flexibility of the system.

On marketplace platforms (Wildberries, Ozon), the rating acts as a direct determinant of the commercial success of sellers, determining the visibility of product positions and transactional activity in the general product list (including based on the position in the general selection in the recommendations for each individual user). In contrast, in the YandexGo taxi aggregator service and on the Avito ad platform, the rating primarily performs the function of controlling access to the service, where critically low ratings can lead to suspension or complete termination of user service on the platform. At the same time, the severity of sanctions measures is also significantly differentiated. The most rigorous approach is demonstrated by YandexGo, where lowering the rating to a certain threshold entails the immediate blocking of the account. Ozon and Avito apply a more "flexible" system of restrictions, including reducing the priority of ads and submitting written complaints to sellers. Wildberries focuses sanctions on sellers, which translates into potential financial losses for the latter.

Despite the existing sanctions policy for users with low ratings, the systems somehow offer rehabilitation and assessment correction mechanisms. An analysis of the rating correction possibilities shows that Ozon and Avito provide users with more advanced mechanisms to improve their performance by consistently improving the quality of services provided (although this mechanism largely depends on the buyers themselves, who should give sellers high marks based on subsequent interaction). In Wildberries and YandexGo, the rating restoration process is characterized by less transparency and high dependence on internal algorithms, which often become incomprehensible and difficult for the user to understand. For example, Wildberries and YandexGo use unique automated systems, which makes it much more difficult for users to understand the factors influencing their assessment. In YandexGo, for passengers, this is the average rating from drivers over the last 40 trips, and for drivers, in addition to ratings from passengers themselves, there are ratings provided by the aggregator itself. Wildberries operates in a similar way when the evaluation for sellers is formed both on the basis of average ratings from buyers and on the basis of a special evaluation methodology formed by the market place itself. Ozon and Avito, on the contrary, provide more information about the principles of rating formation, although their rating system itself is only the simplest designation of the average rating given by buyers to the seller. Therefore, the risk of unfair sanctions is higher in services with automated rating systems, such as Wildberries and YandexGo, since algorithms are not always able to take into account the context of the situation of each individual case of interaction between users of these services.

Interaction with the support service on rating issues is more developed in Ozon and Avito, where support can review individual cases of conflicts between users. In Wildberries and YandexGo, ranking decisions are more often made by algorithms without the possibility of influence from the support service. Therefore, the "psychological impact" of the rating system is more strongly felt in services with severe consequences for low ratings, such as Wildberries and YandexGo, where users may experience stress due to fear of negative reviews. In Ozon and Avito, however, due to the greater possibility of correcting the situation, the system is perceived as more loyal and flexible.

The analyzed rating systems in Ozon, Wildberries, YandexGo and Avito demonstrate the evolution of quality control mechanisms and interaction in digital commerce. There is a tendency to use ratings not only as a tool for evaluating the effectiveness of user interaction with each other, but also as a lever for controlling the behavior of service representatives and their recipients. At the same time, the balance between the transparency of the system, the fairness of sanctions and the possibility of rehabilitating the rating remains critically important for maintaining user trust and the effectiveness of the platforms themselves. The definition of this balance directly follows from the peculiarities of state regulation of both the rating and evaluation process itself and companies implementing such systems in their work.

4.3 Assessment of the Need to Regulate Rating Processes

Considering the above-described rating cases, we came to an interesting conclusion that most domestic companies developing and implementing rating of their clients are implemented as digital ecosystems (marketplace, bank, analytics services, etc.). This fact has expanded the repeated interest in our past works devoted to the study of modern digital ecosystems, which allowed us to identify a number of key expert opinions on the importance of and the need to regulate social rating systems, especially in the context of their development in large commercial digital ecosystems. Despite the fact that there is no direct focus on social rating in our previous research, expert assessments regarding digitalization, digital platforms and ecosystems allow us to draw informed conclusions about the views on the regulation of rating systems. And the expert opinions on the need to regulate rating systems in this study reinforce and expand the theses of our previous work.

One of the central points that experts emphasize is the scale and functionality of digital ecosystems. They note that "ecosystems are a large digital "mechanism" based, among other things, on various services and platforms that are components of the ecosystem." This definition indicates that it is within such large structures that a significant amount of user data is concentrated, which is a key condition for the functioning of effective rating systems. As noted, "an ecosystem is a complex structure that provides access to various services and providers of various services." Such a variety of services and interactions generates vast amounts of data that can be used to evaluate and rank users according to various criteria.

Experts also make a clear distinction between digital services/platforms and ecosystems in terms of consistency and scale. While services and platforms have "limited functionality," ecosystems are characterized by "the level of internal organization and complexity of implementing mechanisms for the interaction of system elements." It is this complexity and integration of ecosystems that create a favorable environment for the development of multifaceted rating systems that can take into account many parameters of user behavior and interaction.

In the context of regulation, experts express some caution regarding interference in the formation of digital ecosystems in various fields, noting that "the introduction of any restrictions on the formation of digital ecosystems is not advisable, as it may limit their development." When it comes to broader regulation of the digital sphere, experts tend to favor the need for legislative intervention by government agencies. A significant number of experts believe that legislative regulation of the digital sphere is necessary in principle. Moreover, many argue that "Russian legislation is poorly consistent with the current processes of digitalization and requires modernization, taking into account the interests of entities interested in the development of digital ecosystems (including those developed by commercial organizations)." This emphasis on the need to modernize legislation in the digital sphere indirectly indicates that experts are aware of the potential risks and challenges associated with the uncontrolled development of digital ecosystems, including the rating systems that operate in them. Currently, the regulation of rating systems in commercial organizations is usually carried out on the basis of their internal regulatory documents, user agreements and confidentiality policies. However, experts, judging by their general opinion on the need for government regulation of the digital sphere, probably see the need for a broader and more unified approach to regulating rating systems, especially given their potential impact on the lives and capabilities of users.

Experts pay special attention to the risks associated with the use of large amounts of digital user data. Citing examples of constant leaks of users' personal data, experts currently see the introduction and creation of digital ecosystems in the political sphere as unsafe, where the personal data of specific people can be used in illegal activities. This fear of data misuse also directly affects rating systems that use sensitive information about user behavior, preferences, and interactions. Without proper regulation of this area, there is a risk of manipulation, discrimination and violation of citizens' rights to privacy.

Experts also note the opacity of many modern digital systems, especially the "digital ecosystems of large commercial organizations." This opacity can also extend to the algorithms of rating systems, making the criteria for evaluating and ranking users unobvious. In such circumstances, there is an even greater need for government regulation that could ensure greater transparency and accountability of rating systems. Some experts also express the opinion that the development of digital ecosystems is outpacing the reaction of authorities, which makes it difficult to introduce regulatory measures in a timely manner. "The development of digital ecosystems is outpacing the reaction of authorities who are unable to respond in time to changes in digitalization and digital transformation," experts say. This highlights the need for a specialized regulatory approach based on a deep understanding of the principles of rating systems and their potential impact on society, including the prevention of potential risks to society.

Summarizing the opinions of experts, it can be concluded that, despite the recognition of the importance of developing digital ecosystems and the potential inexpediency of unnecessarily limiting their formation, there is a clear understanding of the need for government regulation of the digital sphere as a whole. This regulation should take into account the risks associated with big data processing, ensure transparency in the operation of complex digital systems, including rating systems, and protect the rights and interests of citizens. While the regulation of rating systems in commercial organizations is still limited to internal documents, experts have traced a request for a more systematic and governmental approach to this area, due to the significant impact of ratings on the opportunities and social status of users in the digital space, which is increasingly based on large-scale commercial digital ecosystems. It is the concentration of huge amounts of data in these ecosystems that makes the issue of regulating rating systems particularly relevant and requires government attention.

5 Discussion

Despite the extensive possibilities of studying the rating processes of modern Russian digital services, this work has revealed a number of deficits that may hinder the disclosure of certain aspects of social rating. The first of these is limited access to the internal documentation of Russian companies and the specifics of their algorithms. Our research was based on publicly available information (both posted by them on the Internet and obtained during calls to the support services of these companies), when access to internal documents could strengthen the interpretations obtained as part of the analysis of the main body of regulatory documents. Also, this study presents a limited set of cases that demonstrate only the most well-known rating practices of large Russian companies. There are many non-public social rating systems focused on regulating various aspects of interactions between citizens and organizations that we have not been able to access. Studying them would contribute to a deeper understanding of existing methods for collecting, analyzing, and compiling ratings, which in itself would expand the range of existing rating practices in the digital environment. Also, this study could support data on the psychological impact of rating processes on individuals, which could provide more expanded conclusions about the impact of rating processes on the behavior of citizens.

Despite the above-mentioned deficits in studying the specifics of the regulation and functioning of social rating systems for Russian companies, we see a certain prospect of studying this phenomenon in the future. As an example, we find it interesting to study foreign social rating practices. Conducting comparative studies of social rating systems in various countries and industries could identify best practices and general trends.

6 Conclusions

To summarize, it is necessary to focus on several key points that determine the current state and prospects of rating development in the domestic commercial environment. Firstly, the study demonstrated that rating has ceased to be a unique mechanism and has become firmly established in the practice of large Russian digital platforms, covering various areas – from marketplaces to taxi aggregators. Companies see these systems as a powerful tool for improving the quality of service, optimizing internal processes, and creating a more trusting environment for interaction between market participants. Secondly, the variety of approaches to the construction and application of rating systems indicates the lack of uniform standards in this area. Each company develops its own model based on the specifics of its business, target audience, and strategic goals. This leads to significant differences in evaluation criteria, rating mechanisms for users, and dispute resolution procedures. Such differentiation can create certain inconveniences and misunderstandings on the part of users who are faced with different rules of the game on different platforms. Thirdly, despite the obvious benefits that companies receive from the introduction of rating systems, our research has revealed the potential risks associated with their operation. These include issues of algorithm transparency, the possibility of subjective and biased ratings, insufficient feedback and appeal mechanisms, and the potential for unjustified discrimination against users with low ratings. These risks are particularly relevant in the context of the growing dependence of citizens on digital services in their daily lives. Fourth, the analysis of expert opinions clearly indicates the urgent need for more active involvement of the state in the process of regulating social rating systems. Of course, this is not about total control or the creation of unnecessary barriers to the development of innovations, but about the formation of common principles and standards that would protect the rights and legitimate interests of citizens, enhance transparency and accountability of these systems, and minimize the risks of their misuse. In an environment where rating systems are increasingly penetrating into various aspects of society, the lack of a clear legal framework can lead to undesirable social and economic consequences. Thus, the further development of social rating systems in Russia requires a balanced approach that combines business initiative in the search for effective quality management and interaction tools with a responsible government attitude to protecting the rights and interests of citizens in the digital environment. The formation of an open dialogue between all stakeholders – companies, users, the expert community and authorities – is a key condition for creating fair, transparent and effective social rating systems that contribute to the development of the digital economy and improve the quality of life of society.

Acknowledgment. The research was funded by Russian Science Foundation, research project No. 24-28-00728, https://rscf.ru/en/project/24-28-00728.

References

1. Tiwari, V., Omar, A.: The impact of the hotel star rating system on tourists' health safety and risk perceptions: study based on tourists' vacation experiences. J. Vacat. Mark. **31**(1), 157–173 (2025). https://doi.org/10.1177/13567667231188880

2. Abell, A., Morgan, C., Romero, M.: The power of a star rating: differential effects of customer rating formats on magnitude perceptions and consumer reactions. J. Mark. Res. **61**(6), 1041–1057 (2024). https://doi.org/10.1177/00222437241240694
3. Chen, J., Xu, A.J., Rodas, M.A., Liu, X.: Order matters: rating service professionals first reduces tipping amount. J. Mark. **87**(1), 81–96 (2023). https://doi.org/10.1177/00222429221098698
4. Cicognani, S., Figini, P., Magnani, M.: Social influence bias in ratings: a field experiment in the hospitality sector. Tour. Econ. **28**(8), 2197–2218 (2022). https://doi.org/10.1177/13548166211034645
5. Konopiy, A.S.: The social credit rating system in China: law and practice. Bull. Fac. Law Southern Federal Univ. **8**(1), 20–24 (2021). https://doi.org/10.18522/2313-6138-2021-8-1-3
6. Zhu, Y.: Privacy cynicism and diminishing utility of state surveillance: a natural experiment of mandatory location disclosure on China's Weibo. Big Data Soc. **11**(2), 1–17 (2024). https://doi.org/10.1177/20539517241242450
7. Naumenko, T.V., Sekretareva, K.N.: The Chinese social credit system: dystopia or a factor of social well-being? J. Soc. Policy Res. **20**(3), 419–432 (2022). https://doi.org/10.17323/727-0634-2022-20-3-419-432
8. Hou, R., Fu, D.: Sorting citizens: governing via China's social credit system. Governance **37**(1), 59–78 (2022). https://doi.org/10.1111/gove.12751
9. Szwajnoch, E.: Regulatory capture of the Chinese social credit system: bureaucratic self-interests in project implementation. China Information **38**(3), 309–330 (2024). https://doi.org/10.1177/0920203X241259431
10. Blomberg, M., Yu, H.: Shaming the untrustworthy and paths to relief in China's social credit system. Modern China **49**(6), 744–781 (2023). https://doi.org/10.1177/00977004231152138
11. Trauth-Goik, A, Chuncheng, L.: Black or fifty shades of grey? The power and limits of the social credit blacklist system in China. J. Contemp. China **32**(144), 1017–1033 (2023). https://doi.org/10.1080/10670564.2022.2128638
12. Kartashova, Y.V., Mityashin, G.Y., Plotnikov, V.A.: The social rating system as a form of state control over society: prospects for implementation and development, threats to implementation. Manag. Consult. **2**(146), 100–109 (2021). https://doi.org/10.22394/1726-1139-2021-2-100-109

Author Index

M. Bakaev et al. (Eds.): IMS 2025, CCIS 2671, pp. 409–410, 2026.
https://doi.org/10.1007/978-3-032-04958-2